Force and Understanding

ALSO AVAILABLE FROM BLOOMSBURY

Force and Understanding

Writings on Philosophy and Resistance

HOWARD CAYGILL

Edited by Stephen Howard
Afterword by Jacqueline Rose

BLOOMSBURY ACADEMIC
LONDON • NEW YORK • OXFORD • NEW DELHI • SYDNEY

BLOOMSBURY ACADEMIC
Bloomsbury Publishing Plc
50 Bedford Square, London, WC1B 3DP, UK
1385 Broadway, New York, NY 10018, USA

BLOOMSBURY, BLOOMSBURY ACADEMIC and the Diana logo are
trademarks of Bloomsbury Publishing Plc

First published in Great Britain 2021

Cover design by Charlotte Daniels
Cover image: According to the Laws of Chance (Selon les Lois du Hasard) by
Jean Arp, 1933, Sugar paper on plyboard (© Tate Images / DACS 2019)

A catalogue record for this book is available from the British Library.

A catalog record for this book is available from the Library of Congress.

ISBN: HB: 978-1-3501-0786-1
         ePDF: 978-1-3501-0785-4
         eBook: 978-1-3501-0788-5

Typeset by Integra Software Services Pvt. Ltd.

To find out more about our authors and books visit www.bloomsbury.com
and sign up for our newsletters.

Contents

List of Illustrations

Acknowledgements

The editor would like to thank friends and colleagues who have read the introduction and parts of the manuscript; Nigel Tubbs, unofficial archivist of Caygill's writings, who provided pieces that Caygill himself thought were forever lost; and, at Bloomsbury, Lucy Russell, Liza Thompson and Lisa Goodrum for seeing the book through to publication. I am grateful to Jacqueline Rose for generously writing the Afterword. Last but certainly not least, thanks to Howard Caygill for the new pieces collected here and for his enthusiastic involvement in all aspects of the project.

Thanks to the following publishers for permission to republish articles and chapters:

Chapter 2: Howard Caygill, 'The Return of Nietzsche and Marx', in Paul Patton ed., *Nietzsche, Feminism and Political Theory*, London: Routledge, 1993, pp. 189–203. Reprinted with permission of Taylor & Francis.

Chapter 3: Howard Caygill, 'Violence, Civility and the Predicaments of Philosophy', in D. Campbell and M. Dillon eds., *The Political Subject of Violence*, Manchester: Manchester University Press, 1993, pp. 48–72. Copyright © Manchester University Press 1993. Reproduced with permission of The Licensor through PLSclear.

Chapter 4: Howard Caygill, 'Politics and War: Hegel and Clausewitz' from Caygill, *Hegel and the Speculative Community*, UEA Papers in Philosophy, Norwich: University of East Anglia, 1994, pp. 22–38.

Chapter 5: Howard Caygill, 'Perpetual Police? Kosovo and the Elision of Police and Military Violence', *European Journal of Social Theory* 4(1) (2001): 73–80. Reprinted with permission of SAGE Publishing.

Chapter 6: Howard Caygill, 'The Consolation of Philosophy; or "Neither Dionysus Nor the Crucified"', *Journal of Nietzsche Studies* 7 (1994), pp. 131–50. Copyright © 1994 The Pennsylvania State University Press. This article is used by permission of The Pennsylvania State University Press.

Chapter 7: Howard Caygill, 'Philosophy and Cultural Reform in the Early Nietzsche', in Keith Ansell Pearson & Howard Caygill eds., *The Fate of the New Nietzsche*, Aldershot: Avebury, 1993, pp. 109–22. Reprinted with permission of Taylor & Francis.

Chapter 8: Howard Caygill, 'Affirmation and Eternal Return in the Free-Spirit Trilogy', in Keith Ansell Pearson ed., *Nietzsche and Modern German Thought*, London: Routledge, 1991, pp. 216–39. Reprinted with permission of Taylor & Francis.

Chapter 9: Howard Caygill, 'Under the Epicurean Skies'. *Angelaki: Journal of the Theoretical Humanities* 11(3) (2006): 107–15. See https://www.tandfonline.com/ and https://doi.org/10.1080/09697250601078793. Reprinted with permission of Taylor & Francis.

Chapter 11: Howard Caygill, 'Drafts for a Metaphysics of the Gene', *Tekhnema* 3 'A Touch of Memory' (Spring 1996), pp. 141–52.

Chapter 12: Howard Caygill, 'Liturgies of Fear: Biotechnology and Culture', in Barbara Adam, Ulrich Beck and Joost Van Loon eds., *The Risk Society and Beyond: Critical Issues for Social Theory*, London: Sage Publications 2000, pp. 155–64. Reprinted with permission of SAGE Publishing.

Chapter 13: Howard Caygill, 'Life and Aesthetic Pleasure', in Andrea Rehberg and Rachel Jones eds., *The Matter of Critique: Readings in Kant's Philosophy*, Manchester: Clinamen, 2000, pp. 79–92.

Chapter 14: Howard Caygill, 'Soul and Cosmos in Kant: A Commentary on "Two Things Fill the Mind"', in Diane Morgan and Gary Banham (eds.) *Cosmopolitics and the Emergence of a Future*, Basingstoke: Palgrave Macmillan, 2007, pp. 213–34. Reprinted with permission of Springer Nature.

Chapter 15: Howard Caygill, 'Life and Energy', *Theory, Culture & Society* 24(6) (2007): 19–27. Reprinted with permission of SAGE Publishing.

Chapter 16: Howard Caygill, 'The Topology of Selection: The Limits of Deleuze's Biophilosophy', in Keith Ansell Pearson ed., *Deleuze and Philosophy: The Difference Engineer*, London: Routledge, 1997, pp. 149–62. Reprinted with permission of Taylor & Francis.

Chapter 17: Howard Caygill, 'The Force of Kant's *Opus postumum*'. *Angelaki: Journal of the Theoretical Humanities* 10(1) (2005): 33–42. See https://www.tandfonline.com/ and https://doi.org/10.1080/09697250500225123. Reprinted with permission of Taylor & Francis.

Chapter 18: Howard Caygill, 'Technology and the Propitiation of Chance', *Parallax* 13:4 (2007): 78–91. See https://www.tandfonline.com/ and https://doi.org/10.1080/13534640701682834. Reprinted with permission of Taylor & Francis.

Chapter 19: Howard Caygill, 'Bataille and the Neanderthal Extinction', in Will Stronge ed., *Georges Bataille and Contemporary Thought*, London: Bloomsbury Academic, an imprint of Bloomsbury Publishing Plc, 2017, pp. 239–63.

Chapter 21: Howard Caygill, 'Kafka's Exit: Exile, Exodus and Messianism', in Peter De Bolla and Stefan H. Uhlig eds., *Aesthetics and the Work of Art: Adorno, Kafka, Richter*, Basingstoke: Palgrave Macmillan, 2008, pp. 126–46. Reprinted with permission of Springer Nature.

Chapter 22: Howard Caygill, 'The Fate of the Pariah: Arendt and Kafka's "Nature Theatre of Oklahama"'. Copyright © 2010 West Chester University. This article was first published in *College Literature* 38.1 (2011): 1–14. Reprinted with permission by Johns Hopkins University Press.

Chapter 23: Howard Caygill, 'Benjamin's Natural Theology', in Colby Dickinson and Stéphane Symons eds., *Walter Benjamin and Theology*, New York: Fordham University Press, 2016, pp. 144–63. Reprinted with permission of Fordham University Press.

Chapter 24: Howard Caygill, 'Levinas's Silence', in Marinos Diamantides ed., *Levinas, Law, Politics*, Abingdon: Routledge-Cavendish, 2007, pp. 83–92. Reprinted with permission of Taylor & Francis.

Chapter 25: Howard Caygill, 'Tableaux for a Massacre: Shatila, Thursday–Sunday 16–19 September 1982', in Christopher Stewart and Esther Teichmann eds., *Staging Disorder*, London: Black Dog Publishing, 2015, pp. 29–33. Reprinted with permission of Black Dog Press.

Chapter 26: Howard Caygill, 'Philosophy and the Black Panthers', *Radical Philosophy* 179 (May/June 2013), pp. 7–13. Reprinted with permission of Radical Philosophy.

Chapter 28: Howard Caygill, 'The Spirit of Resistance and Its Fate' in Rebecca Comay and Bart Zantvoort eds., *Hegel and Resistance: History, Politics and Dialectics*, London: Bloomsbury Academic, an imprint of Bloomsbury Publishing Plc, 2018, pp. 81–99.

Chapter 31: Previously unpublished in English. Howard Caygill, 'Resisting Escalation: The Image of Villa Amalias' published in Greek in Maria Kakoyianni ed., *To Helleniko Symptoma, He Krisi, To Chreos, Ta Kinimata kai He Aristera*, Nissos, 2014.

Chapter 32: Howard Caygill, 'Strategic Intervention and the Digital Capacity to Resist', in Howard Caygill, Martina Leeker and Tobias Schulze eds., *Interventions in Digital Cultures: Technology, the Political, Methods*, Lüneburg: meson press, 2017, pp. 45–60. Licenced under CC BY-SA 4.0 https://creativecommons.org/licenses/by-sa/4.0/. Available at https://www.mediarep.org/handle/doc/3100.

Chapter 33: A previous version was published as 'Slow Violence and the Limits of Eco-Resistance' in *The Philosophical Journal of Conflict and Violence*, 3.1 (2019).

Chapters 1, 10, 20, 27, 29 and 30 are previously unpublished.

Introduction

Howard Caygill's philosophical practice

Cultural history, political theory, aesthetics, sociology, literary criticism? Howard Caygill's work over the past three decades defies categorization. He is best understood as a philosopher in the continental tradition, but, given that his is an original voice in the already wildly diverse field of modern European thought, this leaves everything still to be explained.

Caygill is known for the innovative and sophisticated readings of major thinkers in his books on Kant (*Art of Judgement* (1989)), Benjamin (*Walter Benjamin: The Colour of Experience* (1998)) and Levinas (*Levinas and the Political* (2001)). His *A Kant Dictionary* (1995) provides uniquely thoughtful and historicized glosses on Kant's terminology that have helped scores of readers navigate the works of this most canonical of philosophers. In 2013, Caygill reached a wider public through *On Resistance: A Philosophy of Defiance*, a timely exploration of the philosophical-political notion of resistance. His work on resistance will form a trilogy: the second instalment is *Kafka: In the Light of the Accident* (2017) and the third book, *Aesthetics of Madness*, will examine madness, art and psychiatry.

It is less well known that over the last thirty years, Caygill has written close to a hundred articles and book chapters on an astonishingly wide range of topics. These are not merely drafts that were later collected in his books. Caygill treats his books as self-sufficient works, writing each from scratch, and his essays form a separate body of work in their own right. A glance at the subjects treated in the essays shows that Caygill is a different breed of thinker to the blinkered hyper-specialist typically produced by modern universities. Topics on which he has written include Berlin's Potsdamer Platz, Italian-Egyptian poet Guiseppe Ungaretti, Shakespeare and nihilism, Husserl, theories of memory, the Ottoman Baroque, Karl Popper's ontology, Naples, the seventeenth-century Dutch painter Saenredam, graffiti, the historians

Fernand Braudel and Arnaldo Momigliano, Scholem and Taubes on Sabbatai Zevi, and many more.

The present collection brings together for the first time a selection of Caygill's most significant philosophical essays. It presents pieces originally published in a range of journals, edited collections, magazines and pamphlets, now often difficult to find, alongside new and previously unpublished texts. In order to showcase his work on philosophical themes, I have left out Caygill's essays on art, architecture and cities (including, in fact, all those on the topics listed above). Despite this limitation, the essays collected here have a range that is unique in contemporary philosophy. As well as engaging more deeply with themes in Kant, Benjamin, Levinas and Clausewitz, we see Caygill pursuing surprising and provocative interpretations of Hegel, Nietzsche, Darwin, Marx, Maxwell, Arendt, Fanon, Derrida, Deleuze, Rose and many others. The essays provide insight into the philosophical roots of Caygill's 'resistance' project, illuminating and supplementing the theoretical frameworks of *On Resistance* and *Kafka*. Moreover, each individual piece has intrinsic philosophical interest and testifies to Caygill's belief in the value of close, critical reading.

Although Caygill's work has an unparalleled scope, it does not fall prey to an arbitrary eclecticism: it is unified by a complex but coherent approach to interpreting the history of philosophy, ideas and culture. The present introduction aims to provide coordinates for understanding this methodology, which I will call Caygill's 'philosophical practice'. I sketch these coordinates in what follows under the headers of *the speculative*, *aporia*, *philosophizing*, *philology* and *history*.

It is apt to consider Caygill's philosophical method in the light of his essays, as he might be considered first and foremost an essayist. Even *On Resistance* can be read as a coordinated set of essays that identify the strengths and test the limitations of a series of practical and theoretical conceptions of resistance. Ever since it was inaugurated by Montaigne, the essay form has been characterized by its openness, its probing and assaying, and its preference for local, provisional explorations over grand, definitive claims. Adorno writes in his classic analysis that, in the essay form, 'thought's utopia of hitting the bull's eye unites with the consciousness of its own fallibility and provisional nature' (Adorno [1958] 1984, 164). This deliberate, thematized tension between thought's striving towards fixed conclusions and its inability to attain full satisfaction – a key Kantian idea to which Caygill often returns – is one reason that the essay is such a fitting vehicle for Caygill's philosophical practice.

The essay, in another apposite formulation proposed by Adorno, can be thought to occupy a space between the conceptual work of philosophy and the freedom of art. Neither attaining scientific results nor creating artistic forms, the 'effort of the essay reflects a childlike freedom that catches fire, without scruple, on what others have already done' (Adorno [1958] 1984, 152). Adorno's description fits the way that Caygill's essays arrange intellectual materials from the past as kindling on which something new can ignite. For Caygill, the necessity of thinking through the history of philosophy and culture nevertheless provides the freedom to bring to life new conceptual and political possibilities, by interpreting, 'without scruple', past philosophers and forms of thought. This is a qualified freedom, for, as we shall see, he is intensely conscious of the risk of unduly emphasizing freedom or possibility over Kant's other modal categories of actuality and necessity. Moreover, a comment by Gillian Rose indicates a further way in which the essay is an appropriate vehicle for Caygill's thought: 'the essay form … corresponds to the method of speculative engagement' (Rose 1993, xi). We can now turn to Rose's conception of speculative thought, as the first methodological coordinate for grasping Caygill's philosophical practice.

The speculative

Gillian Rose (1947–95) was Caygill's doctoral supervisor in the sociology department at the University of Sussex, with whom he wrote his thesis, 'Aesthetics and Civil Society: Theories of Art and Society 1640–1790', which developed into his first book, *Art of Judgement*. The two were close friends and philosophical interlocutors; Caygill became Rose's literary executor after her untimely death in 1995, and he edited and published the notebook jottings from the last weeks of her life and her unfinished work-in-progress *Paradiso* (Rose 1998, 1999). His moving memorial lecture for Rose at Sussex is published here for the first time (Chapter 1).

Rose was perhaps the most important British continental philosopher of the twentieth century. This does not mean that she was in any way an epigone of the French 'poststructuralist' thinkers whose ideas swept through Anglo-American humanities departments in the 1970s, 1980s and 1990s: she was a vociferous critic of her fashionable French contemporaries.[1] Her books are highly original contributions to post-Hegelian thought, tracing a line from Hegel through Marx, Kierkegaard and Nietzsche to a reconceived Judaic philosophy, all in service of a sophisticated examination of contemporary social and political reality. Rose sought a deliberately 'difficult' renewal of the Hegelian notion of the absolute, while dissolving any hope of dialectical resolution of the irredeemable contradiction (the 'aporia' that we will consider in the next section) that she identified therein. For Rose, politics *is* the attempt to think the absolute.[2] Such an attempt requires a distinction between dialectical and speculative thought, a distinction also significant to Caygill's early work.

Whereas Hegel's philosophy is usually primarily understood through the dialectic – an organic process in which conceptual contradictions are negated, preserved and raised up in higher forms – Rose stresses its speculative side. Hegel presented speculative thought as a higher mode of philosophy than dialectic: the latter is negative reason, which traces the movement of fixed determinations, but only speculative thought can be positive reason and a true philosophy of spirit.[3] Rose foregrounds Hegel's notion of a 'speculative proposition', in which the subject and predicate are at once non-identical and identical. The key Hegelian speculative proposition, for Rose, affirms the identity of religion and the state.[4] This proposition is misunderstood if read as containing a stable subject and predicate. Instead, both terms – in this case, 'religion' and 'the state' – are initially empty and problematic, and they must be filled out over the course of a philosophical development – here, Hegel's philosophy – through a series of changing relations between them. As Caygill puts it, 'The "is" of a speculative proposition ... does not mark a present identity, but rather the promise of a future meaning that will arise out of unforeseeable experiences' (Caygill 1998a, 23). The echo of the *specular* in the term 'speculation' is relevant: a speculative proposition *foresees the result* of a series of encounters between the subject and predicate, although the specific encounters are themselves unforeseeable.[5] This struggle between chance experiences and a speculatively affirmed rationality remains an undercurrent of Caygill's thought, up to and including his recent work on Kafka and the 'accident'.

The paradigmatic case of the speculative proposition for Rose, the identity of religion and the state, is not central to Caygill's work. Rather, he expands on Rose's broader point that, in his words, 'the task of philosophy is to rehearse the trauma of reason – to tarry with the negative and to work through its brokenness in an interminable analysis' (Chapter 1). Whereas Rose's analysis of the trauma of reason increasingly came to focus on the intersection of philosophy, politics and theology, Caygill arguably shifts the analysis to philosophy, politics and *history*. This historicized attention to the travails of modern reason will be discussed below.

Caygill develops Rose's notion of the speculative in further ways, which align with his increasingly sharp critique of Hegel in the mid-1990s. In 1994, he published three essays on 'Hegel and the Speculative Community': the second of these contrasts Hegel and Clausewitz (Chapter 4). With the notion of a speculative *community*, Caygill develops the idea that, unlike the dialectic, speculative thought assumes responsibility for its destructive moment. A speculative community thus recognizes and is accountable for the fact that its civic freedoms are inevitably qualified by violence: it is a community marked by the difficult but necessary awareness of its speculative identity with violence. According to Caygill, Hegel shrinks back from his early awareness of this mutual implication of violence and civility; in failing to theorize this in his philosophy of right, Hegel opens the space for Clausewitz's philosophy of pure violence. Although not yet foregrounding the notion of the capacity to resist in Clausewitz's concept of war, the 1994 text is a first iteration of ideas that appear in *On Resistance* thirty years later.

Caygill's 1998 book on Benjamin revolves around the notion of the speculative, arguing that Benjamin consistently seeks to present a 'non-Hegelian speculative experience'. Benjamin's concept of experience has a speculative character in its 'sensitivity to the indirect manifestations of the absolute in space and time' (Caygill 1998b, 120). Unlike Hegel, but echoing ideas of German Romanticism, Benjamin considers the absolute or infinite to be folded into the spatiotemporal totality of the present. The absolute manifests itself *indirectly* in that it can be discerned 'in those things that the present regards as insignificant, absurd and unwanted' (Caygill 1998b, 8). For Caygill, Benjamin's work is characterized by a tension between, on the one hand, properly conceiving of speculative experience as a methodological principle, guiding us to unearth the traces of the absolute in the 'neglected detail and the small nuance', and, on the other hand, succumbing to a dogmatic belief that this method might yield timeless truths or redemption (Caygill 1998b, 152). Only the former, regulative notion of speculative experience is, in Caygill's view, to be affirmed.

Caygill's transformation of the speculative thus takes a path that increasingly diverges from Rose's Hegelianism. For Caygill, speculative thought is oriented towards the immanent totality of experience and the absolute that indirectly and partially manifests itself in the overlooked debris of everyday culture. On a very abstract level, this orients Caygill's philosophical practice throughout his work and throughout the essays collected here. Among Rose's ideas to which Caygill nevertheless remains faithful, however, perhaps one is key: that our reading of philosophy and culture must attend to the broken, aporetic nature of speculative experience.

Aporia

Caygill has developed an aporetic approach to the history of philosophy that remains an underappreciated methodological innovation. Aporia is foregrounded by Rose in her 1992 book on Kierkegaard, but the aporetic approach developed in conversations between Rose, Caygill and the artist and mathematician Greg Bright around their respective projects in the 1980s and 1990s. For Rose, aporia is a consequence of reason's 'broken middle' that is buried between the irreconcilable oppositions of speculative thought. Caygill emphasizes this connection between speculative thought and aporia in an essay on Rose: he contends that she affirms 'Hegel's speculative experience as intrinsically damaged and aporetic' (Caygill 1998a, 23). Against dialectic, which even in its Adornian, negative form employs determinate oppositions and objects of knowledge, speculative thought wrestles with the challenging, irresolvable aporia of the simultaneous identity and non-identity of its objects.

In Rose's work, aporia is generally aligned with speculation, against the hasty solutions of dialectical thought. However, she also points to an aporetic *method*, writing in *Mourning Becomes the Law* (1996) that philosophical works can be read either deterministically or aporetically. According to a deterministic reading, they are 'fixed, closed conceptual structures, colonising being with the garrison of thought', but an aporetic reading is sensitive to 'the difficulty which the conceptuality represents by leaving gaps and silences in the mode of representation' (Rose 1996, 8). Rose's formulation nicely captures the way that Caygill transforms the theme of aporia into a fully fledged approach to reading the history of philosophy.

Art of Judgement, Caygill's first book, presents Kant's treatment of judgement as an example of an aporetic method. Faced by the difficulty of explicating the human faculty of judgement, Kant adopts a singular procedure according to which 'the outcome of unravelling the problem is not a clear solution – the revelation of a principle, as in the first *Critique* – but a statement or report of its difficulty' (Caygill 1989, 2). The aporetic approach thus seeks to sufficiently attest to the complexity of a problem rather than feign to solve it. Caygill has cited books by Harry Wolfson (*The Philosophy of Spinoza: Unfolding the Latent Processes of His Reasoning* (1934)) and Edward Booth (*Aristotelian Aporetic Ontology in Islamic and Christian Thinkers* (1983)) as important sources for an aporetic history of philosophy. This approach does not seek syntheses and neat solutions in past thinkers but scrutinizes the historical emergence of philosophical problems and questions, which remain open-ended and unresolved.

Caygill thus focuses on the historical *genesis* of concepts, arguments and fields of inquiry. He carefully attends to the intellectual and social context of philosophical works in order to unsettle the standard narratives about the problems and solutions at stake. This entails a particular affinity for unfinished philosophical projects: Kant's *Opus postumum* (see Chapter 17), Nietzsche's *Zarathustra* and his 'ghostly, unwritten magnum opus on philosophy and culture' (Chapters 2 and 7), Marx's *Capital* (Chapter 2) and Benjamin's *Arcades Project*. From the perspective of the aporetic approach, such unfinished works are valuable in that they may be *unfinishable*: they reveal a difficulty without jumping to a hasty, facile solution.

As Benjamin writes of Baudelaire, we must be aware of the 'historical scars' that the history of interpretations has inflicted on past thinkers. Caygill identifies these scars in the reception of Benjamin's own work: in 'bringing out a particular feature or phase of Benjamin's authorship and discreetly tucking away the others', this reception has led to an 'inevitable levelling of Benjamin's work, and the reduction of its constituent paradoxes into stages of a developmental narrative or *Bildungsroman*' (Caygill 1998b, xi). Caygill seeks to replace comfortable teleological narratives about progress or decline within or between bodies of thought with the more complicated reality of partial achievements, chance occurrences and unforeseen consequences. The 'constituent paradoxes' of a philosopher's work can be seen in its aporetic quality, the philosophical problems that it opens without resolving. This leads the aporetic historian to focus on the indecipherable parts of an oeuvre. As Caygill notes of Benjamin, 'These difficult, opaque and often unreadable texts are crucial to any interpretation of Benjamin's thought' (Caygill 1998b, 1). The necessity of reading the unreadable might be said to reveal the 'constituent paradox' of Caygill's own philosophical practice. The key moments in a philosopher's *oeuvre* are precisely those that must be read because of their unreadability, their resistance to being fixed and categorized.

Philosophizing

If philosophy can be productively seen as aporetic, as a series of attempts to adequately state problems in their complexity rather than provide final answers, then our focus shifts from the stately monuments that are philosophical *works* and *philosophies* onto the ongoing and messy process of *philosophizing*. Caygill foregrounds the process of philosophizing throughout his work, and particularly in the introductions and entries in *A Kant Dictionary*. The latter book, as Caygill acknowledges, is 'by no means only a dictionary' (Caygill 1999, 8). It is more a study of Kant's conceptual inventiveness understood as a point of sophisticated interplay between tradition and modernity, a case study of the developmental and contextual nature of philosophical terminology, packaged, for strategic purposes, in the form of a dictionary.

Caygill elucidates his account of Kant's conceptual creativity through the latter's own easily overlooked distinction between axioms and acroamata. For Kant, philosophical concepts are not axiomatic but acroamatic, which means they are 'the discursive outcome of an open-ended process of reflection upon philosophical problems. Unlike geometrical axioms, philosophical concepts are for Kant less the indisputable products of definition than the equivocal outcomes of a process of indirect presentation resting ultimately on analogy' (Caygill 1995, 2). Philosophical concepts are therefore not fixed in advance and directly intuitable but are rather the equivocal – so to some extent aporetic – results of a *discursive* process in which they are legitimated through language and always open to further discursive challenge (Caygill 1995, 46–7). This linguistic field in which philosophical concepts are developed and contested in an open-ended process is the space of philosophizing.

The distinction between philosophy and philosophizing is one made by Kant himself, who claims that one cannot learn philosophy, only to philosophize.[6] Against the grain of 250 years of Kant scholarship, Caygill insists that Kant was more interested in the process of philosophizing than in its end result, an ossified philosophy. He points out that Kant took a surprisingly casual attitude to his published works and, for example, often delegated to his students the correction of the proofs of his books. An emphasis on this feature of Kant's work distinguishes Caygill's dictionary from Rudolf Eisler's 1930 *Kant Lexicon*, as he notes: 'Instead of presenting a concept as a fixed, axiomatic element of Kant's *philosophy* in the manner of Eisler, the entries stress the problematic, exploratory character of his *philosophizing*'. Caygill thus offers a highly unfamiliar picture of Kant that foregrounds 'the studied equivocations and sensitivity to aporia which characterize his philosophizing' (Caygill 1995, 3).

Consistent with his stress on philosophizing over the philosophical works that offer mere snapshots of this process at a standstill, Caygill has a strong antipathy towards schools and -isms, which fossilize fertile and open explorations into dogmas, whether Kantian, Hegelian, Marxist or Nietzschean. Such followers fail to heed Nietzsche's call to think beyond good and evil or, otherwise put, fail to adhere to Kant's model of critique, which neither damns nor endorses, but tests the proper limits and identifies the conditions of legitimacy of its object. Caygill therefore approves of readings of Marx and Nietzsche that overcome the opposition imposed by Marxists and Nietzscheans (Chapter 2) and affirms what he sees as Rose's overcoming of the opposition between left and right Hegelians (Caygill 1998a, 22).

Caygill's emphasis on philosophizing over philosophy has various further consequences. One is the dissolution of disciplinary boundaries that, for historically contingent reasons, have separated philosophy from art and the various sciences; this will be discussed below. Another is the affirmation of an interpretative practice that seeks to keep works as *open* as possible. In the book on Benjamin, Caygill outlines this practice in terms of Benjamin's conception of immanent critique, which does not apply external standards of judgement but finds its criteria within its object:

> Immanent critique, sensitive to the incompleteness of a work and the negotiability of its formal limits, was dedicated to revealing the unrealized futures inherent in the work. Such critique did not apply criteria of judgement, but sought strategically to maximise the possible futures of a work. It did so by showing the restrictions of existing interpretations – the ways in which they foreclosed on the work's possible futures – and by attempting to keep open these futures for critical invention. (Caygill 1998b, 79)

Interpretation, on the model that Caygill develops in tandem with Benjamin's thought, philosophizes by keeping open the possibilities latent in works and the resources they offer for reimagining the culture from which they emerged and in which we read them. This attempt to activate 'unrealized futures' proceeds immanently within the history of thought, through a practice of *reading*, to which we can now turn.

Philology

Nietzsche, whose work is a constant touchstone for Caygill, trained as a classical philologist. Although he left his professorship in philology at Basel due to ill health to become the nomadic freethinker of philosophical myth, Nietzsche recognized that his philological training continued to shape his thought:

> It is not for nothing that I have been a philologist, perhaps I am a philologist still, that is to say, a teacher of slow reading. ... – this art does not so easily get anything done, it teaches to read well, that is to say, to read slowly, deeply, looking cautiously before and aft, with reservations, with doors left open, with delicate eyes and fingers ... My patient friends, this book desires for itself only perfect readers and philologists: Learn to read me well! (*D* 5)

Nietzsche demanded that his readers read him as well as a philologist would: carefully, sceptically, attuned to delicate nuances of tone and irony, and 'with doors left open': aware of the infinite perspectives that can be brought to bear on any text. He remained a philologist, a teacher of close reading, because philologists 'are the destroyers of every faith that rests on books' (*GS* §358). Careful, critical attention to texts is anathema to any kind of faith, including the faith inherent in lazy philosophical dogmatism.

Nietzsche's call for philological readers informs Caygill's philosophical practice as much as does the German thinker's specific ideas. Caygill adopts the philologist's approach, not only in his careful readings but also by scrutinizing the provenance, editions and textual variations of texts to a degree unusual in modern European philosophy. This includes attention to manuscripts, as in the reading of the two versions of Kafka's story 'Description of a Struggle' in *Kafka*. Through a painstaking comparison of the variations between the manuscript versions, Caygill identifies two different responses to the Nietzschean predicament of living after the death of God: a nihilistic collapse into *ressentiment* grounded on a latent Platonic nostalgia, and a Nietzschean affirmation of the unrealizable desire for eternity (Caygill 2017, 23–45). The reading is moreover part of Caygill's broader aim to undermine the prevailing critical view that 'The Judgement', with its 'claustrophobic father–son conflict', is Kafka's first important story and an interpretative key to his writings (Caygill 2017, 47, 10–11). Such philological claims identify a process of philosophizing *between* manuscript versions, which opens an 'unrealized future' of Kafka's work, beyond the themes of law, domination and punishment.

Alongside this attention to manuscript variations, Caygill reveals the philosophical significance of publication history: for example, the sequence in which Kafka wrote his novels. In influential essays, Arendt and Benjamin take the order in which Brod published the novels to be their order of composition, and as a result they erroneously read a redemption narrative and even a 'happy ending' into Kafka's trilogy (Chapter 22). Such philological care leads Caygill to identify overlooked breaks in philosophers' oeuvres – such as that between Nietzsche's 'yes-saying' and 'no-saying' works (Chapter 8) – as well as continuities – for example, between Kant's well-known critical philosophy and his relatively ignored late drafts (Chapter 17). In each case, attention to the textual and historical conditions of philosophical production allows Caygill to expose new interpretative possibilities that creatively resist the standard accounts of the thinkers and ideas he treats.

History

In an inaugural lecture given in 1999 to mark his appointment as Professor of Cultural History at Goldsmiths College, Caygill stated,

> In my work I have tried to intensify the critical history of philosophy through the methodology and disciplines of cultural history, with the hope that a more thoroughgoing use of historical evidence and materials will intensify the critique of philosophy. (Caygill 1999, 2)

Caygill here aligns his project with the young Marx's critique of philosophy, where the demonstration that philosophy is one more element of culture, ultimately underpinned by economic relations, goes hand in hand with the self-formation and self-overcoming of the proletariat class. Caygill acknowledges the contribution that what he calls the 'critical histories' of philosophy presented by Heidegger, Deleuze, Derrida, Irigaray and Levinas make to this project of situating philosophy within broader culture and undermining its universal claims. He contends, however, that these critical histories rely on an insufficiently rigorous or detailed conception of history, which is a failing also evident in Rose's work (Caygill 1999, 2, 5). Caygill thus diverges from both Rose and post-war French thinkers in the care with which he historicizes philosophy, emphasizing its relations with non-philosophical discourses, scouring archive material and employing the philological resources noted above.

While broadly instructive, the claim in the inaugural lecture is a little hasty, no doubt a result of the momentary strategic need to stake out a position between the fields of cultural history and history of philosophy. In fact, Caygill's project is far from an orthodox Marxist critique of self-sufficient philosophy. It rather redefines philosophy as a practice of careful, historicized reading of cultural texts to enable an infinite philosophizing that unsettles ossified categories and opens up new, unforeseen possibilities that are not transcendent but remain strictly immanent to culture as a speculative totality.

Caygill's foregrounding of history, understood in a broad cultural sense, nevertheless undermines philosophy's traditional claim to provide an autonomous, 'master' discourse. This results in a blurring or dissolution of the disciplinary boundaries marking off philosophy from other elements of culture. Again, this aspect of Caygill's method emerges within his reading of Benjamin. The latter's recasting of Kant's concept of experience enables him to recognize that 'philosophizing need no longer be confined to "philosophy"' and 'could move beyond classical philosophical problems and texts into the critical reflection upon literature, art, and culture in the broadest sense' (Caygill 1998b, 23). Such boundary-breaking is most evident in the essays in section four, below, which stage confrontations between figures generally considered philosophers – Deleuze, Kant and Warburg – and figures considered scientists – Darwin, Newton and Maxwell. In these cases, the 'scientists' are often more philosophical than the philosophers (see particularly Chapters 16, 18 and 19), according to Caygill's conception of philosophy as philosophizing: that is, they refuse easy answers and fearlessly face new and disconcerting ideas.

Caygill has consistently refused to respect the distinction between philosophy and literature, as is most evident in his work on Kafka (Chapters 21 and 22) and his long-running interest in Shakespeare. This results in no straightforward encounter, however: the Kafka book revolves around the collision between fiction, philosophy and, remarkably, insurance-writing; the book's most extended 'reading' examines Kafka's photographs and descriptions of quarries, produced in his day job at the Prague Workers Accident Insurance Institute (Caygill 2017, 6, 101–21). Further heady disciplinary admixture is evident in an essay that brings together a Papal encyclical letter, a report from the British Medical Association and the work of the performance artist Stelarc (Chapter 12).

Moreover, Caygill's work remains broadly within the wake of Marx's critique of philosophy in its consistent orientation towards a political horizon. The opening of *Levinas and the Political* illustrates Caygill's conception of genuine political engagement. Levinas's work is approvingly depicted as possessing a 'chilling ... unsentimental understanding of violence and power almost worthy of Machiavelli', 'ruthless political clarity' and 'an intensity and a bleakness unrivalled in philosophical writing' (Caygill 2002, 1). This runs counter to the view, dominant in the prevailing 'sentimental commentary', of Levinas as an irreproachable but unthreatening ethicist of alterity. This misconception, Caygill contends, is encouraged by the troubled place of politics in Levinas's thought.

Throughout his work, Caygill approves of thinkers whose philosophical confrontations with politics are unflinching, implacable and honest. He consistently criticizes sentimentality as a duplicitous, self-comforting failure to face up to bleak realities. The contrast between a merciless honesty and the failure to broach cold political truths is most evident in Chapters 24 and 25 below, which sharply juxtapose Genet's response and Levinas's non-response to the violent acts of the contemporary State of Israel. Caygill's view of the appropriate philosophical approach to political reality recalls his reference to the 'pre-modern doctrine of the virtues' when characterizing resistance as the demand for *justice* pursued with *fortitude* and *prudence* (Caygill 2013, 97).

This call for unsentimental and courageous witness to political reality has its philosophical basis in a reading of Kant's table of categories. Kant identifies three modal categories, which are forms through which we as subjects relate to objects or to experience: possibility, actuality and necessity. Caygill's reading of Clausewitz as an innovative post-Kantian philosopher turns on his proposal that, whereas the German idealists emphasized the modal category of possibility and therefore freedom – a bias whose philosophical consequences extend into our present – Clausewitz offers an alternative line of thinking grounded in the category of actuality (Caygill 2013, 17–18, 97–8; see also Chapter 29). This trajectory is not concerned with desirable possibilities to be realized by ideally free subjects, but with the difficult strategic decisions of subjects compromised by their actual circumstances.

Alongside actuality, Caygill also foregrounds the third modal category, necessity, and its correlate, contingency. Faced by a bleak political reality, we might dream of possibilities or alternatively consider ourselves in a situation governed by necessity, where we *must* act, and by contingency, in which chance occurrences can be co-opted by either warring party. Caygill thus affirms Clausewitz's non-Hegelian conception of history: accidents cannot be retroactively understood as moments of a rational historical sequence, but rather 'history is understood as the realm of chance and accident that resists easy subordination to rational sequences or progressions' (Caygill 2013, 18). This clarifies the place of the Kafka book, no straightforward work of literary criticism, in Caygill's project. Caygill conceives of his three resistance books – *On Resistance*, *Kafka* and the forthcoming study of madness, art and psychiatry – as a 'perverted critical philosophy', that is, analogous to Kant's three critiques. *On Resistance* takes the place of Kant's practical philosophy, the *Critique of Practical Reason*; the forthcoming book on aesthetics and madness that of the

Critique of Judgement. This means that, counter-intuitively, *Kafka* is Caygill's *Critique of Pure Reason*.

How might this be understood? The clue is that *Kafka* presents an 'ontology of the accident' (Caygill 2017, 1). The *Critique of Pure Reason* proposes that the proper replacement for ontology is Kant's critically renewed metaphysics, in the form of an analytic of the understanding; analogously, Caygill's *Kafka* offers a new ontology. But far from delineating the categories and forms of intuition necessary for stable, law-governed experience, the ontology in *Kafka* contends that our historical actuality is the result of a play of accident and necessity. For example, a landslide, the focus of much of Kafka's insurance work, is at once necessary on the level of the population (because we know statistically that landslides will affect a certain proportion of quarry workers) yet, for individuals, contingent (an unforeseen and unforeseeable accident). When an accident randomly befalls unfortunate victims, the struggle begins to identify a necessity governing the chance event: the insurers, managers and quarry workers battle to secure a particular story of the series that ineluctably determined the event, whether the bad practice of the workers or the negligence of the managers.

Caygill extends this ontology of the accident to a general account of political reality. The bureaucrats in the Castle of Kafka's novel are incapable of taking decisions: instead, pressure to resolve a case builds up until it explodes and the bureaucratic apparatus randomly arrives at a resolution. After this happens, and as the decision rolls around like a thunderclap, the bureaucrats must find a way 'to make what happens appear necessary' (Caygill 2017, 180). There is therefore no transcendent law. There are only chance events, but the bureaucracy is set up to retroactively appropriate these *as* its decisions and to strategically use them for its ends. This explains the embattled nature of resistance movements against institutions formed to capture accident by necessity.

The ontology of *Kafka* thus urges us not to shrink back from this bleak actuality. Although Kafka is a writer with the singular fortitude to recognize that the Nietzschean death of God and the collapse of the values of good and evil could lead to a world of pure evil (Caygill 2017, 188), there is nevertheless light at the end of the tunnel. Caygill's reading of *Before the Law* at the close of *Kafka* clarifies his suggestion in *On Resistance* that this classic short story should be read as a parable of resistance (see also Chapter 21). In *Kafka*, Caygill emphasizes that it is only the man from the country who mentions the law; the gatekeeper 'seems oblivious to its existence' (Caygill 2017, 205). The law is therefore merely a story that the man from the country tells himself in order to avoid the awful alternative conclusion: that his being there is a mere accident. The only truth of the law is that 'it had to happen to someone and this time it just happened to be him' (Caygill 2017, 206). This radical affirmation of contingency bears a further Kantian echo in that it entails that law is not 'out there', in the things themselves, but is prescribed by subjects to their experience. In contrast to Kant's universal and necessary subjective law, however, Caygill stresses the individual and contingent character of what we take to be political necessity: as affirmed in *On Resistance*, we err if we succumb to being individualized and to pursuing the law rather than properly seeking our fellow resistants (Caygill 2013, 211). This may be the ultimate political horizon of Caygill's philosophical practice: a call to indefatigably engage in implacable resistant readings of the texts of contemporary culture to reopen the contingent accidents that have been retroactively ossified as necessary, guided by the speculative principle that defiant philosophizing can realize philosophies of defiance.

Overview: Force and understanding

The essays collected here are arranged thematically. I have avoided ordering them chronologically, as this would impose a sense of teleological development that is anathema to Caygill's own conception of the history of philosophy, which as we have seen is characterized by discontinuities, unfinished projects and unintended consequences. Likewise, an arrangement by thinker would obscure the unified nature of Caygill's thought, which follows threads through diverse thinkers and across disciplinary boundaries in service of a coherent political-philosophical project. My thematic arrangement should be taken only as a suggestion, and the reader is encouraged to draw their own criss-crossing connections between the essays and with Caygill's books.[7]

The collection is divided into two: part one, 'Conditions', provides an overview of the philosophical conditions of possibility for Caygill's work on resistance. It reveals the complex intellectual backdrop to the 'resistance trilogy' of books.[8] Part two, 'Resistance', collects key examples of Caygill's ongoing work on resistance, supplementing *On Resistance* and *Kafka* with extended and updated reflections on the theory and futures of defiance.

Section one, 'Starting points', presents early pieces determinative for the development of Caygill's thought. These statements of intent introduce the importance of Rose's thought, the productive affinity between Nietzsche and Marx, and philosophy's implication in the violence underpinning civility. A first examination of Clausewitz shows Caygill's increasing distance from Hegelianism, and the political stakes of this early work appear in a reflection on NATO's intervention in Kosovo. Section two, 'Affirmation', presents a series of Caygill's writings on Nietzsche and Nietzschean themes. Although Caygill has not devoted a book to Nietzsche, the latter may be the strongest single influence on his work. Faithful to its subject, Caygill's work on Nietzsche reaches no simple conclusion but opens productive aporia, through Nietzsche's ambivalent relation to Epicurus and, in Chapter 6, a powerful response to Rose's illness, in a reflection on the possibilities of philosophical consolation and the pre-emptive mourning of 'what will be lost'.

Section three turns from Nietzschean affirmation to the ecstatic supplement that resists philosophical capture: the notion of life. This is explored through the metaphysics of genetics, responses to biotechnology, the awkward place of 'life' in Kant's critical philosophy and the physiological concept of energy. Section four continues in this vein, presenting pieces that undermine the distinction between philosophy and its scientific others: as noted above, the 'scientists' often turn out to be more philosophical than the 'philosophers'. Section five collects essays in which Caygill rejects appeals to a transcendent realm in favour of a determined insistence on immanence. Two essays on Kafka's uncompromising vision of modernity are followed by a cosmological reading of Benjamin, in which Caygill continues to counter the transcendent messianism foregrounded by many interpreters, and Levinas's ambivalent attempt to distance himself from violence committed by the State of Israel is put into stark relief by being paired with Genet's unblinking witness to the Shatila massacre.

Part two collects key pieces on the theme of resistance, four previously unpublished and one, a text- and photo-essay on the anarchist squat Villa Amalias in Athens, only published in Greek. Figures key to *On Resistance*, such as Clausewitz, Hegel, the Black Panthers and Fanon, are treated at length, and Caygill's ongoing engagement with our present is showcased in inquiries into the indebted subject, digital resistance and ecological activism. The final essay remarkably explores the limits of the discourse of resistance 'at the end of the world' in contemporary ecological struggles, reminding us of the Nietzschean roots of Caygill's notion of resistance: resistance is, properly understood, beyond good and evil, demanding our constant attention to its changing connotations and strategic valencies.

This collection presents Caygill's theorization of resistance and the philosophical conditions out of which it emerged. This is captured in the title, *Force and Understanding*, which Caygill himself proposed. It is drawn from a chapter of Hegel's *Phenomenology of Spirit* that is particularly resistant to analysis. Between the more straightforward dialectics of 'sense-certainty' and 'perception' and the famous 'master-slave dialectic', Hegel's 'Force and Understanding' chapter has received little attention in comparison with the chapters that bookend it. However, it contains a vital transition from consciousness to self-consciousness, via a dialectical movement between force and law, in which the Kantian distinction between appearances and the supersensible emerges, only for the opposition to parodically collapse in the 'inverted world'. Caygill makes use of Hegel's dialectic of solicited and soliciting force at the opening of *On Resistance* to set out the complex situation of opposed forces in the Parisian riot that Sartre failed to adequately describe (Caygill 2013, 1–5; see also Chapter 28). But other themes yet more significant to Caygill's work are foreshadowed in Hegel's attention to the given, necessary but unpredictable forces that the understanding tries but ultimately fails to codify through laws, and to the collision between different modes of knowledge, here mathematical physics and transcendental philosophy. Hegel's bewildering, often overlooked and yet centrally important chapter thus anticipates key aspects of Caygill's philosophical practice, which can be read as a sustained interrogation of the unresolvable dialectic between force – political, aesthetic, physical, vital – and philosophical understanding.

Notes

1   Indeed, Caygill has criticized Rose's harsh treatment of thinkers like Deleuze and Derrida, which primarily appears in her *Dialectic of Nihilism* (1984): see Caygill 1998a, 24. A sympathetic but critical dialogue with modern French philosophy runs through Caygill's work: see Chapters 8, 10, 16, 19 and 24, below.

2   Rose [1981] 2009, 45, 98, 218. See Caygill 1996, 56.

3   See Hegel's letter to Niethammer, November 1812, discussed in Rose 1993, 53–63, and Caygill 1994, 6.

4   In Hegel's *Philosophy of Religion*, quoted in Rose [1981] 2009, 51.

5   For examples of Caygill's work on the theme of visibility, see the role of chromatic differentiation in his reading of Benjamin in *The Colour of Experience*, his essay 'Agitation and the Visible' (2005) and the closing meditation on the light of defiance in *Kafka*.

6   *CPR* A837/B865; Kant 1902–, 9:25 (*Jäsche Logik*).

7   Alternative thematic readings might follow the theme of 'chance', mentioned above, through Chapters 6, 9, 11, 16, 18 and the Kafka book's 'ontology of the accident'; or the theme of the 'cosmic' through Chapters 9, 14, 18, 23, and the closing reflection on the light of Nietzsche's dancing star in *Kafka*.

8   Based on this groundwork, Caygill quickly wrote *On Resistance* after teaching a seminar on the topic at Université Paris 8. By contrast, he had been working on *Kafka*, the second volume of the trilogy, for fifteen years by the time it was published.

PART ONE

Conditions

Section one: Starting points

1

Gillian Rose 1947–1995: Art, justice and metaphysics

It is both an honour and a heavy responsibility to give the first memorial lecture for Gillian Rose, especially here, at the University of Sussex, where she spent much of her working life in the School of European Studies as Lecturer and Reader in Sociology. There is something uncanny in speaking of her as past in a place that for me remains haunted with her presence. Arriving at Falmer Station today felt little different from late winter (or was it early spring?) eight years ago, when I came to listen to the series of carefully crafted lectures that later became the book *Judaism and Modernity*. Those lectures exemplified Rose's generosity and lack of pretentiousness: she would speak for an hour and then retire to the 'European Common Room' to argue with a motley following of students, colleagues and friends from the town, many of whom – like Gillian – are now dead.

Not only Gillian Rose has died but also the unique intellectual circumstances of the University of Sussex of the 1970s and 1980s that sustained the development of her thought. The writings she left from her Sussex period – *The Melancholy Science* (1976), *Hegel Contra Sociology* (1981) and *Dialectic of Nihilism* (1984) – are memorials to that unique institution and cultural moment. And in a sense, Rose's move to Warwick University was her acknowledgement that the form of life in which she had lived and worked had passed; her later books *The Broken Middle* (1992), *Judaism and Modernity* (1993) and of course *Love's Work* (1995) were the retrospective flights of her beloved Owl of Minerva reflecting on a world tormented by the shades of Hitler and Stalin – one which seemed, after 1989, to have passed. None of these books would have been possible without the paradoxically liberal climate of political, cultural and, more inconspicuously, religious severity that characterized the institution in those years.

The Sussex University of the late 1970s was not only the last redoubt of student radicalism – with anarchist student occupations shadowing the rise of Thatcher – but was also home to a generation of scholars marked by the direct experience of Nazism, the Second World War and the Stalinist fate of Marxism. The pipe-smoking Professor of Sociology Tom Bottomore, who appointed Gillian, served in Vienna after the war as a member of the Allied Control Council. He brought back with him a passion for German-language social theory and a commitment to Austro-Marxism as a radical democratic socialist alternative to both Stalinism and Social Democracy. Also in the Sociology Department were Gillian's friends, the melancholy Romanian exile and theorist of totalitarianism Zev Barbu and Julius Carlebach, the criminologist and scholar of modern Judaism who left Germany as child in the 1930s. Other exiled scholars who provided a human link with the traditions of European thought were the Czech Kafka scholar Eduard Goldstücker and the student of the Hungarian Marxist Georg Lukács, István Mészáros. The presence of these and others – Norman Cohn, Marie Jahoda – gave the ideas with which Gillian was working a sense of urgency and risk: they were not just academic exercises.

For Rose, the human individual embodiment of the radical, intellectual response to the violent events of the twentieth century extended beyond the professoriat. She found it in her friend Yvette Stone who worked here as a secretary – a woman of the first generation of native modern Hebrew speakers who preferred French and was engaged in an endless re-reading of Proust. Gillian's account of Yvette in *Love's Work* is paradoxically both perceptive and extremely unjust. She also found this direct experience in her friends and students – refugees from Chile, Sri Lanka, South Africa and Northern Ireland. The intellectual responses to this violent century were for Gillian part of the climate in which she lived and worked. Even her next-door neighbours in Richmond Road, Brighton, the modest street near Sainsbury's where she lived for most of her time at Sussex – who had no idea what she did when she went to work and were puzzled by why she spent so much time reading books out in the garden – confided in her and spoke at length about their experience of the Blitz and the class struggle between squaddies and officers during the Battle of El Alamein.

What exactly was it that she did at work – what was the point of Gillian Rose's reading and thinking? I don't think she would object to it being described as an exploration of what it means today to be an Hegelian. Her finest book for many of her readers – *Hegel contra Sociology* – more than any other questions the scission in the Hegelian heritage between 'left' and 'right' Hegelianism. This was the division already evident on Hegel's death in

1831 between the Godless, political development of speculative thought that emerged in the form of Marxism and the theological, ethical version which fed into the late nineteenth-century British idealist tradition (and remains a skeleton in the cupboard of Oxford philosophy). One of Rose's most perceptive early critics, the Hungarian political theorist I. M. Birki, recognized that her book rendered obsolete the artificial separation of political and theological aspects of Hegel's thought and that this in its turn put on the agenda a radical reassessment of the post-Hegelian tradition of European philosophy and political thought. Gillian herself was clear about the significance of the book and, in her preface to the 1995 reprint, brings together Hegel and those alleged anti-Hegelians – Kierkegaard and Nietzsche – into a shared intellectual and political adventure:

> By reassessing the relation between the early and the mature works of Hegel, the experience of negativity, the existential drama, is discovered at the heart of Hegelian rationalism. My subsequent reassessments of Nietzsche and Kierkegaard, which challenges the tradition of regarding them as radically nihilistic or existential alternatives to Hegel, draw on this exposition of Hegel … the dilemma of addressing modern ethics and politics without arrogating the authority under question is seen as the ineluctable difficulty in Hegel, Nietzsche and Kierkegaard's engagement with modernity. (Rose 2009)

This holds also for *Love's Work*, which addresses the same dilemma of setting an existential drama – the experience of imminent death – within 'objective spirit' or social and political institutions. By what authority did she do this; by what authority did she justify her often tough judgements of her life and those who shared it? But even in this last book the question still remains of why turn to Hegel, why continue to be an Hegelian after almost two centuries of Hegelian thought?

The question brings us to the themes of 'art, justice and metaphysics'. What is it that gathers together these three terms, what is it that they share, and why does it seem so natural to unite them in a single phrase? One of the answers is historical: the trinity of art and beauty, justice and the good, and metaphysics and the true refer to three of the four 'transcendentals' of medieval philosophy. The transcendentals denote the extra-categorial attributes of beings – unity, truth, goodness, beauty (adding, in some classifications, thing and something) that are prior to any act of perception: they provide the horizon for meaningful human action or categorial judgement, whether intellectual, moral or political, or aesthetic. In the tradition the 'transcendentals' were thought to constitute a system, to be 'convertible': the one was true, good and beautiful; the good was beautiful, true and one …

The structure of medieval transcendental philosophy persisted into the modern period in the architecture of Kant's transcendental philosophy presented in the three critiques: *The Critique of Pure Reason* (1781) was Kant's critique of metaphysics and 'truth'; *The Critique of Practical Reason* (1788) Kant's critique of the 'good', and *The Critique of Judgement* (1790), Kant's critique of the beautiful. What is striking in Kant – whom Gillian always referred to in Moses Mendelssohn's words as 'the great destroyer' – is that, in the modern, critical age, the true, the good and the beautiful are no longer convertible. The unity of reason is something that has to be justified; we can no longer comfortably move from the true to the good, or in modern terms, from is to ought. What is in question in all three critiques is precisely the fourth transcendental of unity. Kant can no longer repose in unity but has to pursue it – in the transcendental unity of apperception of epistemology, in the unity as universal of morality and in the unity in plurality of the *sensus communis* that judges the beautiful.

Gillian Rose believed that Kant's work of creative destruction was constitutive of our modernity and left us the task of rethinking the transcendentals, especially unity. The range of possible and actual responses to the fractures identified by Kant defines for Rose the parameters of modern thought and largely consisted in trying to relocate the transcendental unity. We can seek it in truth, developing a philosophy in which 'the real is rational' and in which the claim to truth will inform our moral, political and aesthetic choices. The problem with this position is that it can become ideological and dogmatic – the truth may be that of religion, of atheism, of a political ideology. We are in danger of converting the good and beautiful into an ideology – committing terrible deeds in the name of partial truths and producing terrible works of art in the name of the unity of the nation or of the international unity of the proletariat in socialist realism.

Alternatively, we can convert the one, the true and the beautiful into the good, saying that what we do and how we act are fundamental. This for Gillian was represented by the alternative of pragmatism; it can even combine with the claims for the truth in social theory such as sociology which grounds our knowledge and affects in the scientific truth of the social determination. This is the burden of the argument of the difficult first chapter of *Hegel Contra Sociology*. A third position with respect to the fractured transcendentals would be to unite them under the sign of the beautiful, an operation carried out as early as Schiller's influential *Letters on the Aesthetic Education of Mankind*. Here it is the experience of beauty that opens the possibility of unifying the true and the good, but it runs the risk of aestheticizing both truth and politics, making truth a matter of sentimental affect and the good a matter of looking rather than being good.

Gillian Rose began and ended her reading and teaching of modern European thought with the fractures of transcendental philosophy. She insisted on staying with the fractures, with the brokenness. She placed herself in a tradition begun by another of Kant's contemporaries – Heinrich von Kleist – who drew the ultimate consequences of the critical philosophy: the modern age is one of fracture and loss of transcendental horizon and has to be shown to be such. Gillian counted Kleist's *Marionettentheater* and *Michael Kohlhaas* among her favourite texts which she constantly returned to – the one exploring the destructive effects of consciousness on grace and beauty, the other the destructive effects of the single-minded pursuit of justice. Kleist developed a form of writing which showed that the unity of reason was shattered and that now reason itself was the site of a personal, existential drama; in the words of *Judaism and Modernity*, there is a 'trauma within reason itself'.

Kleist's combination of 'existential *eros*' and 'philosophical *logos*' provided a model of authorship which Gillian adopted and pursued further. It provided an analytic of despair, a response to the brokenness of the 'unity of reason' that did not seek to restore a transcendental unity to it – whether through ideology, through action or through art. Instead, the task of philosophy is limited to rehearsing the traumas of reason – to 'tarry with the negative' and to work through its brokenness in an interminable analysis. She found the model for this authorship in Hegel's *Phenomenology of Spirit*, a work which ends – in the spirit of Kleist – on Golgotha, one of the most equivocal, broken moments of the Christian tradition. She did not find in Hegel the unification of reason on the basis of speculative thought – the alleged 'real is rational' of the *Philosophy of Right* – but interpreted this phrase in conformity with Hegel's own gloss in his lectures that the 'real is often broken and bad' – extending perhaps the brokenness and badness to reason itself. So Gillian's Hegel was less the triumphant unification of the good and the beautiful under the rational unity of philosophy's absolute than a staging of the traumatization of philosophy by the attempt to think the absolute.

This reading of Hegel brings him very close to Kierkegaard and Nietzsche, whose authorships are also dedicated to working through the trauma of a broken reason. Kierkegaard's 'teleological suspension of the ethical' in the demand of faith marks a limit to philosophy, an inconvertible moment which traumatizes the unity of reason and seems to evacuate the good and the beautiful of any content. Nietzsche's death of God, announced in the marketplace by the madman in the *Gay Science*, totally disorients reason and introduces the parodic tragic drama of Zarathustra that followed. For Rose it made no sense to read Kierkegaard as offering the opposition of faith to Hegelian reason, or Nietzsche the innocence of becoming to the cynical experience of Hegelian metaphysics: they were all authors of the trauma of reason.

Gillian Rose had a passionate distrust of innocence, claiming in *Love's Work* that she was not an innocent child, and by implication disbelieving anyone who thought they were. This sense of responsibility for the trauma of reason led her to criticize very forcefully what she saw as an attempt to find in Jewish thought a refuge from the trauma of reason. She saw this as characteristic of a contemporary current of thought which appealed to Jewish thought as the Other of the modern, Christian nihilist tradition without knowing very much about it. In the wonderful opening to *Judaism and Modernity* she wrote:

> Yet, suddenly, in the wake of the perceived demise of Marxism, Athens, for a long time already arid and crumbling, has become an uncannily deserted city, haunted by departed spirits. Her former inhabitants, abandoning her justice as well as her reason, have set off on a pilgrimage to an imaginary Jerusalem, in search of difference or otherness, love or community, and hoping to escape the *imperium* of reason, truth and reason. (Rose 1993, 1)

There is no escaping Rome to either Athens or Jerusalem, but what is left is the task of working through the heritage of law, philosophy and prophesy. Gillian did so in philosophy, but while paying due libations to the claims of the others. For her it was not possible to inhabit Athens without being mindful of Rome and Jerusalem.

In Rose's work there is no attempt to re-establish the convertibility of the one, the good, the true and the beautiful, but rather the constant effort to stage their brokenness. It was more difficult for an author to do this than to claim the spurious authority of any one of them and to convert. The transcendental unity of reason which might have grounded the true, the good and the beautiful is a broken middle, one that does not occupy a particular site – neither Rome, Athens nor Jerusalem – but which is always restless but vigilant.

I would not want to leave you with the impression that the author of this difficult thought of the broken middle regarded her work as a sad or even tragic philosophy. It was certainly one of its time, but to be an author for Gillian was more an ecstatic than a melancholy condition. This is evident in the drama of reason at its limit that is played out in *Love's Work*. That author recognized her Guardian Angel in Klee's *Angelus Dubiosus* not the tragic, traumatized *Angelus Novus* of Walter Benjamin or the angry angels of Simone Weil and Levinas. The dubious angel is one of those burly Kafkaesque angels, a very Rosean

> hybrid of hubris and humility – who makes mistakes, for whom things go wrong, who constantly discovers its own faults and failings, yet who still persists in the pain of staking itself, with the courage to initiate action and the commitment to go on and on, learning from those mistakes and risking new ventures. The dubious angel constantly changes its self-identity and its relations to others. Yet it appears commonplace, pedestrian, bulky and grounded – even though, *mirabile dictu*, there are no grounds and no ground. (Rose 1993, 10)

Gillian's last work, *Love's Work,* is the drama of a life lived under the sign of this angel – a very knowing book, a paradoxical statement of what it means to be a Hegelian in the broken space between Rome, Athens and Jerusalem. I'd like to end as she ended – with her voice in the present tense – both weighty and light, with a puckish joke shared with the *Angelus Dubiosus* that brings her momentarily back to us:

I like to pass unnoticed, which is why I hope that I am not deprived of old age. I aspire to Miss Marple's persona: to be exactly as I am, decrepit nature yet supernature in one, equally alert on the damp ground and in the turbulent air. Perhaps I don't have to wait for old age for that invisible trespass and pedestrian tread, insensible of mortality and desperately mortal.

I will stay in the fray, in the revel of ideas and risk; learning, failing, wooing, grieving, trusting, working, reposing – in this sin of language and lips. (Rose 1995, 144)

2

The return of Nietzsche and Marx

The probity of a contemporary intellectual, especially a contemporary philosopher, can be measured by their attitude toward Nietzsche and Marx.

– MAX WEBER

When Nietzsche observed that some are born posthumously, he might have added that some meet their significant contemporaries only after their deaths. He and Marx, for instance, were largely unaware of each other's existence, yet both were called back in the twentieth century to engage in a dialogue *d'outre-tombe*. Their debate has been one of the most consequential intellectual confrontations of twentieth-century thought, provoking some of its highest as well as its lowest moments. The names 'Marx' and 'Nietzsche' have come to carry an ideological and political charge that, when combined, has the power either to open or close debate. For the energy that motivates the profound reflections upon the question of the relation between Nietzsche *and* Marx is the same that drives it into the impasse of the choice between Marx *or* Nietzsche.

The history of the twentieth-century confrontation between Nietzsche and Marx moves between the two questions, with the either/or on the whole prevailing. The grotesque use of Nietzsche against Marx by the National Socialists in the 1930s is but an exceptionally grisly moment in a consistent history of pitting the two thinkers against each other. Other unedifying episodes include the image of Nietzsche propagated by the *nouveaux philosophes* of the 1970s and the imagined Nietzsche whose works now fill the spaces in east European bookshops previously reserved for the 'classics' of Marxism-Leninism. In both cases Nietzsche is cast as an alternative to Marxism, the thinker whose work would exclude and supersede that of Marx.[1]

The inverse holds for Lukács's *The Destruction of Reason* (1980, esp. chapter 3) and other orthodox Marxist readings that cast Nietzsche as a bourgeois intellectual who prefigured and contributed to the rise of fascism. In the words of one of the last books to be published by the philosophical section of the late East German Academy – *Moderne-Nietzsche-Postmoderne* (Buhr 1990) – Nietzsche's philosophy is but 'an anticipation of the bourgeois imperialist barbarism of our century'.[2] This philosophy is naturally contrasted with Marx's anticipation of twentieth-century socialist internationalist civilization. Both the Nietzschean anti-Marxists and the Marxist anti-Nietzscheans are clear that a choice has to be made between either one or the other; the main point, however, is to read neither attentively. For the choice between Nietzsche or Marx is largely the reflex of an opposition between Marxists and Nietzscheans, one which has very little to do with the differences between two bodies of work produced in relative isolation during the second half of the nineteenth century.

The most interesting and important reflections upon Nietzsche and Marx have been beyond good and evil, beyond the Manichean opposition of saint and Satan. They have not necessarily been written by those who attempted a 'synthesis' – such as the 'left-Nietzscheans' of the early twentieth century – but rather by those who reflected upon what is implied in the 'and' of Marx and Nietzsche. Their attitude is exemplified by Max Weber in a comment made towards the end of his life in 1920:

> Whoever claims that they could have accomplished the most important parts of their own work without the work done by both [Marx and Nietzsche] deceives themselves and others. The world in which spiritually and intellectually we live today is a world bearing the imprint of Marx and Nietzsche.[3]

For Weber, the character of the imprint left by Nietzsche and Marx combined the features of an insight into power and its inversions and the materialist conception of history. Later in the 1930s Walter Benjamin and Georges Bataille regarded Marx and Nietzsche as the pre-eminent thinkers of revolutionary excess and 'active nihilism';[4] while for other readers, particularly those critically engaging with the thought of Heidegger, such as Levinas and Irigaray, they are the last metaphysicians whose thought ultimately cannot contain ethical exteriority.[5]

Two shared themes emerge from the reading of Nietzsche *and* Marx: both are taken to analyse the nihilistic condition of modern subjectivity, and both explore the possibility of an excessive return or 'revolution'. They are both thinkers of crisis, but crisis thought not only in the pathological sense of the critical moment in the progress of a disease, but also in the sense of a moment of judgement or decision. The texts of both Marx and Nietzsche are informed by an often unbearable tension between crisis as condition and crisis as decision, or in other words, the diagnosis of the critical condition of nihilistic subjectivity and the prescription of its decisive over-turn.[6]

The crisis they explore is that of the Kantian autonomous, legislative subject of modernity. This is the subject that would give itself its own laws, the subject for whom the claims of traditional values have been stripped of their legitimacy by the 'critical tribunal', who is free but nevertheless subjected, one who is dissatisfied and locked into oppressive and exploitative relations of its own making.[7] It is the crisis of this subject – for whom 'all that is solid melts into air' and for whom 'God is dead' – that is the object of Marx and Nietzsche's analysis; they analyse both the aetiology of the crisis and the conditions under which the subject may return to or beyond itself.

Central to both Nietzsche and Marx's analysis of crisis is the concept of return. Indeed, it is this concept which, in various guises, has informed the entire twentieth-century reception of their thought. 'Return' is the site of the 'and' which cleaves the thought of Marx and Nietzsche. The affinities and differences between their analyses of return can already be detected in the word they choose for the concept: Marx, in the *Grundrisse* and *Capital*, uses *Wiederholen*, while Nietzsche, in *The Gay Science* and *Thus Spoke Zarathustra*, uses *Wiederkehren*. Both words signify return, and both are used reflexively of a subject (*sich wiederkehren, sich wiederholen*), but with a subtle difference of emphasis in each case. *Wiederholen* implies repetition, going over the same old thing, fetching back again and again in the manner of Freud's repetitive *Fort/Da*, while *Wiederkehren* implies return as a turning back. Yet in spite of these slight differences, the deployment of the notion of return by the two thinkers is strikingly similar. For both Nietzsche and Marx, 'return' signifies not only a crisis in the subject, but also an excessive or 'revolutionary' 'return' or 'conversion' which transforms the subject.

The problem of return has implicitly determined both the depths and the heights of the twentieth-century understanding of Nietzsche and/or Marx. Even the lower reaches of the either Marx or Nietzsche 'debate' is informed by the distinction between the 'revolutionary' and 'reactionary' character of the preferred thinker, overlooking that both terms are compounds of the Latin equivalent of *wieder*, namely re-: re-action, re-volution.

The more profound reflections on the 'and' of Nietzsche and Marx are almost without exception conducted in terms of an analysis of their concepts of return. For Benjamin and Bataille the return of both thinkers is excessive: 'revolution' or 'eternal return' is open and cannot be contained within restricted economies of circulation. Conversely, for Levinas and Irigaray, Marx and Nietzsche's return is ultimately closed – there is no exteriority or excess, only what is given can return. For these readers, Nietzsche and Marx's notions of return can give rise only to closed, unethical or matricidal regimes.

Both Marx and Nietzsche depict the crisis of modern subjectivity in terms of the experience of time, finding the locus of this crisis in the uncanny experience of return. But by taking as their theme the tension between analysing and provoking a crisis (crisis as diagnosis and decision), between return within a closed and restricted economy and return as open and excessive, Nietzsche and Marx encountered great difficulties in realizing their texts. The most striking of these is their oft-remarked inability to complete: neither was able to finish his main work.[8]

Marx could complete only the first volume of *Capital*. We have reconstructions from his notes of volumes two and three by Engels: the planned volumes on legislation and the state were never realized. The reason for this inability to complete was not simply Marx's growing ill health (which in his and Nietzsche's case may be seen more as a symptom than a cause), but rather the impossibility of completing a text that would both analyse and evoke a crisis of return. This will be illustrated through the analysis of some crucial passages from the *Grundrisse*, a text which comes closest to an overall conspectus of Marx's project. The situation is similar with *Thus Spoke Zarathustra*, which also remained incomplete because uncompletable.

Zarathustra begins with the protagonist's descent from the mountains to the cities in order to teach the eternal return of the same. Most of the first and the second book of *Thus Spoke Zarathustra* traces the systematic misunderstanding of this philosophy by Zarathustra's contemporaries and disciples. The third book ends with Zarathustra acknowledging the defeat of his address and retreating to the mountains where, in an *opera buffa* sequel, he is visited in the fourth book by the 'higher men'. Nietzsche envisaged continuing to address them as contemporaries, in a way they would understand. But it was impossible to write this conclusion, since the doctrine of eternal return was both a diagnosis of the nihilistic culture of the 'last man' and an attempt to evoke a decision. The evocation of this crisis was the task [*Aufgabe*] of the 'fish hook' texts of Nietzsche's last four years of sanity.[9] Zarathustra itself remains incomplete – we are left not knowing how he would have spoken – thus or thus.

Neither Marx nor Nietzsche could finish: their main texts remained open and remain so in spite of the efforts of some Marxists and Nietzscheans to close them. And significantly, both texts are interrupted at the same moment, at the cross between crisis as diagnosis and prescription, between the analysis of a condition and the provocation of a decision. Both texts founder at the moment of legislation, the moment of giving a law which is also the subject's 'autonomous' taking on of law. And the paradoxes of this moment – aptly described by Irigaray as the 'attempt to square the circle' (Irigaray 1985, 212) – emerge in the difficulty of thinking return, a difficulty framed in terms of time and subjectivity. What is at stake in this difficulty may be exemplified by briefly considering Kant's analysis of the return of the law and its relation to time.

Time for Kant is neither the frame within which events occur, nor the relation between events. We can best understand his view if we look at his early text from 1763, *The Only Possible Proof for the Existence of God*.[10] Here Kant makes the celebrated claim that being is not a predicate, but the position of predicates. He uses the term *Setzen* for position, which should be read actively as the act of putting, positioning or placing. This term is significantly the one Marx uses to name the operation of that particular relation between being and time that he calls 'capital'.[11]

Kant distinguishes between relative and absolute *Setzung*: relative *Setzung* is the ascription of a predicate to a subject, but such ascription can be accomplished only if both subject and predicate have *already been* posited absolutely.[12] We are able to predicate being of an object only if we have already 'posited the relation' which makes such predication possible. Kant designates this positing of the relation as time and gives it certain formal properties. Time cannot be derived from the relation between events or appearances, nor may it be regarded as their frame, receptacle or horizon; it is an event of absolute position which is the 'condition' of the events and appearances of relative position (judgement).

Kant further defines this absolute event in terms of schema. In an earlier text, the *New Exposition of the First Principles of Metaphysical Knowledge* (1755), Kant introduced the term 'schema' – crucial to the later *Critique of Pure Reason* – as the continuous activity of divine intelligence, 'the origin of all existents' and their mutual relations. Although the divine subject of the schema has been effaced and has become an 'unknowable' by the time of the first *Critique*,[13] the character of its activity remains constant – it both *realizes* and *restricts*. Time allows events and appearances to be realized but restricts the way in which they may occur and appear. Kant went on in the third *Critique* to develop the movement of 'realization and restriction' into a theory of culture in which communities are the agents of realization and restriction, thus anticipating the union of philosophy and social theory that became axiomatic for Marx and Nietzsche.

According to Kant we are victims of a transcendental illusion or paralogism around time; from the appearance of objects and the occurrence of events *in time* we infer that time may be thought and measured in terms of 'appearances' and 'events'. Against this Kant suggests that we should think of events and appearances as posited *through* and not *in* time; in this way we become aware of time as a schema, as an absolute position which determines the relations between events and appearances. If we persist in reducing absolute position to the terms of relation, we shall be led into the kinds of antinomy and paralogism diagnosed by Kant in the 'Dialectic' of the first *Critique*.

For Kant time is originary (*ursprunglich*): it does not appear or occur in time but is a schema of the event of absolute position which allows appearances and events to take their place in the temporal order. Yet with the notable exception of the third *Critique*, the subject of the act of *Setzung* is usually disavowed by Kant. The schematizing God of the *New Exposition of the First Principles of Metaphysical Knowledge* is transformed into the 'mysterious art' whose works and ways are closed to us. This is entirely consistent, for Kant argues that it is impossible to think the foundation of thought without falling prey to dialectical inferences. Whether this dialectic can be mobilized to think the absolute is the Hegelian wager whose implications still have to be fully grasped and worked through. But according to the Kantian account 'we' are not in a position to accept responsibility for the absolute positing of time: we may become aware of it in the progressive development of culture and the 'signs of history' but qua absolute it cannot be said to be in our power.

Both Nietzsche and Marx are heirs to Fichte and Hegel's challenge to this disowning of time. Indeed this challenge continues to haunt post-Kantian philosophy in the guise of thinking the difficult relation of being, time and subjectivity. Nietzsche and Marx take their place within this heritage: both develop the distinction between the absolute and the relative aspects of the position of time and its relation to being and subjectivity. This heritage forms the condition of the 'and' of Marx and Nietzsche, and it is analysed in terms of the concept of 'return'.

Nietzsche's question of eternal return in *The Gay Science*, provoked by the demon's words 'life as you now live it and have lived it, you will have to live once more and innumerable times more' (*GS* 273), can be answered in relative or absolute terms. It is this which makes the answer a judgement on the answerer, as is spelt out in *The Gay Science*:

> If this thought gained possession of you, it would change you as you are or perhaps crush you. The question in each and everything, 'Do you desire this once more and innumerable times more?' would lie on your actions as the greatest weight. Or how well disposed would you have to become to yourself and to life to crave nothing more than this ultimate eternal confirmation and seal. (*GS* 273)

In Kantian terms, the question of eternal return reveals the work of the schematism of time by driving it to its limit where it yields to paradox (eternal return). Faced with these limits the questioner may either become stiflingly aware of its restriction and be paralysed by the 'greatest weight' – or become realized and return to themselves in an 'eternal confirmation' that accepts responsibility for giving the time within which things and events return anew.[14]

The question of eternal return challenges Kant's disowning of time – it proposes that we take absolute responsibility for time – that we cease to accept time as given but instead repeat the event of the giving of time, its absolute position. We must return the gift of time, finding time to give it back. The implications of this return for subjectivity are developed through the imagined *Übermensch* who in refusing the gift accept responsibility for the giving of time. The *Übermensch* do not act as if they have time, are in time or are measured by time but posit time through every act and, by so doing, change themselves and their experience of events and objects. They are no longer restricted to 'taking place' in time but realize themselves in an originary positing of time.

As Nietzsche acknowledges, such a view of time and experience is nightmarish, but he nevertheless insists on posing the stark alternatives: either we own the foundation of time or are owned by time. If we are owned by time, then our actions and our possessions are not ours, the meaning they seem to have and which we seem to bestow on them is illusory. Nietzsche is not proposing in place of this experience of the crisis of meaning a 'modern' full, authentic possession of the meaning of our actions and things, nor a 'postmodern' embrace of their meaninglessness; rather he is calling the subjectivity that finds itself in this condition to judge itself and come to a decision, one whose outcome he leaves open. There arises a 'struggle for time' which Nietzsche casts in terms of a nihilistic subjectivity crushed by meaninglessness and seeking revenge on time and another that is transformed by accepting responsibility for its time. The former are the modern and postmodern subjectivities who oscillate between the desire to possess meaning and the vengeful celebration of its absence, while the latter are the *Übermensch*, those who beyond measure accept the responsibility for the giving of measure: they are those who have become what they are – 'the unique, the incomparable, the self-legislating, the self-creating' (*GS* 266 – the reference to extraneous 'human beings' deleted from Kaufmann's translation).

Nietzsche saw socialism as the epitome of the vengeful subject, the one taking revenge on the order of time within which it is restricted.[15] However, if we return to Marx with the question of time and return, we shall find an analysis of time and subjectivity that in crucial ways both questions and supplements the one provided by Nietzsche.

In the later sections of the *Grundrisse* Marx makes some fascinating comments about time and capital. In them capital is presented as doing the work of the Kantian schematism. He writes that capital 'posits' not only the commodities which are produced and circulated (relative position), but also the time within which their circulation takes place (absolute position). Furthermore, the time of production and circulation is posited 'restrictively' as repetition in an already given time through which capital realizes itself. The time of capital may be thought relatively, in terms of motion/process/turnover, or absolutely, as their position:

On the one side labour time, on the other circulation time. And the whole of the movement appears as unity of labour time and circulation time, of production and circulation. This unity itself is motion, process. Capital appears as this unity-in-process of production and circulation, a unity which can be regarded both as the totality of the process of its production, as well as the specific completion of *one* turnover of the capital, *one* movement returning into itself. (Marx 1977a, 620)

Capital then both founds the time of the unity of production and circulation (the 'totality of the process') and yet eternally returns to itself as a 'specific turnover' in this time. Capital performs the Kantian paralogism: it is driven to overcome its disowned absolute position of time by repeating the act of relative position, increasing the speed of turnover within the time posited by capital, an enterprise which is prone to self-destructive crisis. In this condition of crisis there is no decision regarding the absolute position of time, only an adaptation to the relative position of things and events as commodities.

Marx outlines how capital strives to overcome the interval between absolute and relative position of time by nihilistically accelerating its returns, in relative time:

the sum of values which can be created in a given period of time depends on the number of repetitions of the production process within this period. The repetition of the production process, however, is determined by circulation time .... The more rapid the circulation, the shorter the circulation time, the more often can the same capital repeat the production process. (Marx 1977a, 627)

The acceleration of the turnovers of capital in relative time leads to the 'abolition of time' – a form of eternal return which evokes all the paradoxes of the thought: '*Circulation without circulation time* – i.e. the transition of capital from one phase to the next at the speed of thought – would be the maximum, i.e. the identity of the renewal of the production process with its termination' (Marx 1977a, 631, see also 671). This abolition of difference, in which production, circulation and consumption approach the limit of simultaneity, recalls Nietzsche's nightmare of eternal return thought restrictively as a return *in* time rather than *of* time. This is a closed temporal economy, a regime of the identical in which time and difference are dissolved in simultaneity, a moment at which time collapses upon itself.[16]

Implied in both Nietzsche and Marx's thoughts on time and subjectivity is the Kantian distinction of relative and absolute positing of the events and appearances in time. In the words of Marx, capital does not posit the time of 'merely *one turnover*, one circulation; but rather the positing of turnovers;

positing of the whole process [*Es ist nicht mehr nur Ein Umschlag, eine Zirkulation; sondern Setzen von Umschlägen, Setzen des ganzen Verlaufs*]' (Marx 1974, 532; 1977a, 639). The various turnovers of capital are really eternal returns of the same, since for capital everything is *Gleichzeitig*, at the same time; the nihilistic truth of capital is its abolition of difference at the limit. Yet capital does not ask itself the question of eternal return, does not assume responsibility for its time but nihilistically strives to abolish time and difference within the limits of a disowned event of time.[17]

The absolute time of capital is a condition for the appearance of objects and events – capital is their schema which realizes and restricts them – but it is a disowned founding of time. Capital, says Marx, posits itself as its own measure and breaks down other measures of time such as the seasons, day and night, the 'working day'. Yet it does not behave responsibly towards this founding of time but instead tries to overcome itself in terms of the events and appearances which it realizes and restricts. In the face of this crisis Marx analyses the emergence of a different subjectivity which resists capital's measures of time. One of the uncanny features of the *Grundrisse* is Marx's dual diagnosis of the crisis of capital: he takes the abolition of time under capital to mean either the destructive end of human life or the possibility of a decision to reconstitute the conditions of subjectivity.[18] In the terms of Nietzsche's question of eternal return, capital may be the 'greatest weight' that crushes the subject or the chance for the subject to transform itself into an *Übermensch* capable of giving itself time.

As with Nietzsche, Marx puts the struggle for time at the centre of his work. It is a struggle which may be confined to the time of capital, as with the struggle over the length of the working day described in *Capital*, or it may involve the question of capital's positing of time as such. Both mark the struggles of a subjectivity striving to constitute itself through taking responsibility for its constitution of time – initially in the vengeance of sabotage and resistance, but increasingly in terms of autonomous organizations such as trade unions and political parties.[19] Yet Marx's inability to complete the sections of *Capital* concerned with legislation suggests that he was well aware of the difficulties in constituting a political subjectivity free of a vengeful relation to the time of capital. The passage from the proletariat as constituted by capital in opposition to the bourgeoisie to the proletariat as constituting a new time, a new relation to subjectivity and a new relation to being became literally unthinkable once Marx abandoned the early humanist logic of a return to a human 'species being'. As with Nietzsche's *Übermensch*, this 'new' or 'original' subjectivity cannot be described in terms of existing categories, nor may it be presented as a return to something that has been alienated or lost. The 'return' is intended to provoke a crisis and a decision of subjectivity: it does not prescribe or give a utopian image of a future subjectivity.

Both Nietzsche and Marx sought to provoke the emergence of a subjectivity responsible for its constitution of time, the one by posing the question of eternal return to the nihilistic time of modernity, the other by evoking a subjectivity that would challenge the repetitions of capital with another founding of time. Both thinkers reject a return to full possession or self-presence, but this leaves them with the difficulty of a return which is original, one which involves the return *of* time rather than return *in* time. Both see intimations of a new subjectivity inhabiting its own time, the one in the 'free spirit', the other in the nascent forms of proletarian political organization, but neither of them prescribed the forms which this return to time might take.

Both Marx and Nietzsche were unable to complete their work, but this should not be regarded as their failure. Their texts remain open and in question, partaking of the crisis of subjectivity which is their theme. The inability to end, or worse, the sense of never having begun that haunted both authors, evokes the experience of a subjectivity that is not responsible for its own time, and can find no meaning in the things and events that it encounters in time.

Their response to this condition was to recommend neither a return to the possession of time, self and meaning nor an apocalyptic celebration of its loss, but instead to return constantly to the difficult question of what it means for a subject to assume responsibility for time. It is this return to the difficulty of modern subjectivity and its experience of time that haunts the 'and' of Marx and Nietzsche.

Notes

1   A particularly clear example is supplied by *The Times*, which drew an extravagant connection between the 1989 Revolutions and the foundation of the Nietzsche Society of Great Britain: 'Recent events may not have treated Karl Marx very kindly, but the formation of the new Nietzsche society reflects the upturn in the reputation and fashionability of another 19th century German philosopher, Friedrich Nietzsche.'

2   Robert Steigerwald, 'Die Wahrheitskonzeption im Werk von Friedrich Nietzsche' (Buhr 1990, 46).

3   Uttered to students on the Ludwigstrasse in Munich following a depressing evening's debate with Spengler, cited in Baumgarten 1964, 554–5. For a recent discussion of Nietzsche and Weber see 'The traces of Nietzsche in the works of Max Weber' (Hennis 1988).

4   See especially Georges Bataille, 'Nietzsche and the Fascists' (Bataille 1985) and Walter Benjamin, 'Theologico-political fragment' and 'The destructive character' (Benjamin 1979) and 'The work of art in the age of mechanical reproduction' (Benjamin 1977a).

5   For programmatic statements see Levinas's 'Ideology and idealism' (Levinas 1989, 236–48) and Irigaray's 'The poverty of psychoanalysis' (Irigaray 1991a, 79–104). Their fundamental positions are worked through in Levinas 1969 and Irigaray 1991b.

6   The two-sided character of crisis is explicated in Heidegger's reading of Nietzsche's sentence 'The doctrine of eternal return; as fulfilment of it [i.e. nihilism] as *crisis*' (Heidegger 1991, 159): 'Seen from this vantage point, the thinking of the thought of eternal recurrence, as a questioning that perpetually calls for decision, is the fulfilment of nihilism .... The doctrine of eternal return is therefore the "critical point", the watershed of an epoch become weightless and searching for a new centre of gravity. It is the crisis proper.'

7   For a detailed exposition of this reading of Kantian subjectivity see my *Art of Judgement* (Caygill 1989, chapters 4 and 5).

8   The temptation to read this failure superficially is too often indulged. One exception is Irigaray, whose analysis of the sufferings of the philosopher legislator is never superficial but overemphasizes the 'greatest weight' of the eternal return, its interiority, over its exteriority: 'But now everything has moved inside the house the subject has made, or is. And whether the scene seems set inside, or outside, whether in his room or in his study, sometimes enjoying a fire fancied to be burning in baroque coils of smoke or else gazing out through the/his window at the still in(de)finite space of the universe, the action is always inside his house, his mind. And what or who can now put it outside? Only a messenger of revolution perhaps? Or else the fact that this hearth is made of glass and that those glasses – rather tarnished by age, their brilliance dimmed, having always in fact been unsilvered or blackened by smoke – mirror so deadly a boredom that, whatever one's firm intent, one might finish by wishing to die – to die of love, were that still possible – rather than have things just go on. Forever' (Irigaray 1985, 212).

9   The 'fish hook' texts, for which there were no fish, were dedicated to 'conjuring up a day of decision' (*EH* 22).

10 See my discussion in *Art of Judgement* (Caygill 1989, 220–2).

11 The concept of *Setzen* became one of the central concepts of post-Kantian idealism and was especially prominent in Fichte's *Doctrine of Science*. Marx's usage in the *Grundrisse* follows Hegel's exposition of it in the *Science of Logic*. For a sustained critique of the implications of this concept for Hegel and subsequent social and political theory see Gillian Rose [1981] 2009.

12 See Kant [1763] 1979, 58–9.

13 In the *New Exposition* (1755) Kant describes 'the schema of divine intelligence, the origin of all existents' as God's 'constant activity' (Kant 1986, 110); in the *Critique of Pure Reason* schematism is described as 'an art concealed in the depths of the human soul, whose real modes of activity nature is hardly likely to allow us to discover, and have open to our gaze' (*CPR* A141/B181).

14 In this reading the eternal return is neither a cosmological thesis of the return of all events and appearances that have ever taken place in the

universe, nor a version of the categorical imperative 'will so that your actions will return eternally'. Rather it is intended as a call to responsibility for the subject's positing of the time in which it acts and experiences, a time which appears to it as if it were distinct. In this way it may be contrasted with the cosmological and psychological readings of Löwith and Klossowski.

15 In a fragment from the *Nachlass* Nietzsche explicitly contrasts the socialism of the nihilistic 'last man' with the eternal return of the *Übermensch*: it is available in 'Translations from Nietzsche's *Nachlass* 1881–1884', trans. K. Ansell-Pearson and R.J. Hollingdale (1991) *Journal of Nietzsche Studies* 1: 6.

16 Marx offers some fascinating insights into how the moment of crisis may be deferred by the institutions of credit but adds presciently that these institutions will themselves eventually exacerbate the crisis. On the first point: 'The necessary tendency of capital is therefore circulation without circulation time, and this tendency is the fundamental determinant of credit and of the capitalist's credit contrivances' (Marx 1977a, 659). For a philosophical reading of Marx sensitive to the importance of time and credit see Lyotard 1988b, 171–9; for an apocalyptic interpretation of the acceleration of turnover, see Virilio 1986.

17 This emerges in a compulsion to accelerate circulation, a movement Marx consistently describes 'as a spiral, as an expanding circle' (Marx 1977a, 620) but one which can preserve itself only by constantly increasing its speed of circulation until it reaches a self-destructive point of collapse in crisis.

18 Marx develops a double reading of this crisis: on the one hand, 'The violent destruction of capital not by relations external to it, but rather as a condition of its self-preservation, is the most striking form in which advice is given to it to be gone and to give room to a higher state of social production' and on the other – in contrast to its internal violence of devaluation of commodities and the suspension of labour power – a 'violent overthrow' which would lead to the development of a subjectivity able to 'grasp its own history as *process*, and to recognise nature (equally present as practical power over nature) as its actual body' (Marx 1977a, 749–50).

19 The most sustained Marxist analysis of the organizational conditions for the formation of a new subjectivity was conducted by Lukács in the early 1920s. He gives Lenin's distinction of trade union and political 'consciousness' from *What Is to Be Done* a Nietzschean twist, seeing in the former a vengeful subjectivity, in the latter a new subjectivity embarking upon a refounding of time and space. See 'Towards a methodology of the problem of organisation' (Lukács 1971).

3

Violence, civility and the predicaments of philosophy

They both, for the first time, became aware that they lived in conditions where the unusual may be dangerous, and that there was no power on earth outside of themselves to stand between them and the unusual. They became uneasy, went in and loaded their revolvers.

– JOSEPH CONRAD, *AN OUTPOST OF PROGRESS*

The violent constitution of world society under the auspices of European modernity raises some very hard questions for philosophy. As the epochal event of modernity, world society was forged by means of political and economic institutions, as well as technological developments, deeply informed by philosophically grounded notions of reason and subjectivity. Philosophy has had to reflect upon its share of the responsibility for the 'real-existing-world-society' of international capital, systematic inequality and the potential for species threatening violence. Is this world the 'realization' of philosophy's universalist aspirations; is philosophy complicit with the European project of violent, imperial expansion; or is the course taken by world society nothing to do with the ideals of philosophy, at worst their grotesque perversion?

The process of reflecting on its involvement in the emergence of world society has profoundly shocked philosophy's notions of rationality and subjectivity. It has led to proclamations of the 'end of philosophy' and the conviction that the object of world society now exceeds its categories of understanding and renders irrelevant its accounts of human subjectivity and action.

The response of philosophy to world society is not recent but was central to the self-definition of philosophical modernity. The project of managing the crisis of reason and subjectivity provoked by the violent, imperial expansion of Europe contributed decisively to the development of modern philosophy. Indeed, the current upset in the certainties of European reason and subjectivity – registered under the titles of 'postmodernism' or 'deconstruction' – is in many respects a response to the collapse of an earlier attempt at crisis management. This project, inaugurated by Descartes, sought to ground reason in the self-certainty of an autonomous subject, but self-certainty itself – issuing from *cogito ergo sum* – was largely a response to the corrosive effects of sceptical doubt. Such scepticism was not peculiar to philosophy but articulated an intense and widespread culture of doubt that had its correlate in the early-modern European expansions and their encounters with the 'unusual'.

The medieval expansions of Europe in the Crusades were widely perceived as the recovery of Christendom's lost territories and intellectual resources. They stimulated efforts systematically to present the sum of all Christian knowledge in order to assert and define a Christian identity *against* the Moslems and the Pagans without, and the Jews and Heretics within, the bounds of Christendom.[1] This project of recovery is exemplified by Aquinas's (c.1225–74) first systematic treatise *Summa Contra Gentiles*, which combines scriptural exegesis with a claim for Christianity to represent the 'natural reason' common to humanity.[2] But the Atlantic explorations and expansions unsettled what were thought to be the divinely secured intellectual and territorial possessions of Christendom. The expansions were not the recovery of lost possessions, but the acquisition of new, unforeseen ones. The temporal and spatial limits which enabled the medieval *summas* confidently to present the comprehensive knowledge of God, the World, and the Soul were shaken. The medieval attempt to create a Christian identity through external expansion and internal, bureaucratic-ecclesiastical control was not sustainable, and its collapse was sealed with the Reformation.[3]

It was succeeded by the complementary formations of the nation state and the creation of a Protestant subject uncertain of its salvation and, as a consequence, of the self within, the world around and the God above it. This subject was discovering certainty within itself, but such discovery could only take place within the fragile and contradictory civility established within the borders of the nation state.[4]

The experience of crisis and uncertainty was managed philosophically in three ways. The first, taken by Montaigne (1533–92) in his *Essays*, was to open philosophy to the experience of the destabilization of Christian reason and subjectivity. His exploration of the impact of the 'unusual' on knowledge and subjectivity embraced the paradoxes of the experience of doubt and finitude.[5] The second response accepted the uncertainty of all knowledge of

God, the world and the self but took this uncertainty along with the certainty of death as the occasion for a leap of faith. For Pascal (1623–62), the first and still the most unsettling exponent of this thought, God is the power that stands between us and the unusual, and through faith in God the dangers of finite existence may be faced with a tortured equanimity.[6] The third response was to pursue doubt and finitude until it was finally banished in the attainment of subjective certainty. The subject returned from thence not only with the certainty of its own existence, but also with the correlative certainties that in spite of all doubt, God and the world *did* exist. This strategy – consummately realized by Descartes (1596–1650) – contains the unusual by establishing a fixed subjectivity which, certain of its possession of itself, can set itself to surveying and possessing the world around it.[7]

The three responses to the predicament of doubt and uncertainty have overwhelmingly determined the development of modern, European philosophy. The Cartesian reduction of certainty to the self-certainty of the subject has been dominant but continually accompanied by the sceptical and the religious arguments. The arguments formed some of the most influential intellectual constellations of European philosophy, such as those of Hamann, Hume and Kant in the eighteenth, and Hegel, Friedrich von Schlegel and Kierkegaard in the nineteenth century. Their common denominator, what characterizes them all as 'modern', is the centrality of the experience and management of doubt. This experience differed from its classical, sceptical precedents in being concerned with the management of the anxiety and doubt of possession. The claims to possess knowledge of the world, or of God, or of the self – even to possess or be responsible for the actions of the self – are all uncertain, all racked by doubt.

Why then is modern European philosophy so obsessively devoted to the management of doubt, and why is doubt constantly figured in terms of *guilt regarding the legitimacy of possession*? A teleological history of philosophy would assume that the exploration of doubt testified to the superior ability of European reason to free itself from the shackles of uncritical tradition. This freedom contributed to the development of scientific knowledge and the institutions and technologies characteristic of European modernity. This narrative was widely used to legitimate the 'civilizing mission' of the European colonial adventure, effacing its origins. For doubt was less the means for liberating modern philosophy from religious tradition and regulation than a reaction to the re-configuration of Christendom into competing nation states. Doubt emerged as a strategy for managing an unacknowledged violence; expressing the anxiety that those possessions are usurped whose legitimacy is so anxiously surveyed and justified. The search for a strategy to justify possession stimulated great feats of philosophical invention, producing texts whose persuasiveness has sometimes obscured their idiosyncrasy.

Descartes's reduction of the world to substance as bare extension appropriable by coordinate geometry may be narrated teleologically as the great act of philosophical abstraction that permitted Newton and Leibniz to develop the mathematical calculus crucial for the advance of European science and technology. But it can also be read as the violent extinction of the unusual or immeasurable other in the interests of surveillance and control. Substance as uniform extension abolishes all other understandings of space; it denies a voice to any claim but its own, for nothing may validly contest reason's claims unless it be couched in the language of reason.[8] This act of abstraction, however, was not accomplished with a clean conscience: there always remained the doubt that the world is not what we want it to seem and that it may even be the work of a malevolent demon.

Doubt is not just a theoretical luxury indulged in a warm Bohemian retreat during a lull in campaigning but figures the guilt and anxiety surrounding possession secured by violence. Such a displacement of violence into doubt can be accomplished only on the condition that the violence is past or banished to the periphery of a protected, sovereign space. Philosophy was above all the exercise of reflection upon and within this assured, sovereign space of rational civility, but such reflection could not wholly insulate itself from the violence which established and sustained this space. In philosophy, the violence of doubt could remain covert for only as long as the border held between internal civility and external barbarity.

The violence of imperial expansion inhabited a liminal realm between what is known and securely possessed, and what is unknown but desired. The border was an object of anxiety, sustained by a lawless violence reflected back into civil society as doubt and insecurity. The possibility of feats of extravagant and unrestrained violence at and beyond the border contrasted with the constraints of the rational management of violence within the borders of the nation states. Here civility was achieved through consensual social contracts and the management of differences between citizens by means of the rational institutions of law and 'policy' (welfare and social security).[9] But the rational management of violence within the nation state was only possible when potential and actual violence had been displaced to the border, whether through the export of refractory elements of the population or the import of plundered wealth to support the welfare institutions of the metropolis.

With the achievement of world society the character of the border changes. It is no longer a 'natural', external frontier to a space which is other – yet to be colonized – but has itself become internal. There is no longer any space for the apparent distinction between the sovereignty of reason within, and violence at and beyond the limit. With the limits for territorial expansion themselves reaching their own limit with the achievement of world society, reasoned civility and sovereign violence threaten to collapse into each other. With world society, the potential for violence displaced to the periphery returns to the centre with increasing speed, or more properly, periphery and centre collapse into each other.[10] Instead of the uniform space of reason being sustained by the violence of its expansion, violence recoils, and the shock of its return warps the space of reason making it complex, characterized by unfamiliar and inexplicable folds, gaps and tears. The predicament of reason itself has changed.

In the twentieth century the acknowledgement of the violence underlying 'doubt' and 'possession' has become part of the philosophical agenda. With the experience of the Holocaust and of warfare on a world scale the progressive certainties of European reason lost their lustre and became objects of suspicion – doubt itself became an object of doubt.[11] Yet this is not simply the shocked response of an innocent philosophy to events on the 'slaughterboard of world history'. For modern philosophy was itself complicit with the European imperial project, whose collapse, as Hannah Arendt has shown, was an immediate cause of the event of rationally planned and technologically executed mass death. It was part of the recoil of the violence of imperial expansion upon the culture and the institutions of the metropolitan states which followed the exhaustion of territory available for expansion.[12] The transition of European reason from doubt to violent madness had been anticipated in Conrad's colonial novels, which stage the nihilistic return of imperial violence to the heart of reason or darkness. The direct, violent encounter with the colonized other recoils on the colonizer not as doubt, but as the horror of total and ultimately self-destructive disorientation.

Arendt develops Conrad's prescient theme of the return of imperial violence to the metropolis in *The Origins of Totalitarianism*. In it she shows that the twentieth-century crises of European modernity, along with its cultural refraction in modernism, marked the return of imperial violence to the metropolitan states. This return took the guise of total war, the use at home of colonial administrative technologies such as concentration camps and the mobilization of alterophobic legitimatory ideologies such as racism. The distinction between a 'civil' space occupied by 'civilian' populations, with its rational management of violence, and the exercise of unrestrained violence at the frontier breaks down and is succeeded by 'total domination', one which indifferently employs both reason and violence in securing its continued movement of inner, self-destructive 'expansion'.

With the establishment of world society the characteristically modern doubt over the legitimacy of possession becomes an acute if not pathological horror. In such circumstances doubt as a focus for the management of guilt is transformed into the open management of violence. The move from a problematic of doubt to one of the suppression and repression of violence was first analysed by Marx, Nietzsche and Freud and subsequently by Heidegger and the philosophers of postmodernism and deconstruction. They are responding to a radical change in what it means to 'possess' either the world or the self. We can no longer coolly survey the world as if it were a uniform extended substance, with ourselves poised above it with compass and rule. For the world no longer possesses the boundaries which would make it into a plane surface. When the plane becomes a globe, the boundary becomes immanent to the world, no longer marking the border between what is possessed and not possessed, but between what is possessed by some and not by others.

The border between civility and violence is no longer to be found at the limit of a sovereign, territorial space, but now traverses that space. It can no longer be located or fixed at a particular place and time, since the world can no longer be imagined in such spatial and temporal terms. Every act of violence at an imagined border returns in predictable and unpredictable ways to an imagined centre, whether in the guise of images,[13] traumatized veterans, economic distortions or the effects of environmental damage. The border no longer insulates the 'inside' of the civil from the violent 'outside'.[14] There is no position from above or without the scene of violence from which it is possible to doubt that possession can be the issue of anything but violent occupation.

As the theoretical displacement of the violence of possession, the project of philosophical doubt was inseparable from the achievements of European civility. However, with the collapse of this civility into world war and genocide, the problem of doubt has changed into that of managing violence. With this move, the political and ethical issues of practical philosophy assume central importance. Yet practical philosophy is also in difficulty, since its notion of the acting, human subject is deeply informed by the heritage of European civility. Its notion of subjectivity assumes the validity of individual human actors who 'own' their actions and behave in a self-controlled and rationally predictable way within the limits of civility. The originally violent establishment and preservation of these limits is taken to be 'exceptional' and the behaviour of actors called to participate in military violence 'on the border' clearly distinguished from their behaviour as civilians within the border.

When these distinctions break down or become fragile, then violence ceases to possess its privileged, exceptional aura. When it becomes ubiquitous, then the models of subjectivity associated with the space of civility, with its managed and displaced violence, are thrown into crisis. With the possession by states of unprecedented instruments of destruction targeted upon 'civilian' populations, the economic power of the military, and the insidious permeation of civil and military institutions – whether through intelligence, defence contracts or 'academic contacts' – it is anachronistic to consider practical reason in terms of an actor in 'civil society'.

With the achievement of world society many of the distinctions between reason and violence informing European theoretical and practical philosophy become questionable, if not even wholly unsustainable. The very mise en scène of philosophy has changed, the scene within which it performed its theoretical and practical judgements. Previously this scene was imagined as a secured, uniform space and time traversed by self-evident distinctions such as 'identity and difference', 'inside and outside', 'agreement and opposition', and 'matter and form' – the basic predicaments of theoretical and practical reason. It was a scene of civility, common sense and self-evidence, with violence only interrupting the play of reason as the 'noises off' of sundry 'Alarums and Excursions'. Now the scene has changed; it possesses the complex topology of a structure that has been shaped and riven by an omnipresent violence and one in which the existing predicaments of thought no longer 'self-evidently' hold.

The inquiry into theoretical and practical reason cannot avoid attending to the implications of change in the predicaments of thinking. This means coming to terms with the unprecedented violence under which modern world society has been realized, and to explore the impact this has had upon the rational ground on which philosophy establishes its theoretical and practical structures. For the very space of its universal claims – its unquestioned civil cosmopolitanism – was itself ever partial and warped, constituted by a violence which was imagined as being without reason, experienced only in doubt. Philosophy has to reorient itself in this new space, beginning with an acknowledgement of the violence of its predicaments. If it does not do so, then its theoretical and practical judgements can only be further disoriented, leading it into the utopian and dystopian extravagances which have characterized the uglier moments of its twentieth-century history.

This work of reorientation has led many philosophers, beginning with Heidegger, to proclaim the end of philosophy and the search for new predicaments of thought and being.[15] Others such as Macintyre have attempted to restore pre-imperial utopias of virtue or with Baudrillard to indulge dystopic analyses of the futility of thought and action. We however will try to continue the critical exploration of the predicaments of global thinking by analysing the impact of the violent constitution of world society on the predicaments of theoretical and practical philosophy. It begins with an examination of the fate of the categories of theoretical judgement under the predicament of global thinking and proceeds to explore some of the implications for the practical issues of subjectivity, alterity and the ethical negotiation of violence.

The theoretical predicaments

The question 'what happens to our categories of explanation when we try to think globally?' has proved explosive for modern philosophy, if not terminal. For some philosophers, above all Heidegger, this question led to the 'end of philosophy' as the attempt to think being within the topoi of metaphysics. With the extension of 'global technology' the nihilism of metaphysical reason becomes manifest in such phenomena as 'world wars' and the subjection of nature as a 'resource' for productive activity. And yet, in a paradox already discerned by Marx and Nietzsche, metaphysical thinking is no longer capable of understanding the world that it has brought into being. Our categories and their conditions of application (the predicaments) are no longer adequate for a proper understanding of world society; the reason they embody has been dispossessed of its world. It has become necessary in the wake of this dispossession to inquire into the conditions of the possibility of a global thinking and acting informed by a non-metaphysical topology of being, one which does not rest on the possession of an object or a self-thought to be present in space and time.[16]

The ways in which we make sense of the world are still deeply indebted to the structures of categorial knowledge inaugurated by classical Greek philosophy. We are often unwitting, even unwilling, heirs to an economy of thought and action bequeathed us by the imperial Greeks, one that persistently determines the ways in which we think and act. We are indebted to this tradition whenever we appeal to 'reason', 'logic', 'being', 'structure', 'system', 'meaning', 'causality' …. The force and compass of these and other terms which we use to make sense of the world and to give meaning to our actions within it were initially determined by Greek philosophy. Greek concepts and modes of thought provide the setting for our thoughts and actions and, moreover, determine the shape of the space in which we locate and employ our concepts – it determines the topology of thoughts and actions.[17]

This space is above all that of categorial judgement: the necessity to make such judgements informs all the ways in which we create and adapt concepts, the ways in which we establish a presence or sense of objectivity appropriate to them, and the ways in which we bring these concepts together with present objects and actions into judgements. For moderns the nature of this objectivity and its relation to concepts is fraught with difficulty. The key to the legitimate possession of knowledge (and self) is what Kant called a 'deduction of the categories', the establishing of a title to their use, one which would connect de facto possession with its justification de jure. But the deduction itself is riven with problems and difficulties that arise from the assumption of a particular understanding of categorial and objective space.

These points may be clarified by a closer characterization of categorial thinking. It would not be unreasonable to describe much scientific activity as the work of categorizing objects and events, bringing them within frameworks of concepts which are themselves continually refined, improved and even occasionally rejected. This view of scientific method was first laid out by Aristotle in his *Categories* (part of the *Organon* or 'toolbox' for thinking), who extends it to reasoning as a whole. Aristotle tries to organize all our acts of classification and naming under generic headings or 'categories' (literally, 'accusations'); he suggests ten: substance, quantity, quality, relation, time, place, position, condition, action and affection. He illustrates them by outlining the categorial structure of what can be said of a warrior on horseback in a city square:

> To sketch my meaning roughly, examples of substance are 'man' or 'the horse', of quantity, such terms as 'two cubits long' or 'three cubits long', of quality, such attributes as 'white', 'grammatical'. Such terms as 'double', 'half', 'greater', fall under the category of relation; 'in the market place', 'in the Lyceum' under that of place; 'yesterday', 'last year' under that of time. 'Lying', 'sitting' are terms indicating position; 'shod', 'armed' indicate condition; 'to lance', 'to cauterize' indicate action; 'to be lanced', 'to be cauterized' indicate affection. (*Categories* 1b26-2a4 in Aristotle 1941, 8)

The categories for Aristotle provide the structure of our thought and our knowledge; everything that may legitimately be thought must be thought through them. Much of the history of philosophy has consisted in the refinement of Aristotle's categorial programme. So, for example, 2000 years later Kant offers in the *Critique of Pure Reason* a 'deduction of the categories' that inform modern, scientific knowledge. He groups them under four headings: quantity, quality, relation and modality, and each heading contains three categories: quantity contains unity, plurality and totality; quality contains reality, negation and limitation; relation contains inherence, causality, reciprocity; and modality contains possibility, actuality and necessity. If we can justify the application of these categories to the world, then we would be in legitimate possession of knowledge of the world.

In spite of the enormous differences between them, both Aristotle and Kant claim that whenever we make a judgement about an action or an object we have recourse to some kind of categorial structure. Yet Kant is modern in that he has severe doubts about the limits and validity of categorial thought, and these arise largely from the failed attempts to extend it to such 'global objects' as God, the World and the Soul in time and space.[18] He realizes that the categorial structure, in spite of its universal pretensions, remains dependent upon a specific and possibly parochial topology of being and time. What is more, this understanding of space and time – one which fuses categorial and objective space – does not itself seem open to justification, being the condition for the use of the categories. The possession of such an understanding of space and time offers plenty of potential for doubt. At its most radical, Kant's critical project set to questioning the restricted topoi within which the categories were deployed. Indeed, the prime motivation of the critical philosophy, what makes it 'critical', is the recognition that we cannot simply deploy our existing categories globally – we cannot extend them without a careful examination of the limits within which they may be used. For Kant it is necessary to establish with precision the limits of the categories' validity – the bounds within which it is meaningful to use them or the limited predicaments of categorial thought. The question then arises: why should these particular limits be established in this particular way? This question haunted not only Kant's work, but also that of his successors, from Fichte and Hegel to Marx and Nietzsche.

Kant exposed the parochial character of the predicaments of categorial thinking in two ways. The first insisted on the temporal limitation of thought, the fact that categorial judgements are made not by Gods in the eternal heaven of thought, but by finite human beings in time. The temporal character of a finite being's judgement severely qualifies its claim to be universal and necessary, throwing it into doubt, if not despair. However, this claim, while itself radical, had further implications which Kant only began to explore: these involved the number of dimensions used to characterize the space of categorial judgement. Introducing time effectively adds a fourth dimension to the three spatial, geometric dimensions, yet Kant also intimates that the dimensions need not be restricted to four let alone three. The first argument holds that categorial judgements must be made in a time and space which are meaningful for human beings; the second that the topology of categorial judgement must not necessarily be restricted to the limits set by human finitude.

Kant rested the critical philosophy on the first position, that categorial judgements be limited to the human experience of space and time. Even such a formal logical principle as the law of contradiction – which claims that X cannot both be and not-be Y – was subject to the condition of time. The principle appears a self-evident basis for good argumentative practice, yet Kant exposed the limited understanding of being and time that it assumes. He pointed out that the principle only holds if it is supported by a tacit temporal qualifier, i.e. X cannot both be and not-be Y *at the same time.* There is nothing to prevent X *becoming* Y in the course of time.[19]

What is in question here, and elaborated in the 'transcendental logic' of the *Critique of Pure Reason,* is the way in which being thought as 'presence' is privileged over being thought as an event in time. The law of the excluded middle assumes that X and Y are things which persist over time rather than events taking place in time; they are set within an understanding of being as an eternally present space never subject to violent change. In the 'transcendental logic' Kant redefines the largely static and spatial categories bequeathed by Aristotelian metaphysics, adapting them to the time of human finitude. He shifts the scene of categorial judgement from a three-dimensional space to a four-dimensional space/time.

The enterprise of 'transcendental logic' was dedicated to supplementing the categories of 'formal logic' with temporal 'principles'. These gave the categories a temporal setting, allowing them to be 'schematized' or made meaningful for the forms of intuition of finite human beings. The categories thus adapted to a human space/time were presented in the 'Analytic of Principles' as 'axioms of intuition', 'anticipations of perceptions', 'analogies of experience' and 'postulates of empirical thought'. Between them they presented an attempt systematically to reorient the categories according to the space/time of finite human beings.

In addition to elaborating the temporal character of the categories, Kant also developed a second important strand of argument for the human predicament of categorial judgement. Not only were the categories themselves temporally oriented, but they could only be used in the context of certain basic orientations of thought which must be assumed in making categorial judgements. These are effectively pre-adaptations of the world to human judgement – making it the kind of place that could be possessed by human judgement. This form of argument goes back to Aristotle and consists in revealing the undisputed conditions for predication, the 'predicaments' of categorial thought. The Aristotelian tradition itself recognized the incomplete character of the supposedly fundamental categories and supplemented them with a further set of relations which underpinned categorial determination and were 'axiomatic' or self-evident to any rational citizen. These became known as the 'predicables' and duly resurfaced in Kant as the 'Concepts of Reflection'.

The 'Concepts of Reflection' offer an extra-categorial order indispensable for making categorial judgements and form the basic orientation of thought, the matrix of judgement. Like the 'principles of judgment' they serve to limit the validity of the categories to the range of human experience, but unlike the principles, they are not aligned with particular categories as their spatio-temporal schema but form the basic predicament of categorial judgement. They consist of the four oppositions, each with a privileged term, of identity and difference, agreement and opposition, inner and outer, form and matter.

For Kant the concepts of reflection presented an ineluctable predicament of judgement; there seemed to be no alternative to orienting our judgements within the four oppositions. Yet we do not possess means to justify orientating our judgements in these ways. We adopt them – or are adopted by them – through an act of violence without which we would be unable to secure our judgements. They presuppose a prior occupation of being and an adequation to our forms of judgement, but one which we cannot justify and certainly not through our categorial structures. As finite beings we are in the predicament of making judgements in accordance with identity and difference, agreement and opposition, inner and outer, form and matter. All that the categories can do is calibrate and refine our judgements within the original predicaments – they tell us how we might modify the predicaments in terms of quantity, quality, relation and modality. Yet, disturbingly, our possession of this original matrix of judgement cannot itself be justified theoretically, nor can our assumption that it corresponds in any way to the shape of being.

The operation of the matrix of judgement may be illustrated by running through the table of categories. Judgements according to the categories of quantity can tell us *how much* A, at a certain time, is identical or different to B, is in agreement or opposition to B, is within or without B, form or matter of B. The quantitative categories, in other words, establish the quantitative determination of the original matrix of the four sets of predicaments. The same mode of argument holds for the remaining groups of categories, those of quality, relation and modality. The judgements according to the categories of quality tell us *whether* at a certain time A is identical or different to B, in agreement or opposition to B, within or outside B, and whether it is form or matter of B. Judgements according to the categories of relation determine the manner in which A and B are related at a certain time, while those of modality determine whether at a certain time A is possibly, actually or necessarily identical or different, in agreement or opposition, inside or outside, and matter and form of each other. All the categories can do is specify the original matrix in some way; they cannot justify its particular structure. They allow us to measure, manipulate, exchange objects within this structure, but not to justify how it is we came into possession of it in the first place.

This rather abstract *Kategorienlehre* can be illustrated with some brief examples from the analysis of global society, showing how pervasive categorial thinking is not only in mainstream work, but also in its radical critiques. In examining a global society composed of 'nation states' there is a tendency to privilege identity over difference – the state is constituted as a spatially defined identity that acts to further and protect its interests vis-à-vis other similarly structured identities. Here the differences between states follow from their initial definition as pre-existent identities.

The predicaments orient our judgements with respect to being, as may be illustrated by the ways in which the remaining predicaments may be adapted to world society. Do we privilege agreement between states over their opposition or vice versa? Similarly with inner and outer, does the external world system have priority of the internal agenda of unit states or do the internal agendas determine the world system? This familiar question may be identified as a modification of the inner/outer predicament by the category of quality; we could modify it quantitatively by asking 'to what degree does the world system determine the unit state, or *vice versa*?' We could also modify it by the categories of relation by asking, 'by what means does the unit state determine the world system or *vice versa*?', or by the categories of modality with the question, 'does the world system necessarily, actually, or possibly determine the unit state or vice versa?'. In these cases all we have done is play the categorial variations upon an assumed predicament. But this kind of work – the stuff of a thousand theses – requires the tacit assumption that this predicament and its fellows (identity and difference, inside and outside, agreement and opposition, matter and form) offer a useful and justified ordering matrix for making judgements about global society. As will be seen, it is by no means the case that the world occupies the kind of space appropriate to the predicaments; these, and in particular the first three, are adapted to a space of civility, along with everything else that this space brings with it.

There is a tension in Kant's work between the concepts of reflection and his effort to adapt the categories to the limits of finite intuition in the 'Analytic of Principles'. The four concepts of reflection clearly make sense only within a three-dimensional space; they assume that the objects of categorial knowledge obey oppositions defined by the nature of that space. By introducing a fourth temporal dimension, Kant substantially complicated the picture by making the concepts of reflection themselves flexible and open to transformation over time. Worse still for the predicaments, the introduction of a fourth dimension did not only make possible a far richer and more concrete account of categorial judgement, it also raised the question of 'why only four dimensions?'

On a few occasions Kant came close to realizing that the character of the space within which judgement took place could be extended not only from three to four, but to several dimensions. There are intimations in his work of an analogy between the parochial character of categorial determination and the three-dimensional space of Euclidean geometry. Kant was one of the first philosophers to realize that three-dimensional space offered only a very particular and restricted model for the organization and conception of spatial relations: the world need not be confined within it. On one occasion he even anticipated the possibility of a multidimensional geometry, which broke the spatial limits established by Greek geometry.[20] However, this realization implied not only a transgression of the boundaries of Euclidean geometry, but of reason itself, since much of the prescriptive force of reason rested upon the self-evident certainty of the axioms of geometry. Kant's intimation of different structures of space carried with it a threat to a structure of categorial thinking dependent upon a predicamental matrix determined by the particular characteristics of Euclidean space.

The problem then becomes: how can we justify a given categorial and predicamental organization of being? We cannot do so empirically, because the categories and the predicaments cannot be legitimated by abstraction from concrete experience; indeed Kant gives some examples (incongruent counterparts) where concrete experience does not obey the predicaments. In order to think categorially we have to 'anticipate' an order of relations between concepts and their objects and between the subject and its concepts and objects. This order gives meaning to the categories but is itself extra-categorial; it can be justified by recourse neither to the categories – since it forms the condition for categorically justified argument – nor to experience, since it is a condition of experience. By realizing that this extra-categorial order is indebted to a specific, yet unjustified conception of space, Kant severely threatens not only the authority of categorial judgement, but also reason itself; can judgements securely assume legitimacy within a space whose character and limits are secured by something other than reason?

The critical philosophy is strung between the vertiginous consequences of abandoning the extra-categorial order or attempting to re-establish it on the basis of the human experience of space and time. If we radically question the validity of the extra-categorial order and attempt to extend it, then we are in danger of speaking nonsense. If, for example, we propose that the world inhabits a space of more than four dimensions then, although we can argue rigorously in N dimensions, we have, for Kant, left the realm of human significance since objects in more than four dimensions exceed human intuition. We cannot legitimately possess, because we are not the kind of being that can meaningfully possess things or ourselves in the fifth dimension. Even when we extend possession from three to four dimensions we run into difficulty, because finite beings cannot fully secure possession for all time.

A similar problem arises if we replace the quantitative, dimensional ordering of the predicaments of judgement with predicaments of a qualitatively different order such as Derrida's 'trace' or 'vomit'. In such a situation we once again risk speaking nonsense, making judgements which exceed the capacity of human intuition. Such predicaments would entail a thorough recalibration of meaning, one which would be violent while certainly opening us to different ways of being and relating to other beings. In spite of his intimations of an N-dimensional geometry, Kant was of course not in a position fully to develop its implications. Instead he sought to secure the predicaments of judgement by aligning them with a human space and time, one in which judgement would make sense in terms of the structure of human intuition.

Yet this move itself, with all the subtlety and passion which Kant brought to it, rests on a philosophical *fiat*. The human space and time decreed by Kant is tainted by violence and insecurity – it is a space of insecure possession and a time of insecure finitude. Kant's enterprise is dedicated to securing our possessions within this condition, assuaging our doubts by means of his critical tribunal. Possession in this condition – which Kant figures as a civil republic in contrast to sceptical nomadism and dogmatic despotism – is insecure but not impossible; we may doubt the legitimacy of our possessions, but not despair over them.[21] Such an attempt to maintain human meaning for the categories was subsequently judged insupportable by Marx, Nietzsche and Heidegger. They claimed that it was no longer possible to understand world society within the compass of traditional humanism. The space and time of human occupation and finitude was simply no longer appropriate to a global society organized according to such ahuman forces as 'capital', 'will to power' and 'global technology'. These forces determine their own configurations of space and render notions of human possession and self-possession sentimental and irrelevant. With this thought, they began the reconsideration of the character and shape of the predicaments of judgement which was extended by their twentieth-century successors.

For Marx, Nietzsche and Heidegger the establishment of world society put the predicaments of theoretical and practical judgement into crisis. The human predicaments proposed by Kant seemed increasingly inefficacious in understanding the 'world' let alone in acting to change it. In Marx's work from the 1850s there is a growing realization that the worldwide expansion of capital increasingly renders human measures of time and space inappropriate. Capital is inherently expansive and destructive; it breaks down the predicaments of identity and difference, agreement and opposition, inside and outside, and matter and form. To make judgements within these predicaments is to misunderstand the nature of world society; it no longer takes place within a human space of civility, but in an ahuman space of perpetually expanding destruction/creation.

Not only does capital exceed the predicaments of judgement, but it does so at a speed which bears little relation to human measures of time. In the *Grundrisse* Marx consistently describes capital as a process of establishing and overcoming limits, positing its predicaments in order to exceed them. He even regards it as approaching the nihilistic limit of abolishing its own time and space in an instantaneous act of production, circulation and consumption.[22] Human finite judgement and its predicaments are no longer appropriate measures for understanding the world society of capital. The latter tends to a condition in which the differences between identity and difference, agreement and opposition, inside and outside, and matter and form are no longer respected; nor are the temporal limits established by human finitude. Capital does not leave any space for such judgements; within its limits all judgements have to obey the law of capital – the 'Moses and all the Prophets' of 'accumulate, accumulate' – or else be dismissed as irrelevant.

The impact of the self-expansion of capital on the predicaments is analogous to the effects Nietzsche saw arising from the global extension of the will to power. He argues that the establishment of an order of predication is itself a violent act, the manifestation of a will-to-power in which a subject violently establishes its conditions of meaning. Kant's finite subjects, insecure in their possessions and fearful of death, are the products of a history in which human beings have 'become what they are'. In the course of this history they have settled on certain ways of judging, which must themselves be brought under genealogical scrutiny. Nietzsche's investigation proceeds by translating the predicaments into questions. Instead of assuming the predicaments as self-evident, the genealogist asks such questions as who or what is identical or different to me/us, who or what is in agreement or opposition to me/us, who or what are within me/us or without me/us, who or what are matter and who or what form to me/us?[23] The theoretical predicaments are shown to be founded in certain practices of exclusion, practices of forming a subjectivity that does not recognize the violence of its acts of exclusion, but instead couches them in the language of reason. The predicaments of such a subjectivity, which Nietzsche designated 'nihilistic', are revealed, through genealogy, to have originated in the suppression of alterity. Such unowned violence increasingly characterized what Nietzsche described in *Daybreak* as the 'power hungry societies of Europe and America' for whom he presciently predicted a century of inhuman and ultimately uncathartic warfare on a world scale. If human actors persist in reading the world in terms of their limited perspectives, then the world will become an increasingly strange and terrifying place; they must become *Übermensch* by establishing new measures and perspectives of judgement appropriate to an ahuman world.

Both Marx and Nietzsche saw the advent of world society as severely qualifying the universalist claims of reason. Judgements according to the categories and their predicaments were increasingly inappropriate for understanding world society. The world was no longer the kind of object that could be confined within the limits of oppositions appropriate to a historically specific kind of possession. The renunciation of the old, civil notions of possession of self and world was systematically worked through by Heidegger in his account of the end of philosophy in the face of 'global technology'. The world dominated by 'global technology' marks the end of philosophy in two senses. In the first, philosophy has ended in so far as its system of categorial judgements and their predicaments are no longer appropriate to world society: the rational is no longer appropriate to the real. But in another sense 'global technology' was the end or 'realization' of philosophy.[24] The largely spatial organization of the world by the predicaments – which thought of their objects as 'present' – was itself a 'violent assault' on being.

The conditions for judgement lay outside of reason in an unjustifiable ordering of the 'real' which made it present for the manipulations of the categories. The world became a present or 'standing resource' for the technical manipulations of the categories, and these manipulations, when conducted on a world scale, could dispense with the original human agent. Heidegger moved from an attempt in *Being and Time* to radicalize Kant's project of qualifying the categories according to human finitude to realizing that the conditions of global technology required a fundamental rethinking of the topology of being.

The legacy of Marx, Nietzsche and Heidegger's questioning of the predicaments of judgement has been a crisis in thinking the relation between reason and violence. World society can no longer be thought within a matrix of judgement constituted by the oppositions of identity and difference, agreement and opposition, inner and outer, form and matter. For these four predicaments occupy a topologically limited space, analogous to the three-dimensional space of Euclidean geometry. They are, however, no longer self-evident, no longer to be taken for granted when thinking globally. Forcing an object such as world society to occupy such a matrix of judgement is like trying to describe a three-dimensional world in two dimensions. If we retain these predicaments we are effectively reducing an (at least) four-dimensional world of space and time to a three-dimensional matrix of judgement. The result is unavoidable distortion and disorientation.

Yet if we abandon these predicaments, as we must, further difficulties arise about how to conceive the relation between the world and the subject. This relation can no longer be thought in terms of limited space and finite time: the privileged space of the predicaments, one in which violence was banished to the frontier, is succeeded by one in which the potential for violence is ubiquitous. We cannot from within 'identity' violate the 'different' and manage our guilt through doubt concerning the legitimacy of our usurped possession. The consequences of this violation are omnipresent and have to be managed directly. The carefully policed distinction between violence and reason – between establishing de facto possession and legitimating it de jure – has collapsed upon itself.

In consequence there is no longer any privileged or 'civil' space on the globe free from the traces of violence. Judgement can no longer be automatically justified within the space of the predicaments but now involves the open and continuous management of violence; each judgement must be accompanied by a decision regarding the character of the site upon which judgement is taking place. The attempts to secure the possessions of theoretical reason involved displacing the violence of expropriation to the margins and judging within the privileged space of sovereign civility. This violence has now returned to the heart of judgement, putting an ethical question mark beside each theoretical claim to possession. Rethinking the predicaments of world society beyond the protected, sovereign space of civility has become an ethical problem, one requiring an analysis of the practical predicaments.

The practical predicaments

So far the predicaments have been analysed in terms of their role as the matrix for theoretical judgements. The four 'concepts of reflection' were shown to be appropriate to a specific understanding of space, one which was uniform, not subject to violent, qualitative change, one indeed whose main qualitative features were inscribed by the predicaments themselves. It was a space in which distinctions such as identity and difference, agreement and opposition, inside and outside, matter and form were able to hold undisputed sway. Within this space it was possible to survey, calculate and manipulate all forms of motion and change by means of the categories. These determined whether, how much, why and in what ways change had occurred.

On the basis of such knowledge it was possible to imagine rational utopias in which human beings would adjust their actions with respect to their knowledge of each other and of nature. This theoretical knowledge, once adequately secured, would serve as the basis for practical judgement; by its means not only personal conduct, but the conduct of a state could be rationally determined. Knowledge of the true would tend, in other words, to the realization of the good. However, these rational utopias were precisely 'utopian' – of no place – they certainly did not inhabit a world of human finitude, one in which the occupation of space was an occasion for constant anxiety and doubt. They proposed a civility without violence, forgetting that civility was based on the repression of violence and its export to the frontier.

The introduction of 'time' into the predicaments thoroughly complicated the nature of both space and the predicaments, prompting instabilities that had to be negotiated. What was different might become identical, what was inside may find itself outside; the very boundaries of the predicaments might become unstable, open to negotiation. But when the boundaries of judgment themselves become an object of judgement, the problem arises of establishing adequate criteria for judging them. It appeared as if the predicaments were not simply the neutral framework of beings in space, but also corresponded to the particular experience of particular beings in time. They can be regarded as inseparable from the experience of a finite subjectivity, one which is unsure of its possession of itself – poised between being and not being – and seeking security in the possession of things and territory.

Although this subjectivity found security in the objects which it possessed and the territory over which it was sovereign, it also discovered a fresh insecurity in the limits to its possessions. These limits were established not only by the possibility of losing possession at death, but also having them removed by 'others'. The search for a stable identity in possession was always accompanied by the sense that this possession and this identity were always under threat. The threat could be met by expansion, but this paradoxically only yielded further insecurity at the extended borders. The theoretical introduction of finitude into the predicaments did not just bring with it the finite subject but also the question of violence.

These formal arguments which make the move from theoretical to practical reason were anticipated by Kant and worked through by his successors, most starkly by Nietzsche. Kant's insistence that knowledge must respect the limits of finite, human intuition was not simply an epistemological argument. By showing how the application of the categories could be adjusted to finite intuition through schematism and the principles, Kant made Being into a temporal event – it was no longer present in space but was continually being presenced. Furthermore, the mode of presencing itself was by implication directly ethical since it took place in accord with the intuition of a finite subjectivity in the throes of suffering its insecurity and fear of death.

It was Nietzsche who showed not only that experience was temporal, that the categories were the perspectives of a 'human, all too human' understanding, but that the predicaments themselves were but the ways in which finite subjectivities, or 'sick animals', went about ordering themselves, others and the world around them. The clue to the origins of the predicaments lies in the fact that they take the form of oppositions, that they are in some way internally contested. The predicaments are not simply the ways in which we organize being but are the issue of a struggle over this definition. This is further attested by the existence of a privileged term in each of the oppositions – one prevailing over the other – as identity over difference, agreement over opposition, within over without, form over matter. These privileged oppositions, going back to the Pythagorean Table, assumed a new urgency in modern philosophy. They point to the fact that the predicaments are intrinsically practical, evidence of a struggle, but additionally, that the world has this kind of being, is thought and acted upon in this kind of space, because it is violently made to be and do so.

The oppositions of the 'Concepts of Reflection' obey a deeper logic than the one which is conducted through the categories on their surface. The oppositions themselves seem to have inscribed within them the confrontation between violence and limitation which defines human finitude. The privileging of one term in the opposition over the other suggests an adversarial logic of friend/foe, life/death, while the fact that the vanquished term persists suggests either that it has not been fully subdued or that it cannot be overcome. In the latter case, the existence of 'identity', 'inside', 'agreement', 'form' is only possible with their other of 'difference', 'outside', 'opposition', 'matter'. What would have happened if everything was identical without difference, if everything became inside with no outside, everything agreement with no opposition, all form, no matter? In such a condition there would no longer be any need for categories to manage the oppositions, since there would no longer be any doubt, only certainty. Nor in such a condition would there be any place for finite subjects in the throes of negotiating their finitude through controlled violence.

The analysis of the theoretical predicaments suggested that with the achievement of world society these oppositions folded in upon themselves. The kind of space within which these oppositions made sense was one in which the oppositions coexisted on a single stage: the identical and the different in opposition, but on the same stage; within and without but again in terms of the same stage. In order to contain the violence of these encounters the stage had to be continually expanding, the violence deferred to its border. When this is no longer possible, when there is no longer a border, then the space changes; it is no longer appropriate to manage the oppositions by expanding the stage, since this expansion has itself reached its limit.

In this situation, the problem of practical philosophy becomes one of changing the stage, or the predicaments, on and through which violence in the modern period has been managed. This requires the rethinking of the predicaments of ethics and politics, trying to imagine an ethics and a politics informed by a different involvement with, for example, the problems of identity and its correlates possession and security. This need not necessarily take the shape of dystopias of speed or simulation, which remain radical gestures within the existing predicaments, but might consider reformulating the predicaments or even developing new ones more appropriate to world society.

One example of a renegotiation of the predicaments is represented by postmodern thought. In its various guises this relies on inverting the privileged term in the oppositions of the 'Concepts of Reflection'. It privileges difference over identity, opposition over agreement, the excluded over the included, the material over the formal. So, for example, in the analysis of the state, the postmodern analysis does not regard the state as self-identical subject but as an identity constructed through the negotiations of differences. The state, in other words, does not act as an identity but is constituted as identity through its acts with respect to what is perceived as 'foreign' or 'other'.[25]

Another strategy is to propose a number of new candidates for the predicaments of being and acting. The most striking precedent is offered by the later works of Heidegger. He sought a new understanding of being in terms of its presencing and withdrawing, thus giving the thought of being a strong temporal accent. He provisionally sketched a matrix of predicaments appropriate to a world dominated by global technology: *Ereignis*, dwelling, favour. A similar strategy is pursued by Derrida, who proliferates fresh predicaments in order to avoid subordinating them to a hierarchical principle. This may be the proper strategy for a world in which the subject can no longer prescribe the terms in which the world will appear and the other will act towards it.[26]

A further approach consists in reconsidering the adversarial basis to the oppositions of the predicaments, rethinking the basis of the friend/foe structure. This has been ventured by Levinas in his work on ethics, where the ethical encounter with the Other does not take place on the terrain of theoretical reason. There is no 'opposition' between self and other because their encounter is not staged within the uniform, limited space of theoretical reason. It opens a qualitatively distinct ethical 'space' and 'time' which is not involved with the oppositions of the predicaments.[27]

A further influential critique of the oppositions informing the predicaments has been developed by feminist philosophers. They question the gendered quality of the space of theoretical and practical reason, in which women are cast as the differential other to a fixed male identity. The work of Luce Irigaray, for example, is dedicated to opening new predicaments of thought and practice in which the 'identity' of women may be constituted beyond the predicament of identity and difference. This questions not only the parasitic character of male identity, but also the entire oppositional scenario in which negotiations of identity and difference, agreement and opposition, inside and outside, and matter and form have previously been staged.[28]

The various beginnings of attempts to rethink the predicaments can be seen as responses to the collapse of the old predicaments upon the advent of world society. With this event, the space of reason co-extensive with civility can no longer be accepted as self-evident. Yet philosophical modernity has largely confined itself *within* this space, concerning itself with securing the categories of knowledge in the face of theoretical doubt and elaborating an ethics and politics of civility; it is ill suited for reflection *upon* this space. The self-possessed, self-disciplined and 'rational' subject of ethical and political civility is internally divided between civil and military identities; rational discipline is its norm in civilian life, disciplined violence the exception, used on and beyond the border and in times of emergency. The space and time of the categories and the predicaments was secured by the coexistence of violence and reason, one which was made possible by the deferral of violence spatially to the frontier, temporally to a time of emergency. This deferral was informed by a sovereignty which defined the limits of violence and civility – defined the place of ethical and political judgement. But with the collapse of these limits, the place of judgement is no longer secured from the question of the implication of violence and reason. Philosophical reflection conducted within the bounds of civility is thrown into crisis when faced with the mutual implication of reason and violence.

The collapse of the spatial and temporal limits of violence with the advent of world society does not lead automatically to the rule of violence in totalitarian politics, nor does it necessarily entail the suspension of the ethical. The new space that has been opened no longer defers violence, no longer attempts to manage it in the old ways of doubt and securing the possessions of the categories. New predicaments can be seen to be taking shape, which raise the possibility of an ethical management of violence.

This could not be based upon the neutral space of civility – the 'level playing field' – protected by sovereign violence, a space in which judgements are made within predicaments accepted by 'common sense'. The new practical judgements require predicaments which are not fixed or protected by an external sovereign violence but which acknowledge the ways in which they are informed by that violence.

Under these circumstances, a political or an ethical judgement has to invent for itself anew its own 'concept of reflection' – it has to include within itself a reflection on the site or the place from and in which judgement is made. The exercise of violence in judgement is no longer deferred to the borders of the space of judgement but is placed in the act of judgement itself. This reorientation of judgement and its predicaments is appropriate to a world in which violence has no place, in which it is ubiquitous ranging beyond oppositions such as identity or difference, agreement and opposition, within and without, matter and form. If the problems resulting from the ubiquity of violence continue to be thought within these obsolete predicaments, the result will be an intensification of violence, not only in the guise of military conquest, but also as global pollution, poverty and hunger.

Notes

1   The themes of identity and 'self-assertion' in early modern Europe are discussed in Blumenberg 1983.

2   For example, 'against the Jews we are able to argue by means of the Old Testament while against heretics we are able to argue by means of the New Testament. But the Mohammedans and the Pagans accept neither one nor the other. We must, therefore, have recourse to the natural reason, to which all men are forced to give assent' (Aquinas 1975, 62).

3   For various aspects of the origins, operation and breakdown of the medieval system of control see Brundage 1987; Moore 1987; Morris 1989; and the classic Southern 1981.

4   On 10 December 1520 Luther and the students of the University of Wittenberg retaliated for the burning of Luther's books with their own *Auto-da-Fe* of the books of Canon Law and the Papal Constitutions. By doing so they symbolically turned their backs on the medieval system of social regulation, without having fully elaborated a replacement. The ad hoc way in which the forces and anxieties released by this revolution were managed by the elaboration of civility within the nation state is of course the subject of two sociological classics, Weber 1977, and vol. 2 of Elias 1973.

5   This attitude informs the essay 'Of coaches', The Third Book, Chap. VI, where Montaigne declaims against the Spanish Conquests of Peru and Mexico: 'Our world hath of late discovered another (and who can warrant whether it

be the last of his brethren, since both the Damons, the Sibylles, and all we have hitherto been ignorant of this?) no lesse-large, fully-peopled, all-things-yeelding, and might in strength, than ours … yet have we not whipped and submitted the same unto our discipline, or schooled him by the advantage of our valour or naturell forces, nor have wee instructed him by our justice and integrity; nor subdued by our magnanimity' (Montaigne 1938, 141–2).

6   The contrast between Pascal and Montaigne is at its starkest with regard to death. For Montaigne, in the essay 'That to philosophie is to learne how to die', death 'is the condition of your creation: death is a part of yourselves: you fly from your selves. The being you enjoy is equally shared betweene life and death' (Montaigne 1938, vol. I, 87). In contrast to his view that 'the profit of life consists not in the space, but rather in the use' (Montaigne 1938, vol. I, 89), Pascal is extremely anxious about the infinitesimally tiny space of his life, terrified by its insignificance before the immense territories of death: 'When I consider my short life, absorbed in the eternity of before and after, the little space that I fill and can see plunged into the immense infinities of spaces which I don't know and which don't know me, I am frightened and astounded to see myself here rather than there for there's no reason why here more than there, why now rather than then' (Pascal 1909, Section III, no. 205). His fear is not only of *Le silence eternel de ces espaces infinis* but is also more concretely, and perversely, echoing Montaigne, a fear of 'the many kingdoms which do not know of us' (nos. 206 and 207).

7   In the *Discourse on Method,* part II, Descartes employs a series of parallels between the reform of law, architecture and philosophy. His diffident claim to having only designed to 'reform my own opinion and to build on a foundation which is entirely my own' is undermined by its contiguity with earlier reflections on the 'prudent legislator'. There is a clear analogy between laying the foundations of philosophical knowledge in certainty and giving the law to half-savages: 'Thus I imagined that those people who were once half-savage, and who have become civilized only by slow degrees, merely forming their laws as the disagreeable necessities of their crimes and quarrels constrained them, could not succeed in establishing so good a system of government as those who, from the time they first came together as communities, carried into effect the constitution laid down by some prudent legislator' (Descartes 1969).

8   See Heidegger's provocative reading of Cartesian substance in chapter 3 of *Being and Time* and the commentary on this chapter by Hubert L. Dreyfus in Dreyfus 1991, chapter 6.

9   For discussions of the role of the post-reformation *Polizei* in securing the civility of civil society, see my *Art of Judgement,* Caygill 1989, 103–9, along with Oestreich 1982 and Raeff 1983.

10   Paul Virilio makes the same point when he writes 'Fascism is alive because total war, then total peace, have engaged the headquarters of the great national bodies (the armies, the forces of production) in a new spatial and temporal process, and the historical universe in a Kantian world. The problem is no longer one of a historiality in (chronological) time or (geographic) space, but in what space-time?' (Virilo 1986, 117). However, his turn to speed and the strategic war for time in a dromology does not adequately answer his crucial question – what space-time? – what is the current condition of the dromos?

11 See Bauman 1989.

12 Edith Wyschogrod's otherwise thoughtful *Spirit in Ashes: Hegel, Heidegger, and Man-Made Mass Death* (Wyschogrod 1986) overlooks the specific contribution made by imperialism to the rise and fall of civility; she thus overemphasizes the role of 'technology' in abstraction from its social and political setting.

13 Caygill points the reader to the chapters by Der Derian and Shapiro in the volume in which this piece was originally published [editor's note].

14 Caygill points the reader to the chapter by R. Walker in the original volume [editor's note].

15 Heidegger's thought exemplifies this disorientation, veering between National Socialist utopia and technological dystopia, waiting on a God to save us and some most radical and important destructions of the metaphysical tradition and statements of a new topology of being. It is not fortuitous that the debate around the 'Heidegger Affair' has become the site for some of the most sustained reflections on the relation between philosophy, violence and the political. See the contributions from Derrida 1989, Lacoue-Labarthe 1990, Lyotard 1988a, and the stimulating collection, Brainard et al. eds. 1991.

16 For a sustained and rigorous presentation of Heidegger's development of a non-metaphysical topology of Being see Schürmann 1987.

17 This 'setting' emerged with the invention of philosophy in the colonial cities of Ionia and its return to Athens; it coincides with the political effort to distinguish between the civil space within the *polis* from that of the barbarians without.

18 These 'destructions' of the global pretensions of cosmology, psychology and 'theology' are carried out in the 'transcendental dialectic' of the *Critique of Pure Reason*.

19 Kant exposes the tacit introduction of a temporal qualifier in the first critique: the principle of contradiction asserts 'A thing = A, which is something = B, cannot at the same time be not-B, but may very well in succession be both B and not-B. For instance, a man who is young cannot at the same be old, but may very well at one time be young and at another time not-young, that is, old. The principle of contradiction, however, as a merely logical principle, must not in any way limit its assertions to time-relations' (*CPR* A152/B191).

20 In the opening pages of his first published text from 1747 – *Thoughts on the True Estimation of Living Forces* – Kant is already speculating on spaces with more than three dimensions. He derives three-dimensional space from the inverse square law of motion and argues for the possibility of other laws of motion in other forms of space with 'different properties and dimensions'. He goes on to say, 'A science of all these possible modes of space would unmistakably be the highest geometry that a finite understanding could undertake. The impossibility we note in ourselves of representing a space with more than three dimensions seems to me to arise from our soul perceiving external impressions under the law of the inverse square, and because it itself so constituted that it is not only affected, but also acts outside itself in this way' (Kant 1982, 34). In 1747 Kant observed that such thoughts 'could serve as a programme for an inquiry which I am considering', and they are hinted at in *Universal Natural History and the Theory of the Heavens,* but not properly developed until his text on topology of 1768 – 'Concerning the ultimate foundations of the differentiation of regions in space' in Kant 1968. Here Kant attempts to develop further Leibniz's programme for a proto-topology outlined in 'Analysis situs'. This sought to extend geometry by the analysis of figure and its properties of similarity and congruence. Kant extends this analysis to a questioning of the limitations of Euclidean space. He begins with a phenomenology of three dimensionality which relates the dimensions to the human body's experience of above and below, right and left, front and back (Kant 1968, 38). He then shows how the experience of the world in these spatial terms nevertheless succumbs to perplexing 'difficulties' such as incongruent counterparts and directional orderings which point to a broader notion of space within which three-dimensional human space must be set. Kant calls this excessive space 'absolute space'. Although these comments are set within a theistic framework, they clearly show Kant not only relating three-dimensional space of human, finite intuition, but also considering other forms of space and their appropriate geometries.

21 This is the task of the 'critical tribunal' which 'will assure to reason its lawful claims … not by despotic decrees but in accordance with its own eternal and unalterable laws'. *CPR* A xii.

22 For textual details supporting these points, see my article 'The Return of Nietzsche and Marx' [Chapter 2 above – editor's note].

23 Nietzsche saw these oppositions originating in a will to power, as in this passage from *Thus Spoke Zarathustra*: 'One neighbour never understood another: his soul was always amazed at his neighbour's wickedness. A table of values hangs over every people. Behold, it is the table of its overcomings; behold it is the voice of its will to power' (Nietzsche [1883/85] 1975), 84.

24 See the two main collections of Heidegger's essays on these themes, Heidegger 1972 and Heidegger 1977. See also Zimmerman 1990.

25 This form of argument is impressive worked through with respect to US foreign policy in Campbell 1992.

26 Derrida's term *différance* is an example of a new predicament which refuses the opposition implied in the tradition predicament of identity and difference; see *'Différance'* in Derrida 1982. Derrida has recently explored some of the political questions of the opposition of identity in Derrida 1992.

27 The an-archical implications of refusal to ground ethics in the principles of theoretical philosophy are concisely presented in 'Humanism and An-archy', in Levinas 1987, 127–39. The position is developed in more programmatic detail in Levinas 1969. For an illuminating analysis of both Derrida's and Levinas's practical philosophy, see Critchley 1992.

28 See Irigaray 1985; and Margaret Whitford's convincing presentation of Irigaray's work in Whitford 1991.

4

Politics and war: Hegel and Clausewitz

In one word, the Art of War in its highest point of view is policy,
but, no doubt, a policy which fights battles instead of writing notes.
– CLAUSEWITZ, *ON WAR*

Hegel's presentation of a speculative community fails at the point where he was required to reflect on the relationship between military violence and the ethics and politics of civility. The book *On War* by his Berlin contemporary and fellow victim of the cholera epidemic of 1831, Carl von Clausewitz, can however serve as a means of driving Hegel's *Philosophy of Right* beyond its limits of right and civility. The philosophies of war and of right, taken together, recover Hegel's early insights into the inextricability of violence and property in *The German Constitution* and the *System of Ethical Life*, while Clausewitz's demonstration of the inextricability of war and politics and his call for a 'tact of judgement' is an essential supplement to the *Philosophy of Right*, without which it will fail to comprehend modern *Sittlichkeit* or speculative community.[1]

Political and moral philosophy since Kant has been conducted within the limits of the ethics and politics of civility defined by the European nation state.[2] The idea of freedom at the beating heart of Kant and Hegel's theoretical and practical philosophies is essentially a civil freedom of possession, action and exchange. Such a philosophy is ill-suited for reflecting on violence since the very context of civility is established by the *exclusion* of violence. Violence for civil freedom is the exception, whether as a sign of the breakdown of civility or as the potential force securing the borders of civility. The notion of civil freedom requires violence to be concentrated in the state, preferably in the hands of professionals such as police and military. Modern civility has as a result many contradictory features: dependent on the massing of an extreme and concentrated potential for violence at its borders, it nevertheless pathologizes any violence that emerges within these borders. The overall effect is to remove responsibility for violence from civil society and to obscure its complicity with civil freedom.

The absence of any sustained reflection upon the violence informing civility is a noteworthy feature of modern philosophy. It is most obvious in the disappearance of the institution of military violence from modern philosophy, a process which can be observed in the development of Hegel's political philosophy. The exclusion of violence from the development of the institutions of civil freedom in the *Philosophy of Right* is complemented by its extravagant return as the truth of civility in Clausewitz. For at the very moment that violence retreats from Hegel's political philosophy to become a moment of the philosophy of spirit under the title 'philosophy of right' it returns in all its extravagance in Clausewitz's *On War*. For although they appear opposed, both analyses of the modern, post-revolutionary social order focus upon the problem of freedom, with Hegel analysing it in terms of freedom and right and Clausewitz in terms of freedom and violence.

Are the philosophies of right and of war diametrically opposed, or is there a relationship between them, and if so, what is its character? The first step towards a speculative answer to these questions is to inquire into the conditions for the separation of right and war, which are found in the peculiar structure of modern civility. The scission of civility and the violence which sustains it is expressed in the separation of the philosophy of civility or right from the philosophy of violence or war. And yet each element is unthinkable without the other: the internal pacification of modern civility is secured by the concentration of violence at the periphery of civil society, while modern war is only possible with the support of the productive resources of civil society. To paraphrase Adorno, 'The philosophy of right and the philosophy of war are torn halves of an integral freedom which do not add up.' The inability to 'add up' or the failure of the modern concept of freedom to achieve an internal recognition of the violence of civility has repeatedly wrecked the consistency of the ethical and political judgements of both liberals and Marxists. Both traditions either deny the complicity of violence and civility, or else they pull away from working through its consequences in favour of the crude, almost eschatological opposition of means and ends. The latter is exemplified by Lenin, who perceptively criticized the theorists of the Second International for not understanding either Hegel or Clausewitz, only himself to produce a forced reconciliation which led to bureaucratic/military dictatorship and the destruction of civility.[3]

The ethical politics of the 'speculative community' is characterized by the recognition and assumption of responsibility for its own violence. This requires that the philosophy of right include at least a moment of reflection on the violence of its apparently peaceful and free acquisitions, and exchanges. This is signally lacking in the *Elements of the Philosophy of Right* (1821) and is a symptom of its failure to develop a morally and politically adequate notion of community or *Sittlichkeit*. In this respect the text of 1821 marks a retreat from the insights gained in such early writings as *The German Constitution* (1801–2) and the so-called *System of Ethical Life* (1804–5).[4] It will be argued, indeed, that these texts do not represent stages in the development of Hegel's political philosophy towards the *Philosophy of Right* but are part of a lineage leading to the *Phenomenology of Spirit* (1807) and its thematic of the recognition and misrecognition of violence. This insight seems to be abandoned in the *Philosophy of Right*.

Hegel's *Philosophy of Right* was published as a manual for students to accompany part of his annual Heidelberg lectures on the philosophical encyclopaedia. He claims in his preface that it presents 'a more systematic exposition of the same basic concepts which, in relation to this part of philosophy, are already contained in a previous work designed to accompany my lectures, namely my *Encyclopedia of the Philosophical Sciences*' (PR 9). He is referring to Sections 400–452 of the 1817 *Encyclopedia* on 'Objective Spirit' which moves from the notion of free will in abstraction – 'free will which for itself is free will' – to the ways in which it actualizes itself. It does so in terms of three moments: as immediate concept (*Begriff*) or free will as expressed in the laws of property and contract; as reflected concept or free will as expressed in the laws of morality; and as actualized concept or community (*Sittlichkeit*). These moments of actualization drawn from the *Logic* are carried over into the architectonic of the *Philosophy of Right*, which begins with the 'abstract right' of possession, contract and crime, moving to 'morality' as the analysis of responsibility, intention and the good and ending with *Sittlichkeit* or the analysis of family, civil society and state. What is crucial about this structure is that it *begins* with abstract 'free will' and proceeds to an exposition of its becoming concrete in actuality, while the earlier texts begin with a freedom already heavily implicated in, and qualified by, violence. The freedom of the *Philosophy of Right* has been purified of its violence at the outset, with serious consequences for the analysis of community.

The caesura between Hegel's early and later political writings is most evident in the inversion of argumentative procedure which has taken place between them. The early writings begin with the existing constitution acknowledging itself as being in a state of war; here a community or ethical life *(Sittlichkeit)* is constituted by its preparedness to unite in self-defence. Freedom is not a 'free will' actualizing itself in possessions and contracts but is constituted as something that the community is prepared to defend. Accordingly, in §1 of *The German Constitution* on the 'Concept of the State' Hegel writes, 'If a multitude is to form a state, then it must form a common military and public authority.'[5] Only after the union for common defence has been attained can the state proceed to assign legal status and property rights to its citizens. This is an inversion of the liberal, social contract theory of the state, which begins the assignment of property rights in private law and then derives relations of public law from them. Under Hegel's early definition of the state, freedom is qualified; it is not the property of an abstract 'free will' but is defined by its relation to a potential enemy, at once implicated in violence and recognizing this implication.

Hegel's early texts begin by recognizing the place of violence in the foundation of the state, while in the *Philosophy of Right* there is no mention of military violence until the final paragraphs concerning the external sovereignty of the state. Hegel's early account begins with the mutual implication of freedom and violence, while the *Philosophy of Right* relegates violence to the borders of the state and the state's relation with other states. For the latter the state is founded in an abstract freedom which proceeds from possession through contractual exchange and then to morality and finally the familial, occupational and public constitution of ethical life. In this exposition, which moves from relations of private to public law, the state is above all a realm of civility in which violence has no place. The development from The *German Constitution* to the *Philosophy of Right* may be characterized as one of the effacement of violence, its displacement from the core of the state to the periphery of civility. But this banishment of violence from the site of civil and political judgement provokes severe distortions in Hegel's later text, which open the space for a philosophy of pure violence in Clausewitz. By removing the recognition of violence from the foundation of the state, violence becomes the abstract reflex of an abstract freedom put to the service of the largely amoral, technical manipulations of experts.

What is at stake in the claim for the mutual implication of freedom and violence may be drawn out from a closer consideration of the role of the military in the early writings. In §5 of *The German Constitution* Hegel makes the claim, shocking to liberals of all persuasions, that 'The change from the mailed fist to politics is not to be regarded as a change from anarchy to constitutionalism. There is no real change in principle but only on the surface' (*HPW* 188). This passage claims no less than the continuity of war and politics, but not in a Clauswitzian sense that politics is war. It serves to point towards the mutual implication of violence and civility or the fact that a civility without the collateral of military violence is unsustainable:

A mass of people which, owing to this dissolution of military power and lack of finances, has not been able to erect a public authority of its own, is incapable of defending its independence against foreign enemies. It must of necessity see its independence disappearing, if not at once then gradually. (*HPW* 173)

Hegel puts this point even more clearly when he subordinates the political economy of civility to the modes of common defence, as when he claims that 'The strength of a country consists not in the number of its inhabitants, nor in its fertility, nor in its size, but solely in the manner whereby all these things can be used for the great end of common defence' (*HPW* 179). However, it must be stressed that such comments do not serve to elevate violence above civility, but rather to underline their mutual implication.

The distance between Hegel's early understanding of the mutual implication of right and violence and a liberal or a Clauswitzian separation of them is underscored by Hegel's uncompromising attack on the notion of a standing army. Instead of professional administrators of violence, Hegel calls for citizen militias or rather, and more fundamentally, for citizens who recognize the violence of their civility. Such a state can count on the 'free devotion, the self-respect, and the individual effort of the people' or the 'all powerful and invincible *spirit*' (my emphasis) of the citizens which is opposed to the 'hierarchical system' adopted by modern states. Hegel remarks of the latter:

> How dull and spiritless a life is engendered in a modern state where everything is regulated from the top downwards, where nothing with any general implications is left to the management and execution of interested parties of the people. (*HPW* 163–4)

Hegel gives post-revolutionary Imperial France and Prussia as examples of states without spirit; they are ruled from above with commands relayed from state to society by means of a hierarchy of what Lenin would call 'transmission belts'. Society is a blank sheet on which is inscribed the will of the ruler, a uniform field subject to the violent impositions of the state, rather than one already informed by the traces of local negotiations of right and violence.[6]

The issue of the mutual implication of right and violence is taken up again in the *System of Ethical Life*, but with the added clarification that the people who recognize the violence of their civility are not necessarily members of a particular state. Violence is not simply directed from a civil 'inside' towards a hostile 'outside' – and preferably by means of professional soldiers – but is the predicament of civility itself. This involves the recognition that freedom has been and continues to be secured violently, a recognition which is shattering. The experience of 'absolute ethical life' presented in the *System of Ethical Life*, albeit in Platonic terms, is the destruction of the apparent fixity and taken-for-granted character of civility – possession, production, exchange – through the recognition of the violence which they entail. Anticipating the *Phenomenology of Spirit*, this experience of recognition is described as the *Bildung* of spirit, 'for in what is eternal lies the real and empirical destruction of all specific things, and the exchange of all of them. It is absolute unselfishness, for in what is eternal nothing is one's own' (*SEL* 147).

The process of recognizing the nothingness of ownership entails no less than the dissolution of the *proper*, the undermining of all claims to legitimate possession. Each claim to possession is disrupted by the violence which it entails, both in its origin and in the continuation of its enjoyment. The recognition at stake entails qualifying each act of possession, production and enjoyment with what Hegel calls the 'humiliation of not being dead and of still having the selfish enjoyment of singularity'. The selfish enjoyments of civility are qualified by the recognition of the violence which they entail; such a recognition is an intimation of the 'speculative community'.

What is of particular interest in the *System of Ethical Life* is the way in which the speculative community of 'absolute ethical life' is presented in terms of a radical inflection of Kant's language of judgement. Hegel mobilizes Kant's aporia of judgement which emerges between concept and intuition (the 'what' and the 'that') into a phenomenology of judgement which explores the ways in which concept and intuition appear to appropriate and make themselves appropriate to each other. He avoids the hierarchical relationship of concept as law to intuition by pointing to the movement of ethical life which 'runs through all the virtues but is fixed in none. In its movement ethical life enters difference and cancels it; its appearance is the transition from subjective to objective and the cancellation of this antithesis' (*SEL* 147). This phenomenological *Bildung* is not about putting the violence to work, as is maintained in Kojève's influential reading of Hegel, for it 'does not look to a product but shatters it directly and makes the emptiness of specific things emerge' (*SEL* 147).

It is precisely this *Bildung* of spirit which reveals the unacknowledged violence of the possessions of civility which is the subject of the *Phenomenology of Spirit* but which is conspicuously absent from the *Philosophy of Right*. The fact and the implications of this change can be illustrated first by looking at the notion of freedom informing the *Philosophy of Right*, then at the distinction developed in that text between the internal and external power of the state, and finally at the expositions of colonization and military violence. Following this I will look briefly at Clausewitz's radical turn of the Kantian aporia of judgement into a philosophy of war. It is proposed not only that the *Philosophy of Right* fails to sustain the phenomenological recognition of violence ventured in the Jena writings, but also that its focus upon abstract *right* (civility) to the exclusion of violence opens the theoretical space for an abstract philosophy of *war*.

In the *Vorlesungen über Rechtsphilosophie* 1823–4, an elucidation of the 'elements' presented in the *Philosophy of Right*, Hegel offered the following commentary on the definition of right given in §29: 'our vocation is freedom, which must realize itself, and this realization is right ... freedom gives itself existence *[Dasein]*; this is the necessary content, this definition will be elucidated by examples, and the entire treatise is such an example'.[7] The entire *Philosophy of Right* is revealed as an example of freedom giving itself existence, but in utter contrast to the *Phenomenology of Spirit*, the form in which and the site on and through which it does so is unthematized. The violent character of freedom's donation remains unacknowledged in the exploration of the examples of its coming to existence in property, contract, crime, morality, family, civil society and state. In these examples the entailments of freedom, the form and site in, on and through which it is given existence, are manifest only symptomatically and no more obviously than in the implication of these examples of freedom giving itself existence in violence.

First of all, it is noteworthy that freedom gives itself existence in terms of the institutions of Roman law, presented in the *Philosophy of Right* as *modes* of freedom. It is by means of this transformation of received legal concepts into modes of freedom that Hegel distinguishes his philosophical jurisprudence from the historical version of Savigny and the German Historical School. Yet as was then already well known, the concepts of property, contract and legal personality used by Hegel were elaborated by the Romans in order to apportion the conquered lands taken into the possession of the Roman state – the *ager publicus* – among the soldiers and citizens of Rome. They are the precipitates of the Roman state's attempt to manage the impact of the return of imperial military violence and colonial occupation upon Roman society itself. Just to provide such a genealogy does not in itself question Hegel's exposition, but it does underline the point that the concepts of private law through which freedom allegedly gives itself existence are themselves implicated in the past violence of the state. In other words, the concepts of abstract right which constitute civility are ineluctably qualified by the imperial violence of a historic state; they are not pure concepts. The traces of violence which inhere in them return repeatedly, as for example in the 'absolute right of appropriation which all human beings have over all things' (*PR* 75) which is a 'right' prior to all other rights, one in which freedom gives itself the freedom to give itself existence. It is a rationally unjustifiable, 'absolute' right to appropriate, one whose necessary violence is never thematized or questioned in the *Philosophy of Right*.

Following the exposition of 'Abstract Right' in terms of Roman law, Hegel proceeds to present conscience and morality in terms of concepts drawn from Christianity. Both 'Abstract Right' and 'Morality' are concerned with the exposition of the forms in which 'subjective freedom' gives itself existence. The donation of freedom has two basic aspects: one is its 'external form' in the Roman Empire and its laws and the other its 'internal form' in the moral concepts of the Christian religion. But while the *Phenomenology of Spirit* pursues this split in the concept of freedom into external and internal forms by showing how Christian moral freedom becomes militant and violent in the Crusades, the *Philosophy of Right* refuses to scrutinize or challenge this division. In the account of 'Culture' in the *Phenomenology of Spirit*, Hegel describes how Christian moral freedom can only become certain of itself and its inner spiritual possessions by means of the violent subjugation of the infidel at the borders of Christendom.

By contrast, in the *Philosophy of Right* the genealogy of Christian moral concepts is played down, and the internal form of freedom's giving itself existence unproblematically accepted. Hegel here claims that the 'essence of the modern state is that the universal should be linked with the complete freedom of particularity and the well-being of individuals' (*PR* 287). But this linkage between the universal and individual is presented unproblematically as the union of 'Abstract Right' and 'Morality' in the 'Ethical Life' of the family, civil society and state. In this text freedom simply gives itself existence in the forms of internal and external right without reflection on the violent freedom which first gave itself the 'right' to give itself existence in the form of 'right'. Hegel presents instead a smooth transition from the inner to the outer, from morality to ethical life, from private familial and civil life to the public life of the state.

The argument for the continuity between the forms by which freedom gives itself existence is carried over to the discussion of military violence in the *Philosophy of Right*. In an addition to §271 Hegel distinguishes between the 'civil power' or the 'inward aspect of the state' and the 'military power' or 'outward aspect'; he immediately qualifies this distinction by describing the latter as 'a specific aspect within the state itself' (*PR* 304) thus making it both inner and outer. In the *German Constitution* and *System of Ethical Life* Hegel saw the mutual implication of the inner and outer orientation of military violence as constitutive of the state; now, however, he seeks a mechanical balance or equilibrium between them. The passage continues:

> The equilibrium of these two aspects is an important factor in the history of the state. Sometimes the civil power is completely defunct and based exclusively on the military power, as at the time of the Roman emperors and praetorians; at other times, as in the modern period – the military power is solely a product of the civil power, as when all citizens are eligible for conscription. (*PR* 304–5)

In this passage Hegel introduces the liberal argument that the military is subordinate to the civil power which is developed in the remaining pages of the *Philosophy of Right*. The military power is an effect of the civil, and not a constitutive moment; the internal civility of the state deploys military violence instrumentally and does not recognize it as a constitutive feature of civility. It is both inside and outside the state, with the consequence that citizens do not have to recognize the intrinsic violence of their civility. They possess and exchange their goods and services according to the laws of 'Abstract right' with a clean moral conscience; they do not possess their well-being with the conscious 'humiliation of not being dead' which recognizes that their possession is someone else's violent dispossession. Their possession and enjoyment are sustained by means of concentrating violence in the discreet hands of the bureaucrats of violence who with their mechanical weaponry have given violence an 'abstract form'.

In the final sections of the *Philosophy of Right* Hegel presents violence as the exception from civility. Rather than being recognized as an engrained feature of everyday moral and commercial life of family and civil society, it has become abstract, external and removed from civil society. Yet the everyday violence required to sustain civility remains unthematized, and the price of the freedom to pursue civil freedom remains unacknowledged. For example, Hegel takes it for granted that the freedom and civility of the modern European state can only be sustained on the premise of colonial expansion: 'civil society is driven to establish colonies' (*PR* 269) in order to divest itself of surplus population and to give itself 'a new market and sphere of industrial activity'.

While Hegel is far from sanguine about the outcome of such expansion, he does not consider the effect it will have on the balance between military and civil power in the metropolitan states, let alone its impact on the colonized. Furthermore, he does not draw the implications of such expansion for corruption of what remains of civility in the metropolitan states. The metropolitan populations have become clients of their military and civil bureaucracies; their freedom and enjoyments depend upon the military and commercial expansion on the colonial frontier, but since this is carried out by bureaucrats, they do not have to recognize their direct moral and political responsibility for it. They are spared the humiliation of not being dead.

In the *Philosophy of Right* Hegel does not fully face the implications of the inextricable link between civility and violence. He can only conceive of violence either as the dissolution of civility in military dictatorship, as when 'the entire state has thus become an armed power' (*PR* 363) or as the work of bureaucratic specialists barracked outside and apart from civility as in the case when 'the armed power of the state becomes a standing army' (*PR* 363). He does not give an exposition of the way in which the freedom which gives itself existence in civility is already qualified by violence. In consequence, the insistence on freedom as an absolute 'abstract free will' has no immunity to the claim that violence is an absolute, as made by Clausewitz.

It is evident from the *System of Ethical Life* that Hegel's political philosophy is largely a radical development of Kant's language of judgement, one which stressed the role of freedom in the equation of concept and intuition which comprises judgement. Clausewitz too developed a radical version of

Kant's aporia of judgement, but one which overwhelmingly stressed the role of violence. Kant's forms of intuition – space and time – for Clausewitz represent limitations of violence; judgement itself is intrinsically violent since it always exceeds the terms of concept and intuition. At several points in *On War* Clausewitz equates judgement with the violence of imagination (see, for example, *OW* 117, 153); at one point under the heading 'Difficulty of separating perception from judgement (Art of war)' he follows Kant in making even perception a judgement which is accomplished by imagination beyond the limits of logic:

> Where the logician draws the line, where the premises stop which are the result of cognition – where judgement begins, there Art begins. But more than this: even the perception of the mind is judgement again, and consequently Art; and at last, even the perception by the senses as well. (*OW* 201–2)

The art of war is a branch of the art of judgement that it involves making decisions without the aid of logic. Clausewitz also suggests that these logically unjustifiable judgements gain validity from the exercise of power. This power is originary, cannot be logically justified, and is therefore violent. Judgement in this view becomes the management of violence and is carried through from perception, to cognition, to ethical feeling and to political decision. The sheer consistency of Clausewitz's philosophy of war is highlighted by the way in which it translates all of the transitions made by Hegel in his philosophy of right into the language and world of the philosophy of war.

In Clausewitz the institutions of modern society can be interpreted as modes of an abstract violence 'giving itself existence'. Its modes are not those of civility, not those of Roman law and its interior analogue of Christian morality, but military tactics and strategy. These all derive from the deferral of what Clausewitz calls the 'decisive blow' or the 'form of absolute war' in which the tactics of intuition and the strategies of the concept are compressed into a moment of pure expenditure of violence (*OW* 344). Civility itself is but a deferral of the 'decisive blow' or act of absolute violence and, just as in the *Philosophy of Right*, violence is removed to the periphery of civility, so the inverse holds of *On War* where civility is cast as the periphery of violence. War here is not the instrument of policy or its outer direction, because policy is but a tactic employed to the end of successful warfare. Yet in their discussions of modern warfare Hegel and Clausewitz arrive at similar conclusions: either war dissolves civility, or it is separated off from it. But Clausewitz is closer to the insights of the early Hegel in his recognition that civility is a mode of violence which cannot recognize itself as such. It is the violent appropriation, of colonial or neo-colonial wealth, that cloaks its violence in the commercial language of fair and equal exchange.

The exclusion of violence to the borders of civility in the *Philosophy of Right* disengages it from any but the most formal ethical and political regulation and provides the condition for its potential return as an absolute. By not properly acknowledging the violence in its freedom, the philosophy of right can be inverted into a philosophy of pure violence. By not owning their violence, the legal, moral and political categories of right are made vulnerable to it; instead of integrating the management of violence into civility, it is freed from civil control by being made the province of experts who are in but not of civil society. The peculiar relationship between violence and civility requires that violence be marginalized, with the danger that by so being it becomes abstract and a potential threat to civility. Clausewitz's *On War* is but the logical outcome of an account of civility which abstracts violence from its context in civil society and allows it to become a force with its own purposes.

The separation of civility and violence presented in the *Philosophy of Right* proved a problematic legacy for the Hegelian tradition, especially in the case the relationship between freedom and violence. If the two are considered in abstraction from each other, then the achievement of freedom and the exercise of violence can be separated and cast in terms of freedom as an end, and violence as the means to achieving it. The potential for moral and political adventurism is correspondingly great, bringing the possibility that the state may violently subjugate family and civil society in the name of their own freedom. The synthesis of Hegel and Clausewitz intimated by Lenin not surprisingly arrived at this outcome; freedom and violence remained separate, with the latter employed by the vanguard party to realize freedom in some distant future. Abstract freedom and abstract violence are thus brought into what Hegel would describe as an 'external relation' and one, moreover, with the potential to destroy civility itself.

Notes

1   See *OW* 402 for 'war is nothing but the continuation of political intercourse, with a mixture of other means' and 162 and 375 for 'tact of judgement'.

2   See 'Violence, Civility and the Predicaments of Philosophy' [Chapter 3 above – editor's note].

3   At one point Lenin described Clausewitz as an Hegelian; Clausewitz however regarded himself as a Kantian.

4   I accept Gillian Rose's arguments for this dating of the text; see Rose [1981] 2007, 63–77.

5   *HPW* 153. This definition of the origin of the state is directed explicitly against the social contract tradition; see the essay *Natural Law* for a more sustained theoretical critique.

6   This sentence develops the point made by Hegel with respect to Imperial legislation; see Hegel 1964, 182.

7   Cited in *PR* 402.

5

Perpetual police? Kosovo and the elision of police and military violence

In the present age it came very near to this, that a battle in the economy of war was looked upon as an evil rendered necessary through some error committed, as a morbid paroxysm to which a regular and prudent system of war would never lead: only those generals were to deserve laurels who knew how to carry on war without spilling blood ... Contemporary history has destroyed this illusion.

– CARL VON CLAUSEWITZ, *ON WAR*

Kant refers the title of his philosophical sketch *Perpetual Peace* (1795; in Kant 1980) to the inscription on a Dutch inn sign commemorating the Treaty of Westphalia (1648) that concluded the Thirty Years' War: it accompanied the picture of a graveyard. The satire became even keener in the age of thermonuclear warfare, when the sole prospect of a post-war peace was indeed that of a global graveyard. Yet Kant's text belies its pessimistic opening by laying out the conditions for a perpetual peace emerging from within the European state system codified in the Treaty of Westphalia. He proposed a number of 'preliminary articles' intended to govern future peace treaties between sovereign states and sufficient to ensure 'perpetual peace'. These included articles forbidding states to reserve the possibility of future warfare, to acquire other states by any means, to institute standing armies and national debt for military purposes and to interfere in other states. The preliminary articles also stipulated the future legal regulation of the conduct of warfare. Kant argued that the public observation of these articles by sovereign states would make it possible for perpetual peace to succeed perpetual war as if it were a mathematical problem 'which gradually working out its own solution, steadily approaches its goal' (Kant 1980, 135). Perpetual peace is thus the outcome of an asymptotic process, but of what happens in the meantime (which is the only time we have) between war and peace, Kant remains silent. Perhaps this silence should direct reflection away from the Manichean opposition of war and peace and towards the institution of a 'perpetual police'.[1]

The inquiry into the nature of the relationship between war, peace and police is not an antiquarian exercise dedicated to understanding texts of the Enlightenment but is crucial to understanding the causes, conduct and the outcome of the conflict in Kosovo. The sixty-eight days' 'war' that commenced during the night of 24–25 March 1999 provoked by the excesses[2] of a Serbian 'police' operation against the Albanian separatist guerrilla organization, the UCK, coincided with the ratification of a 'new strategic concept' for NATO on 24 April 1999. The conflict in Kosovo was regarded by many commentators and participants as a police operation; in fact it was more than one. The conflict can plausibly be regarded as a struggle between two rival police forces and concepts of police, the Serbian 'police' operating to restore order within their claimed sovereign territory and the international 'police' of NATO's new strategic concept.

Before looking more closely at these claims and their implications for the management of violence in the era after the Cold War it is necessary to clarify the concept of police and the relationship between the police and the military exercises of violence. This preliminary is especially prudent in the wake of the political and media rhetoric of the Kosovo conflict as a peacekeeping operation or even, extremely unfelicitously, as a 'postmodern crusade' in the name of human rights. Unfortunately, the social theory of police is underdeveloped, largely restricted to reflections on the practice of civil policing and the implementation of criminal law. The lacuna is particularly striking given the growing public prominence of discourses of police in the national and international arenas (the EU's Schengen agreement, NATO's new strategic concept), yet the concept of police was not always so neglected. In the eighteenth century the concept of police was much broader and had its own university discipline, *Polizeiwissenschaft* (police science). The origins of police science can be traced to the same Treaty of Westphalia which not only ratified the doctrine of external sovereignty but also tied it to the internal cultural homogeneity of the sovereign state with the maxim *cuius regio, eius religio*. The link between external sovereignty and internal uniformity was to have a long history, of which the attempt to create ethnic uniformity of their populations by the sovereign states in the Balkans is only the latest episode.

The combination in the new Protestant states of sovereignty and cultural uniformity in the absence of the bureaucratic and capillary structures of the Catholic Church contributed to the emergence of the institutions and the theory of police. Early statements of the new architecture of the state can be found in von Seckendorff's mid-seventeenth-century theory of the Christian princely state, with the princely state undertaking to perform welfare functions previously the domain of the church, and at the end of the century in Leibniz's theory and diplomatic practice in favour of a European police state based upon the reform of the institutions of the German empire. The concept of police that emerged was thus extremely broad, concerned with security, welfare, economic development and cultural uniformity, in many ways attributing to the state the millennial mission of the church to secure peace on earth and to care for the bodies and souls of the faithful. Put provocatively, the theory of police was the modern replacement for medieval practical and speculative theology.[3]

Perhaps like Edgar Allan Poe's purloined letter, the ubiquity and the sheer scale of the police have made both it and its principles invisible. In some respects the occlusion of police was achieved by means of its transformation into a theory of civil society, evident in the German context in its transformation at the beginning of the nineteenth century into jurisprudence and national economy. The same process is evident in one of the unrecognized masterpieces of police science, namely Adam Smith's *Wealth of Nations*, which shifted the focus of police work to the economy and wagered upon wealth as the solvent for the social and political problems previously the concern of police. Similarly, Kant's *Perpetual Peace* may be read as part of his broader liberal critique of police science, providing a response – and not a very strong one – to the millennial claims of perpetual police and replacing the administrative structures of the police state with the self-regulating structure of the public sphere. The transformation of police theory at the end of the eighteenth century into a theory of the liberal economy and public sphere did not mark the end but rather the displacement of its problems.

The narrow concept of police as the force responsible for ensuring public order that emerged in the early nineteenth century accompanied the displacement of its earlier comprehensive concerns with the economy and the public sphere. However, a trace of the earlier breadth of the concept persisted in the problem of the relationship between police and military violence, often inaccurately understood in terms of the internal and external exercise of violence. In order to clarify the relationship between the two modalities of violence, a relationship that is once more prominently on the political agenda, it is helpful to consider Clausewitz's definition of the military violence proper to the modern sovereign state. The passage from *On War* used as an epigraph concerning 'the regular and prudent system of war' that does not resort to military violence has classically been understood in terms of Clausewitz's critique of diplomacy, but it can also be read as directed against the police 'theory of war'.[4] Indeed, the work of the Berlin theorists of the German war of liberation – Clausewitz, Fichte, Hegel – can be understood as one of the last sustained reflections on the relationship between war and police, many of whose insights remain timely, especially after Kosovo.

Although long regarded as the founding text of realism in international relations, Clausewitz's *On War* in fact proposes a rigorous view of human action as the expenditure of force in decisions guided by what he calls 'the tact of judgement'. As in any dynamic model based on forces – whether fluid dynamics or violence dynamics – temporality is more important than spatiality, movement more important than territory. Clausewitz's famed maxim that 'War is nothing but the continuation of political intercourse, with a mixture of other means' should be read as a dynamic expression, with war and policies signifying different modalities of force. He describes these modalities in terms of the temporality of violence or, in his words, the time of the 'blow'. War at one extreme, 'the form of absolute war', is characterized as the instantaneous expression of violence – 'In one point of space and time all action is here pressed together' (*OW* 344). The compression of time and violence in the act of war is contrasted by Clausewitz with politics and police, which are characterized by deferral and the endeavour 'to avoid the decisive battle'. The latter characteristic, deferral, takes its means from police and involves a 'system of war' or strategic disposition of forces that Clausewitz considered to have become obsolete, following Napoleon and Jacobin military doctrine.

In spite of his attention to the different temporalities of military and police violence Clausewitz regards both as strategic dispositions of force that can complement or obstruct each other according to occasion. His position is close to that of his contemporary Hegel or at least to his 1802 *The German Constitution*.[5] Here Hegel claims even more forcefully than Clausewitz that politics is war by other means. While his later *Outline of the Philosophy of Right* departs from freedom and its actualization in the institutions of property and contract (civil society) moving to the *Sittlichkeit* of the state, this earlier work begins with the establishment of 'a common military and public authority' (*HPW* 153). The latter position is closer to Machiavelli than to Rousseau in regarding the origins of the state to lie not in a free contract but in an organized response to military insecurity. On this basis Hegel makes the claim: 'The change from the mailed fist to politics is not to be regarded as a change from anarchy to constitutionalism. There is no change in principle, but only on the surface' (*HPW* 188). This extreme claim for the continuity of war and politics is largely abandoned in the *Philosophy of Right* where war is relegated to the colonial frontier (whence Hannah Arendt was to bring it back in *The Origins of Totalitarianism* (1951)).

Yet even in the *Philosophy of Right* what takes the place of the identity of war and politics is not the spontaneous and pacific harmony of civil society proposed in different ways by Smith and Kant, but the deferral of civil war by means of the police. Civil society, whether national or international, is for Hegel ineluctably conflictual, and the postponement of war – which is not the same as the attainment of peace – is police work.

Hegel and Clausewitz between them shift the point of difference between war and police from the topological distinction of the exercise of violence inside and outside the sovereign state to that of temporality. War is a present and compressed, police a deferred and distended expression of violence. From this perspective, the distinction between war and police is not just territorial but involves the modality of the exercise of violence, modalities that are different but not necessarily incompatible. It was axiomatic for Hegel that the object of police was national and international civil society and its task was to manage the inevitable turbulence and insecurity that accompanied them. Thus as opposed to war, the object of police action was not an enemy but a *condition* of turbulence or instability; the notion of the enemy is only significant in so far as the cause of turbulence may be identified with a particular person or group. With respect to the police there is for Hegel 'no clear boundary between what is harmful and what is harmless, between what is suspicious and what is not suspicious, or between what should be prohibited or kept under surveillance and what should be exempted from prohibitions, surveillance and suspicion, inquiry and accountability' (*PR* §234). The role of police in managing turbulence implies surveillance and the capacity for flexible and limited response; it addresses a *condition* of turbulence or disorder that may have many causes rather than an identifiable enemy. On occasion, as in Kosovo, the condition of turbulence may crystallize into a definable enemy, prompting a shift in the exercise of violence from deferral of conflict to war, even if this is conducted under the guise of the police and by agents identified as police.

The distinction between military and police violence is thus paradoxically firm – the one an immediate response to an enemy, the other a deferred response to a turbulent condition – and flexible, with the unstable condition crystallizing under specific circumstances into an enemy. This ambiguity has become almost constitutive for what may be described as the postmodern exercise of violence. In many ways the focus upon the proper response to social turbulence rather than war that is characteristic of influential theorists such as E. N. Luttwak and institutions such as the RAND Corporation is a reprise of the broader concept of police which concerned itself with the entire condition of the population rather than with a particular identifiable threat. This means that police action may assume a variety of guises dedicated to easing the causes of turbulence and instability, including surveillance, economic assistance and political intervention, but not excluding warfare.

These distinctions between police and military action are helpful for understanding the chain of events in the Kosovo crisis, as well as the confusion and crisis of judgement that beset commentators who were not sure whether the crisis indeed added up to a war. What took place were a number of crystallizations of potential sources of turbulence into identifiable enemies – some more contrived than others – with the consequent transformation of police into military violence.

The Kosovo region was itself long regarded as a source of turbulence within Yugoslavia.[6] Subordinated under the Serbian Federal Republic for historical and political reasons, the repressive policing of Kosovo until 1966 ensured the creation of a tradition of resistance to what was seen as Serbian governance. The concession of the status of an Autonomous Socialist Province under the 1974 Yugoslav constitution permitted a number of reforms and a degree of autonomy that lasted until after Tito's death in 1980. During the 1980s the autonomy was revoked and increasingly repressive police measures were reinstated in Kosovo, amounting to a system of apartheid. These moves were largely driven by the Serbian pursuit of cultural uniformity and the phantasm of a greater Serbia. The repression produced a cycle of resistance that provoked enhanced repression. In this case the police action itself provoked turbulence and an escalation of the severity of police violence. In 1996–7 the largely reformist initiative of the Kosovo Albanian leadership was succeeded by a call to armed resistance and the formation of a liberation army, the UCK. The initial success of the resistance permitted the identification of an enemy as the cause of turbulence in Kosovo and an escalation of police violence to the point of war. In 1997 the police were supplemented by Serbian Ministry of the Interior 'Special Forces' who began to manage the turbulence in the Kosovo region by means of a dirty war against the UCK and its supposed sympathizers. The murderous excesses of this technically legal police operation provoked the international Contact Group in ex-Yugoslavia to call for a withdrawal of the Special Forces in March 1997, using the threat of sanctions and other possible interventions. It was at this point that NATO began to study options for armed intervention in the territory of ex-Yugoslavia.

The elision of police and military violence represented by the Special Forces in Kosovo eventually provoked a response from NATO that also elided police and military violence. The NATO interventions in Bosnia and Kosovo were the first real acts of the 'new NATO' and marked the ambiguous and contradictory transformation of the military alliance into a police organization. Following the loss of its main military role as the defender of the Atlantic alliance against the Warsaw Pact with the collapse of the socialist states, NATO moved steadily during the 1990s towards a redefinition of its mission as dedicated to the exercise of police – managing turbulence – rather than exclusively military violence directed against an identifiable enemy. Instead of combating an enemy, the object of NATO now became the management of any turbulence that might be assumed to affect the security and interests of its members, even if this was of mere regional significance such as the events in Kosovo.

The shift towards a police rather than exclusively military strategy was prepared in the early 1990s by a number of think-tank discussions and policy papers that identified the condition of turbulence and crisis rather than a discrete enemy as the main threat to the interests of the Atlantic alliance. These considerations clearly surfaced in speeches by President Clinton in spring 1997 which spoke of 'constructing a new NATO', one no longer directed against 'a hostile bloc of nations' but rather oriented to 'providing security' to its members.[7] The police role of the alliance was ratified by its new strategic concept adopted in the middle of the NATO police action/war in Kosovo in April 1999. The new strategic concept recognized that the main threat to the security of NATO members was no longer an identifiable *enemy* but rather an insecure and unpredictable *condition*. It stated: 'The security of the Alliance remains subject to a number of risks military and non-military, of various origins and difficult to predict.' Accompanying this shift was a focus on instability whose origins could lie outside the NATO area, but with potential impact on the security of NATO members. Like most police forces, NATO reserved to itself the right to judge when and where its interests were threatened. At the NATO summit it remained only for Tony Blair to provide a moralistic window dressing for the new strategic concept as the 'defender of the values of liberty' for the ideological and strategic remodelling of NATO to be complete.

Although a little premature, the Kosovo intervention marked the formal shift of NATO from a predominantly military to a police organization. However, this was less the complete institutional transformation of the organization than an elision, with its police and military roles blurring into each other. The result was a war masquerading as a police action and a police action masquerading as a war; in short, an intervention characterized by extreme ambiguity, notoriously without clear war aims and objectives. The regional turbulence crystallized into an enemy, Serbia, but it was not clear what Serbia consisted in. The ambiguity confused even external commentators, above all many intellectuals, who felt impelled by the appearance of a logic of war – friend or enemy – to take up positions for or against an ambiguous police *and* military action. Similar ambiguity characterizes the post-war situation in Kosovo, with KFOR, ambiguously a police and military force, presiding over the creation of a process of ethnic cleansing. The lack of an enemy – for different reasons neither the remaining Serbs nor the UCK can qualify for this role – and the continuing turbulence is currently provoking renewed crisis and disturbance in the region and perplexity in the eyes of Western commentators. After the compressed temporality of sixty-eight days' military action, the deferral of violence that is the mission of KFOR fades into a sordid future of perpetual police.

The increasing importance of the concept of police in national and international discourse demands a theoretical response of the part of philosophy and social theory. Without such a theoretical response the intellectual débâcle of Kosovo is certain to be repeated with respect to the next police action undertaken by NATO or under the terms of the Schengen agreement. In many respects the concept of police, in spite of its early modern pedigree, qualifies as a postmodern theoretical category par excellence. The object of police is not a discrete subject but a condition of turbulence; the modality of police violence is decentred, becoming centralized only when it elides with the modality of military force, and finally, police action is not directed to a particular goal and cannot be a subject of a grand narrative, in spite of Blair's efforts to accord moral prestige to the new strategic concept of NATO. The Manichean opposition of war and peace proposed by Kant at the end of the eighteenth century that has since governed the rhetoric of international relations is now deflated into the deferred future of perpetual police.

Notes

1   Kant's faith in the role of the public sphere in achieving perpetual peace mirrors that mentioned in his essay *Answering the Question – What Is Enlightenment?* But there the link between the police and the public sphere is explicit: it is the public sphere of the Prussian self-proclaimed police state to which Kant refers, under whose enlightened monarch Frederick II it was required to 'argue as much as you will about what you will, only obey' (Kant 1980, 10).

2   It has been alleged that the toll of deaths caused by the special police units of the Serb Ministry of the Interior in the later phase of their operation against the UCK was exaggerated, on one occasion to a factor of 100, in Western media coverage immediately before the NATO intervention. See the analysis in *Le Monde diplomatique*, n.3, VII, March 2000.

3   For more detailed discussion see Caygill 1989, chapter 2.

4   The work of Leibniz testifies to the close relationship that exists between the theory of diplomacy and the theory of police, one that would repay further investigation.

5   For a more sustained comparative reading of Hegel and Clausewitz, see Chapter 5 above.

6   For a reliable analysis of the background to the Kosovo conflict see the editions of *Limes – Rivista Italiana di Geopolitica*, 'Il triangolo dei balcani', vol. 3, 1998, 'Dopa la guerra', vol. 2, 1999, and the special issue on 'Kosovo, l'Italia in guerra', 1999.

7   President Clinton's comments may be found at www.whitehouse.gov. For a broader discussion to the background of the change in the strategic concept see Mortarello 1999.

Section two: Affirmation

6

The consolation of philosophy or 'neither Dionysus nor the crucified'

Perhaps what is to be found here is largely the care of the 'burned child', of the disappointed idealist; but there is also another, superior component: the jubilant curiosity of one who formerly stood in his corner and was driven to despair by his corner, and now delights and luxuriates in the opposite of a corner, in the boundless, in what is 'free as such'.

– NIETZSCHE, 'WHY WE LOOK LIKE EPICUREANS' (*GS* §375)

What is the consolation of philosophy? Can philosophy console in the face of utter loss, or is it all that is left, a consolation prize for the losers? Enobarbus's comment in *Anthony and Cleopatra* that 'this greefe is crown'd by consolation'[1] is typically double-edged, for such consolation crowns grief by fantasies of restitution and profit at the same time as it marks the ineluctable sovereignty of loss. Thus the consolation of philosophy consists as much in the hope of finding an unexpected trump in a losing hand as in laying down a forfeit in full expectation of loss.[2] What is more, the loss at stake in the consolation of philosophy is the loss of everything in death, whether in the imminent deaths of the jailed Socrates and Boethius or the more drawn out deaths of Kant and Nietzsche. In each case, philosophy consoles by crowning death with fables of restitution while at the same time acknowledging and preparing for utter loss. But where are the love and the wisdom in this consolation? Is it in the desire for, and knowledge of, the certain return of what will be lost or in knowing and desiring its irretrievable surrender, or even, impossibly perhaps, in both?

Unlike mourning, consolation is not simply for those who have lost, but also for those who fear to lose. This accounts for its ambiguous character: while certainly commemorative, it is also driven by the fantasy of what it would be to lose and so must engage with this anxiety. Philosophy must console the one in fear of loss, whether by maintaining that nothing will be lost or that everything has already been hopelessly lost, or even both, with the proviso that whatever returns is a blissful and unexpected gift. Unlike mourning, then, the consolation of philosophy can affirm love and wisdom and is capable of producing a sense of elation and affirmation, however temporary, in the consoled.[3]

This consolation is addressed not only to the dying philosopher, but also to their friends and, even, to philosophy itself. In each case, the one to be consoled is torn between remembered and anticipated loss. The ambivalent consolation of philosophy is repeatedly figured in terms of an innocent suffering the anxieties of the experienced. Time and again, from Plato to Nietzsche, the consolation of philosophy is addressed to the 'burnt' and 'frightened' child in every adult.[4] Indeed, in Boethius, philosophy herself appears both childlike and yet 'so ancient that none would think her of our time'; she is 'shrouded by a kind of darkness of forgotten years, like a smoke blackened family statue in the atrium'. The philosophy that would console and be consoled has herself been blasted by the experience and fear of loss and yet returns to give consolation to the disconsolate Boethius.

The consolation of philosophy can be a mixed blessing, for when it meets the fear of death with fables of restitution it makes life liveable by devaluing it; yet when it is 'absolute for death' it can intensify the sense of what is being lost. Moreover, on some bleak occasions the consolation of philosophy manages *both* to devalue life and intensify the fear of losing it, a movement exemplified by Plato's *Phaedo* and, more tangentially, by Epicurus's reply to him in his *Letter to Menoeceus*. In the former – the paradigmatic text of philosophical consolation – the promise of restoring what has been lost intensifies the despair, if not for Socrates, then certainly for his friends. While the consolations of Platonism tend to feed the fear that they would assuage with their promise of life beyond death, Epicurus's anti-Platonic meditations on death would, in being absolute for death and utter loss, refuse both the fear and its antidote. Yet both he and Plato are inconstant lovers of death: both find love of life in the love of death, but while Plato's wisdom finds, in loving death, a life beyond it, Epicurus's would, in madly loving death, turn back and love life. Their differences arise from how their choreographies of consolation stage the movement of loss and return to life.

Because death is at stake in the consolation of philosophy, the point of departure for its love and its wisdom is the body. Even a text as opposed to the body as the *Phaedo* nevertheless stages the restoration of the soul from the body in terms of the corporeal metaphors of medicine and the 'cure' of law and the freedom and 'purity' of the soul. Philosophy here is a saving wisdom, one which loves life by denying the body and redeeming the soul. There emerges in this dialogue a complex complicity between the fear of loss and the consolation offered by redemption, one whose parameters define the consolation of philosophy and which recur throughout its tradition.

In the *Phaedo*, Socrates is portrayed spending his final hours in the condemned cell, consoling his friends with a discussion of philosophy and death. Since the mood of his friends is volatile, veering between despair and elation, Socrates would console them by saying that he meets death without resentment. He tells them that he does not fear it, for it is no stranger to him, he and death are already well acquainted. He asks them, are not philosophers 'always engaged in the pursuit of dying and death' and since 'they have had the desire of death all their life long, why when their time comes should they repine at that which they have always been pursuing and desiring?' (Plato 1969, 64a). The philosopher pursues death in the guise of a wisdom which is not distorted by the experience of the body: death is the wisdom that he would love.

Socrates bases the case for the philosopher's desire of death on the denial of the body. His consolation requires that the body be separated from the soul, and its pleasures regarded as an obstacle to the soul's attainment of knowledge. For this reason, says Socrates, 'it is characteristic of the philosopher to despise the body; his soul runs away from his body' (65d). The search for absolute knowledge, whether of justice, the good, the true or the beautiful, is impeded by the body; it blinds us to the world of ideas, filling 'us full of loves, and lusts, and fears, and fancies of all kinds, and endless foolery, and in very truth, as men say, takes away from us the power of thinking at all' (66c). If we would have 'pure knowledge of anything we must be quit of the body' (66d); the wisdom we now desire as philosophers can only be attained through death, when the soul is purified of the body and the pure 'lays hold of the pure' (67b). The love the body fills us with is not the love of wisdom; to be worthy of this we must be cured, freed or otherwise purified of the body.

It seems that it is not possible to be a lover of both wisdom (philo-sophy) and the body (philo-soma). If we would love wisdom then we must purify ourselves of our bodies, freeing our souls from their bodily prisons and allowing them to ascend to the world of ideas. This liberation, so desired by the lover of wisdom, is the same as death, leading Socrates to the conclusion that 'true philosophers, Simmias, are always occupied in the practice of dying' (67e). Once more the body is cast as the adversary of love and of wisdom and the source of distraction, anxiety and the fear of death. Socrates, about to die, considers himself on the eve of being liberated from the prison of his body. His last words bring together medical cure and religious redemption: 'Crito, I owe a cock to Aesculapius; will you remember to pay the debt' (118). Since for Socrates life in a body is a disease for which death is the cure, it is wholly appropriate for him to mark his demise with a thanksgiving sacrifice to the God of medicine.

In conversation with Cebes, Socrates attempts to bolster his argument for the separation of soul and body by appealing to the theme of recollection. He offers proofs which Cebes politely accepts, while clearly remaining unconvinced. His attempt at consolation failing, Socrates offers 'to probe the argument further' before changing tone and saying to his listeners, 'like children, you are haunted with a fear that when the soul leaves the body, the wind may really blow her away and scatter her' (77d). Cebes answers with a smile, 'Socrates, you must argue us out of our fears' and then adds, 'they are not our fears, but perhaps even in us men there is a child to whom death is a sort of hobgoblin: him too we must persuade' (77e). The body and the soul addressed earlier in Socrates's abstract soliloquy are suddenly transformed into the man and the frightened child before him, both fearing death and the scattering of the ashes of the soul, and trying to unlearn this fear by the charms of argument and persuasion.

The frailty of argument in the face of death is sadly exposed when Socrates gives his advice to the frightened, and frightening, children who haunt his friends. He says, 'Let the voice of the charmer be applied daily until you have charmed away the fear.' Cebes replies, 'And where shall we find a good charmer of our fears, Socrates, now that you are abandoning us?' (78a). At this moment, when the consoling effect of the charm of reason is under most threat, Socrates advises his friends to look for another charmer: 'Hellas is a large place ... and has good men.' At this intimation of Socrates's departure, Cebes abruptly returns the dialogue to its rational thread, after which it continues with repeated interruptions as the children in the listeners fail to be persuaded by its charm. Socrates asks repeatedly 'in what respect is the argument insufficient' but the question masks the realization that it is not the particular argument, but argument itself which is failing to console. The dialogue attempts to cure both speaker and listeners of the fear of death, a charm which was both successful and unsuccessful, meriting a sacrifice to Aesculapius, but one given by a substitute.[5]

In his final conversation Socrates sacrifices 'the body' for the sake of consoling his friends before the prospect of his imminent death. His arguments were a charm which, in the guise of denying the body and celebrating death as a liberation, were to confirm his friends in their resolve to live. The obligation to continue living still held, even though Socrates in his argument was 'absolute for death'. In this dialogue, philosophy is indubitably the art of dying, but not in the way it immediately seems. It is no less than the attempt to master the fear of death by appearing to make it an object of knowledge. Such making sense of death is held to free life from the aura of senselessness which death casts over all human actions and ambitions. Making sense of death is a way of redeeming life, but in the case of Socrates's account, it seems that life can only be redeemed by staging the sacrifice of the body. In making sense of his death by telling the story of the struggle between body and soul, Socrates redeems his life as that of a philosopher engaged in dying, as well as that of his witnesses who will go on to live after him. As a spoken charm, the story of the body and the soul was perhaps of some consolation, but as a written doctrine it is transformed into the charm, or ambiguous consolation prize, which creates the illness – fear of death – which it purports to cure.

The Platonic view of philosophy as the attempt to master the fear of death by making it an object of knowledge and desire persisted in Aristotle's account of the origins of philosophy in wonder. In the *Metaphysics* he claimed that 'it is owing to their wonder that men both now begin and at first began to philosophize' (982b, 13) and described the objects of wonder as the moon, the stars and the genesis of the universe. However, the wonder aroused by these objects is only possible 'when almost all the necessities of life and the things that make for comfort and recreation have been secured'. The satisfactions of life are always only almost secured; it is the awareness that this enjoyment is provisional and under threat that can provoke wonder and interest in the universe (it can also provoke melancholy). The need to secure the satisfactions of life against the threat of death makes us want to know death, for wonder, says Aristotle, implies a desire to know its object (1371a, 32). And yet possession of such knowledge 'might be justly regarded as beyond human power; for in many ways human nature is in bondage' (982b, 29); such knowledge can only be pursued, never possessed. Aristotle remains with the Platonic pursuit, unlike Epicurus, who regarded the bondage of human nature as an effect and not a cause of the desire to know death. The wisdom of Plato and Aristotle is informed by the desire to restore what will be lost, while that of Epicurus strives to lose the desire to restore.

In the *Letter to Menoeceus*, Epicurus explored the same themes as the *Phaedo* – the nature of philosophy, its relation to death, pleasure, knowledge and the body – but pointed to a different path of consolation, one which may be described as an antidote to Plato.[6] The mise en scène could hardly differ more: the condemned cell of the Socratic meditation on death, the body and philosophy is succeeded by Epicurus's thoughts in a garden. The meditations of the imprisoned philosopher on the eve of death are countered by those of a philosopher in the midst of life, the one's spoken testament by the other's written council. Where Socrates argued that love of wisdom and love of the body were irreconcilable, Epicurus maintained that to practise love of wisdom – philosophy – *is* to practise philosoma – love of the body.

Philosophy for Epicurus is dedicated to showing the absurdity of fear for the future, especially fear for the future of the body. He begins by refusing Plato's account of knowledge as recollection, as well as its entailment of the separation of body and soul. We can only know through sensation: our souls (*anima* and *animus*) are corporeal and thus inseparable from the body; the death of the body is the end of sensation and the death of the soul. The ashes of our souls will be scattered by the wind, but why be haunted by this hobgoblin, why not embrace it? This fear need not be the greatest weight that it was for Socrates. Epicurus advises Menoeceus to 'Accustom thyself to believe that death is nothing for us, for good and evil imply sentience, and death is the privation of all sentience; therefore a right understanding that death is nothing to us makes the mortality of life enjoyable, not by adding to life an illimitable time, but by taking away the yearning after immortality' (X, 124). As with Plato, but how differently, knowledge diminishes the fear of death not by making it the purification or liberation of the soul from the body, giving it absolute significance, but by making it insignificant. Instead of regarding life in the body as a disease and death the cure, fear of death is the disease for which love of the body and its pleasures is the cure. Death indeed, reputed 'the most awful of evils, is nothing to us, seeing that, when we are, death is not, and when death is, we are not' (X, 125). Wisdom consists neither in deprecating life nor fearing its end; indeed, the one is the cause of the other: we fear death because we deprecate life. In affirming the loss of everything – body and soul – we gain life.

In place of the Platonic jail of the body, haunted by phantoms of an ideal world from which the soul imagines it has fallen into the distractions of guilty bodily pleasures, the Epicurean body is a garden. The care to live well is the same as the care to die well, which means to die without fear and without resentment. The ultimate good for Epicurus is 'health of body and tranquillity of mind', that is, the union of philosoma and philosophy. The two are not opposed, since one is not gained at the price of the other, but health of the body consists in tranquillity or absence of fear. There is no realm of ideas to negate the body and its pleasures, nor is there an intelligible soul set to revenge itself on its jailor body. What is more, this wisdom is for both the child in the adult and the adult in the child:

> both old and young ought to seek wisdom, the former in order that, as age comes over him, he may be young in good things because of the grace of what has been, and the latter in order that, while he is young, he may at the same time be old, because he has no fear of the things that are to come. (X, 122)

In place of the return of the terrified, and terrifying, child in the adult we find an equipoise between youth and age: in seeking wisdom the adult in us affirms what has been, while the child in us affirms what is to come. Yet perhaps this balance is but a more intensely pitched version of the consoling moments of loss and restitution. By affirming the past, the old suddenly receive everything back and are young in 'the grace of what has been' while the young lose their fear by renouncing what is to come. The Epicurean affirmation of loss conceals within it the desire for grace and with this loses its absolute character, opening the way for fear and dereliction.

The contrast between love of wisdom and love of the body returns in Nietzsche's staging of his physiological opposition to Kant's 'idealism': he would liberate the body from its despisers and jailors, and especially from Kant. Yet Kant like Nietzsche can be read as the attempt to 'liberate' the body from the resentment against time which infallibly accompanies the fear of death,[7] and both thinkers may be read as condemning the body to be ferried back and forth between jail and judgement. This movement in and out of prison informs Nietzsche's critique of Kant in *The Gay Science* §335, where he claims that Kant's 'thing in itself' and 'categorical imperative' 'led him astray – back to "God", "soul", "freedom" and "immortality", like an old fox who loses his way and goes astray back into his cage. Yet it had been his strength and cleverness that had broken open the cage'. The 'all destroying Kant' of the *Critique of Pure Reason* breaks open the cage of God, the World, and the Soul in which metaphysics had bound the body only to return to it with the postulates of pure practical reason in the *Critique of Practical Reason*. This reading has much to recommend it, except that Kant wrote three critiques and that with the *Critique of Judgement* he once more escapes from the cage, perhaps ultimately to return to it, but by a quite different route.

Kant's movements in and out of the metaphysical cage follow both Platonic and Epicurean precedents. Within the first *Critique*, Epicurean concepts and vocabulary abound, as in 'canon' and 'organon' (staging the opposition of Epicurean and Aristotelian philosophy), but also more fundamentally in the basic arguments of the transcendental analytic and dialectic. The negotiation between concept and intuition throughout the analytic follows Epicurean epistemology even down to such details as the use of Epicurean prolepsis in the 'Anticipations of Perception'. Kant's critique, in the dialectic, of the three main objects of metaphysics – God, the World and the Soul – is likewise indebted to Epicurus. In the Platonic tradition, the consolation of philosophy would free us from anxiety and fear by pursuing knowledge of the metaphysical trinity, and yet Kant shows that we cannot know them. This is not a counsel of despair since the fear in question may arise from reason's invention of such objects. In Epicurean fashion, Kant shows us that we are perplexed and anxious about things we cannot possibly know; knowledge of the limits of our knowledge is the way to tranquillity. As with Epicurus, Kant consoles us for the fear of God, our finitude and the immensity of the universe through the knowledge of the futility of seeking knowledge of such things.

The destructive serenity of the first *Critique* was persistently haunted by an opposition between the real and apparent world; this was put to the service of the destruction but was not an altogether reliable ally. In the second *Critique* it returns in Kant's restoration of the entire apparatus of the *Phaedo*: the glimpse of a world without God, world and soul fades with the return of the distinction between the ideal and the present world along with its correlate of the autonomy of the pure practical will and the heteronomy of the body and the related postulates of immortality, freedom 'affirmatively regarded', the causality of a being inhabiting an intelligible world and the existence of God. Yet Kant did not remain confined in the second *Critique*, as Nietzsche suggests, but with the *Critique of Judgement* achieved his most considered Epicurean position, apparently escaping the need to escape. Here the body and its pleasures are thought beyond the Platonic antitheses, with the body's pleasure not opposed to, but closely aligned with the power of judgement.[8] The opposition of soul and body is dissolved into a single term – *Gemüt* – which partakes of both and provides the site for the interplay of pleasure and judgement. While the character of this site is far removed from the Platonic dissonance of body and soul, is the consolation it offers beyond the fear of death, or but its most subtle modulation?

The complex character of *Gemüt* may be illustrated by the following passage from §29 of the third *Critique*:

> We must even admit that, as Epicurus maintained, gratification and pain though proceeding from the imagination or even from representations of the understanding, are always in the last resort corporeal, since apart from any feeling of the bodily organs life would be merely a consciousness of one's existence, and could not include any feeling of well being or the reverse, i.e., of the furtherance or hindrance of the vital forces. For, of itself alone, the *Gemüt* is all life (the life principle itself), and hindrance or furtherance has to be sought outside it, and yet in the person themselves, consequently in the connection with their body. (*CJ* 5:277–8)

This passage systematically undoes the Platonic elevation of the soul over the body. Imagination, representation and the affects are inseparable from the body, and the 'soul' or *Gemüt*, as with Epicurus, is life itself, inseparable from the body. The life force may be furthered or hindered in various ways, but never in abstraction from the body. This Epicurean account of body and soul, with its emphasis upon life and the relationship between pleasure and the power of judgement, supplements the critical destruction of the intelligible objects of God, the World, and the Soul ventured in the first *Critique*. The alignment of corporeal affect and the power of judgement within the *Gemüt* suggest possibilities of an Epicurean alliance between love of the body and love of wisdom. This does not seek to redeem the body from judgement, since this would merely invert the structure of the *Phaedo* while leaving its terms intact in seeking to release the body from the thrall of the soul instead of the soul from that of the body. With hardly any trace of redemptive pathos Kant begins in the third *Critique* to explore a terrain which no longer recognizes a distinction between body and soul nor one between affect and judgement.

With the third *Critique* it becomes possible to imagine a philosophy which neither jails the body nor seeks to redeem it from its idealist captor. The consolation of this philosophy, like that of Epicurus, consists in recognizing the mortality of the soul and the inevitability of total loss. The desired result is not utter dereliction and the ruin of life, but an openness to life's gifts and pleasures. Here the consolation of philosophy consists in affirmation, a thought more usually associated with Nietzsche than with Kant. However, is it possible to affirm this utter loss without any trace of hope for restitution? The consolation of philosophy is intrinsically ambivalent, defined by instability and a lack of equipoise veering between loss and restitution. This was evident not only in Plato but also in Epicurus; it also informs the definition of life as the play of affirmation and negation proposed by Kant in the third *Critique*. While the third *Critique* makes it possible to imagine a love of wisdom which is also the love of the body, a love of death which is a love of life, it remains within this ambivalence even while staging it.

The inextricable entanglement of the affirmation of loss and the desire for redemption is unmistakeable in Nietzsche's work, provoking an ambivalence staged in terms of the figure of Epicurus. The latter haunts the historic choice offered by Nietzsche in *Ecce Homo*: 'Have I been understood? – *Dionysus versus the Crucified* … '. The Dionysian and the Christian are defined against the Epicurean, while remaining complicit with it: Epicurus is neither Dionysus nor the Crucified and is yet both. Epicurus becomes for Nietzsche a point of intense equivocation, rejected by Dionysus and Christ and yet part of them both. Reflecting on the malice of philosophers in *Beyond Good and Evil* Nietzsche asks, 'It took a century for Greece to find out who this garden God Epicurus had been. – Did it find out?' (*BGE* §7). Did anyone know who the 'eternal Epicurus' had been, he who had 'been alive at all times and is living now, unknown to those who have called and call themselves Epicureans' unknown even to himself, having 'forgotten his own name: it was the heaviest pack he ever threw off'?[9] In explaining 'Why we look like Epicureans' Nietzsche aligns the cautious mistrust of the burned child with the jubilant curiosity of the liberated adult in order to evoke an Epicurean pride in ambivalence, one figured in terms of the 'self control of the rider during his wildest rides'.[10] Neither Dionysian nor Christian, Nietzsche nevertheless finds Epicurus in both.

Nietzsche evokes Epicurus in such most beautiful moments of affirmation as *'Et in Arcadia ego'*:

> The beauty of the whole scene induced in me a sense of awe and adoration of the moment of its revelation; involuntarily, as if nothing were more natural, I inserted into this pure, clear world of light (in which there was nothing of desire or expectation, no looking before and behind) Hellenic heroes: my feeling must have been like that of Poussin and his pupil: at one and the same time heroic and idyllic. – And that is how individual men have actually lived, that is how they have enduringly *felt* they existed in the world and the world existed in them; and among them was one of the greatest of men, the inventor of an heroic-idyllic mode of philosophizing: Epicurus.[11]

Epicurus is here cast as the philosopher who affirms the moment, without resentment of past nor fear of future time. And yet earlier in this text Epicurus had appeared in the less elevated guise of the 'soul soother of late antiquity' who, perhaps taking the place of Socrates, addressed his consoling charms to those tormented by fear. This Epicurus did not affirm the moment but gave consolation by negating 'fruitless and distant disputation' upon ultimate questions. The moment of Dionysian affirmation is thus qualified by this reactive moment of negation. In recognizing his affirmative character, Nietzsche believed himself to 'experience the character of Epicurus quite differently from perhaps everybody else' but saw also that it was born of fear, 'continual suffering' and thus negation (*GS* §45). For this reason Epicurus was for Nietzsche both a Dionysian 'garden god' and a romantic decadent or the 'opposite of a Dionysian pessimist' (*GS* §370).

Just as Epicurus was for Nietzsche both Dionysian and the opposite of the Dionysian, so too was he both Christian and anti-Christian. In *Daybreak* and *The Anti-Christ* Nietzsche develops a genealogy of Christianity which emphasizes its battle with Epicureanism – the Garden God versus the Crucified. In *Daybreak* Nietzsche presents Epicurus as the enemy of the 'idea of punishment' after death developed by the 'secret cults' of the Roman Empire and which resurfaced as Christianity.[12] Epicurus is here the enemy of Christianity who 'triumphs anew' in the guise of modern science which rejects 'any other idea of death and of any life beyond it'.[13]

In *The Anti-Christ* Nietzsche gives a more detailed version of the claim that Christianity is the outcome of a historic choice between Epicurus and the Crucified. He describes the culture of late antiquity as riven by the conflict between Epicureanism and Platonism, the latter in both its elite form[14] and its popular manifestation in the secret mystery cults of first Mithras and Isis, and later Christianity. He describes in *The Anti-Christ* how Christianity marked the victory of Platonism over the Epicureans; Epicurus, he says, 'opposed the subterranean cults, the whole of latent Christianity – to deny immortality was already in those days an actual *redemption*. – And Epicurus would have won, every mind of any account in the Roman Empire was an Epicurean: *then Paul appeared*.[15] For Nietzsche, Christianity or the 'Platonism of the masses' was a redemptive religion which negated life in order to justify its promise of salvation; it had first to secure the 'corruption of souls through the concept of guilt, punishment, and immortality' to then be able to save them (*AC* §58). Epicurus, in this reading, challenged the corruption of the soul by Platonism of all kinds by affirming life and the moment against the melancholy prison of sin, the afterlife and punishment.

Epicurus seems here to be unequivocally cast as the opposite of Christianity, as the enemy of God and the gods,[16] of Platonism, the mystery cults and Christianity. Yet this is compatible with his being described by Nietzsche as Christian. In the same sentence from *The Gay Science* in which he says he learned to understand Epicurus as the 'opposite of the Dionysian pessimist' he also identifies the Christian as 'actually only a kind of Epicurean – both are essentially romantics'. This is because both Epicurus and Christ offer consolation for 'those who suffer from the *impoverishment of life*' and who, like the friends of Socrates, seek 'a god who would be truly a god for the sick, a healer and saviour; also logic, the conceptual understandability of existence – for logic calms and gives confidence' – anything, any charm in short, which can 'keep away fear' (*GS* §370). For Nietzsche, Epicurus and Christ offer consolation[17] with an emphasis upon redemption, and so must both be opposed: the Anti-Christ must also be the Anti-Epicurean. In his critique of redemption in *The Anti-Christ* Nietzsche describes Epicureanism as 'the redemptive doctrine of the pagan world' and Epicurus as a '*typical decadent*, first recognised as such by me'. Epicureanism, in this readings, flows smoothly into Christianity: 'The fear of pain, even of the infinitely small in pain – *cannot* end otherwise than in a *religion of love*' (*AC* §30).

Against both forms of redemptive consolation, Nietzsche pits the Dionysian affirmation born of the '*over-fullness of life*' or a 'desire for *destruction*, change, and becoming [that] can be an expression of an overflowing energy that is pregnant with the future' (*GS* §370). Yet this affirmative destruction in its turn is revealed as another consolation: 'I have presented such terrible images to knowledge that any "Epicurean delight" is out of the question. Only Dionysian joy is sufficient: *I have been the first to discover the tragic*' (*WP* §1029). Here Dionysian affirmation is shown to be reactive: only it can offer consolation for the 'terrible images' which Nietzsche's philosophy has frightened itself with.

The shifts in the identity and affiliations of Nietzsche's Epicurus are bewildering: Epicurus versus the Crucified, Epicurus versus Dionysus, Dionysus and Epicurus versus the Crucified, Epicurus and the Crucified versus Dionysus. These movements and transformations testify to the ambivalent consolation of philosophy, its inability to redeem itself from the desire for redemption. The wisdom that would love death and the wisdom that would love life merge into each other; redemption is revealed in destruction and destruction in redemption. To give consolation philosophy must find the wisdom both to 'close the open hand out of love' and yet allow the erratic stream of love to 'plunge into impassable and pathless places!'. For this reason the consolation of philosophy, even at its limit in Nietzsche, is constantly in danger of its ambivalence turning into mourning, of its wisdom turning gloomy.

To end with two dreams of frightening children. In the first, interpreted by Freud, a father mourning his dead child 'had a dream that his child was standing beside his bed, caught him by the arm and whispered to him reproachfully: "Father, don't you see I'm burning?"' (Freud 1985, 652). In the face of utter loss, the father stages the desired return of the child, even if this means dreaming the child in pain and in need of help: even this is better than letting the child be lost. In this haunting, the mourning of the lost child is undone by the residual hope of its impossible return. In 'The Child with the Mirror' Zarathustra too is haunted in his sleep by an uncanny child.[18] He awakes in fear from a dream in which the child visits him with a mirror. The child bids him look at himself in the mirror. He looks and cries out with a shaken heart. He cannot see himself in the sneer and grimace of the devil that looks back at him but interprets this image as the work of enemies who have distorted his teaching. He cannot bear to think that seeds he sowed might have been weeds and not wheat, that the gifts he gave might have been something to be ashamed of. He cannot bear losing his friends, or the thought that they might want to be lost to him, and decides that the hour has come to seek them again. Did Zarathustra 'understand the dream's omen and warning all too well'? He does and he does not. When he reflects to himself immediately following the dream, he mourns and desires redemption in the return of what has been lost, but when he then speaks with his animals he changes, and bliss comes to him 'like a storm wind'. He is consoled and, embracing ambivalence, affirms what will be lost by evoking the image of a secluded lake which out of love flows down and loses/finds itself in the sea.

Notes

1   *Anthony and Cleopatra*, I, ii, 176.
2   According to the *OED*, a consolation is not only 'an alleviation of sorrow or mental distress' but also the stake in a game of cards 'which is always paid by those who lose to those who win'.

3   Consolation may thus be distinguished from both mourning and melancholia, the latter's distinguishing features described by Freud as 'profoundly painful dejection, cessation of interest in the outer world, loss of the capacity to love, inhibition of all activity, and a lowering of the self-regarding feelings to a degree that finds utterance in self-reproaches and self-revilings, and culminates in a delusional expectation of punishment'. Sigmund Freud, 'Mourning and Melancholia', in Freud 1987, 252. At its rare best, the consolation of philosophy can produce feelings of elation, enhanced interest in the 'wonder' of the world, love, activity and an affirmation which is not based on guilt and fear of punishment.

4   The relationship between mourning, fire, death and the child is explored in Freud's analysis of the dream of the 'Burning child' in Freud 1985, 652–4.

5   Derrida's reading of the frightened child in *Phaedo* ('Plato's Pharmacy' in Derrida 1981), to which I am deeply indebted, moves to *Crito* (46c) in order to discover the antidote for the fear of death to lie in training in dialectics. However, it is possible to read *Phaedo* as directly complicit with the mutual implications of *pharmakon* and *alexipharmakon*, with the charm producing the very fear which it soothes. Socrates reflects on this risk when he admits that he is trying to convince himself of his arguments and not only his listeners. He must be convinced of their truth, and his listeners must bear witness to this truth (and his conviction). He would not deceive himself and his listeners, and 'like the bee leave my sting in you before I die' (91c), and yet perhaps this sting and his death are a necessary part of the cure.

6   The two main surviving sources for Epicurus's ideas are Book X of Diogenes Laërtius's *Lives of Eminent Philosophers* (Laërtius 1991), which reproduces three letters concerning physics, celestial phenomena, God and death, along with forty Epicurean 'maxims', and the majestic *De rerum natura* of Lucretius.

7   This is a suitable point to mention Marx's redemptive reading of Epicurus in his doctoral dissertation. Marx regards Epicurus as a philosopher of freedom, one who liberates humanity by freeing it from the fear of punishment after death. He too includes Epicurus in the ranks of the redeemers, while acknowledging that without fear of punishment there is no place for redemption.

8   This is the case in spite of Kant's use of the table of logical judgements to present his 'logic of pleasure'. It is not that pleasure is forced into the schema of logical judgement, but that there is an affinity between pleasure and the power of judgement which permits it to be presented in this way. For a more detailed reading, see Caygill 1989, chapter 5.

9   *The Wanderer and His Shadow* in *HH*, §227. In a letter to Peter Gast of 3 August 1883, Nietzsche writes that the 'world has paid [Epicurus] back … for *allowing* himself to be taken for someone else'. But how can anyone presume not to be taken for someone else, why would anyone want to be taken for what they are?

10   *GS* §375. The ambivalence is heightened in the concluding sentence of the aphorism which claims that 'when we hesitate it is least of all danger that makes us hesitate'.

11 *The Wanderer and His Shadow* in *HH*, §295, a characteristically ambivalent passage, for if the scene is so perfect, why clutter it with Greek heroes?

12 *D* §72; see also *The Will to Power*, §196.

13 *D* §72; for the latter point see also *HH* §68.

14 See *BGE* §7 for Nietzsche's analysis of Epicurus's attack on the Platonists as the 'flatterers of Dionysus' (both the tyrant and the God of the theatre).

15 *AC* §58. It is notable that even here, at the point of maximum vituperation, Nietzsche cannot resist translating Epicurean philosophy into the redemptive language of Christian Platonism. However ironic the implied contrast between an apparent and an actual redemption, the desire for salvation remains uppermost.

16 See, for example, *GS* §277.

17 *The Wanderer and His Shadow* in *HH*, §7: 'he who wishes to offer consolation – to the unfortunate, ill-doers, hypochondriacs, the dying – should call to mind the two pacifying formulae of Epicurus, which are capable of being applied to very many questions. Reduced to their simplest form they would perhaps become: firstly, if that is how things are they do not concern us; secondly, things may be so for us, but they may also be otherwise'.

18 This section of Zarathustra is a presentiment of Joyce's *Finnegans Wake*, with its river of love running to the sea and the advent of 'new ways and new speech'.

7

Philosophy and cultural reform in the early Nietzsche

All the early philosophers took pains to alter the concept of the
polis and to create a Panhellenic way of thinking.
– NIETZSCHE, 'THE STRUGGLE BETWEEN SCIENCE AND WISDOM' (*SSW* 145)

In his preface to *The New Nietzsche* David Allison describes Nietzsche's thought as 'at once the most philosophically critical project since Kant's *and* the one that bears the greatest urgency'. He sees the urgency as arising from the disquieting challenge it is held to pose to 'the very validity of our contemporary forms of intelligibility' (Allison 1985, ix). This sense of danger surrounding Nietzsche's thought accurately describes the context of the post-war European reception of the relationship between Nietzsche's critical philosophy and its cultural impact.

In the shadow of the National Socialist appropriation of Nietzsche's philosophy, the authors of the 'New Nietzsche' addressed themselves to the question of the cultural significance of Nietzsche's thought and in particular to why its challenge to the limits of philosophy posed, and should continue to pose, such a threat to the validity of the organizing principles of modern culture. The exploration of this question led unavoidably to the more fundamental issues of the meaning of 'philosophy' itself and its significance for projects of cultural transformation.

Nietzsche himself was deeply concerned with these themes, indeed the reflection upon the relationship between 'philosophy' and culture formed the matrix of his authorship. This is evident above all in the writings from the formative period of the early 1870s, the period which saw the publication of the *Birth of Tragedy* (1872) and the *Untimely Meditations* (1873–6). These texts are but the outcrops of an archipelago of reflections dedicated to exploring the significance of the practice of 'philosophy' for cultural reform. His thoughts in these early writings pursue two intersecting routes: the first passes through the relationship of philosophy to 'non-philosophy' (art, science, religion and politics), the second through a genealogy of philosophy or the search for its origins or 'birth' in the cultural revolutions of Ancient Greece.

The two projects are complementary, since for Nietzsche the origins of a phenomenon are always to be found in what it is not, what it has negated in order to become what it is. Thus the origins of philosophy are to be traced to non-philosophy and, in the specific case of Ancient Greek philosophy, to its relations with tragic art, science, religion and political reform. But enciphered within the search for the 'birth' of philosophy and the cultural significance of the first philosophers is a concern for its 'death' and the significance of the last philosophers. For according to Nietzsche, 'Since Kant, philosophy is dead' (*KGA* III/4, 105; but cf. Nietzsche 1979, 153) and like tragedy before it, it died suicidally. Nietzsche maintains that both episodes – beginning and end – can only be understood in the context of the programmes of cultural reform which, although inspired by philosophy, created, and destroyed, the *need* for it.

The 'birth' of philosophy was inseparable from the reform of the cultic myths associated with the *polis* and the creation of a Panhellenic culture, while its death was inexplicable without the reform of Christianity and the rise of the nation state. Even though the two themes are inextricable, I will stay for now with the birth of philosophy, leaving its death for another time.

The themes of birth and death loom large in *The Birth of Tragedy* which, in spite of its title, is overwhelmingly concerned with the death of tragedy. The centre of the book, sections 11–15, had been published privately a year before (1871) as 'Socrates and Greek Tragedy' and the complete text itself developed the theme of the death of tragedy already announced in the 1870 lecture 'Socrates and Tragedy'. Without becoming involved in the details of Nietzsche's inquest on tragedy – his working back from its tragic death to the circumstances of its birth – it is necessary to emphasize two points that emerge from his narrative. The first is that the death of tragedy was an immense *cultural* catastrophe: 'when Greek tragedy died, there rose everywhere the deep sense of an immense void' (*BT* 76). The experience of void and disorientation following the death of tragedy is akin to that predicted by the madman in *The Gay Science* to follow the death of the Christian God. In both cases the event is cast as a cultural disaster of incalculable scope and consequence.

The second point concerns philosophy's involvement in the death of tragedy. Nietzsche evokes Euripides's tormented incomprehension of the old tragedy and describes how, detached from the tragic culture of his fellow spectators, 'he found that other spectator who did not comprehend tragedy and therefore did not esteem it' (*BT* 81). With this other spectator he could now venture from his solitude to begin the tremendous struggle against the art of Aeschylus and Sophocles (*BT* 81). The other spectator was Socrates, and in his person philosophy became involved not only in the suicide of an art form, but in the death of an entire culture. For it is not only the suicide of tragedy but 'The self-destruction of the Greeks [that] is accomplished in Socrates' (*SSW* 136). From the standpoint of *The Birth of Tragedy* philosophy appears in the person of the unmusical Socrates as the deadly adversary of tragedy and of tragic culture. To the 'Cyclops eye' (*BT* 89) of the 'mystagogue of science' neither the effects without clear causes of tragic art nor the cultural 'forms of intelligibility' which it sustained made any sense.

The moment of the death of tragedy coincides for Nietzsche with the birth of a philosophy dedicated to the unrestrained pursuit of knowledge. This was not the first birth of philosophy, but its rebirth through Socrates out of the spirit of knowledge. Yet this too, at its moment of 'birth', already contained within it a limitation that would prove fatal. This is not to deny the immense power and longevity of Socratic philosophy and the culture of knowledge of 'science' which succeeded it and thrived for two millennia, on the contrary:

> the hunger for knowledge reached a never-suspected universality in the widest domain of the educated world, became the real task for every person of higher gifts, and led science onto the high seas from which it has never again been driven altogether ... this universality first spread a common net of thought over the whole globe, actually holding out the prospect of the lawfulness of an entire solar system. (*BT* 96)

Nevertheless, Nietzsche did see this entire development as fated to destroy itself, for 'science, spurred by its powerful illusion, speeds irresistibly towards its limits where its optimism, concealed in the essence of logic, suffers shipwreck' (*BT* 97). When science reaches its limit, and is compelled by its knowledge drive to look further, it discovers that 'logic coils up at these boundaries and finally bites its own tail – suddenly the new form of insight breaks through, tragic insight which, merely to be endured, needs art as a protection and remedy' (*BT* 98). Thus the suppression of tragedy present at the birth of Socratic philosophy returns at its death. The unrestrained knowledge drive pushed beyond what it can know finds itself suffering its limits, unable to resign itself to not-knowing. For Nietzsche, Kant's attempt to chart the limits of knowledge marks the death of a philosophy dedicated to satisfying the drive for unlimited knowledge and is potentially the beginning of a new, self-limiting tragic wisdom.

The new tragic wisdom is cast as the repetition of an older, pre-Socratic 'philosophy' which promised a different relation to tragic art than that embodied in Socrates. *The Birth of Tragedy* is an account not only of the birth of Socratic philosophy out of the death of tragedy, but also of the birth of a tragic philosophy, one which died at the same time as tragedy and tragic culture. Indeed, without this account *The Birth of Tragedy* would be incomplete, for the life story of tragedy is inseparable from the emergence of a tragic culture, and in this the role of philosophy was crucial. The antagonistic relationship between Socratic philosophy and tragic culture presented in *The Birth of Tragedy*, along with the narrative of philosophy distinguishing itself from non-philosophy in terms of its knowledge drive, is only part of the story. It rests on another narrative of the birth of philosophy, one in which philosophy participates in the formation of a tragic culture and is not invested in distinguishing itself as science from the claims of art, religion and politics.

Nietzsche's pursuit of this other birth of philosophy can be traced through his letters and notebooks from the early 1870s. It was his abiding preoccupation, manifest at first in his attempts to write a supplement to *The Birth of Tragedy* on the subject of the birth of philosophy. Later it informed his reflections first on the 'free spirit' and then on the tragic philosopher or 'artistic Socrates' of the future, both of whom would cease to police the boundaries between philosophy and non-philosophy and commence the cultural reformation of the revaluation of values.

The writings of the early 1870s are haunted by the presence of the ghostly, unwritten magnum opus on philosophy and culture. It manifests itself in the notebooks and letters as the 'Philosopher's Book' [*Philosophenbuch*] described as 'The Birth of Tragedy from another viewpoint. Its confirmation by the philosophy of its contemporaries' (*KGA* III/4, 144). It is also described as a 'companion piece' which would complement the story of the birth and death of tragedy with that of philosophy. The historical research into the early Greek philosophers partially presented in *Philosophy in the Tragic Age of the Greeks* was crucial to this project, but it was set in the context of the broader issues of the meaning of philosophy and its role in cultural transformation. The latter themes were explored in their own right in the lectures 'On the Future of Our Educational Institutions' in 1872 and the *Untimely Meditations*, one of which was to have been on the theme of 'Philosophy under Pressure' and material from which appears in the published texts. Yet Nietzsche repeatedly stressed that the cultural and historical inquiries were inseparable, writing to Rhode (22/3/1873) that 'I am concerned with a fine general problem and not merely with a historical one' (cited in Nietzsche 1979, xxiii). The question of the relationship between philosophy and culture informed the historical research, which in its turn determined the direction taken by the exploration of the cultural question. This is reflected throughout the notebooks, where historical, conceptual and cultural themes are inextricably linked, often appearing together in the same sentence.

In his notebook Nietzsche poses himself the question: 'What can a philosopher do in regard to the culture of the people?' (*KGA* III/4, 221) and answers:

[The philosopher] is unable to create a culture,
but can prepare it, remove restraints,
or moderate and thus preserve it,
or destroy it. (*KGA* III/4, 222)

All three options are bracketed with the qualifications that they are 'always only negative'. The philosopher stands in a negative relation to culture and must always challenge its 'forms of intelligibility', whether by preparing and removing their constraints, moderating and preserving them or even bringing about their destruction. Yet for Nietzsche these options are not necessarily alternatives: philosophy can do all these things at once. What it cannot do by itself is be culturally formative: 'It is not possible to found a popular culture [*Volkskultur*] on philosophy. Philosophy can never be fundamental with respect to a culture, it will always have a marginal significance. What is this?' (*KGA* III/4, 140). To answer this question Nietzsche has first to establish philosophy's effect on culture and then to ask what philosophy is, that is, how it relates to, and distinguishes itself from, non-philosophy such as science, art, religion and politics.

Philosophy's effect upon culture is equivocal, and this equivocation is closely related to its relationship with non-philosophy. The philosopher, Nietzsche insists repeatedly, is both a destroyer and a preserver. The philosopher 'destroys and dissolves everything positive in a culture or a religion (even as he tries to found one)' (*KGA* III/4, 222). The philosopher destroys not only what is positively esteemed, but whatever is 'positive' in the sense used by Hegel in his early essay on 'The Positivity of the Christian Religion' (1795–6), that is, whatever is fixed and instituted. Yet the philosopher is also described as a preserver, serving as 'the brake-shoe on the wheel of time' for 'There are times of extreme danger in which philosophers appear – when the wheel rolls with increasing speed – they, with art, take the place of a disappearing myth' (*KGA* III/4, 9). Thus, philosophy may precipitate a crisis in culture, in this case the mythical culture or 'form of intelligibility', and/or it may, in alliance with art, serve as the brakeshoe to slow down the course of the crisis. It is the alliance with art that is crucial in these circumstances, but entering such an alliance decisively contributes to shaping the meaning and identity of philosophy.

The crisis Nietzsche associates with the disappearance of myth refers to the specific event of the collapse of the pre-classical culture of Greek city states. But this specific crisis serves as a paradigm for general cultural crisis, including that of the death of the Christian God. In times of cultural crisis the identity assumed by philosophy – its relation to non-philosophy – is crucial in determining the character of its cultural impact. And while the character of philosophy determines its effect upon the culture, the state of a culture reciprocally determines the character of its philosophy. This mutual relation between a culture and its philosophy is adverted to by Nietzsche in the first section of *Philosophy in the Tragic Age of the Greeks*; there he wrote, 'That the Greeks philosophized at such a time teaches us as much about what philosophy is, and should be, as it does about the Greeks themselves' (*KGA* III/2, 299). Philosophy is the key to Greek culture as much as this culture is the key to ancient Greek philosophy.

One of the main clues to discerning the cultural significance of philosophy is the nature of its relationship to non-philosophy. Philosophy, Nietzsche writes, 'has nothing in common [*nichts Gemeinsames*], it is sometimes science, sometimes art' (*KGA* III/4, 136). This is not to say that philosophy is the *Aufhebung* or suspension of the differences between art and science, but rather to point to the anomalous position it occupies between them. It may become the site for the negotiation between the knowledge and the art drives, but it can just as easily be the means by which one is vanquished by the other. What then is its place? This question returns us to Nietzsche's observation that philosophy has 'marginal significance' for culture. The place of philosophy with regard to non-philosophy serves as an index for the condition of a culture, but it also determines the cultural significance of philosophy.

Nietzsche enquires into the meaning of philosophy – what it 'is' – by demarcating it from, and situating it with respect to, science and art. He points to the 'Great difficulty, whether philosophy is an art or a science' and proceeds to say it is both and neither:

> It is an art in its aims and its productions. But its means, presentation by concepts, are shared with science. It is a form of poetic invention [*Dichtkunst*]. It can't be placed [*nicht unterzubringen*] and as a result we have to invent and characterize a species for it. (*KGA* III/4, 27)

Even the classification of philosophy requires the exercise both of artistic invention and scientific characterization. Nietzsche goes on to invent such a characterization: philosophy is the site for the *Agon* or struggle of science and art; the philosopher 'knows in that he invents, and invents in that he knows'. Philosophy possesses an artistic power, a 'continuation of the mythical drive' of 'invention beyond the limits of experience' (*KGA* III/4, 27). This allows it to master its other drive, the drive to knowledge: 'We see in nature itself mechanisms against absolute knowledge; philosophy recognizes the language of nature and says "we need art" and "we require only a part of knowledge" (*KGA* III/4, 23). Philosophy is both between and beyond science and art, and it occupies this anomalous position both at its beginning and at its end. For

Heraclitus and Kant, both of whom Nietzsche often mentions in the same breath, philosophy consists in the 'Overcoming of knowledge through the powers that create myths' (*KGA* III/4, 27).

These abstract reflections on philosophy and non-philosophy and the cultural impact of philosophy are developed and modified with regard to the historical events surrounding the birth and death of philosophy. Nietzsche aligns the birth of philosophy with the cultural reforms of Panhellenism and claims first that this 'tragic philosophy' died with Socrates and then that Socratic philosophy in its turn died with the Christian reformation and the founding of cultural modernity. Thus when discussing the birth of philosophy, Nietzsche attends to its relations with non-philosophy in the guise of science and art but stresses its place within the political and religious reforms of pre-classical Greek culture. From the general question of how to 'invent and characterize' a species for philosophy, he now turns to the historical analysis of how 'they' – the early Greek philosophers – themselves set about inventing and characterizing the anomaly that was early Greek philosophy.

Nietzsche locates the invention of philosophy within the conditions of the transition from a mythical to a tragic culture. He first addresses the difficulty of appreciating what was at stake in this cultural reform from the surviving source materials. The texts of the early Greek philosophers were transmitted by philosophers working after the collapse of the attempted cultural reform. Nietzsche figures the fate of the early thinkers by means of a metaphor of a group of statues dismembered by posterity:

> they were plundered, and soon an arm here from Parmenides, a shoulder-blade there from Heraclitus, a foot from Empedocles, [appeared] in Plato's Academy as well as in the Stoa and the garden of Epicurus. To understand them as a whole, one must recognize in each of them an effort towards and an accompaniment to the Greek reformers; for they should have prepared the way for these, they should have gone before them like the dawn before the sun. But the sun didn't come, the reformers failed, and so that dawn remained a wraithlike illusion. (*KGA* III/4, 133)

Early Greek philosophy is thus aligned with an unsuccessful project to reform Greek culture. The questions then arise of what Nietzsche understood these reforms to be, what he saw as the role of philosophy in them and what he identified as the reasons for their failure.

The answers to these questions regarding the circumstances surrounding the birth of philosophy are inseparable from those attending the birth of tragedy. For the early Greek philosophers were 'ruled in part by a drive similar to that which created tragedy' and the reforms centred upon the creation of a tragic culture:

> That something new was in the air is shown by the simultaneous emergence of tragedy, yet the philosopher and the legislator who could have understood tragedy never appeared, and so this art too died, and the Greek reformation became forever impossible. (*KGA* III/4, 133)

The Greek reformation would only have been possible if it was supported by an alliance between the artist, the philosopher and the legislator: but the ancient Greeks did not find their philosopher and reformer and as a result 'the spirit of reformation was sustained by a [single] group of phenomena – the development of tragedy' (*SSW* 134).

Nietzsche does not attempt to base the failure of the Greek cultural reformation on a single factor such as the frailty of the philosophers or the absence of legislators but seeks instead a constellation of causes. However, underlying these is a consistent historical tendency towards centralization, one which moves from the attack upon the parochial myths of the Greek cities to the establishment of Athenian domination. Instead of a reformation which would unite Greece without establishing a dominant political centre, the attack upon local myths issued in Athenian hegemony:

> The tendencies to centralization produced by the Persian wars: Sparta and Athens seized upon them. In contrast no such tendencies existed between 776 and 560, when the culture of the *polis* blossomed. I think that if it had not been for the Persian wars, they would have hit upon the idea of centralization through spiritual reform. Pythagoras? (*SSW* 138–9)

Here Nietzsche regards the potential for a reform of the mythic culture associated with the cities as lost in the course of the Persian Wars. The reform expressed in the move from a mythical culture based in the *polis* to a Panhellenic tragic culture presided over the births of tragedy and philosophy. This development, however, was brought to an end by the 'domination of Athens' and the emergence of politics to the exclusion of a reformed *cultural* Panhellenism.

Nietzsche did not share the adulation of Periclean Athens almost endemic among classical German philosophers. He made little attempt to conceal his hostility towards and even contempt for Athens, and his unremitting attacks on Athenian domination clearly echo and parallel his hostile comments on the new German Reich. In his essay on the Greek (read Athenian) state he draws explicit parallels between contemporary German and ancient Greek politics, both of which smothered the possibility of cultural reform. For him Athens meant no less than the ruin of the Greeks. After a litany of complaints about Athens, including its 'philosophical unproductivity' and the mediocrity of its musicians and tragedians – 'The Athenian tragedy is not the highest form which one might be able to imagine' – he concludes:

> It was the spiritual domination of Athens which prevented this reformation. One really has to imagine what it was like before this domination existed. It was not something that had to happen; it first became necessary as a consequence of the Persian wars: that is to say, not until after the necessity of such domination was demonstrated by physical and political might. Miletus, for example, was more talented, as was Agrigentum. (*SSW* 137)

The unification of Greece under the Athenians destroyed the Greek reformation and led eventually to the death of tragedy at the hands of Euripides and to the more protracted rebirth and death of philosophy through Socrates. And with them also ended the attempt to found a tragic culture based upon an alliance of art and philosophy. Only in Plato's *Republic* is the distorted external face of Athenian politics transcended and the cultural vocation of the state recognized in the 'relationship between state and genius' or in its goal to promote 'the Olympian existence and the ever-renewed creation and preparation of genius' ('Der Griechische Staat', *KGA* III/2, 270).

Nietzsche describes the failed tragic culture which would have informed, and been informed by, tragedy and philosophy in terms of the unity of festival and cult. It is in this unity that the

> reform would have begun. The thought of a Panhellenic tragedy: an infinitely more fertile power would have then developed. Why did this not happen? (*SSW* 139)

The local cults of the *polis* would have been 'unified' in a festival focusing upon a Panhellenic tragedy. The move from the local, mythical culture of the *polis* to the Panhellenic tragic culture of the festival would be accomplished by the alliance of tragic art and philosophy. Philosophy would dissolve and destroy local mythical cults from the standpoint of the universal claims of knowledge but would then with tragedy preserve them in the tragic festivals. But this alliance of philosophy and art did not take place – 'Greek philosophy and music developed side-by-side' but did not achieve the symbiosis necessary securely to found a tragic culture.

Nietzsche saw the Greek philosophers as successful in destroying the local, mythical cults but less successful in finding a form through which to invent a Panhellenic culture in association with tragedy. The early Greek philosophers were united in their destructive struggle against myth – Nietzsche refers to 'the struggle of them all, but especially of Democritus, against myth' (*SSW* 134) – but divided as to the direction of the reform or 'new interpretation of myth' which would succeed it. Thus Nietzsche returns repeatedly to the relationship between the attempts of the Greek philosophers to distinguish philosophy from myth and their proposals for the Panhellenic reforms of Greek culture (for examples from 1872 and 1875 see Nietzsche 1979, 149–50 and 146). His discussion and judgement of the individual philosophers are firmly set within this context.

Nietzsche distinguishes between the early Greek philosophers in terms of the steps they took towards inventing a new form of culture. On this criterion he was especially impressed by the contributions of Thales, Heraclitus and above all Empedocles. He does not find in the surviving fragments of the other philosophers that he analyses comparable visions of a Panhellenic culture capable of succeeding the destruction of the mythical cultures of the *polis*. Anaximander recognized the dangers of myth for Greek culture 'insofar as myth coddles people and makes then superficial' (*SSW* 146) but does not develop an alternative. Similarly with Parmenides, who 'struggles against the fanciful and unstable character of the entire way of looking at the world' but who instead of directing those passions towards new cultural ends 'wishes to grant mankind rest from political passion' (*SSW* 146). Pythagoras too is criticized for turning his back on Panhellenism and pursuing cultural reform in small groups and sects, while the cultural alternatives proposed by Anaxagoras and Democritus are deemed nostalgic and reactionary, looking back fondly to the culture of the *polis* while destroying its mythic and cultic foundations (*SSW* 146).

For Nietzsche it is Thales, Heraclitus and Empedocles who fully understood that the destruction of mythic culture made it imperative to elaborate new, Panhellenic cultural alternatives. It is they who sought 'to replace the popular picture of the world with a new one' (*SSW* 141). Yet even they failed because they did not appreciate the cultural potential of tragedy and thus missed the chance to establish an alliance between philosophy and tragic art. With Thales 'for the first time the man of science triumphs over the man of myth, and then the man of wisdom triumphs in turn over the man of science' (*SSW* 145). That is, after having destroyed the culture of myth as a 'man of science' he proposed a new culture as a 'man of wisdom'. Nietzsche continues with a reconstruction of Thales's process of thought:

> If the *polis* was based upon myth, then abandoning myth meant abandoning the old concept of the *polis*. Now we know that Thales proposed, though he did not accomplish, the foundation of a league of cities: he ran aground on the old mythical concept of the *polis*. At the same time he had a foreboding of the enormous danger to Greece if this isolating power of myth continued to keep the cities divided. (*SSW* 145)

Although Thales recognized the need for a Panhellenic league of cities, his replacement of mythical aetiology with the thought that 'water is the source and maternal womb of all things' (*SSW* 145) was insufficient for a new cultural unity. Philosophy by itself, as Nietzsche observed, could not create a *Volkskultur* out of its own concepts but required the aid of art. In the absence of a convincing principle of Panhellenic unity, Thales fell back upon the idea of a federation of existing cities, seeking to found an alliance between them rather than a cultural unity that would both exceed and contain them. He did not envisage the possibility of a Panhellenic culture transcending the *polis*, and thus he too, in Nietzsche's eyes, fatally underestimated tragedy.

For Nietzsche the cultural ambition and imagination of Heraclitus far exceeded that of Thales, it even exceeded the bounds of Panhellenism. Once again there is 'the struggle against myth' and the culture of the *polis*, but this time because 'myth isolates the Greeks and opposes them to the barbarians' (*SSW* 146). Nietzsche claimed that Heraclitus was aware of the dangers of producing Panhellenic unity in the guise of expanded *polis*, shut off from what it defined as 'barbarians'. For this reason, 'Heraclitus even appears to have torn down the barrier separating the barbaric and the Hellenic in order to create greater freedom and to broaden narrow points of view' (*SSW* 146). However, this was not a programme which could have gained popular support, and Nietzsche saw Heraclitus retreat from the *polis* into solitude as a confirmation of the impracticability of his proposed cultural reform.

If Thales's ideal of cultural reform remained too bound up with the *polis* and if Heraclitus's was too cosmo- or ultrapolitan to inspire popular support, then the philosopher who for Nietzsche came nearest to formulating a viable programme of Panhellenic cultural reform was Empedocles. Nietzsche continues the note from 1872–3 in which he says that 'the philosopher or legislator who could have understood tragedy never appeared' with some thoughts about Empedocles:

> One can never think about Empedocles without deep sadness; he was nearest to the image of one of those reformers, and that it also went wrong for him and he disappeared prematurely, who knows after what terrible experiences and in what despair – that was a Panhellenic destiny. (*KGA* III/4, 133)

Politically, Nietzsche describes Empedocles as 'the democrat with social reform up his sleeve' (*SSW* 141). His Panhellenic reforms were directed towards creating a new mythology which, in the guise of 'the great Hellenic festivals', would pursue the 'republic – transformation of life – popular reform' (*SSW* 134) on the basis of 'Love, democracy, communal property' (*SSW* 146). But this democratic renewal of Greek culture did not ally itself sufficiently with tragedy, and whenever Nietzsche mentions Empedocles the comparison with tragedy is never far away. After mentioning Empedocles's attempt to transform Greek culture by means of the Panhellenic festivals, Nietzsche quietly observes, 'Tragedy likewise was a means' (*SSW* 134), but one whose power was not fully appreciated by Empedocles. He pursued reforms in isolation from tragedy and is thus 'the unsuccessful reformer' and 'when he failed, all that remained was Socrates' (*SSW* 134). And with Socrates, as we have seen, the potential for a constructive alliance between philosophy and tragedy was finally lost to Greek culture.

Nietzsche's accounts of the births of tragedy and philosophy are set within the context of a failed cultural reform. Philosophy and tragedy emerged with the crisis of the mythical culture of the *polis* but neither alone was able to institute the required Panhellenic popular, tragic culture. Philosophy and tragedy shared a common interest but remained apart; when they finally came into contact it was under the destructive auspices of Socrates and Euripides. Thus *The Birth of Tragedy* is an analysis of a failed cultural revolution, one in which art and philosophy failed to achieve the alliance which might have founded a *Volkskultur*. It is also a text which notoriously promotes the new tragic art of Richard Wagner. From the perspective of the complementary accounts of the births of tragedy and philosophy, the text can be read less as an adulation of Wagner than as a warning of the necessary perversion and failure of a cultural reform led by art alone. In the face of the modern crisis of Christian culture and the perceived need for new festivals following the death of God, the alliance of tragic art and philosophy became all the more urgent.

The identity of the philosopher Nietzsche had in mind as the 'artistic Socrates' who would complement Wagner's tragic art is not too difficult to guess. Yet with the renunciation of his fantasy of an alliance with Wagner the problem of the relationship between philosophy and cultural reform became even more urgent. With the example of the unsuccessful Greeks before him, Nietzsche tried a variety of strategies to provoke the crisis of nihilism, to destroy but at the same time preserve Christian culture. The evocation of the 'free-spirits', the various strategies employed by Zarathustra to carry his message down from the mountain and initiate cultural reform, and finally the 'fish-hook texts' of the mid- to late 1880s (for which, he lamented, 'there were no fish') all testify to Nietzsche's preoccupation with the role of 'philosophy' in cultural reform. The initial exploration of the nature of philosophy and its cultural impact during the early 1870s is thus crucial for understanding Nietzsche's insight into the power of philosophy both to destroy and preserve a culture. It also informed his prescient sensitivity to the capacity of a culture to adapt a philosophy to its own ends. Philosophers may supply both the brakeshoe and the dynamite with which a culture can arrest or destroy itself, but it is other hands that pull the emergency cord and light the fuse.

8

Affirmation and eternal return in the Free-Spirit Trilogy

Shall we do this, friends, again? Amen, and auf Wiedersehn!
– EPILOGUE, *HUMAN, ALL TOO HUMAN*

The question of where the thought of eternal return belongs continues to haunt the reading of Nietzsche's philosophy. There is some doubt whether it belongs to him at all, or if it does, where it stands with respect to his other thoughts of 'will to power' and 'overman'. It is a thought difficult to place, one which disturbs any attempt to gather his thinking under the traditional titles of theoretical and practical philosophy. And while it appears in some respects marginal to the development of his philosophy, eternal return is claimed by Nietzsche in *Ecce Homo* as its centre – the 'highest formula of affirmation' and the 'basic thought' of *Also Sprach Zarathustra* (1883–5).

One response to the difficulty of placing eternal return is to expel it altogether. This option was taken by Alfred Bäumler in *Nietzsche der Philosoph und Politiker* (1931) where the thought is relegated to the realm of biographical idiosyncrasy, so clearing the field for an alignment of will to power and overman congenial to a National Socialist understanding of Nietzsche. Although few would today admit to following Bäumler's reading, its consequences are evident in many contemporary critiques and defences of 'Nietzscheanism'.[1]

A more subtle form of relegation casts eternal return as an esoteric doctrine whose hidden ubiquity may be established by a scrutiny of what Nietzsche wrote but did not publish in the manuscripts and notebooks from the 1880s. This approach combines the pleasures of close textual scholarship with the virtue of leaving an open verdict on where to place eternal return. But it also threatens to divert the search for eternal return into unravelling the philological difficulties posed by Nietzsche's projects, notebooks and jottings.[2]

In this essay eternal return will be located as an outcome of the crisis of judgement rehearsed in the 'Free-Spirit Trilogy' of *Human, All Too Human* (1878–80), *Daybreak* (1881) and *The Gay Science* (1882). This approach, recommended by Nietzsche in *Ecce Homo*,[3] emphasizes the difficult, aporetic character of the doctrine over its systematic ties with 'will to power' and 'overman'. In this reading eternal return becomes, in Kantian terms, a 'statement' of the 'enigma' or 'puzzle' of liberation, and not its 'solution'.[4] The difficulty of placing eternal return marks its resistance to the classic topic of philosophy and an intimation of new philosophical spaces.

I

The translation of Nietzsche's philosopheme into the classic distinction of theoretical and practical philosophy informs many readings of his work. Theoretical philosophy is discovered in the relation of will to power's 'becoming' and the 'being' of eternal return, while practical philosophy is found in the 'legislative' will to power of the 'sovereign' overman. Such a translation informs Heidegger's designation of Nietzsche's philosophy as the 'end of metaphysics' in the text of his Nietzsche lectures from the 1930s.[5] However this text, whose importance for reading Nietzsche cannot be overestimated, becomes extremely apprehensive when thinking about eternal return and its relation to 'will to power' and 'overman'. It constantly exceeds its own interpretative limits in a movement later thematized in the non-metaphysical reading of Nietzsche developed in *What Is Called Thinking* (1954).

One of the subtexts of Heidegger's lectures is the restoration of eternal return in the wake of its dismissal by Bäumler and company.[6] He does so by 'including' eternal return within will to power, suggesting that they say and think the same thought:

> We call Nietzsche's thought of the will to power his sole thought. At the same time we are saying that Nietzsche's other thought, that of the eternal return of the same, is of necessity included in the thought of will to power. Both thoughts – will to power and eternal return – say the same and think the same fundamental character of beings as a whole. (Heidegger [1954] 1968, III, 10)

Nietzsche's 'other thought' is 'included in' the thought of will to power by virtue of the metaphysical dichotomy of being and becoming. The terms of this theoretical inclusion were later described by Heidegger as 'the way of continuance through which will to power wills itself and guarantees its own presencing as the being of becoming' (Heidegger [1950] 1984, 22). So while eternal return is recovered from the oblivion decreed by Bäumler, it is 'included' in a metaphysical dichotomy which it cannot but disrupt.

Another defence of eternal return offered in the lectures is practical and involves the inclusion of eternal return in a metaphysics of the temporality of *Dasein*. The moment of eternal return is a 'collision' of past and future in the resolute decision:

> Whoever stands in the Moment is turned in two ways: for him past and future *run up against* one another. Whoever stands in the Moment lets what runs counter to itself come to collision, though not to a standstill, by cultivating and sustaining the strife between what is assigned him as a task and what has been given him as his endowment. (Heidegger 1991, II, 56–7)

Heidegger correctly and profoundly identifies the key to understanding this moment – a moment of the greatest weight or the greatest liberation – as the manner in which it is affirmed. It is how we say yes to the return of 'every pain and every joy' that determines the meaning of the moment.[7] He distinguishes the affirmation of a spectator (the dwarf in *Zarathustra*) from one who stands resolutely in the moment and decides between past and future. But the choice Heidegger offers between irresolute and resolute affirmation does not exhaust all the options. There is also the affirmation of one who is in the moment but free from the choice which it poses, the free spirit, whose yes neither affirms nor negates the times of past, present and future.

The way in which Nietzsche came to this yes through the 'historical philosophy' announced in *Human, All Too Human* will be examined below. It involves liberation from judgement rather than grasping the freedom to judge and decide resolutely. In Heidegger's reading, the moment of liberation occurs when eternal return and will to power cross each other in the resolute decision which affirms ecstatic temporality: 'Strange – are we to experience something that lies behind us by thinking forward? Yes, we are' (Heidegger 1991, II, 135). Such affirmation characterizes authentic *Dasein*; we forfeit liberation if we avoid this decision of the moment since

> we no longer ponder the fact that as temporal beings who are delivered over to ourselves we are also delivered over to the future in our willing; we no longer ponder the fact that the temporality of human being alone determines the way in which the human being stands in the ring of beings. (Heidegger 1991, 136)

But perhaps there is another form of avoidance,[8] one which is not inauthentic but whose affirmation is beyond the past and future of the moment of *Dasein*;

perhaps the strange thought is not exhausted by past and future united in the moment of willing? For eternal return points beyond man and time, beyond *Dasein* and ecstatic temporality, perhaps beyond the ontological difference of being and beings. The complexity of Heidegger's narrative at this point, his admission that 'Nietzsche knew and experienced a great deal more than he sketched out or fully portrayed', points to an uneasiness with the proposed practical alignment of the moment of eternal return with ecstatic *Dasein*.

The interruptions of the lecture's narrative by apprehensions of the excess of eternal return are transformed into the rhythmic tropes of *What Is Called Thinking*. Here Heidegger lets his reading of Nietzsche sway in and out of metaphysical dichotomies. One trope makes eternal return 'the supreme triumph of the metaphysics of the will that eternally wills its own willing' (Heidegger [1954] 1968, 104) while the other makes it rehearse the *difficulties* of such thinking. In the latter, 'Nietzsche's attempt to think the Being of beings makes it almost obtrusively clear to us moderns that all thinking, that is, relatedness to being, is still difficult' (Heidegger 1968, 110). In the first trope eternal return is included within metaphysical dichotomies as a supplement to a philosophy of the will, while in the second it breaks their bounds and becomes the site for the crisis of thinking. With the second thought Nietzsche is no longer the philosopher of will to power who completes the metaphysics of presence, but the thinker who turns thinking into thanks – not recompense but devotion – one whose difficult thought is a remembrance of 'what is unspoken', of what has not been sent down or destined to be present.

The example of Heidegger's subtle rhythmic movement between immanence and externality in the later reading has until recently had few imitators. His 'inclusive' reading of the 1930s has been more influential, even in a text as unsympathetic to Heidegger's general project as Deleuze's *Nietzsche and Philosophy* (1962). This text locates Nietzsche's philosophy as a 'radical transformation of Kantianism', one in which the Kantian problematic of synthesis in judgement is transformed into the synthesis of forces effected through will to power and eternal return:

> He understood the synthesis of forces as the eternal return and thus found the reproduction of diversity at the heart of synthesis. He established the principle of synthesis, the will to power, and determined this as the differential and genetic element of forces which directly confront one another. (Deleuze [1962] 1983, 52)

The principle of will to power and the principle of eternal return achieve the synthesis of judgement, but at the cost of closure, for 'Return is the being of becoming, the unity of multiplicity, the necessity of chance' (Deleuze 1983, 189). Eternal return is thus brought under judgement as the supplement necessary to bring the becoming of will to power to presence or to stabilize it in synthesis. This is to 'include' eternal return within will to power and to subordinate both to the oppositions of metaphysical thinking.

While Deleuze's reading of Nietzsche stabilizes eternal return in a synthetic judgement, Derrida's reading develops Heidegger's later thought that eternal return marks the crisis that destabilizes judgement. In his reading of *Ecce Homo* in *Otobiography* (1982), eternal return is less the metaphysical negotiation of being and becoming than the difficult attempt to think beyond metaphysical dichotomies. Reading Heidegger against Heidegger, Derrida writes:

> The point is that the eternal return is not a new metaphysics of time or of the totality of being, et cetera, on whose ground Nietzsche's autobiographical signature would come to stand like an empirical fact on a great ontological structure. (Here, one would have to take up again the Heideggerian interpretations of the eternal return and perhaps problematize them.) The eternal return always involves differences of forces that perhaps cannot be thought in terms of being, of the pair essence-existence, or of any of the great metaphysical structures to which Heidegger would like to relate them. (Derrida [1982] 1988, 46)

Derrida turns Heidegger's late reading of Nietzsche against the early lectures, preferring the 'difficulty' of eternal return to the 'solution' of the will eternally willing itself. For Derrida, as for Heidegger in *What Is Called Thinking*, this enigma poses itself in the uncontainable affirmation of eternal return.

Derrida's return to Heidegger's later reading of Nietzsche underlines the way in which the difficulty of eternal return forces a return to the question of Nietzsche's affirmation. In both cases the 'yes' of eternal return is thought as a 'yes' before 'yes and no', an Affirmation before affirmation and negation. It is not a resolute yes, nor a yes spoken in judgement, but a yes that both enables and disturbs judgement. The character of this unspoken yes before yes and no – a yes that is not of the logos – is beautifully described by Rosenzweig in *The Star of Redemption* (1921) as 'the silent attendant of every sentence, the confirmation, the "so be it", the "amen" behind every word'.[9] This affirmation is not willed, it is before the subject and its willing; nor is it a judgement but is before, and yet confirms and upsets, the giving of judgement.

The readings of eternal return intimated by Heidegger and developed by Derrida are confirmed when the thought is read as the summation of the Free-Spirit Trilogy. The trilogy is concerned with evoking a crisis of judgement, of achieving a liberation from the measures of 'man' while respecting them, of affirming while paying a penance for yes and no. It develops the thought of eternal return as the 'highest formula' of an affirmation which both conserves and disrupts. This affirmation and disruption is contained in Nietzsche's analysis of the 'calling' (*Aufgabe*), an idea central not only to the trilogy, but to the whole of his authorship. Indeed, the notions of return and originality developed in the context of the 'calling' of the 'free spirit' are crucial to understanding Nietzsche's presentation of eternal return as something which 'if it took hold of you would transform you as you are or would lie on your actions as the greatest weight' (*GS* 341).

II

In *Ecce Homo* Nietzsche describes how he signed the receipt for the thought of eternal return, some time in August 1881, with the phrase '6000 feet beyond Man and Time'. His signature states the condition and consequence of receiving the affirmative formula of eternal return as an elevation beyond 'man and time', one which is both task and achievement. It was the projective and retrospective character of the formula that impelled Nietzsche to return to the Free-Spirit Trilogy in the prefaces he wrote to each volume in 1886[10] and in his 'autobiography' (*Ecce Homo*) of 1888. I shall begin with the autobiographical return.

The presentation of the Free-Spirit Trilogy in *Ecce Homo* challenges the assumption that Nietzsche's authorship was progressive. Far from tracing a development through his writings before and after *Zarathustra*, Nietzsche insists on a qualitative break in his authorship. The writings before and including *Zarathustra* represent the 'yes-saying *part*' (*der jasagende Teil*) and the later writings the 'no-saying, no doing *half* [*neinsagende, neintuende Hälfte*] of my calling [*Aufgabe*]' (*EH* 310). This division of the 'calling' is crucial to understanding Nietzsche's view of his authorship. For the yes-saying part is not the simple complement of the no-saying half, as if they added up to some integral calling, but belongs to a completely different order of affirmation.

The texts of the no-saying half have become the canonical sources for Nietzsche's philosophy. Yet they were described by their author as mere 'fish hooks' intended to catch those who 'would offer their hands for destroying' and contribute to 'conjuring up a day of decision' (*EH* 310). The second half of the calling, in other words, engages on the terrain of previous and current values and attempts to institute a state of crisis and decision. Their manifesto character distinguishes them from the texts of the 'yes-saying' part of his authorship which Nietzsche described as 'monuments', as sites for the return and remembrance of his calling.

Far from being the positive propaedeutic for the later negative texts, the affirmation of the trilogy and *Zarathustra* emerges from a working through of a crisis of yes and no. They do not complement the later texts since they already contain the *whole* of Nietzsche's philosophy. The return of negation in the writings after *Zarathustra* is not defined against the affirmation achieved in eternal return but is tied to the same crisis of yes and no which the free spirit had overcome. The 'fish hook' texts were addressed to the 'agitated, power-hungry society of present-day Europe and America' (*D* 148) in a language they would understand and in a manner intended to provoke the return of the liberating destruction already experienced by the free spirit.

Human, All Too Human, the first book of the Free-Spirit Trilogy, is described in *Ecce Homo* as the 'monument of a crisis'. One of its preconditions was its author's 'profound alienation from everything that surrounded' him at the first *Bayreuther Festspiel*, when Wagner descended among the Germans and draped himself in 'German virtues' (EH). The alienation was experienced as a break between memory and actuality, with Nietzsche waking up to feel that he was dreaming. As he 'leafed' through his memories he could find 'no shadow of similarity' between the Wagner before him and the Wagner of Tribschen. There was no discernible relation between the present and the past.

The shock of 'recognizing nothing' led first to a general impatience with the forgetting of self or 'selflessness' of 'idealism' and then to an 'inexorable decision' against 'yielding, going along, and confounding myself'. Wagner had become for Nietzsche the 'opiate' of the *Reich*, and Bayreuth the place where Germans could 'forget themselves, be rid of themselves for a moment – what am I saying? For *five or six hours*' (*EH* 287). Against this Nietzsche determined to 'return to myself', 'to recall and reflect on myself', to liberate his self from what did not 'belong' to him. He presents his negation in terms of recovering possession: the free spirit is one 'that has *become free*, that has again taken possession of itself' or one which has 'recovered' itself.[11]

The recovery of what was his own required 'rigorous self-discipline' on the part of Nietzsche, but here an ironic note enters the triumphant autobiographical narrative. The 'self-discipline' required is passive, that of a patient '*commanded*' by sickness to be still; it is a discipline 'of lying still, of leisure, of waiting and being patient. – But that means, of thinking' (*EH* 287). Nietzsche introduces a complication into the classic schema of loss, struggle and recovery through which he seems to describe the genesis of *Human, All Too Human*. The complexity of his autobiographical narrative is underlined by his claim to have avoided 'the little word "I"', which exemplified the 'monstrous sureness [with which] I got hold of my task and its world historic aspect' (*EH* 288). The book which seemed to be about the recovery of the 'I' becomes the book in which the 'I' is to be avoided.

The avoidance and the recovery of the 'I' are not necessarily incompatible, nor does self-discipline rule out lying still and being patient. But these movements are quite different from the classic dialectic of loss, self-disciplined labour and recovery. In *Human, All Too Human*, 'idealism's' trope of recovering the 'I' is arrested and brought to a standstill:

This is war, but war without powder and smoke, without warlike poses, without pathos and strained limbs: all that would still be 'idealism'. One error after another is coolly placed on ice; the ideal is not refuted – it *freezes* to death. (*EH* 284)

This 'dialectic at a standstill' confirms the description of the book as the 'monument' at once to a 'crisis' (*EH* 283) and to 'rigorous self-discipline' (*EH* 288). It is monumental in the sense of placing the movement of loss, struggle and recovery in a different time, one beyond loss and recovery. The attempt to remember the lost 'I' is made into a monument or object of remembrance, and in doing so it changes its significance. What is recovered in remembrance is new and original, even if it had always been present.[12]

The same refusal to move from loss to recovery informs Nietzsche's autobiographical recall of *Daybreak*, the second volume of the trilogy. The 'effect of the book is negative' but 'this in no way contradicts the fact that the book contains no negative word, no attack, no spite' (*EH* 290). The self-discipline required to execute this 'campaign against morality' imitates the languor of a 'sea animal basking among rocks'. Nietzsche teases his reader with the suggestion that the book might be read as a 'liberation from all moral values, in saying yes to and having confidence in all that has hitherto been forbidden, despised, and damned'. But he ends a beautiful description of how the yes of this negative book expels 'morality' in an outpouring of 'light, love and tenderness', by freezing the yes with the question 'Or?': 'This book closes with an 'or?' – it is the only book that closes with an 'or?'.

Nietzsche remembers that it was with *Daybreak* that he began his 'campaign against a morality that would unself man' (*EH* 292). But this negative campaign did not imply a positive one which would reself man, return him to himself. The yes and the no of the campaigns for and against 'man' are disturbed by the question 'or?' – or is there something more than saying yes and no? Must the no to the priestly memory which 'conserves what degenerates' imply a yes to a memory which conserves what regenerates? For Nietzsche this implication would confine thought to an 'idealistic' movement of loss and recovery, of negation and affirmation. Against this particular trope he affirms the need to avoid solutions and to conclude with questions: the 'no' to morality and the 'yes' to the forbidden, despised and damned are equally questionable.

What is recovered or affirmed is not necessarily that which was lost but might be something new and original. This is how Nietzsche recalls *The Gay Science* where the 'highest hope' or the freedom won was not what was sought, but 'something incomparable' (*EH* 296). From it emerged the beginning of *Zarathustra*, and, in the penultimate paragraph (§341), the first and most perfect expression of the thought of eternal return.

In remembering the Free-Spirit Trilogy in *Ecce Homo* Nietzsche shows how the liberation achieved in these texts was not the recovery of a self that had been lost and forgotten. The autobiographical narrative of *Ecce Homo* transforms the movement of self-discovery characteristic of its genre to a movement of questioning, one which reinvents the meaning of the signature 'Nietzsche'. When Nietzsche does his duty and asks, 'Above all do not mistake me for someone else' he is not presenting his real self against the mistaken self, but in asking that the question of his signature, of what he meant, of what belonged and did not belong to him, be kept open – *Nietzsche oder?*

A similar insistence on the questionable nature of his work informs Nietzsche's earlier return to the trilogy in the prefaces he wrote for each of the works in 1886. Here the ironic undermining of the autobiographical trope of *Ecce Homo* is anticipated in a magisterial contribution to the venerable genre of the self-destructing philosophical preface. The return of the trilogy announced and performed by these texts once again puts the character of Nietzsche's calling in question.

III

Nietzsche added prefaces to the books of the Free-Spirit Trilogy several years after they were completed. They were retrospective prospects for books which were, he said, already dated when he wrote them.[13] Nevertheless, their reissue remained timely, and what he said in the preface to *Daybreak* applies to them all: 'This preface is late but not too late – what, after all, do five or six years matter?' (*D* 5). He does not return to deliver his own or philosophy's funeral oration – as in Hegel's painting 'grey in grey' in the preface to the *Philosophy of Right* – but to announce the recovery of his calling; he returns to announce his return.

In the preface to Part One of *Human, All Too Human* dated 'Nice, Spring 1886', he describes his 'recovery' as 'a temporary self-forgetting' (*HH* 5). The preface to Part Two, written in Sils Maria in September 1886, offers a more startling image of the author's departure and return: while his pessimistic anti-romantic insights 'have often made him jump out of his skin' he has 'always known how to get back into it again' (*HH* 210). Similarly, in the 'belated' preface to *Daybreak* dated 'Ruta, near Genoa, in the Autumn of 1886', he assures his friends that the 'underground man' will return and that 'in this late preface which could easily have become a funeral oration' he is pleased to announce, 'I have returned and, believe it or not, returned safe and sound' (*D* 1). The preface to *The Gay Science*, written at the same time and the same place, assures us that Herr Nietzsche has recovered and returned from profundity to superficiality. In all the prefaces Nietzsche seems to depart and return – he does not stay still long enough to watch with Hegel as a shape of life grows old.

The prefaces are full of gratitude for the return and unanimous in claiming that what has returned is something new, something unprecedented. The preface to Part One of *Human, All Too Human* presents this return of the new as the 'riddle of liberation', and it will be examined at length below. But what is it that can return as new? In the preface to Part Two of the same book Nietzsche describes it as 'the return of our calling' (*Aufgabe*) and praises this return as 'the *greatest* of life's gifts, perhaps the greatest thing it is able to give of any kind', its reward.

The return of the calling is the discovery of something new and original. But discovery simply renames the calling's property of being both a process of discovery and the object discovered, the way and the goal. Nietzsche's calling is both what he is and the search for what he is; there is no distinction between them. But the calling is also other, strange, a tyrant without a name: 'That concealed and imperious something for which we for long have no name until it proves to be our calling – the tyrant in us takes a terrible retribution for every attempt we make to avoid or elude it' (*HH* 211). Nietzsche goes on to say that there can be 'no return to health', no recovery unless we 'burden ourselves more heavily than we have ever been burdened before'. The calling has always been there, but in 'alleviated' form;[14] with its return the tyrant is named and while still demanding satisfaction it ceases to exact retribution.

Nietzsche's description of the calling as 'nameless' but effective anticipates the terms of his later description of 'originality' in §261 of *The Gay Science*. Originality is the ability 'to see something that does not bear a name and can still not be named even though it stares us all in the face'. The calling, or the nameless, is both revealed and concealed and can only be named in its return – which is always too late. The return is always questionable, and this burden of the question must be borne to the extent of becoming *the greatest weight*.

Nietzsche ends his preface by claiming that he holds this 'novel and strange' perspective 'as much for myself as, occasionally at least, *against* myself' (*HH* 214). But even this statement of the calling is questionable and provokes the further question, 'do you want me to prove this to you? But what else does this long preface – prove?' What else indeed – the reply is a return of the question.

The return of the calling as something new and questionable also informs the preface to *Daybreak*. The same 'concealed and imperious something' drives the single-minded, unalleviated excavations of the 'subterranean man':

> Does it not seem as though some faith were leading him on, some consolation offering him compensation? As though he perhaps desires this

prolonged obscurity, desires to be incomprehensible, concealed, enigmatic, because he knows what he thereby also acquires: his own morning, his own redemption, his own *daybreak*? (*D* 1)

Yet this faithful excavator – worthy pioneer – is engaged in investigating and digging out an ancient faith – faith in morality. If this seems contradictory, then 'you do not understand me?' For this excavation of faith in morality, even faith in reason, is undertaken '*out of morality!*'.

It is the calling of faith and 'men of conscience' *not* to want 'to return to that which we consider outlived and decayed, to anything "unworthy of belief", be it called God, virtue, truth, justice, charity'. There is a return to the tradition of 'German integrity and piety of millennia' but one which makes it new and strange. The questionable descendants of this tradition, 'its heirs and the executors [*Vollstrecker*] of its innermost will' are those who deny with joy and achieve 'the *self-sublimation of morality*'. The return is an execution of tradition in both senses of the word, as the fulfilment of its testament and as its destruction. This questionable execution, with its destructive fulfilment of tradition, is both the calling of faith and its sublimation into something new and unprecedented.

The questionable calling is renamed 'philosophy' in the preface to *The Gay Science*. Philosophers are perpetually jumping in and out of their skins, for they

> have traversed many kinds of health, and keep transversing them, have passed through an equal number of philosophies; they simply *cannot* keep from transposing their states every time into the most spiritual form and distance: this art of transfiguration *is* philosophy. (*GS* 35)

The philosopher returns from the exercise of the calling as something new, informed with the question, 'a different person, with a few more question marks – above all with the *will* henceforth to question further, more deeply, severely, harshly, evilly, and quietly than they had questioned heretofore' (*GS* 36). The joy in the question is the privilege of those 'knowing ones' who 'learn to forget well, and to be good at *not* knowing'. They 'return *newborn* having shed their skin ... with a second dangerous innocence in joy, more childlike and yet a hundred times subtler than they had ever been before' (*GS* 37). The modality of the calling – the return anew of the question – has now become that of philosophy.

The question of the return of the calling is directly addressed in the preface to Part One of *Human, All Too Human*. The first edition of the book was not prefaced but carried the subtitle: 'A Book for Free Spirits'. These free spirits, Nietzsche explains in the preface, were his 'invention' – in both senses of fabrication and discovery – for 'free spirits of this kind do not exist, did not exist' (*HH* 6). Yet he is in no doubt that they could exist and will exist in the future 'physically present and palpable and not, as in my case, merely phantoms and a hermit's phantasmagoria' (*HH* 6). Indeed, he will provoke their advent by describing the ways by which they will appear: 'I see them already coming, slowly, slowly; and perhaps I shall do something to speed their coming if I describe in advance under what vicissitudes, upon what paths, I see them coming' (*HH* 6). Once again it is a question of originality, of naming what can be seen, and in so naming to create new 'things' (*GS* §58).

The free spirit is called to undergo the experience of the 'great liberation', a vocation which Nietzsche unfolds in four stages. The first stage is a release from the fetters of obligation. Under the tyranny of the calling the free spirit learns contempt for its past – 'the youthful soul is all at once convulsed, torn loose, torn away – it does not know what is happening. A drive and impulse rules and masters it like a command' (*HH* 7). The contemptuous glance back points to this first stage of the calling as being an 'enigmatic, question-packed, questionable victory' (*HH* 7). For the cruelty of this immoral wilful stage – the stage which has come to typify vulgar 'Nietzscheanism' – is a destructive sickness, a vengeful inversion of values.

This stage is followed in Nietzsche's genealogy of the free spirit by the two stages of *ataraxia* – the suspension of judgement. The first marks a distance from judgement:

> One lives no longer in the fetters of love and hatred, without yes, without no, near or as far as one wishes, preferably slipping away, evading, fluttering off, gone again, again flying aloft; one is spoiled, as everyone is who has at some time seen a tremendous number of things beneath them. (*HH* 8)

The second stage of the suspension of judgement is a return to 'what is close at hand'. The free spirit looks back in gratitude, and 'only now does he see himself'. The calling becomes manifest and is repulsed in favour of the 'happiness that comes in winter, the spots of sunlight on the wall' (*HH* 9). And yet this suspension of judgement in the convalescent's *dolce fa niente* is not the end of the calling, merely its abeyance. For the calling returns in 'the riddle of the great liberation which had until then waited dark, questionable, almost untouchable in memory' (*HH* 9) and returns as something new and terrible.

The return of the calling is itself the 'great liberation'; in recognizing it the free spirit is freed of the past, present and future. Nietzsche describes the temporality of the calling in the following terms:

> The secret force and necessity of this calling will rule among and in the individual facets of his destiny like an unconscious pregnancy – long

before he has caught sight of this task itself or knows its name. Our calling commands and disposes of us even when we do not yet know it; it is the future that regulates our today. (*HH* 10)

However, this is not the ecstatic temporality which Heidegger discerned in the eternal return. For the return of the calling is not in time, nor does it negate or affirm judgement. This is underlined at the point in the preface when Nietzsche has the calling name itself in recalling the free spirit's vocation:

You shall get control over your for and against and learn how to display first one and then the other in accordance with your [calling]. You shall learn to grasp the sense of perspective in every value judgement – the displacement [*Verschiebung*], the warping [*Verzerrung*], and apparent teleology of horizons and whatever else pertains to perspectivism; also the bit of stupidity in every opposition of values and the intellectual penance that must be paid for every for and against. (*HH* 9)

The calling of the free spirit is imperious – it makes itself known as the task which is, has been and is to be followed. And this is no less than judgement's questioning of judgement, which for the free spirit manifests itself as 'the problem of the order of rank' (*HH* 10).

Before further pursuing the problem of the 'order of rank' it might be well to close this section on Nietzsche's prefaces by returning to Hegel's preface to the *Philosophy of Right*. Both thinkers consider their prefaces to be late additions to a delayed philosophy. For Hegel philosophy is too late to 'give instruction' because its shape of life has grown old: 'By philosophy's grey in grey it cannot be rejuvenated but only understood. The owl of Minerva spreads its wings only with the falling of the dusk.' So too for Nietzsche, the return of philosophy's calling is always too late and remains in question. But it is this remaining in question which marks the *daybreak* of philosophy, its originality and its beginning. The return of the calling marks a new day, a renewal and is what prevents the Nietzschean preface from becoming a funeral oration.[15]

IV

The itinerary of the free spirit transformed the problem of judgement into the problem of rank. The free spirit began its calling with the yes and no of 'human, all-too-human' judgement. These were refused in the first, evil stage of the free spirit's liberation, and their opposites revalued. Then the free spirit refused to judge for or against – it deemed judgement to be below it and even unhealthy for it. But judgement returned in the problem of rank – but this return established a new non-human measure, a new for and against which did not simply invert or ignore the old yes and the old no, but which 'sublated' them. It was beyond human measure and inhabited a penitential time, remembering and mourning the necessary injustice of its measure. Its affirmation was 'beyond man and time'.

In the preface to *Human, All Too Human* Nietzsche describes the calling's return in the demand to pay penance for the ineluctable displacement and warping of judgement: 'you must learn to understand the necessary injustice in every for and against'. The free spirit must affirm a judgement which warps and displaces is unjust, one which would normalize originality, measure the immeasurable, compare the incomparable and identify the different. And it must do so because it recognizes that there can be no originality without repetition, no immeasurable without measure, no incomparability without comparison, no difference without identity. There is a necessary violence and injustice in judgement which manifests itself in law. But it is open to the judgers to recognize this violence and to pay penance for it, and this is what is *more* than human.

Nevertheless, Nietzsche's penance calls for more than the recognition of the necessary injustice of judgement. Like the calling it executes the traditional oppositions of judgement by destroying while fulfilling them. The penance of the free spirit is an affirmation of judgement which is beyond and before its yes and no. This is underlined in section 32 of *Human, All Too Human* where Nietzsche suggests, 'We are from the beginning illogical and unjust beings and are able to recognize this: this is the greatest and unresolvable discord of Being' (*HH* 28). The possibility of recognizing that we are illogical and unjust rests on two modalities of discrimination, one within and one beyond judgement. In the case of logical judgement, there is an illogic that says no to logic, but there is also an alogic that is beyond logical affirmation and negation. In the case of justice, there is an injustice that says no to justice, but also an ajustice beyond the affirmations or negations of just judgement. The penance of the free spirit is directed beyond such oppositions as logic/illogic, justice/injustice to their realization and destruction. Nietzsche describes the *via negationis* of penance as a purification, and his model, cited approvingly in *The Gay Science*, is Ekhardt's saying 'I ask God to rid me of God' (*GS* §292). It is the prayer of a creature to God to rid him of having to think God in terms of the opposition creature/God.

The character of the Nietzschean penance – what Heidegger later called 'devotion' – is developed in the discussions of logic/illogic and justice/injustice in the Free-Spirit Trilogy. The no-saying half of his calling simply inverts the conventional privilege enjoyed by one term over its other, while the yes-saying part affirms and destroys the very opposition of the terms by putting them into question. Remaining with *Human, All Too Human*, Nietzsche writes in §18 on the 'Fundamental Questions of Metaphysics':

> The first stage of the logical is the judgement: and the essence of judgement consists, according to the best logicians, in belief. The ground of all belief is the sensation of the pleasurable or painful in relation to a perceiving subject. (*HH* 21)

He approaches this 'fundamental question' by systematically undermining the notion that judgement can have a ground or a foundation. The basis of the belief that founds logic is the distinction of pleasure and pain, but this itself is not fundamental since it is based on the further distinction of perception and non-perception. This distinction in turn surrenders to the more fundamental belief that everything is one. But the one depends on the distinction between identity and plurality, which depends in its turn on those of existence and non-existence, uniqueness and repetition. But these distinctions themselves are already derived, and foundations appear as displaced oppositions.

The exposure of the displacements of judgement is pursued in section 32 in terms of evaluation. All evaluations are partial, and we have no logical right to a total evaluation (the right to employ logic cannot be derived logically) because

> the standard by which we measure our own being is not an unalterable magnitude … and yet we would have to know ourselves as a fixed standard to be able justly to assess the relation between ourself and anything else whatever. (*HH* 28)

Logically and justly, 'we ought not to judge at all' – but it would not be human to live without judging, since the name '*Mensch*' for Nietzsche means the measurer and the judger.

Nietzsche goes on to reverse his previous founding of logical evaluation on pleasure/pain by saying that 'all aversion [*Abneigung*] is dependent on an evaluation, likewise partiality [*Zueignung*]' (*HH* 28). Nietzsche makes the prefixes *Ab* (away) and *Zu* (toward) in *Abneigung* and *Zuneigung* denote the operation of a drive: 'A drive [*Trieb*] toward something or away from something … without some kind of knowing evaluation of the worth of its objective does not exist in man.' The disposition of the drive towards and away (a modality which constitutes good and evil in *ressentiment*) is itself based on an evaluation, but this in its turn is founded on the drive. In this passage Nietzsche drives the human notion of measure into distraction, showing that it is necessarily aporetic. And far from seeking a solution to this aporia, as Habermas claims, Nietzsche insists that we recognize and pay penance for it.

In *Daybreak* Nietzsche further twists the tangles of judgement by introducing the problem of the 'other' or 'neighbour'. In section 118 on the question 'What then is our Neighbour?' Nietzsche anticipates the discourse on the thousand and one goals in *Zarathustra*. The border which marks the difference between my neighbour and I cannot be thought in terms of the simple opposition of inner and outer:

> What do we understand to be the boundaries of our neighbour, I mean that by which he so to speak engraves [*einzeichnet*] and impresses [*eindruckt*] himself on to [*auf*] and into [*an*] us … our knowledge of him is like a hollow but informed space. (*D* 118)

The neighbour is both engraved and impressed *on to* us as if we were surfaces but also impressed and engraved *into* us – the operation anticipates the punitive inscription of the offence in Kafka's story *The Penal Colony*.[16] In place of Kafka's archaic machinery of the law, Nietzsche's inscription of the boundary *is* the boundary; its action cannot be thought since it is the condition of thought. The simultaneously constituting and constituted border can only be known as a 'hollow but informed space', neither inner nor outer, 'World of phantoms in which we live. Inverted [*verkehrte*] upside down, empty world, yet dreamed as *full* and *straight*' (*D* 118).

To fill the informed void by postulating a 'theory of power' to effect the inscription of the boundary is less a solution than an avoidance of the difficulty. The difficulty has to be recognized and then atoned for in an affirmation which is not one of judgement. The previous paragraph of *Daybreak* entitled 'In Prison' describes the boundary as both a prison wall and a web, simultaneously enclosing and extending:

> it is by these horizons, within which each of us encloses his senses as if behind prison walls, that we *measure* the world, we say that this is near and that far, this big and that small, this is hard and that soft … We sit within our net, we spiders, and whatever we may catch in it, we catch nothing at all except that which allows itself to be caught in precisely our net. (*D* 117)

Our various systems of distinction fall within definite limits; the limit or prison wall is reflected back and constitutes a network of differences which determine what can appear. However, it is with the knowledge of the neighbour that this otherwise invisible limit becomes perceptible as an informed void.

The breakdown of our knowledge of the neighbour manifests the injustice of our measure and judgement. The experience of the 'informed void' brings the illogic and injustice of human measure and judgement into recognition. The recognition of the collapse of measure and its network of differences is at the core of Nietzsche's conception of the yes-saying free spirit. Returning to Kafka's *In the Penal Colony*, the name of the crime being expiated is written on to and into the flesh of the prisoner. For Nietzsche the return of the injustice of measure is in the recognition of the proper name 'human' inscribed on and in the body. In the section of *Human, All Too Human* on 'Man as the Measurer' Nietzsche writes:

> Perhaps all the morality of mankind has its origin in the tremendous inner excitement which seized on primeval men when they discovered measure and measuring (the word *Mensch* indeed, means the measurer, he desired to *name* himself after his greatest discovery!). With these conceptions they climbed into realms that are quite immeasurable and unweighable but originally did not seem to be. (*HH* 310–11)

The recognition of the collapse of measure has two possible consequences. The first remains within measure and is the all-too-human yes and no of nihilism, while the other exceeds measure and is the unmeasured affirmation of the free spirit.

The relation between the penance for the all-too-human yes and no and the affirmation of the more than human is worked through in the well-known aphorism section 335 of *The Gay Science*, 'Up with Physics'. Here Nietzsche distinguishes between the Kant of synthesis in judgement and the Kant who having 'broken open the cage' of moral judgement was led back into it by the postulates of God, Soul, Freedom and Immortality. Kant's escape from the cage through critique and legislation is the paradigm for Nietzsche's demand for penance and legislation. The critical project of establishing the 'extent and the limits' of understanding through critique presupposes the transcendence of limit, not in terms of the metaphysical postulates, but in terms of legislation. The philosopher 'is not a worker in the field of reason, but the lawgiver of human reason' (*CPR* A839/B867) and it is because philosophers give the law that they can establish its limits.

For Nietzsche, the legislative giving of limit avoids becoming simply another founding of judgement if it is accompanied by penance: 'Let us therefore limit ourselves to the purification of our opinions and evaluations and to the creation of new, proper tables of the good' (*GS* 265–6). Both purification and legislation, the 'intellectual penance' for yes and no and the giving of new law tables, are themselves already limited: *Beschränken wir uns*. The law of *this* limitation, the giving of the giving of law, is beyond-law. It is not measured in terms of the yes and no of a normalizing subject but is the creative and original affirmation of law.

Such an affirmation cannot be made within the 'prison wall' or 'cage' of judgement except in terms of the paradoxes into which the prisoner's language falls when driven beyond its web of distinctions. One such an occasion is the celebrated call for the return of what we are. Here Nietzsche clearly refers to the notion of the calling which informs the Free-Spirit Trilogy: 'We, though, want to become those we are – the new, unique, the incomparable, the self-legislating, the self-creating' (*Wir aber wollen die werden, die wir sind, – die Neuen, die Einmaligen, die Unvergleichbaren, die Sich-selber-Gesetzgebenden, die Sich-selber-Schaffenden*) (*GS* 266). Walter Kaufmann humanizes this passage in his translation by introducing 'human beings who are new ..., etc.', but they are absent in Nietzsche. It is not 'men' (*Mensch*) who are called to give themselves law and create themselves but those whose calling is to fulfil and destroy human measure. The 'we' want to return, to become what 'we' are called to be, yet the 'we' are not measurers; 'we' affirm and act beyond the distinctions of new/old, unique/repeated, incomparable/comparable, legislating/legislated, creating/created. The giving of the free spirit in each case 'executes' the limit of these oppositions.

The new, the unique, the incomparable cannot be named; 'their' calling is not the affirmation of a given limit but a limitless giving which exceeds the bounds of human measure. With this Nietzsche both fulfils and destroys the tradition of judgement. The classical doctrine of judgement was inseparable from a doctrine of invention, and it was the suppression of this relation in early modernity which led to the warps and displacements of judgement first identified as such by Kant.[17] His transcendental logic and its phenomenological development by Hegel tried to rethink the relation of judgement and invention. For judgement to take place there must be an appropriation or a giving of place which is more than judgement and which cannot be described in its terms. This giving, which does not bear a name but which stares us all in the face, is the yes for judgement which is before and beyond its yes and its no. By returning to the human, all-too-human act of judgement, Nietzsche fulfils this tradition in the 'creative legislation' of the free spirit which liberates affirmation from the opposition of judgement's yes and no.

The penultimate aphorism of the first edition of *The Gay Science*, 'The Greatest Weight', speaks of this '*Ja-und Amen*' before yes and no. When the demon whispers that everything in life must return 'all in the same series and sequence' he is stating something which stares us all in the face – that judgements must both return and be made anew. Such a thought becomes overwhelming, able to transform or destroy, when it is made into a question: 'Do you desire this once more again and innumerable times more?' (*GS* 274) or, in other words, 'do you want to judge?'. The question itself is a judgement on whoever is asked it, since it shows that the yes and no of wanting *this* rests on a yes and amen before every yes and no. To want this yes is to want a singularity which cannot be generalized, cannot be named, and which exceeds the limits of judgement.

The extreme statement of *eternal* return – one beyond time – leads paradoxically to an affirmation of singularity. To affirm the yes before yes and no leads beyond the universal and particular of judgement. A portrayal of this affirmation is the 'Yes saying, Yes laughing' of Zarathustra in '*das Ja-und Amen-Lied*' which closes Part III of *Also Sprach Zarathustra*. The double yes would have everything return in order to release it from time. To affirm the judgement of eternal return, to answer yes to its question (yes, saying) is to make a nonsense of the generalizations and measures of judgement (yes, laughing). The rigorous affirmation of eternal return pays penance for judgement by executing its original sin of generalization. Judgement is the return of measure to the singular, but when this return is made eternal it is driven to its limit in absurdity. And at that wicked moment of parody, the 'greatest burden' changes into the greatest joy.

With the statement of the eternal return at the end of the Free-Spirit Trilogy Nietzsche recovers his calling, he recapitulates '6000 feet beyond Man and Time' what had already been said 'lying back amid the grasses' in the 'epilogue' 'Among Friends' to *Human, All Too Human*. The folly of this 'fools-book' is but 'Reason coming to its senses', and it does so in the repeated refrain:

Shall we do this, friends, again? Amen, and *auf Wiedersehn*!

Notes

1   As when Jürgen Habermas criticizes Nietzsche for positing will to power as a 'solution' to the aporia of judgement: 'If all proper claims to validity are dissolved and if the underlying value judgements are mere expressions of claims to power rather than validity, according to what standards should critique differentiate? It must at least be able to discriminate between a power which *deserves* to be esteemed and a power which *deserves* to be disparaged. Nietzsche's *theory of power* is intended to provide a way out of this aporia' (Habermas 1982). This reading of Nietzsche, whose provenance lies in Bäumler's emphasis on will to power, has become an *idée reçue* of commentators and textbook writers: one example: 'Nietzsche pressed his case against both Kant *and* Hegel by arguing for a yet more radical scepticism, one that treated all the truth claims of philosophy as mere emanations of an arbitrary will-to-power' (Norris 1985).

2   See David Farrell Krell's 'Analysis' of Heidegger 1991, vol. II, 268. 'The very worst thing that could happen is that the *thinking* of eternal recurrence, a thinking which Nietzsche and Heidegger share, should get lost in the barren reaches of the philological debate.'

3   See below, section II.

4   In the Preface to *The Critique of Judgement-Power* (1790) Kant wrote, 'Yet even here I venture to hope that the difficulty of unravelling a problem

so involved in its nature may serve as an excuse for a certain amount of hardly avoidable obscurity in its solution, provided that the accuracy of our statement of the principle is proved with all requisite clearness.'

5   Heidegger's lectures were published in 1961 and are translated in four volumes: I *The Will to Power as Art*, II *The Eternal Recurrence of the Same*, III *Will to Power as Knowledge and Metaphysics*, IV *Nihilism*. The 'new' Nietzsche is largely the outcome of Heidegger's engagement. David B. Allison prefaces his collection (Allison ed. 1985) with the claim that Heidegger was the first to recognize Nietzsche as 'one of the prodigious thinkers of the modern age' and to show that 'what remains to be considered within Nietzsche's own thought somehow stands as a model for the tasks and decisions of the present generation' (ix). The power of Heidegger's reading of Nietzsche is such that reading Nietzsche today is almost inseparable from reading Heidegger.

6   Heidegger situates his reading of eternal return in this way: 'No wonder commentators have felt it to be an obstacle and have tried all sorts of manoeuvres to get round it, only grudgingly making their peace with it. Either they strike it from Nietzsche's philosophy altogether or, compelled by the fact it obtrudes there and seeing no way out, they list it as a component part of that philosophy. In the latter case they explain the doctrine as an impossible eccentricity of Nietzsche's, something that can count only as a personal confession of faith and does not pertain to the system of Nietzsche's philosophy proper' (Heidegger 1991, II, 5).

7   The classic *loci* for the moment of eternal return are *The Gay Science* section 341 'The Greatest Weight' and *Thus Spoke Zarathustra* 'Of the Vision and the Riddle' and 'The Second Dance Song'.

8   For a profound analysis of Heidegger's 'avoidance' see Derrida 1989.

9   '*Ja ist kein Satzteil, aber ebensowenig das kurzschriftliche Siegel eines Satzes, obwohl es als solches verwendet werden kann, sondern es ist der stille Begleiter alter Satzteile, die Bestätigung, das "Sie", das "Amen" hinter jedem Wort*' (1921, 29). Rosenzweig's discussion of the exteriority of the 'yes' beyond yes and no in the section '*Gott und sein Sein oder Metaphysik*' has been crucial for contemporary French thought, notably Levinas 1969 and Jacques Derrida 1987, 122.

10   Nietzsche wrote four prefaces in 1886, one each for the two volumes of *Human, All Too Human* (1878–80), one for *Daybreak: Thoughts on the Prejudices of Morality* (1881) and one for *The Gay Science* (1882).

11   For an excellent discussion of the circumstances under which the Free-Spirit Trilogy was conceived and composed, see Bergmann 1987, esp. chapters 4 and 5.

12   Walter Benjamin's work is the most significant and rigorous deployment of Nietzsche's view of remembrance; see his *Theses on the Philosophy of History*, especially Thesis XVII on the 'messianic cessation of happening' which both preserves and destroys.

13   'All my writings, with a single though admittedly substantial exception, are to be *dated back* – they always speak of something "behind me"' (*HH* 209).

14 'Strange and at the same time terrible! It is our *alleviations* for which we have to atone the most!' (*HH* 212).

15 It is of course by no means clear that Hegel is pronouncing a funeral oration, or if he is, for whom. The flight of Minerva's owl in the Roman dusk is seen by Gillian Rose as heralding a philosophy of the Greek morning: 'Minerva cannot impose herself. Her owl can only spread its wings at dusk and herald the return of Athena, freedom without domination' (Rose [1981] 2009, 91). What is indisputable though is that both Hegel's and Nietzsche's prefaces are extremely questionable invitations to what follows them.

16 In Kafka 1975.

17 See my book *Art of Judgement* for details of the history of invention and judgement and Kant's diagnosis of the 'aporia of judgement'.

9

Under the Epicurean skies

*Whatever it is, bad weather or good, the loss of a friend, sickness,
slander, the failure of some letter to arrive, the spraining of an
ankle, a glance into a shop, a counter-argument, the opening of
a book, a dream, a fraud – either immediately or very soon after
it proves to be something that 'must not be missing'; it has a
profound significance and use precisely for us. Is there any more
dangerous seduction that might tempt one to renounce one's
faith in the gods of Epicurus who have no care and are unknown,
and to believe instead in some petty deity who is full of care and
personally knows every little hair on our head and finds nothing
nauseous in the most miserable small service?*

– NIETZSCHE, *THE GAY SCIENCE* (§277)

Nietzsche's interpretation of Epicurus anticipated certain of the directions of the twentieth-century reception of the Epicurean philosophy, while weaving them together in an original and still not fully appreciated pattern. His concern with the nature of the Epicurean gods and friendship anticipated the focus of André-Jean Festugière's controversial *Épicure et ses dieux* and the focus on Epicurean prescriptions for leading a blessed life intimated the reading of ancient philosophy as 'a way of life' developed by Pierre Hadot.[1] His interpretation nevertheless remained curiously distant from the preoccupation with the ontological status of atomism and the problems of the theory of knowledge and the *eidôla* that were to dominate Anglophone Epicurean scholarship. One of the reasons for the orientation of Nietzsche's interests in Epicurus is his acceptance of Epicurean cosmology and its distinction between world and universe.[2] The focus on the world – the sky under which we find ourselves – rather than the universe or sum of possible worlds allowed Nietzsche to collect the themes of Epicurean divinity, blessedness, friendship and philosophical regimen around the focus of the ancient science of this world or 'meteorology'. His reading of Epicurus thus takes place under the sign of the weather, identifying its significance in Epicurus's texts and assigning it a key role in Epicurus's conception of blessedness.

In Aphorism 277 from *The Gay Science* on 'personal providence' the interpretation of the significance of the weather appears first in Nietzsche's list of events that might seduce one to renounce a belief in the Epicurean gods. Interpretation of the meaning of good or bad weather can turn us away from the gods of Epicurus 'who have no care and are unknown' and prompt us 'to believe instead in some petty deity who is full of care and personally knows every little hair on our head and finds nothing nauseous in the most miserable small service' (*GS* §277). The 'significance and use' of the weather 'for us' tempts us to believe that, whether good or bad, it nevertheless signifies the providential care or anger of the petty god rather than a series of chance events in which the gods have no interest or involvement and which consequently have no intrinsic or providential meaning.

The seemingly casual reference to weather in Aphorism 277 forms part of a broad and systematic mobilization of meteorology throughout the writings of Nietzsche, one so ubiquitous as to become nigh invisible, literally the climate of his thought. It nevertheless assumes thematic importance in his notoriously ambivalent readings of Epicurus, which moves between warm approval and harsh critique. Nietzsche began his career as a philologist with a study of the *Epicurea*, and references to Epicurus appear throughout his writings. Yet these references show such stark inconsistencies that it is at first glance difficult to understand what precisely was the importance of Epicurus for Nietzsche and in what sense he not only seemed but was an Epicurean.[3]

Nietzsche considered himself to at least share Epicurus's enemies, or rather he mobilized Epicurus as part of his own attacks on Platonism and Christianity. The opposition between the Epicurean gods and the Christian god implied in Aphorism 277 is repeated in a number of instances that combine to make Epicurus a formidable opponent of Platonism and by extension Christianity, the latter being for Nietzsche the 'Platonism of the people' (*BGE* Preface). Thus, in *Beyond Good and Evil* Aphorism 7, Nietzsche describes Epicurus as perhaps writing out of 'rage and ambition against Plato?' and his followers (the flatterers of Dionysus the tyrant). In Nietzsche's reading, Epicurus opposed not only Plato and Platonism but also the 'subterranean cults, the whole of latent Christianity' that they would inspire and that entombed themselves, hidden from the skies and the changing effects of the weather (*AC* §58).

The proleptic critique of Christianity that Nietzsche finds in Epicurus was in its turn overcome by Paul, who knew how to accommodate Christianity 'to already existing and established anti-paganism'.[4] Nietzsche claims that but for Paul, 'Epicurus would have won'. This Epicurus stands not just for the thinker of the indifferent gods but also for the critic of the immortality of the soul, a doctrine Nietzsche associates with the tomb and the underground cults, dark and gloomy and hidden from the bracing effects of the sun and winds.[5] Yet in a note from spring 1888, Epicurus's proleptic critique of the 'pre-existing Christianity' of the cults is identified more generally as directed not just against the doctrine of the immortality of the soul but also against the 'moralization' of the world, a struggle 'against the old world grown senile and sick, already gloomy, moralized, soured by feelings of guilt' (*WP* §438).

On other occasions, Epicurus is described less favourably as a model to be avoided. He features alongside Pyrrho as an example of 'sagacious weariness', 'naïve, idyllic grateful' (*WP* §437). Epicurus exemplifies the danger of 'relaxation' of placing ethics above knowledge and regarding philosophy as nothing more than 'the art of living'.[6] Here, Epicurus runs the risk of becoming himself a saviour figure, one who trades upon the movement between rejecting the world and offering salvation from it, nurturing the illness of world-rejection in order to justify the cure of salvation. Even if such salvation is attainable within this world, in the Epicurean garden, it remains for Nietzsche a doctrine of salvation and as such an expression of decadence.[7] With this step, Nietzsche sets out upon a reading of Epicurus as a proto-Christian, no longer the enemy of Christianity but its ally in rejecting the rigours of the world in favour of the consolations of a promised salvation.

The argument for the affinity of Epicurus and Christ appears again later in *The Gay Science* in Aphorism 370, 'What Is Romanticism?' Nietzsche introduces Romanticism in medical terms, judging it in terms of its contribution to 'growing and struggling life'. He describes 'every art, every philosophy' as a medicine, as 'remedy and an aid' (*Heil und Hilfsmittel*) in the struggle for life. Consistent with Greek medical doctrine, he identifies complaints of *plethora* (excess) and dearth. Those who suffer from 'overfulness of life' need a Dionysian art as remedy for plethora, while those who are poor in life 'seek rest, stillness, calm seas, redemption from themselves through art and knowledge, or intoxication, convulsions, anaesthesia, and madness'. Those who suffer poverty of life require

> above all, mildness, peacefulness, and goodness in thought as well as deed – if possible, also a god who would truly be a god for the sick, a healer, a saviour; also logic, the conceptual understandability of existence – for logic calms and gives confidence. (*GS* §370)

When situated within this medical model, the 'optimistic horizons' of Epicurus reveal him to be the 'opposite of a Dionysian pessimist'; Nietzsche 'gradually learnt to understand Epicurus' as a saviour figure, providing mild remedies for those poor in life, arriving at the inevitable conclusion that the 'Christian' 'is only a kind of Epicurean'. This judgement is confirmed by Nietzsche in *The Anti-Christ*, where, working from the same medical premises or 'physiological reality', he identifies Epicureanism as a medicine ('the redemption doctrine of the pagan world') and Epicurus as a 'typical decadent' adding that 'The fear of pain, even the infinitely small in pain, cannot end otherwise than in a religion of love' (*AC* §30). Yet there is another Epicurus to be found in the pages of Nietzsche, one whose doctrine of pleasure entails more than the avoidance of pain and which tends not towards a religion of love but to a celebration of friendship.

In both *The Gay Science* and *The Anti-Christ*, Nietzsche presents an ambivalent image of Epicurus as both friend and enemy of Christianity. The question mark he left beside the name of Epicurus was deliberate, for the figure of Epicurus was for him a herm, facing both ways – 'It took a hundred years until Greece found out who this garden God, Epicurus, had been – Did they find out?'.[8] Yet perhaps there is more to Nietzsche's ambivalence with respect to Epicurus than the deliberately anachronistic question of his pro- and anti-Christianity.[9] For Epicurus is also placed in an ambivalent relationship with Dionysos: he is the 'opposite of a Dionysian pessimist' in offering consolation for suffering but also, like Dionysos, is able to transfigure existence. In the idyllic landscape of 'Et in Arcadia ego', where the 'pure world of light (in which there was nothing of desire or expectation, no looking before or behind)'[10] anticipates the moment of eternal return, the philosopher who is cited as arriving beyond the Dionysian struggles is 'the inventor of the heroic-idyllic mode of philosophising: Epicurus', not just the philosopher of the idyllic consolations of looking away from a world of suffering, but one who combined the idyll with heroic struggles of transfiguration.

It is not a coincidence that the Christian side of Epicurus is always associated by Nietzsche with medicine, with the soul doctor, while the Dionysian is inseparable from idyllic weather conditions – the landscape of 'Et in Arcadia ego' is cloaked in 'a veil of sunlit vapour'. Nietzsche's ambivalence with respect to Epicurus resolves into that between the medical and the meteorological perspectives that he saw as intrinsic to Epicurus's work. From the standpoint of the former, Epicurus remains a 'soul doctor', a saviour close to Christianity, a saviour figure himself afflicted with dearth and suffering.[11] This Epicurus offers ways to live with suffering, while the other offers images of a transfigured existence much closer, but not fully identical with the Dionysian *plethora*. Viewed from both perspectives, Nietzsche's Epicurus emerges as a distinct figure, encompassing and exceeding the opposition of Dionysos and the Crucified.

Nietzsche's most sustained reading of Epicurus in terms of the medical model of offering a cure for the sufferings of both body and soul appears in Aphorism 7 of *The Wanderer and His Shadow*. There, Epicurus, described as the 'soul soother of later antiquity', is praised for his 'wonderful insight' that 'to quieten the heart it is absolutely not necessary to have solved the ultimate and outermost theoretical question'. Instead, it suffices to apply logical formulas, like medicines, that serve to neutralize the damaging effects of such questions on body and soul. Nietzsche then refers to the celebrated Epicurean *tetrapharmakon*, maintaining that

> he who wishes to offer consolation – to the unfortunate ill-doers, hypochondriacs, the dying – should call into mind the two pacifying formulae of Epicurus, which are capable of being applied to very many questions. Reduced to their very simplest form they would perhaps become: first, if that is how things are they do not concern us; secondly, things may be thus but they may also be otherwise.[12]

The phrase 'pacifying formulae' refers to the consolations for suffering offered by the *tetrapharmakon*, reduced here to its two basic principles.

The *tetrapharmakon* has its most economic formulation in Philodemus's summary: 'Don't fear God. Don't worry about death; what is good is easy to get, and what is terrible is easy to endure' (see *ER* vi). The formulas abstract the essence of Epicurus's *Letter to Menoeceus*, which opens with thoughts on the value of philosophizing for both young and old. The letter to Menoeceus resembles in many respects medical advice; he is advised by Epicurus to follow the regimen or way of life that he recommends, 'Do and practice what I have constantly told you to do, believing these to be the elements of living well' (*ER* 28; *EHU* 170–1). The first of the elements or principles [*stoicheia*] is not to fear god. God is an 'indestructible and blessed animal [*zöion*]' who is not to be ascribed any qualities apart from indestructibility and blessedness. He (subsequently they) is not to be feared or loved but respected in his/ their remoteness from human concerns. The second recommendation is to develop the habit of thinking that death is nothing to us, making mortality a matter of contentment. The prescription turns around the non-presence of death: when we are, it is not; when it is, we are not. The third prescription concerns the management of desire, distinguishing first between natural and physical desires, and then between necessary and merely natural desires. Every expression of desire, every 'choice and avoidance' should be directed as much to the 'health of the body' as to the 'imperturbability [of the soul]' (*ER* 30; *EHU* 180). Such aims form the goal of the 'blessed life'. Finally, Epicurus adds to the three prescriptions the fourth, that 'the limit of bad things has a short duration or causes little trouble' completing the *tetrapharmakon* and supplementing it with recommendations against believing in fate and luck.

The *Letter to Menoeceus* closes with Epicurus's recommendation to 'practice these and related exercises day and night' once again underlining the therapeutic value of exercising the principles for health of the body and soul. The *tetrapharmakon* will ensure health and tranquillity, 'day and night', but then Epicurus adds that Menoeceus, by following the exercises, will also then 'live as a God among men' emphasizing this by adding a final principle or precept, supplementary to the *tetrapharmakon* to the effect that 'a man who lives among immortal goods is in no respect like a mere mortal animal' (*ER* 31; *EHU* 184). While much of the *Letter to Menoeceus* would confirm Nietzsche's diagnosis of Epicurus as a 'soul doctor' the final principle or supplement to the *tetrapharmakon* points beyond this to a transfiguration or living like god among men – indestructible and blessed. The latter may of course be interpreted as confirming the soteriological mission of Epicurus, the promise of living like a god, but it may also point beyond this to a notion of a transfigured life in a transfigured nature.

Nietzsche's appreciation of the Dionysian aspects of Epicurus evident in 'Et in Arcadia ego' is strikingly confirmed in Aphorism 45 ('Epicurus') of *The Gay Science*. Nietzsche begins by expressing his pride, repeated consistently elsewhere, that he experiences 'the character of Epicurus quite differently from everybody else'. When he reads him, he experiences 'the happiness of the afternoon of antiquity' which he evokes by a description of a transfigured landscape and a transfigured gaze upon it: 'I see his eyes gaze upon a wide, white sea, across rocks at the shore that are bathed in sunlight, while large and small animals are playing in this light, as secure and calm as the light and his eyes.'[13] The contemplation of the play of the little (mortal) and large (immortal) animals in the sun transfigures both the seascape and the eye, which gazes upon it without resentment or fear. Yet Nietzsche continues:

> Such happiness could be invented only by a man who was suffering continually. It is the happiness of eyes that have seen the sea of existence [*Dasein*] become calm, and now they can never weary of the surface and the many hues of this tender, shuddering skin of the sea.

The calm of the sunlit sea and of Epicurus's gaze upon its 'tender shuddering skin' joins in an image of serene weather following a storm.

In Aphorism 45, Nietzsche leaves open the character of the calm enjoyed by Epicurus. It follows a storm, for this is the happiness of an eye '*vor dem das Meer des Daseins stille geworden ist*', for whom the sea of existence has grown calm. The rough weather, the continual suffering has passed, but is this only a respite, or is it the achieved transfiguration of both seascape and gaze? The reading of Epicurus as tending towards Christian consolation for suffering would see this as a consolation, a momentary illusion created by the eye as a tranquilizer or respite from suffering. The state of achieved outer and inner calm will break down with the renewed onset of suffering.

The Dionysian reading of Epicurus would agree, but with a slight change of emphasis: the Epicurean state of outer and inner calm must once more be surrendered by welcoming the Dionysian, the 'sudden winds' or 'cool spirits of the afternoon', and ultimately the dance on the back of the tempest.[14] Here, the idyllic calm is also a temporary respite, prologue to the renewed embrace of suffering. Yet there is a further sense in which Epicurus is beyond the opposition of Dionysos and crucified, for the transfigured gaze and nature are in agreement, an agreement figured by meteorological conditions. Images of the weather and the specific use of meteorology to describe the parallels between inner and outer states are an important if underestimated feature of Epicurus's thought, one in which the individual medical prescriptions of the *tetrapharmakon* are succeeded by the transfiguration of 'nature' and the place of the human creature within it through meteorology.

Epicurus's passionate interest in meteorology alluded to and shared by Nietzsche has been neglected in favour of 'epistemological' and 'ontological' investigations of his thought. A certain resistance to his meteorological discourses may be detected in the long-standing controversy over the authenticity of the *Letter to Pythocles*, one of the three major surviving epistolary epitomes of his philosophy whose content is largely meteorological.[15] A persuasive point in favour of its authenticity are the references to meteorology in the *Letter to Herodotus* and in other surviving fragments as well as the meteorological climate of Lucretius's *De Rerum Natura*.[16] Taken together, the references to weather and meteorology suggest two considerations worthy of further examination, first the nature and scope of ancient meteorology, and second the use Epicurus makes of it.

The scope of ancient meteorology was far broader than its contemporary heir, which is preoccupied above all with prediction, even though metaphysical and theological issues are never far removed from contemporary meteorology, which is unusually aware, for a modern techno-science, that it cannot intervene in the processes it tries to understand and predict. The range of classical meteorology was immense:[17] it involved the reading and interpretation of signs, the place of living beings in nature, providence and the control of the heavens, the responsibilities of the polis in prediction of seasonal change, as well as scientific explanation of natural phenomena. Aristotle's introduction to his *Meteorology* summarizes the scope of a particular, philosophically oriented branch of the ancient science. He situates meteorology between the study of the 'first causes of nature and every natural movement' and the study of 'problems relative to animals and to plants in general and in particular' (Aristotle 1952, 338a21, 339a8). Meteorology studies the links between the movements of celestial and terrestrial bodies, generation and corruption and the life of animals and plants; its objects include 'all those phenomena that occur by nature but not with the regularity that characterizes the first elements of bodies' (Aristotle 1952, 338a20). The science is explicitly cast as one that links cosmic and living processes, looking at the place of living beings within the irregular manifestation of terrestrial natural movements.

In the *Letter to Herodotus* on physics, Epicurus moves from a discussion of the shape of the *cosmoi* to some reflections on meteorology that give a context to the extended meteorological discussions in the *Letter to Pythocles*. The most striking feature of these reflections is the insistent allusion to the link between blessedness and meteorological knowledge. The discussions of physics and meteorology in the *Letter to Herodotus* are directed towards the achievement of blessedness beginning with the recognition that the gods are not involved in meteorological phenomena (which include celestial movements) and that these do not reflect their own desires and intentions (*ER* 17 and 18; *EHU* 108 and 114). Epicurus insists that

> when it comes to meteorological phenomena, one must believe that movements, turnings, eclipses, risings, settings and related phenomena occur without any [god] helping out and ordaining or being about to ordain [things] and at the same time having complete blessedness and indestructibility; for troubles and concerns and anger are not consistent with blessedness, but these things involve weakness and fear and dependence on one's neighbours. (*ER* 17; *EHU* 110)

Similarly, the phenomena themselves cannot be in a blessed state if we attribute to them intentions, as if the heavenly bodies 'adopt these movements by deliberate choice'. The error of attributing intention, whether divine or natural, to meteorological phenomena not only detracts from their solemnity but compromises our own striving for blessedness. Epicurus insists that we 'preserve the complete solemnity implied in all the terms applied to such conceptions, so that we do not generate from these terms opinions inconsistent with their solemnity; otherwise the inconsistency itself will produce the greatest disturbance in our souls' (*ER* 17; *EHU* 110). For this reason, 'blessedness lies in this part of meteorological knowledge' and is to be pursued for the sake of achieving an 'undisturbed and blessed state' (*ER* 17; *EHU* 110).

The question remains of whether meteorological knowledge functions as a therapeutic prescription in the same way as the *tetrapharmakon* or whether it points to something more substantial. Epicurus seems to incline to the former, for this is a letter of consolation to his disciple Pythocles, emphasizing freedom *from* the disturbances provoked by inadequate knowledge. In claiming that it is not necessary for the purposes of tranquillity (*ataraxia*) to have definitive knowledge of meteorological phenomena, Epicurus proposes a degree of knowledge sufficient to achieve tranquillity or the removal of fear; for the latter involves only 'a recollection of the general and most important points' (*ER* 18; *EHU* 116). Yet beside and beyond the achievement of ataraxia is the blessed state of *makaria* in which humans approximate to the gods. As in the conclusion to the *Letter to Menoeceus*, blessedness consists in living as a god among men, and the path to it lies in *ataraxia* or liberation from care and anxiety. However, blessedness is not identical to *ataraxia* but is the state beyond 'troubles, concerns and anger and gratitude' and the 'weakness and fear and dependence on one's neighbours' that these involve.

Epicurus's *Letter to Pythocles* initially introduces meteorology with the therapeutic claim that there is no 'other goal to be achieved by the knowledge of meteorological phenomena, whether they are discussed in conjunction with [physics in general] or on their own, than imperturbability and a secure conviction' (*ER* 19; *EHU* 124). The theatre of meteorology is the world or *cosmos*, 'a circumscribed portion of the heavens … separated off from the unlimited and terminates at a boundary that is either rare or dense' (*ER* 20; *EHU* 124). Ours is one of many possible worlds separated by an '*intercosmos*', and while physics reflects on the generation and constitution of the worlds, the specific science of events and movements within our given world is meteorology. Consistent with the argument of the *Letter to Herodotus*, it is thus of direct ethical significance for the possibility of living a blessed life in this world. Correct knowledge of the causes of meteorological phenomena will prevent the fear and disturbance of the soul that may be provoked by incorrect interpretations, 'for our life does not now need irrationality and groundless opinion, but rather for us to live without tumult' (*ER* 20; *EHU* 126). Epicurus's strategy is to pluralize possible explanations of meteorological phenomena, avoiding exclusively divine/mythical explanations that would create fear and disturbance by misinterpretation. Thus, in the case of thunderbolts, Epicurus maintains they 'can be produced several different ways – just be sure myths are kept out of it! And they will be kept out of it if one follows rightly the appearances and takes them as signs for what is unobservable' (*ER* 24; *EHU* 146). By removing such interpretations, Epicurus neutralizes the disturbances of the soul provoked by involving the gods in the weather but also intimates the image of a transformed, non-mythical nature. Not only are the gods' 'divine natures' to be freed from 'burdensome service' (*ER* 23 and 27; *EHU* 160) but nature itself including the human part of it is similarly to be liberated from the burdens of service.

The letters hint at a blessed state in which nature has been demythologized, and both humans and gods liberated from the burdens of service. However, since they are written with therapeutic intentions, the letters tend to emphasize the path to liberation through *ataraxia* rather than the nature of *makaria* or the state of blessedness. There are, however, hints at the nature of this in other fragments, above all in the Vatican Collection of Epicurean sayings discovered in 1888. Vatican Saying 52 is translated by Inwood and Gerson as 'Friendship dances around the world announcing to all of us that we must wake up to blessedness' (*ER* 38; *EO* 151). The language of this sentence, with a personification of friendship dancing around the world calling us to wake up to blessedness, was related by Festugière to the language of the mysteries.[18] What is equally important is the dance of friendship and the universal character of the call, calling all to wake up to blessedness. The suggestion that the herald – *philia* – is joyfully calling everyone to wake up to the blessed state of friendship is confirmed by the constant return to the theme of friendship in the Vatican Collection. However, while most of the aphorisms on friendship (Sayings 23, 28, 34 and 39) are sententious injunctions balancing the advantages and risks of friendship, the gravity of Vatican Saying 52 is best gauged by reflecting on the universality of its claim to friendship and the contrast between friend and neighbour.

The call to blessedness by means of universal, cosmopolitan friendship complements the other reference to the cosmopolitan to be found in the Vatican Collection: Vatican Saying 31 advises: 'One can attain security against other things, but when it comes to death all men live in a city without walls' (*ER* 37; *EO* 149). The shared predicament of death provides a backdrop to the call to blessedness through friendship; the dawn call of friendship accepts that there can be no security but that the night of the fear of death can be overcome. Living in a city without walls, without security, implies a relationship with the other beyond that of the 'weakness and fear and dependence on one's neighbours' diagnosed in the *Letter to Herodotus*. Following the overcoming of the troubles and anxieties through *ataraxia* – the distancing from the security afforded by the neighbour in the shadow of the city walls – there arises the possibility of *makaria* or a friendship not based on anger and gratitude. It appears to be a friendship not only of humans, based on their shared mortality, but also of humans and gods and nature.

The intimation of the blessed state of friendship situated by Epicurus beyond the therapeutic consolations of *ataraxia* is an apt moment to return to Nietzsche's self-proclaimed Epicureanism. It is not part of a religion of love, with its impregnable City of God that succeeds the mortal city of the humans, but a star friendship, with the implacable sense of risk and exposure that for Nietzsche attends such friendship. But it is also a friendship of humans, nature, and the gods, a blessed state before and after the storm, the *makaria* of Aphorism 45 ('Epicurus') of *The Gay Science* where the sage gazes upon a white sea bathed in the sunlight where great and small creatures play together in the fine weather which is not all for them, or forever, but just for now.

Notes

1   See Festugière 1946; Hadot 1995; Hadot 2002.

2   A distinction clearly described by Jones 1989, 37.

3   The aphorism of *The Gay Science* that seems to promise an answer, §375 'Why we look like Epicureans', is addressed to a 'we' of 'modern men' whose Epicureanism is restricted to a combination of mistrust and 'jubilant curiosity'.

4   *WP* §196 (Nov. 1887–Mar. 1888); see also *The Anti-Christ*: 'Christianity as the formula for outbidding all the subterranean cults, those of Osiris, the Great Mother, of Mithras for example, and for summing them up: it is in this insight that the genius of Paul consists' (§58).

5   Nietzsche's view of the Platonic inspiration of the 'subterranean cults' seems indebted to Johann Jakob Bachofen's 1867 work *Die Unsterblichkeitslehre der orphischen Theologie auf den grabdenkmalern des Altertums nach Anleitung einer vase aus Canosa im besitz des Herrn Prosper Biardot dargestellt*.

6   *WP* §449, a view exhaustively developed in Pierre Hadot's readings of Epicurus, readings which are close to the medical model of philosophizing put into question by Nietzsche.

7   'As decadence: pendant to "Epicureanism" – Paradise, as conceived by the Greeks, also only the "garden of Epicurus"' (*WP* §225).

8   *BGE* §7; in *The Wanderer and His Shadow* (in *HH*) §227 'Eternal Epicurus,' Nietzsche reports that Epicurus is alive and well, having forgotten his own name and enjoying no reputation among the philosophers.

9   An opposition that informs the traditional perspective of Christian Epicureanism that begins with Gassendi continues to inform Festugière's classic *Épicure et ses dieux* first published in 1946.

10   *The Wanderer and His Shadow* in *HH*, §295.

11   See the 'Attempt at a Self-Criticism' to *The Birth of Tragedy* §§1 and 4.

12   *The Wanderer and His Shadow* in *HH*, §7.

13   *GS* §45: 'Ich sehe sein Auge auf ein weites, weissliches Meer blicken, uber uferfelsen hin, auf denen die Sonne liegt, wahrend grosses und kleines Getier in ihrem lichte spielt, sicher und ruhig wie dies Licht und jenes Auge selber.'

14   See 'The Sun Sinks' in *Dithyrambs of Dionysus*, trans. R.J. Hollingdale (London: Anvil Press Poetry, 1984) 49, and note also 'To the Mistral: A Dancing Song', in *The Gay Science*. The *Dionysos Dithyramben* are replete with weather metaphors, from the 'abgehellter Luft' of the opening *Nur Narr! Nur Dichter!* to the 'regenloser Land' of the closing *Von der Armut des Reichsten*.

15   For a summary of this complex philosophical debate, see the introductory note to the *Letter to Pythocles* in Ilaria Rarnelli's edition, *EHU* 123–7. Current consensus inclines towards accepting its authenticity.

16 Lucretius's opening evocation of Venus is cast in terms of the fertility occasioned by fine weather.

17 My understanding of ancient meteorology is indebted to Taub 2003.

18 Drawing attention in an important footnote (Festugière 1946, 57, n. 3) to the themes of the herald and the call, relating both to hermetic and Mithraic sources.

10

That perhaps abused word ...

errida concludes *Punctuations: The Time of a Thesis* – his *soutenance de thèse* before a jury for the *doctorat d'État* at the Sorbonne on 2 June 1980 – with an apology for using once more 'a word I have perhaps abused in the past', one he suspects his jury and readers have already 'heard too much talk of ... ' (Derrida 2004, 128). The setting for this apology is curious: we are at a *soutenance de thèse* – something Derrida notes with amusement is called in English a 'thesis defence' – but of a thesis that did not exist, even though it had a title: *The Ideality of the Literary Object*. And this defence is collected in a dossier of texts dedicated to a vindication of the right to philosophy. Instead of a thesis he proposes to defend the stages of an incomplete itinerary. And that perhaps abused word? Well, the reasons he found himself defending an unfinished thesis were many and part of an 'interminable deliberation' concerning institutional politics that led him to resolve to prepare for a 'new kind of mobility'. This decision was accompanied by an awareness that 'Perhaps because I was beginning to know only too well not where I was going but where I was, not where I had arrived but where I stopped' (Derrida 2004, 127). No question of going straight to a defence of the right to philosophy here, but then, 'philosophy' was never the abused word in question.

The defence closes with many iterations of the word 'perhaps' – the Nietzschean leitmotif – but that did not mean that 'perhaps' is the perhaps abused word. Anyway how could 'perhaps' be abused, except by squeezing a dialectical result out of perhapsing, perhaps ... But there is the further question of how Derrida of all people could 'abuse' a word. Did he not teach that a word could be used only with the prefix ab-use and can such abuse consist in twisting its meaning, employing it in an inappropriate context, using it 'in-appropriately' as a weapon? Also, who is entitled to decide whether a word has been abused – who can judge between use and abuse (again the Nietzschean register of use and abuse is sounding through these closing words)? Derrida's apology emerges at the end of his address when he admits that up to now he has been speaking in code, that what he has said is not all that was to be said – it is in a sense encrypted and that perhaps he has been abusing his words to another end. For 'above all, above all' he repeats, which is to say, above all talk of 'above all', 'it has sounded too much like the totting up of a calculation, a self-justification, a self-defence' (Derrida 2004, 127) according to the equation: *Margins of Philosophy* + *Glas* + *Truth in Painting* + X (any work by Derrida) = a thesis. Has he perhaps been all along abusing his jury, calculating the moves necessary to secure a *doctorat d'État*?

He attempts to defuse any such suspicion with a disarming gesture, confessing the word that he had abused in the past: 'You have heard too much talk of strategies. "Strategy" is a word that I have perhaps abused in the past' (Derrida 2004, 128). Surprisingly, 'strategy' is the perhaps abused word in question – but why does he make it his last, defensive word? Derrida suspects he has abused it because 'it was always to specify *in the end*, in an apparently self-contradictory manner and at the risk of cutting the ground under my own feet – something I almost never fail to do – a strategy without any goal (*finalité*)'; it was in short the 'aleatory strategy of someone who admits that he does not know where he is going' (Derrida 2004, 128). But is this not just a strategic admission, a final throw of the dice in abusing strategy itself here? Suddenly the final words of the *soutenance* assume a peculiar gravity, for knowing they are spoken by a self-confessed strategist we cannot trust them, even, or *especially* when they are uttered in all sincerity among philosophical friends. He assures us that 'This, then, is not after all an undertaking of war or a discourse of belligerence' (Derrida 2004, 128) but we must read this remembering that strategists such as Sun Tzu and Clausewitz – Mao's Eastern and Western 'masters of strategy' – insist that the best strategy is to claim there is no war – it disarms the enemy. So perhaps he is using strategy at the very moment that he claims to be abusing it – there is a war, but I tell you, my institutional friends and enemies, there is no war. The same holds for the final flourish of *Punctuations* or the declaration of unilateral disarmament; it is the declaration of a 'headlong flight straight towards the end', a 'joyous self-contradiction, a disarmed desire, that is to say, something very old and very cunning, but that has also just been born and delights in being without defence' (Derrida 2004, 128). Is this nothing but a strategic feint? Might that proclaimed defencelessness be – perhaps, strategically – the ultimate aggression?

Now the perhaps abused word has been identified as 'strategy' we should perhaps look at it more closely, but with a strategic gaze, not frontally, but from various angles. Let's begin with some formal characteristics of strategy and its relationship to philosophy and ask how this word and practice was understood in France at this time. Then we can consider two instances of Derrida's use or perhaps even abuse of the word: one with respect to his understanding of 'thinking' hinted at earlier in *Right to Philosophy* in 'Privilege' and the other his manoeuvres as part of what he openly described as a thirty years war – his war with Antonin Artaud.

While Derrida may confess to having abused the word 'strategy', it is certain that he never deconstructed it – even in his readings of the strategist Clausewitz in *The Politics of Friendship*. Perhaps because strategy is the condition of possibility of deconstruction: perhaps even because deconstruction *is* strategy. This would be astonishing, since philosophy has always defined itself against strategy as the practice of the *strategos* or soldier. Philosophy pursues the love of wisdom and truth; strategy pursues victory by all means, including deceit. Philosophy has a strong concept of friendship; strategy urges the eminence of the enemy. Philosophy is sincere and open; strategy is cunning and secretive. Philosophy is Greek and ultimately democratic; strategy is Roman and inseparable from hierarchical military command. Finally, the Kantian Clausewitz will define strategy as the intelligent conduct of the war of resistance: one that obeys the categorical imperative to act according to the strategic maxim that enhances your own and compromises your enemy's capacity to resist. Now, to be very summary, some strands of post-war French philosophy associated with the resistance – Raymond Aron and Jean-Pierre Vernant, especially the latter – began to question whether there was indeed any great distance between strategy and philosophy. Indeed, Vernant's work into the origins of philosophy emphasizes its proximity to hoplite warfare and strategic reason: philosophers were not dedicated to pure argument; they liked above all to *win* arguments; victory not truth is their supreme value. Nietzsche had already suspected that the appeal to truth was above all a winning tactic and that any claim to free dialogue is but a strategic device to dominate the interlocutor. This implies that free democratic debate is a strategic ruse of hierarchy and that freedom and 'rights' are but permissions granted by the powerful or the state. According to this view Socrates didn't die for the truth or out of respect of the laws of Athens, but because he was a poor strategist who underestimated his enemy.

We can pick up echoes of this view of strategy throughout Derrida's work, but especially in the reflections on academic and institutional politics that make up the 'Right to Philosophy' collection. In the opening reflection 'Privilege: Justificatory Title and Introductory Remarks' Derrida subtly aligns strategy with thinking, claiming that 'deconstruction forces us to *think* differently the institutions of philosophy and the experience of the right to philosophy' (Derrida 2002, 13). It should be noted at the outset that it *forces* us to think differently, implying a resistance that has to be overcome by force, that is, strategically. But what is meant by 'thinking', let alone thinking differently here? For Derrida, thinking has never 'taken the form and function Heidegger gives it' and he specifies, 'Here less than ever is *thinking* opposed to science, technique, calculation and strategy' (Derrida 2002, 13). Far from being opposed to thinking, strategy seems to join science, technique and calculation by its side; but perhaps this is only its strategic proximity as a calculative discipline whose interests remain close to those of technique and science. This becomes clear later when we return to 'thinking' in the context of the non-binding contract between philosophy and the state at issue in these deliberations. Here we will see resistance emerge as the key value associated with strategy.

But before looking at this strategic doctrine more closely, I'd like to point to a potential strategic weakness (or strength, it is always difficult to tell). This involves the relationship between right and resistance, remembering that a right is always a privilege, an immunity or permission granted by the state; there can never be an uncomplicated 'right to resist'. And yet in the discussion of right midway in 'Privilege: Justificatory Title and Introductory Remarks' Derrida gives the state the tasks of (a) not impeding the exercise of the right *of* and (b) making possible the exercise of a right *to* philosophy through *active intervention*. While establishing this distinction between rights *of* and rights *to* Derrida introduces a parenthetical sequence of analogous rights: '(rights of property, rights of speech, writing, publishing, resisting oppression)'. The last right, however, is problematic: can I really expect the state to not impede the exercise of my right to resist it (maybe within certain limits but who determines those if not the state?) and can I really expect it to 'intervene actively' and 'prepare conditions favourable' for my exercise of the right to resist it? This leaves open the question of whether the right to resist is a strategic right, or whether it is here called right strategically. Is Derrida strategically insinuating the right to resist and the right to philosophy into a list of rights familiar from the American and French revolutionary constitutions or has he made the strategic error of believing these to belong to that same family of rights?

This brings us then to the other strategic right, one that we can either say is in a weak sense analogous to the right to resist or in a strong sense that it is the same right, or even that the two anomalous rights can enter into a close strategic alliance – since both rights are strategic. Derrida continues by arguing that 'a right to philosophy could not be one right among others' (Derrida 2002, 41) and that even if the state provided conditions favourable for the exercise of the right to philosophy

> no contract would bind philosophy itself and institute this philosophy as a reciprocal and responsible partner of the state. If this were demanded of philosophy, even implicitly, philosophy would have the right, a right it only gets from itself, this time, and in no way from the state, to match wits with the state, to break unilaterally every agreement, in a brutal or cunning, declared or, if the situation demands, surreptitious fashion. (Derrida 2002, 41)

That is, philosophy must exercise its right strategically in resisting the state – this strategic thinking is even identified as being more than philosophy and even its responsibility to itself: 'This irresponsibility toward the state can be demanded by philosophy's responsibility to its own law – or the responsibility of what above called *thinking*, which can, in analogous conditions, break its contract with science or philosophy' (Derrida 2002, 41). So, to paraphrase Nietzsche, the strategic animal is the one with the right to break promises, especially those made to the state. Thinking is therefore clearly strategic and is characterized by the features of strategy in general – cunning, enmity, pursuit of victory and the enhancement of its capacity to resist.

Let me add to this some thoughts on the revealing case of Derrida's conducting open war, although this time not with the state. He might have pursued his *soutenance* by means of his writings on Artaud from the early 1960s, which seem closely associated with the 'Ideality of the Literary Object' research project. This is particularly relevant for underlining the strategic gesture of the close of *Punctuations* – the 'disarming' gesture. This was always part of Derrida's strategic defence doctrine with respect to the enemy Artaud and the source of his Artaud-immunity developed over decades of struggle with the work of the Mômo, a struggle whose strategic options were already set in the opening skirmish *La parole soufflée*, first published in *Tel Quel* in 1965 and collected in *Writing and Difference*.[1]

Derrida in that first essay professes a naïveté which, in case we had not realized it, 'was not a stipulation of style' (Derrida [1967] 1978, 175) – it was always that defensive strategy that consists in the calculated lowering of defences. This throwing away of the defence doctrine of Rivière and the Neo-Rivièrians provoked one of the first intense bursts of strategic reflection that emerged from Derrida's Artaud wars.[2] He muses on the importance of never underestimating the Mômo, for he is engaged in a war of *absolute* resistance:

> If Artaud absolutely resists – and, we believe, as was never done before – clinical or critical exegeses, he does so by virtue of that part of his adventure (and with this word we are designating a totality anterior to the separation of the life and the work) which is the very protest itself against exemplification *itself*. Both critic and doctor are resourceless before an existence that refuses to signify, or by an art without works, a language without a trace. (Derrida [1967] 1978, 175)

Derrida recognizes that Artaud was already well advanced in his war of resistance against 'the history of dualist metaphysics which more or less subterraneously inspired the essays invoked above [by Blanchot, Foucault and Laplanche]' (Derrida [1967] 1978, 175). This war was conducted against a structure of *theft* by the invisible *souffleur* or prompter in the theatre who ensures the actor's fidelity to the text being played and who was one of the main targets of Artaud's theatre of cruelty.

Derrida describes the function of the invisible prompter with one of the earliest uses of a neologism that would become one of his signatures: 'it ensures the indispensable *différance* and intermittence between a text already written by another hand and an interpreter already dispossessed of that which he receives' (Derrida [1967] 1978, 176). Ensuring the respect of *différance* is the strategy pursued by Artaud's enemy, but had not Artaud already pre-empted the protection offered by *différance* and the *souffleur* whom he compromises by implicating them in the metaphysical scene? In defending *différance* against Artaud, the *souffleur* or prompter cannot simply repeat the metaphysical text since this is already compromised, but if he does not, then he is no longer a *souffleur*, no longer an invisible guardian of the text – he has been conscripted into the theatre of cruelty. How then can the *souffleur* ensure respect of *différance* without cruelty? He must begin by recognizing more clearly than the others that his adversary is not to be underestimated:

> Artaud desired the conflagration of the stage upon which the prompter [*souffleur*] was possible and where the body was under the rule of a foreign text. Artaud wanted the machinery of the prompter [*souffleur*] spirited away [*soufflé*], wanted to plunder the structure of theft. To do so, he had to destroy with one and the same blow, both poetic inspiration and the economy of classical art, singularly the economy of the theatre. And through the same blow he had to destroy the metaphysics, religion, aesthetics etc., that supported them. (Derrida [1967] 1978, 176)

Derrida will return Artaud's blows thirty years later, when he will be just as clear that these blows were also addressed against him and that they had to be parried with force and cunning.

Just what is it that Artaud proposes to put in the place of the security and protection offered by the *souffleur* – the invisible guarantor of the text and protector of the actor against the lapse of memory? Derrida, looking out from his little booth at the front of the classical stage of metaphysics, can immediately appreciate the gravity of the threat: 'He would thus open up to Danger a world no longer sheltered by the structure of theft. To restore Danger by reawakening the stage of cruelty – this was Antonin Artaud's *stated* intention at the very least' (Derrida [1967] 1978, 176). And it is here that Derrida perceives a weak point in Artaud's metaphysical immunity, his Artaud-immunity in self-disabling his own lines of defence in the name of exposure to (upper case) Danger: Derrida detects a 'calculated slip' in this opening to Danger but is sure enough of his enemy to be unsure whether this 'slip' is a weakness or a trap. This is Artaud's need to restore un-metaphysical danger, a procedure that has two steps – disabling the self-defences offered by text and prompter (autoimmunity) and affirming Danger or exposure. Artaud has first to lower his defences and abandon the protection they seem to offer: 'Loss, precisely is the metaphysical determination into which I will have to slip my works if they are to be understood within a world and a literature unwittingly governed by the metaphysics for which Jacques Rivière served as a delegate' (Derrida [1967] 1978, 176–7). Having to lower defences, to claim silence and irresponsibility prior to affirming danger, opens a chink where the *souffleur* can intervene. It is at the very moment that Artaud evades the ramparts of metaphysics manned by Rivière and his protégés that it is possible to intervene and to become dangerous. And Derrida does so – for who else is the 'I' slipped into this passage as if in the person of Artaud ('I will have to slip ... '), whose role is to evade the rational metaphysics called upon by Rivière in his defence against the madman, than the *souffleur who is* speaking *for* Artaud, prompting Artaud to break with metaphysics and escape stage right? The lowering of defences (auto-immune cruelty) and the opening to danger still require a negotiation of protection in which the prompter can step in to ensure that Artaud properly performs Artaud, that is to say, betrays himself at the very moment of being true to himself, obeying the voice that tells him how to be Artaud.

Derrida's is not a critical or clinical assessment of Artaud, but an infiltration, a viral overriding of Artaud-immunity that protects it while proclaiming its exposure to danger. Artaud's cruelty is faithfully performed on the proscenium stage of metaphysics guarded over by the invisible *souffleur* who gives permission for and approval of the performance. But is it at all certain that Artaud's apparent vulnerability at the moment of lowering defences is not already feigned, a decoy in the spirit of Sun Tzu's *Art of War* that makes a noise in the east before attacking from the west? Derrida gives the possibility a full airing but only to expose the strategic weaknesses of the *souffleur*. Speaking as ever for Artaud by giving him the right/permission to speak and prompting him here in the name of his true desire, Derrida mimes his opposition to the scenario of loss imposed by having to disable his metaphysical defences. He (the *souffleur* is now giving him the words), *he* 'wants to explode it. He opposes to this inspiration of loss and dispossession a good inspiration, the very inspiration that is missing from inspiration as loss' (Derrida [1967] 1978, 179). And yet 'he', by saying so, is recaptured by the metaphysical opposition between good and bad inspiration. In making Artaud speak in this way Derrida nevertheless underestimates the poet's capacity to resist, his Artaud-immunity. For Derrida can only imagine the self-disabling of defences according to the gesture of suicide followed by rebirth: 'This is why – such is the concept of true suicide according to Artaud – I must die away from my death in order to be reborn "immortal" at the eve of my birth' (Derrida [1967] 1978, 181). Yet, ever the *souffleur*, the prompts by which Derrida leads Artaud into this onto-theological trap are not entirely apt, and they forget Artaud's direct and sustained attacks on the gesture of suicide: the celestial poet was never suicided by the cosmos. His objections – to take his voice against Derrida's – maintain that the embrace of danger by suspending defences only appears suicidal from the secure standpoint of metaphysics. Indeed, Derrida's consistent alignment of auto-immunity with suicide – the self robbing itself of its own life – in his later thinking of auto-immunity, above all in *Rogues*, originates in this moment of translating Artaud-immunity into the despised Latin *sui-cide*.

With this we can see that Derrida's first line of defence against Artaud is largely engaged and consolidated through reflections on the theatre of cruelty and the impossible *restoration* of danger; it is a strategy sustained up to the closing constellation identifying Artaud and Heidegger's contemporary destruction of metaphysics. From his deconstructive redoubt Derrida observes that neither Heidegger nor Artaud effects the 'simple surpassing of this history' and especially not the latter who is at the limits of this history: 'the metaphysics which Artaud destroys and which he is still furious to construct or preserve within the same movement of destruction' (Derrida [1967] 1978, 194). Artaud acts at this limit, and Derrida, abandoning the prompt, or rather prompting himself now as the first-person plural, adds, 'we have attempted to read him at this limit' (Derrida [1967] 1978, 194). Or even to keep him at this limit, standing on the edge of the stage looking out towards a new stage without metaphysics.

In this last paragraph of *La parole soufflée* Derrida reveals his strategy and the line of fortification he has erected against Artaud. It comprises a cruel sequence of manoeuvres in which the erstwhile prompter metamorphoses into a choreographer, producing the spectacle of Artaud walking a line between self-murder and resurrection: 'One entire side of his discourse destroys a tradition which lives *within* difference, alienation, and negativity without seeing their origin and necessity. To reawaken this tradition, Artaud in sum, recalls it to its own motifs: self-presence, unity, self-identity, the proper etc.' (Derrida [1967] 1978, 194). After de/prescribing these *actions* Derrida identifies the force of their character: 'Artaud's "metaphysics", at its most critical moments, fulfils the most profound and permanent ambition of Western metaphysics' (Derrida [1967] 1978, 194). But in a twist away from this, Derrida detects at work a cruel 'law of difference' which constitutes a fixed line of defence where Artaud abandons 'metaphysical naïveté'. The restoration of defences, the abandoning of the defenceless posture that Derrida feigned at the outset of his essay, thus finally renders Artaud's defensive and offensive strategy transparent to his enemies, announcing his imminent defeat that may also be his victory.

Derrida explicitly identifies these movements as part of a devastating stratagem on Artaud's part that is the deadlier for never explicitly disclosing itself: 'The duplicity of Artaud's text, simultaneously more and less than a stratagem' (Derrida [1967] 1978, 194). It is one that has 'unceasingly obliged us to pass over to the other side of the limit' (Derrida [1967] 1978, 194). Yet this disarming avowal is not all it would seem, since Derrida is not just maintaining a bipolar offensive posture with respect to Artaud, as recommended by the Maoist doctrine close to the editors and readers of *Tel Quel* where he published this essay – when Artaud destroys, Derrida preserves; when Artaud preserves, Derrida destroys – but is setting himself to reveal that strategy is in play in what appears to be naïveté. He will reveal the tactic deployed in Artaud's denunciation of the 'naïve implications of difference' from a position that feigns 'the closure of presence' and he will claim that this exposure compromises Artaud's immune strategy. So while admitting that he might seem to be 'criticizing Artaud's metaphysics from the standpoint of metaphysics itself', this is but a feint since his strategy consists in 'delineating a fatal complicity' in Artaud. But fatal for whom? For with this delineation we return to his earlier formulation of his post-Rivière resistance strategy. The complicity is 'fatal' in giving rise to precisely that hiatus between the moments of lowering defences and affirming danger that was earlier probed as the most vulnerable point of Artaud-immunity, namely 'a necessary dependency of all destructive discourses: they must inhabit the structures they demolish, and within them they must shelter an indestructible desire for full presence, for nondifference, simultaneously life and death' (Derrida 1967, 244). But we already saw that this simultaneous life and death – understood as the suicidal gesture – was a weak line of defence against Artaud since, for Artaud, immunity is anything but suicidal. At the end of this essay Derrida retreats, for now, but with a sense that his strategy – of revealing the tactical deployment of complicity – while much more supple and apparently effective than the clinical/critical distinction of Rivière et al., had nevertheless already been anticipated by Artaud. But then perhaps the *souffleur* never really believed that performance of Artaud just concluded has ended in the life that chooses death or suicide.

The work on Artaud is exemplary for understanding Derrida's use and abuse of strategy in other contexts. It is that 'very old and very cunning' discipline that has just been born and that delights in the impregnability of appearing to be without defence. The much 'abused word' describes his thinking and reading as well as the field of force and understanding within which it makes its parries and feints. The resistance implied in the right to philosophy recognizes that philosophy is at war but without admitting it. Just as Artaud forcefully requested permission from Jacques Rivière for the gift of the right to speak by publishing his poetry, so too Derrida petitions state power for the right, that is to say, permission to practise philosophy. And yet in both cases, permission is requested as a feint – as appearing in the position of a weak adversary in order to be granted rights and so secure victory, but over what, or whom?

Notes

1   Derrida's Artaud wars begin with 'La parole soufflée' 1965, continuing with 'The Theatre of Cruelty and the Closure of Representation' 1966, 'To Unsense the Subjectile' 1986 and largely culminate in 'Artaud the Moma' of 1996. For more on Derrida's attempts to secure Artaud-immunity, see Caygill 2015.

2   On the war of resistance and counter-resistance between Artaud and Jacques Rivière, see Caygill 2015.

Section three: Life

11

Drafts for a metaphysics of the gene

These drafts for a metaphysics of the gene explore the theme of the 'touch of memory' from a number of diverse aspects. They propose an analysis of contemporary culture in which the locus of heritage is figured in terms of 'the gene' but suggest that the latter figures less as a biochemical than as a metaphysical expression. While there is indubitably an elective affinity between the science of genetics and metaphysics, the popular science of genetics prevalent, or virulent, in contemporary genetic culture is dominated by metaphysics. Our contemporary genetic culture can be described in Nietzschean terms as a 'nihilistic' culture insofar as it replaces Christianity as a 'Platonism for the masses' with 'popular science'.

The culture of popular science veers between the nihilistic extremes of naturalism and idealism, a movement figured in representations of 'the gene'. The gene, first definitively named as such in 1909 by Wilhelm Ludwig Johannsen, is at once an intelligible unit of 'information' – part of a digitalization of Platonism inaugurated by Leibniz – and a part of physical nature subject to chance and natural selection. This instability within the gene – whether it is to be understood idealistically or naturalistically – also contributes to the fear of genes prevalent in genetic culture. The fear of the manipulation of the intelligible gene by science reaching the limit of the abolition of nature and the flesh in the totally genetically engineered species of human being is accompanied by a fear of the uncontrollable consequences of genetic interventions in some future test of 'fitness' in natural selection. Neither the fear of the abolition of chance in a technical order of necessity nor that of the revenge of chance against the same order has any real basis in the science, but both have assumed considerable weight in the culture of genetics.

The following five drafts explore the dilemmas posed by genetic culture through reflections informed by the writings of Plato and Nietzsche, for some the first and the last metaphysician. In the first – *The Slave Revolt of Popular Science* – Nietzsche's claim that Platonism survived the proclamation of the 'death of God' in the shape of 'faith in science' is interpreted as the emergence of a nihilistic, post-Christian culture of metaphysical 'popular science'. The second – *The Expulsion of the Physicians* – enquires into Plato's view of the future priests of genetic culture, namely the physicians, seemingly expelled, with the artists, from the Republic. The third reflection – *Chance, Necessity and Techne* – explores the role played by *techne* in Plato's overcoming of the tragic play of chance and necessity, while the fourth – *Digital Platonism* – begins to draw out the Platonic paradigm informing the science of genetics. The final reflection – *The Nihilism of Genetic Culture* – speculates on the metaphysical refraction of the science in genetic culture and some of the implications this has for the experience of birth, embodiment and death. The possibility of another rebirth of tragedy is also raised here and left open.

The slave-revolt of popular science

> Certain ingenious lots, then, I suppose, must be devised so that the inferior man at each conjugation may blame chance and not the rulers. Yes indeed, he said.
>
> – Plato, *The Republic* V, 460

Book V of *The Gay Science*, published in the second edition of 1887 after *Also Sprach Zarathustra* and *Beyond Good and Evil*, begins at §343 with a reflection on the proclamation of the 'death of God'. The madman of §125 proclaimed this event in the market place and called for 'festivals of atonement' to create the humanity capable of living with the responsibility of this deed. In Book V Nietzsche returns to this proclamation and reflects on what it must entail: the change of trust into distrust, the collapse of faith in morality and the 'monstrous logic of terror' that will unfold in an impending 'plenitude and sequence of breakdown, destruction, ruin and cataclysm'. In spite of this gloomy prophesy Nietzsche still finds cause for cheerfulness, affirming the horizon that is opened by the death of God. The shadows of the dead God haunting the madman have now given way to 'a new and scarcely describable kind of light' which promises a future open to chance and unimaginable inventions.

The affirmative analysis of 'The meaning of our cheerfulness' in the face of the death of God is followed in §344 by an analysis of the negative, reactive response to deicide. The reactive response takes the form of *faith in science* or the development of a metaphysical scientific culture in the place of Christian culture. Such a culture is 'still pious' in that it rests upon a faith in truth and a trust in mistrust. Such 'faith in science' substitutes itself for faith in God and draws out the ultimate consequence of this faith which is not just an 'hostility to life' but even a 'concealed will to death'. The proclamation of the death of the Christian God was perhaps premature, for God takes a long time to die. Instead of the 'festivals of atonement' and their new light 'there may still be caves for thousands of years in which his shadow will be shown' (*GS* §108).

Such a cave is represented by the popular culture of science that for Nietzsche translates science into a moralistic metaphysics. He sees the 'faith in science' that defines the modern, post-Christian culture of 'popular science' as resting upon a '*metaphysical faith*'. This governs even the work of the most 'godless anti-metaphysicians' who still take their fire 'from a flame that is lit by a faith that is thousands of years old, that Christian faith that was also the faith of Plato, that God is the truth, that truth is divine' (*GS* §344). The faith in science is more than a principle informing the work of scientists; it is the founding principle of a culture which believes in science, in the efficacy of scientific solutions to questions of life and death.

The post-Christian culture that is governed by metaphysical faith in science, that trusts science, is for Nietzsche another version of a Platonic culture: metaphysics, he writes in §347, 'today discharges itself among large numbers of people in a scientific-positivistic form'. The interest in the development of metaphysical popular cultures informs much of Nietzsche's authorship. His early work from the late 1860s on the impact of philosophy upon the formation of a popular culture culminated in his view of the struggle in late antiquity between the popular cultures of Platonism and Epicureanism. The former was victorious in the shape of Christianity as 'Platonism for the masses'. For Nietzsche such popular Platonism represented a slave revolt of the masses against an Epicurean imperial aristocracy, a revolt whose members negated the world and fantasized a blissful future based on the punishment of the powerful. The 'death of God' does not necessarily entail the end of the slave revolt of morals, but its move into a new and crueller phase of its history. The modern culture of science for Nietzsche rests on the same faith, the same affirmation of the 'other world' and the negation of its counterpart 'this world, *our* world'.

The slave-revolt of popular science takes up the flame dropped by Christianity but turns it upon this world. The faith in science looks to science not only for guidance as to who is to be saved and who is to be damned in the next but also in this world. The world of 'life, nature, and history' is now subject to a metaphysical and moralistic discipline far more rigorous than that ever imagined by the most dedicated inquisitor. Faith in science and its attendant moralism can now justify who is to live and who is to die; indeed, with scientific culture the slaves achieve power and wield it with a vengeance.

The ambiguous consequences of the 'death of God' – a liberation from Platonism or its intensification in popular science – inform Nietzsche's work above all. *We too* are still too pious – we too, the Godless anti-metaphysicians are Platonists in imagining that we possess the light to lead others out of the shadows of the cave, 'we still have to vanquish his shadow' (*GS* §108). The ambiguity is expressed most clearly in the contrast between the third in the sequence of aphorisms opening Book V and the contemporary Preface to the second edition of *The Gay Science*. After the cheerfulness of the affirmation of the death of God and the diagnosis of the nihilism of faith in science follows an analysis of the revenge of the weak in §345, 'Morality as a Problem'. Morality is born of revenge, even if it dissembles its origins in the guise of science, and in particular the science of medicine.

Nietzsche describes morality as 'the most famous of all medicines' and proposes to question it as such, that is to question both morality and medicine. This, however, sits uneasily with his call in the Preface for a 'philosophical *physician*' 'who has to pursue the problem of the total health of a people, time, race, or of humanity' (*GS* Preface §3). The philosopher-physicians are not in a position to question the metaphysics and morality of popular science since their power depends on this faith. The philosopher-physician indeed seems to represent the dictatorship of the slave revolt of popular science, its executive arm.

In 'Morality as a Problem' Nietzsche claims disingenuously that 'nobody up to now has examined the *value* of the most famous of all medicines which is called morality'. However, precisely this questioning was one of the constant preoccupations of Plato, who arrived at a similar result to Nietzsche. In the *Republic* the legislator appears in the guise of the philosophical physician, but only after having been expelled with the artists. However, it also becomes apparent in the *Republic* that the philosophical physician possesses in addition the ability of the artist to dissemble reality, to 'devise certain ingenious lots', which, in the name of science and *technē*, executes the legislation of who may be born and who must die.

The expulsion of the physicians

But what have you to say to this, Socrates? Must we not have good physicians in our city?

– Plato, *Republic* III, 408

It is often forgotten that the artists were not the only ones to be expelled from Plato's *Republic* – they were joined by the physicians. Yet in *Republic* III 407–9 the physicians are expelled only to return in the guise of the legislators. The philosophical physician is precisely the one who will legislate, but only after having been expelled as physician. The philosophical physician will create a new *technē* of medicine capable of combining justice and medicine in the care of the body and the soul.

The artists are expelled from the city for practising an imitative art; the physicians for practising an art that supplements nature. It is the ambiguous quality of medicine between art and science that gives it the uncanny quality of cheating chance and the necessity of nature. Socrates cites Pindar's description of Asclepius, the God of healing, being struck by lightning for healing a man on the point of death, that is, for cheating the necessity of nature. Furthermore, the physician achieves this perverse end by applying knowledge to the body – Asclepius is the son of Apollo and healed both through knowledge and through the laying on of hands and oneiric visitation. For these reasons the physicians must be expelled with the artists as chimerical creators of chimeras.

Socrates continues the case against the physicians by arguing that their skill combines knowledge of 'the principles of the art' and a familiarity with 'the greatest possible number of the most sickly bodies' (III 408e). What is more, a good physician for Socrates would have to experience illness in order to have sufficient knowledge to treat it. Yet this experience would be such that they could not cure by touch, since their bodies would be corrupt, nor could they treat the body with the mind since 'it is not competent for a mind that is or has been evil to treat anything well'. What is required is a philosophical physician who has been trained from childhood to philosophize and who possesses the idea of justice and virtue. Such a philosopher-physician would be able to combine health and justice in the Republic.

The expulsion of the physicians as chimerical is succeeded by their return as guardians. Indeed, it is precisely their ability to overcome chance and necessity by means of *technē* that qualifies them for the task of legislation. The latter is the supreme *technē* but is now applied not in the case of the life and death of an individual, but with respect to the life and death of the Republic. Socrates accordingly calls for the establishment by law of 'an art of medicine' in conjunction with the institution of justice. In the Republic the philosopher-physician will combine the arts of medicine and legislation to ensure the life of the Republic against the attrition of chance and necessity. This will require them to apportion life and death: 'these arts will care for the bodies and souls of such of your citizens as are truly well-born, but those who are not, such as are defective in body, they will suffer to die, and those

who are evil-natured and incurable in soul they will themselves put to death'
(III 410a). The philosopher-physicians' care for the total health of the Republic
requires them to decide who will die and who will be born, according to the
knowledge of the just and the possession of the *techne* sufficient to execute
this knowledge.

The Platonic fusion of knowledge and *techne* in the philosopher-physician
may be understood as an answer to the question of tragedy. The latter
concerns the limits of human action and skill in the face of chance and
necessity. The philosopher's knowledge of the true and the just and the
physicians' possession of the *techne* required to cheat nature combine to
produce the legislator or precursor of Nietzsche's philosophical physician. Yet
the legislator who would overcome tragedy must also be an artist, able to
dissemble the legislation and make the art of legislation appear as an aspect
of necessity. Ultimately, Plato brings together knowledge, *techne* and art
in a comprehensive overcoming of tragedy, a fusion which is subsequently
both welcomed and refused by Nietzsche. However, the latter left open the
question of the place of tragedy in the modern metaphysical culture of popular
science, whether it be confined to art or whether it could find a place within
the prevailing 'faith in science'.

Chance, necessity and *techne*

Then destiny and its own inborn urge took control of the world again and
reversed the revolution of it.

– Plato, *Statesman* 272e

The intertwining of chance and necessity which drove the action of tragedy
continued to haunt Plato in spite of his attempt to resolve the tragic condition
by means of *techne*. In tragedy the attempt to master fate through *techne*
provoked collision and catastrophe while in Plato there emerges the promise
that fate can be mastered through knowledge and skilful action. This promise
remains haunted by the possibility of *hubris* – that the *techne* of the philosopher-
physician is always qualified, whether by the absolute master necessity or by
chance. Indeed, Plato's attempt to smother tragedy initiates a classically tragic
predicament in which the technical alleviations of chance and necessity defer
only to intensify the tragic crisis.

In Books IV and X of the *Laws*, 'The Athenian' compasses the entirety of
being – past present and future – within the limits of chance, necessity and
techne. This predicament of being is presented most clearly in X 888e, where
techne is placed between the necessity of nature and chance:

we are told, you know, that whatever which comes, has come, or will come into existence is a product either of nature [*phusei*], or of chance [*tuche*], or of art [*technē*]. (X 888e)

Technē is thus exercised within the tragic predicament of necessity and chance, and yet the estimation of its capability is far from unambiguous. Across Books IV and X *technē* is at once capable of arresting the catastrophic play of chance and necessity while remaining ineluctably subject to its rhythms. At stake in this indecision surrounding *technē* is the very possibility of a legislator, especially a legislator such as the one proposed in the *Republic* in the guise of the physician.

In Book IV of the *Laws* (709a–c) Plato has the Athenian speculate on the threat to legislation posed by chance: 'I was on the brink of saying that man never legislates at all; our legislation is the work of chance and infinitely various circumstance' (709a). Innovations may be forced on us by disease or environmental conditions, provoking the thought that 'no law is ever made by a man, and that human history is all an affair of chance' (709b). Such a view of chance converts it into its opposite, necessity, since 'God is all, while chance and circumstance, under God, set the whole course of life for us' (709c); chance, in other words, becomes the law or 'ultimate legislator' subjecting on occasion even the Gods. Plato then introduces a third element into this play of opposites: 'Yet we must allow for the presence of a third and more amenable partner, *technē*' (709c). The exercise of the third is apparent not only in legislation, but also in 'seafaring, navigation, medicine or strategy' (709b) which is the knowledge of contingency or, the same thing, the knowledge of how to propitiate necessity, namely 'what form of fortune to pray for' (709d). Here *technē* seems able to overcome the tragic predicament of chance and necessity, offering the possibility of orientation and eventually propitiation.

In Book X, 'The Athenian' ironically entertains the position that *technē* is feeble before chance and necessity, maintaining that 'all the grandest and fairest of things are products of nature and chance, and only the more insignificant of *technē*' (889a). There follows a reprise of the argument from the *Republic* against mimetic art, those 'certain toys' such as painting and music which only imitate nature and are 'as perishable as their creators' (889d). To these may be added the productive arts such as medicine, husbandry, gymnastics and perhaps statesmanship which 'lend their aid to nature' but which are nevertheless subject to it. In the final analysis even these are 'unreal' because, like their makers, they are subject to death, unlike chance and necessity which preside over life and death.

The limits to *technē* drawn by chance and necessity legislate even over legislation, which is but a *technē*. It may lend its aid to nature but will eventually succumb to it. The limits drawn by chance and necessity thus point to the finitude of *techne* and corrode its appearance of invincibility. They also leave in question its claim to have solved the tragic question – the Platonic fusion of knowledge and technique itself yields to the tragedy it would overcome and the project of deciding who is to live and who to die collapses in *hubris*. Perhaps this is the destiny of the metaphysical culture of popular science which succeeded the death of God and which in the shape of genetics has restated the Platonic attempt to inaugurate a legislation based upon the knowledge and *techne* of the philosopher-physician.

Digital Platonism

And having been created in this way, the world has been framed in the likeness of that which is apprehended by reason and mind and is unchangeable, and must therefore of necessity, if this be admitted, be a copy of something.

– Plato, *Timaeus* 29a

The play of chance and necessity takes on its modern form in the language of evolutionary biology and genetics. The tension between Darwin's theory of natural selection and Mendel's study of variation crystallized in the late nineteenth century in the attempt to reconcile the chance of mutation (the source of variants in a population) with the necessity of selection (the elimination of some variants). The biometric analysis of this tension by Galton, Weismann and de Vries was pursued and taken a step further by the Danish biologist and philosopher Wilhelm Ludwig Johannsen. It was he who introduced metaphysical concepts into population genetics and by doing so forged a vocabulary and structure of research which persists in contemporary genetics, even though functionally the science of genetics has developed beyond its confines. It is his metaphysical concepts however which continue to structure the popular science of genetics.

Johannsen's achievement was to transform population genetics and its purely quantitative, functional descriptions of variability into qualities and substances. Functional terms for description of variation (itself an index of the play of chance and necessity) such as 'fluctuation', 'continuous' and 'discontinuous' magnitudes were converted into qualities. This search for metaphysical causes underlying described regularities was owned by Johannsen by his citation of Goethe at the end of his 1903 *Über Erblichkeit in Populationen und in reinen Linien* (*Heredity in Populations and Pure Lines: A Contribution to the Solution of Outstanding Questions in Selection*):

Dich im Unendlichen zu finden
Musst unterscheiden und dann
Verbinden
To find yourself in the eternal
You must first separate
and then rebind.

From the observation of variation in populations Johannsen discerned the presence of a *Typus* or pure line, a discovery which pointed to a distinction between hereditary (necessary) and non-hereditary (chance) variation. In the final pages of his 1903 work, Johannsen cited a number of attempts to give substance to the regularity in variation, whether 'determinant' (Galton), 'hereditary corpuscle', 'hereditary particle' or 'pangene' (de Vries). Mendel himself had used the term *Merkmal* or unit character to describe such regularity but left it metaphysically undetermined. Johannsen also used a functional term drawn from accounting – *Rechnungseinheit* – unit of account, but attempted to give it some metaphysical substance.

This was definitely achieved with the invention of the term 'gene' in the 1909 *Elemente der exakten Erblichkeitslehre* (Jena) (*Elements of an Exact Doctrine of Heredity*). This work was extremely successful (three editions up to 1926) and is accepted to have been the most influential textbook in genetics, giving a vocabulary and structure to the science that were adopted by genetic scientists of the early decades of the century and bequeathed to their successors. The *Elements* move from population genetics to a metaphysics of the gene, not only in the sense of giving the gene substance, but also by situating it within an extremely well-defined Platonic context of argument. The most significant is the distinction between *genotype* and *phenotype*, with the former denoting the totality of genes that inform an organism and the latter how these are manifest in the appearance and actions of the organism. This Platonic distinction remains widely accepted if increasingly challenged in the science of genetics and universally acknowledged in the popular science of genetic culture.

Part of the explanation for the persuasive power of Johannsen's terminology was its combination of biometrics and philosophy. The distinction of genotype and phenotype clarified a number of issues in genetics and opened a field for further investigation of the aetiology of variation. Many of the results of this research have now outlived their original Platonic paradigm, but this has persisted as the framework for the presentation of popular genetics and the experience of its truth. The genotype, as substance, has become the truth of the phenotypical appearance of the body and of its actions (also evident in the distinction between germ line and somatic cell interventions). The ideal truth of the gene is the source of necessity, which is then assailed by chance at the level of phenotypical characteristics.

Such a metaphysics of the gene has the potential to become the source of a new legislation – with philosopher-physicians intervening in the name of a genotypical truth. With the extension of the range of the genotype by sociobiology to include even such phenotypical actions as economic, sexual and criminal behaviour, the Platonic dream of uniting biology and justice begins to seem feasible. However, this is precisely a *Platonic* dream, one which seeks to control the play of chance and necessity (variability) by means of knowledge and *technē*. The result of this new Platonic idol taking the place of the dead God may be a new, resentful dictatorship of popular science, which ignores the genetic scientists' arguments for the value of geno- and phenotypical diversity and uses the Platonic elements of their science to once again make the selection as to who may live and who must die.

The nihilism of genetic culture

When this has been determined, the whole citizen body must do public sacrifice to the destinies and the entire pantheon at large, and consecrate each hymn to its respective god or other patron by solemn libation.

– Plato, *Laws* VII, 799b

One of the extraordinary features of the Christian culture which Nietzsche saw as progressively replaced by a culture of popular science was its underdeveloped conception of *technē*. While it was certainly heir to the Platonic distinction of real and apparent worlds it also developed a sophisticated technology of legislation or, rather, of revenge. Its sacramental and liturgical machinery offered a technology of salvation and damnation which, accompanied by the development of disciplines of the soul, convincingly offered a cure for anxiety in the face of chance and necessity. This structure encompassed both the chance of birth and the necessity of death by creating a sacramental economy of reward and punishment which alleviated anxiety. However, the death of God and the twilight of this structure created a form of hyper-Platonism in which knowledge, *technē* and legislation reunite in a nihilistic culture which has difficulty in recognizing the sources of its own anxiety.

The anxiety characteristic of this culture is one of ambivalence before the imagined ambition to overcome chance and necessity by *technē*. There is on the one hand the anxiety that genetic technology will abolish chance and with it spontaneity; that the manipulation of the genotype will produce *true* human beings who no longer possess the capacity for self-creation through mutation. On the other hand, however, it is precisely with this ability to technologically control who is to live and who is to die that the genotype itself becomes a source of anxiety, since it raises the spectre of the return of necessity in the shape of a future selection. Purified of its capacity to mutate, humanity might find itself unfit to meet a future selection. These projections are not themselves scientific, but effects of the metaphysical and moralistic discourse of popular science which both desires and fears the philosopher-physicians in the contemporary guise of the genetic technologist intervening in the name of health and justice.

The nihilism of genetic culture, what Nietzsche would see as the desire for death located in its refusal to accept the limits of chance and necessity, is now played out at the level of *techne*. It is the issue of the technical working through of the metaphysical truth of the gene which constitutes a major source of cultural anxiety. For precisely this reason it is difficult to see how Christianity, with its underdeveloped conception of *techne*, can provide the necessary 'festivals of atonement'. Perhaps for this reason a reinvention of tragedy is now a possibility, for tragedy possesses a strong conception of *techne* and of its limits. The Platonic festival of the overcoming of the limits of chance and necessity in *techne* may give way to the rebirth of concepts of *hubris*, *fate* and *destiny* through the limits of knowledge, and *techne* may be recognized and once again mourned and celebrated.

12

Liturgies of fear:
Biotechnology and culture

During the 1980s the locus of anxiety regarding the technological threat to the future of human life shifted from nuclear technology in its civil and military guises to biotechnology. In many respects this shift marked the reprise of an earlier, pre-Cold War cultural anxiety focused upon eugenics and biological control of populations. The earlier anxiety was sufficient in the case of Germany (and in other ostensibly democratic societies) to mobilize support for political movements and legislative initiatives dedicated to biologically selecting the character of future human populations. The recent wave of anxiety, in some respects, repeats the unstable fusion of fear and desire that characterized the earlier culture of eugenics, with the difference that the current object of concern is less the survival of a particular 'race' or 'nation' than the human species itself. Developments in biotechnology are perceived to pose a potentially irreversible threat to the future of human life, producing a culture of anxiety, which is framed and debated within the limits of existing religious, political and aesthetic culture – even while exceeding and challenging them.

Whatever the accuracy of the perceived risk to human life posed by biotechnology, the anxiety that surrounds it is proving a central and productive feature of contemporary culture. The positive and negative fantasies that constitute this anxiety manifest themselves in the actions and proclamations of such public institutions as the state, the Church and the medical profession, as well as in art, popular science, film, music and fiction. Together, these internally inconsistent and often competing versions of the biotechnical imaginary aspire to create a culture capable of reflecting upon, assessing and perhaps even managing the risks posed by biotechnological intervention.

The range of perspectives contained within this emergent culture can be illustrated by three ideal-typical responses to the threat of biotechnology: the

1995 encyclical letter of Pope John Paul II, *Evangelium vitae: The Value and Inviolability of Human Life*; the 1992 report of a Working Party of the British Medical Association, *Our Genetic Future: The Science and Ethics of Genetic Technology*; and the work since the late 1980s of the Australian performance artist Stelarc. All three works – religious, scientific and aesthetic – are devoted to framing the risk to the future of human life posed by biotechnology but do so in ways which, while predictably diverse, display some surprisingly convergent features.

Each of these texts and works attempts to frame the threat posed by biotechnology in terms of an existing repertoire of cultural interpretation and resistance but finds that these are themselves transformed in the process. Each presents an imagined future for the human species and from this dream (or nightmare) attempts to frame cultural responses that will either counter or promote the feared/desired future. The ambivalence with respect to the future may be registered in the ambiguous cultural strategies that each of the texts contrives in order to manage the effects of anxiety, strategies which oscillate between the retreat to a religious, scientific-professional, or artistic culture, and the megalomaniacal ambition to inaugurate a wide-ranging cultural revolution.

Evangelium vitae

In the encyclical letter addressed to 'Bishops, Clergy, Monks and Nuns, the Faithful Laity, and all Persons of Good Will', Pope John Paul II called on behalf of the Catholic Church for a 'culture of life' opposed to the prevailing, secular 'culture of death'. The letter defines the culture of death in terms of an extension of the 'crimes and attacks against human life' detailed in a document of the Church Vatican Council (1965), which encompassed a depressing range of violations of the human body and human dignity. After citing the conciliar document, John Paul II extends its list of violations to include recent scientific and technological developments: 'Unfortunately this disturbing panorama, far from being reduced, has been extended: with the new perspectives opened by scientific progress and technology are born new forms of attack on the dignity of human beings' (John Paul II 1995, 8).

The threat posed by biotechnology is thus aligned with those actions identified by the Church as injurious to the flourishing of human life. Biotechnology is a central feature of the 'culture of death', which in the wake of liberal individualism and moral relativism has made it 'difficult to maintain a grasp on meaning of the human, its rights and obligations' (John Paul II 1995, 19). The unqualified value of human life in itself is succeeded by 'the conception of an efficient society' (John Paul II 1995, 20) in which all other values are subordinated to those of economic and political efficiency.

For the encyclical letter, the concept of efficiency is an insidiously disguised exercise of violence on the part of the economically and politically powerful – a form of 'conspiracy against life'. The victims of the 'culture of death' are the 'inefficient', namely the poor, the ill and those with a 'handicap', and the key agents of their persecution are those who decide what constitutes an efficient life. These are above all the scientists and the biotechnologists who pursue their research within the parameters of a naturalistic understanding of human life. Those engaged in genetic research and the development of techniques of artificial reproductions are in the vanguard of this culture, especially insofar as they regard their object of research – human embryos – as raw material for research or technological manipulation:

> Embryos are produced in numbers greater than are necessary for implantation in the wombs of women and these so-called 'surplus embryos' come to be destroyed or used for research which, under the pretext of scientific or medical progress, in reality reduce human life to a simple 'biological material', which may freely be disposed of. (John Paul II 1995, 23)

The encyclical letter declares such research, 'the expanding field of biomedical research legally permitted in some states' (94), as thoroughly inconsistent with human dignity. This is because the 'life and integrity of the embryo' is injured when it is treated naturalistically as raw material for the production of efficient human beings. The document aligns this treatment of the fertilized egg with prenatal screening and selective abortion of 'abnormal embryos'.

The position adopted by the document is consistent with the Church's doctrine regarding the integrity of the human person at the moment of conception. Yet even while reiterating the position sustained by the 'Christian tradition' regarding the spiritual integrity of the embryo, the encyclical letter resorts to citing the 'precious confirmation furnished by modern genetic science' (John Paul II 1995, 90). It is difficult to imagine how the 'individuality' of a fertilized cell as conceived by genetics can accord with the traditional position of the Church regarding the integrity of human personality. For the former, the fertilized cell is individual insofar as it is a product of a singular combination of the genetic heritage of the parents. Unless this moment of chance combination is made the unfathomable, perhaps divine origin of the singular being, then the positions of the Church and genetics are not compatible. Indeed, such individual combinations of genetic material cannot support a definition of the singularity of a human life since such unique combinations characterize all the products of sexed reproduction, not solely those of human beings.

Before the fact of the 'culture of death' – whose scientific ideology seems to have penetrated even the documents of the Vatican – *Evangelium vitae* proclaims a culture of life. Yet this cultural politics is extremely ambiguous and takes a number of forms in the final part of the encyclical letter. At its broadest, the promotion of a 'culture' of life entails a wide-ranging cultural politics entailing a 'general mobilization of conscience and a common ethical effort to put into action a grand strategy in favour of life. Everyone must join together to create a new culture of life' (139). This entails a mobilization of believers and non-believers as well as an institutional cultural politics directed against medical scientists and practitioners (John Paul II 1995, 131), educational practitioners, intellectuals and 'workers in the mass media' (John Paul II 1995, 145).

In this version of the revolutionary culture of life, 'everyone has an important role to play' (John Paul II 1995, 144). Against the hegemony of the culture of death, a broad alliance of forces has to be united to pursue a counter-hegemonic culture of life. But as in the Gramscian cultural politics of the Italian Communist Party, whose experience uncannily informs this document, the dangers of a sectarian retreat of the true believers to their own churches, or party cells, are omnipresent. Consequently, alongside the calls for a broad cultural politics can be found those recommending a retreat to the narrow, sacramental culture of the Church and the 'celebrating of the liturgical year' (John Paul II 1995, 125). In many respects, the pursuit of both a grand and a modest cultural strategy has been a characteristic of the Church and ecclesiology since Augustine's description of the two cities in the *City of God*. In the case of biotechnology, the implications even for believers are so considerable that the Church's universal mission is accentuated, almost to the point of reducing to insignificance its sectarian mission of providing a sacramental liturgy for the benefit of believers. This tension is evident in the appeal to the evidence of genetics, which marks an attempt to mediate between the Church's sacramental role and the terrain of secular ideology (genetic science) with which it must engage if it is to pursue a broader cultural strategy.

Evangelium vitae recognizes the role of the medical professions as central to any cultural politics of life:

> These professions serve and protect human life. In today's cultural and social context in which the science and art of medicine risk losing their native ethical dimension, they may be occasionally strongly tempted to transform themselves into tools for the manipulation of life or even into the workers of death. (John Paul II 1995, 131)

The encyclical letter reminds medical practitioners of their ethical obligations under the Hippocratic Oath, but the force of this oath has already been considerably qualified in modern medical practice. This is recognized in the British Medical Association's (BMA) working party report (1992), *Our Genetic Future: The Science and Ethics of Genetic Technology*, which addresses and embodies many of the concerns of the Papal encyclical letter.

Our Genetic Future

Our Genetic Future begins in a similar way to *Evangelium vitae*, except that the spectre of the body and soul threatened by sin is succeeded by that of the physical body beset by genetic illness. The threat to life posed by the 'culture of death' is in its turn replaced by a culture of ignorance, which surrounds gene therapy. The culture of ignorance, and thus, at least for this enlightenment document, of anxiety, produces the typical effects of uncritical support and uncritical rejection of biotechnology. In the face of such widespread 'ignorance' and anxiety, the report maintains that the increased knowledge of genetics and a broader diffusion of its results will create a culture or community capable of making informed assessments of the risks involved in a given genetic therapy. However, this enlightenment confidence in the liberatory potential of knowledge is qualified by a sceptical undertone that doubts whether sufficient knowledge will ever be attained to make an accurate prediction of the potential effects of a particular genetic intervention.

The BMA report provisionally resolves this potentially paralyzing ambiguity by postulating that 'biotechnology and genetic modification are in themselves morally neutral. It is the uses to which they are put that create dilemmas' (British Medical Association 1992, 4). Yet this neutrality is almost immediately qualified by the self-evident admission that the increase in biological knowledge and its biotechnical application will create 'some new ethical dilemmas' but their main effect will be 'to magnify existing ethical problems in medicine' (5). Here the BMA follows the same strategy as the Vatican, regarding the developments in biotechnology as on balance intensifying existing problems rather than creating new ones. However, this stated view is qualified on several occasions throughout the document when it appears as if the new biological knowledge will indeed create unprecedented ethical dilemmas. The ambiguities in the text offer a clear example of what Adorno and Horkheimer (1979) described as the 'dialectic of the enlightenment', that is to say, the way in which the promise of liberation offered by science creates new and novel forms of subjection.

Underlying the argument about the intensification of existing 'ethical dilemmas' is the deeper concern over the possibility of ever accumulating sufficient knowledge to minimize the risk produced by the same increase in knowledge. If the dilemmas remain the same, and are only magnified by the increase in knowledge and its application, then it may theoretically be possible in the future to gain sufficient knowledge to minimize the risks of its technological application. Yet if the very increase in knowledge and its application produces new areas of risk, then the pursuit of knowledge becomes at best asymptotic, at worst catastrophic. It may never be possible to achieve sufficient knowledge to outweigh the risks generated by the technological applications of existing stocks of knowledge; indeed, scientific discoveries may exponentially increase risk, making it potentially unimaginable. As the BMA's report ingenuously admits, 'no one is yet [sic] in a position to forecast accurately either the benefits or the risks from some of the developments of genetic modification' and 'the totality of scientific knowledge which we would like to have available when making judgements about the future is rarely [sic] available' (British Medical Association 1992, 5). It may well be that the deficit of knowledge available for making assessments of risk (judgements of the future) is paradoxically enhanced by the very increase in knowledge.

In the light of this fundamental dilemma of scientific knowledge the 'challenge which faces us' of how 'to achieve an optimal future: one which maximises the benefits of genetic modification and minimises the harms' (British Medical Association 1992, 4) is more complex than can be answered in a cost-benefit analysis. Yet any possible objection to the principle of pursuing genetic research as such, a position which is approached in *Evangelium vitae* in the name of the 'totality of *theological* knowledge' is pre-emptively neutralized by the claim that biological research and biotechnology is in itself ethically neutral, regardless of how it is conducted or its potential effects. Thus, for example, the 'abuse' of prenatal diagnosis – which 'can be used to prevent children being born with seriously incapacitating disease' (it is not clear from this whether they will be born without disease or not born at all) – is cultural and not generated by the research and technology. Nevertheless, the report finds it necessary to elaborate a principle that can serve as a criterion for assessing levels of future risk, not to an individual but to a population conceived as the species as a whole.

For this principle, the report has to resort to the distinction commonplace in popular genetics between genotype and phenotype. The distinction was first elaborated by the Danish geneticist Wilhelm Ludwig Johannsen not only better to describe the phenomena of descriptive population genetics, but also to provide a metaphysical legitimacy to the descriptive science of genetics (see Chapter 11 of this volume). By introducing a platonic distinction between timeless essence and time-bound appearance, Johannsen was able to confer metaphysical dignity upon the 'science' of genetics, making it into the practice of neutral scientific investigation and separating it from the less-than-neutral ideological positions of some of its other earlier eugenic practitioners such as Galton. In addition, the distinction serves many further purposes, notably that of inserting genetics within a powerful paradigm of religious and scientific experience. The axiom of a genotype or genetic substance underlying but separate from the phenotype or appearances provided a potential terminus for the pursuit of genetic knowledge as well as moral even theological legitimation for genetic researchers and biopolitically oriented politicians.

The recommendations proposed by the report all assume the legitimacy of the axiomatic distinction between geno- and phenotypes, translated into the therapeutic correlate of germ and somatic cell therapies. In the case of gene therapy, this translates into the ban upon 'interfering with DNA in egg cells or spermatozoa (germline therapy), as in the production of transgenic animals' ('at least in the foreseeable future') but support for 'altering genes in particular tissues of the body (somatic cell gene therapy)' (British Medical Association 1992, 116). The latter affects only the individual subject of therapy, while the former is bequeathed to subsequent generations and thus poses an incalculable risk. The report shies away from such risk on the grounds that interventions may prove irreversible and produce unanticipated effects in future generations (British Medical Association 1992, 231).

On occasion, the report seems to qualify the distinction, but only tangentially. Yet if it were to remain consistent with its broad enlightenment premises, then it should assume that any defect in current germline therapy will be corrected in future generations by vastly improved genetic knowledge. Furthermore, biological risk does not simply involve an individual organism but the interaction between organism and environment. Somatic cell interventions are also capable of producing catastrophic effects in their interaction with the environment, but in the present and without the (questionable) insurance policy of the superior knowledge of future generations. In this light it would appear as if somatic cell therapy potentially holds greater risk than germ line. Whether it does or not, what is important is the point that acceptance of the distinction between somatic cell and germline therapy as a criterion for assessing risk is itself a decision fraught with risk.

Our Genetic Future is beset by ambiguity, notably in its view that genetic research and its biotechnical applications are culturally neutral, while at the same time posing a fundamental threat to existing culturally founded understandings of the body and human life. The existence of the document itself marks an attempt to address a cultural anxiety with the enlightenment panacea of improved knowledge. Yet the attempt to create an informed culture cannot go so far as to question its own premises, and so becomes apologetic, seeking to minimize the risk already taken in genetic research and its therapeutic applications by neutralizing their impact. The report concludes with a dual cultural strategy similar to that adopted by the Vatican in *Evangelium vitae*: ignorance rather than sin has 'given rise to fear and opposition to new developments' (227), which should be countered by the creation of an 'informed' popular culture of genetics:

> The scientific community, both in academia and commerce, has a duty to inform the general public of new developments in the applications of genetic modification in a manner comprehensible to lay people. Schools, radios, television, and publishers of books, journals, and newspapers also have an important role to play in achieving this end. (228)

At the same time as informing the public about the science of genetics, the report recommends that scientists and medical practitioners be informed of 'the link between the ethics and the practice of medicine' (228). The cultural strategy involves remedying both the knowledge deficit of the lay public and the ethical deficiency of the medical profession. The title *Our Genetic Future* consequently expresses the aspiration of creating a community of compromise between the future feared by the lay public but desired by the scientific and medical professions: the grounds of the compromise are established through an exchange between the professions' knowledge and the public's ethical *sensus communis*. The very terms of this exchange are unfortunately endangered by the threat that the increase in knowledge may produce unprecedented dilemmas, which render the ethical culture of the community inflexible or obsolete. In this case, the perplexity of the ethical culture is supposed to be remedied by the increase in knowledge, an unconvincing appeal to what Nietzsche described as the new religion following the death of God, namely, 'faith in science'.

Fractal flesh

One of the leading practitioners of 'faith in science' is the Australian performance artist Stelarc. Since the late 1980s his work has moved increasingly towards a quasi-liturgical staging of the possible features opened by developments of biotechnology. Performances such as the 1986 and 1990 *Amplified Body, Laser Eyes and Third Hand*, the 1992 *Host Body/Couples Gestures: Event for Virtual Arm, Robot Manipulator and Third Hand* and the recent *Fractal Flesh* explore the possibilities of prosthetically reorganizing the body and redefining the limits and character of human life. In these works, Stelarc reorganizes the body's flows of information by linking his stomach muscles with motor prostheses such as a third arm and in the later work with remote signals from the Internet processed through STIMBOD software (see Armstrong 1996, 24–7).

In both the work and theoretical reflections upon it, Stelarc stages a faith in science as uncompromising in its formulation as the opposed position of the Vatican in *Evangelium vitae*. His deliberately clumsy prostheses are deliberate liturgical anticipations of a transformation of human life through the micro-prostheses made possible by developments in nanotechnology. The possibility of technologically manipulating molecules and atoms – producing self-replicating machines that operate at a molecular level – promises to transform the human body, making it the host of micro-technological devices, which can effect changes not only at the level of the cell, but also at the level of the proteins that make up the cell. The locus of Stelarc's work is the organism and not the genetic code informing its reproduction. Indeed, Stelarc seems to refuse the distinction between information and organism, which informs genetics and the medical distinction between somatic and germline cell therapies. By turning the external prostheses already ubiquitous in human life into the interior of the body and imagining them operating at a sub-cellular level, he envisages the possibility of a totally prosthetic body which would no longer be subject to the limits of human life: 'Thus life would no longer commence at birth and end with death! Life would become a digital experience and no longer a development, a maturation and a decline as in an analogue experience' (Stelarc 1992, 28). This is a view of the future which embraces and takes to an extreme the tendency, feared in the encyclical letter and discreetly overlooked in the BMA report, of the human body becoming the raw material of technological manipulation.

Stelarc's work performs an uncompromising inversion of the Christian view of the value of life and the uniqueness of the individual. In a gesture of extreme naturalism he imagines the technological reorganization of the body made possible by biotechnology. He imagines, for example, the creation of a 'human' skin capable of photosynthesis:

> With such a skin we would no longer have need of a mouth to chew, of a throat to swallow, of a stomach to digest, of lungs to breathe. We would be able to leave the human and replace useless organs with technologies. Ha-ha-ha-ha-ha-ha-ha-ha-ha-ha-ha! (Stelarc 1992, 29)

By driving the logic of biotechnology to its inhuman extreme, Stelarc affirms both its ultimate tendency and the modern aesthetic fantasy of a *Gesamtkunstwerk* in which the human body becomes the raw material of an irreversible scientific and aesthetic reorganization. As a consequence of his extreme naturalism, the future imagined by Stelarc is devoid of risk. If the human being and human life are simply particular forms of organized matter, then their transformation or even destruction is a matter of indifference. This is expressed in his view that the process of evolution ends with the development of biotechnology:

The end of the Darwinian concept of evolution through organic change. From now on, with nano-technology, mankind can absorb technology. Thus the body must no longer be considered as the seat of the spirit or as the instrument of human relations but must be considered as a structure. Not as an object of desire, but as an object to be redesigned. (Stelarc 1992, 27)

Extreme naturalism combined with the ambition to produce a *Gesamtkunstwerk* thus gives rise to a secular eschatology of the end of the human body.

The staging of the ultimate direction of tendencies feared in the Vatican document and informing that of the BMA is also dedicated to the formation of a culture. Stelarc regards his work as provoking a wide-ranging cultural debate by means of the liturgical staging of a possible future *in extremis*:

There are of course social, ethical, and religious arguments to oppose to what I am proposing. But these ideas are the result of what I am doing. At first these are not clearly ideas easy to accept. When I began to have these sort of ideas I also questioned myself about their problematic nature. But they are my contribution. (29)

The view that the work of art can provoke wide-ranging debate and contribute to the formation of a culture is questioned by the location of a Stelarc's practice within the institution of avant-garde art. While his work goes further than any other in using a fantasy of biotechnology to challenge the limits of art and aesthetic reflection, it still remains within the view of art as effecting an aesthetic transformation of life, which has informed avant-garde theory and practice since its beginnings in Schiller's *Letters on Aesthetic Education* (1796). The solemn liturgy of Stelarc's performances anticipates a future in which the human body itself, and not just this exemplary human body of the artist, will have become an object of technological and artistic manipulation.

Evangelium vitae, Our Genetic Future and *Fractal Flesh* all attempt to frame the threat to human life posed by biotechnology in terms of existing cultural codes, whether those of religion, medical professional ethics or avant-garde art, but in each case the codes are themselves challenged and transformed. Each of these responses to biological research and its biotechnical applications attempts to create a culture capable of negotiating the risk perceived to be posed by biotechnology. In each case, moreover, this culture is anticipated in liturgical terms, as a staged transformation of the meaning of everyday life by the implications of biotechnology.

At the one extreme, the Papal encyclical letter asserts the uniqueness of an individual human life in the face of its biological transformation into a naturalistic combination of genetic information and proteins. However, even this extreme formulation of the uniqueness of human life finds itself appealing to the evidence of genetics, thus undermining the purity of its own position. With this, the encyclical letter approaches the position of the British Medical Association Working Party, which attempts to find a compromise position between a naturalist and a religious-moral understanding of human life. Stelarc's position, finally, is located at the affirmative extreme of naturalism, where the human body is conceived technologically, and life is considered as a 'digital' rather than an 'analogue' experience.

The differences in positions adopted by the Church, the BMA and the avant-garde artist regarding the understanding of the future of human life are reflected in their cultural strategies. The encyclical letter establishes a Manichean opposition between the cultures of life and death, regarding future developments of biotechnology as representing an absolute danger to human life. The response is ambiguous, with a militant call for cultural politics (or a cultural crusade) dedicated to creating a new civility immediately tempered by a call for a retreat of believers to the arms of the Church and the celebration of the liturgical year. The British Medical Association's document is also ambiguous, staking compromise positions on both the tension between genetic research and its therapeutic applications and that between the ethical culture of the community and the scientific culture of the profession. The key to the compromise is increased knowledge, so the report concludes by urging the creation of a cultural and institutional climate favourable to continued research and technological development. Stelarc's position, at the extreme opposite pole to that of the Church, inversely replicates its stance. The future is imagined eschatologically as the end of evolution in the realization of a new form of post-human life, although the cultural strategy adopted by the artist is strangely liturgical, performing a small anticipation of the future in the secular retreat of the art world.

Between them, the three documents bear witness to the diverse ways in which contemporary culture positions the risks posed by biotechnology. They show both the extent to which this culture is inconsistent and internally divided, as well as the ways in which the various fantasies of the future at risk affect each other. Not only do all the texts show the ways in which religious, professional/moral and aesthetic discourses borrow from each other, but also the ways in which together they mark the creation of a divided but creative culture which stages and reflects upon the anxieties that drive and motivate its development.

13

Life and aesthetic pleasure

The ubiquity of the concept of life in Kant's *Critique of Judgement* has been accompanied by a striking absence of any critical discussion of it.[1] Not only is 'life' put under direct and sustained scrutiny in the largely ignored *Critique of Teleological Judgement* but it also directs, or rather disrupts, the progress of the argument in the *Critique of Aesthetic Judgement*. Pleasure in the beautiful is there defined in terms of the 'feeling of life' or 'a feeling of the furtherance of life' (*CJ* 5:204, 244). The critical neglect of Kant's concept of life not only obscures many aspects of his account of aesthetic pleasure but serves also to mask a fundamental shift in the critical philosophy between the first and the third *Critiques*, one that Kant himself was reluctant openly to acknowledge. This involved the movement away from the representational model of consciousness that dominated the first *Critique* to the more dynamic and corporeal model of vital experience that emerges episodically in the third. It is a shift signalled by a change in the conduct of the critical argument from a juridical concern with the legitimacy of possessing representations to what might be described as an economic concern with the distribution (promotion and hindrance) of the forces that constitute life. This shift entailed the extension of the dynamic concept of matter to life itself and, while providing a solution to the riddle of aesthetic pleasure, raised for Kant the spectre of hylozoism and with it, for him, the death of philosophy.

Kant's growing realization that the concept of life troubled the representational model of consciousness can be traced through the pre-critical *Lectures on Metaphysics*, but it is only in the third *Critique* that he admits its full implications. Yet even here the concept emerges episodically alongside and in competition with the representational model, occasionally even grafting itself on to and scrambling the language of representation. This process of interruption and scrambling is most evident in Kant's discussions of aesthetic pleasure, where the nature of the experience described most resists the representational model of consciousness. Kant's analysis of aesthetic pleasure has always provoked problems for understanding the critical philosophy, seeming to point to an experience that resists formalization but which nevertheless can be broken down into an analogue of the table of categories. It will be suggested that the difficulty with aesthetic pleasure stems from the relationship Kant insists upon between it and a non-representational concept of life.

Three important *loci* in the *Critique of Judgement* for the alignment of aesthetic pleasure and life are to be found in §§1, 23 and 29. The first, at the very beginning of the 'Analytic of the Beautiful' (§1), offers a fine example of Kant's scrambling of the language of representation by a concept of life that exceeds it. Kant begins by distinguishing between the cognitive representation of a 'regular, purposive building' and the 'conscious representation' of it attended by 'a sensation of delight' (*CJ* 5:204). His analysis of the latter – the debut of aesthetic pleasure – constitutes one of the most obscure sentences in the third *Critique*. In it the non-cognitive representation at issue 'is tied [*bezogen*] wholly to the subject, indeed to the feeling of life itself, under the name of the feeling of pleasure and displeasure'. The latter feeling 'grounds a quite particular capacity for distinguishing and estimating' that compares 'the given representation in the subject with that whole capacity for representations of which the *Gemüt* in feeling its state, becomes conscious' (*CJ* 5:204). The transfers carried out in this passage by means of the conjunctives 'tied', 'founds' and 'compares' are dizzying: the representation is referred to the subject and the feeling of life, the latter to the feeling of pleasure and displeasure and this in turn to a capacity of discrimination that returns the original representation to a comparison with the 'capacity' of representation of which the *Gemüt* (a term inconsistently translated as 'mind' or 'soul' but having a far more complex meaning that will emerge below) becomes conscious when feeling its condition.

Before referring this movement of representation to an aporetic reflexivity it would be well to look at the other passages aligning life and aesthetic pleasure. In §23, the first section of the Analytic of the Sublime, Kant distinguishes between the satisfaction provided by the beautiful and the sublime in terms of a dynamics of vital forces. While the beautiful 'directly brings with it a feeling of the furtherance of life', the sublime provokes an 'indirect' pleasure in 'the feeling of a momentary checking of the vital powers and a consequent stronger outflow of them' (*CJ* 5:244–5). The difference in the modality of the pleasures arises from the immediate promotion of the feeling of life produced by the beautiful and the interruption and subsequent reactivation of vital forces by the sublime. What remains unexplained is the feeling of life or vital force itself and what it might mean for it to be promoted or hindered.

The term 'feeling of life' is common to both §1 and §23, but it is not used in the same sense in the two passages. In the first passage it is couched in the language of representation and aligned with terms such as 'subject', 'faculty of distinction' and 'whole faculty of representations' (*CJ* 5:204), while in the second it is inseparable from the language of dynamics. While a linking argument between the two passages might be contrived in terms of the feelings of pleasure and pain and direct/indirect pleasure, this would not fully explain the operations of the feeling of life and thus leaves unexplained the very aesthetic pleasure that is the focus of the analysis.

The chase of the 'feeling of life' is sent off in yet another direction by the reference in §29 where Kant explores the different effects sensible and intelligible representations can have on 'the feeling of life'. Referring ambiguously to Epicurus, he concedes that 'all *gratification* or *grief* may ultimately be corporeal' for the reason that 'life without a feeling of bodily organs would be merely a consciousness of existence, without any feeling of well-being or the reverse, i.e. of the furthering or the checking of the vital powers' (*CJ* 5:277–8). Here life is tied to the bodily organs and the feeling of corporeal well-being to the promotion of the vital powers. Kant continues with the intriguing definition that 'the *Gemüt* is by itself alone wholly life (the principle of life itself), and hindrances or furtherances of it must be sought outside it and yet in man, consequently in union with his body' (*CJ* 5:278). The *Gemüt* is identified with life, but the dynamic of life is located inside and outside man, consequently in the body which for Kant seems to be simultaneously interior and exterior.

The third passage adds to the previous pair the thoughts that the *Gemüt* is life and that promotion and furtherance of it involve the body. From this it may be seen that the *Gemüt* forms the link between the discussion of representation in §1 and that of vital dynamics in §§23 and 29. In the former, when the *Gemüt* is affected by its condition it becomes aware of the whole faculty of representations. This awareness permits a given representation to be compared with the whole faculty through the discriminations provided by the feeling of pleasure and pain. Yet these in their turn are but the name given to the 'feeling of life'. If the results of §§23 and 29 are factored into this account the result is even more confusing: in these the *Gemüt* is life, and pleasure and pain the effect of its promotion or hindrance. Perhaps pleasure and pain are diagnostic aids for assessing the impact of a given representation on the life of the organism, but this would require a very special concept of representation which would be governed less by its relation to an object than to the feeling of life in general. If not, there seems no obvious way of reconciling the accounts founded in representation and in vital dynamics.

It is hard to avoid the suspicion that the difficult linkage between the concept of life and aesthetic pleasure indicates a fault line running across Kant's philosophy. The suspicion is both confirmed and complicated by an analysis of the origins of these concepts and arguments in Kant's earlier work.

The pre-occupations that surface in the third *Critique* may certainly be traced to the lectures on anthropology and theology,[2] but more revealingly to the *Lectures on Metaphysics*, appearing in an already developed state as early as *Metaphysik L1* from the mid-1770s (*LM* 17–106; 28:195–301). From this and later transcripts of Kant's *Lectures on Metaphysics* it can be shown that the discussions of life in terms of representation and dynamics emerged from different parts of the lecture course and were set in different argumentative contexts and directed to very different ends. The tension between them was intensified when they were brought into proximity with each other as in the analyses of aesthetic pleasure.

Kant lectured on metaphysics according to Baumgarten's *Metaphysics*, a text officially approved for instruction in the Prussian universities.[3] Baumgarten was a follower of the influential early Enlightenment philosopher Christian Wolff and was orthodox in most respects except in his view of the relationship between reason and sensibility. In this he was closer to Leibniz than to Wolff, maintaining a continuum between sensibility and reason and claiming that sensible knowledge is not simply the corruption of rational knowledge but has its own *aesthetic* perfection. Baumgarten illustrated these laws by means of the example of art in his *Reflections on Poetry* (*Meditationes philosophicae de nonnullis ad poema pertinibus;* 1735) and his incomplete *Aesthetica* (1750–8).[4] In the *Metaphysics* he largely follows the Wolffian architectonic established in Wolff's *Rational Thoughts on God, the World and the Human Soul as Well as Things in General* (originally published in 1719), which organized the materials of metaphysics according to the headings of ontology ('things in general'), cosmology ('the world'), empirical and rational psychology ('the soul') and theology ('God'), a pattern that persisted into Kant's first *Critique*. The main discussions of life and aesthetic pleasure are to be found in the commentaries on empirical and on rational psychology. The former consists of a description of the parts and functions of the representational power of the human soul according to cognition and appetition while the latter considers rational attributes of the soul such as its relation to the body and its immortality. The character and extent of Kant's discussion of empirical as opposed to rational psychology shows his preference for the former, as does his carrying over of much of its material into his lectures on anthropology and theology.

The extended commentary on Baumgarten's discussion of the appetitive faculties and functions of pleasure and displeasure (*Metaphysica*, §§655–62), recorded in *Metaphysik L1* (mid-1770s) and later transcripts such as *Metaphysik Mrongovius* (1782–3) and *Metaphysik Vigilantius* (1794–5),[5] can be identified as the matrix of the link between pleasure, representation and life established in §1 of the *Critique of Judgement*. The transcript of the *Lectures on Metaphysics* from the 1770s anticipates the *Critique* in proposing a 'faculty for distinguishing things according to the feeling of pleasure and displeasure, or of satisfaction and dissatisfaction' apart from the faculty of cognition (*LM* 62; 28:245). It serves as a supplementary faculty insofar as it is interested in the affective sense of representations already given by the cognitive faculty – as a faculty of sense it relies on the cognitive faculty for its representations: 'All pleasure and displeasure presupposes cognition of an object' (*LM* 62; 28:246). However, the predicates pleasure and displeasure do not refer to the object of representation, but rather to 'the faculty in us for being affected by things' (*LM* 62–3; 28:246). At this point Kant insists on departing from Baumgarten's view that pleasure is the outcome of the sensible perception of a perfection, thus establishing the position presented over a decade later in §1 of the *Critique of Judgement.*

In *Metaphysik L1* the intent of Kant's disagreement with Baumgarten and the motivation of his original position on pleasure are much more apparent. The difference between his and Baumgarten's position is stated in terms of quality and modality: Baumgarten's aesthetic rests on the quality of an object (its perfection) while Kant's concerns the relation of an object to the subject, in his terms, its modality: 'With pleasure and displeasure what matters is not the object, but rather *how* the object affects the mind' (*LM* 63; 28:246). The faculty of pleasure and displeasure, he continues, distinguishes objects 'not [according to] what is met with in themselves, but rather [according to] how the representation of them makes an impression on our subject, and how our feeling is moved there by [*sic*]' (*LM* 63; 28:246). While the stress upon the modal operation of the faculty illuminates the passage in the third *Critique*, it does not solve the problems of the vital sources of pleasure and displeasure or the nature of the judgement couched in terms of life.

Kant attempts to clarify the modality of pleasure in the next paragraph of *Metaphysik L1*. He states that representations are 'two-fold' – of the object or the subject – which means that they are comparable 'either with the objects or with the entire life of the subject' (*LM* 63; 28:247). The twofold character of the representation is asymmetrical, with objects on the one side and 'the entire life of the subject' on the other. Kant gives an important clue to the modal character of pleasure when he describes pleasure and displeasure as the 'subjective representation of the entire power of life for receiving or excluding objects' or again 'for either most inwardly receiving them or excluding them' (*LM* 63; 28:247). The movement of reception into the power of life, or exclusion from it, mirrors Kant's understanding of matter in terms of the forces of attraction and repulsion.[6] The power of life either attracts and is attracted to the object – so much so that it would incorporate it – or it is repulsed by the object. At this point Kant disappointingly announces that 'More cannot be said of this here' (*LM* 63; 28:247), only to go on and, indeed, to say more, but prefaced by a cautionary elision of objective and subjective cognition with Baumgarten's theory of logical and aesthetic perfection.

In the following two paragraphs of the lectures Kant gives an extended development of what will become the compressed thought of §29 of the *Critique of Judgement*, namely that the *Gemüt* is the life principle. He begins by defining life as the 'inner principle for acting from representations' and then modulates it first into the 'principle of life' and then into 'the entire power of the *Gemüt*' (*LM* 63; 28:247). If a given representation 'harmonizes' with this principle/power of life/*Gemüt* 'then this is *pleasure*'; if, however, it 'resists' the principle/power then 'this relation of conflict in us is *displeasure*' (*LM* 63; 28:247). The account of pleasure here suppresses a stage in the argument revealed in that of displeasure. This is the stage of the receptivity of the representation by life/*Gemüt* which produces harmony and then pleasure just as the resistance and exclusion of a representation produce conflict and thus displeasure. Yet the movement of representation – reception/exclusion – harmony/conflict – pleasure/displeasure remains difficult to follow, given the lack of definition of life itself. Kant replays the argument in reverse: objects are not intrinsically beautiful but only '*in reference to living beings*', a phrase he repeats in order to fix the ground of the predicate '*in the living being*' or that faculty in the living being 'for perceiving such properties in objects' (*LM* 63; 28:247). The *explanandum* – the peculiar faculty of discrimination – has now become the *explanans*, only for it in its turn to be once again explained in terms of the 'agreement or ... conflict of the principle of life with respect to certain representations or impressions of objects' (*LM* 63; 28:247).

The peculiar circularity in the argument between faculty of discrimination, the affects of pleasure and displeasure, and the principle of life seems to arise from treating the life principle as a state with which a representation can harmonize or come into conflict with rather than as a dynamic movement of attraction and repulsion. If life is a given state – as it is whenever the *Gemüt* is described in terms of the faculties of intuition, imagination, understanding and reason – then there is need of a faculty to adjudicate whether a given representation does or does not accord with the organization of the life principle into faculties. However, Kant repeatedly undermines this understanding of life by returning to the view that it is a dynamic process of reception and expulsion.

Such a return is evident in the subsequent paragraph where Kant attempts to sharpen the dynamic view of life already intimated. He begins with another definition. Instead of the earlier definition of life as the 'inner principle for acting from representations' which privileges representation and implicitly objectivity, he now defines life as simply 'the inner principle of self-activity' without privileging representation. Self-activity is governed by an inner principle, and while Kant concedes that this must 'act according to representations', this conformity is now secondary to the dynamics of life (*LM* 63; 28:247). The principle at issue is no longer thought in terms of representation, but in terms of an immanent self-activity which might involve representation but is not defined by it. Kant examines this 'inner principle' more closely, rephrasing the modality of this self-activity – earlier described in terms of reception/expulsion – as the promotion or hindrance of life. While in the earlier paragraph the representation remained important as the spur to the activity of life – it could either be received or expelled – now it simply supplements an existing movement, either promoting or hindering the activity of the life principle. From this point of view the 'feeling of the promotion of life is pleasure, and the feeling of the hindrance of life is displeasure' (*LM* 63–4; 28:247). From this he moves to the more audacious claims, first that pleasure and displeasure are grounds of activity and the hindrance of activity, and then that pleasure 'consists in desiring', displeasure 'in abhorring' (*LM* 64; 28:247). With the introduction of desire the receptive/exclusionary movement returns, but this time not in terms dictated by the digestive movement of reception/ exclusion but in terms of a promotion/hindrance of life which is ultimately determined by the future continuation or cessation of the activity of life itself.

At this point in the development of his argument Kant breaks off and turns instead to an illuminating discussion of the three forms of life: animal, human and spiritual, which he maps on to the distinctions between the agreeable, the beautiful and the good, later to become prominent in the architectonic of the third *Critique*. While this discussion offers some fascinating insights into the motivation underlying the argument of the 'Analytic of the Beautiful', it is notable that in the latter the discussion of life per se all but disappears. It persists in terms of the grades of activity provoked by the agreeable, the beautiful and the good, but the issue of the vital sources of the pleasure so distributed remains shelved. The concept of life will return later in the lecture series in the context of a discussion of death in the section on rational psychology.

The discussion of life and aesthetic pleasure provoked by the commentary on Baumgarten's empirical psychology moved beyond the confines of aesthetic perfection but did not provide a full and satisfactory account of Kant's alternative. Pleasure and displeasure are referred to life, but the concept remains undeveloped. *Metaphysik L1*, however, shows that Kant's views on the subject of life were already highly developed before the critical philosophy. There the argument moved from the comparison of a representation with a static vital principle through a faculty of discrimination to a working of the vital principle, first according to a modality of reception/expulsion and then to one of promotion/hindrance. It is the latter, the second dynamic model, that persists into the third *Critique*, evident both in §§23 and 29, where it supplements the version founded in representation based on a problematic faculty of discrimination proposed in §1.

Kant's position on life and aesthetic pleasure does not show signs of having developed substantially in the subsequent transcripts of his comments on empirical psychology in his *Lectures on Metaphysics*. In *Metaphysik*

Mrongovius from 1782–3 (after the publication of the *Critique of Pure Reason* in 1781), the discussion of life is largely avoided, reduced to one cryptic reference. The assumption that this reflects a change in the content of Kant's lectures rather than the quality of Mrongovius' note-taking is supported by the usually reliable and exhaustive character of Mrongovius' transcript and the omission of the discussion from the transcript of 1790–1, the *Metaphysik L2* (*LM* 297–354; 28:531–94). The transcript from 1794–5, *Metaphysik Vigilantius*, shows evidence of the results of the third *Critique* in its distinction between sensible gratification/pain and reflective pleasure/displeasure, but it avoids the problem of determining the ground of reflective aesthetic pleasure. As in the third *Critique*, so here too Kant refers reflective aesthetic pleasure to the harmony of the *Gemütskräfte* or the notorious free play of the imagination and the lawfulness of the understanding (*LM* 481; 29:1011), which here, as also on occasions in the third *Critique*, masquerades as an *explanans* rather than an *explanandum*. Yet it was already evident in *Metaphysik L1*, as also throughout the *Critique of Judgement* that there is a level of explanation for aesthetic pleasure and displeasure anterior to the harmony of the *Gemütskräfte*.

The development of this level of argument is to be found in the *Lectures on Metaphysics* during Kant's reflections on rational psychology, but here the dynamic conception of life appears in a context quite distinct from that of the lectures on empirical psychology. In his comments on Baumgarten's paragraphs on the state of the soul after death (*Metaphysica*, §§782–91), which address the question of whether the soul will continue to live after the death of the body, Kant offers some fascinating clarifications of his concept of life, but in abstraction from the particular problem of the nature of aesthetic pleasure and displeasure.

Kant's discussion of life in the context of rational psychology is consistent with the discussion earlier in the lecture course of pleasure and displeasure, characteristically clarifying and extending it in some ways while complicating it in others. Life is initially defined as 'a faculty for acting from an *inner* principle, from spontaneity' (*LM* 94; 28:285). This faculty or 'source' that 'animates the body' is described as an *actus*. The *actus* of life animates the matter of the body which is itself 'lifeless' and indeed serves as a 'hindrance to life that opposes the principle of life' (*LM* 94; 28:285). Here matter serves the same function as the displeasurable representation earlier in the empirical psychology, that is, of hindering life. Life itself is an *actus* independent of the body. While the soul is the principle of life, the body is its tool or *organon*. The discussion of rational psychology in the lectures deriving from pre-critical, critical and post-critical stages of Kant's authorship remains faithful to the broad project of Baumgarten's metaphysical textbook. There rational psychology departs from the a priori distinction between two substances – soul and matter – and seeks to combine them in a *commercio*.

Kant's fidelity to the rational metaphysical tradition goes as far as describing the corporeal *organon* as a cart and the *commercio* between soul and body as analogous to that of 'a human being ... fastened to a cart' (*LM*, 95; 28:286). Even given the parody of Plato's *Phaedrus*, the latter analogy is rather surprising, since it might be expected for the soul to occupy the position of the driver rather than the horse, but Kant's analogy is ruthlessly consistent. The cart's motion proceeds from the human being who pulls it: best for that human would be liberation from the cart, but failing that, the lot of the human horse would be improved if 'the wheels on the cart [were] greased' (*LM* 95; 28:287). The effects of greasing or not greasing the wheels are described in terms, familiar to us from another context, of the promotion or hindrance of life: 'if the soul is once bound to the body, then the alteration of the hindrances is a promotion of life; just as motion is easier when the wheels on the cart are greased, although it would be even easier upon liberation from the cart' (*LM* 95; 28:287). Life, or the *actus* of the soul, becomes the motive power of the body, which as 'lifeless matter ... is a hindrance to life' and for which 'a good constitution of the body is also a promotion of life' (*LM* 95–6; 28:287). In this view, death is the maximum promotion of life, being 'not the absolute suspension of life, but rather a liberation from the hindrances to a complete life' (*LM* 96; 28:287).

Although Kant destroyed the foundations of rational psychology in the 'Transcendental Dialectic' of the *Critique of Pure Reason*, he continued to teach the analogy of the human horse and cart. In *Metaphysik Mrongovius* (1782–3), the unfortunate human is even 'welded' to the cart and its death described as the 'promotion of the life of the soul' (*LM* 278; 29:913–14), while in *Metaphysik K2* from the early 1790s (that is, after the publication of the *Critique of Judgement* in 1790) the human is still welded to the cart, but the latter is now significantly described as a 'support' of life and not simply an obstacle to it (*LM* 393–413; 28:753–75 and *LM* 403; 28:763). This modification is taken further in *Metaphysik Vigilantius* (1794–5), reflecting a change in Kant's understanding of life provoked by the composition of the third *Critique*.

Before looking more closely at these changes it is necessary to review the tension between the accounts of life given in the two parts of the *Lectures on Metaphysics* and their persistence into the third *Critique*. The work of the pleasant representation in promoting life in the empirical psychology is undertaken in the rational psychology by the application of grease to the body/ cart that must be dragged forward by the soul. Given the linkage between aesthetic pleasure and the promotion of life pursued in the third *Critique*, the implication here is that the work of art serves as the grease for lubricating the *commercio* between soul and body. This is an intriguing implication, with its possible intimation of a 'materialist aesthetics', but it is not entirely consistent; nor is the further implication that the representation which most promotes life is the one that ends it, although this is admittedly a position not far removed from the characterization of the sublime in the third *Critique*.

The view of promotion and hindrance of life in the lectures on empirical psychology rested on a movement of reception and expulsion wholly inconsistent with the analogy of a rickshaw used in the lectures on rational psychology. The former view implied that this movement is internal to life itself, that life relates to matter in terms of an immanent movement or *actus* of incorporation and expulsion but not in terms of the interaction or *commercio* of distinct substances. The view of life as immanent movement fundamentally questions the opposition between life partaking of the spontaneity of the soul in opposition to the dead materiality of the body and its corollary that the two substances may enter into *commercio* only through representation. While the concept of life developed in the empirical psychology brings together corporeality and consciousness in an expanded *Gemüt*, that of the rational psychology opposes soul to matter.

Kant sketches an outline of his expanded concept of *Gemüt* in the passage from §29 of the *Critique of Judgement* that identifies *Gemüt* with an immanent life principle and suggests that its hindrance and promotion are to be sought 'outside it and yet inside man, consequently in union with his body' (*CJ* 5:278). The body is no longer external dead materiality, fit only to be expelled by life, but the site of the movement of life in receiving and expelling, a movement distributed topologically in terms of an identical inside/outside. While further specification of this concept of the *Gemüt* must be sought outside of the *Critique*, in the *Lectures on Metaphysics* from the 1790s, it is clear that it is quite distinct from any view of the representational 'mind' or 'soul' as the site of *commercio* between opposed material and intelligible substances. The move towards a corporeal concept of life announced in a preliminary way in §29 of the third *Critique* is developed a little further in *Metaphysik K2* with the notion of the body as a support for the soul, but most fully in *Metaphysik Vigilantius*. Here Kant qualifies the tenets of rational psychology by first rehearsing the demonstration that life may be hindered by matter and then moving to a fundamental distinction between '*the principle of life*' and the '*<actu> of life itself*' (*LM* 504; 29:1039). The *actus* is inseparable from the body, not in the sense of being 'welded' to it as its implacable adversary, but as a corporeal manifestation of life – or, to use Kant's word, as *Gemüt*. The cooperation of the body with the *actus* of life 'visibly manifests itself' – makes what is internal external – 'through sensation as the consequence of these actions of life' (*LM* 504; 29:1039). Appropriate to the context, Kant's examples are largely negative, involving the 'sacrifice of powers', such as fatigue (*LM* 504; 29:1039), but the argument also holds for other sensations of life, such as pleasure. In this, too, the *actus* of life visibly manifests itself through the medium of the body, a movement implied in the pleasure of the aesthetic judgement of taste. Here the beautiful representation promotes the actualization of life by a homeopathic dose of the hylozoic union of soul and matter.

In *Metaphysik K2* Kant described hylozoism as 'the death of all philosophy', but this in a context that already foresaw a qualification of the lifeless materiality of the body (*LM* 405; 28:765). The latter only holds if opposed and complemented by a 'principle of life', and not if life is thought as an *actus* or *Gemüt* that for Kant is both inside and outside the body. The externality of the *actus* of life to matter is thus qualified in a way that makes sense of the relation between life and pleasure but at the cost of abandoning the basic platonic structure of the 'philosophy' that would meet its end through hylozoism. This problem tormented the *Opus postumum* where Kant distinguished between matter and living or organic bodies, mainly in terms of the presence of ends and thus of desire in the latter. Yet time after time in the late notes Kant confronts the forces of attraction and repulsion that govern matter with the forces of life, or the movement of organic bodies, only to resist any transition from the first to the second through the interplay or transposition of forces. He insists on viewing living bodies as absolutely spontaneous and governed by ends given by means of representation. The emphasis on the representation of ends necessary to protect philosophy from hylozoism is ultimately destructive of pleasure, perversely locating the promotion of life in death. Even at the end of Kant's authorship, and in spite of his most astute intuitions, the experience of pleasure and its link to the concept of life remained a question that could not be explicitly answered.

Notes

1   Citations of the *Critique of Judgement* (*CJ*) are guided by J.H. Bernard's translation (Kant [1790] 1951) but frequently modify it.
2   See Caygill 1989, chapter 4.
3   See the selections from the *Metaphysica*, in Baumgarten 1983.
4   Baumgarten 1954 and *Aesthetica* in Baumgarten 1973.
5   *LM* 107–286; 29:747–940 and *LM* 415–506; 29:943–1040.
6   See Kant, *The Metaphysical Foundations of Natural Science*.

14

Soul and cosmos in Kant: A commentary on 'Two things fill the mind ...'

Two *things fill the mind with ever new and increasing wonder and awe, the more often and constantly reflection concerns itself with them:* the starry heavens above me and the moral law within me. *I need not seek or intimate them beyond my horizon, shrouded in darkness or clothed in exaltation; I see them both before me and tie them immediately with the consciousness of my existence. The first begins from the place I occupy in the external world of sense, and extends the ties in which I stand into the unfathomable immensity of worlds beyond worlds and systems within systems and then into the limitless times of their periodic motion, their beginning and continuation. The second begins with my invisible self, my personality, and shows me in a world that has true infinity, but is discernible only through the understanding and with which (through which but at the same time with all those visible worlds) I know myself to be tied in a universal and necessary and not just, as there, in a contingent way. The first view of a countless multitude of worlds annihilates my significance as an* animal creature, *which must give back to the planet (a mere point in the universe) the matter from which it came, the matter which is for a little time provided with vital force, we know not how. The latter, on the contrary, infinitely raises my worth as that of an* intelligence *by my personality, in which the moral law reveals a life independent of all animality and even of the whole world of sense – at least so far as it may be inferred from the final destination assigned to my existence by this law, a destination which is not restricted to the conditions and boundaries of this life but reaches into the infinite.* (CPrR 169)

The most-cited sentence from the works of Kant is found in the conclusion of *The Critique of Practical Reason*. Apparently relaxing after the rigours of sustained reflection on the moral law, Kant mused on the 'Two things that fill the Mind ...' Yet this seemingly perspicuous and innocent soliloquy contains within it many layers of significance and points of perplexity that have been overlooked in its celebratory citation. A meditation upon the perplexities of the text offers a point of entry into a Kantian physiology that links soul and cosmos in ways far stranger than would be expected from the author of the paralogisms of psychology and the cosmological antinomies in the 'Transcendental Dialectic' of the *Critique of Pure Reason*. It also provides a point of departure for an examination of Kant's medical philosophy, whose influence on early nineteenth-century romantic medicine and even upon the allegedly anti-romantic pathology of Rudolf Virchow is enormous but still little understood.

The infinite analogy

In order to motivate the close work of commenting upon the paragraph and analysing how it works and what its tropes and terms mean, it might be useful to stress the completely overlooked perversity of Kant's parallel between the 'starry heavens' and the 'moral law'. It is necessary to ask what exactly it was that Kant saw when he looked up at the night sky. From his subsequent description of the heavens in the same paragraph it would appear that Kant saw something that was seen by very few others in his century. From his place in the 'external world of sense' Kant moves from his vision of the stars – 'I see them before me' – to an '*unabsehlich Große*', an unsurveyable magnitude of 'worlds beyond worlds and systems within systems and then into the limitless times of their periodical motion, their beginning and their continuation' (*CPrR* 166). Apart from the evocation of what in the *Critique of Judgement* will be called the experience of the 'mathematical sublime' and beyond the contrasting tropes of worlds *beyond* worlds and systems *within* systems that intimate their periodic motion, the description of the infinite universe is clear and definite. Yet this was very much a deviant view, one for which Giordano Bruno was burnt to death at the stake. Kant is thus comparing the moral law with a deviant and heretical view of universe, one not widely accepted among scientists and philosophers at the time, let alone the general public (and would not be for at least another century), and one that would have been met with sensations of distaste and even horror. The question then arises: why should Kant want to compare the majesty of the moral law that he has just reverently described in the *Critique* with what many contemporary readers would have regarded as an abhorrent and even despised view of the heavens?

One possible approach to an answer lies in the analysis of the aesthetic structure of the sentence and the paragraph that follows it. Following the analysis developed by Kant in the *Critique of Judgement*, it is possible to ask whether the sentence and paragraph obey the rules of the beautiful or the sublime. In the case of the beautiful, one whose logic seems to have been automatically assumed in most readings of the sentence, the relationship between the two terms – starry heavens and moral law – is understood in terms of an analogy. According to section 59 of the *Critique of Judgement* the hypotyposis of symbol and analogy was identified as one of the structures underlying the experience of the beautiful. In section 59, Kant distinguishes between two species of hypotyposis: schema and symbol – both share the generic characteristic of 'presentation' but differ according to mode. The schema presents intuitions to concepts, whereas the symbol presents them to reason 'according to analogy'. In analogy, judgement has a double function, 'first in applying the concept to an object of a sensible intuition, and then, second, in applying the mere rule of its reflection upon that intuition upon quite another object' (*CJ* 222, §59).

As an analogy, the moral law stands in the same relation – applies the same rule of reflection – to the finite subject, as do the starry heavens. In this case, it is infinity which serves as the rule of reflection applied analogically to both the starry heavens and the moral law.

The analogical experience has for Kant a number of specific characteristics. It is usually associated with the beautiful, the analogy being identified etymologically as 'proportion' and in the tradition issuing specifically from Baumgarten, with harmony. For Kant, the beautiful consists in the experience of harmony, whether this is located in the object or, more commonly for Kant, in the harmony of the *Gemütskräfte*. However, when the rule of reflection in question is infinite, then strange things happen to the analogy. Proportion is established on the basis of disproportion – neither infinity being commensurable with the other – and indeed points to an antagonistic relation between the rules of relationship. The analogy of infinity loses its proportioned, harmonic quality and begins to approximate more fully to the sublime. The sublime is characterized by a pulsar movement, described in the *Critique of Judgement* in terms of inhibition and discharge or repulsion and attraction. At infinity, the beautiful becomes sublime, and the movement of the sublime stabilizes in the harmony of the beautiful. Returning to the specific analogy of the conclusion to the *Critique of Practical Reason*, the terms of the analogy are the 'starry heavens' and the 'moral law' and the predominant rule of relation is 'infinity'. Both the starry heavens and the moral law relate to the finite subject as 'things' which 'fill the mind with ever new and increasing wonder and awe'. The analogy is clear, but every term in it is far from being so. We shall return below to what Kant means by 'mind' (*Gemüt*) and the extent to which it is empty and can be filled, as we shall with the by no means self-evident notions of the 'ever new', 'increase' and of course 'wonder and awe'. The analogy also consists in both the moral law and the starry heavens possessing the property of being immediately visible to a finite subject – '*ich sehe sie vor mir*', 'I see them before me'. By virtue of this visibility the finite subject can '*verknüpfe sie unmittelbar mit dem Bewußtsein meiner Existenz*', 'tie them immediately with the consciousness of my existence'. Yet at this point the analogy begins to complicate itself again, especially with the reference to '*Bewußtsein meiner Existenz*', a formula which brings the *Gemüt* back into the equation, 'consciousness of my existence' being one of its defining properties. The complications emerging from the infinite rule of reflection are compounded by the second analogy according to which 'immediate visibility' and 'consciousness of my existence' – the *Gemüt* – forms the governing rule of reflection that sustains the analogy. It is also the *Gemüt* that would be filled by the infinities of the starry heavens and the moral law.

Before examining the meaning of *Gemüt*, it is necessary to look more closely at the work of infinity as a rule of reflection. This requires putting into question the character of the analogy at work in the passage under discussion. The notion that the moral law and the starry heavens are the equivalent terms of an analogy is shaken by the horrific character of the infinite starry heavens that Kant saw before him. In place of the harmonious experience of the beautiful, the analogy between the starry heavens and the moral law emerges as rather more perverse, being driven by a polar opposition between its terms. This experience brings the analogy into the orbit of the sublime, with its pulsatory movement described in the *Critique of Judgement* in terms of a *Hemmung* (inhibition following repulsion) of the vital forces and their *Ergießung* (discharge following attraction) (section 23), a movement which gives increase, since for Kant overcoming an inhibition provokes a greater discharge. Read in these terms, the passage in question may be situated within the corporeal experience of polar pulsation of the sublime rather than the harmonizing experience of the beautiful. The terms of the analogy possess a reversed polarity,[1] with the experience moving between disgust at the infinity of the universe and reverence for the moral law: the *Hemmung* provoked by the disgusting spectacle of the infinity of unlimited 'worlds beyond worlds and systems within systems' enhances the *Ergießung* achieved when the gaze turns to the integrated consistency of the moral law. In this view, consciousness of existence, or *Gemüt*, is 'filled' by 'new and increasing wonder and awe' with each enhanced experience of inhibition and discharge.

Suspending the prejudices of two centuries of reading of this paragraph as a beautiful analogy, it does indeed seem as if it is structured in terms of a sublime pulsation. Indeed, the overall organization of the paragraph is pulsar. Kant provokes a series of pulses between the starry heavens and the moral law that are staged in terms of 'the first' (the starry heavens) and 'the second' (the moral law) and which produce an effect of emptying and filling that, we shall see not coincidentally, echoes that of the *Anfang* and *Fortdauer* of the infinite and repeatedly new universe. This same pulsar movement of 'the two things' 'fills' the *Gemüt* with 'ever new and increasing wonder and awe' precisely in so far as it provokes its *Hemmung* and *Ergießung*. The pulsar experience also takes the form of repulsion, an emptying or shying away of the *Gemüt* before the object, and attraction, the filling of the *Gemüt*, even to the point of overflowing in *Ergießung*.

The first pulsar movement is evident in the successive sentences beginning '*Der erste fängt von ... an*', 'The heavens begin ...' and '*Der zweite fängt von ... an*', 'The moral law begins ...'. The first sentence effects a movement of reduction and limitation – literally *Hemmung*. The place where I stand gazing up at the heavens and whose ties I extend to the universe is rendered insignificant before what Leopardi would call the 'sterminatory' scale of the cosmos. Kant describes this experience of disorientation more vividly in his discussion of the breakdown of measurement in the sublime of section 26 of the *Critique of Judgement*. There he moves from the measurement of a tree by the scale of the human body, to that of a mountain by the tree, to that of the earth by the mountain, to that of the solar system by the earth, to the milky way where the comparative measurement breaks down before '*die unermeßliche Menge solcher Milchstraßensysteme unter dem Namen der Nebelsterne* [the immeasurable set of such milky ways that are called nebulae]'. The breakdown of human measure before the starry heavens would itself be a demoralizing and disorienting experience, one compounded by Kant by adding to the intimations of spatial infinity, the limitless temporal repetitions of the universe. Arriving at this extreme *Hemmung*, where the limitless of the starry heavens disrupts the tranquillity of the stargazer, Kant provokes a shocking switch in polarity, akin to that described with respect to the starry heavens in his essay 'What Is Orientation in Thinking'.

At this point of repulsion and self-loss before the immensity of the starry heavens, Kant summons up the moral law. The latter begins from the invisible self, the 'person' – the stage of development that in the *Religion within the Limits of Reason Alone* is held to succeed animality and humanity (Kant 1960, 21). The point of view of personality reveals a 'true infinity', one implicitly opposed to the 'false infinity' of the starry heavens. The true infinity is discernible by the understanding through the presence of 'universality and necessity' – the fundamental quantitative and modal properties of any legitimate judgement of the understanding according to Kant. In this movement, the repulsion provoked by the false infinity of the starry heavens is countered by the true infinity of personality (here playing the role adopted by imagination in the third *Critique*). Before the starry heavens, consciousness of existence is disrupted by the infinite vastness of the universe and its contingent links with it; from the standpoint of the moral law, however, consciousness of existence is experienced as universal and necessary. In the sublime movement between the two, consciousness of existence is emptied and filled, each time anew and with increase. It is a movement to which Kant, in the *Critique of Judgement*, gives the name 'life'.

In the subsequent two sentences of 'Two things fill the mind ...' Kant augments the pulsar movement of the analogy by repeating it at an enhanced level, at the same time making explicit the links between the analogy and the stages of animate life. The first glimpse of countless world sets 'annihilates my significance as an animal creature'. The extreme case of *Hemmung* annihilates the significance of my animal life in a peculiar way, namely by reminding me that the matter of my animated body must be restituted to the planet: 'the matter out of which it came must be returned to the planet (a mere point in the universe)'. The sight of the starry heavens reminds the stargazer of their mortality and their return to matter. The prospect of this reduction to matter, the annihilation of animal life provokes a small turn in the sentence towards the question of life. The matter of the animate body must be returned to the planet (without increase it would seem) 'which is for a little time provided with vital force [*Lebenskraft*], we know not how'. The sight of the starry heavens intimates the annihilation of this life and the reduction of stargazer to matter but at same time raises the question of the meaning of that life and the mystery of animate matter or 'life'. With this second reflection, nested within the annihilation, the *Hemmung* begins to turn towards *Ergießung*.[2]

From the repulsive intimations of annihilation, loss of animal life, reduction to matter and death provoked by the spectacle of the starry heavens, Kant turns to their opposite. Annihilation of my significance is succeeded by the contrary 'raising of my worth'. The sterminatory sense of the fragility of my matter-bound animal life is succeeded by 'personality' or my worth as an 'immortal intelligence', a sense that reveals a 'consciousness of existence' or life that is 'independent of animality and from the sensuous world'. Yet instead of remaining with this exalted *Ergießung*, Kant begins the turn back towards limitation by qualifying the 'purposive determination of my existence through this law' that is not 'limited to the conditions and limits of life' but reaches into the infinite, with the phrase 'as least in so far as'. The cycle of *Hemmung* and *Ergießung*, repulsion and attraction, is thus set to recommence, as the exaltation of personality begins to be shrouded by the shadows of the limits of animal life.

The recommencement of the movement between the starry heavens and the moral law is part of the ineluctable movement of human life between the repulsion of *Hemmung* and the attraction of *Ergießung*. For the polar opposites of the starry heavens and the moral law oscillate between animality and personality – there is not a direct location of the human in this paragraph. The human is not mentioned since it provides the setting upon which the movement between animality and personality is played out – indeed, the human is this playing out. The *Gemüt* that is filled and emptied by the movement between animality and personality is the human soul, which can never be entirely emptied or filled, but is itself the movement of emptying and filling, the mysterious 'vital force'. Cosmos and the soul are closely linked in this movement, with the starry heavens prompting the gaze 'above me' and the moral law 'within me'. This perplexed gaze, turning in and out of the body, sees itself as at once animal and immortal, is confused in turn by the shadows and the exalted light. Repulsive strophe prompts attractive counter-strophe whose unstable excess provokes repulsive counter-strophe, an unstable polar oscillation oriented towards infinity but ever failing that point where the sublime oscillation would settle into the harmony of the beautiful.

It is precisely such perplexities of the soul that the critical philosophy was supposed to relieve us of. The section of the *Critique of Pure Reason* on the 'System of Cosmological Ideas' – 'The Antinomy of Pure Reason' – showed that the cosmos could not be an object of experience. Why be terrified by the infinite universe in 1786 if it had been shown in 1781 that it could not qualify as an object of experience? The therapeutic contribution of the *Critique* was intended to liberate the soul from concerns about the temporal and spatial beginnings and ends of the universe, its atomic or non-atomic composition, and its implications for freedom. An enlightenment thinker such as Christian Wolff could comfortably link the soul and the cosmos with a phrase such as 'Before we can understand what the soul is … we must first learn what the constitution of the world is', thereby taking for granted that both soul and cosmos were possible objects of experience and thus knowledge (Wolff 1719, section 540). In contrast, Kant's position is far less secure. Disqualifying the cosmos and the soul as objects of experience in the 'Transcendental Dialectic', he acknowledged their peculiar character arising from their links with the infinite. Wolff's understanding of the cosmos as finite permitted it to be an object of knowledge from which could be deduced the knowledge of the soul; Kant's understanding of the cosmos disrupted both its own status as an object as well as that of the soul. What emerges in the *Critique of Practical Reason* is that the universe is a peculiar 'thing' – not a possible object of experience but nevertheless present through the affects of wonder and awe. The universe, like the moral law, is an impossible object of experience that Kant can nevertheless 'see before me'. Perhaps it is this spectral quality of the cosmos that contributes to the uncanny affects it provokes in the soul, abnegation before and exaltation above it. In order to understand this better it is necessary to move the focus of the commentary from the infinite and its sublime analogies to an inquiry into the notion of seeing that which is not a possible object of experience.

Light and the cosmos

The starry heavens are infinite, but within my horizon; neither shrouded in darkness nor exalted they are an object of vision – I see them before me and tie them immediately with 'the consciousness of my existence'. We may return to the question posed earlier of what it was Kant saw when he looked up at the night sky, but now inflecting it from *what* he saw to *how* he saw it. What enabled Kant to see the stars before him if not their light? It is light that linked his perception of the stars and the infinity of the cosmos; light is both of the object – it is that which is shown – and of the subject, being the medium in which it is seen. It is light, also, that allows for the 'immediate consciousness of my existence' that is *Gemüt*, suggesting further that the relationship between light and *Lebenskraft*, the cosmos and the soul, between cosmology and physiology, is more intimate than has been suspected. Kantian 'enlightenment' is not simply a question of knowledge but involves an understanding of the nature of the cosmos and the closely related mystery of the soul or how matter came to be infused with life.

The inquiry into the link between seeing the light of the stars and the 'consciousness of my existence' that it provokes raises again the question of the relationship between soul and cosmos. This is a complex and a little-explored area of Kantian research that reveals a physiological dimension to his thought that, although inconspicuous, continues to inform the critical philosophy. A preliminary outline of the mutual implication of cosmology and physiology hinted at in the 'Two things fill the mind …' passage may be sketched by a reading of the early and much-neglected text, *Universal Natural History and the Theory of the Heavens* (1755), whose conclusion anticipates that of the second *Critique* and the late, and also much-neglected *Opus postumum*. The comparison reveals a startling continuity in Kant's thought regarding the soul and the cosmos that tacitly informs the analogy between the starry heavens and the moral law.

The *Universal Natural History and the Theory of the Heavens* finds Kant looking to the night sky, with Thomas Wright's *An Original Theory and New Hypothesis of the Universe* (1750) in hand. This time he is concerned by the discrepancy between the regularity established in the motions of the planets and the apparent spatial disorder of the stars. The apparent disorder of the stellar skyscape is a function of the Copernican revolution that has bestowed order upon the movement of the erstwhile wandering planets only to set the stars adrift from the 'hollow spheres of the heavens'. For the starry heavens are no longer, as claimed in our passage, 'above us' but all around us. What is more, for Kant, departing from observations on the Milky Way, not only we, but also the stars and even the galaxies are in motion. The scale of the universe is also disorienting, since Kant entertains the conjecture that the Milky Way is just one of a vast number of galaxies and that the visible nebulae might themselves be distant galaxies (or 'world orders'), all of which are in motion. Kant anticipates his observation in the *Critique of Practical Reason* with the thought of the infinity of the cosmos:

> If the greatness of a planetary world edifice, in which the earth as a grain of sand is hardly noticed, moves the intellect into admiration, with what astonishment will one be enchanted if one considers the infinite amounts of worlds and systems which fill the totality of the Milky Way; but how this astonishment *increases* when one realizes that all these immeasurable star orders again form the unit of a number whose end we do not know and which perhaps just as the former is inconceivably great and yet again is only the unit of a new minute system. (*UNH* 108, my emphasis)

From this experience, Kant tries to derive this infinite object from an infinite cause operating through a single 'divine presence' expressed in the three cosmological principles of matter and the forces of attraction and repulsion.

Kant resumes the theme of what it is we see when we look at the night sky in the fascinating section VII of part II, 'From the Creation in the Entire Extent of Its Infinity According to Space as Well as Time'. Here Kant argues that light – the what and how of seeing – is made up of fine matter impelled by the movement of the forces of attraction and repulsion. The forces of attraction and repulsion working upon matter not only constitute 'the systematic constitution among the fixed stars of the Milky Way' but also the mode by which this constitution is made visible. Force and matter are not only the ontological constituents of the cosmos, but also the condition of the possibility of their being visible. However, this visibility also has within it invisibility. For the play of forces is not only constitutive but also potentially destructive – an imbalance of the forces of attraction and repulsion can either scatter the universe through infinite space or bring it into a concentrated singular collision: they can 'remove [world orders] from their positions and bury the world in an inevitably impending chaos' (*UNH* 150). The periodicity of the universe mentioned in the conclusion of the second *Critique* is none other than the destructive and constructive work of the forces of attraction and repulsion, correcting and disrupting the amassing of matter in the cosmos. For force in general is a quality of matter, and attractive force is 'precisely that universal relation which unites the parts of nature in one space; it also stretches out over the entire extension of that space into all the reaches of its infinity' (*UNH* 150). Kant then makes the physical claim that underlies his later metaphysical proposition in the *Lectures on Metaphysics*: 'Light is reality, darkness is negation, shadow is limitation, for it is a darkness that is bounded by light' (*LM* 232). For given that light is fine matter, its motion towards us is subject to the forces of attraction and repulsion. If the attractive force of its object exceeds the attractive force of the rest of the cosmos, then the light will not escape the object and will not be visible to us. Kant relates light to the constant dispersal of matter that constitutes the universe. We cannot see chaos since it emits no light; we can only see creation through the emission of matter of which we are ourselves a part. Kant appears in the *Universal Natural History* to endorse two incompatible positions. The first concerns the acceleration of light on its journey through the universe, arriving at a limit of absolute speed or divine presence. According to this version, the cosmos is the 'infinite space of divine presence – buried in a silent night'. This version of the cosmos offers a physical correlate to intelligible 'personality' whereas that of material dispersal corresponds to what Kant in 1755 called 'this Phoenix of nature'. In this view, light is the fine part of the matter thrown off from the burning stars that is scattered by the force of repulsion and then re-gathered by the force of attraction, to be scattered again. For 'the unification of so infinite an amount of fire store-houses as are these burning suns ... will scatter the stuff of their masses, dissolved by the unspeakable glow ... and the materials become available through these mechanical laws for new formations' (*UNH* 160). According to this view, the universe explodes and collapses; all we can see is the explosion – as the fine matter of light rushes through us. As one system begins collapsing, its phosphorescent fine matter is not impelled sufficiently to reach us, although another, in creative explosion, impels its light through us – we can only by definition see 'reality' or creation; we cannot see destruction because the emission of light is a condition of creative explosion.

    In the first account of the cosmos light is impelled by divine grace; in the second it is fine matter impelled into motion through the emission by a burning sun. Kant does not make a decision for either one of these positions but leaves them both in place, offering the cosmological equivalent for the distinction between personality and animality that structures the conclusion of the *Critique of Practical Reason*. Indeed, and here we anticipate somewhat the discussion of the next section, Kant also situates the soul within this cosmic history. There is the immortal soul of the cosmos viewed as the space of divine presence and the other soul that is a part of the movement of the cosmos. Kant asks at one point, 'With what kind of awe must not the soul look at her own being when she considers that she still has to live through all these changes?' In this view the soul too is part of the movement of matter driven by the forces of attraction and repulsion. The movement between attraction and repulsion located in the soul as the movement of *Hemmung* and *Ergießung* is also the movement of the cosmos, with the *Ergießung* of matter through combustion that generates sufficient repulsive force for matter – fine and otherwise – to escape the attractive force of the star and be drawn by that of the cosmos always restricted by the *Hemmung* of attractive force that would contain the emission of matter. The former (i.e. the *Ergießung*) is the death of the star, its protracted departure from the order of reality, while the latter (i.e. *Hemmung*) its life, the reconstitution of its matter.

Kant's claim in the conclusion to the *Critique of Practical Reason* that we must return our matter to the planet needs to be situated in this context. The destruction of death is but one part of the periodic movement through which the soul too must live. The possibility thus emerges of reading the affects of the soul in terms of the movement of repulsive and attractive force that constitutes the dynamic of the universe. Thus, the gaze oriented without into the starry heavens and the gaze oriented within, into the soul, are but two views of the same cosmic dynamic. Whereas the version of the unity of soul and cosmos is relatively crudely expressed in the early *Universal Natural History*, it is nevertheless clear that Kant is willing to see animate life and the soul as part of the wider, cosmic history of the expansion and contraction of matter through the play of attractive and repulsive forces. This is perhaps even clearer in the late *Opus postumum*.

Before moving to consider the cosmological dynamic in terms of the soul and the sophisticated medical physiology to which it gives rise in the *Opus postumum* it is necessary to consider again the account of light, which, although consistent with the earlier version, has undergone a further development. Once again, whenever Kant looked to skies, whether in the 1750s, 1780s or 1790s, he saw fiery storehouses burning themselves out and casting their matter and light across the universe for reconstitution into new worlds – the starry heavens above present the monstrous glow of self-destructive, fire-creating matter. However, Kant's account of light has changed somewhat, since it is no longer consistently identified with fine matter (and consistency should not be expected too much from the jottings that make up the *Opus postumum*) but with the oscillation of fine matter. Kant indeed sways between a particle and wave account of light, inclining on the whole more towards the latter. Light is carried on waves through the fluid matter of ether but is also the cause of the patterns adopted by ether. In the case of the starry heavens, 'since the generation of all cosmic bodies requires a preceding fluid state, and, since this latter is now preserved (at least) by the light of the sun, one may regard the fire-element as a type of matter which moves and is

contained by all bodies; by means of heat and light it is the cause of all fluidity'
(*OP* 20–1).[3] Light is characterized by 'free progressive and oscillatory motion'
transmitted as a wave through the ether. It is a wave, however, that moves
by means of a pulsar movement of attraction and repulsion yet one which is
incremental, constantly augmenting itself. Here Kant points to a combination
of the two views of the cosmos opposed to each other in the *Universal
Natural History*. For now the motion of light is continuous, its attractive and
repulsive forces proportioned: 'That light be no discharging motion (*ejaculatio*)
of a matter but an undulatory motion (*undulatio*)' (*OP* 174). Light no longer
obeys the sublime restriction and discharge – *Hemmung* and *Ergießung* – but
is a continuous and augmentative oscillation. The universe thus obeys both
physical laws and the laws of divine presence as a self-augmenting proportion;
this unified cosmology has its equivalent in the soul with the experience of the
beautiful. The latter, as Kant will later show in the third *Critique*, is manifest in
the augmentation of the feeling of life.

The life of the soul

The subject of the conclusion to the *Critique of Practical Reason* is the
Gemüt, a term often translated as 'mind' – especially in its ubiquitous use
in the *Critique of Pure Reason* – but whose meaning was by no means so
restricted or even fixed. Since the term is drawn from medieval mysticism,
one of the earliest recorded uses being by Master Eckhart, and given Kant's
own differentiated use of the Latin equivalents *anima* and *animus*, even the
translation 'soul' is to be preferred over mind.[4] However, it too does not do
full justice to the properties of the term, and Kant is careful to distinguish
Gemüt from *Seele* or the hypostatization of the soul as substance (*anima*)
by describing it as *animus* or the 'capacity to effect the unity of empirical
apperception' and spirit (*Geist*).[5] This capacity is exercised by the *Gemütskräfte*
or powers of the *Gemüt*, variously classified but always involving sensibility,
imagination, understanding and reason. Yet more than this, *Gemüt* is a
physio-philosophical concept that does not obey the distinction of sensibility
and intelligibility, mind and body, but is itself identified as life. In the *Critique
of Judgement*, *Gemüt* is described as 'all life (the life principle itself), and
its hindrance or furtherance has to be sought outside it, and yet in the man
himself, consequently in connection with his body' (*CJ* 131, section 29).[6]
The *Gemüt* as 'life principle' is also described as the *Inbegriff of* knowing,
desiring and affect (Kant 1977b, 429) and has two origins, leading to the
'receptivity of impressions' and the 'spontaneity of concepts' and the two
affects of the *Gemüt*, sensation and reflection (*CPR* A50/B74). An example of

its operation is the affect of pleasure in the beautiful in which the experience of a beautiful object, illustrated by Kant with the example of 'a regular and appropriate building', 'quickens' the subject's 'feeling of life' or awareness of its own existence.

The filling of the *Gemüt* with wonder and awe at the sight of the starry heavens and the moral law is to be understood in terms of quickening the 'consciousness of existence' of the 'life principle'. Its operation in the key of the beautiful is signalled by the combination of the properties of escalating repetition of the (receptive) perception and (spontaneous) reflection (*je öfter und anhaltender sich das Nachdenken damit beschäftigt* ...) experienced in terms of 'constantly new' and augmentative affect (*mit immer neuer und zunehmender Bewunderung und Ehrfurcht*). The association of the *Gemüt* with the 'life principle' is evident not only from the rehearsal of its properties in the first two sentences – from augmentative repetition of affect to 'consciousness of existence' – but also in the fact the two objects that it contemplates resolve by the end of the paragraph into two understandings of life. The final paragraph unfolds the spectacle of the life principle moving from the vision of impossible objects to reflections on life itself. Through the reflection of the *Gemüt* the 'starry heavens' resolve into a reflection on animality and the restitution of the body's matter to the planet and the departure of its inexplicable *Lebenskraft*; the reflection upon the 'moral law' in its turn is expressed in terms of personality and a life 'independent of the world of the senses', one that, determined by the moral law, is infinite, unlimited by the 'conditions and limits of this life'. But the life of the *Gemüt* that has these reflections is neither of these, neither animality nor personality, yet somehow the scene of the play of both conceptions of life.

The conclusion to the *Critique of Practical Reason* ties sensible and intelligible life in the human *Gemüt* or 'principle of life'. Yet this tie involves a relationship to the cosmos, since the *Gemüt* itself is a part of the cosmos. Kant remains an heir to the close alignment of physiology and cosmology established by Paracelsus. His interest in animal economy – the connection between the outer and the inner relations of soul (evinced in the 'starry heavens' and 'moral law') – is evident in both the *Universal Natural History* and the *Opus postumum*. It gives rise, in both texts, to a sustained discussion of 'animal economy' or physiology in the narrow sense, a discussion that provides the conditions of the possibility for medical therapy. In the former it appears in the guise of the fantastical reflection on life that makes up the third and final part of the text, one organized in terms of a reflection upon the life of the inhabitants of the various planets/stars.

Kant uses the theme of terrestrial and extra-terrestrial life as a conceit through which to explore the relationship between physiology and cosmology. He claims that the distances of the celestial bodies from the sun embody certain relationships which in turn entail a decisive influence on the various characteristics of thinking natures that are found there; whose manner of operating and feeling is bound to the condition of the material with which they are connected. (*UNH* 183)[7]

The reference to the restitution of the matter of the body to the planet in the passage from *Critique of Practical Reason* is thus founded in the general claim that the characteristics of the matter of the body – its operations and affects – are inseparable from the material conditions of the planet, and these in turn are inseparable from the material conditions of the cosmos. Kant correlates these characteristics with the 'measure [intensity] of the impressions which the [external] world evokes' in the body and these in turn with 'the properties of the relation of their habitat to [the sun], the centre of attraction and heat' (*UNH* 184). The sun's gravity – its force of attraction – and the 'repulsive force' of its heat together provide the conditions for the propagation of fine matter (light) (Kant is writing before the crucial invention of the concept of energy), which determines the life of the body. Kant is 'certain that this heat produces specific relationships in the materials of those celestial bodies in proportion to their distance from the soul' and thus experiences of body and soul on the different planets.

Kant takes as his 'general reference point' the variant with which he is most familiar: human life on earth. Abstracting from the 'physical construction' of human beings or their 'moral traits', he restricts his investigation to 'what limitations his ability to think and the mobility of his body, which obeys that [former] would suffer through the properties of the matter to which he is linked and which are proportioned to the distance from the sun' (*UNH* 186). He then restates this physio-cosmological proposition even more emphatically:

> Whatever the infinite distance between the ability to think and the motion of matter, between the rational mind and the body, it is still certain that man – who obtains all his notions and representations through the impressions which the universe through the mediation of bodies evokes in his soul, both in respect of their meaning and of the readiness to connect and compare them, which man calls the ability to think – is wholly dependent on the properties of that matter to which the Creator joined him. (*UNH* 186)

Both the reception of the universe into the *Gemüt* and thinking is 'wholly determined' by the properties of matter – the particular balance of attractive and repulsive force (gravity and heat) that obtains in our part of the universe. This balance is, of course, not uniform throughout the cosmos, thus raising the possibilities of other forms of life, other forms of thinking and movement and of course other *Gemüts*.

Kant discusses human physiology in terms of states and relations: the former comprises an amalgam of traditional and innovative medical concepts, the latter the notion of their interrelation or 'animal economy'. The units of human physiology are the Hippocratic fluids and fibres (sometimes 'nerves'). These are subject to the prevailing physical forces of attraction and repulsion, although the balance between them is different in the case of each individual. Human nature is characterized in terms of the 'unbending of the fibres, and in the sluggishness and immobility of fluids which should obey its stirrings' (*UNH* 187). The resistance of matter expressed in fibral inflexibility and the sluggishness of the humoral fluids stiffens the 'forces of the spirit into a similar dullness'. But the intensity of life – the degree of vivacity as opposed to dullness – depends upon 'excitation' expressed as 'animal economy' or the relationship between the 'forces of the human soul' and the matter to which 'they are most intimately bound'. He continues, 'this specific condition of the stuff has a fundamental relation to the degree of influence by which the sun in the measure of its distance enlivens them and renders them adapted to the maintenance of the animal economy' (*UNH* 188). This consists in the 'necessary relation to the fire, which spreads out from the centre of the world system to keep matter in the necessary excitation' (*UNH* 188). Life thus consists in the excitation of the matter that makes up the body, present in the forces of the soul and in the relations between the bodily humours and the suppleness and flexibility of its fibres.

In the *Universal Natural History* the concept of life and of animal economy is relatively underdeveloped, but its leading characteristics are clear. The character of life is intimately tied with the attractive and repulsive properties of matter that prevail on the planet Earth. The excitation of matter expressed as heat and light determines both the motion of the body and of thought. Thus, when Kant at one point in his discussion compares reason and the ability to judge with 'flashes of sunshine when thick clouds continually obstruct and darken its cheerful brightness', he is not mobilizing a standard Enlightenment metaphor but is being literal.

In the *Universal Natural History* Kant's understanding of terrestrial animal economy is framed in terms of humours and fibres. The concept of life is relatively imprecise, even though he is prepared to mitigate the rigour of his physio-cosmology by appeals to the hope of a 'future life'. In the *Opus postumum* the concepts of soul and life are far more fully developed and conducted almost entirely in the language of contemporary physiology with explicit reference to the 'life principle' of Paracelsus.[8] The references to humoral fluids have disappeared, and the discussion of life, soul and cosmos is conducted almost entirely in modern terms.

One of the leitmotifs of the *Opus postumum* is the transition from metaphysics and transcendental philosophy to the discipline of physics. By the latter, however, Kant intends what previously had been known as 'physiology'. Thus Kant's 'physics' comprises both the 'moving forces of matter' in general – physics in the narrow sense – and the influence of these forces 'on the subject', 'In which, the body is thought of as animated and matter as animating' (*OP* 145). In this physics, questions relating to life and the soul thus form a major consideration. These considerations are framed in terms of the new understanding of the cosmos outlined above. The plenum of the ether oscillates through waves of attraction and repulsion, and the vital force is understood in terms of the 'concussive motion of an all-penetrating matter' (*OP* 66).[9] Kant does not wish fully to embrace the mechanistic understanding of life in terms of physical forces that he identifies with the physiologist Hildebrandt (author of the *Lehrbuch der Physiologie*, 1799) but nor does he wish wholly to adopt the Stahlist (ultimately Paracelsian) view of a completely immaterial vital principle. Living bodies contain a 'vital principle' but one which is connected in some way with ether. Kant reflects upon this principle in terms of Paracelsus's and Van Helmont's notion of the vital principle as the '*archeus*' – a term that was later re-adopted by Virchow. Kant noted that 'Life, however, stems from a distinct substance, from an *archeus* (animated matter is contradictory), and organic bodies stand, through the ether, in the relation of a higher organ toward each other' (*OP* 184). The orientation of the *archeus* or 'life principle' according to the ether accords it a polar, oscillatory character of attraction/repulsion. This is described at one point in the context of the 'transition to physics' in terms of an oscillation between the life/death, sickness/health polarities: 'the [characteristic] phenomenon of a species which preserves itself in space and time is the continuation of the genus and the alternating death and life of its individuals. Sickness forms the constant transition between the two' (*OP* 118).

In a subsequent note Kant reflects upon the polar character of the life principle at greater length. He writes that 'One can think of *health* and *sickness* with regard to organic bodies (not organic matter) since they possess a vital force, be it vegetative or animal, and for this reason also death or decay' (*OP* 197). The vital force moves between attraction and repulsion that is transmitted through the ether.[10] The vital principle is joined to the cosmos, physiology to cosmology, although Kant is no longer convinced about the way in which this is achieved. Life is linked to an 'inner final cause' but its relationship to the cosmos is left open: 'It remains undetermined whether this encompasses the entire universe and hence underlies [everything] in cosmic space – as a world soul, as a unifying principle of all life (which thus must not be called *spirit*) or whether several be arranged hierarchically' (*OP* 197). The old relationship of soul and cosmos is no longer valid – life is now both animated and animating – life generates life. In Kant's terms 'by the word "soul" is understood not merely a living or animated substance, but something which animates another substance (matter)' (*OP* 182). Whether this property is a cosmic world soul, or whether it is product of individual life in interaction with matter, the new view of life is consistent with the new view of the cosmos explored in the *Opus postumum*. Life is interactive and augmentative; like the oscillations that make up the flow of ether, its movements do not consume but enhance each other. Vital force, consistent with the understanding of human physiology at time, is no longer, as in *Universal Natural History*, a product of excitability, but its cause.[11]

The implications of these changes in the understanding of the life principle and its relationship to the cosmos are apparent in the changed understanding of 'animal economy' or *zoonomy* evident in the *Opus postumum*. In the context of another of the many discussions of the transition to physics, this time from the 'metaphysical foundations', Kant is unambiguous concerning the physiological dimension to his new physics. He defines physics as 'the empirical science of the complex of the moving forces of matter. These forces also affect the subject – man – and his organs, since man is also a corporeal being. The inner alterations thereby produced in him, with consciousness, are perceptions; his reaction on, and outer alteration of, matter is motion' (*OP* 103). The new physics has four divisions that relate closely to the schema of physiology proposed by Campanella and adopted to some extent by Descartes. The first concerns 'matter and bodies, according to their moving forces'; the second, the formal elements of the forces (mechanical or dynamic); the third 'organized and organizing matter'; and the fourth 'will power'.

Zoonomy comprises the third part of the new physics and is classified twice, according to the four *animalische Potenzen* or three *Lebenspotenzen*. The first three elements are common to both classifications – the animal powers add a fourth 'on the organization of a whole of organic beings of different species'. The three main parts of zoonomy depend 'on nervous power as a principle of excitability (*incitabilitas Brownii*); on muscular power (*irritabilitas Halleri*); on a force which preserves all the organic forces of nature as a constant alteration of the former two of which *one* phenomenon is heat' (*OP* 103). Here, excitation and irritation – identified with the medical doctors and physiologists Brown and Haller – provide the polar opposition whose play constitutes life – one expressive, the other reactive. Both in their turn are situated cosmologically according to what is identified in the second classification as the ether: the third vital power 'which brings both forces into active and reactive, constantly alternating, play; one all-penetrating, all moving etc., material, of which heat is one phenomenon' (*OP* 103). Thus the physiological and cosmological are linked in Kant's new physiological physics into a polarized vital principle whose oscillation is informed by the cosmic ether and whose play, like that of the ether, does not consume but augments itself.

Yet even in the *Opus postumum* Kant places above the order of life a divine order in which we participate in a higher form of life, the life of *spirit* rather than the life of *soul*. At this point he self-consciously distinguishes his position from that of Spinoza, for whom the order of God and World – spirit and soul – are inseparable. Kant however, although sometimes touching upon the notion of God as the plenum of the world, ultimately separates them, insisting upon 'the necessity of the division of the complex of all beings (of everything that exists): *God and the world*' (*OP* 214). This separation modulates into one between soul and spirit, for 'In man there dwells an active principle, arousable by no sensible representation, accompanying him not as soul (for this presupposes body) but as spirit, which, like a particular substance, commands him irresistibly according to the law of moral–practical reason' (*OP* 214). The assertion of the distinction between God and the world clearly shows Kant's extreme reluctance to move towards a rigorous physiology, a step that would be taken by his radical successors – Virchow in pathological medicine and Nietzsche in philosophy. But his awareness of the problems arising from such a division was acute. It is in the context of this awareness that the apparent analogy or contrast between the starry heavens above and the moral law within, soul and spirit, world and God should begin to be read anew.

Notes

1   Kant's fascination with the properties of polarity and the experience of its reversal has been little noted. It is however central and thematized as such in *What Is Called Orientation in Thinking* and is implicitly at work in a number of other places in Kant's work.

2   The contrast with Leopardi is again constructive, since for the poet of *la ginestra* there is no second reflection but only the annihilation. For more extended readings of Leopardi, see Caygill 2000.

3   In the *Opus postumum*, Kant returns to the Cartesian view of the importance of heat in stimulating the motion of matter. At one point he even supplements the ether with 'caloric': 'matter without gravity and not displaceable, but which moves all matter internally, renders matter elastic but also cohesive ... it is extended in the whole of cosmic space' (*OP* 37).

4   Etienne Gilson described *Gemüt* in terms of disposition and stability, the 'stable disposition of the soul which conditions the exercise of its faculties' (Gilson 1955, 444).

5   This is most clearly carried through in Kant's 1796 letter to the medical doctor Sömmering on his *The Organs of the Soul*, an early attempt to localize cerebral functions (Kant 1977a, 255–9).

6 The explicit Paracelsian and thus medical-physiological provenance of 'the life principle itself' will be shown below.

7 Here Kant anticipates some of the themes of recent anthropic cosmology; see Barrow and Tipler 1986.

8 Kant was extremely well informed about contemporary debates in medicine and human physiology. This is apparent above all in the discussions of Georg Ernst Stahl (1660–1754) and Friedrich Hoffmann (1660–1742) and their respective vitalist and mechanical views of human physiology as well the controversial medical doctrine of John Brown (1733–88), all discussed in his address 'On Philosopher's Medicine of the Body' in Kant 1986, especially 231–2.

9 In this view Kant is even prepared to view heat less as the cause of the repulsive force that 'expands and disperses matter' but as 'the mere effect of the repulsion of a matter set in motion' (*OP* 215).

10 See *OP* 197 for Kant's mapping of the polar characteristics of life onto sexual reproduction.

11 See *OP* 142 for Kant's qualification of the generally augmentative nature of the interactions of vital force in the case of sexual intercourse which uniquely 'erodes', *aufreibt*, vital feeling.

15

Life and energy

The association of life and energy is culturally ubiquitous, pervading breakfast cereal packages, ecological politics and a host of energy/life enhancing products and programmes. The nexus of life and energy is moreover axiomatic for contemporary research in biology and the neurosciences which are developing extremely sophisticated accounts of life and consciousness in terms of energy transfers, conservation and degradation. Yet in spite of the centrality of energy to the contemporary cultural and scientific *doxa*, the concept itself remains strangely unanalysed in contemporary philosophy and theory. Here, work continues to be pursued in terms of such archaic concepts as force and power. While such concepts may serve to introduce a dynamic element into contemporary theory – evident in such theoretical couplings as 'corporeal force' or 'bio-power' – they are historically anachronistic and conceptually limited in comparison with the concept of energy. Philosophy, however, very rarely reflects directly on the concept of energy, let alone the nexus between the concepts of energy and life.

One of the exceptions to the philosophical oblivion of energy is the series of works produced by Alfred North Whitehead between 1920 and 1934. *The Concept of Nature* (1920), *Science and the Modern World* (1925), *Process and Reality* (1929) and *Nature and Life* (1934) all criticize the conception of nature as a sum of objects and their relations (conceived in terms of force and power) and outline a new concept based on the premiss of a set of events. In *Process and Reality*, Whitehead begins very tentatively to link the 'event' with quantum expressions of energy, while in *Nature and Life* he proposes that 'the deficiencies in our concept of physical nature should be supplied by its fusion with life' (Whitehead 1934, 58) – in other words, that the physical concept of energy should be supplemented by the physiological concept of life. This audacious and necessary proposal remained largely unexplored in Whitehead's subsequent work and was largely ignored by posterity. His own conclusion that 'the energetic activity considered in physics is the emotional intensity entertained in life' (Whitehead 1934, 96) does not fully escape from the reliance on analogy in *Process and Reality*, where the physical transformation of energy into quanta is related to 'its analogues in recent neurology'. The reliance upon parallels and analogies between the expressions of energy in physical nature, life and consciousness is testimony, even in the radical work of Whitehead, to the difficulty of framing a unified philosophy of energy.

Whitehead's attempt to bring together the physical account of energy in nature and the physiological account of it in life and consciousness is provocative even if unrealized. His challenge still remains open, but the obstacles facing any attempt to meet it are formidable. Here a few preliminary steps may be ventured respecting the historical conditions for the emergence of a discourse of energy and its division into physical and physiological dimensions. If the historical basis of the separation is better understood it might then become possible to appreciate the nature of the difficulties facing any attempt at unification. A pivotal figure in any such consideration is Hermann von Helmholtz, one of the pioneering contributors to the invention of the concept of energy in the nineteenth century. Beyond its acknowledged debt to the philosophical tradition and in particular to the work of Kant, Helmholtz's work was also remarkable for its preoccupation with both physical and physiological approaches to the problem of energy. It has recently been argued most forcefully and elegantly by Peter Harman that the physical side of Helmholtz's theory of energy has precedence over the physiological, that his concept of energy is overwhelmingly a physical hypothesis. Harman's account for the precedence of physics is philosophically and scientifically sophisticated but I do not intend to scrutinize it in detail at this point. I would, however, like to reflect more generally on the validity of separating the physical and the physiological reflections of energy, especially since it is this separation that Whitehead attempted to overcome in *Nature and Life* (1934).

Some idea of what might be questionable about giving the physical discourse of energy priority over the physiological may be gained from a brief reflection on the concept of work. If the physical definition of energy as the 'ability to do work' is translated to the physiological, then 'life' is defined as the 'ability to do work', and indeed, the assumption that to live is to do work informs modern economic, social and political institutions.[1] Yet it may be objected that such a translation from the physical to the physiological depends on the sophism of equivocation – that the term 'work' in thermodynamics is not the same as the term 'work' in wage labour. However, there are historical grounds for insisting on the univocity of the term, and that work understood in terms of the product of force, mass and distance does not differ in essence from work as the accomplishment of wage labour.[2]

The example of work is important for illustrating some of the issues facing a philosophy of energy and a genealogy of its sources. The physical account of energy forms a largely discrete tradition emerging from the theoretical reflection upon engineering problems encountered by early nineteenth-century capitalist production. These problems involved the inefficiency – that is, the relative unproductivity – of heat engines, quite literally the steam-powered engines of the first industrial revolution. The 'losses' that occurred in the transformation process of matter, heat, liquid, gas and motion that made up steam power (coal heating water to produce vapour to produce motion) stimulated a number of important reflections on the theory of heat in the early decades of the century by Carnot, Davy, Joule and Watt.[3] The emergence of the idea of the conservation of heat, in the context of a concern to minimize the loss of heat in the transformation process and thus maximize the efficiency or 'ability to work' of the steam engine, provided an important condition for its theoretical elaboration into the concept of energy in the 1840s and 1850s. The minimization of heat loss maximizes the translation of heat into mechanical motion – i.e. work – which in turn maximizes productivity and profit. Thus the work of the definition of energy emerged from the same context as industrial wage labour and is not inconsistent with the productivism of the capitalist mode of production and with the view of the body as an analogue of the engine understood above all as a vehicle for the performance of work.

It is at this point that it might be useful to point to a contrast between the context for the emergence of the physical concept of energy and the physiological perspective. The differences between them may be highlighted by their differing conceptions of heat. For the physical argument, heat signifies loss of work – energy that is not translated into motion – while for the physiological tradition, of which I will say more below, heat is identified with life. For the one, the maximization of heat is the minimization of work, while for the other it is maximization of life. The physical tradition understands heat in largely mechanical terms drawn from the context of practical engineering problems, while the physiological tradition understands it as a source of vitality, with Lavoisier, for example, working in the physiological tradition at the beginning of the nineteenth century, regarding heat as the 'material soul' or animating principle of life. It may not be too exaggerated to see the concept of energy as driven by these contrasting perspectives on heat.[4]

The differences between the physical and the physiological traditions may be illustrated by their interpretation of a key concept from Leibniz – *vis vita* – living or vital force. This is a concept used not only by contemporary historians of science[5] but also by the main protagonists in the invention of the concept of energy – Helmholtz, Thompson and Maxwell. It forms a part of Leibniz's dynamics where it serves as an element in his explanation of the possibility of motion. Newton answered the question of why objects move under conditions of gravity by postulating a contrary force – *vis insita* – inherent force which is then defined as *vis inertiae* or inertial force. In a cancelled insertion Newton defines this as the 'power of resisting' but none of this satisfied Leibniz who proposed instead *vis vita* as an active source of movement.[6] What was meant by this was the subject of considerable controversy – one in which the 24-year-old Immanuel Kant made his philosophical debut in 1746 with the massive *Thoughts on the True Estimation of Living Forces* (Kant [1746] 2012). The purely physical understanding of *vis vita* emphasized the *vis* or force capable of resisting the tendential stasis of gravity while the vitalist understanding emphasized the *vita* or its living character.

Leibniz was very well acquainted with the physiological tradition that can be traced to Paracelsus, Telesio and Campanella in the sixteenth and early seventeenth centuries which had developed a theory of life as heat.[7] The physiological tradition inaugurated by Campanella as a modern revision of Aristotelian philosophy had an important influence upon the development of experimental and medical physiology, which nevertheless continued to identify life with heat.[8] This tradition understood heat as *vis vita* or the animating force that resisted the force of gravity, an understanding that Kant extended in his *Metaphysical Foundations of Natural Science* (1786) – a crucial influence on Helmholtz – into the distinction between the attractive force of gravity and repulsive force, identifying the latter in the *Opus postumum* (1993) as cosmic heat (caloric) and vital heat.

For the physical tradition, *vis vita* is a force that tends to movement, and the attrition or loss of that force – its useless expenditure – is heat (that which is neither conserved nor translated into motion or mechanical work). For the physiological tradition, *vis vita* is vital force that animates matter by means of heat – it is always conserved and never lost. From the two traditions emerged the discourse of energy or 'thermodynamics', but within it the physical tendency was dominant and the physiological recessive. It is not possible here to describe fully the development of the two sources of the concept of energy – nature and life in short – but some idea of its complexity may be gained indirectly by some comments on François Jacob's *The Logic of Life* (1973), a classic account of the history of heredity – and biology – during the nineteenth and twentieth centuries.

In many respects the subtext of Jacob's history of biology is the transformation of the broader physiological tradition into biology, narrowly understood as the attempt to apply physical concepts to the understanding of life.[9] The momentous force of this transformation is elegantly summarized in Jacob's description of the emergence of the biological field. Departing from the concept of *vis vita*, he explains:

> If vital force became a concept of such importance at the beginning of the nineteenth century, it was because it then played a role subsequently assumed by two new concepts. Today, living organisms are seen as the

site of a triple flow of matter, energy and information. In its early days, biology was able to recognize the flow of matter, but, lacking the other two concepts, it had to postulate a special force. (Jacob 1973, 95)

In many ways this statement is both rich and strange. The triple flow of matter, energy and information is in fact a single flow, matter and information being but modes of energy. The emergence of the science of biology, in other words, depends on replacing the concept of vital force with that of energy. This replacement was by no means straightforward, as Jacob goes on to show. He reflects on three ways in which the concept of *vital force* is replaced by energy, thus underlining the complexity of the passage from one to the other. The first consists in a parallel between the emergence of the concept of population in Darwin's evolutionary biology and Boltzmann's statistical thermodynamics. The parallel is suggestive but only works if its terms are inverted: evolution tends through natural selection towards the increasing organization of a population while thermodynamics through entropy tends towards the increasing disorder of a population of molecules. Jacob's second and third routes out of physiology and its central concept of vital force point to the persistence of the concerns of the physiological tradition. The first is the centrality of cell theory to nineteenth-century biology. Jacob is unequivocal in his assessment of the significance of this development:

With the advent of cell theory, biology was given a new foundation, since the unity of the living world was no longer based on the essence of beings, but on their common materials, composition and reproduction. (Jacob 1973, 128)

The cell thus provides a molecular unit according to which all living beings can be unified – it provides a basis for the unicity of life. Yet it is not quite what it seems, since it too is situated within the triple flow mentioned above: it has a common material basis; its composition is governed by the laws of energy exchange and its reproduction by information (genetics).

The central figure in the elaboration of the cell doctrine was Rudolf Virchow, whose role is curiously understated in Jacob's account of the emergence of the cell doctrine.[10] Virchow was a pathologist and a political revolutionary who, while sternly criticizing the concept of *vis vita* and its extravagant development in Romantic medicine, nevertheless remained close to the physiological tradition. He was very careful to distinguish the cell from the atom, and indeed the distinction points to the distance between the physical and the physiological traditions. For Virchow, the cell possesses properties that were not characteristic of physical atoms, properties that made it into a vital rather than a mechanical phenomenon. Jacob, however, attempts to establish the emergence of a parallel between the cell and the atom – and their sciences biology and physics – during the nineteenth century, claiming that

> The cell theory drew the living world closer to the inanimate world, since both were constructed on the same principle: diversity and complexity built up of combinations of simple components. The cell became a 'centre of growth' in the same way as the atom represented a 'centre of force'. (Jacob 1973, 128)

The analogy that is drawn here to underline the similarities equally serves to emphasize the differences between the cell and the atom. For the parallel between 'growth' and 'force' is by no means apparent and conjures up the ancient tension, evident in Aristotle, between motion and generation. While the parallel is intended to point to the proximity of biology and physics to the advantage of physics, it might equally work in the opposite direction, to the advantage of biology.

The first two explanations provided by Jacob for the emergence of biology out of physiology rely on parallels and analogies that are by no means self-evident. The third argument differs in so far as it addresses the revolution in scientific thinking represented by the concept of energy and points to the pivotal significance for both physics and biology of the work of Helmholtz. Jacob sums up the nineteenth-century revolution in biology in an extremely crisp formulation: 'At the beginning of the nineteenth century, an organism expended vital force in order to perform its work of synthesis and morphogenesis; at the end of the century it consumed energy' (Jacob 1973, 195). The description of the replacement of vital force by energy no longer relies on analogy but instead focuses on the figure of Helmholtz. Jacob once more:

> There were two generalizations that brought biology nearer to physics and chemistry: the same elements compose living beings and inanimate matter; conservation of energy applies equally to events in the living and inanimate worlds. Those who, like Helmholtz, grasped the universality of these principles, drew a simple conclusion: there is no difference between the phenomena occurring in living beings and in the inanimate world. (Jacob 1973, 194)

Thus Helmholtz's texts signify a point of decision respecting the nature of the 'no difference' between the physical and the vital. Is the choice simply between subordinating the vital to the physical and the physical to the vital, or are there other possible options? Helmholtz himself tended to vacillate on this question. His seminal text from 1847 'The Conservation of Force: A Physical Memoir' reflects on *vis vita* and heat and presents itself as a physical hypothesis for physicists (Helmholtz 1971, 3–55). The essay moves towards the reduction of vital to physical phenomena – animate bodies consume 'chemical tensional forces' and produce heat and movement. However, in a later address to the Royal Society in 1861 on 'The Application of the Law of the Conservation of Force to Organic Nature' (Helmholtz 1971, 109–21), Helmholtz makes the parallel between the human body and a steam engine only to claim that the human body is a far better machine than a steam engine, so much so that the laws of the conservation of force demand a different understanding in the context of vital phenomena. They may not simply obey the laws of work and the efficient transformation of heat into motion (Helmholtz 1971, 121).

In the address Helmholtz leaves open the question of the relationship of life with what was being recognized as the concept of energy. It remained so in spite of enormous advances in physics and biology until Whitehead. Since then, the theme has not been properly explored, leaving the question of the nexus of life and energy still philosophically unresolved. Perhaps this should be recognized by eliding the two terms – life/energy – and trying philosophically to understand what the implications are of their relationship without reducing one to another. It is perhaps necessary to discover a perspective on life/energy that is neither a revival of vitalism nor an endorsement of a purely physical understanding of life. This perspective can be sought first of all in a genealogy of the concepts and the recognition of their mutual tension.

Notes

1   Such a definition was central to National Socialist biopolitics and its murderous campaign against 'unproductive' life, but it remains a powerful source of values in contemporary societies.

2   The Marxist critique of wage labour is remarkably close to physical and physiological considerations. Indeed, a fascinating point of proximity between physiology and the critique of political economy can be located in Marx's critique of Feuerbach, who in the 1840s moved increasingly towards a physiological definition of matter and action.

3   See the historical accounts of the links between steam technology and the discourse of energy in Angrist and Hepler 1967 and Cardwell 1971. Smith 1998 offers a divergent perspective, focusing upon the cosmological and theological contexts of the emergence of the 'science of energy'.

4   Enrico Bellone's (2004) recent history of physics situates energy discourse as a second scientific revolution, continuous with the concerns with heat and caloric that emerged from the first. Bellone is among the few contemporary writers who attempt to describe the entirety of Helmholtz's project and to bring into proximity physical and physiological discourses; see Bellone 2004, 5–6, with its explicit acknowledgement of debt to Helmholtz.

5   Harman (1982) makes considerable use of the concept, developing a powerful argument for its exclusively physical relevance. I will try to show that it also involves other considerations drawn from the physiological tradition.

6   See Harman 1982, chapter 3.

7   In Campanella's work this almost went so far as the identification of the sun – as source of heat and life – with divinity. See for example his most famous work, the physiological utopia *The City of the Sun*. For a statement of Campanella's physiological position see Campanella 1999.

8   Read in this context Harvey and Descartes are extremely clear examples of medical and experimental physiologists working in this tradition, Harvey with respect to his work in embryology and Descartes with his understanding of the role of the heart in the circulation of the blood. For the beginnings of a comparative analysis of Campanella and Harvey, see Brissoni 2002.

9   This perspective was anticipated by Everett Mendelsohn (1964) in *Heat and Life: The Development of the Theory of Animal Heat*: 'The whole history of biological thought can be outlined as a transition from a period when men were willing to attribute a living phenomenon to a "vital force" to that stage when they demanded a description of the conditions and a search for the material causes of all living activities.' Jacob, however, is far more precise in identifying such conditions and causes in the discourse of energy.

10 Jacob confines his assessment of Virchow's contribution to the development of the cell doctrine to the latter's critique of Schleider and Schwann's views of the spontaneous generation of cells, a neglect paralleled in Canguilhem [1953] 1965.

Section four: Philosophy/science

16

The topology of selection: The limits of Deleuze's biophilosophy

Le selezioni si sentono arrivare. 'Selekcja': la ibrida parola latina e polacca si sente una volte, due volte, molte volte, intercalata in discorsi stranieri; dapprima non la si individua, poi si impone all'attenzione, infine ci perseguita.

– PRIMO LEVI, *SE QUESTO E UN UOMO*

In the final section of *Spinoza: Practical Philosophy* Deleuze describes a biophilosophy or 'ethology' whose field of study would be the 'relations of speed and slowness, of the capacities for affecting and being affected that characterize each thing'. The 'thing' – be it body, animal or human – is specified by the composition or distribution of such relations and capacities as well as by the modes through which they 'select what affects or is affected by the thing, what moves it or is moved by it' (*SPP* 125). This definition of the thing locates Deleuze's ethology as a combination of the philosophical themes of 'relation' and 'capacity' with the biological themes of 'distribution' and 'selection'. In this ethology the kinetics of 'relation' and the dynamics of 'capacity' that shape the 'thing' are shaped in their turn by the orders of 'distribution' and 'selection'. Deleuze's explicit elaboration of ethology progressively privileges the theme of the topology of the distribution of 'relations and capacities' in the 'plane of immanence' over that of the theme of selection. It is this decision – what may be described as the avoidance of Darwin – that establishes the limits of Deleuze's biophilosophy and the politics which it informs.

The combination of philosophy and biology – a powerful tradition in French thought – informs Deleuze's seminal text *Difference and Repetition*. Here the outlines of his ethology are already discernible, as is the tension between the themes of distribution and selection. The focus on the theme of selection which characterized *Nietzsche and Philosophy*, where the thought of the 'eternal return' is read as a principle of selection, increasingly shifts in favour of distribution. The reason for this shift may be sought in the key role played by the reading of Spinoza in the development of Deleuze's ethology, specifically the concept central to the *Ethics* of the 'common notion'. Deleuze understood the Spinozian 'common notion' to be 'more biological than mathematical' (*SPP* 55) and used it as the keystone of his biophilosophy. Deleuze understands 'common notions' as 'physico-chemical or biological ideas' which 'present nature's unity of composition in its various aspects' (*SPP* 115); that is to say, they are topological 'relations of composition' such as 'foldings' which may be traced according to their distribution in a single 'plane of immanence'. What is striking about this development is the emphasis upon the *topology* of distribution and the apparent surrender of the theme of selection central to the Darwinian natural philosophy. It is as if in the passage from philosophy to biophilosophy or ethology Deleuze flinched before the full implications of the inhuman concept of selection and its role in the biological immanence of the Victorian naturalist.

Nevertheless, the issue of selection inevitably remains central to Deleuze's ethology, even though he carefully avoids a full and explicit analysis of its implications. This is apparent from the tension between the biological concepts of distribution and selection which informs *Difference and Repetition* and its implicit presence in later works. Indeed, Deleuze's ethology is not only compatible with the Darwinian concept of selection but is unthinkable without it. This will be shown in the first section – 'Distribution and Selection' – as will its subsequent resolution in favour of distribution and a topology of the common notions in the Spinoza books. Then in the second section – 'The Law of Selection' – the same tension will be shown to be at work in Darwin's *On the Origin of Species by Means of Natural Selection*, but there, as is well known, it is resolved in favour of selection. In the third section – 'The Eternal Return of Selection' – it will be shown that the principle of selection remains crucial but unacknowledged in Deleuze's ethology, forming its limit and the starting point for a critique of the bio-ethics and politics that are associated with it.

Distribution and selection

In 1968 Deleuze published *Difference and Repetition* and *Expressionism in Philosophy: Spinoza* as his principal and secondary theses for the *Doctorat d'Etat*. At first sight there would seem to be little in common between one of the founding texts of the 'philosophy of difference' and a reading of Spinoza's philosophy of unitary substance, although on closer inspection the two texts share many common features. The main point connecting them is the exploration of the relationship between the themes of selection and distribution. In *Difference and Repetition* this is undertaken by confronting Spinoza as the thinker of distribution with Nietzsche as the thinker of selection, with the Darwinian revolution figuring at one sole point in the text as a possible resolution of the relationship between distribution and selection. This possibility was not further explored by Deleuze, whose subsequent work followed the direction of the topology of the 'common notions' proposed in the final three chapters of *Expressionism in Philosophy: Spinoza*.

The first important bridge between the two books of 1968 appears in the context of a discussion of the ontology of distribution in chapter 1, 'Difference in Itself'.[1] This discussion in turn forms an important part of the general critique of Hegel and Hegelianism under the sign of the philosophy of representation. Against such a philosophy and its grotesque theatre of the movement of the concept Deleuze proposes a theatre of repetition in which

> we experience pure forces, dynamic lines in space that act without intermediary upon the spirit and link it directly with nature and history, with a language which speaks before words, with gestures that develop before organized bodies, with masks before faces, with spectres and phantoms before characters – the whole apparatus of repetition as a 'terrible power'. (*DR* 10)

The distinction between the philosophies of representation and difference/ repetition is played out at various levels throughout the text, but most significantly at those that are established between equivocal and univocal being and between sedentary and nomadic patterns of distribution.

For Deleuze, the ontology of equivocal being informs the philosophy of representation. In this ontology, whose origins he discovers in Aristotelian logical metaphysics, being cannot be said in the same way of all beings; there is a difference between the being of finite and infinite being such that the concepts for one can only be used equivocally of the other.[2] One of the consequences of the equivocal conception of being for Deleuze is the emergence of a philosophy of transcendence which, in the words of the later Spinoza book, 'always has an additional dimension; it always implies a dimension supplementary to the dimensions of the given' (*SPP* 128).[3] This supplementary dimension – infinite as opposed to finite being – permits the exercise of judgement or the 'proportioning [of] the concept to the terms or to the subjects of which it is affirmed' (*DR* 33). This is made possible by means of the 'two essential functions' of judgement, namely *distribution* and *hierarchization*. These functions characterize for Deleuze 'every philosophy of the categories', but above all the work of Kant, Hegel and their successors.

The distribution and hierarchy of equivocal being are later specified in terms of a 'dividing up of that which is distributed', a division which 'proceeds by fixed and proportional determinations which may be assimilated to "properties" or limited territories within representation' (*DR* 36). Such distribution within a demarcated field is sovereign and thus hierarchical; its principal characteristics are best conceived in accordance with the definition of the plan of transcendence given in the later Spinoza book:

> Any organization that comes from above and refers to a transcendence, be it a hidden one, can be called a theological plan: a design in the mind of a god, but also an evolution in the supposed depths of nature, or in a society's organization of power … it will always be a plan of transcendence that directs forms as well as subjects, and that stays hidden, that is never given, that can only be divined, induced, inferred from what it gives. (*SPP* 128)

This form of distribution of 'limits and lots' is contrasted with another form of distribution which Deleuze aligns with a univocal definition of being. In this tradition, which Deleuze traces back to Duns Scotus, there is no distinction between finite and infinite being – both are spoken of in the same way. Univocal being is unitary and immanent, in contrast to the divided and transcendent equivocal being. It is this concept of univocal being which for Deleuze informs the philosophy of difference/repetition and makes possible a pattern of distribution other than the plan of transcendence of equivocal being.

The 'completely other distribution' is described by Deleuze as 'nomadic'. In this distribution 'there is no longer a division of that which is distributed but rather a division among those who distribute *themselves* in an open space – a space which is unlimited, or at least without precise limits' (*DR* 36). In such a distribution there is no 'additional dimension' which could found a sovereign plan of transcendence (and its appropriate topology), but an immanence which resists the forms of representation:

> It is an errant and uneven 'delirious' distribution, in which things are deployed across the entire extensity of a univocal and undistributed being. It is not a matter of being which is distributed according to the requirements

of representation, but of all things being divided up within being in the univocity of simple presence (the One-All). (*DR* 39)

In this distribution of being, the categories which order representation, such as those of quantity, quality, relation and modality, are succeeded by an 'enveloping measure' which is the 'same for all things'.[4] In place of the sedentary hierarchy of equivocal being, 'Univocal being is at one and the same time nomadic distribution and crowned anarchy' (*DR* 37).

Deleuze proposes three moments in the history of univocal ontology – Duns Scotus, Spinoza and Nietzsche. Spinoza is thus in a crucial position between Scotus's still theological (Franciscan) conception of univocal being thought in terms of a divine immanence in nature and Nietzsche's Godless conception. Spinoza's presentation of the substance, attributes and modes of being maps a distribution of being in which each is folded upon the others in an 'enveloping measure' which resists any hierarchization:

> Any hierarchy or pre-eminence is denied in so far as substance is equally designated by all the attributes in accordance with their essence, and equally expressed by all the modes in accordance with their degree of power. (*DR* 40)

Yet at this stage Deleuze finds that Spinoza's topology of univocal being is still afflicted by an inequality between substance and its modes and attributes: the latter stand in an asymmetrical relation of dependence to the former. This inequality results from a decision to privilege substance within the plan of immanence, one which marks a selection prior to distribution. Nietzsche, however, folds even this selection into the plane of immanence with the test of eternal return:[5]

> Repetition in the eternal return, therefore, consists in conceiving the same on the basis of the different. However, this conception is no longer merely a theoretical representation: it carries out a practical selection among differences according to their capacity to produce – that is, to return or to pass the test of the eternal return. The selective character of eternal return appears clearly in Nietzsche's idea: it is not the Whole, the Same or the prior identity in general which returns …. Only the extreme forms return – those which, large or small, are deployed within the limit and extend to the limit of their power, transforming themselves and changing one into another. (*DR* 41)

Here the selection which informs the distribution of being is wrapped into being itself, but not in the name of a principle or privileged instance, but rather in the name of a test of becoming – in Deleuze's words, 'production of repetition on the basis of difference and selection of difference on the basis of repetition' (*DR* 42). It is at this point that Deleuze's text is in close proximity with Darwin, for whom 'Any variation which is not inherited is unimportant' (Darwin 1993, 115). Such differences have failed the test of selection and have been unable to repeat or reproduce themselves.

The importance of selection within a philosophy of difference/repetition operating within the plane of immanence of univocal being is acknowledged in Deleuze's brief discussion of Darwin in *Difference and Repetition*. This moment, in chapter 5, 'Asymmetrical Synthesis of the Sensible', marks a possible transformation of Nietzsche's thought of the eternal return into a biophilosophy. Here Deleuze initially recognizes the 'essential role' of natural selection as 'the differentiation of difference (survival of the most divergent)' but then loses sight of the implacable rigour of Darwinian Selection by conceiving of moments when 'selection does not or no longer occurs'. This allows him to regard difference as either the 'primary matter of selection or differenciation' or as 'indeterminate variability' (*DR* 148). Consequently, while acknowledging the 'Copernican Revolution of Darwinism' Deleuze misses the at once radically immanent and exterior character of its concept of Selection.[6]

The reasons for Deleuze's underestimation of Darwinian natural selection are diverse, but prime among them is his approbation of the work of the pre-Darwinian Etienne Geoffroy Saint-Hilaire. Darwin himself criticized Geoffroy's emphasis upon the '*mode ambiant*' as the cause of change of an organism and by implication of the role played by the reciprocal relation between the composition of the organism and the environment. Deleuze, however, discovers a possible rapprochement between Geoffroy and Spinoza through the latter's concept of the 'common notions'. He concludes *Difference and Repetition* by repeating the call for a combination of Spinoza's topology of the distribution of univocal being with Nietzschean selection, but without fully specifying the character of this topology of selection:

> All that Spinozism needed to do for the univocal to become an object of pure affirmation was to make substance turn around the modes – *in other words, to realise univocity in the form of repetition in the eternal return.* (*DR* 304)

Yet this turn folds selection back into distribution, retreating from a Darwinian to a pre-Darwinian biology. To turn substance around the modes through eternal return is precisely to obscure the character of difference and repetition as a succession through the test of selection. It modulates the thought of selection into one of distribution by means of a formula, obscuring the law of distribution through selection by an appeal to the 'crowned anarchies' of 'nomadic distribution'.

It is in the complementary *Expressionism in Philosophy: Spinoza* that Deleuze establishes the conditions for his collapse of selection into a topology of distribution. This study of Spinoza further develops the univocal ontology informing *Difference and Repetition* through the concept of expression. Expression offers the condition of the possibility for a topological analysis of the distribution of being since it 'involves and implicates what it expresses, while also explicating and evolving it' (*EP* 16). The complicated folds which express univocal being resist any move to transcendence; they define what Deleuze will later call a 'plane of immanence'. In the words of *Spinoza: Practical Philosophy*, the plane of immanence 'has no supplementary dimension; the process of composition must be apprehended for itself, through that which it gives, in that which it gives' (*SPP* 128). Expression, or the 'process of composition', is not a form applied to matter, but a 'composition' or 'structure' of being, the mode in which it distributes itself.

Deleuze's careful description of the Spinozan machinery of expression – substance, attributes and modes – culminates in an analysis of the 'common notion' or 'idea of a similarity of composition in existing modes' (*EP* 275). The 'common notions' in Deleuze's reading are not abstractions such as 'transcendental terms' or 'universal notions' but the structural constituents of bodies, their 'composition' (*EP* 277–8). Deleuze argues that 'Spinoza's "common notions" are biological rather than physical or mathematical Ideas. They really do play the part of Ideas in a philosophy of nature from which all finality has been excluded' (*EP* 278). The 'common notions' are expressions of a univocal being, providing, in Deleuze's words, the beginnings of a topological analysis of 'the great principle of compositional unity' in which 'Nature as a whole is a single animal in which only the relations between the parts vary' (*EP* 278). The analysis of the 'common notions' is accordingly immanent, a description of the dynamics of 'the laws of production of essences' and the kinetics of 'the laws of compositions of relations' (*EP* 293) of univocal being.

At a crucial point in his analysis of the obscure 'common notions' Deleuze describes Spinoza as 'a forerunner of Geoffroy Saint-Hilaire'. He expands on this comment in a significant footnote which reveals the pre-Darwinian character of his biophilosophy. He applauds Geoffroy Saint-Hilaire's anti-Aristotelian method, which for Deleuze proposes

> a determination of the variable relations between fixed anatomical components: different animals correspond to variations of relation, respective situation and dependence among those components, so that all are reduced to modifications of a single identical animal as such. For resemblances of form and analogies of function, which must always remain

external, Geoffroy thus substitutes the intrinsic viewpoint of compositional unity or the similarity of relations. (*EP* 393)

Yet while this view of nature is consistently immanent, seeing 'animals' as modifications of a 'single animal', it still conceives of these modifications in terms of distribution, namely 'variations of relation', 'respective situation' and 'dependence'. The implications of this *adaptive* view of the 'common notions' are spelt out more fully in *Spinoza: Practical Philosophy*, as is their link to a bio-ethics and politics. There each body is defined as a relation of motion and rest; different bodies compose new relations with other bodies in their environment. The 'common notion' is accordingly 'the representation of a composition between two or more bodies and a unity of this composition' (*SPP* 56). Through the 'common notions' it is possible to apprehend the composition of bodies

as they are, that is, as they are necessarily embodied in living beings, with the variable and concrete terms between which they are established. In this sense, the common notions are more biological than mathematical, forming a natural geometry that allows us to comprehend the unity of composition of all of Nature and the modes of variation of that unity. (*SPP* 57)

This focus on the modes of variation – the pattern of their distribution – is indebted to both Geoffroy and Spinoza and forms the basis not only of Deleuze's ethology, but also of a bio-ethics and politics.

In their encounters with each other, bodies agree or disagree with each other, leading to the augmentation of the bodies' composition or its destruction. Deleuze reads from these vivifying or destructive relations the affects of joy or sadness, a move which allows him to make with Spinoza the passage from a biophilosophy to a bio-ethics and politics. The purpose of such a bio-ethics and politics is to select joyful encounters, and accordingly in both Spinoza books such selection/composition of joyful encounters is central. In *Expression in Philosophy: Spinoza* Deleuze describes four stages in the formation of an ethics of active joy. The first stage, passive joy, follows from desires and passions based on inadequate ideas; this stage issues in the formation of 'common notions', which form the basis of the active joys which in the fourth stage combine with the passive joys in an affirmative joy of reason (*EP* 284). Crucial to the formation of active joy is the concept of selection, as becomes clear in the subsequent discussion of the passage through the stages of joy.

The passage from the first to the second stage of active joy – the formation of 'common notions' – is encouraged by the joy produced by our body encountering 'another body that agrees (or some other bodies that agree with it)' or impeded by 'the sadness or opposition produced in us by a body that does not agree with our own' (*EP* 287). The passage from the second to the third stage – action according to 'common notions' – is accomplished by the selection of joyful and the avoidance of sad encounters. In the passage from the third to the fourth stage, selection is raised a power by the realization that sad encounters cannot necessarily be avoided but can be experienced selectively as occasions for the active joy that understands their necessity. The 'common notions' are thus biological – concerning the encounter of bodies with each other – and selective, permitting the choice of joyful or sad encounters.

Such a concept of selection fuses biology and philosophical ethics and politics, but perhaps in a way that sentimentalizes selection. Darwinian Selection is not an analogue of judgement, replacing truth and falsity with joy and sadness, but is an implacable selection of those bodies capable of repeating or reproducing themselves. The distance between this concept and Deleuze's concept of selection may be shown by means of a brief conspectus of Darwin's concept of selection, which shows that the topology of selection is more complete than that entertained by Deleuze. Selection is immanent for Darwin, but implacably exterior, favouring a 'law' which admits no exception.

The Law of Selection

In the first sentence of the introduction to *On the Origin of Species by Means of Natural Selection* (1859) Darwin remembers how 'When on board I I.M.S. "Beagle" as a naturalist, I was much struck with certain facts in the distribution of the inhabitants of South America, and in the geological relations of the present to the past inhabitants of that continent'.[7] This opening, of extraordinary economy and beauty, locates the observer at a specific time and place within a vast spatio-temporal continuum. What is observed from this point is a number of facts about 'geographical distribution' and 'geological succession' that together pose a question about the link between the present and past patterns of distribution. The question posed by these facts is then claimed to throw light on the 'mystery of mysteries' that is the 'origin of species'. The answer to the question of the linkage between present and past distributions is to be found neither in an act of creation nor in adaptation to the environment, but in Selection.

For Darwin, Selection links the spatial order of distribution with the temporal order of succession. This linkage is conceived in two ways – through an analogy between 'domestic' and 'natural' selection or through the analysis of those characteristics proper to natural selection. Darwin sees in the argument by analogy 'the best and safest clue' to understanding natural selection, but solely in terms of the insight it gives into the accumulation of successive (and irreversible) variations. The fascination with the patterns of distribution created by the accumulation of successive, infinitesimally small changes was already evident in Darwin's work on the geology of coral reefs. His book of 1842 – *The Structure and Distribution of Coral Reefs* – begins in the same way as the *Origin of Species*, that is, by explaining the origins of the forms of coral reefs from the observation of their distribution.[8] The 'species' in the book of 1859 are like the 'coral reefs' of 1842 not only in terms of the link between the two being conceived as the accumulation of infinitesimally small changes. The polypifers whose remains accumulate to form the coral reefs map by analogy onto the individuals whose accumulated variations accumulate into the species.[9]

It is the accumulative aspect of selection that constitutes the analogy between domestic and natural selection, and not the teleology of domestic selection. The latter is but the human attempt to channel an inhuman process, or in Darwin's words, 'nature gives successive variations; man adds them up in certain directions useful to him' (Darwin 1993, 127). Yet after establishing this analogy in chapter 1 of the *Origin of Species* Darwin totally destroys it in chapter 4 on 'Natural Selection'. Here he dissolves human actions into the inhuman Selection that he calls nature. What is more, he regards this Selection as more rigorous and implacable than any that can be conceived of by analogy to human schemas and purposes. It cannot, for example, be understood in terms of the execution of a ruthless law, since even this analogy would qualify the immanence of nature by a transcendent law or teleology which nature merely executes. Darwin reduces the significance of human interventions by comparing the time of human with that of geological selection: 'How fleeting are the wishes and efforts of man! how short his time! and consequently how poor will his products be compared with those accumulated by nature during whole geological periods.' Such Selection exceeds human understanding not only in terms of its quantity but also in terms of its rigour. Darwin continues:

> It may be said that natural selection is daily and hourly scrutinising, throughout the world, every variation, even the slightest; rejecting that which is bad, preserving and adding up that which is good; silently and insensibly working, whenever and wherever opportunity offers, at the improvement of each organic being in relation to its organic and inorganic conditions of life. (Darwin 1993, 162)

'We' can only imperfectly perceive the results of these changes; we cannot, however, have full insight into the combination of chance and necessity that makes up Selection. The infinitesimally small variation that will pass the scrutiny of Selection and be bequeathed to successive generations cannot be perceived or predicted by human understanding. Selection, indeed, is rigorously exterior to human purposes and yet also immanent in them and in nature.

What is important for Darwin is not so much the patterns of distribution – whether they be those of coral reefs or of species of animals – but the incremental process of selection through which they are formed. In Selection, a minute variation is put to the test of its environment and bequeathed if successful obliterated if not; adaptation is consequently a long-drawn-out play of chance and necessity, one far beyond the time and the purposes of human beings. Consequently it is temporal succession through Selection which ultimately determines spatial patterns of distribution. Deleuze, on the contrary, follows the pre-Darwinian Geoffroy Saint-Hilaire in focusing on patterns of distribution and composition rather than upon selection. In his ethology, distribution would determine selection, except that as Darwin had already observed in his critique of Geoffroy, selection returns to test all patterns of distribution.

The eternal return of Selection

Deleuze's biophilosophy seeks systematically to replace concepts with affects, a programme for which Spinoza's work provides a powerful precedent. Spinoza is situated by Deleuze in a 'great lineage that goes from Epicurus to Nietzsche' (SPP 72) in which the order of concepts such as good and evil is subordinated to an order of active and passive affections. The latter order produces a distribution of organisms whose folds and convolutions are mapped by ethology (SPP 27). Yet the stress upon the biological character of active and passive affections maps awkwardly with the ethical motif of maximizing active and minimizing passive encounters. Deleuze writes with great philosophical pathos:

> It is a disgrace to seek the internal essence of man in his bad extrinsic encounters. Everything that involves sadness serves tyranny and oppression. Everything that involves sadness must be denounced as bad, as something that separates from our power of acting; not only remorse and guilt, not only meditation and death (IV, 67), but even hope, even security, which signify powerlessness. (SPP 72)

While the rhetoric is perhaps admirable, what it hides is the fact that a bio-ethics or politics does not consist in choosing encounters that encourage active affections. For Darwinian biology, such affections would be the result of passing or failing the Selection and not a criterion of that selection itself.

In *Expressionism in Philosophy: Spinoza*, Deleuze presents what can only be described as a humanized account of selection. In the concluding paragraph of his chapter on 'Beatitude' he appears to align Spinoza with a Darwinian naturalism, saying, 'There are no such things as the moral sanctions of a divine Judge, no punishments or rewards, but only the natural consequences of our existence' (*EP* 319). Existence for Deleuze as for Darwin is a test, but for the latter this test is an implacable test of fitness to reproduce, while for the former the test of existence consists in the ethical requirement that 'while existing we must select joyful passions'. The implication of choice and value in Selection persists even in the harder account of selection given in *Spinoza: Practical Philosophy*. There, as already mentioned above, each 'thing' in nature 'selects what affects or is affected by the thing, what moves it or is moved by it'. Deleuze gives as an example the selection pursued by an animal in the world.

> What does it react to positively or negatively? What are its nutrients and its poisons? What does it 'take' in its world? Every point has its counterpoints: the plant and the rain, the spider and the fly. So an animal, a thing, is never separable from its relations to the world. The interior is only a selected exterior, and the exterior, a projected interior. (*SPP* 125)

Here selection is clearly understood in terms of positive and negative affections, a philosophical perspective far from that of natural selection in Darwinian biology. It is a perspective which humanizes nature, at the same time as brutalizing human ethics and politics. The biological and the human orders cannot be so quickly confused without the risk of reducing ethics and politics to the image of a humanized nature.

Deleuze's ethology in the final analysis employs a biological rhetoric to evoke an anti-human, anti-ethical, anti-political, anti-philosophical pathos which sentimentally avoids the implications of biological selection. The immanence of the *Origin of Species* remains far more rigorous and implacable than that of *Difference and Repetition* and *A Thousand Plateaus*. These texts moralize selection, linking it with the active or passive affective relations of an organism to its environment. They provide by default a strong case for maintaining the separation of the biological and the philosophical, especially in respect to their use of the concept of selection. Indeed, there is no place for philosophy with its active and passive capacities and relations within a rigorously defined Darwinian world. Any biophilosophy, consequently, will reduce not only the philosophical to the biological, but also the biological to the philosophical. Certain conceptions of action and classification will be applied to nature and then refracted back into philosophy. In an earlier version of biophilosophy these conceptions were those of race and fitness, while now they are those of passive and active affections. In both cases, nature and politics are sentimentalized and brutalized. By refusing the full rigour of Darwinian Selection, Deleuze is left with a sentimentalized nature and a brutalized ethics and politics.

Notes

1 This discussion forms the kernel of the immediately following collaborations with Guattari – *Anti-Oedipus* and *A Thousand Plateaus*. Both texts are notable for their philosophical *timidity*, for in spite of their rhetorical radicalism each avoids a full reckoning with the implications of Darwinian Selection, preferring to luxuriate in a thematics of distribution.

2 In *Expressionism in Philosophy: Spinoza*, Deleuze elaborates upon equivocation and its two species – eminence and analogy. In the former, infinite being is defined in terms of its excess over finite being, while in the latter it is defined in terms of an internal similarity of relation between the two beings.

3 The opposition of the 'plan of transcendence' and the 'plan of immanence' in this text is the apparent heir to the earlier distinction between the philosophies of representation and difference/repetition.

4 The contour of this 'enveloping measure' will subsequently be traced through the kinetics and dynamics of Deleuze's ethology.

5 [Note by editor of original volume, Keith Ansell-Pearson] As Robert Hurley, the translator of Deleuze's 'little' *Spinoza* book, points out, the French word *plan* covers nearly all the meanings of the English words 'plan' and 'plane'. Hurley proposes that 'plane' should be used only for Deleuze's *plan d'immanence* and *plan de consistance*, not for the notion of *plan de transcendance* or *plan d'organisation*, since the word 'plane' is suggestive of the kind of conceptual-affective continuum that Deleuze has in mind when writing of the *plan d'immanence*. The reader might wish to bear in mind this distinction in navigating the trajectory of Caygill's reading of Deleuze on Spinoza.

6 'Selection', like 'God', is always capitalized by Darwin

7 From the introduction to the first edition reprinted in Darwin 1993, 107. By the sixth edition, the 'inhabitants' had become 'organic beings inhabiting' – see Darwin 1956, 17.

8 'The object of this volume is to describe from my own observation and the work of others, the principal kinds of coral reefs, more especially those occurring in the open ocean, and to explain the origin of their peculiar forms. I do not here treat of the polypifers, which construct these vast works, except so far as relates to their distribution, and to the conditions favourable to their vigorous growth' (Darwin 1993, 72).

9 Darwin himself uses the analogy at the end of the fourth chapter of the *Origin of Species:* 'As buds give rise by growth to fresh buds, and these, if vigorous, branch out and overtop on all sides many a feebler branch, so by generation I believe it has been with the great Tree of Life, which fills with its dead and broken branches the crust of the earth, and covers the surface with its ever branching and beautiful ramifications' (Darwin 1956, 194).

17

The force of Kant's *Opus postumum*: Kepler and Newton in the XIth fascicle

The *Opus postumum* is what remains of a work in progress that occupied Kant for much of the last decade of his life. It survives as a collection of fascicles or bundles of manuscripts that begin in the early 1790s and continue until 1803, shortly before its author's death. Although not able to bring this last work to publication, Kant nevertheless regarded it as completing 'the task of the critical philosophy' and thought sufficiently highly of his achievement to refer to it as 'his chief work, a *chef d'oeuvre*'.[1] Despite its author's own commendation, the text as a whole remained unpublished until G. Lehmann and A. Buchenau's edition for the Prussian Academy of Sciences in the mid-1930s.[2] The tormented publishing history of the manuscript began with doubts among Kant's contemporaries concerning his state of mental health in the last years of his life. The view that any attempt to put into question the major achievements of the critical philosophy was a symptom of mental decline was implicitly shared by later generations of Kantians, notoriously voiced by Kuno Fischer, who insisted that the critical philosophy was completed by the *Critique of Judgement*.[3] Reticence concerning the *Opus postumum* continues, with the text remaining one of the least interpreted of the Kantian oeuvre. Yet, with even a minimal degree of interpretative charity, the *Opus postumum* can be seen to mark a number of important departures for the critical philosophy, especially with respect to the philosophy of science. These are admittedly obscured by the note-like character and apparent absence of structure that characterizes this (or any) work in progress, but once past these obstacles it quickly becomes apparent that the *Opus postumum* proposes a revolutionary – but also consistent – departure for Kant's thought.

One of the most provocative aspects of the *Opus postumum* is its apparent polemic against Newton – perhaps surprising given the ancillary role the critical philosophy is often held to play with respect to the *Mathematical Principles of Natural Philosophy*. The scale of the differences with Newton is evident even at the level of the structure of the *Opus postumum*, as has been shown by the reconstruction of its architecture proposed by its Italian translator Vittorio Mathieu. The 'gap' in the critical philosophy addressed by Kant is located between the 'metaphysical principles of natural science' and 'physics', the work in progress itself constituting a 'transition' between metaphysical principles and physics. Mathieu shows that this transition was to be accomplished in two parts: a 'System of the Elements of the Motive Forces of Matter' and a 'System of the World'. The first comprised a 'division of forces' and a transition to the system of the world by means of the concept of ether, while the second was to comprise a cosmology and a further transition or 'return from metaphysical principles to transcendental philosophy as a system of the ideas of pure reason', providing an astonishing and affirmative return to the concerns of 'special metaphysics' (God, world and the soul) that were subject to critical scrutiny in the transcendental dialectic of the *Critique of Pure Reason*.

The parallel between the structure of Kant's projected text and that of Newton's *Mathematical Principles of Natural Philosophy* is striking, and certainly not accidental. The first two books of Newton's work concern the motion of bodies in a vacuum and in a resistant medium while the third book presents a 'system of the world' concluded by a 'General Scholium' on God and the world. The suspicion that Kant's *Opus postumum* represents his attempt to rewrite the *Mathematical Principles of Natural Philosophy* is corroborated by the methodological critique of Newton developed most fully in the XIth fascicle dating from 1800 but anticipated throughout the *Opus postumum*. In the XIth fascicle Kant scrutinized the relationship between the work of Kepler and Newton in order to question the historical claim that Newton's concept of force offered a physical and metaphysical account of the mathematical regularities in celestial motion detected by Kepler.

The discussion of Kepler and Newton in the *Opus postumum* was not Kant's first thought on the character of the relationship between the two scientists. In the *Idea for a Universal History with a Cosmopolitan Purpose* (1784) he alludes to a particular view of the historical relationship between the work of Kepler (1571–1630) and Newton (1642–1727). In illustrating the difference between discovering the 'guiding principle' of a 'purpose in nature behind the senseless course of human events' and writing the history of such a purpose, Kant produces an analogy to the different achievements of Kepler and Newton: 'Thus nature produced a Kepler who found an unexpected means of reducing the eccentric orbits of the planets to definite laws, and a Newton who explained these laws in terms of a universal natural cause' (Kant 2007,

109). Reversing the direction of Kant's analogy it is evident that Kepler is cast as discovering the 'purpose in nature' of the wandering motions of planets, while Newton provided an account or causal history that explained them. While there remains some question as to what precisely Kant might mean by Kepler's 'unexpected means' (*unerwartete Weise*) – whether he is referring to the discovery of the laws of planetary motions by means of mathematical and musical mysticism or to the laws themselves – the point of the analogy is transparent: Kepler achieved a kinematic description of planetary motion that was subsequently expanded by a Newtonian dynamics of force. This is a view that has been questioned by historians of science such as Dijksterhuis, who argued that Kepler had at the end of his life moved towards dynamics of force, and Koyré, who read Newton's *Principia* as a defence of the 'Copernican-Keplerian system' rather than simply its extension.[4] Kant, too, would have his doubts in the *Opus postumum*, but implied in these were wider concerns regarding the relationship between philosophy and science in general. Remaining within the terms of the analogy posed in *Ideas for a Universal History from a Cosmological Viewpoint*, in the later work Kant questioned not so much the *fact* of Newton's dynamic history of planetary motion as its philosophical or scientific character.

The XIth fascicle, which contains the most extensive discussion of Kepler and Newton, is located by Mathieu at the point of transition between the system of the elements of the motive forces of matter and the system of the world (Kant 1984, 59). In this fascicle Kant concerns himself with such questions as 'what is physics?', 'how is physics possible?' and 'what is the transition from the metaphysical foundations of natural science to physics?' This set of questions is typical of the entire *Opus postumum* but is given a particular inflection at this point in the compositional history of the work (1800) and by its place within the overall structure of the work in progress. The general problem of the *Opus postumum* – namely the transition from metaphysical principles of natural science to physics – required a firm understanding of the difference between 'metaphysical principles of natural science' and 'physics'. While 'metaphysical principles of natural science' referred specifically to Kant's 1886 text of the same name, his earlier elaboration of such principles in terms of attractive and repulsive force is extended in *Opus postumum* into a more elaborate account of force and its medium, ether and/or caloric. The question 'what is physics?', however, required a fresh approach, and much of the XIth fascicle comprises repeated attempts at a definition, moving through subjective and objective definitions of the science to the emergence of a definite outline to the science when Kant begins to distinguish between philosophy and mathematical natural science. It becomes most clear when he begins to take a distance from the approach to the mathematical principles of natural philosophy represented by Newton.

In one of his efforts to define physics in the XIth fascicle, Kant draws a number of unexpected distinctions. The most surprising of these, in retrospect, is his attempt to distinguish physics from natural science. The Latin expression *scientia naturalis* contains the danger, according to Kant, of its content and method being opposed to (and thus brought into proximity with) 'artificial' and 'revealed' science. Yet for Kant the 'natural' of 'natural science' signifies more than an alternative to artificial or revealed science, and to avoid such misunderstandings Kant prefers the expression 'science of nature' to 'natural science' when describing physics as 'the universal doctrine of experience of the objects of both outer and inner senses (insofar as it forms a doctrinal system)' (*OP* 137–8). This distinction, however, is but the prelude to a further attempt to assign the territory of physics, one contained in the lapidary claim that 'physics belongs to philosophy'. The claim is justified by physics being 'philosophical, not merely empirical, not mathematical'. In this case the title 'natural philosophy' is also to be shunned, but for different reasons than that of 'natural science'.

Natural philosophy, and specifically that practised by Newton, combines – illegitimately in Kant's eyes – philosophical and mathematical reasoning. Newton's 'immortal work *philosophiae naturalis principia mathematica*' is described as creating 'a bastard (*conceptus hybridus*)' that is neither legitimately philosophical nor mathematical (*OP* 138). The *Principia* performs the amphiboly of making philosophy and metaphysics into a branch of mathematics, rather than recognizing that philosophy 'must set metaphysical foundations prior to mathematical ones', since the former concern reason in its 'unconditional employment' while the latter concern reason in its 'conditional employment as a tool for a particular purpose' (*OP* 138). Metaphysics, the revival of which is intimated in the last section of the *Opus postumum*, should not be subordinated to the technical procedures proper to mathematics. The two approaches to knowledge may complement each other in a 'natural science', but not in the philosophy of nature. Physics belongs to the latter with respect to its object and its 'formal element' (the laws of nature), a discipline to which Kant also gives the name – following Campanella's late Renaissance anti-Aristotelian philosophy of nature – of physiology.[5] These reflections culminate in a proposal to re-title Newton's 'immortal work': 'The title should be *scientiae naturalis principia mathematica* (not *philosophiae*)' – that is, mathematical principles of natural science rather than natural *philosophy* (*OP* 140). The latter is not amenable to mathematical principles, requiring instead metaphysical principles which in their turn have to be related to physics – hence the problem of the 'transition' from one to the other with which the entire *Opus postumum* is concerned.

The *Opus postumum* – or, as it may be re-titled, *The Metaphysical Principles of Natural Philosophy* – is no less than a fundamental challenge to

Newton. Kant is explicit about this in a reflection on 'what is physics?' later in the fascicle. The reflection repeats the scruple concerning the term 'natural science' (now opposed to 'supernatural' science, but with less interest). Kant is more concerned now to distinguish between the illegitimate natural philosophy according to mathematical principles and the legitimate contender,

> a certain work with the title: *Metaphysical Foundations of Natural Science* [wherein] philosophical principles of the latter were developed. For metaphysics is a part of philosophy, and nothing but metaphysics could be at issue in the transition from philosophy to the science of nature, if it is a matter of knowledge from concepts. (*OP* 151)

The author of the same work sees himself as having a rival – a *Nebenbuhler* – 'no less a man, indeed, than Newton himself in his immortal work **Philosophiae** *naturalis principia* **mathematica**' (*OP* 151). Kant sees this title now as 'self-contradictory', since analytically, for him, natural philosophy cannot be conducted by means of mathematical principles. After generously repeating the offer to his rival to change his title to 'Mathematical principles of natural science', Kant insists that the relationship between the metaphysical principles of natural philosophy and the mathematical principles of natural science is not associative. Natural philosophy, implicated in the absolute ends of reason, can make legitimate use of 'technical' mathematical principles, but natural science cannot legitimately subordinate metaphysical principles in the way allegedly performed by Newton: 'One can <indeed,> also make philosophical use of mathematics, <but only indirectly> as an *instrument*; remaining on the track laid down by the transition from the metaphysical foundations of natural science' (*OP* 151). Kant now introduces further precision into his account. A mathematical account of nature would depart from the fact of motion and its laws in space and time and derive from them dynamic forces, while in an account developed according to metaphysical principles 'the moving forces must precede in order for motions to take place' (*OP* 151). A philosophical transition from metaphysical principles of natural science departs from notions of force to arrive at descriptions of motion and the space and time in which they are set, while a mathematical transition would begin with descriptions of motion and move towards metaphysical reflections upon force.

With the question of the nature of the legitimate transition from metaphysical principles to physics, and the existence of rival illegitimate transitions from mathematical principles to physics, Kant begins a chain of reflections on the nature of Newton's immortal achievement by means of a comparison with Kepler. In a marginal note to the above discussion he observes that mathematics can act *indirectly* to establish philosophical principles. Echoing the discussion of the main text, where philosophy could make indirect use of mathematics, Kant now suggests that mathematical principles can 'establish problems which point in the direction of physics and the moving forces of matter (and hence, also, toward philosophy)' (*OP* 151). He thereby opens the possibility of an indirect transition from the laws of motion to the dynamics of forces which he identifies with the work of Kepler. Newton, however, represents the precipitate and illegitimate leap from the mathematical identification of a problem to its 'philosophical' solution:

> Kepler's three famous analogies led to a coup on Newton's part, in which he declared gravitational attraction by a bold but inevitable hypothesis for physics; in this way mathematics was endowed, for the sake of the science of nature, with the ability to prescribe laws to nature *a priori*, laws which it could by no means have made use of for philosophy in the absence of such a capacity [*Organ*]. Yet this transition was a step [*breaks off*]. (*OP* 151)

The passage offers a number of important clues for identifying Kant's scruples with respect to the achievement of Newton compared to that of Kepler.

In using the term 'analogy' to describe Kepler's laws, Kant is carefully insisting that what became known as 'laws' were analogies – mathematical ratios or proportions – discovered in the course of astronomical observation (although the third law emerged in *De Harmonices Mundi* in the context of Pythagorean speculation). The first analogy or ratio related the changing distances of the planets from the sun in terms of their elliptical orbits, the second related motion and time through the discovery that a planet swept equal areas of its orbit in equal time, while the third related the square of the true period of the planet's orbit to the cube of its average distance from the sun. Kepler also possessed metaphysical or dynamic 'explanations' for these analogies (if they did precede their discovery) – locating them in the *anima motrix* or later *vis motrix* of the sun – but Kant did not subject these to analysis. He was more interested in the way that Newton explained Kepler's ratios. Ironically referring to the 'hypothesis' of gravitational attraction (Newton famously claimed not to make hypotheses), Kant saw Newton as investing mathematical ratios with a dynamic explanation. Yet for Kant, although this seemed to give mathematics 'the ability to prescribe laws to nature *a priori*' – a capacity previously reserved for philosophy – this was achieved by the subreptive use of the metaphysical principle of force; Newton, Kant observes, 'made his most important conquest by means of philosophy, not mathematics' (*OP* 151). The *Nebenbuhler* was successful by means of smuggling metaphysical principles in a mathematical guise.

Turning from the question of 'what is physics?' to that of 'how is physics possible?', Kant goes deeper into the question of the metaphysical principles of natural science. As if explaining why his 1786 *Metaphysical Foundations of*

Natural Science seemed to have remained unsuccessful in comparison with its centenarian *Nebenbuhler*, Kant points to its limitation in defining matter as the moveable in space. In place of this limited version he offers another, more radical definition of matter as 'that *which makes space an object of the senses*' (*OP* 152). It is immediately apparent that this move from a mechanical to a dynamic definition of matter had radical consequences not only for the immediate question of the possibility of physics but also for the fate of the critical philosophy as a whole. For that which makes space into an object of the senses – matter – is itself *force*. Kant notes in the margin of the manuscript that 'it is matter which makes space into an object of experience (perception); that is, the moving forces outwardly in space and internally in sensation. For sensation and feelings also belong to physics' (*OP* 152). Force thus traverses both movement in space and internal sensation, yet it is important for Kant that it possesses its own dynamic. The transition from the discussion of the elements to the system of the world pivoted on the existence of an ether or caloric – explicitly echoing the *pneuma* of Stoic physics – which provided the medium for the dynamic play of attractive and repulsive force. According to Kant, this dynamic play of the two original forces is not fully developed by Newton, who precipitately rests his dynamics on 'attraction, as cause of gravity'. Kant suggests that by emphasizing only attractive force, Newton's explanation remains committed to the priority of motion and to a notion of its taking place in empty space – attraction is only 'conditionally given a priori, as a moving force' (*OP* 152). Against this view Kant argues for a plenum articulated in terms of the absolute a priori opposition of attractive and repulsive force: 'for, without attraction and repulsion, infinite space would remain empty' (*OP* 152). The critique of Newton is thus engaged on the terrain of force, and the difference rests ultimately on the metaphysical character accorded to force.

In the ensuing discussion of Kepler and Newton, Kant's position becomes rather more nuanced: Newton's 'coup', or his 'step' across from mathematics to physics, becomes an exercise in bridge building between them, but without, according to Kant, achieving a full and reasoned transition. Continuing to explore the question of 'how is physics possible?', Kant reasons that 'motion can be treated entirely mathematically' because it is 'nothing but concepts of space and time' presented in intuition but made by the understanding.[6] However, discussion of the efficient causes of such motion requires philosophical principles of moving forces:

All mathematics, then, brings one not the least bit nearer to philosophical knowledge unless a causal combination such as that of the attraction or repulsion of matter by its moving forces is first brought on the scene and postulated for the sake of appearances. As soon as the latter occurs, the transition to physics has taken place, and there can be *philosophia naturalis principia mathematica*. (*OP* 153)

A causal history of motion requires the postulation of forces – a postulate for Kant being a form of *prolepsis* or anticipation of perception. For Kant, such postulation should not be derived from motion but anticipates it; in short, it has to be justified *metaphysically*. Newton's practice, however, was to postulate force on the basis of mathematical description, but without offering a full metaphysical justification of the postulate – that is, without offering a systematic account of the transition from the metaphysics to the physics of force.

Bringing force onto the 'scene' of the mathematical description of motion and postulating it 'for the sake of appearances' – that is, using it to explain appearance – is a form of transition to physics and one that makes possible the 'mathematical principles of natural philosophy'. But for Kant it is not a fully justified transition: it is a philosophical transition, but one that does not justify itself philosophically. Newton's postulate of force is thus philosophical, but for Kant not *sufficiently* so. It both postulates force as prior to motion but allows the principle of force to remain too close to the description of motion. Regarding the passage to 'mathematical principles of natural philosophy', Kant writes:

> This step was taken by Newton in the role of a philosopher who brings new forces onto the scene; not, indeed, as forces derived from pre-supposed motions (centripetal and centrifugal) which would contain only mathematical principles, but original forces (*vires primariae*) in which mathematics is only used as an instrument for the moving forces (whereas philosophy is required to ground them primordially). (*OP* 153)

Newton, while making 'his conquest' by means of philosophy, did not do so *philosophically*: putting to use the a priori concepts of 'original forces', he did not respect the philosophical requirement to 'ground them primordially'.

Kant is not only engaged in trying to save the honour of natural philosophy before the opportunism of Newton but is also concerned that the absence of primordial grounding of dynamic concepts may generate unnecessary philosophical and scientific problems. The absence of a reasoned and justified transition from metaphysical principles to physics may lead to the diversion of physics. He reflects on this by returning again to the question of Kepler and Newton. Newton's step – his rushed transition – occurred because 'once Kepler's three analogies had grounded all the mathematically determined laws of the rotation of the planets by sufficient observation, there yet remained the question for physics regarding the efficient cause of this appearance' (*OP* 153–4). Kepler's role has now changed subtly. The analogies (proportions/ratios) discovered by observation of planetary orbits are transformed by their confirmation in a further act of observation of 'mathematically determined laws'. The analogies, by means of observations, are invested with necessity or the character of physical law. But it is in Kantian terms a mathematical necessity –

concerning quantity and relation – and not a dynamic one concerning quality and modality. The 'mathematically determined laws' of planetary motion – law at the level of appearance – left open the question 'of the efficient cause of this appearance'. It is a question that was also experienced as a 'difficulty', as witnessed by Kepler's own attempts at dynamic solutions.

Kant saw Newton as responding to the predicament bequeathed by Kepler but described this response in hardly complementary terms: 'Newton, in order to find a way out of this difficulty, built a bridge from mathematics to physics, namely, the principle of an attractive force, penetrating all bodies through empty space, according to the inverse law of the square of the distance' (*OP* 154). Instead of working through the difficult transition by metaphysically justifying dynamic principles, Newton in Kant's reading sought to evade the difficulty by building a bridge between mathematics and physics, exploiting philosophical principles at the same time as avoiding their full and reasoned exposition. Newton was philosophical in so far as 'he did not, thus, rest content with appearances, but brought into play a primordially moving force' (*OP* 154), but without philosophically justifying it: Newton's primordial force, in other words, remains an hypothesis.

At this point in his argument, Kant's critique begins to change direction. He wishes to argue at the outset that Newton proposed only a single force but changes his view in mid-thought. Continuing the thought of the 'primordially moving force', his notes 'on the one hand' break off before arriving at the other hand:

> on the one hand [primordially moving force] presented universal reciprocal gravitation [as] merely forces striving towards one another according to Kepler's law; and in the end, however, it presented these forces as a universal attraction in infinite space of bodies and of the matter in general which fills the universe. As hypothesis [*breaks off*]. (*OP* 154)

The uncertainty as to the relationship between the plurality and unicity of forces that Kant detects in Newton is taken up immediately afterwards, when Kant has Newton proliferating the number of forces at play in the physical universe. Kant is trying to show that Newton's use of force – because it is not justified by a full philosophical transition – is subject to internal instability. It relies on both a unity and plurality of force/forces:

> As regards, *firstly*, the relations of the moving forces (in space) Newton made use of the concept of the *attraction* of all cosmic bodies in infinite space, and their motions by means of those forces in time. **Secondly**, [he makes use of the concept of] the *repulsion* of parts of matter, which [extends] itself in cosmic space, according to the same law, by means

of light and its laws of motion in colours (imponderable, incoercible, incohesible, inexhaustible); all of which is thoroughly mathematical. Then, however, also of fluidity and solidity [*breaks off*]. (*OP* 154)

Kant will subsequently return to elaborate the details of this passage.

In the succeeding paragraph Kant recapitulates the basic claim of the first part of the *Opus postumum*, namely that 'Attraction and repulsion are the acts of the agitating forces of matter, which contain *a priori* a principle of the possibility of experience and the transition to physics' (*OP* 154–5). This states that neither experience nor the objects of experience are possible without the play of the forces of attraction and repulsion: they are conditions of the movement of matter as well as of the 'possibility of perception in it'. Importantly, it is the relationship between the two forces that provides the '*a priori* principle' that in Kant's judgement Newton lacked. The concept of attractive force was more fully developed in Newton than that of repulsive force, but for Kant both are of equal dignity. After this restatement of the doctrine of force in the first part of the *Opus postumum*, Kant returns to Kepler and Newton:

to [proceed] from Kepler's forms (his three analogies) to the moving forces which act in conformity with them; [to develop] the system of universal gravitation from original attraction or motion from repulsion (in [the form of] which light and sound [are given] for optics and acoustics); and thus to found physics, in conjunction with other relations of force. (*OP* 155)

This recapitulation then leads to the most explicit statement of his critique of Newton and of the underlying motivation of the *Opus postumum*:

It is noteworthy that Newton's propositions in his *Principia philosophiae mathematica* are not developed systematically, from a principle, but had to be compiled empirically and rhapsodically. Consequently, they led to the expectation of ever new additions, and, hence, his book could not contain a philosophical system. (*OP* 155)

The reference to the absence of a principle being filled by an empirical and rhapsodic compilation echoes Kant's critique of Aristotle in the *Critique of Pure Reason*. There, Kant described his own table of the categories as 'developed systematically from a common principle, namely, the faculty of judgement', comparing his systematic procedure with Aristotle's rhapsodic approach. His division of the categories 'has not arisen rhapsodically, as a result of a haphazard search after pure concepts, the complete enumeration of which, as based on induction only, could never be guaranteed' (*CPR* A81/B106). He continues, 'it was an enterprise worthy of an acute thinker like Aristotle to make a search for these fundamental concepts. But he did so on no principle, he merely picked them up as they came his way.' Rhapsodic procedure is fully consistent with empiricism; Aristotle, for example – the 'chief of the empiricists' (*CPR* A855/ B882) – enumerated his categories according to induction 'after a haphazard search'. The link between poetic rhapsody and empiricism is filled out later in the closing pages of the *Critique* in the 'Architectonic of Pure Reason'. There, discussing the predicament of a 'founder of a science' (referring to Aristotle, Newton and perhaps also to himself), Kant notes that the foundation of a science involves 'the rhapsodic collection of materials according to an idea hidden within us' (*CPR* A835/863). As in poetry, the aesthetic idea (in this case of a possible science) is not directly visible but guides the selection of material. After a period of time and assembly it is possible to view the idea 'in a clearer light' – if it has not, that is, already fallen to ruin. The problem with rhapsodic assemblies of materials is that their coherence 'could never be guaranteed'.

What held for Aristotle's categories and the foundation of metaphysics in the *Critique of Pure Reason* now holds in the *Opus postumum* for Newton's forces and the foundations of physics. Newton's founding of a science on the basis of dynamics obeyed a not entirely transparent idea of such a science, but his procedure, according to Kant, could not guarantee the systematic coherence of a philosophy of nature – the *Principia*, in other words, 'could not contain a philosophical system' and could not guarantee its assemblage of forces. To do so would require a *deduction* of these forces, one which was ventured by Kant in the discussion of the transition from the metaphysical principles of natural science to physics in the *Opus postumum*. Kant's motivation in criticizing Newton was in a real sense that of completing the foundation of physics by making explicit the notion of force that, returning to the general problem of the foundation of sciences explored in the 'Architectonic' of the first *Critique*, formed the 'schema, nay even the definition which, at the start, he first gave of the science [but which] is seldom adequate to his idea' (A834/862). The transition may be understood as the systematic exposition of the unstable inspiration prompted by the idea of a dynamic physics.

The unfolding of the idea of a dynamic physics is evident in Kant's subsequent and fuller account of the transition from Kepler to Newton, from mechanics to dynamics. After recapitulating his exposition of force, Kant returns to the history of modern physics, beginning: 'The *laws* of motion were sufficiently established by Kepler's three analogies. They were entirely mechanical' (*OP* 157). From the discovery of the mechanical laws he then describes the emergence of the idea of a dynamic explanation of these laws, continuing: 'Huygens knew also of composite yet derivative motion, forces fleeing from the midpoint or constantly driving towards it (*vis centrifuga et centripetal*)' (*OP* 157). Although for Kant both Kepler and Huygens came close to postulating a universal force of gravitation – already anticipated by Galileo's 'law of the gravity of falling bodies at heights which led to an approximately equal moment in their fall' – all their efforts remained 'empiricism in the doctrine of motion' (*OP* 157). What the science lacked was a 'universal principle', 'a concept of reason from which it would be possible to infer *a priori* a law for the determination of forces' (*OP* 157). Newton made a step towards this principle with the force of attraction, but it remained for Kant partial, action at a distance across empty space. The idea of succeeding mechanical by dynamical explanation was sound – attraction was dynamic, not transmitted mechanically by means of motion between bodies – but left the force in question to operate in ways not fully understood. Kant's response, prepared in the first part of the *Opus postumum*, was to propose a counter-force to attraction: 'To this Newtonian principle of universal attraction through empty space there corresponds a similar principle of repulsion (*virium repellentium*), which, likewise, cannot be an object of experience in itself, but is only necessary in order to present space as an object of the senses' (*OP* 157). Both forces make up ether or caloric, which is not matter but the condition of possibility for matter and its experience. With this, Kant closes with the justification for his critical completion of Newtonian physics, which is also the physical completion of the critical philosophy – 'We are here concerned only with the problem of transcendental philosophy: how is synthetic knowledge *a priori* possible?' (*OP* 158) or, in the words of the statement of the highest principle of all synthetic judgement in the first *Critique*, 'the conditions of the *possibility of experience* in general are likewise conditions of the *possibility of the objects of experience*' (*CPR* A158/B197).

With the return to the fundamental problem of transcendental philosophy, Kant looks forward to the second major transition to be accomplished in the *Opus postumum*. After the philosophical completion of Newtonian physics by means of the transition from metaphysical principles to physics, Kant prepares to move from physics to transcendental philosophy as a system of pure reason. The completion of the Newtonian physics whose example presided over the critical enterprise thus also entailed the completion of metaphysics and the return of the ideas of pure reason. For these reasons Kant's own high view of the ambition and achievement of the *Opus postumum* should be considered more sympathetically. Its own rhapsodical assemblage – even if it fell into ruin before its completion – announced the season of systematic philosophy in Germany, one in which philosophers such as Schelling and Hegel attempted to reconcile the work of science with the philosophy of the absolute idea.

Notes

1   Citations from the Introduction to Eckart Förster and Michael Rosen's translation, *OP* xvi–xvii. When citing the main text, Kant's later additions are marked with angle brackets.

2   Kant 1902–, vols. XXI and XXII (1936–38). Gerhardt Lehmann subsequently wrote some of the most intelligent commentary on the text, relating its concerns to those of the *Critique of Judgement*; for a collection of his articles spanning several decades, see Lehmann 1969.

3   For a helpful account of the publishing history of the *Opus postumum*, and in particular the dispute between Albrecht Krause and Fischer concerning its significance or otherwise, see the Introduction to *OP* esp. xvi–xxix. Förster is also the author of the most sustained attempt at commentary upon the *Opus postumum* in English (Förster 2000).

4   See Dijksterhuis 1986, 310, for Kepler's replacement of the word *anima* by *vis* (force); and Koyré 1965, 30.

5   For Campanella's definition of physiology as the science of the things of nature in so far as they are generated and corruptible, see Campanella 1999, 36.

6   He notes that although the concepts of space and time are 'presented *a priori* in pure intuition, the understanding *makes* them' (*OP* 153).

18

Technology and the propitiation of chance

And why do they bother to throw their bolts in the desert?
Is it for exercise and to tone up their muscles?
Why do they waste their ammunition on earth
Instead of keeping it for the old man's enemies?

– LUCRETIUS, *DE RERUM NATURA*, BOOK VI

It is hardly necessary to add, that it is not advisable,
during a thunder storm,
to stand on the roof of a house so protected,
or to stand on the ground outside and lean against the wall.

– JAMES CLERK MAXWELL, 'ON THE PROTECTION OF BUILDINGS
FROM LIGHTNING' (*SP* 540)

In his essay 'On the Protection of Buildings from Lightning', James Clerk Maxwell (1831–79) applies his research into electromagnetic force to the problem of protecting a 'gunpowder manufactory' from being struck by lightning. His largely forgotten essay makes a contribution to the ancient problem of how to propitiate and hopefully avoid the chance event of being struck by lightning. The ancient solution of divinizing chance, by making lightning the weapon of Zeus and its avoidance a matter of prayer and sacrifice, was fundamentally questioned in Epicurus's meteorological *Letter to Pythocles* and the last book of Lucretius's *Poem on Nature*.[1] Both show that lightning is a natural event explicable without any reference to divinity, yet this knowledge alone does not necessarily liberate us from the fear of chance. At the other end of the same tradition, Aby Warburg closes his 1923 lecture *Images from the Region of the Pueblo Indians of North America* with a reference to 'The lightning imprisoned in wire-captured electricity – [that] has produced a culture with no use for paganism', decrying the hubris of the technological civilization made possible by Maxwell's discoveries that considered itself to have overcome chance by means of technology (Warburg [1923] 1997, 54). Warburg's diagnosis of the optimism of technology, however sound, nevertheless underestimates the persistent threat of chance in Maxwell's work and, by extension, in the technological civilization that it made possible.

Maxwell's approach to the technology of protection from lightning by no means assumes that chance can be overcome. It consists in identifying lightning as an electrical discharge and trying to prevent it by minimizing conduction between two charged bodies. The theme of movement across a medium – conduction, diffusion – was central to many aspects of Maxwell's work and provided the scenario for his celebrated thought experiment known as 'Maxwell's demon'. The question of the identity of Maxwell's demon secretly haunts any discussion of the propitiation of chance by technology. Like all demons, Maxwell's has a secret, and like most demonic secrets, this one involves life and death. Much of the passion aroused by Maxwell's 'thought experiment' is driven by an intimation of this secret, the suspicion that the demon somehow achieves the impossible by overcoming the second law of thermodynamics, arresting or even reversing the process of entropy, making the bolt of lightning return to the sky. Nineteenth-century reflection on the second law imagined maximum entropy or the state in which the universe's energy has been converted into heat, in terms of death, the 'heat death of the universe'. Maxwell's demon, by virtue of using information to arrest or reverse the process of entropy, becomes a crypto-saviour figure who stands behind many contemporary assumptions that entropy can be contained by information and information-based technologies.

James Clerk Maxwell himself never used the term 'demon' and, for interesting philosophical reasons, was always very specific and precise about the scenario and the cast of his parable or 'thought experiment'. He is remembered, perhaps anachronistically, as a physicist whose discovery of the laws of electrodynamics was described by Richard Feynman as the 'most significant event of the nineteenth century',[2] providing the foundations for the technological revolution of the twentieth century. He was best known initially among his contemporaries for his research into the nature and consciousness of colour, producing the first colour photograph and anticipating the principles of colour television. However, his work in what became known as science and his commitment to technological experiment and application was rooted in philosophical and even religious speculation at the core of which lay a very radical cosmo-anthropology with classical antecedents.

The summoning forth of Maxwell's 'demon' is inseparable from the broader context of his scientific, philosophical and cultural interests. At the end of 1867 Maxwell was asked by Henry Tate to comment on his draft of a treatise on thermodynamics. In reply Maxwell raised some questions about the status of the second law in the form of a 'thought experiment'. Two vessels A and B of equal volume are separated by a diaphragm, one containing 'elastic molecules' with a 'greater energy of motion' than the other. Maxwell continues:

> Now conceive a finite being who knows the paths and velocities of all the molecules by simple inspection but who can do no work except to open and close a hole in the diaphragm by means of a slide without mass. Let him first observe the molecules in A and when he sees one coming, the square of whose velocity is less than the mean square of the molecules in B, let him open the hole and let it go into B. Next let him watch for a molecule in B, the square of whose velocity is greater than the mean square velocity in A, and when it comes to the hole let him draw the slide and let it go into A keeping the slide shut for all other molecules. Then the number of molecules in A and B are the same as at first but the energy in A is increased and that in B is diminished, that is the hot system has got hotter and the cold colder and yet no work has been done, only the intelligence of a very observant and neat fingered being has been employed.[3]

Maxwell ends this evocation of what seems to be a perpetual motion machine of the second type fuelled by intelligence with the comment that human beings cannot achieve this result, 'not being clever enough'. The movement between A and B was thus not entirely predictable; it was only possible for a very special kind of being, one neither human nor technological. In principle, however, the thought experiment suggested that a finite intelligent being was capable of arresting the necessary execution of the Second Law of thermodynamics. Maxwell's intent in formulating this fictional scenario was complex: he wanted above all to argue for the limited statistical validity of the Second Law of Thermodynamics, showing it to have no 'mechanical basis'. This was a thinly veiled reply to James Thomson's objection to his notion of the electromagnetic field proposed in the 1864 *A Dynamical Theory of the Electromagnetic Field* where his notions of the field and primacy of waves seemed to break with classical mechanics (Maxwell [1864] 1983). However, the emergence of a demonology out of this scenario was entirely the work of Thomson in his response to the thought experiment. Maxwell commented ironically on this interpretation in a parodic catechism 'Concerning Demons' in which he asks:

1   Who gave them this name? Thomson.

2   What were they by nature? Very small BUT lively beings incapable of doing work but able to open and shut valves which move without friction or inertia.

3   What was their chief end? To show that the 2nd law of thermodynamics has only a statistical certainty.

4   Is the production of an inequality of temperature their only occupation? No, for less intelligent demons can produce a difference in pressure as well as temperature by merely allowing all the particles going in one direction while stopping all those going the other way. As such value him. Call him no more a demon but a valve like that of the hydraulic ram, suppose.[4]

The character of the demon is open to dispute. Crosbie Smith understands Maxwell not to object to Thomson's use of the term 'demon' and perhaps even to consider a human candidate for the role of demon, while Peter Harman argues against his acceptance of the term 'demon' maintaining that the function of the latter could be performed technologically by a valve or 'self-acting device'.[5] Maxwell does indeed distance himself from the demonization of the 'small but lively being' who can intervene against the Second Law of Thermodynamics at a molecular level, but this did not prevent the emergence of a lively demonological discussion in the twentieth century. Leo Szilard in 1929 and Brillouin in the 1950s challenge Maxwell's scenario by insisting in different ways that the demon performs work, thus contributing to an increase in entropy, whether by the work of opening and closing the aperture, in measuring velocity and location or, more recently, by erasing accumulated information on past locations and velocities.

Yet it is important to insist that the demon is not Maxwell's. His descriptions of the agent in his scenario are very precise, as in 'conceive a finite being' – a demon is not a finite being. He also distinguishes the agent from a machine, restricting the automatic selection to a gatekeeper function which is not the active choice of the 'finite being'. The agent is neither demonic nor technological, but its action should not in any simple way be anthropomorphized. Some idea of the subtle complexity of Maxwell's position, and its extreme philosophical radicalism, may be gathered from his 1878 *Encyclopaedia Britannica* article on 'Diffusion'. Here Maxwell puts into question the entire entropic scenario by way of a reflection on 'finite beings', one which has been neglected in the previous underestimation of Maxwell's philosophical interests. Maxwell argues that a certain understanding of the relationship between knowledge and energy is assumed in the entropic scenario into which the demon was introduced:

It follows from this that the idea of dissipation of energy depends upon the extent of our knowledge. Available energy is energy we can direct into any desired channel. Dissipated energy is energy which we cannot lay hold of and direct at pleasure, such as the energy of the confused agitation of molecules which we call heat. Now confusion, like the correlative term order, is not a property of material things in themselves, but only in relation to the mind which perceives them. A memorandum book does not, provided it is neatly written, appear confused to an illiterate person, or to the owner who understands it thoroughly, but to any other person able to read it appears to be inextricably confused. Similarly the notion of dissipated energy could not occur to a being who could not turn any of the energies of nature to his own account, or to one who could trace the motion of every molecule and seize it at the right moment. It is only to a being in the intermediate stage who can lay hold of some of the forms of energy while others elude his grasp, that energy seems to be passing from the available to the dissipated state. (*SP* II, 646)

This remarkable concluding paragraph to Maxwell's article develops a critique of the human, all too human notion of the concept of entropy, underlining that this concept is the product of a being with limited potential to know, direct and control energy. The entropic scenario in which the 'demon' intervenes is already the product of a limited being and perhaps even the fantasy of such a being overcoming its limits. If we follow through Maxwell's argument we can see emerge a far grander philosophical landscape than is usually imagined to be present in the founder of contemporary technoscience, one ignored by both philosophers and historians of science (with the salient exception of Alfred North Whitehead) and one that anticipates and exceeds the twentieth-century alignment of energy and information entropy. Maxwell suggests that it is not only the idea that the dissipation of energy depends on 'the extent of our knowledge' but that it is the latter which allows us 'to take hold of and to direct at pleasure' energy. Knowledge is entropy; it is at once the premise and the outcome of our interaction with energy. That energy which 'we cannot take hold of and direct at pleasure' we call heat, dissipation and, Maxwell implies but does not say, death. It marks the limit of a finite being, that 'small BUT lively being' capable of interacting with energy, of living.

It is only by being able to 'take hold of and direct' some energy that we become aware of the energy that is not so available and try to make it available, even in the guise of entropy. We call unavailable energy – energy beyond our grasp and power – confused, dissipated, deathly, the negation of the energy we can lay hold of. Maxwell illustrates this with the provocative analogy of a memorandum book, that is, a store of abbreviated written memory. A being who does not possess the capacity to read will not find its content confused but will regard it as a visual object; the author has almost full access to its meaning, being able to grasp a large part of its content, while one with the power to read will find its mnemonics confused and will be restricted to a partial interaction with the meaning of the words, aware of the limits to what can be known. Maxwell thus moves in this analogy from the parochial character of energy entropy to that of information entropy and then back. The notion of dissipated energy – entropy – could not occur to either a powerless being 'who could not turn any of the energies of nature to his own account', that is, a being who does not interact with energy, nor to an omniscient/ omnipotent being 'who could trace the motion of every molecule and seize it at the right moment', who completely masters energy. Such a notion is only available to beings in the intermediate stage, who can take hold of some forms of energy with others still eluding their grasp, opening them to events beyond their grasp and control, to chance.

Maxwell places great emphasis on the quality of a being's relation to energy, recognizing that this relation is itself an energetic expression. After locating entropy as an entropic response of a limited being towards energy, Maxwell expresses the question of the relation to energy in terms of *how* a finite being interacts with energy, especially with energies that exceed our power to interact with them. It is possible to discern in Maxwell an intimation of the Nietzschean distinction between noble and resentful responses to superior energy. To call energy that is not available to us 'confused' or 'dissipated' or 'heat death' is to adopt a resentful relation to it: if it is not for us, then it is to be negated and consigned to the realm of death. According to this view – the entropic scenario – we cannot both preserve and enjoy our available energy – our life – while at the same time opening ourselves to energies that exceed us – the latter are taken to threaten our lives. Against this Maxwell proposes a different relation, 'Now conceive a finite being who knows the paths and velocities of all the molecules'; that is, we can conceive of a finite being who has more energy than us; indeed the act of conception of such a being, whom Nietzsche will call the Overman, is a step towards its realization. In terms of the anthropology adumbrated at the close of the 'Diffusion' essay, we can conceive of a finite being who is potentially ever approaching completion, that is, a relation to energy that makes all energy available to a being for work and for pleasure in work, even if that being is not us, not yet and perhaps never will be. It is the energy released by this capacity to imagine such an energetic state that Thomson and other Christians fascinated by the thermodynamic proof of the end of the universe found 'demonic' – only a demon could have such a thought. In Nietzsche it is of course a demon that whispers a similar thought to Zarathustra in the guise of the eternal return and the marriage with chance.

The parallels between Maxwell and Nietzsche are not fortuitous – there is a common denominator in their shared admiration for Lucretius. Both admired the role played by chance in Lucretius's poem as well as the model of noble interactivity figured by Venus and Love in the *Poem on Nature*, but Maxwell more than Nietzsche subscribed to Lucretius's Epicurean commitment to the liberatory significance of scientific knowledge. The latter affirmation, however, goes far beyond the technological dehumanizing of nature criticized by Warburg, pointing to ways in which a being 'who can lay hold of some forms of energy while others elude his grasp' can cease to suffer this predicament as a negative one. It is necessary to adopt a different relationship to 'energy we cannot lay hold of and direct at pleasure', not feeling threatened or weakened by it.

The radical character of Maxwell's cosmo-anthropology can be highlighted by comparing his work with one of Nietzsche's most important heirs and open critic of the technological and cultural implications of the technological revolution that followed Maxwell's discovery of the laws of electromagnetism. At the centre of the apparent differences between the thought of Maxwell and the cultural historian Aby Warburg is a shared appreciation of the predicament of a finite being before cosmic necessity and chance, figured in both cases by the planet Saturn and the bolt of lightning.

Both Maxwell and Warburg were fascinated by the figure of the planet Saturn, both for reasons ultimately motivated by Epicurean or Lucretian commitments. Maxwell's 1857 essay 'On the Stability of the Motion of Saturn's Rings', and Warburg's work on astrological symbolism culminating in the collaborative work *Saturn and Melancholy*, both implicitly ask the Epicurean question of how it is possible to be liberated from the influence of the old Gods.[6] Of these, of course, Saturn was the most malign and maleficent, the astronomical God of time who eats his own children and who provokes melancholy and catastrophic change. For Warburg the influence of Saturn was literally demonic, and much of his work was dedicated to showing and therapeutically defusing this influence – making difficult the conduction of the God's influence. Warburg literally reads the 'memorandum book' of an entire culture that experienced its inability to master time and to accept the limit marked by death as a catastrophe. Saturn was a mnemonic for this incapacity, largely because of the limits to classical astronomical knowledge.

Saturn is the most remote visible planet; located at the limit of what the human eye can perceive, it was by definition imperfectly visible. Following Maxwell's logic, had it been wholly invisible then we could not have been troubled by it nor would we have been so if it had been completely visible; it was its partial visibility that made it threatening. Its evil character was evident in its famous changes of complexion; it seemed to bulge and change colour as if enraged. Its threatening aspect was confirmed by the shadows that seemed to move across its face, signifying planetary wrath. It was the most threatening of the planetary Gods, and interaction with it had to be conducted with care and precaution. It was still not fully understood even by Galileo, whose telescopic examination attempted to account for the changes in planetary complexion by postulating satellites. As Warburg and his colleagues showed, Galileo's observation was part of a broader cultural change in the significance of Saturn, from open to ambiguous threat, with a growing predominance of the aspects of Saturn as God of genius and technology. Such change allowed Saturn to be viewed with new eyes, literally in the case of Christiaan Huygens who in 1655, before he could fully benefit from Spinoza's lens, revealed the threatening planet to possess a ring. The long-feared changes in planetary complexion were but confused perceptions of the ring, invisible with the naked eye. Science would seem to have liberated humanity from the evil God and indeed went far in now emphasizing the aspect of the 'age of Saturn' as a utopia or paradise.

In his comments on the rings of Saturn in the 1755 *Universal Natural History and Theory of the Heavens*, Kant – another admirer of Lucretius – spoke of the state of wonderment provoked by the spectacle of Saturn's rings and gave a molecular explanation for them that in some respects anticipates Maxwell's 1857 account. However, beside the 'mechanical explanation' lay another speculation that brought together one of the affirmative aspects of the classical Saturn – the Golden Age of Saturn – with the proposal that the Earth too once possessed a ring-like Saturn. Its loss marked a catastrophic change registered in Greek myth and the Bible:

> A ring around the Earth! What a beauty of a spectacle for those who were created for inhabiting the Earth as a paradise […] This ring without doubt consisted of watery vapours and, in addition to the advantages which it could provide for the first inhabitants of the Earth, one could still let it break up on a needed occasion to punish with floods the Earth which made itself unworthy of such a beauty. (*UNH* 146)

The catastrophic loss of the Earth's ring was the product either of the chance passing of a comet or of ineluctable changes in the Earth's climate.

> Either a comet, whose attraction brought its regular movements into confusion, or the cooling of the region of its locality united its scattered watery parts and [made them] crash in one of the most gruesome cloudbursts down to the Earth's surface. (*UNH* 146)

The result of this catastrophe is recorded in the Bible, the ring of Earth forming the biblical 'water of the firmament' and its catastrophic dissolution described in the story of the flood and its aftermath.

> The whole world went down in the water and in addition imbibed in these foreign and fleeting vapours of the unnatural rain that slow poison that

brought creatures closer to death and destruction. The form of a pale and light bow had now disappeared from the horizon, and the new world that could never remember that sight without a feeling of fright of that fearful instrument of divine wrath, saw perhaps with no less bewilderment in the first rain that colourful arch which seemed according to its shape to imitate the former, but was to be through the assurance of a reconciled heaven, a sign of grace and a monument of a lasting maintenance of the new transformed surface of the Earth. (*UNH* 146)

Kant himself immediately retreated from this extravagance, but his cosmo-theological digression marks a significant moment in the Lucretian tradition of natural philosophy, a combination of science and myth that distantly persists even in Maxwell and the technoscientific culture he helped inaugurate. For Kant in this passage, the advent of mortality coincided with the crashing down of Earth's planetary ring, while the rainbow of the new covenant promised the possibility of a renewed planetary paradise signalled by the emblem of the ring of Saturn. The change in the status of Saturn into the image of a transformed earth was inflected by the technological developments of the nineteenth century, which, however ironically, was manifest in Grandville's technological vision of the technological paradise of the rings of Saturn ironically noted by Walter Benjamin in his *Arcades Project* (see Benjamin 1999, 18).

While Maxwell's essay on the rings of Saturn was a considerably more sober effort, its underlying cultural concerns are by no means remote to those of Kant. It is an early work which anticipates many later discoveries, notably the emphasis on waves that would reappear in the context of electromagnetic waves. In the light of the technological impact of this discovery on the modern world, it may be said that in a way Kant was right in claiming that the rings of Saturn contributed to transforming the surface of the Earth. Maxwell proceeds by showing that the solid or liquid explanations for the constitution of the rings of Saturn were impossible and that consequently the only plausible hypothesis was the atomic one: the rings were composed of miniscule units of matter. Given this hypothesis, he had to show how the micro interactions of the particles with each other and with the gravitational field of the planet created the relatively stable macro phenomenon of the rings. But the move from an aggregate of particles to stable phenomenon required a number of important and difficult steps of argument, the most significant being the use of the concept of intersecting waves – Maxwell looks at four – that combined together to produce the effect of stability. The atomic hypothesis, combined with an account of wave patterns, characterized the explanation of Saturn's rings and would reappear in the context of the theories of electromagnetism, heat and gas. Hidden within it was the possibility or otherwise of a 'resisting medium' in which waves move, the existence of ether or the possibility of waves producing effects without a physical medium.

The essay begins by describing the rings as having no 'practical significance' for 'astronomy or navigation' but nevertheless posing a problem for the future of science: 'We must either explain the motion on the principles of mechanics or admit that, in the Saturnian realms, there can be motion regulated by laws which we are unable to explain' (*SP* I, 291). The latter would mark the defeat of the modern aspiration to produce universal physical laws and a return to Aristotelian patterns of explanation. Maxwell illustrated the complex wave motions that created the appearance of stable rings 'by means of a small mechanical model made by Rumage of Aberdeen', but it would be mistaken to consider this explanation as the technological demystification of Saturn's rings and thus the role of the planet as harbinger of catastrophic change, for better or worse (*SP* I, 291). For Maxwell draws close to Kant's cosmogonic concerns in his speculative interpretation of changes in the dimension of rings. He closes his essay with the thought that if these changes are confirmed by observation

> it will be worthwhile to investigate more carefully whether Saturn's rings are permanent or transitory elements of the Solar system, and whether in that part of the heavens we see celestial immutability, or terrestrial corruption and generation, and the old order giving place to the new before our own eyes. (*SP* I, 374)

The ambiguous place of Saturn between permanence and change, between immutability and corruption and generation, and between old and new orders, shows that the necessity of its planetary influence has been succeeded by chance and indeterminacy. For human observers, Saturn remains an equivocal planet, but even if only partially understood it is no longer an object to be feared.

The passing of the age of Saturn to the age of Jupiter alluded to in the closing lines of Maxwell's treatise, and the qualification of divine necessity, returns us to the theme of Jupiter's lightning bolts. In place of the continuous malign influence of the one planetary God arises the sudden and unpredictable deadly force of another. In his 1923 lecture, delivered in the unpropitious circumstances of the Bellevue mental hospital, Warburg mused on what it means to come into contact with forces greater than our own, or more specifically by what means is it possible to interact with lightning. Drawing on fieldwork conducted among Pueblo native Americans in Arizona in the 1890s,[7] the lecture is replete with Warburg's reflections on demonology, astrology, art, culture and modernity, all framed within the problem of interaction with forces beyond human power, exemplified by the case of lightning. The lecture ends, as noted earlier, with a warning concerning modernity's hubris or inability to interact with the non-human, exemplified in the technology released by Maxwell's discovery of electromagnetic waves.

Much of the lecture describes the liturgical and visual expressions of a snake ritual conducted by Pueblo Indians in order to summon the lightning and rains essential for their agriculture. At the centre of Warburg's account is an extremely complex description of the interactions between humans, earth, animals, sky and Gods, one conducted by means of the obliteration of drawings executed in sand:

> The snake is treated like a novice of the mysteries, and notwithstanding its resistance, its head is dipped in consecrated, medicated water. Then it is thrown onto a sand painting done on the kiva floor and representing four lightning snakes with a quadruped in the middle. In another kiva a sand painting depicts a mass of clouds from which emerge four differently coloured lightning streaks, corresponding to the points of the compass, in the form of serpents. Onto the first sand painting, each snake is hurled with great force, so that the drawing is obliterated and the serpent is absorbed into the sand. I am convinced that this magic throw is intended to force the serpent to invoke lightning or produce rain. This is clearly the significance of the entire ceremony, and the ceremonies that follow prove that these consecrated serpents join the Indians in the starkest manner as provokers and petitioners of rain ... The ceremony culminates as follows: approach to the bush, seizing and carrying of the live serpents, dispatching of the snakes to the plains as messengers. (Warburg [1923] 1997, 36)

Warburg describes the ritual as the disrupted inscription of lightning, moving from the snake as a demon intervening malefically in human affairs through its consecration to the status of ritual ally. The human attempt to control lightning through drawing it in the sand is surrendered to the snake who, destroying the human image, becomes an ambassador for the humans to the weather Gods. From being at the prey of the superior force of nature, the serpent ritual opens a space and a time in which extra-human energies can be propitiated. This is not a bid for control or mastery – it consists in the renunciation of the mastery of the lightning diagram – but rather in recognizing and propitiating a superior force. Warburg recognizes in the ritual a respect for non-human power and the impossibility of controlling it ('chance'), one that he contrasts with 'Uncle Sam' and his 'technological culture' that serves him as a precision weapon against the forces of nature. In his amusing description of his allegorical photograph of 'Uncle Sam' in San Francisco – 'the conqueror of the serpent cult and of the fear of lightning' – Warburg sees him strolling beneath an electric wire and comments that 'In this copper serpent of Edison's, he has wrested lightning from nature' (Warburg [1923] 1997, 53). In his closing thoughts Warburg reflects on the intellectual and technological achievements of Maxwell and the technological culture that these made possible. Overwhelming 'natural forces' are now regarded as 'infinite waves obedient to human touch' and with them 'the culture of the machine age destroys what the natural sciences, born of myth, so arduously achieved: the space for devotion, which evolved in turn into the space required for reflection' (Warburg [1923] 1997, 54). Warburg here carefully distinguishes between the achievements of scientific enlightenment with respect to myth, the conversion of the space of devotion into that of reflection, with the abolition of distance achieved in Warburg's view by modern technology.

The discoveries most closely associated with Maxwell – telegram and telephone – in Warburg's eyes destroy the distance necessary to propitiate non-human powers, with the threat of consequent 'chaos'. The destruction of the distance of devotion or reflection surrenders humanity to the working of chance; precisely the hubristic belief to have overcome chance surrenders humanity to the most terrible exposure to chance. The catastrophic abolition of distance represented by the lightning bolt once again hangs over humanity. The alternative foreseen by Warburg is not encouraging: 'mythical and symbolic thinking strive to form spiritual bonds between humanity and the surrounding world, shaping distance into the space required for devotion and reflection: the distance undone by the instantaneous electric connection' (Warburg [1923] 1997, 103). With this, Warburg is advocating less a return to mythical thinking than the rethinking of myth and symbolic form achieved by Ernst Cassirer, whose work and person assumed great significance for Warburg during the 1920s.[8] However, the appeal to symbolic form seems a weak alternative to the alleged monolithic destruction of distance achieved by modern technology. This alternative is perhaps exemplified by Walter de Maria's *The Lightning Field* (1977) in New Mexico which gives aesthetic form to the same meteorological effects witnessed by Warburg in neighbouring Arizona (where the artist developed a prototype). Viewing the work is an aesthetic ritual, whose sacred character is emphasized by the ban on photography and whose risk of chance and deadly exposure to lightning is foreseen in Dia Foundation's liability waiver clause that must be signed by all visitors to the work.

Warburg's critical diagnosis of the cultural impact of a technological civilization both overestimates its monolithic character and underestimates the respect for distance and chance that informs Maxwell's work and the technology to which it gave rise. Maxwell's essay 'On the Protection of Buildings from Lightning' never underestimates the element of chance that remains even in the most technologically protected building and advises respect and distance for lightning in its invaluable advice not to tease chance by leaning against the wall of a protected building during a thunder storm. However, the complexity of his Lucretian approach to modern science and technology is most evident in his paper 'The Telephone' describing the performance of the new technology in Cambridge (*SP* II, 742–55). His view of the telephone and its potential is far indeed from that of the destruction of distance that it embodied for Warburg: for him the telephone permits the emergence of new dimensions of chance and reflection previously unimaginable. The paper and the event it describes mark a fascinating moment in the development of Maxwell's thought where he reflects on the technological application of some of his ideas on electricity, namely the 'transmission of the articulate sounds of the human voice' (*SP* II, 742). In the company of Mr Garnett, who collected and constructed some of the apparatus, Mr Gower who brought along his 'telephone harp' (on which he subsequently played a transmission of 'Men of Harlech' from the Geology Museum) and the instruments of Mr Middleton, Maxwell reflected on the implications of this new technology.

Speaking from within the university, Maxwell contrasts the gathering of individuals in the same room with the gathering embodied in and promised by the telephone. The latter is both the chance product of intersecting paths of knowledge and the promise of a new kind of knowledge and of new chance discoveries:

> I shall, therefore, consider the telephone as a material symbol of the widely separated departments of human knowledge, the cultivation of which has been led, by many converging paths, to the invention of this instrument by Prof. Graham Bell. (*SP* II, 742)

The telephone not only emerged from an unprecedented and unpredictable intersection of various paths of knowledge but will also enable a fundamental change in the technology of knowledge, with a move from depth to width. Maxwell refers to existing technologies of knowledge as based on a model of depth, emphasizing the storage and retention of information, embodied in the university: 'We are too apt to suppose that we are congregated here merely to be within reach of certain appliances of study, such as museums, laboratories, libraries and lecturers' (*SP* II, 742). In place of this, the telephone symbolizes and enables width of knowledge and with it the proliferation of new chance encounters, an understanding of knowledge that Maxwell illustrates with a lovely analogy that subtly introduces Epicurean atomism into a botanical scenario:

> I suppose that when the bees crowd around the flowers it is for the sake of the honey that they do so, never thinking that it is the dust which they are carrying from flower to flower which is to render possible a more splendid array of flowers and a busier crowd of bees, in the years to come. (*SP* II, 742)

The chance encounters between the dust of different spheres of knowledge will enable the emergence of unexpected hybrids such as the telephone itself. Maxwell illustrates this by developing the distinction between telegraph and telephone and recognizing that there was no inevitable progression from one to the other. He imagines an acceleration of the discrete units of the telegraph message to the point where 'the ear ceases to distinguish [the signals] as separate signals, but begins to recognize the impression it receives as that of a musical tone' (SP II, 745). For Maxwell, full of the excitement of the discovery of analogue technology, the transmission of voice requires not only pitch but also shape or the envelope of a sound. Without this, the sound transmitted would be 'like playing a violin with a saw instead of a bow' as opposed to the electrical induction between transmitter and receiver (SP II, 745). Maxwell's enthusiasm allows him to imagine amplification, multiple receivers and even medical consultations at a distance.

Maxwell's account of what made this technology possible emphasizes the unpredictable idiosyncrasy of Bell's formation, and while it appears at first glance an example of Victorian humanism, it is subsequently revealed to be much more. The cross-fertilization of the sciences that made possible the telephone and that the telephone in turn makes possible is

> an operation which cannot be performed by merely collecting treatises on the different sciences and binding them together into an encyclopaedia. Science exists only in the mind, and the union of the sciences can only take place in a living person. (SP II, 751)

Bell, for example, was 'not an electrician who has found out how to make a tin plate speak, but a speaker who, to gain his private ends, has become an electrician' (SP II, 751). Maxwell then describes Bell's background: his father was a pioneer of phonetics and speech therapy and thus 'the inventor of the telephone was prepared by early training in practical analysis of the elements of speech' (SP II, 751). Bell experimented with his father's system of visible speech in the Boston School for the Deaf and Dumb, and thus for Maxwell was able to develop his new technology in an absolutely singular therapeutic context. The invention of the telephone could be anticipated, but not predicted; it required the chance conjunction of a therapeutic approach to speech and the science of electromagnetism.

Maxwell notes in passing that he 'cannot conceive a nobler application of the scientific analysis of speech' than the therapeutic assistance of those deprived of it (SP II, 751). However, this aside becomes more significant in the context of his speculation upon the implications of the results of the Helmholtz School of Experimental Physiology in Germany, especially their exploration of the neurology of sensation and consciousness. After reflecting on the use of technology to 'produce the sounds of the human voice by means of artificial apparatus', Maxwell moves immediately to the new physiology, and implicitly the possibility of a technologically augmented body, an area that he considers to have the highest 'truly scientific or science producing consequences' (*SP* II, 753). When placed in the context of his earlier view of the malleability of the human and its potential to develop, the view of the therapeutic extension of human powers also intimates the general technological extension of human powers. Yet this development remained within limits; Maxwell did not foresee the possibility of the human becoming omniscient and omnipotent like the demon and thus saw it as always subject to chance and to the necessity of death.

In many respects Warburg's desperate view of the hubris of modern technology is recognizable and even familiar. Yet it is his understanding of the total claim of technology to overcome chance and insecurity that allows him to develop the equally familiar catastrophic scenario of its failure and total exposure to chance and disaster. His thought is governed by a familiar, tragic movement between hubris and nemesis. However, the work of James Clerk Maxwell shows a quite different understanding of the relationship between technology and chance. It recognizes that technology may open new dimensions of chance, both baleful and beneficial, and that it emerges within a context of limited human powers and finitude. Nevertheless, as opposed to Warburg, Maxwell seeks to understand the predicament of technology from a place beyond resentment at inevitable powerlessness. In this way, his natural philosophy parallels the thought of Nietzsche in its attempt, inspired by Lucretius, to respond to vulnerability before superior and non-human forces and the insecurity and danger they bring by simply loving chance.

Notes

1   For an overview of ancient debates on lightning, see Taub 2003, esp. 127–30.
2   Cited as an epigraph to a recent biography of James Clerk Maxwell: Mahon 2003, 1.
3   Letter to Tait, cited in Smith 1998, 251.
4   Letter to Tait, in Smith 1998, 252.
5   Smith 1998, 252; Harman 1998, 139.
6   *SP* I, 288–376; Klibansky, Panofsky and Saxl 1964.
7   For the circumstances and the results of this field work, see Michael P. Steinberg's 'Interpretative Essay' added to the English translation of the lecture, 'Aby Warburg's Kreuzlingen Lecture: A Reading', in Warburg [1923] 1997, 59–109; and Guidi and Mann eds. 1998.
8   See the collection of letters and other documents in Ghelardi ed. 2003.

19

Bataille and the Neanderthal extinction

The Accursed Share (1949) extends a fascination with paleo-anthropology already evident in Bataille's work from the early 1930s and intensified by his book and series of articles and lectures prompted by the discovery of the cave paintings of Lascaux in 1940.[1] The conjuncture of an interest in the discipline dedicated to studying the origins of the human species and the discovery of cave art led Bataille to his central paleo-anthropological but also philosophical hypothesis that the phase of human development achieved by 'Lascaux Man' was inaugurated by the invention of art. He saw the violent bid for transcendence expressed in the majestic images of hunted animals as an act of human self-definition against animality, but also, we shall see, against other humanities. His reflections upon 'animality' often explicitly refer to the uncanny human-animals encountered by *Homo sapiens* on their migration into northern Eurasia. Perhaps this is the reason why his paleo-anthropological meditations return insistently to a link between the emergence of the kind of human capable of producing art and the extinction of 'prior' 'Neanderthal' humanity. The remorseless haunting of his paleo-anthropological and philosophical texts by the Neanderthals points to unanswered even unasked questions concerning the relationship between the emergence of a single humanity and the Neanderthal extinction.

Bataille's hypothesis assumes the chronological coincidence between the arrival of *Homo sapiens*, the departure of *Homo neanderthalensis* and the beginnings of art. While the fossil record broadly supports the first coincidence, with the arrival of *Homo sapiens* coinciding with the Neanderthal extinction, the second coincidence is not quite as certain. The surviving examples of cave art, including Lascaux, point to them being made between 15,000 and 20,000 years *after* the Neanderthal extinction, making the artists of Lascaux closer to us than they were to that event. The sculptures of female figures Bataille discusses alongside the cave paintings are admittedly older, ranging back as far as 35,000 years, which is to say 4,000 years after the extinction. Bataille's exemplary female sculpture – the *Venus of Willensdorf* – dates back 28,000 years, which locates it 10,000 years after the extinction.[2] This dating was not known to Bataille, who believed that a date of 40,000 years ago for the birth of art was 'unquestionable' (*CH* 145). It is on the contrary very questionable, although most recent debate is moving back to proposing far older dates for some of the work, consistent with Bataille's hypothesis.[3] However, my intention is not to refute his hypothesis by pointing to disputed chronology but to explore its conceptual limits by showing that, even assuming his chronology, Bataille's response to the hypothesis is confined by the limits set by then prevailing paleo-anthropological knowledge.

The science of human origins

By responding to the question 'What is human?' with an enquiry into the origins of humanity, paleo-anthropology emerged in the mid-nineteenth century under the dual auspices of Darwin's *Origin of Species* (1859) and the discovery of problematically 'human' fossilized remains in the Neander valley of the River Düssel slightly earlier in 1856. The new discipline confirmed and strengthened geology and palaeontology's earlier challenge to biblical chronology and the creation narrative with the proposition that humanity not only had a prehistory, but also, as Nietzsche quickly deduced, that this history was not yet finished. Any answer to the question 'What is human' had now to account not only for where humans came from and where they had arrived, but also where they were going. But the very possibility of the existence of paleo-anthropology had been bitterly disputed and most forcibly from within the emergent science of fossil life – palaeontology – with Cuvier famously declaring 'fossil humanity does not exist' ('*l'homme fossile n'existe pas*'). While there may have been myriad forms of life that emerged and sank back into the obscurity of the sedimentary strata, human life was considered qualitatively distinct from the fossil life studied by palaeontology. Acknowledging the existence of human fossils required not only accepting that humans emerged from animal life but also that the species *Homo sapiens* had a beginning and, by inference, must also have an end.

It was for these reasons that paleo-anthropology would prove such an important point of reference for Bataille's thinking on the nature of the human and its (im)possibilities. His fascination was part of a broader philosophical interest in the question of the origins of the human shared by Blanchot and Leroi-Gourhan, among others, but it was an interest enabled but also restricted by the then state of paleo-anthropological knowledge. Less than a century old when Bataille and his contemporaries began to reflect on the significance of its findings, the attempt by the discipline of paleo-anthropology to establish the distinctive factors contributing to the emergence of contemporary humanity was ensnared by the assumptions of colonial anthropology. And, in spite of the peculiarly French inflection contributed by the pioneer Paul Broca and later Abbé Henri Breuil, such assumptions persisted until the late twentieth century. The spatial colonialism of comparative anthropology was played out in the temporal colonialism of paleo-anthropology. In the case of the latter it was manifest above all in the concern to distinguish *Homo sapiens* from another known form of fossil humanity – *Homo neanderthalensis* – and to justify the existence of an evolutionary and/or *species* distinction between the two humanities.

The existence of a strong distinction between *Homo sapiens* and *Homo neanderthalensis* structures Bataille's reflections on paleo-anthropology and is a condition of possibility for his thinking in *The Accursed Share*. It informs and disrupts his hypothetical distinction between restricted and general economy. Yet working with the paleo-anthropological distinction brought with it assumptions and blind spots that would return to haunt Bataille's broader enquiry. These converged on the problem of the causes of the Neanderthal extinction and its possible role in the formation of *Homo sapiens*. To appreciate how this problem played through in Bataille to emerge in suspicions of a paleo-genocide it is necessary to review the role played by Neanderthal humanity in the formation of the discipline of paleo-anthropology and the ways in which they became – and remain – problematic objects of knowledge.

In August 1856 two quarry workers preparing the ground for the extraction of lime in a complex of caves overlooking the Düssel river came across some bones, which they unceremoniously threw on to the spoil heap.[4] They were seen by the quarry owner, Wilhelm Beckershoff, who – in the first of a line of misidentifications – suspected them to be the fossilized remains of cave bears. Aware of the lively market for such fossils, he collected the sixteen fragments and invited the opinion of a local teacher and scientist, Johann Carl Fuhlrott. Fuhlrott immediately rejected the cavebear hypothesis but was perplexed by the morphology of the fossilized bones. They *seemed* human but were thicker and stronger with the fragments of arm and leg bones slightly curved and the skull displaying an unfamiliar morphology. His perplexity was understandable. In the first place, contemporary palaeontology held that human bones were not supposed to exist in a fossilized state, and, what is more, these human bones displayed peculiar deviations from the anatomical norm. Fuhlrott's initial announcement of the find in the local newspaper subsequently carried in a Bonn regional newspaper cautiously referred to similarities with Native Americans – the uncovered bones 'belonged to humans of the race

(*Geschlecht*) of flat-heads who still live in the American West' (Harf and Witte 2014, 44). From being identified as cave bears, the bones moved into comparative anthropology as Native Americans, an identification that, even if quickly dropped, prepared the ground for investing the bones with fantasies of colonial and even genocidal violence.[5]

The transformation of the Neanderthal bones into objects of knowledge provides a case study in the generation of accredited knowledge in nineteenth-century science but also made them hostages to competing hypotheses, interests and broader cultural conflicts. Fuhlrott's article was noted by an anatomy professor at Bonn, Hermann Schaafhausen, who had previously published an article arguing the case for the possibility of human fossils and saw the bones as confirmation of his thesis. With Fuhlrott, he toured the bones around various scientific societies and in 1857 jointly published an article, 'Human Remains from a Cave in the Valley of the River Düssel', in the 'Proceedings of the Natural Historical Society of the Prussian Rheinland and Westphalia' that set the bones in a number of contradictory contexts. From one perspective, calculated to placate religious critics, they were proposed as evidence for the existence of humanity before the Flood while from another more scientific but not yet Darwinian point of view they were said to have belonged to an 'ur-typical individual of our race' (*Geschlecht*).[6] A visit by Charles Lyell, author of the prodigious *Principles of Geology*, to survey the scene of the discovery in 1860 and to take a cast of the enigmatic skull introduced the bones to Darwinian circles in Great Britain where they stepped forth yet again, this time in the guise of the long-sought evolutionary link between humans and apes. Darwin's indefatigable public champion Thomas Huxley situated them in a series of evolutionary transitions from the skull of the ape to the human skull, predicting the discovery of more fossilized bones of even more or less humanized apes.

At this point the bones were still known as the 'Human Remains from a Cave in the Valley of the river Düssel' and only in 1864 were they given a dubious honour of belonging to a distinct species – *Homo neanderthalensis* – by William King. The name has since entered into popular legend as designating the 'Neanderthals', but while identifying the bones as part of the human genus it left undecided whether the bones belonged to humans who once lived in the Neanderthal or whether they belonged to a distinct species of humanity. The question of whether they belonged to a distinct species remains disputed, perhaps surprisingly given the now-established biological definition of a species in terms of the possibility of its members successfully reproducing that we shall see in the case of *Homo neanderthalis* and *Homo sapiens* has now – but not in Bataille's time – been proved incontrovertibly to have been the case.[7]

A series of further finds in nineteenth and early twentieth centuries extended the fossil record of what became known as 'Neanderthal man' but in spite of the discovery of the larger brains possessed by Neanderthal humanity (1520 cm³ compared to *Homo sapiens*' 1400 cm³) and evidence of developed sociality extending to care for the infirm and wounded, funerary practices, ornamentation and (disputably) musical instruments, they were quickly identified as bestial, stupid and no match for the astute, better-armed and colonizing *Homo sapiens*. Which is to say, they were cast not as another humanity, but as an evolutionary stage to be overcome, an alien species to be vanquished and their territory and possessions appropriated. In many respects, Neanderthal humanity was drawn into a European colonial narrative as a paleo-colonized population possessing the characteristics lent by contemporary colonial discourse to native peoples to justify their dispossession. Neanderthal humanity functioned as a cipher for contemporary colonized peoples and their apparent fate presaged that of the colonized. In short, Neanderthal humanity was drawn into an emergent racial discourse associated with colonialization and a vulgarization of Darwin regardless of the improbabilities and immense ironies attending such capture.[8]

Apart from the anatomical evidence of the remains themselves, the distribution of the fossil discoveries of the late nineteenth and twentieth centuries allowed for a chronological and geographical description of Neanderthal humanity. Fossilized remains associated with Neanderthal humanity were found across Northern Europe, from Gibraltar[9] and the south of Italy to France and Germany. Finds were also made in the Near East and as far north-east as the Caucasians and Siberia. The finds dated from 200,000 to 39,000 years ago, when – with some disputed exceptions – they cease, marking the disappearance of Neanderthal humanity. They are thus almost strictly contemporary with *Homo sapiens*, whose earliest fossil remains have been dated to 195,000 years ago in Ethiopia.[10] The fossil record also attests to a spatial and temporal movement of *Homo sapiens* arriving in the Near East 55,000 and Southern Europe 45,000 years ago and entering Northern Europe soon thereafter. The arrival of *Homo sapiens* in the territory occupied by *Homo neanderthalensis* coincides with the near definitive disappearance of the latter from the fossil record 39,000 years ago. The stark coincidence generated (and continues to generate) speculation concerning the relationship between the arrival of *Homo sapiens* and the extinction of Neanderthal humanity. Until recently, this question obsessed paleo-anthropology and historically inspired some of Bataille's darker thoughts about the formative past of humanity.

Bataille's humanity

Bataille's distinction between general and restricted economy in *The Accursed Share* should not only be understood as the emancipatory 'Copernican turn' of political economy from scarcity towards the thinking of plethora, but also as the encrypted inscription of a potentially genocidal logic. It is one that he intuited and even begins to address explicitly in later work but nevertheless remains at play not only in his view of an excessive humanity but also in the basic conceptual architecture of the two economies. It is in this spirit that we should approach the 'basic fact' with which *The Accursed Share* opens:

> The living organism, in a situation determined by the play of energy on the surface of the globe, ordinarily receives more energy than is necessary for maintaining life; the excess energy (wealth) can be used for the growth of a system (e.g. an organism): if the system no longer grows, or if the excess cannot be completely absorbed in its growth, it must necessarily be lost without profit; it must be spent, willingly or not, gloriously or catastrophically. (Bataille 1991, 21)

The 'basic fact' establishes a scenario in which the globe is bathed in an energy whose excess over the needs of life drives an organism *or* system *either* to expand or expend. The scenario of global expansion and the first either/or of expansion or expenditure leads to a question of the nature of expenditure: if expansion is not possible then excess energy must be spent *either* willingly or unwillingly, gloriously or catastrophically. However, this is not a scenario in which either/or is a real option, for limits to expansion provoke expenditures that are at once glorious *and* catastrophic. From the standpoint of *The Accursed Share*'s 'basic fact' the future lies with an organism that can both expand and expend – as Bataille will equivocally define *Homo sapiens* – and not with organisms whose systems cannot grow or expend. For Bataille and his contemporaries and colleagues in the *Collège de Sociologie* (including on its margins Walter Benjamin in 'The Work of Art in the Age of Its Technical Reproducibility'), *Homo sapiens* is such an organism and system, with its colonial adventures tending towards global domination, possessed of an overwhelming sense of transcendence and a creativity or ability gloriously to expend excess energy in the creation of art. But also, it should not be forgotten, in its capacity to induce catastrophe.

Bataille's convictions regarding the origins of the human developed during the 1930s were confirmed and intensified by the discovery of the cave art of Lascaux, whose images of animals and hunting scenes would prove of such importance to Bataille and his views on expenditure and sacrifice developed in *The Accursed Share*. The imagery of Lascaux confirmed Bataille's understanding of how humanity distinguished itself from nature and animality in an act he describes in an early note on 'The Frobenius Exhibit at the Salle Pleyel' of 1930 as one of 'inconceivable violence' (*CH* 46). The rest of this note, saturated in the discourse of colonial anthropology, is dedicated to understanding sacrifice and art as ways of conceiving this apparent inconceivability. Bataille's first methodological step is to propose a parallel between African and European Palaeolithic civilizations: 'This civilization, which disappeared thousands of years ago in our region, was interrupted in South Africa only several centuries ago by the invasion of the Bantu, a people infinitely more advanced in ironwork' (*CH* 45). The parallel between the disappearance of the European and African Palaeolithic humanity implicitly extends to the cause of disappearance in the arrival of a technologically superior invader. In this early note, Bataille constructs a scenario that he will return to in the case of Neanderthal humanity, one which sees the South African bushmen as 'typologically ancient men' whose art 'from the point of view of life' 'surpasses in interest that of the European caves' (*CH* 45), but who, like them, were violently supplanted.

With the reference to the caves and cave art Bataille is carefully referring to ancient *Homo sapiens* but the mise en scène of the destruction of a form of life and humanity by a technologically superior human invader will be carried over into his view of a civil war within humanity between *Homo sapiens* and *Homo neanderthalensis*. In this early note, however, Palaeolithic humans 'born of nature' appear as a 'kind of waste': 'Man's first movement amid animals and trees had been to conceive of the existence of these animals and trees and to negate his own' (*CH* 45). Animals and trees served the 'unhappy waste' that is humanity in the same way as 'houses, churches, and administrative buildings do around us', but instead of submitting 'to these buildings, these churches' early humans killed them to 'eat their meat' (*CH* 46). This intimates an act of sacrifice – glorious and catastrophic expenditure – that restores what has been separated by 'inconceivable violence' and engenders 'not only man but his rapport with nature' (*CH* 46). But there is something evasive in this Hegelian account of the emergence of humanity in a negation of the negation or violent sacrificial response to an inconceivably violent exclusion from nature. For the bushmen have already been described as victims of a *human* violence directed against them: they are 'negated' by (and themselves originally 'negated') not just nature and animality, but other humans. Human beings were not only surrounded by elephants, zebras, trees and grass, but also by other humans with violent designs on their lives and their bodies without the alleviation offered by an Hegelian struggle for recognition. The violence expiated by sacrifice and art described in this and Bataille's succeeding essays on cave art is not just directed by and against 'nature' and animality, but also against other humans. In looking at the ancient art, Bataille is also forced to see something else, the possibility barely tangible and difficult to coax into visibility that the original violence was 'inconceivable' because it was directed not just against nature or other humans in some Palaeolithic struggle for recognition, but was part of an exterminatory gesture directed against another kind of humanity.

The question of the Neanderthal extinction, possibly prefigured in the fantasy of the violent extinction of the bushmen by the Bantu in the note on Frobenus, becomes increasingly prominent in Bataille's work. Contemporary paleo-anthropology provided Bataille with two ways of understanding the coincidence of the arrival of *Homo sapiens* in Europe and the disappearance of *Homo neanderthalenis*.[11] One explained the coincidence in terms of Neanderthal humanity meeting a violent end at the hands of an invading *Homo sapiens* as victims of a literal and successful paleo-genocide. The other maintains that the two humanities entered into sexual relations that led to the emergence of a new humanity or hybrid *Homo sapiens–neanderthalensis*.[12] The options in short involve violence and sexuality, both of which, it hardly needs to be said, are fundamental concerns not only of *The Accursed Share* but of Bataille's wider thought. Although Bataille is initially reticent to discuss violence directed against or sex with (or a combination of both) Neanderthals, he will eventually incline towards the thesis of a Neanderthal genocide at the hands of *Homo sapiens* – the tool-using, art-making, genocidal animal – even if he does not pursue the full implications of this position and its implications for the erotic life of ancient humanity.

When *The Accursed Share* is read in the context of Bataille's paleo-anthropological writings it is difficult to avoid the suspicion that it repeats at the level of the concept the very genocidal gesture by which he thought *Homo sapiens* became synonymous with humanity. Indeed, it appears as if *The Accursed Share* depends not only on a parallel between the two species of humanity and the two forms of economy – with *Homo neanderthalis* exemplifying restricted and *Homo sapiens* general economy – but also, albeit ambivalently, on situating *Homo neanderthalis* at a lower point of the scale between animality and humanity than *Homo sapiens*.[13] Yet there is also a sense that Bataille believes contemporary humanity is falling back from the art-making excessive creature that was Lascaux man to a Neanderthal condition of ceaseless labour driven by fear of death. For him Neanderthal man may be the future of contemporary humanity, certainly if the restricted economy associated with the Neanderthal condition continues to prevail. The enquiry into the origins of humanity is quickly transformed into speculation on its future and the kind of production and labour discipline associated with industrial capitalism.

In a remarkable and revealing essay from 1959, 'The Cradle of Humanity: The Vézère Valley', Bataille provides a testament to the abiding importance of paleo-anthropology for his thought. He fully endorses its search for the 'essential element' in the birth of the human in 'a characteristic *unique* to humanity' (*CH* 143). The unique characteristic is less the creation of tools or the possession of speech and consciousness than 'the power to create a work of art' (*CH* 145). It is with the discovery of this power that 'humanity decidedly distanced itself from the animal, unleashed itself in a way, risking the full gamut of its richness'

(*CH* 145). The time and place Bataille assigns this event – the region of Southern France and Northern Spain during the Pleistocene but specifically the Vézère Valley 40,000 years ago[14] – immediately provokes conjecture: it coincides with the arrival of *Homo sapiens* but also with the disappearance of all trace of *Homo neanderthalensis*. Bataille's last contribution to paleo-anthropology is haunted by what he took to be a coincidence between the birth of art and the death of *Homo neanderthalensis* and an answer to the unasked question nevertheless ineluctably emerges in the course of his meditation.

Bataille proposes a dramaturgy of the birth of humanity that fully conforms to the Aristotelian unities of time, place and action: the 'coming of humanity' is 'a drama in two acts' (*CH* 145), the first interminably slow and the second accelerated and sudden – a glorious catastrophe. The pace of the two acts is governed by their prevailing economies – the first act conforms to the regime of restricted, the second to general economy. In addition, the cast of players also differs between the two acts: the cast performing the restricted economy of production according to scarcity, need and fear of death are made up of *Homo neanderthalensis* who are succeeded in Act 2 by the glittering, sovereign performance of the excessive general economy of *Homo sapiens*. Act 3, of course, has yet to be written; whether it will be a dramatic synthesis of the first two acts, a return to the Neanderthal condition following the short and catastrophically glorious eruption of *Homo lascauxensis*, or something completely different cannot be foreseen for we are still enmeshed in the unfolding drama. Bataille is not afraid of exaggerating the significance of the drama he saw played out in the arena of the Vézère Valley: 'Some tens of thousands of years ago, this small valley was the theatre of changes whose consequences are the origin of everything that follows' (*CH* 146). But what exactly were these changes that manifested themselves in the origin of the work of art and why does Bataille understand them in terms of birth, awakening and glorification?

Once again, the chronology provides an important clue: Bataille refers to the thriving population of the Vézère Valley over a period 'that began around 120,000 years ago' and its occupants who

> differ profoundly from us. They are not as close to the monkeys as those from earlier periods, but we must locate them midway on the path that goes from the *Pithecanthropus* or the *Sinananthropus* to *Homo sapiens*, who resemble us precisely and populated the valley only at the dawn of art, at the end of the Mousterian period. (*CH* 149)

Bataille is referring, of course, to *Homo neanderthalensis*, further from animality than their predecessors but not yet one of 'us'. In the text of a lecture delivered on 18 January 1955, Bataille stated absolutely explicitly that

'Neanderthal man was of the same genus as us but not of the same *species*', adding 'the human species in the strict sense of the word made works of art' (*CH* 89). But there is nothing strict at all about this use of taxonomy and the word *species*. If we return to the passage on the pre-colonial occupants of the Vézère Valley we can trace the emergence of a major problem involving Bataille's definition of humanity as a species in the wording of the second part of the sentence. For, of course, *strictly* speaking, the existence of *Homo sapiens* as a *species* predated the invention of art by over 150,000[15] years; as a *species* they too played out the long first act of Bataille's drama in distant East Africa. The invention of art did not distinguish them as a *species* and did not make them genetically *us*. Bataille's wording 'they resemble us precisely' registers this difficulty – what is the difference between identity and 'precise resemblance'? The latter can only mean that *Homo sapiens* both are and are not us. Something happened to *Homo sapiens*; what exactly it was is quickly passed over in the bland description of their 'populating' the valley 'only at the dawn of art' at the end of the 'Mousterian period', i.e. the epoch of *Homo neanderthalensis*. The question of how the three events are conjoined – *Homo sapiens* populating the valley 40,000 years ago, experiencing the birth of art and becoming human with the end of the restricted economy of Neanderthal humanity – remains unasked.

At this point in 'The Cradle of Humanity' Bataille introduces the 'race of the Neanderthals', identifying them now as a race and no longer a species and placing them vaguely out of history as a force of nature 'appearing just about everywhere at the same time, with the exception of America' (*CH* 149). While he is fascinated by the physiognomy of this humanity – the large but low skull, arched eyebrows, thick neck and overall 'animal appearance' – he is most concerned to fix its *character* as *Homo faber* or the proponent of a productive restricted economy of scarcity. Bataille is too Hegelian to deny consciousness to *Homo neanderthalensis*; on the contrary, he urges us 'to never lose sight of the fact that work expanded consciousness … work is the intellectual operation that changed the brain of the animal that man initially was into a human brain' (*CH* 150). The experimentation of the action of chipping flint to create a tool, the use of that tool in a collective project, usually the hunt, and finally the consciousness of death – the death of the animal but also of the hunter – were all properties of *Homo neanderthalensis*. Bataille describes the funerary practices of this humanity as evincing consciousness of death and even a terror before the fact of death requiring ritual propitiation. Neanderthal humanity possessed consciousness, contrary to a widely accepted assumption; for Bataille it was not *this* that distinguished it from *Homo sapiens*.

The 'first act' of the birth of humanity – both *sapiens* and *neanderthalensis* – was the era of restrictive economy, the era of an industrious but death-obsessed humanity. Bataille describes this era – which has by no means irretrievably ended – in terms of the conflict between 'two orders of possibility'. In the first, 'Man responded to the harshness of the climate through industriousness' (*CH* 151), preparing animal skins, working wood and developing 'the capacity to overcome human difficulties through continual activity and work [that] undoubtedly made the Mousterian man feel that he would carry the day' (*CH* 157). Except that, 'Like us, he had to bow down before death; death completely sabotaged his industrious efforts'; the Neanderthal was not master in his own cave but subject to 'the radical, terrifying negation of what he essentially is' (*CH* 152). Consciousness is made up of these two orders of possibility, work and the absolute negation of death, the latter of which is equally an order of impossibility. It is 'not only consciousness of objects and actions' but also of death as 'designating the limit of the power of human action' (*CH* 153). It is this consciousness rent between possibility and impossibility with its consequent 'mobile and ambiguous state of mind' that is shared by *Homo neanderthalensis* and *Homo sapiens*; it is the shared predicament of humanity, but one that Bataille believes can be lived in different ways.

The mise en scène of the second act of Bataille's drama forcibly inaugurates general economy under the sign of invasion and violence. In a trope that would be often repeated with respect to the encounter of *Homo sapiens* and *Homo neanderthalensis* he imagines the apparition of travelling *Homo sapiens* from the standpoint of the sedentary Neanderthals: 'One day, at a twist of a road, perhaps in a group, perhaps alone, a new kind of man appeared' (*CH* 153). Bataille focuses immediately on the differences in physical appearance between the two humanities, emphasizing height (*Homo sapiens* is on average fifteen centimetres taller than *Homo neanderthalensis*) and the physiognomy of the neck (for Bataille, that of *Homo sapiens* resembles a swan and *Homo neanderthalensis* significantly a bull). Bataille then moves to a short series of questionable deductions that can only be described as symptomatic of the problems besetting his narrative of the second act of the birth of humanity. The first is that *Homo neanderthalensis* is only an 'approximation of a human being, still crude', the second that 'the newcomer was man himself; his skeleton hardly differed from our own: meaning that of the European' (*CH* 153). We it seems are the descendants of the newcomer, and we are the Europeans. But what does it mean to claim that we are descendants of the more perfect human? Is Bataille emphasizing that 'we' Europeans are of African origin (as in a longer perspective are all humans), or is he diverting attention from this by suggesting the multi-regionalist position that 'Apparently he came from a central point in Eurasia' (*CH* 153) and that Europeans had consequently always been Europeans? In any case, the severe reduction of chronological perspective is noteworthy: the fossil record of *Homo sapiens* does indeed show an approach from the East of what is now Europe, but this was but the final phase of repeated journeys out of East Africa by way of the Southern and

Eastern Mediterranean. The fossil record also suggests that the encounter between the humanities – and there were not only two – took place on the southern Mediterranean corridor and if at all then most improbably in Western Europe.[16]

The focus of Bataille's dramaturgy now shifts from appearance to disappearance – enter *Homo sapiens* stage left, exit *Homo neanderthalensis* stage right. Yet the interval between entrance and exit remains obscure: 'We know nothing about the transition period except the final result: the Neanderthal man disappeared' (*CH* 155). Bataille at this point makes a symptomatic and immediately disowned return to the position of the Frobinus essay, noting, 'He disappeared so completely that beyond the appearance of the new man, more than fifty thousand years before us, we no longer have any trace of his existence' (*CH* 155). What then are the traces Bataille allows to survive in Southern Africa? They are certainly not Neanderthal fossils and seem to be the bushmen Bataille mentioned earlier as victims of a Bantu invasion. But this introduces a variant of the problem we encountered earlier of *Homo sapiens* existing over 100,000 years before inventing art and becoming *Homo sapiens*. Bataille is clear that all surviving humanity is *Homo sapiens* and that *Homo neanderthalensis* has been completely extinguished: 'No race today represents him' (*CH* 155). But, according to him, 'we' are 'closer' to the 'primitive humanity' that invented art than we are to contemporary

> Bushmen, the Australian Aborigines, and the Eskimoes who endure ... [who] present us with a tableau approximate to that of the life of the inhabitants of the Vézère valley in the period of the painted caves. However, these modern primitives lack this outpouring, this upsurge of creative awakening that makes Lascaux man our counterpart and not that of the Aborigine. (*CH* 159)

In a complex transposition, Bataille transfers the colonial relation of the colonist to the contemporary native peoples on to that between *Homo sapiens* and *Homo neanderthalensis* complete with a justification for the cultural superiority of the former.

The problem remains of how a relation between *Homo sapiens* and *Homo neanderthalensis* becomes for Bataille a relation within *Homo sapiens*. It is as if he is edging towards proposing a new species emerging from within *Homo sapiens* – Lascaux Man *Homo Lascauxensis* or 'we' Europeans – as opposed to the South African *Homo sapiens* who are allegedly culturally closer to *Homo neanderthalensis*. Certain *Homo sapiens* remained (and it seems still remain for Bataille) repeatedly playing out the 'first act' of the restricted economy of Neanderthal humanity – working under adverse conditions of scarcity, oppressed by fears of death and responding with rudimentary chthonic liturgies of burial – while other *Homo sapiens* have entered the 'second act' and respond creatively and artistically to the same predicament. Bataille then sketches an evolutionary schema explaining this development within *Homo sapiens* based on 'Similitudes between Aboriginal life and prehistoric life [that] allow us to represent the dawning of humanity in a concrete way' (*CH* 159). The aboriginal peoples have 'tools and stone weapons' and live as 'hunter gatherers'; 'as in pre-historic times, they place their hands on the cave walls and surround them with paint'. From the similarities between paleo-anthropological and contemporary aboriginal mark-making Bataille draws the questionable inference 'that the human beings of the upper Palaeolithic had reactions similar to those of the Aborigines, that these human beings had, like the aborigines, a religion, and that this religion was not altogether very different from that of the aborigines' (*CH* 159). But this religion of art is very different from that Bataille imagines for Neanderthal humanity. Aware too of death, their response was one of avoidance – Neanderthal burial is interpreted by Bataille as a gesture of protection: 'to escape the threat the dead represented, they made them disappear below the earth' (*CH* 154). Apart from liturgical gestures such as burial with the feet towards the sun, Neanderthal religiosity was for Bataille restricted to avoidance; the religion of *Homo lascauxensis* was quite the opposite, dedicated more to appearance than to disappearance. The paintings of animals on walls, for instance, were not a simple prophylactic gesture of holding them at a distance but were intended to 'bring them to appear before their weapons: to dispose of an apparition was to already make the animal fall into their power' (*CH* 160). This was an expansive and excessive gesture, indifferent to the sense of loss and fear of loss that oppressed Neanderthal humanity; the two humanities in short occupy the worlds of restricted and general economy.

Given the importance of the entry of *Homo sapiens* into general economy as well as the disquieting analogies between their encounter with *Homo neanderthalensis* and the contemporary colonial encounter within surviving *Homo sapiens*, the issue of the Neanderthal extinction becomes salient. Bataille's explanation is ambivalent. After claiming that the extinction of Neanderthal humanity was so complete that 'No race today represents him', he continues: 'Undoubtedly, violence is the only explanation. The more intelligent, more agile newcomer must have effortlessly supplanted him' (*CH* 155). In this scenario, developed further in his 1960 essay 'Unliveable Earth', the Neanderthal extinction was a paleo-genocide, one characterized by a confusion of the sacrificed animal, human and divine represented by Neanderthal humanity. Haunted by the self-destructive technical possibilities of nuclear warfare and the spectacle of excessive festival, 'Unliveable Earth' presents the two acts of the birth of humanity in terms of a continuous disengagement from the animal through work, consciousness and the creation of art. It is in the upper Palaeolithic revolution 'from which man emerged fully formed' that art becomes festive and excessive: 'from the immense crowd of animals, figures that are half human and half animal emerge. They lead, it seems, a musical tumult, a dance of deliverance into intoxication' (*CH* 177). The animal figures represented on the walls of the cave 'were those of the hunt' summoned to appear while the other 'strange – human yet animal – figures were in fact divine: for the undeveloped men, the animal, being essentially man's double, had something of the divine, the very thing he no longer attains except in the prodigious effervescence of the festival' (*CH* 177). The excessive expenditure of general economy seems to summon this conjuncture of human, animal and divine and yet it also seems as if this strange being was physically present in the figure of Neanderthal humanity, the uncanny human who could be killed as if an animal.

Fantasizing a moment when *Homo sapiens* did not kill each other, Bataille notes in a strangely detached way that 'If men killed other men, they were of a different species. Thus Palaeolithic man had to hunt, and it seems he was as capable of killing the Neanderthal man as he was of killing his prey' (*CH* 178). But instead of lingering on this peculiar killing of the men who are animals (and perhaps Gods) and the connection between this killing and the expenditure of the festivals, Bataille moves rapidly into general considerations of animality and the human. Ancient *Homo sapiens* and 'some very primitive savages today' think of themselves as animals 'because animals are in their mind, the most holy, having a sacred quality, which men have lost' (*CH* 178). But another interpretation is possible – it is not that humans have lost a divine/animal quality but that they killed the divine/animal humans that they encountered. The revolution in art associated with Lascaux might, in ways Bataille intimates but does not fully explore, be connected with the killing of Neanderthal humans. If this is plausible – and it is a possibility certainly entertained by Bataille – then the Lascaux humanity defined by this revolution in art is constituted by the genocidal act of killing Neanderthal humans, making them disappear only to reappear in the image of the animal.

There is very little fossil evidence to support this conclusion – some rare bones with marks that might be consistent with injuries sustained by the weapons of *Homo sapiens* – and Bataille himself, on the whole, avoids resorting to it. After evoking violence as the only explanation for the Neanderthal extinction he adds, 'we have no way of imagining it' and, drawing on his view that warfare is associated with sedentary, agricultural social formations, swiftly reverses his violence hypothesis in favour of 'a rather long period of co-existence' that might constitute 'thousands of years' (*CH* 156). On this account, 'the life of the newcomer was not very different from that of the supplanted unfortunate' (note that although coexisting by hypothesis with *Homo sapiens*, Neanderthal humanity has also already been 'supplanted' as per the violence hypothesis). The newcomer peacefully enjoying his newly acquired possessions slowly develops art-making in a way very different to the 'crashing roar that is proper to birth' that only two pages later will describe the same passage into art, identified with the paintings of Lascaux.

Lascaux and the Venus of Willendorf

Bataille's Lascaux is haunted by intimations of the Shoah. Even his description of its discovery by a group of schoolboys in 1940 – commenting in a lecture on a filmed reconstruction – emphasizes that one of them was a Jewish refugee from Paris and that he and his fellow discoverers had originally set out to give another group of Alsatian refugee schoolboys 'a good thrashing'. It is not hard to imagine a possible motivation for this foray against the German-speaking and possibly anti-Semitic children from Alsace. In his discussion of the slaughter of animals in his 1952 lecture 'A Visit to Lascaux', he comments on the industrial slaughter of animals that 'our own kind did as much with other human beings in Germany not so long ago', adding flippantly 'but in the end this was an enormous scandal' (*CH* 48). This reference to the Shoah emerges from a broader argument contrasting the humanity's self-distinction from animality with the 'equality between prehistoric humanity and animals' (*CH* 49). The equality between animality and humanity is Bataille's key to understanding what he will later term the 'enigma' of the cave art of Lascaux, but also of the ancient portable female figurines that feature prominently in Bataille's *Tears of Eros*. Another understanding is possible, however, following from the literal defacement of human self-representation common to both the wall paintings and the sculpture.

In order to describe the distinction between humans and animals in 'A Visit to Lasaux', Bataille resorts to the term 'transcendence' – 'humans see themselves as transcendent in relation to animals. For a human being there is a discontinuity, a fundamental difference between an animal and himself' (*CH* 48). Humans are *esprit* while an animal is only a *thing*. Bataille held to this position and the fascination with the nexus human/animal in spite of its difficulties, implicitly acknowledged but rarely explicitly worked through. The first is that humanity is not one thing – there are many humanities – and the second linked with this is that if Lascaux man did not possess a clear distinction between animality and humanity, when did this distinction emerge and how can we claim to be heirs of the art-making animals? Bataille's explanation seems to entail extending the Hegelian master–slave dialectic to animality with the drama of the emergence of the human played out in art and the confrontation with the animal 'not as though he were confronting an inferior being or a thing, a negligible reality, but as if he were confronting a spirit similar to his own' (*CH* 49). The art records a struggle to the death, a struggle for recognition that issued in the human mastery over the animal. The details of Bataille's audacious argument are pertinent and in their own terms not unconvincing, with the alterity of the animal figuring death and transcendence and the art a practice of atonement for the death and the propitiation of the avenging god-animal. But another logic intimated but not worked through shimmers through this abstract dialectic and radically challenges its terms and its consequences.

Bataille's evidence yields a different understanding if we set the general problem of animality within a context of the presence of different humanities whose very differences seem to be defined in terms of their proximity to animality. Occupying the grottoes previously occupied by Neanderthal humans, the question of the relation between human and animal is posed not so much to the animal but to the questionable animal–human predecessors. This can be seen by paying closer attention to Bataille's account of the 'paradox' or 'enigma' of human self-representation in ancient art and in particular to the non-representation of the face in contexts of killing and sex. Yet how does this account look if we foreground the presence of Neanderthal humanity? In this context, the severely and consistently defaced representations of the human might point to the attempt to distinguish the physiognomy of *Homo sapiens* from the more 'bestial' physiognomy of *Homo neanderthalensis*.

Throughout his reflections on Lascaux and cave art, Bataille consistently affirms the inseparability of the wall art and the portable sculptures as the first 'human' self-representations. But Bataille underestimates how far this art may be used to distinguish between distinct human physiognomies. He notes how in cave art the few humans that appear among the animals 'are often grotesque; they are generally tiresome caricatures, engraved carelessly and without conviction on the cave wall. Women alone were the object of more attentive representations' (*CH* 168). Bataille maintained this position consistently throughout his paleo-anthropological reflections, but without linking the representations to the presence or memory of Neanderthal humans, in appearance 'closer' to the animals. Bataille acknowledges that 'In regard to its own species, humanity first had only the strange feelings evidenced by the figures in the caves' (*CH* 168), but perhaps these feelings concerned not so much the animal in general than the more-animal-humans encountered by *Homo sapiens*. The art does not so much mark a distinction between human and animal than between kinds of humanity and to focus on the former distracts attention from the latter.

The most explicit and complete human representation – what Bataille called the 'Holiest of Holies' – is found in a remote cave in the Lascaux complex. The representation of a human figure is strikingly different from the rest of the art in the complex. It is a graphic almost caricatural or 'schematic silhouette' (*CH* 170) of a fallen male human figure with an avian head lying before an injured bison, a staff with the head of a bird fallen beside him. Although reluctant in his book on Lascaux to over-interpret the 'Holiest of Holies' as a shamanistic image, Bataille is confident that this is more than the representation of a hunting incident. His reading of the image in 'The Cradle of Humanity' emphasizes expiation for the death of the animal and the possibility of overcoming death 'symbolized' by the bird features prominent in the figure. Yet he takes the human physiognomy of the figure for granted, finding its schematic elements tiresome rather than valuable evidence of an act of violent graphic distinction. For this image can be read as the attempt to distinguish an avian from a bovine humanity – Bataille had, of course, on repeated occasions likened *Homo sapiens* to a swan and *Homo neanderthalensis* to a bull. The head of a bird on the fallen human figure and the attacking but dying bovine animal emphasized the different facial and cranial features of the two humanities. By literally identifying the human figure with the pointed face of a bird the artist marked the difference of the sharply defined facial forms of *Homo sapiens* from the broader facial form of the other, vanquished humanity. The fallen figure also possesses the long narrow trunk and the straight limbs and feet of *Homo sapiens* as distinguished from the squat body and curved limbs and feet of *Homo neanderthalensis*, although the left arm is bowed.[17] The image of the human in short is a seemingly caricatural exaggeration of the visible features that distinguished *Homo sapiens* from *Homo neanderthalensis*. If this is the case, then all Bataille says with respect to guilt and expiation holds not so much for the human as killer of animals but as killer of different humans.

The masculinity of the figure is emphasized by the dagger-like form of the erect penis, which seems to form a triangle with the equally pointed but straight feet. The curved feet of Neanderthal humanity gave them a gait and posture different from *Homo sapiens* – Bataille notes ironically that they would have made poor soldiers; the difference in posture emphasized by the straight but pointed feet is visually linked to the sexual excitement of the fallen figure. Bataille links the body 'full of virile force' to 'the convulsive obscurity of the animal world' and 'the act of being suspended, hung over the abyss of death' (*CH* 173). But the rush to identify Eros and Thanatos overlooks the visual link between the penis and the feet or the erotic swoon connected with one of the main physiognomic markers of the difference between *Homo sapiens* and *Homo neanderthalensis*. The question posed by the sign of desire whether in overcoming death or in an erotic swoon directs us to the other genre of art practised beside the cave painting. Bataille regularly juxtaposes the male caricatures that appear in the cave paintings with the 'more attentive representations' of women in ancient sculpture. These sculptures trouble him for a number of reasons, although in the 'Cradle of Humanity' they are passed over quickly in the drive to get back to humans and animals. The first is the 'more attentive' representation that shows the caricatural style of male representation to have been a deliberate choice and not a technical shortcoming. The second is the character of their bodies that 'seem monstrous to us; their hips and breasts are enormous', a characteristic Bataille swiftly reduces to 'the ideal of beauty or at least to the fecundity of human beings during this period' (*CH* 168). The 'attentive representation' then is of a 'monstrous' woman. The third and most striking is the 'absence of a face on these statuettes. Instead of a face, some of them have a smooth or ribbed surface; others have a head whose face and nape have, without human traits, the bumpy appearances of a big blackberry' (*CH* 168). Bataille moves quickly to link this consistent defacement of the erotic object with the obliteration of the face as identifying 'the now-dead living being', thus bringing the sculptures quickly under the sign of his wider reflections on the relationship between death and sexual desire that impatiently dictated his reading of the Lascaux 'holiest of holies'.

In the more extended discussion of the faceless and monstrous representations of women in 'The Passage from Animal to Man and the Birth of Art' Bataille places the sculptures of women in a 'third world' beside those of men and animals. They have no animal characteristics but 'their human aspect is also suppressed' (*CH* 168), notably their facial characteristics, leaving either a smooth polished surface or, in the case of the Venus of Willendorf, a granular sphere. Bataille leaves the question of this defacement unanswered, moving quickly to a connection between women and animality. He overlooks the possibility that while the sculpted female bodies are recognizably human, they are physiognomically closer to Neanderthal female humanity, but with care taken to obliterate the specific identifying marks of this humanity. The Venus of Willendorf is a case in point. Bataille notes that her face is obliterated and replaced with rows of points leaving no trace of facial features but does not comment on other abbreviations of the figure even though he reproduces it from three different perspectives in *The Tears of Eros* (Bataille 2002, 30). He does not note how her short neck corresponds more to his view of the bovine physiognomy of *Homo neanderthalensis* than *Homo sapiens* nor how the compact and powerful body with its perceived erotic exaggerations is consistent with the morphology of female Neanderthal humanity. And significantly not only the face but also the other markers of Neanderthal physiognomy – the bowed arms and the bowed feet – have also been effaced (Bataille did not comment on the Venus of Willendorf having no arms or feet). It is then possible that these defaced objects of erotic desire are women of another humanity to *Homo sapiens*, raising more questions about the character of the desire in play and the formidable ban that attends or incites it and that is expressed in such severe disfiguration.

Reflecting on the meaning of the defacement of the erotic sculptures and the masks in the wall paintings, Bataille's train of thought quickly returns, by way of the ugliness of monkeys, to Neanderthal humanity. He muses on 'the extent to which the monkey's ugliness disturbs us: it never ceases haunting us' and traces the origin of this disturbance to the uncanny apparition of Neanderthal humanity: 'The attitudes I'm talking about surfaced at a time when the sight of a monkey was definitely familiar and were even more important since Middle Paleolithic man certainly looked like a monkey' (CH 73). This train of association leads to the question, 'did Middle Paleolithic man's appearance, which the first men who walked upright had to have known well, cause the same horror in these men that the sight of a monkey induces in us?' (CH 73). Bataille concedes that this question cannot ever be answered and instead modulates it via an alleged aversion for monkeys to the question of humanity's self-distinction from the animal kingdom, very recently we learn later, and the invention of monotheism.

The question is fundamental for Bataille and in many respects reveals the assumptions that vitiate his paleo-anthropology. One line of argument for the source of aversion moves from the monkey to the allegedly monkey-like Neanderthal humanity but it is countered by a phrasing which reveals that the aversion begins with Neanderthal humanity and is only subsequently extended to monkeys and then to the animal kingdom as a whole. It was the encounter with 'previous stooped man' that provoked the aversion for monkeys and 'then the entire animal kingdom' (CH 73). Bataille tries to make the reluctance to represent the human face part of 'prehistoric man's' sense of his own ugliness, but once again his argument runs in a different direction. It is the aversion for the other man, 'what we must call unfinished man', one that was 'loved and killed'.[18] The complex historical and cultural equation linking humanity and animality that Bataille tries to solve always results in a disowned Neanderthal humanity. They are the objects of violence and the expiation of violence, of a sexual desire accompanied by a defacement of the signs of Neanderthal humanity. The problem of animality in short is a cipher for that of a different humanity, one both familiar and alien – an object of murderous desire.

Epilogue: Post-colonial Neanderthals

Bataille's hypothesis made the Neanderthal extinction central to the emergence and sole domination of the human that recognized its own violence with respect to nature, animality and itself through the invention of art. His intuition of a connection between the Neanderthal extinction and the eruption of art-making Lascaux Man rested on paleo-anthropology and saw itself as making a contribution to the discipline. Yet the hypothesis remained underdeveloped and uncertain, transposing a possible violence against another kind of human into a problem of animality. In many respects Bataille's hesitation to explore in depth the relationship between genocide and the invention of art and the human was the outcome of the limits of contemporary paleo-anthropology traceable to its own debts to imperial anthropology.

Recent developments in paleo-anthropology are slowly changing the model of violent invasion and pointing to a far more nuanced understanding of the Neanderthal extinction. The view that the arrival of *Homo sapiens* and the extinction of *Homo neanderthalensis* was a coincidence has been both supported and refuted in recent debate. The very small population of Neanderthal humanity rendered it vulnerable to a number of causes of extinction and reduced the probability of extensive encounters with *Homo sapiens*. The paleo-genetic advances of Svante Pääbo's team reconstructing the Neanderthal genome from fossil mitochondrial and nuclear DNA have confirmed sexual contacts between *Homo sapiens* and *Homo neanderthalensis* that resulted in offspring. Apart from questioning the view that Neanderthals were a different species of humanity, the findings have also revealed significant traces of Neanderthal DNA in contemporary European and Asian populations. The case for the Neanderthals not being extinct but living on in contemporary humanity has also been confirmed by fossil finds after the extinction that might be described as *Homo sapiens–neanderthalensis*. Yet even the genetic evidence does not point to a wide range of encounters between the humanities. It has, however, also confirmed the existence – in one case in the same Siberian cave – of another kind of humanity – the Denisovan – opening the possibility that there were not only two but many humanities coexisting over millennia. It has also shown how developments in the material culture of later *Homo neanderthalensis*, especially in the creation of ornament and (questionably) musical instruments, may be interpreted as a positive outcome of its contact with *Homo sapiens*.

Bataille's interest in paleo-anthropology and the Neanderthal extinction as we have seen throughout was tied to a broader concern not only with the past but also the present and future of the human. His paleo-anthropological hypothesis was also intended as a critique of the current condition of humanity, capable of mass murder, warfare and genocide. The mapping of the distinction between general and restricted economy on to the two forms of humanity was part of this broader project. If current paleo-anthropological knowledge had been available to Bataille he would probably have emphasized the sexual contacts between the humanities, would have been more reticent but not wholly repentant about the chronological lack of fit between the catastrophic

Neanderthal extinction and the glorious birth of art, and would have considered more carefully the implications of an art-making Neanderthal humanity that developed this capacity alongside and perhaps together with *Homo sapiens*.

Notes

1   See Bataille 1979 and Bataille, *CH*.

2   The 'Venus' figurines are associated with the 'Gravettian' culture, which is dated to 37,000 years ago and linked with novel survival strategies that are thought to distinguish them from the Neanderthals. The Venus of Willendorf is thus plausibly a late example of a kind of art-making practised long before and thus within the window of Bataille's chronology. See Papagianni and Morse 2015, 174.

3   The cave of Chauvet discovered in 1994 posed another challenge to the dating of prehistoric art. Some of the images, very similar to those of Lascaux, may be over 35,000 years old. Recent research into the material traces found in the cave has distinguished two phases of occupation – 37,000 to 33,500 and 31,000 to 28,000 – with the art-making confined to the first, older period of occupation. In this case the chronology begins to agree with the older dating of the cave art that underlies Bataille's hypothesis. See Soline Roy's article on Anita Quiles's work on Chauvet (Roy 2016).

4   My account is indebted to Harf and Witte 2014.

5   One of the wilder fantasies proposed by Franz Josef Karl Meyer, Professor of Anatomy at Bonn, departed from the axiom of the impossibility of fossil humanity and identified the bones as those of a Mongolian Cossack who deserted from Napoleon's army and took refuge in the cave; another strategy, pursued by the usually astute Berlin pathologist Rudolf Virchow, identified the 'abnormalities' as consistent with a modern individual suffering from rickets and arthritis (Harf and Witte 2014, 45–6). Both tried to remove the bones from the scene of paleo-anthropology while retaining a sense that they belonged to a victim, whether of war or illness.

6   The term *Geschlecht* recurs throughout German-language discussions of the Neanderthal remains and should be read in the philosophical context enriched by Heidegger's and Derrida's contributions, which see it as essentially equivocal – signifying at once 'race', 'species', 'generation', 'sex'. The flexible ambiguity surrounding the term allowed it to operate in a number of registers.

7   See Svante Pääbo's judicious reflection on the problem of species difference, inclining to a more flexible definition of 'species': Pääbo 2014, 237.

8   Neanderthal humanity unwittingly posed a revaluation of racial values, with the colonizers coming from Africa and the 'primitive' native European peoples being vanquished by them. My thanks to Scott Wilson for alerting me to the continuing reverberations of the late nineteenth-century racial capture of Neanderthal humanity in contemporary racism.

9 A discovery predating that of the Neanderthal and only subsequently identified. The Gibraltar remains are sometimes taken to represent the last surviving group of Neanderthal humans.

10 The two humanities are thought to share a common ancestor in *Homo heidelbergensis*.

11 We shall see below that this picture has been considerably complicated by recent paleo-anthropological research into *Homo neanderthalensis* and its fate.

12 This is the current position, which distinguishes between *Homo sapiens–neanderthalensis* and *Homo sapiens–sapiens*; for Bataille the latter would more properly be described as *Homo sapiens–lascauxensis*.

13 Bataille happily employs the scale to distinguish between grades of humanity. In a discussion of Chinese and European fossil discoveries, he notes parenthetically 'the latter being very primitive; the former, closer to us than more recent humanity, called Neanderthal.' (*CH* 124).

14 'The birth of art, unquestionably more than 40,000 years ago, follows an interminable period of stagnation' (*CH* 145).

15 Recent analysis of fossil remains assigns both *Homo sapiens* and *Homo neanderthalensis* a common ancestor – *Homo heidelbergensis* – with a species lifespan stretching between 150,000 and 200,000 years ago.

16 See Pääbo's *Neanderthal Man*'s deductions from his team's reconstruction of the Neanderthal genome.

17 The apparent possession of an arm characteristic of the two human species invites interpretation of the figure as a hybrid, although on the whole it is elements of physical distinction that are emphasized.

18 Bataille characterizes the human–animal nexus in these terms: 'They loved them and they killed them' (*CH* 75). But the unasked question remains: were animals loved and killed like the other humans, or were the other humans loved and killed like animals?

20

Inhuman destruction: The critique of exterminatory violence

Critiques of violence

What sense does it make to criticize the violence – whether of nuclear war or climate catastrophe – that will result in human extinction? Can we understand such critique as a Kantian transcendental enquiry into the 'conditions of possibility' of exterminatory violence, or is it best understood as a set of normative objections to its contemporary manifestations? And if the former, what might be the conditions of possibility of human extinction? Kant provides a methodological clue in his analytic teaching version of his first critique, the *Prolegomena to Any Future Metaphysics That Will Present Itself as a Science*, when he notes that we have Euclidean geometry and Newtonian physics and then asks: how are they possible? (Kant [1783] 2004, 295). We have the sixth (human) extinction event: how is that possible? What are the conditions of possibility of thinking and talking about extinction violence, let alone venturing a critique of it? One way forward is to read the genitive in 'critique of violence' in both directions: not as just the critique of the object/concept/event of exterminatory violence or discourses on it, but also as the originary epistemological violence of critique itself. Kant described the *Critique of Pure Reason* as a tribunal that judges the conditions of possibility of experience as conditions for the objects of experience. In our case the critique of exterminatory violence is inseparable from the exterminatory violence of critique, and the whole point of critique – the infamous Copernican turn – is that objects fit or are made to fit the conditions of possibility of experience and not the other way around. Are there many critiques of a single concept/object/event of violence – are Clausewitz, Fanon and Arendt talking about the same thing in different ways – or are theirs many critiques of many violences; are they talking about different violences in different ways; and are there, remembering the subjective and objective genitives of 'critiques of violences', many violences of critique? And what happens when the violence we must speak of is absolute exterminatory violence or the violence that destroys its own, that is its human conditions of possibility? Is exterminatory violence continuous with other historical violences and open to critique or is it off the scale, an inhuman violence that erases both the subject and object of critique?

The twenty-first-century critique of absolute violence emerging with the recognition of the exterminatory violence of the Anthropocene and the sixth extinction event has generated a number of diverse but also interrelated critiques of violence, among them the Anthropocene, the 'Copernican Revolution of the Plant' and the post-human or 'Novacene'. They each pursue critique beyond human scales of violence and begin to think the conditions of possibility of an inhuman planetary future. Their critiques of environmental violence are conducted with varying degrees of force and understanding but all exemplify the workings of the Kantian maxim that the conditions of possibility of experience are also conditions of possibility of the objects of experience. However, this is not self-evidently a question of human experience, but also perhaps of the experience of other forms of life, whether vegetal or technical.

Understanding the Anthropocene, the human mass extinction event and the post-human as critiques of violence forces us to confront the question of planetary life and its future. It is a question of increasing urgency given the growing realization that we have irreversibly entered the Sixth Mass Extinction Event. In the last ten years debate has focused on the implications of the violence of mass extinction for five interlocking forms of life: human, animal, vegetal, fungal and technical. What has emerged is a strong thought of future life, but one in which humans are crossing the threshold of what extinction theorist Thom van Dooren in his beautiful 2014 book *Flight Ways: Life and Loss at the Edge of Extinction* has called the edge of extinction, defined less in terms of a single event – the passing of the last human – than as 'a slow unravelling of virtually entangled ways of life that began long before the death of the last individual and continues to ripple forward long afterwards, drawing in living beings in a range of different ways' (van Dooren 2014, 17). What are the parameters of a critique of violence under the conditions of the slow and sometimes rapid unravelling of its human conditions of possibility?

The Anthropocene: 'Last redoubt of the human'?

One of the most forceful and influential twenty-first-century critiques of violence – the Anthropocene – holds that we have entered a geological era in which the human is the dominant force for planetary change, a condition manifest in climate change, changes in the chemical composition of the atmosphere, geosphere and the oceans and the emergence of a noosphere or global communications network. Given the role played by human exterminatory violence in this discourse, it is evident that any 'critique of anthropocenic reason' must also be a critique of the violence of anthropocenic reason.[1] This discourse has existed since the 1980s in the formulation of the Gaia hypothesis by James Lovelock but was formally named and announced by the climatologist Paul Crutzen in a short manifesto, 'The Anthropocene: Geology of Mankind', published in the journal *Nature* in 2002. Since then it has undergone rapid development, forming an interdisciplinary locus across the humanities, arts and sciences that seems to be well on its way to becoming our latest transcendental logic or pure reason. But it is fundamentally a critique of violence, a critique of the violence of human interventions on the working and the composition of the planet and the life that inhabits it. This is evident from the competing chronologies for the beginning of the Anthropocene. Its beginnings are variously dated to the last Ice Age and the extinction of mega-fauna such as mammoths, giant sloths, sabre tooth tigers, or to the creation of the world market after 1492 whether in the Orbis Spike of the Columbian exchange or in the Capitalocene, or to the industrial revolution driven by fossil fuels, or to the explosion of the atomic weapons, or to the post-war 'great acceleration' of population and industrial and agrarian production.[2] It is extraordinary to witness how rapidly this critique developed and ramified – being at once a cognitive critique that would understand and measure anthropogenic change in the environment, a moral and political critique of its effects, and an aesthetic critique of its violent impoverishment of the environment with the emergence of a planet violently dominated by the human.

Paul Crutzen's manifesto, published as a scientific discovery, is revealing in many ways. It begins:

> For the past three centuries, the effects of humans on the global environment have escalated. Because of these anthropogenic emissions of carbon dioxide, global climate may depart significantly from natural behaviour for many millennia to come. It seems appropriate to assign the term 'Anthropocene' to the present, in many ways human-dominated, geological epoch, supplementing the Holocene – the warm period of the past 10–12 millennia.

And it ends:

> Unless there is a global catastrophe – a meteorite impact, a world war or a pandemic – mankind will remain a major environmental force for many

millennia. A daunting task lies ahead for scientists and engineers to guide society towards environmentally sustainable management during the era of the Anthropocene. This will require appropriate human behaviour at all scales, and may well involve internationally accepted, large-scale geo-engineering projects, for instance to 'optimize' climate. At this stage, however, we are still largely treading on *terra incognita*. (Crutzen 2002, 23)

Sandwiched in between this beginning and end of a one-page article is a damning critique of the violence of human environmental depredations that are accused of endangering the very survival of the planet. Disarmingly, and I think with a fair degree of caustic irony, Crutzen maintains that only a global catastrophe – not even a God – can save, not us, but the planet. He even hints that a global catastrophe might save the planet *from* us. Failing that, salvation is the task of engineers and managers who will require 'appropriate behaviour' from the human population and protect them by assuming control and a duty of care for the running of the planet through geo-engineering projects such as seeding the upper atmosphere with sulphur in order to reflect excessive sunlight and so control the greenhouse effect prompted by anthropogenic rises in methane and CO_2.

What Crutzen and, from a slightly different direction, Lovelock mean by 'appropriate behaviour' is a severe reduction in the numbers of humans occupying the planet. So the implications of this critique of violence are considerable, grave and without doubt themselves violent. For this reason alone, and there are others, this critique of violence needs in its turn to be subjected to critique – the critique of anthropocenic reason. In the face of this it is possible to take the analytic path pursued by Kant in the *Prolegomena* and ask, given that we have a discourse on violence, that of the Anthropocene: how is it possible? This does not mean subjecting climate change and environmental violence to critique but rather the discourse that has critically constructed this object of 'environmental violence', namely anthropocenic reason. The study of the anthropocenic critique of violence reveals many interesting features about the use of the concept of violence: most prominently showing it to be an essentially humanist discourse that exaggerates the destructive power of human agency: humanity can destroy itself and its allied species, but not the planet. We err if we believe that the earth's routine self-destruction on a geological scale is at all comparable with the paltry effects of human violence visited upon it.

The anthropocenic critique of violence might qualify as a classic example of the violence of critique. It has had very carefully to construct its object – environmental violence and anthropogenic changes in the structure and functioning of the planetary system – but above all to establish a very specific transcendental aesthetic for this object in order to reshape geological time and space according to human parameters and to create a mis en scène in which the human can *appear* as a geological force. Crutzen's work and that of others associated with Anthropocene discourse, notably Will Steffens, largely work within the parameters of a discipline developed in the 1980s under the auspices of the US government known as Earth System Science. It is the successor to the God-slaying discipline once known as geology and one of the outcomes of the post-war cybernetic revolution carefully cultivated by the US and the Soviet governments. This is a discipline that historically constructed both its own object and the conditions of perceiving it. Its founding document 'Earth System Science: A Programme for Global Change' was published by the NASA Earth System Sciences Committee in 1986 and is remarkable not only for constructing a critical object – the earth system – but also for assembling the technical conditions of possibility – satellites and observation posts – necessary to measure, report and, in Kantian terms, 'experience' it. The conditions of possibility of the experience of the planet as a systematic whole were a condition of possibility of its coming into existence as an object of experience. One of this text's most fundamental achievements is to recalibrate relevant geological time – ostensibly according to protocols of data and accurate measurement – compressing it from 4.5 billion to half a million years.

The sublime construction of the object of geological knowledge through stratigraphy and palaeontology in the long nineteenth century, starting with Kant's contemporary Hutton, through Cuvier and Darwin's inspiration Lyell, divided an earth history of 4500 million years into aions, eras, epochs and ages: the Hadean, Archean, Proterozoic, and our current aion, the Phanerozoic; the Cambrian, Cretacious, Jurassic, up to our Quaternary; and the Eocene, Pleistocene, Holocene and now, disputedly, the Anthropocene. This remarkable genealogy of the earth and its routinely monstrous history is self-consciously and deliberately reduced in much earth systems science to recent geology – at best the Quaternary, but usually the upper Pleistocene and Holocene – the ice age and its interglacial intervals. Relevant geological time is redefined by earth system science as largely the last 500,000 years, not so coincidentally coinciding with the inhabitation of the earth by hominoid and later human species, and so adjusting geological time and the events measured in it to human time. Small variations in climate, sea level, ice coverage – minor variations in terms of a broader geological scale – appear large within this restricted humanized definition of relevant geological time. Earth System Sciences, then, provide the condition of possibility for Anthropocene discourse and its axiom that humans have become a geological force and that they comport themselves violently with respect to the earth. Through the violence of critique enacted by a US government agency in which the transcendental aesthetic of the earth is forced into a human measure, humans can consider themselves capable – in Anthropocene discourse – of inflicting violence on the earth.

But Crutzen's almost involuntary reference to meteorite strikes, world wars and pandemics – to mass extinction events, in short – marks the return of the geological repressed. Because when viewed according to a geological transcendental aesthetic measured in terms of billions of years, the earth routinely engages in acts of extreme destruction and for most of its history operated at temperatures and sea levels incompatible with human life. Not with life as such, but that particular variant we represent. But it would be an unwarranted extension of the concept of violence to describe terrestrial inhuman destruction as violent: this would be an attempt to humanize the very dangerous – for us – planet we inhabit. Any 'violence' we could inflict on the planet is well within its normal, that is to say geological, parameters. Non- or minor violence in this context could include the melting of the ice caps – themselves a recent geological anomaly – the rise of carbon dioxide levels and thus global warming: the worst-case predictions of the Anthropocene discourse, of 400–500 parts per million of CO_2 during this century, should be contrasted with a geological mean of above 4000 ppm. While the risk to the survival of human life is undeniable, the inference that this threatens the planet or more modestly life on the planet is unwarranted. We are, after all, geologically already the sixth mass extinction event and, while perhaps the fastest, the sixth is by no means the worst in comparison with what has already historically taken place on the planet earth.

The violence of the 'critique of anthropocenic violence' consists in reducing geological time and space to a human measure and thus producing the Anthropocene's illusion of planetary and life-threatening human power. It is moreover a violent illusion that licences violent responses such as population reduction and planetary engineering. But while much philosophical discourse on the Anthropocene remains a normative supplement to its critique of human environmental violence limits, there is another philosophical response that violently criticizes the Anthropocene's critique of environmental violence. This emerges out of Gaia theory – the cybernetic precursor and companion of Earth System Science – with James Lovelock himself and more recently Bruno Latour's *Face à Gaïa: Huit conférences sur le nouveau régime climatique* (2015). These texts step out of the Anthropocene critique of violence to claim that the human perpetrators of environmental violence are also its victims. In perhaps one of the most extravagant humanizations of the planet, Gaia is our enemy who acts violently against us, we humans, taking up once more the theme of a state of war between humans and the planet that was already contemplated by Leopardi in *La Ginestra* where 'exterminatory nature' is implacably at war with the human race.

The explicit analysis of the theme of war has been surprisingly restrained in Anthropocene discourse, even though violence without enmity and war – chronic or acute – is hard to conceive. But James Lovelock's 2006 *The Revenge of Gaia* explicitly puts us on a war footing – 'we live on a live planet that can respond to the changes we make either by cancelling the changes or by cancelling us' (Lovelock 2006, 21). He adds that we have made Gaia or the living planet 'our worst enemy'. We are at war; we need ramparts and a strategy to respond to the Earth's violence. Latour goes even further in his *Face à Gaïa*, bringing Schmitt and his concept of the enemy into the discussion. But all this is once more to humanize the earth, to presume that we are capable of being an enemy and that our violence is met by that of Gaia and can respond to it. Perhaps Lovelock was closer to the truth when he speculated on the cancelling out of humanity by Gaia. The inability of humanity even to rise to the level of being a credible enemy of the planet is beautifully captured by the classical geologist Jan Zalasiewicz's proposal in *The Planet after Us* (2008) of a new categorical imperative for humanity: act so as to leave the most interesting sediment layer for the contemplation of future, non-human species of geologists.

The Copernican Revolution of the plant

The most challenging recent thinking of the future of life after the human has emerged within the disciplines of botany and zoology. These debates are moving very fast but their direction is quite clear and their implications for neighbouring discussions concerning the Anthropocene and technical life are considerable. Let's begin with botany and its object plant life and look at two texts on the philosophy of plant life published in 2013. One is backward looking, occupying a restricted philosophical space and proposing a 'weak thought' of plant life; the other is more speculative and employs recent research in the emergent field of neuro-botany to propose a strong thought of plant life as the most likely future for life on this planet. The first, Michael Marder's *Plant Thinking: A Philosophy of Vegetal Life* (2013), presents itself as an exercise in 'weak thought', with a foreword by Gianni Vattimo and Santiago Zabala claiming that this philosophy of plant life 'not only follows a logic of resistance, but also promotes a progressive weakening of the strong structures of metaphysics' (Marder 2013, xii). Pursuing a series of historical studies ranging from Aristotle through Plotinus to Hegel, Nietzsche, Heidegger and Derrida, Marder makes a compelling case for plant life as the unthought of metaphysics. But there is something repetitive about his gesture of pointing to the unthought without trying to think it differently. This might be a result of the almost suffocatingly *philosophical* character of Marder's plant thinking whose arguments remain internal to a narrowly defined philosophical canon. So much so that it is surprisingly innocent not only of the botanical thought of Charles Darwin but also, with some small exceptions, of classical and contemporary botanical literature and debate. His analysis is exclusively directed to the plant as an object of metaphysical inquiry and description, into which, of course, the plant does not and has never really fit. Marder claims 'something in vegetation escapes the objectifying grasp of metaphysics and its politico-economic avatars'; that plants 'accomplish a *living* reversal of metaphysical values ... [and form] the weakest link in the metaphysical chain, where repressed contradictions are condensed into their purest state and where worn out justifications get so thin as to put the entire system on the verge of rupture' (Marder 2013, 55, 56). It is hard to avoid the suspicion that the plant has only been lent visibility here insofar as it has been approached and reduced by metaphysical structures. Even while offering a critique of the metaphysical violence suffered by plant life at the hands of humanity, Marden tacitly affirms human centrality; the conditions of possibility of plant life are none other than the conditions of possibility of our metaphysical experience of it.

A strong contrast to Marden's gesture is proposed by Stefano Mancuso and Alessandra Viola's *Verde Brillante*, also from 2013. Mancuso is the director of the 'Laboratorio Internationale di Neurobiologia Vegetale' at the University of Florence and *Verde Brillante* proposes not so much a weak thought of plant life disrupting metaphysical structures as the strong thought of what he calls a 'Copernican Revolution of the Plant'. For Mancuso and Viola, humans until very recently believed that life and especially plant life rotated around human beings; they surround *us* and form *our* 'environment', planets to our sun. Mancuso and Viola present some fascinating findings and arguments that radically question any anthropocentric assumptions concerning the significance of human life in the life of this planet. One of the most suggestive is the argument from biomass, looking at the contribution of human living matter to the totality of living matter on the planet. The Malthusian assumption that more than 7 billion human beings on the planet constitute a worrying share of the planet's biomass is widely accepted, even as the basis for public policy, but it is one that does not survive close scrutiny.

Mancuso and Viola work with two measures of biomass: weight and percentage, and they interpret share of biomass as providing an index of a species success in adaption to the planetary environment. From an estimated total planetary biomass of living carbon-based matter of 550 gigatons (with gigaton equalling a thousand million tons), animal life makes up a fractional 2 gigatons, with almost 1 gigaton comprising insect life and 0.7 gigatons fish life, leaving 0.3 gigatons for mammals, birds, molluscs and others, including the human population whose biomass measures in at 0.06 of a gigaton.

Mushrooms by contrast have a biomass of 12 gigatons, six times animal biomass, while plants comprise the overwhelming share of planetary biomass with 450 gigatons. Expressed in terms of percentages, plants or majority life represents over 80 per cent of the planet's biomass compared with the human percentage share of 0.01 per cent. We are not even a vanishingly small fraction of the biomass but rather constitute a 'trace element' of plant life according to Mancuso and Viola. From the perspective of the Copernican Revolution of the plant, humans are not even a planet rotating around the plant sun but at best a tiny asteroid following a bizarre and it seems short-lived elliptical trajectory. This radical Copernican Revolution in which we circle plant life and are completely dependent on it – and not the other way round – leads to some fascinating philosophical arguments that complement the temporal arguments concerning the place of human time within geological planetary time: we are completely peripheral to planetary life; in spite of our hubris we cannot extinguish it but it would, or rather it will, carry on in our absence.

Curiously, both Marden and Mancuso follow the examples of the Swiss Ethics Committee on non-human biotechnology in 2008 and the Bolivian constitution of 2010, 'Laws of the Rights of Mother Earth', to present charters of the rights of plant life. The contrast between them is telling. Marden assumes a duty of care on the part of humans: we are obliged to respect and care for plant life; we must become responsible for it, respect its time, consume it responsibly but in the end this duty of care rests on the revealing assumption informing his eighth statement: 'The plant's absolute silence puts it in the position of the subaltern' (Marder 2013, 186). It is weak and we are strong, strong enough either to destroy or to care for plant life: we are the implausible shepherds or dominators of a subaltern vegetal being. By contrast, Mancuso's 2019 *La Nazione delle Piante: Carta dei diritti dei a viventi scritta dalle piante* completely reverses this thought, maintaining with almost Swiftian rigour that it is the plants – the strongest and dominant form of life on the planet – that must assume a duty of care *for us*:

> It is for this reason that the very wise Nation of Plants born hundreds of millions of years before any human nation guarantees to all living beings sovereignty over the Earth, to the end of preventing that any presumptuous single species may extinguish themselves before their time, thus proving that their enormous brains were not an evolutionary advantage but a disadvantage. (Mancuso 2019, 31)

Marden remains confined to the limits of human time and power, succumbing to the transcendental illusion of human dominance, while Mancuso, by setting human significance in a plant-life perspective, places us in a very precarious and humble position: we are not the masters but the supplicants of life on this planet.

What emerges very powerfully in Mancuso's botanical discourse – or phyto-philosophy – is the sense that the very critique of human violence with respect to plant life or the environment is based on the wrong premises or conditions of possibility. Marden's self-professed weak thought tacitly assumes the potentially destructive power of human beings, whereas Mancuso's strong plant thinking assumes the vulnerability and weakness of the human, the fact that they are wholly dependent on plant life for their energy and oxygen and vulnerable to changes in the planetary system beyond their control. While the 0.01 per cent of the biomass may imagine they have the power to destroy the planet and the life upon it, humans are really 'only capable of destroying themselves and those living beings that are useful to its life' (Mancuso 2019) but not life in general nor the planet. The Sixth Mass Extinction Event is literally the human extinction event, condemning only humanity and its vassal species to disappearance.

If Mancuso draws these conclusions from the transcendental conditions of possibility offered by the standpoint of the 80 per cent of living matter made up of plants, debates in zoology have arrived at similar conclusions for the 2 gigatons of animal life. The idea of a human mass extinction event is, in Kantian terms, no more than a transcendental illusion. There have been two stages in the development of this argument within zoology. The first has been elegantly defended by Ursula Heise in her *Imagining Extinction* (2016), which studied the composition of the lists of endangered species. On the 2008 Red List of the International Union for the Protection of Nature, all 5488 known mammal species and 9900 bird species were evaluated for endangered species status; but of the 30,700 then-known species of fish only 3481 had been evaluated for risk; of the 950,000 known insect species only 1250 were evaluated ... The conclusion is that the mass extinction debate has focused on species of direct interest to humans, of interest because implicated in human being and tied to its fate, leaving the vast mass of animals let alone organic life unassessed. Life defined as at risk of extinction is life that had the misfortune of having become objects of human experience. These suspicions have led more recently and perhaps more controversially to a view that human mass extinction event is in fact an event of mass genesis unparalleled since the Cambrian explosion of 530 million years ago. This has been powerfully argued by Chris Thomas – a professor of ecology at the University of York – in *Inheritors of the Earth: How Nature Is Thriving in the Age of Extinction* (2018). After studying unwelcome or invasive species – another way of describing those not of direct interest or use to humans – he comes to this conclusion:

> In the end, the Anthropocene biological revolution will almost certainly represent the sixth mass genesis of new biological diversity. It could be the fastest acceleration of evolutionary diversification in the past half billion

years. Some might discount the new species as weeds and pests, but that is a reflection of the human mind, not a fundamental attribute of these new forms of life. All forms of life simply come into existence on account of their individual histories and take advantage of the resources that are available to them. If some of them thrive at our expense, that is our problem, not theirs. (Thomas 2018, 197)

We have inadvertently provided the conditions of possibility for our supersession as a species, a platform, a *pangaia* or virtual continent that is permitting the flourishing of life but not for us. As the architects of *pangaia* we are also destined to be its victims: the human mass extinction event will be of humans and of species in symbiosis with us, but not of life, which may benefit enormously from our withdrawal.

The Novacene: Age of the post-human

During the early years of the twenty-first century James Lovelock – discoverer of the Gaia hypothesis/principle – warned increasingly of a state of war emerging between humanity and its host planet. In a series of books he warned that Gaia was preparing to rid itself of its most troublesome inhabitant and would do so with extreme violence. It was a position developed further by Bruno Latour who in 2013 gave the Gifford Lectures in Edinburgh with a title that moved from *Facing Gaia: A New Inquiry into Natural Religion* (Lord Gifford–friendly version) to *Facing Gaia: Six Lectures on the Political Theology of Nature* (the version published on Latour's website, subsequently deleted) to *Face à Gaïa: Huit conférences sur le nouveau régime climatique* published in 2015. They are a remarkable performance, not least for the introduction of political theology into ecological and Anthropocene debates, but also for the way in which this is done. His move towards a political theology of nature begins by questioning the unjust 'new age' reputation of James Lovelock's 'Gaia Hypothesis' – itself a case of a cyberbetic planetary systems theory masquerading as the earth mother – by putting us in a state of war with nature/the planet (although Latour's sentimental attachment to the concept of nature weakens his entire approach when compared with Lovelock's own remorseless positions) in his fourth and fifth lectures 'The Anthropocene and the Destruction of the Image of the Globe' and 'War of the Worlds: Humans against the Earthbound'. It is at the end of this fifth lecture that Latour poses the question, 'Under the Pressure of So Many Apocalyptic Injunctions: What Is a Gaian Political Theology?' In a state of planetary civil war, Latour follows Leopardi in his poem *La Ginestra* in imagining new alliances and practices of a humanity united against their common enemy: the unimaginably inhospitable and destructive planet earth evident from even the most elementary knowledge of planetary history.

Whatever the eventual virtues of a Gaian political theology, Latour's own version, in spite of its appeal to dance, art, the Gaia global circus, new alliances etc., is restricted, even stunted. And much of the narrowness of his vision stems from his not putting political theology itself to the test of Gaia and the Anthropocene or, in other words, from his importing Schmitt's political theology almost wholesale into ecological debate. In many ways, Schmitt's emphases on enmity, state of emergency and sovereign order as a hypothetical solution to the theorem posed by religious civil war are appropriate to Latour's proposition that Gaia is the enemy in the planetary civil war of the Anthropocene. But by answering his own question – 'Living in the Epoch of the Anthropocene is to be forced to redefine the political task par excellence: what people will you form, with what cosmology and on which territory' (Latour 2015, 189) – with a sovereign-oriented political theology, Latour dangerously restricts the political and theological task.

Another approach proposes instead that humans learn lessons of how to survive from the majority life of plants and fungi. Anna Lowenhaupt Tsing in the now classic ethnography *The Mushroom at the End of the World: On the Possibility of Life in Capitalist Ruins* (2015) calls on the mushroom, specifically the Matsutake mushroom, for lessons in surviving catastrophe: their 'willingness to emerge in blasted landscapes allows us to explore the ruin that has become our collective home' (Tsing 2015, 3). For Tsing, fungi are our 'ideal guides' for cooperative survival; virtuosi of symbiosis and non-reproductive encounters, they 'have always been recalcitrant to the iron cage of self-reproduction' and of working in and with the ruins of life (Tsing 2015, 143). They are for Tsing at once a model for a global commons, offering lessons in 'how to make a life' amid 'planetary destruction', but also the certain heirs of a post-human planet.

Stefano Mancuso in *The Revolutionary Genius of Plants* (2018) and Barbara Mazzolai in *La natura geniale. Come e perché le piante cambieranno (e salveranno) il pianeta* (2019) also turn to the plants for lessons in how humans should live, but without the apocalyptic edge of Tsing's The *Mushroom at the End of the World*. Mancuso, departing from the premiss that intelligence is 'inherent to life', draws lessons from botany for emergent forms of human organization. For him, 'We are at the very beginning of a revolution that has much to teach us about the true nature of intelligence', one already imperfectly enacted in the Internet: 'today's exemplar of the enormous power of non-hierarchical and diffused organizations that, like plant structures, is multiplying, gaining consensus, and, above all, producing excellent results' (Mancuso 2018, 92). This revolution is one that departs from a critique of the inflexibility of 'animal hierarchical organizations' and moves towards a green cooperative democracy in which 'in addition to imitating the decentralized structure of plants in order to increase the creativity and strength of our organizations, we must imagine new forms of diffused ownership' (Mancuso 2018, 93). This allows Mancuso to imagine a brighter future for the 0.01 per cent of the biomass: 'Three and a half billion more thinking heads is not a problem but a huge resource ... able to solve any problem – as long as they are free to think and innovate' (Mancuso 2018, 93). But, of course, it is also possible that plant life will continue to move from strength to strength if and when humans become victims of their 'animal hierarchical organization'.

The work of Barbara Mazzolai and her colleagues at the Centre for Micro Bio-robotics at Pontedera intensifies some of Mancuso's arguments by translating the intelligence of living organisms into that of artificial systems. Their research into bio-robotics offers two perspectives: 'biorobotics as science, serving to generate new discoveries and thus knowledge ... and biorobotics as engineering employed to invent and generate new technology' (Mazzolai 2019, 11). The union of botany, artificial intelligence and robotics constitutes a 'plantoid' revolution in which robotanic technologies intervene in the processes of life, whether in the management of vegetal life through 'growbots', energy generation and distribution, medical interventions in human life or the development of bio-robotic AI. Mazzolai shares Mancuso's optimism, seeing the potential salvation of the planet in the alliance of botany and AI:

> The many challenges that still await us in the world of robotics and AI will also pass through the development of more efficient energy systems, eco-compatible and sustainable materials, and the ability to learn from and adapt to natural and humanized habitats ... we must make a leap of imagination, try to imagine their future impact on life and on human welfare, and as result develop a global strategic vision in the long term. (Mazzolai 2019, 169)

And although it is certainly part of Mazzolai's vision, the emergent alliance of botany, robotics and AI does not necessarily point to a human future.

The alliance of plant life, technology and AI explored by Mazzolai provides a cue to return to Lovelock's Novacene or a future for AI and artificial, robotic life with or without its human creators. In *Novacene: The Coming Age of Hyperintelligence* (2019), Lovelock decisively rejected his earlier limited horizon of a state of war between humanity and the planet, proposing instead an unexpected alliance between Gaia, the Anthropocene and the post-human or Artificial Intelligence that no longer mobilizes the threat of planetary civil war. The Novacene or geological epoch that for Lovelock has already succeeded the Anthropocene describes the passage of planetary consciousness from the hands of the humans to artificial intelligence. It is precisely this passage that gives Lovelock hope for the end of the paradigm of war to describe the quality of the relation between the planet and its inhabitants. Yet he is also prepared to entertain the possibility that the current symbiosis between animals and plants that constitutes Gaia may be replaced by silicon-based artificial life: 'If, in the Novacene, photosynthesis by plants is replaced by electronic light collectors, the abundance of oxygen in the atmosphere would fall to trace levels within a few thousand years' (Lovelock 2019, 109). Yet while this is a possible, it is not for Lovelock a probable outcome, for

> we do not have to assume that the new artificial life that emerges in the Novacene is automatically as cruel, deadly and aggressive as we are. It may be that the Novacene becomes one of the most peaceful ages of the Earth. But we humans will for the first time be sharing the earth with other beings more intelligent than we are. (Lovelock 2019, 117)

For Mancuso and Mazzolai, we already always have been, and in what Lovelock calls Gaia we possess, a model for this symbiotic existence.

One of the most striking arguments in *Novacene* is couched in terms of the speed of consciousness. Lovelock makes an analogy between the speed of human consciousness and plant consciousness, and that between artificial intelligence and human intelligence: 'They would be likely to see us as we see plants – as beings locked in an extraordinarily slow perception and action' (Lovelock 2019, 119). The physiological limits of humans' neurology will make human perception and consciousness appear to an artificial intelligence as slow moving and apparently insensate as plant intelligence appears to the humans. However, this will not mean that the imagined scenarios of violent singularities, as artificial intelligence or robotics turns against the human, are at all plausible. For Lovelock, humans may provide the agreeable environment or landscape in which artificial intelligences will find it pleasant to live; they will have an interest in preserving the planet for their own forms of life, but also for plant, animal and human forms of life. Post-human life will, perhaps, grow out of and embody its own critique of violence.

Notes

1   This has been argued recently in Kathryn Yusoff's *A Billion Black Anthropocenes or None* (2018), which links the violence of Anthropocene discourse with colonialism, slavery and extraction.

2   For a comprehensive critical review of the chronologies of the Anthropocene see Simon L. Lewis and Mark Maslin, *The Human Planet: How We Created the Anthropocene* (2018).

21

Kafka's exit: Exile, exodus and messianism

Nein, Freiheit wollte ich nicht. Nur einen Ausweg.

– KAFKA, *EIN BERICHT FÜR EINE AKADEMIE*

Ich weiss keinen Ausweg.

– KAFKA, *NACHGELASSENE SCHRIFTEN UND FRAGMENTE*

Theoretical entrances and exits

In his 1934 essay 'Franz Kafka', written for the *Jüdische Rundschau*, Walter Benjamin read Kafka's writings as responses to the predicament of exile. This predicament may be suffered by breathing the air of exile and allowing it to 'gain control' or be resisted through the search for a 'way out' or exodus and/ or the expectation of a messianic setting right of its distortions.[1] Adorno, in his 1953 'Notes on Kafka', locates the condition of exile in the 'middle ground' or 'no-man's-land', where life and death lose their boundaries and where the chance of an exit 'was missed', but for him too the question of the 'way out' is definitive for Kafka's writing.[2] The story 'A Report to an Academy' is crucial for explicitly raising the question of the aesthetic and scientific 'ways out' of captivity: the artist in the vaudeville as the only 'way out'. Yet the predicament of exile remains; the ape continues to breathe the stuffy air of circus, hotel rooms, banquets and learned societies: neither his art nor his scientific report proved to be the desired 'way out'. In contrast to the stories that preceded it in the collection *A Country Doctor*, 'A Report to an Academy' presents an exodus narrative almost without messianism, one which combines art and knowledge as possible 'ways out', but with only the barest hints of the messianic.

The sensitivity of the first generation of philosophical critics to the predicament of exile and the pursuit of a 'way out' in Kafka's stories has largely been forgotten in recent philosophical work concerned with the problem of the 'way in'. The opening question of Deleuze and Guattari's influential *Kafka: Toward a Minor Literature* – 'How can we enter into Kafka's work?' – declares a principle that sits uneasily alongside Kafka's 1917 texts, which return insistently to the question of the *Ausweg* or way out (*ML* 3). The *Ausweg* is central to the ape Rotpeter's descriptions of his passage from ape to human as related first to the journalist and then to the Academy, but it involves more than just 'becoming human'. It registers thematically in the thwarted exits narrated by the hunter Gracchus (so important for Adorno), the imperial messenger and the gravewatcher whose job it is to prevent the dead from finding their way out of the cemetery. Before such repeated searches for an exit, Deleuze and Guattari's methodological 'principle of multiple entrances' (*ML* 3) seems inappropriate, overlooking the essentially fugitive character of this work. Yet their preoccupation with entering and with entrance in Kafka is by no means idiosyncratic but consistent with a climate of philosophical reading for which the guardian of the law in 'Before the Law' is emblematic. The *Türhüter* is assumed to guard the *way in* to the Law rather than the *way out* from the country (exile), assuming the gates to be entrances rather than exits. The *Gruftwächter* or guardian of the grave – whose task is to prevent the opening of an *Ausweg* for the dead – is perhaps a more appropriate emblem for the writings of 1917 among which 'A Report to an Academy', with its central theme of the *Ausweg*, holds a particular place.

The theme of the way out is so prominent in Kafka's writing, in his letters, diaries, and narrations, that it can hardly be overlooked, and yet its messianic significance is often reduced to biographical notions of escape.[3] Certainly even the non-biographical notion of a 'line of escape' that informs Deleuze and Guattari's reading remains dominated by the problem of entrance and the associated movements of 'deterritorialization' and 'reterritorialization' that make up becoming (*ML* 12–14). Their opening paragraph displays a delirium of entrance: they give the Castle 'multiple entrances' and instead of watching for the 'multiple ways out' of the village they claim, ingenuously, that 'only the principle of multiple entrances prevents the introduction of the enemy, the Signifier and those attempts to interpret a work that is actually only open to experimentation' (*ML* 3). The postulation of a *principle* of multiple entrances betrays the hegemony of entrance, one that afflicts even their understanding of Kafka's exit in terms of lines of escape.

Deleuze and Guattari's identification of the three components making up Kafka's writing – letters, becoming-animal stories and the molecular assemblages of the novels – reduces the problem of exit to that of becoming. The 'line of escape' for this machine points to becoming as a deterritorialization of sedentary being, and Kafka's masterpieces of 'failure' are prized for their presentation of the arrest of becoming. *The Metamorphosis* is a paradigmatic of such an arrest and is described by them as 'reterritorialization' or 'oedipal thanatos' since, 'Given over to his becoming-animal, Gregor finds himself re-Oedipalized by his family and goes to his death' (*ML* 39). Yet this principle of becoming, and its movement between territorialized and deterritorialized desire, is not consistent with Kafka's predicament of exile and the torment of exit. Beyond exploring the *theme* of exit, his writings emerge from the *predicament* of having to pursue or await a way out. The novels can be understood as propitiations of exit, attempts to find a way out of the narrative, a condition evident in his recorded dissatisfaction with the endings of *The Metamorphosis* and *In the Penal Colony* and of course the three incomplete novels. They are written within a messianic setting and form explorations of the difficult relationship between exodus and exile, one whose complexity exceeds the philosophical vocabulary Deleuze and Guattari bring to Kafka's texts.

The limits of Deleuze and Guattari's reading are evident in the mobilizations of 'A Report to an Academy' and *In the Penal Colony*, both of which play important but frankly anomalous roles in their descriptions of the workings of Kafka's 'writing machine'. They cite 'A Report to an Academy' as a testimony to Kafka's view that 'it isn't a question of liberty against submission, but only a question of a line of escape or, rather, of a simple *way out*', hastily aligning Rotpeter's 'way out' with their own 'line of escape' (*ML* 6). What is more, Kafka's alleged 'writing machine' is compared with the machine of execution in *In the Penal Colony* (*ML* 29) even if they elsewhere criticize the latter for its excessive mechanism, and its still too Oedipal and thus 'reterritorializing' movement: 'But this machine, which is too mechanical, still too connected to overly Oedipal coordinates (the commandant-office = father-son), doesn't develop at all' (*ML* 39). Yet the focus on the personae of the law leaves unmentioned the messianic voyager [*Reisender*] who is, after all, the main figure of the story and who brings to it a 'development' or perhaps something even more drastic, an exile-exodus, that threatens to open a way out that deflates and compromises the momentum of becoming.[4]

Deleuze and Guattari's readings of these two stories spill over in moments of excess that suggest more is taking place than can be accounted for in their scenarios of writing machines, components of expression and lines of flight. The reference to the 'oedipal coordinates' of *In the Penal Colony* is immediately succeeded by the sentence,

And Kafka can imagine an animal conclusion to this text that falls back to the level of a story: in one version of the 'Colony', the voyager finally becomes a dog and starts running in all directions on all fours, leaping around and hurrying back to his post (in another version a snake-woman intervenes). (*ML* 39)

The significance of the various versions of the ending of the story is quickly brought under control by reducing the variants (and not all are mentioned) to a version of 'a new rebecoming animal' story (*ML* 39). Looking past the messianic exit structure of *In the Penal Colony* allows Deleuze and Guattari to normalize the story and to contain the problems posed by its variant endings.

A similar exercise of containment is pursued in the reading of 'A Report to an Academy' where Rotpeter is literally cast as Kafka's ape – 'As Kafka has the ape in "A Report to an Academy" say' (*ML* 6). Yet they also concede that this ape can provoke disruption in ways that exceed their schema, as becomes evident in the explicit (and acknowledged) torment of their conceptual language and its resort to a concept of force when confronting this story:

The animal captured by the man finds itself territorialized by human force, as the whole of the beginning of 'A Report' tells us. But, in turn, the deterritorialized animal force precipitates and intensifies the deterritorialization of the deterritorializing human force (if we can express it in that way). 'My ape nature fled out of me, head over heels and away, so that my first teacher was almost himself turned into an ape by it, had soon to give up teaching, and was taken away to a mental hospital'. (*ML* 14)

In both stories the disruption accompanying the pursuit of an exit exceeds the model of becoming that informs the 'line of flight'. Their reading overlooks the significance of 'A Report to an Academy' as an experiment in messianic deflation, in presenting the 'way out' as movement between exodus and exile devoid of all but the faintest messianic intimations.

The characteristic feature of this exit may be found in the articulation within Kafka's stories and novels of an entwined exile predicament, exodus pattern and messianic narrative. The three, of course, are closely related, a relation stated most eloquently by David Daube in his classic *The Exodus Pattern in the Bible* where exit or departure is intimately aligned with deliverance from exile in the past towards a hoped-for future. The link of the exile and exodus patterns with messianism is further explored in the topographies of the messianic described by Gershom Scholem and systematized by Moshe Idel in terms of anabatic and katabatic messianism, the former exiting from exile by ascent, the latter by a paradoxical descent into exile. The latter form of messianism, especially in the person of Sabbatai Zevi, opened the possibility in Jacob Taubes's terms of a messianic comedy.[5] The discernment of the central role of the comic messiah in Kafka is the achievement of Max Sebald's readings, above all his essay in *Unheimliche Heimat*, 'Das Gesetz der Schande – Macht, Messianismus und Exil in Kafkas Schloss [The Law of Shame: Power, Messianism and Exile in Kafka's *The Castle*]'. It is the merit of Sebald's essay not only to have recognized the link between exile and messianism in Kafka's work, but also to have intuited the notion of the comic messiah in his identification of K as a messianic figure. For Sebald, Kafka works with an image of the messiah that

> sways iridescently ... between that of the king and that of the beggar, between that of the just and that of the criminal, between the representative and the outsider. The oppositions do not allow themselves ever to be resolved in the realm of morality. Apparent truth and deceptive fraud, violence and patience, such oppositions lose their relevance from the standpoint of messianism. (Sebald 1991, 91)

From this view of the messianic emerges the figure of the abject, even unwitting messiah, a figure whose messianic vocation may be recognized or misrecognized by others. The tension between exile, exodus and messianism takes on very different forms in Kafka's narratives than has perhaps been fully appreciated, making the problem of exit at all levels certainly more complex than any notion of 'becoming' or 'line of flight' can do justice to.

Its recognition does, however, require certain textual and methodological scruples that exceed Deleuze and Guattari's gross anatomy of the body of Kafka's writings. At one point in their analysis of the 'components of expression', Deleuze and Guattari address a problem of method that they, disingenuously, admit will have occurred to many of their readers:

> Someone might say that the break we are instituting between the stories and the novels doesn't exist, since many of the novels are drafts, disjointed building blocks for eventually abandoned novels, and that novels, in turn, are interminable and unfinished stories. But that's not the question. The question is: what makes Kafka plan for a novel and, renouncing it, abandon it or try to close it up in the form of a story, or, on the other hand, say to himself that maybe a story can be the starting point of a novel even if it will also be abandoned. (*ML* 38)

It is, in short, another question of *principle*, one which, like all such questions, blurs and simplifies the real movement and complexity of the material. Kafka's writings are joined in ways that do not conform to genre or to Deleuze and Guattari's 'components of expression'. For this reason it is necessary to situate Kafka's texts within the blocks of writing from which they emerged and to trace internally their complicities. This is especially the case with the writings of 1917, which may be regarded as recording a single campaign of writing.

1917: From the penal colony and back again

In 1919 (or rather 1920), Kafka published with Kurt Wolff Verlag the collection of stories *A Country Doctor*, comprising of fourteen stories written in 1917 and embedded within the reflections and drafts that make up the Octavo Notebooks.[6] Kafka's lists of proposed contents of the collection of stories collated during that year vary but are consistent in *not* including 'A Report to an Academy'. This was published in Buber's *Der Jude* in November 1917, as one of two 'animal stories' ('Zwei Tiergeschichten'); the other, 'Jackals and Arabs', was published in October, having already featured in the two proposed contents lists.[7] The pairing of these two stories is significant, as is their eventual location in the published collection, which closes with 'A Report to an Academy'.[8] 'Schakale und Araber' appears in *Octavheft B* (January/February 1917) following 'Der Jäger Gracchus' and 'Der Kübelreiter' and preceding the 'Dr Bucephalus' drafts for 'Der neue Advocat'. *Octavheft D* (March/April 1917) returns to the hunter Gracchus and then introduces Rotpeter and his address to the Academy. 'A Report to an Academy' is preceded by two fragments describing a visit to Rotpeter and an interview with him. *Octavheft E* (August/ September 1917) contains a letter from a 'reader' of the *Report*, none other than Rotpeter's 'first teacher' complaining about the mention of his 'stay in the sanatorium' in the report. From the latter we learn that the address was given to 'our Academy of sciences' and that the teacher wished to write of other things, but the letter breaks off before he can do so (Kafka 1993, 415–16, my translation).

'Jackals and Arabs' and 'A Report to an Academy' share more than being two 'animal stories'. They are also reports of travel and exploration and, explicitly in the case of the former, accounts of messianic misrecognition. 'A Report to an Academy' is in the style of an oral report of a voyager of exploration reporting back on his travels, in this case from ape to human. This characteristic links the texts directly with *In the Penal Colony*, first written in 1914 but returned to, while still unpublished, on 10 November 1916 at a public reading in a Munich bookshop. Kafka described the reading as a 'grandiose failure' and even, after 'two years of not writing', an 'impudence'.[9] In a later description of the evening in a letter to Gottfried Kolwel (3 January 1917) he wrote, 'I read my dirty story amid total indifference, no empty fireplace can be colder.'[10] Other reports describe a very different reception, with members of the audience fainting and others, repulsed, abandoning the hall.[11] Yet significantly the furious resumption of writing in the octavo notebooks coincides precisely with this reading – In the Penal Colony in other words provoked the series of writings that emerged over late 1916 and 1917.

The second of only two public readings by Kafka – the first was in Prague in December 1912[12] – the reading of In the Penal Colony seems, like the first, to have acted as a catalyst, releasing the stories that would make up A Country Doctor. In an elated letter to Felice on the evening of the first, 1912 reading, Kafka wrote,

> Frankly, dearest, I simply adore reading aloud … As a child – which I was until a few years ago – I used to enjoy dreaming of reading aloud to a large, crowded hall (though equipped with somewhat greater strength of the heart, voice, and intellect than I had at the time) the whole of Education sentimentale at one sitting. For as many days and nights it required, in French of course (oh dear, my accent!), and making the walls reverberate. Whenever I have given a talk, and talking is even better than reading aloud (it's happened rarely enough), I have felt this elation, and this evening was no exception. (Stach 2006, 195)

This elation and the writing released by it also characterized Kafka's public address on the Yiddish theatre and language on 18 February 1912, as well as the reading of 1916. In the case of the latter, the results were evident after a little over a fortnight (November 26) when Kafka took over a new work space in the Alchemistengasse and began work on what became the octavo notebooks. The impact of the public reading of In the Penal Colony on the genesis of the octavo notebooks and subsequently the stories of A Country Doctor has not been fully appreciated, with critics linking Kafka's resumption of writing with the availability of suitable premises. However, the reading reverberates throughout the writings of 1917, culminating in the last story of A Country Doctor, which is the text of a reading, and then the rewriting, at the beginning of August 1917, of the ending of In the Penal Colony. And although Kafka never again read his work in public, 'A Report to an Academy' was read by Elsa Brod in the Klub jüdischer Frauer und Mädchen on 20 December 1917 and became a staple of theatre readings in the 1920s and 1930s.[13]

The octavo notebooks and A Country Doctor are framed at one end by a reading of In the Penal Colony, and the other by several attempts to rework its ending, those preserved in the diary of August 1917 and the further lost attempts he refers to in his letters. Kafka's dissatisfaction with the ending of In the Penal Colony is still evident in September 1917. Writing to his publisher Kurt Wolff on September 4, he describes the 'two or three pages shortly before the end' as 'Machwerk' or substandard work whose 'presence points to a deeper lack, there is somewhere a worm, who hollows out the completeness of the story' (Kafka 1958, 159). Kafka's difficulty with finding the right exit from this story is widely attributed to a problem of redundancy, for once the officer has been executed and 'no sign of the promised deliverance could be detected', the story is assumed to be over (*PC* 58). However, this assumes that the indubitably fascinating machine of execution is the main focus of the story, an assumption that draws attention away from its encrypted identity as a tale of messianic misrecognition. For the problem of exit from an impossible predicament is the worm at the core of this narrative, explicitly thematized in the story and suffered in the repeated rewriting of its ending.

The voyager/researcher or '*Forschungsreisender*' whose experiences in the colonies will undoubtedly supply material for a report to an academy is systematically misrecognized as a saviour figure throughout the story. Indeed, so cunning is Kafka's presentation of these misrecognitions that it has evoked similar responses in many of its readers and critics, who have repeatedly asked why the voyager does not intervene to save either the condemned soldier or the officer. The voyager's adventure on the island penal colony is replete with hints that he is considered as a messianic figure, similar to the voyager who meets the jackals in 'Jackals and Arabs'. This becomes apparent if the reader takes their eyes away from the fascinating and distracting machine, the *Apparat*, of execution and listens to the story of the battle between the old and the new laws in the persons of the old and the new commandants. Following this thread, it becomes clear that the voyager has an unusual role in this story, one that he gradually comes to realize, and with horror, tries to escape.

Sitting on a cane chair at the edge of the pit in the deserted auditorium, the voyager is introduced, in French, not only to the *Apparat*, but also to the history of the penal colony.[14] The presiding officer asks if the commandant has explained the machine to the new voyager and, on hearing that he has not, begins to describe not so much the machine, but the achievements of the former commandant. His description is enigmatic, beginning, 'Well, I'm not saying too much when I tell you that the organization of the entire penal colony is his work.' 'Not saying too much' can mean either remaining modest about the old commandant's achievements, which would be uncharacteristic of the officer, or not revealing everything that can be said. The officer continues by referring to 'we his friends' drawing the voyager into a confidence and perhaps insinuating him among the 'friends'. 'We his friends, already knew at the time of his death that the organization of the colony was so self-contained that his successor, even if he had a thousand new plans in his head, would not be able to alter a thing in the old order, for many years at least.' The friends of the old commandant possessed the knowledge of the immutability of the old order; they knew there could be no escape from the colony, however, many escape plans the new commandant might dream up. This, it then appears, was not simply knowledge but *prophetic* knowledge, for 'Our prediction has indeed come true, the new commandant has had to acknowledge it' (*PC* 37). Yet this prediction, it will become apparent, concerns more than the self-contained character of the organization of the colony and the inviolability of the old law; it also involves the expectation of a messianic saviour figure.

The voyager, looking at the machine, has already been informed of a quasi-secret society of friends of the old order among which the officer is numbered and finds himself being drawn into a complicity. The officer reflects as if the two, commandant and voyager, would have had much in common – 'A pity you never knew the former commandant!' – before excitedly breaking off and turning to the *Apparat*: 'I'm babbling, and his machine is here before us.' The old commandant returns to the discussions after the description of the *Apparat* and the voyager's curiosity about the judgement to be executed by it. Normally the privilege of explaining the judgement is reserved to the commandant, although, to the officer's dismay, this privilege has been neglected by the new commandant. The officer is appalled by the 'innovation' by which so 'distinguished a visitor' (at this point the voyager tries to push away the honour 'with both hands') but controls himself and reflects that he is in fact 'certainly the best person qualified to explain our kind of judgement' (*PC* 39). He then reveals himself to be the custodian of the laws, the first among the 'friends' of the commandant.

The officer describes his qualification, first by virtue of his possession of sacred texts and then in terms of a form of apostolic succession. The sacred texts are the old commandant's hand-drawn designs that the officer carries in a leather wallet in his breast pocket and handles only after washing his hands. Held up at a distance for him to see, they are incomprehensible to the voyager: 'labyrinthine lines intersecting at various points, covering the paper so thickly that it was an effort to detect the white spaces between them' (*PC* 43). It is a script surrounded by many ornaments that is inscribed by the *Apparat* on the body of the condemned over a period of twelve hours. The voyager is struck by the hand-drawn designs and asks whether the commandant 'was a combination of everything? Was he a soldier, judge, engineer, chemist, draughtsman?' (*PC* 39). The officer replies, 'Yes, indeed ... nodding, with a fixed thoughtful stare', before explaining first the mode of execution and the court in which the condemned was tried. His explanation of the basic juridical principle of the court – 'guilt is always beyond all doubt' – shows not only that specific punishment serves as a principle of individuation but also reveals another justification of the officer's status as exegete of the law. He is a judge in the penal colony (despite his *youth*): 'For I assisted the former commandant in all penal cases, and I also know the machine best' (*PC* 40). He stands in apostolic succession to the old commandant, clearly regarding the new commandant as a usurper.

On explaining the function of the machine, the officer 'looked uninterruptedly at the traveller, as if he was trying to read his face for the impression the execution – which he had, after all, explained at least superficially – was making on him' (*PC* 45). He then begins a series of complaints against the new commandant, 'for whom everything serves as a pretext for attacking the old institutions', including giving food to the condemned. At this point the voyager begins to reflect on his role as a highly placed visitor, realizing that his presence at the execution at the behest of the new commandant 'appeared to indicate that his judgement on this court was desired' (*PC* 46). His judgement, in his own eyes and that of the new commandant, was to be framed according to enlightened 'European' notions of fair procedure, the right to a defence, and a revulsion against cruelty and unnatural punishment. Yet the officer too accepts him as a judge, but for what seem to be different reasons.

The officer approaches the voyager, who 'having some sort of presentiment, had taken a step backward' but was not allowed to escape. The officer took his hand, led him aside and asked if he could 'tell you something in confidence'. The voyager accepts the confidence and learns that the procedure and execution just described 'have no open advocates in our colony any longer. I am their only defender and at the same time the only one who defends the old commandant's legacy'. There are, however, many clandestine 'followers' of the old commandant, still numerous according to the officer, but who have gone 'into hiding'. The officer then adds, 'If today, look, an execution day, you go to the teahouse and eavesdrop, you'll probably hear only ambiguous utterances. All of them are loyal followers, but under the present commandant and given his present views, they are totally useless for me' (*PC* 47). It is important to recall this detail since later in the story the voyager will indeed visit the teahouse, here described as full of the old commandant's secret followers, a place of cult where they assemble in secret on days of execution and the place where, it will emerge, the old commandant is buried.

The officer proceeds to propose to the voyager a conspiracy in which both publicly defend the old commandant and the procedure and execution. The traveller realizes that he has been called to judge the procedure and *Apparat* and protests his insignificance. The officer, on the contrary, insists, looking 'not at his face but somewhere at his jacket' as if he had expected such dissemblance, that 'your influence, believe me, cannot be estimated too highly'. The officer then describes a plan in which the voyager publicly disgraces the new commandant, with the officer forcing him to his knees before the voyager's judgement, forcing him to confess, 'old commandant, I bow down before you'. By this point the officer is shouting, 'That is my plan, are you willing to help me carry it out? But of course you are willing, and more than that, you must' (*PC* 53). Whence this certainty, whence the conviction that the voyager must help? The officer clearly regards the voyager as someone who will necessarily join him, who has been expected as a defender of the old law.

There is, of course, a striking irony in the officer's plan to use a public forum and to pursue a public trial of the commandant with speeches for the prosecution and implied right to defence. If the voyager agreed to join the conspiracy, then the old law would be defended not in its own terms according to which guilt is certain, but in terms of the new law and its public procedures. The very defence and justification of the old law in the strategy proposed by the officer would paradoxically be its overthrow and a vindication of the new law. The voyager, of course, refuses to enter the conspiracy but explains that his judgement against the procedure would be executed in private discussion with the commandant, without any opportunity for the officer to defend himself. The overthrow of the old law in favour of the new law, in other words, would be carried out by means of the procedure of the old law: the old law and its judge, the officer, are without doubt guilty. The new law is thus justified by the basic principle and procedure of the old law, paradoxically vindicating while appearing to overthrow it. The extraordinarily intense play of paradox in the conspiratorial conversation leaves the officer unwittingly betraying the old law by attempting its public defence in a trial and the voyager inadvertently confirming it by participating in its apparent overthrow without trial. The voyager will communicate his condemnation of the procedure to the commandant and then leave the island (or at least board his ship): he is, in short, still confident that he has an *Ausweg*.

The judge-officer's subsequent delivery of himself to execution by the *Apparat* following this discussion can be understood in a different light. Kafka writes, 'It did not seem that the officer had been listening'– or that he heard something else behind the traveller's words, smiling to himself and keeping 'his true thoughts to himself behind the smile'. A long-expected eschatological sign has been made, and the officer is ready: 'Then the time has come' – he looks to the traveller 'with shining eyes that held a kind of summons, some call to participate'. The traveller, uneasy, asks, 'The time for what?' (*PC* 53), sensing he is implicated unwittingly in the ritual now taking its course. The prisoner undergoing execution is freed, and the traveller forced to read the condemnation 'be just' (*PC* 54) inscribed in the diagram. The officer will not proceed with the execution until the traveller has reluctantly assented to what is written.

The traveller does not intervene; the reason given in the narration is that he had no right:

> If the legal procedure to which the officer was devoted was really so near to being eliminated – possibly as a consequence of the traveller's intervention, to which the latter, for his part, felt committed – then the officer was acting quite correctly; the traveller would not have acted any differently in his place. (*PC* 55)

The prisoner assumes that the foreign visitor has saved him and condemned the officer, which is true at a certain level, but at another the officer is being executed for his paradoxical but necessary betrayal of the old law by an expected messiah. The traveller's actions are paradoxically and unwittingly consistent with these messianic expectations, confirming the old law by apparently overturning it. He is, then, by condemning and executing the officer, condemning himself to assume the role of the prophetic judge. The macabre death of the officer, with eyes 'calm and full of conviction' (*PC* 58), leaves the unwittingly messianic traveller with the task of finding a way out of his predicament.

In the published ending of *In the Penal Colony*, the traveller, joined by the prisoner and the soldier, returns from the place of execution to the colony. The soldier points to one of the buildings, as if asked to, and says, 'Here is the teahouse.' This is the meeting place for the clandestine followers of the old law, all present on that day of execution, where the traveller is being drawn almost against his will. The tables outside were empty, and the place gave the traveller 'the impression of an historical memory, and he felt of the power of the past'. It is already increasingly difficult for him to escape this, for upon entering the teahouse, he is told by the soldier, 'The Old Man is buried here' (*PC* 58). The traveller asks to see the grave, and both condemned man and soldier (who now turn out to be extremely well informed about the old commandant) take him to see the grave, moving aside the table that covers it. The traveller, who has still not fully appreciated what has happened, described the 'customers' whom the officer has earlier described as clandestine 'followers' of the old commandant, assembled secretly at his grave on days of execution, as 'probably dockworkers, strong men with short, full, shiny, black beards. None of them had jackets, their shirts were torn, they were poor, abused people' (*PC* 59). What happens subsequently reads as the confirmation of a fulfilled prophesy.

The followers of the old commandant rise from their tables, back themselves against the wall and stare at the traveller: '"It's a foreigner", the whisper went around the table; "he wants to see the grave". The traveller went on his knees to read the inscription on the grave, thus presenting the figure of homage and worship before the grave, and read, 'Here lies the old commandant. His followers, who must now be nameless, dug this grave for him and laid the stone. A prophesy exists that after a certain number of years the commandant will rise again and lead his followers from his house to reconquer the colony. Have faith and wait!' There follows an episode of exquisite comedy, with the followers clearly recognizing that the time has come and that they must follow the traveller in the reconquest of the island, and the traveller's growing disquiet and search for a way out. When he rose from his knees, the traveller found the men 'standing around him and smiling' (*PC* 59); he interprets this as an invitation to find the inscription ridiculous, which is a projection on his part, distributes some coins and with polite haste leaves for the harbour.

In the final paragraph, the traveller almost escapes unscathed but is then pursued by soldier and prisoner. They have clearly debated with the other followers their messiah's perplexing behaviour in leaving the teahouse without initiating the prophesied insurrection and have been sent to bring him back. The traveller interprets this as their 'running into acquaintances who delayed them' and assumes that far from wanting to keep him on the island, they want themselves to escape with him. Their threatening approach, silent and rapid, is met by the traveller now in the boat with an active resistance, picking up a tow rope and preventing their leaping onto the boat. The story ends upon this moment of suspension with the traveller neither on nor off the island.

The problem with the ending consists less in the fact that the action of the story seems complete with the death of the officer than that the traveller's way out of the prophesy, which he seems unwittingly to fulfil, is by no means assured. The historical fusion of the messianic and the exodus narratives characteristic of the religions of the book is here set in crisis. The messianic task of liberation or exodus from a state of exile – in short, of providing 'a way out' – has been diverted or even arrested. The journey out of exile is infinitely long and the messianic vocation has itself become an exile: the way out or exodus is far from assured.

The difficulty of securing an exit is performed in the repeated searches for an ending to *In the Penal Colony*. The published version ends with the attempt to escape the predicament of prophesy, the chase to the port and the suspended embarkation. The other surviving drafts of the ending form Kafka's diary entries from 7–9 August 1917 and were written soon after completion of 'A Report to an Academy' in May and June. The 7 August ending finds the traveller lingering before the *Apparat* in a state of paralytic fatigue interrupted by the arrival of the commandant's emissaries and the metamorphosis of the traveller into a watchdog guarding the site of the *Apparat*. The way out explored here consists in a complex series of reparations and substitutions. The traveller's canine metamorphosis echoes the dog-like character of the condemned prisoner introduced as 'so doggishly submissive that it seemed you could let him run freely on the slopes and would only have to whistle at the start of the execution for him to come' (*PC* 36). Indeed the prisoner was condemned for being a bad dog – his task was to guard the door of his master and he not only slept on duty but attacked his master, threatening to 'eat' him 'alive' (*PC* 41). The traveller assumes not only the prisoner's canine posture, but also his duty of standing guard, but now over the *Apparat*. Yet the substitution for the prisoner at the same time substitutes for the executed officer, who in his turn had substituted himself for the prisoner.

The 7 August play of reparation and substitution does not provide a way out for the traveller, who remains trapped, this time by his own prophesy, 'I'll be a damned dog if I allow this', for what he has already permitted (*TB* 822). In the ending tried on 8 August 1917, the traveller assumes his messianic responsibility and the role of leader in exodus, except that this proves an exodus into exile. The spike that killed the officer remains, and with a wave of his hand, the traveller sends away the hesitating soldier and condemned man. He is tormented by having forgotten something, that something has been left awry: 'A crude error in the reckoning, a fundamental misconception, a screaming ink-spurting stroke of the pen runs right through the whole.' Not only is the event described as out of joint, the inscription of the *Apparat* was not supposed to produce a 'screaming ink-spurt', but the narration itself is 'hollowed out'. The traveller asks himself, 'But who will correct it? Where is the man to correct it?', and desperately calls for 'the good old compatriot Müller from the north' who might 'stuff the grinning fellows over there between the millstones'. The evocation of the millstones – a millennial figure of exile – initiates an exodus in which the 'pathfinders and stone breakers' set forth in search of the snake, 'the great madam'. For her arrival, everything 'had to be banged and shattered into dust'. The exodus has become the exile – the business of the marcher or 'snake fodder' is 'to make dust' (*TB* 824), that is, create the very desert they were destined to cross by grinding, banging and by movement itself. The folding of exodus into exile and the expectation of the snake – perhaps the 'worm who hollows out the completeness of the story' mentioned by Kafka in the letter to Kurt Wolff of 4 September 1917 – is accompanied by the traveller accepting the hopeless messianic vocation, transforming himself into the promised, cheerful commandant: 'Hold the lamps high, you up front! You others quietly behind me! Everyone single file. And be still. That was nothing. Don't be afraid. I take full responsibility. I'll lead you out' (*TB* 825).

The failed exits of reverting to a guard dog and of leading an exodus into exile are complemented by the third attempt to exit from the Penal Colony of 9 August 1917. Accepting a complicity with the prisoner and guard around the corpse of the officer even while losing all contact with them, the traveller resists the feeling that 'a perfect order had been established' (*TB* 825). The way out that presents itself now is by means of reversing time through an impossible theatre. The traveller imagines his ship arriving through the 'pathless sands' (*TB* 826) (for the arena of execution outside the colony has now become the limitless desert of 'Jackals and Arabs' and of the exodus). The arrival of the ship in the desert coincides with a reversal of events. Leaning over the railings, the traveller condemns the officer for his execution of the prisoner. As in a theatre (the nature theatre of Oklahoma?) there is a momentary happy ending: the prisoner has not been executed; he is indeed the traveller's luggage bearer.

'"My compliments" the [traveller] would have had to say, and say gladly, "a conjurer's trick?"'. The officer denies this, claiming to have been executed 'thanks to a mistake on your part, on your orders' (*TB* 826–7). The narrative, as in the published version, remains stalled at the point of embarkation with the officer uncovering for the traveller and the crew the fatal spike that killed him.

The drafts for alternative endings to *In the Penal Colony* explore three ways out that differ in many respects from the published version. They differ in the emphasis given to the theme of animality and metamorphosis and to that of spectacle and theatre. All, however, remain in some sense suspended between exodus, exile and the messianic vocation. All four attempts to find a way out of the penal colony share the property of the predicament of exile and captivity overcoming the exodus led by a messianic figure. The exodus is stalled, whether at an impossible moment of embarkation from exile or in a play of repetition and substitution. It has not been possible to achieve a 'line of flight' or to find 'a way out'. The predicament of *In the Penal Colony* remains ineluctable throughout the stories of *A Country Doctor* which were initiated by the return to the penal colony and whose themes and lessons in turn informed the renewed search for a way out of the story in August 1917.

Theatre and animality in 'A Report to an Academy'

The movement between messianic misrecognition, the thresholds between human and animal, and the search for a way out or exodus reverberate through the octave notebooks, but especially in the closely related cluster of stories comprising 'The Hunter Gracchus', 'Jackals and Arabs' and 'A Report to an Academy'. The first does not appear in *A Country Doctor* and before Brod's posthumous editorial work existed as five fragments, the first four appearing in proximity with 'Jackals and Arabs' in *Octavheft B*, the fifth beside 'A Report to an Academy' in *Octavheft D*. The story begins with the arrival of a boat on a still afternoon in Riva, carrying the still living body of the hunter Gracchus who died 1500 years before in the Black Forest.[15] Carried to a room, he is introduced to the Mayor of Riva, and his question 'Who are you?' initiates a series of messianic misrecognitions. The arrival of the hunter Gracchus had been announced to the Mayor – 'Salvatore, that's my name' – by a dove the previous night who had asked him to receive the dead hunter Gracchus 'in name of the city'. Gracchus is always in movement, across the waters of this world and up and down the staircase to the beyond. The hunter asks if he can stay in Riva, but the Mayor replies, 'that I cannot yet say', and then inquires after his fate and his guilt (Kafka 1993, 308). In a subsequent fragment, the hunter Gracchus, who now knows at least that this Herr is not *the* Herr, replies to the Mayor's question whether he thinks of staying in Riva by joking 'I don't think so' for his boat 'is driven by the wind that blows from the deepest regions of death' (Kafka 1993, 310–11). This is succeeded in the octavo notebook by a first-person account of the accident that led to the hunter's death, and then the stories 'The Bucket-Rider' and 'Jackals and Arabs'.

The ingenious interpretations of the hunter Gracchus fragments need not detain us beyond noting the element of messianic misrecognition that structures the encounter of hunter and saviour.[16] The journey of the hunter Gracchus exemplifies the transformation of exodus into exile that appeared in the alternative endings of *In the Penal Colony*. The theme of messianic misrecognition subtly announced in the hunter Gracchus fragments is explicitly explored in 'Jackals and Arabs' in a fusion of traveller narrative and animal story. The European traveller, this time by 'chance' in the desert 'on a brief trip', is accosted at night by the jackals. The oldest jackal welcomes him as the messiah for whom his mother and all mothers 'up to the mothers of all jackals' had been waiting (*JA* 69). The jackals are in exile; they have been 'banished' (*JA* 70) to live among the Arabs and wish the traveller to liberate them from the Arabs with a pair of rusty scissors. The Arab leader of the caravan intervenes, interrupting what he describes as 'a spectacle' (*JA* 71), one moreover that is performed before all Europeans, all travellers from outside. He threw them a carcass and once again affirmed the complicity between Arabs and jackals that the latter experience as their exile.

The tension between exodus and messianism is played through in 'A Report to an Academy', the last of the *A Country Doctor* stories. The themes of exile, exodus and messianism are prominent, as is their framing in terms of travel narrative, animal story and theatrical spectacle. The Academy has invited the ape Rotpeter to speak on his previous life as an ape, a request that he often received and for which he has a practised act. Unlike the traveller of the penal colony, exiled from Europe, Rotpeter is exiled from animality to humanity and from Africa to Europe. The way out or exodus from captivity was achieved through two acts of self-discipline or 'commandments': to give up on thoughts of return and to remain calm. The realization that the way out did not lie backwards is figured in terms of a transformation of the open gateway to a gap or crack. At first, Rotpeter narrates, his return – had 'the world of humans wanted it' – 'was open to me through the entire gateway that the sky forms over the earth'. This vast open gateway so different from Kafka's other gateways became 'lower and narrower under the lash that drove my evolution forward' (*RA* 77). The way out was not through a gateway – there is no promise of any access to 'freedom' (*RA* 79) for Rotpeter; rather the gateway had to be opened through the search for a way out.

The pursuit of an exodus without hope, an exodus that leads further into exile, is driven by 'a draught that cools my heels' blowing through what remains of the gap that remains of the lowered and narrowed sky. Both Rotpeter and the hunter Gracchus are blown in their exodus-exile by this breeze, both hunter and hunted; indeed Rotpeter insists before the gentlemen of the Academy, as he attempts a new way out as a scientist, that 'everyone who walks here on earth feels a tickling in his heels: from the tiny chimpanzee to the great Achilles' (*RA* 77). The vulnerability of this tickling in the heel, signalled by the citation of Achilles and the self-citation of Rotpeter, who later explains his limp as a result of his capture, signals the complicity between comfort in exile and the potential storm that blows from behind. For Rotpeter, this storm emerged from the closing of the gateway of the sky, a closure effected by a change in its significance. The gap and the open return in Rotpeter's description of his early captivity on board a ship, one that, unlike the traveller's in *In the Penal Colony*, has at least embarked on its voyage, but whether it has a destination or is condemned to wander in a mobile exile like that of the hunter Gracchus remains questionable. On board, Rotpeter describes finding a gap, a discovery attended with delight since, if not itself a 'way out' (*RA* 79), it at least pointed to a possibility of exit.

At this point Rotpeter interrupts his narrative in order to distinguish between the way out and freedom. The 'way out' is not a *hope* for a promised objective, freedom on all sides such as the gateway of the sky, but a *demand* for continued movement. This demand entailed the denunciation of hope and its replacement by calm. With this, Rotpeter performs the evacuation of the messianic. Instead of attempting to escape and, if unsuccessful, being recaptured or executed and, even if successful, jumping overboard into the great gate of the ocean and drowning (a way out for enslaved devotees of freedom), Rotpeter chose exodus through exile. His strategy was to pursue a role in the vaudeville, to become an artist and to perform his exodus-exile before a public, to escape 'presupposing that freedom was never an option' (*RA* 83). Yet the chosen option leaves him without cause for complaint, in a comfortable exile, yet also unsatisfied. His goal has 'by and large' (*RA* 84) been achieved, and he does not seek human judgement of his response to his predicament. He stands guard over standing guard, achieving the same position moving from the animal to the human that the traveller would achieve in reverse in the August 7 draft of the way out of the penal colony, moving from the human towards the animal. He, too, plays the man of science, a *Forschungsreisender*, performing his report for the Academy and leaving it unclear whether he is an artist performing the role of a man of science or whether he is exploring the 'way out' provided by knowledge.

The implications of this experiment in messianic deflation and even erasure performed in 'A Report to an Academy' become evident if we look more closely at the comforts of exile described by Rotpeter towards the end of his report. He describes himself without complaint or satisfaction: 'My hands in my pants pockets, the wine bottle on the table, I half-lie, half-sit in my rocking chair and look out the window' (*RA* 83). The rocking chair with its comfortable instability returns us to the swing of Kafka's early story 'Children on a Country Road', with its child poised between the worlds of children and adults, full of expectation. Yet Rotpeter has no expectation and has arrested the movement of the rocking chair by 'half-lying, half-sitting'. Rotpeter's act of looking out of the window contrasts with the same act figured in the messianic story 'An Imperial Message' that appeared a few pages earlier in *A Country Doctor*. That story ends with the coming of evening and the figure of a dreamer at the window, expecting the arrival of an impossible message from a remote and dead Emperor. The message was sent, but its conveyance eternally stalled; yet, waiting and looking out of the window the hope and the expectation remains that it may one day arrive. But what is to arrive for Rotpeter? Apart from the breeze at his heels, there is no message from the outside, no apparent line of escape from his exile-exodus; there seems only guarded calm, breathing the air of exile and playing the role: 'When company comes, I play the host as is proper' (*RA* 83).

The stories of *A Country Doctor* that are initiated by the thwarted messianic exits of the *Forschungsreisender* in *In the Penal Colony* arrive at the 'calm' (*RA* 80) of artist-scientist Rotpeter's 'A Report to an Academy'. The aesthetic way out of exile seems only to return to it, and yet something has changed. The violent gestures accompanying the messianic in *In the Penal Colony* have become reduced to a light breeze, but perhaps this is enough. Even with the reduction of the messianic to the aesthetic, perhaps the breath of wind at the heels is sufficient to stir the air of exile and make it breathable and even, to return to Walter Benjamin's word, *survivable*.

Notes

1   Cf. Walter Benjamin, 'Franz Kafka: On the Tenth Anniversary of His Death', in Benjamin 1977, 126.

2   Theodor W. Adorno, 'Notes on Kafka', in Adorno [1967] 1981, 260, 263.

3   The reduction of the way out to a means of escape from the unbearable biographical predicament of being Jewish in Prague, a version of the Exodus pattern, is performed under the auspices of Deleuze and Guattari by Scott Spector in Spector 2000, 23, and by Marthe Robert in Robert 1979, 52. The escape narrative is bolstered by biographical references to Kafka's 'Spanish Uncle' and by hasty analogical readings of 'A Report to an Academy' in Spector's 'parallel terms' 'Affentum' and 'Judentum' (Spector 2000, 192) and

Robert's claim that 'les jeunes Juifs de Prague tout comme le singe changé en homme de *Rapport pour une Académie* sont obsédés par la recherche d'une "issue"' (Robert 1979, 52).

4   The ubiquity of messianic themes and concerns in Kafka's writing has been shown by Max Sebald in 'Das Gesetz der Schande – Macht, Messianismus and Exil in Kafkas Schloss', where Sebald persuasively links K. with the figure of the abject, unwilling and even unknowing messiah. See Sebald 1991, 91.

5   See Daube 1963; Scholem 1946; Idel 1998; and Taubes 2004.

6   Although *A Country Doctor* carries the date 1919, it was not available to the public before May 1920.

7   Buber chose these from a selection of twelve stories submitted to him by Kafka. His original suggestion that they be published as 'Two Parables' met Kafka's resistance who suggested, without great enthusiasm, the alternative title 'Two Animal Stories'.

8   Also significant is Kafka's placing *Vor dem Gesetz* and *Eine Kaiserliche Botschaft* beside each other in the final collection, the latter's explicit theme of an impossible exit qualifying the former's apparent theme of an impossible entrance.

9   Postcard to Felice Bauer, 7 December 1916, in Kafka 1978, 646.

10 Quoted from Hayman 1983, 214. It was on this occasion that Kafka learnt of Rilke's critical admiration for his work.

11 See Hans Dieter Zimmermann, '*In der Strafkolonie – Die Täter und die Untätigen*', in Müller ed. 2003, 168.

12 The occasion is sensitively described in Stach 2006, 218–20.

13 See Zimmermann in Müller ed. 2003, 176–77.

14 The officer is described as speaking in French, not understood by the condemned, although the reported speech is of course German.

15 A paragraph Kafka reportedly read with great emotion to his friends.

16 See Thorsten Valk, 'Der Jäger Gracchus', in Müller ed. 2003; and Nägele 1974. Valk's is representative of many readings in linking the names Gracchus with Kafka – linking *gracchio* in Italian and *kavka* in Czech for jackdaw – and thus seeing the hunter as an allegory of the artist. A divergent but fascinating interpretation is proposed by Calasso, which follows the thread of guilt and punishment from the animal and human and bears the guilt of this transition (Calasso 2005, 148), while the old commandant marks the same transition, effected by means of the worship of pain (Calasso 2005, 194).

22

The fate of the pariah: Arendt and Kafka's 'Nature Theatre of Oklahama'

Rossmann and K, the innocent and the guilty, both executed without distinction in the end, the innocent one with a lighter hand, more pushed aside than struck down.

– KAFKA, *DIARIES OF FRANZ KAFKA*, SEPTEMBER 1915[1]

One of the many ironies accompanying the early reception of Kafka's writings was the construction of philosophical and political interpretations of his novels based on a mistaken understanding of their order of composition. Max Brod's decision posthumously to publish his friend's novels in a different order from their composition – *The Trial* in 1925, *The Castle* in 1926 and *Amerika* in 1927 – misled an entire generation of readers into assuming that they were written in this order and that they portrayed a development in Kafka's literary and political imagination. This development, abetted by Brod's comments on the supposed redemptive ending of *Amerika*, was understood in terms of a possible optimistic, Utopian solution to the bureaucratic dystopias of *The Castle* and *The Trial* most apparent in the last chapter of *Amerika*, the 'Nature Theatre of Oklahama'.

The distorted order of publication, Brod's change of title from *Der Verschollene* (*The Lost One*) to *Amerika*, and the correction of the 'misspelling' of 'Oklahama' to 'Oklahoma' fatally obscured Kafka's termination of the novel. This cluster of in themselves minor editorial interventions had the incalculable effect of not only shaping the perception of the development of Kafka's *oeuvre* but also of adapting it to, and employing it in, the construction of elaborate philosophical and political narratives. In the case of Walter

Benjamin's powerful and influential interpretation, it led, along with a desire to defend Kafka's writing against Brecht's criticisms,[2] to moments of almost inexplicable blindness otherwise rare in his criticism. The major blind spot was *Amerika* and above all the 'Nature Theatre of Oklahama'. Benjamin read the latter as the culmination of a redemptive history in which the protagonist 'K.' of the 'first' novel gradually assumes his full name, becoming Josef K. in *The Trial* and finally Karl Rossmann in *Amerika*, inexplicably overlooking the significance of Karl Rossmann's entry into the 'Nature Theatre' under the assumed name of 'Negro'.[3] Arendt, too, accepts Brod's ordering of the novels and, following Benjamin, constructs a political narrative of the development of Kafka's work in which, too, the 'Nature Theatre' is raised to the status of a political utopia. Her reading of Kafka is central to her distinction between 'pariah' and 'parvenu' and serves to justify not only the political possibilities of the 'self-conscious' or rebellious pariah but also the Utopian realm of constructed citizenship she sees 'tentatively' described 'at the end, the happy ending of *Amerika*' (*RLC* 108).[4]

Arendt's reading of Kafka is located in two of her important essays, 'The Jew as Pariah: A Hidden Tradition' (1945) and 'Franz Kafka, Appreciated Anew' (1946), although his work remains a constant point of reference throughout her authorship. These two essays are crucial not only for her understanding of Kafka, but also for the formulation of some central categories of her political philosophy subsequently developed in the writings of the 1950s and 1960s. Kafka's work is central to the formulation of her political and historical understanding of modernity, and *Amerika* in particular represents a frail moment of hope for an escape from the grim implications of total domination. What allows it to be read in this way is the hope of future happiness perceived in 'The Nature Theatre of Oklahama' – the supposed last chapter of the supposed last novel: Kafka's last word, so to speak. The readings of the 'The Jew as Pariah: A Hidden Tradition' and 'Franz Kafka, Appreciated Anew' respect the implicit teleology introduced by Brod, both concluding with 'The Nature Theatre of Oklahama' as a potential 'new world' or 'happy ending' to modernity.

In 'The Jew as Pariah: A Hidden Tradition', Arendt constructed an outline of a 'hidden tradition' of cultural exclusion through readings of Heine, Lazare, Chaplin and finally Kafka. Departing from Max Weber's highly disputable formulation of the characteristics of a pariah status group, Arendt revaluates the cultural contributions of Jewish writers and thinkers as 'social outcasts' (Momogliano 1987, 231–7).[5] She contrasts the cultural posture of the Jewish 'pariah' identity with that of the 'parvenu' – the conformist, assimilationist response to social exclusion – and finds in the 'conscious' adoption of the status of pariah a formula for nonconformist rebellion directed as much against the immediate Jewish as against the wider Gentile communities. While admitting that the pariah is an abject and even dangerous 'human type', sharing characteristics with the *ressentiment* of the lumpenproletariat or mass of superfluous peoples, Arendt nevertheless sees political hope in the conscious adoption of this status in the figure of the non-conformist pariah. For Arendt, Kafka is the exemplary writer of this condition, anticipating many of the features of the later, influential evaluation of his work as a 'minor literature' proposed by Deleuze and Guattari.

In the section of the essay devoted to Kafka – 'Franz Kafka: The Man of Goodwill' – Arendt explores two typifications of the pariah type in Kafka's *Description of a Struggle* and *The Castle* (both of which she thought of as early texts). Arendt situates Kafka's depiction of the struggle of the pariah in the context of the late nineteenth-century choice that faced Western Jews of retreating into a boheme or society of pariahs or assimilating into the dominant community. For Arendt, the figure of the conscious, rebellious pariah announced in Kafka's *The Description of a Struggle* and developed in the characters that populate his subsequent writings marks a militant departure for the pariah type: 'Kafka's heroes face society with an attitude of outspoken aggression, poles apart from the ironic condescension of Heine's "lord of dreams" or the innocent cunning of Chaplin's perpetually harassed little man' (*RLC* 84). This preliminary orientation leads into an outstanding reading of *The Castle* as a fable of the rebellious pariah, a political reading of the novel whose subtlety and indebtedness to Walter Benjamin make it an apt companion to Sebald's later political-theological reading of the novel in terms of the abject Messiah (Sebald 1991).

Arendt understands the superfluous land surveyor 'K.' to be 'involved in situations and perplexities distinctive of Jewish life' – strung between the demands of the inaccessible bureaucratic Castle and the village. The choice between parvenu accommodation and assimilation or pariah resistance that is constantly faced by K. assumes an allegorical quality and anticipates Arendt's later historical analysis of the predicament of the Jewish community in the 'Anti-semitism' section of *The Origins of Totalitarianism*. Arendt's reading of *The Castle* rests on a distinction between K.'s individual rebellion – the 'lonely isolation' of his individual claim for 'his minimum human rights' – and the dream of a collective struggle for justice supposedly embodied in the 'Nature Theatre of Oklahoma'. This becomes explicit as she moves towards the end of her essay, when she claims that K.,

unlike the hero of Kafka's last novel, *Amerika* ... does not start dreaming of a new world and he does not end in a great 'Nature Theatre' where 'everyone is welcome', where 'there is a place for everyone' in accordance with his talents, his bent and his will. On the contrary, K.'s idea seems to be that much could be accomplished, if only one simple man could achieve to live his own life like a normal human being. (*RLC* 87)

The assumption of a progression from *The Castle* to *Amerika*, instead of the other way around, allows Arendt to move, seemingly *with* Kafka, towards the collective Zionist alternative to the historical predicament of the Jewish people. The failure of both individual pariah resistance and parvenu assimilation in *The Castle* reveals for Arendt 'a truth that made Kafka a Zionist'. This truth is

> that the man of goodwill is driven today into isolation like the Jew stranger in the Castle. He gets lost – or dies from exhaustion. For only within the framework of a people can a man live as a man among men, without exhausting himself. And only when a people lives and functions in consort with other peoples can it contribute to the establishment upon earth of a commonly conditioned and commonly controlled humanity. (*RLC* 90)

With this culminating proposal Arendt points to the political transcendence of the individual pariah or parvenu in the collective dream and struggle of a people, a proposal she sees anticipated by Kafka in his move from *The Castle* to the 'Nature Theatre of Oklahama' in *Amerika*. Except that he moved in the opposite direction.

The persistence of this interpretative schema is underlined in 'Franz Kafka, Appreciated Anew', which develops a subtle critique of necessity and prophesy inspired by Benjamin's 'Angel of History'. The reading of *The Trial* in terms of necessity, of the law in terms of necessity, presents a powerful case for the impasse of individual resistance. The progression from K.'s death by exhaustion to the shame of Josef K.'s macabre execution is explicitly cited, as is the parallel between the story 'In the Penal Colony' and the 'reality of the gas chambers'. Yet Arendt is careful to separate Kafka from the ranks of the prophets, for she sees catastrophe and ruin as neither necessary nor requiring a prophet's power of prediction. Once again, in the face of catastrophe, 'It is always salvation which is the miracle, not ruin; only salvation, and not ruin depends upon the freedom of man and his capacity to change the world and its natural course'. Kafka's *The Trial* thus becomes an experiment in the consequences of the 'fatal belief – as prevalent in Kafka's time as in ours – that the task of man is to submit to a process predetermined by some power or other' the process that Arendt will describe as 'total domination' in *The Origins of Totalitarianism* (*RLC* 101).

The first appearance of *Amerika* in the essay is as part of a meditation on the distinction between the public and private lives of an official. The Head Porter who mistakes Karl Rossmann for one of his more roguish colleagues working in the Hotel Occidental cannot admit his error. His function is to recognize people's identities, and to maintain his position he must maintain the pretence of infallibly doing so. Here Arendt anticipates for the first time some of the themes of individual responsibility in the context of bureaucratic domination later raised in *Eichmann in Jerusalem*. Obedience to a functional role, regardless of private opinion, 'is the hidden motor that drives the destructive machinery in which Kafka's protagonists are caught' (*RLC* 103). Arendt continues by describing the 'main theme of Kafka's novels' as 'the conflict between the world depicted in terms of a seamlessly functioning machinery of this kind, and a protagonist trying to destroy it' (*RLC* 103). With this she returns to her readings of the novels begun in *The Jew as Pariah* in which, as here, the end of *Amerika* features as a radical departure in Kafka's work.

Before arriving at her analysis of the Nature Theatre as a 'happy ending' Arendt makes a brief but important digression into the character of Kafka's writing. She distinguishes his 'technique' from surrealist 'photomontage' by describing his writings in terms of constructions of 'blueprints' – working diagrams according to which his readers can join him in the work of imagination. Arendt directly cites Kant's concept of the imagination and effectively regards Kafka's writings as schemas, diagrams that enable the free exercise of imagination in reflective judgement.[6] By focusing on the narrative character of Kafka's writing and its diagrammatic relationship to narrated material, Arendt underestimates the proximity of Kafka's work to photomontage. This allows her to exaggerate the a priori, constructivist character of Kafka's technique: for her, his writings are constructions that depart from 'general factors and not out of the experience of any specific event' (*RLC* 106) and in this way, she claims, they reverse 'a tradition reaching back thousands of years, this exceedingly bold reversal of original and imitation suddenly casts what is narrated as the original with reality appearing as an imitation called on to defend itself' (*RLC* 106). This reversal of Platonism in the direction of a Kantian-inspired account of reflective judgement in which reality is judged according to a *sensus communis* of shared narratives is striking but underestimates Kafka's technique, which especially in *Amerika* consists in the kind of imaginative response to photographs later analysed by Benjamin in his *Little History of Photography*. It also uproots Kafka's work from specific historic events captured in photographs and crucial for his narrative in *Amerika*. The underestimation of the role of the photograph in Kafka's authorship and the move away from the photographic to the diagram in understanding it blurs Arendt's understanding of Kafka's writing and, specifically, the central role played by photography, photomontage and history in *Amerika*.[7]

Arendt moves from the sharing of a narrative that constructs reality to a view of Kafka's encrypted utopia as a 'possible world that human beings would construct in which the actions of man depend on nothing but himself and his spontaneity, and in which human society is governed by laws prescribed by man himself rather than by mysterious forces, whether emanating from above or from below' (*RLC* 108). She concludes with the possibility of 'becoming the fellow citizen of such a world' and sees Kafka as tentatively describing such a possibility 'in the end, the happy ending of *Amerika*' (*RLC* 108). She then makes a direct connection between Kafka and Benjamin's 'angel of history' – both contemplate the ruins and rubble left by the destruction of a world. But for her, Kafka superimposes on the catastrophic landscape of history 'the image of man as a model of good will'. It is on the basis of this image or schema that we can narrate and begin spontaneously to construct new, more just worlds.

Arendt returns to confirm her view of the 'Nature Theatre' in her 1946 report on 'French Existentialism'. She introduces it in the context of her critique of the 'seriousness' of the Hotel Porter in *Amerika* who identifies himself with his bureaucratic function. This 'ridiculous and dangerous' identification that anticipates the figure of Eichmann is contrasted with the 'new possibility of authentic life' that Kafka indicated in 'the last chapter of *Amerika*'. In the 'Nature Theatre of Oklahoma' everyone is welcome and everyone's unhappiness is resolved in a theatre: 'Here everybody is invited to choose his role, to play at what he is or would like to be. The chosen role is the solution of the conflict between mere functioning and mere being' (Arendt 2005, 117). In such a theatre, universalized by Kafka into a world, one is able 'to guard one's freedom as a human being from the pretences of one's functions; moreover, only by playing at what he really is, is man able to affirm that he is never identical with himself as a thing is identical with itself' (Arendt 2005, 118). The introduction of theatrical role, of playing with identity and spectatorship, disrupts the literality of fixed bureaucratic roles and opens for Arendt a space for the spontaneous and collective creation of a shared world. This act of spontaneous creation is for her the meaning of the 'Nature Theatre of Oklahoma'.

Yet it is far from Kafka's own view of the 'Nature Theatre', one located within the matrix of the racism of the new world and the transportation and implied extermination of the pariahs. In other words, the 'Nature Theatre' is more appropriately described in terms of Arendt's description of a concentration camp in the *Origins of Totalitarianism* than as a democratic utopia. For not only is *Amerika* or *The Lost One* the first of Kafka's novels written in 1912, followed by composition of *The Trial* in the autumn of 1914, and *The Castle* much later, in 1922 – making it the point of departure of Kafka's work – but the final chapter itself was written later than the rest of the novel, as part of the same writing campaign of autumn 1914 that produced *The Trial* and *In the Penal Colony*. It joins those works as a meditation on capital punishment, and the spectatorship of such punishment, adding to the near-pornographic stories of suburban and colonial executions the spectacle of racist executions in *Amerika*.

The 'Nature Theatre of Oklahoma' arrives at the end of a novel replete with meditations on photography. The opening paragraph of the novel transforms the torch of the Statue of Liberty viewed by Karl Rossmann during his approach to New York first into a photographer's flash gun – Karl Rossmann is photographed on entry – and then into a raised sword of retribution. The opening harbour scene and the subsequent descriptions of Manhattan may be traced to a photo-narrative by Arthur Holitscher, *Amerika Heute und Morgen*, first published in 1912. Not only does Kafka rely on Holitscher's photographs for the topography of his novel, but he makes the photograph itself a protagonist in the novel's action. The narration is driven by loss and dispossession, specifically the repeated loss and restitution of Karl Rossmann's suitcase and the loss of a photograph of his family, his last link with his European identity. Karl Rossmann's exile to America and then his journey down to pariah status, interrupted by short, failed 'parvenu' episodes, are marked by the dispossession of his property – his suitcase – and his link to the past through the photograph.

When Kafka returned to the abandoned manuscript of *The Lost One* in the autumn of 1914 with the seemingly concluding chapter, the 'Nature Theatre of Oklahama', he was very careful to address the main themes of the abandoned narrative. Four elements are of particular importance in the 'Nature Theatre' chapter. The first is the choice of the assumed name 'Negro' when entering the employment of the 'Nature Theatre' at the Clayton Racetrack. Karl Rossmann did not want his real name written down, 'So as no other name occurred to him at the moment, he gave the nickname he had in his last post: "Negro"' (Kafka 2008, 429). Adopting the name given him, a name that identifies him with oppressed Black Americans, Karl passes through the near-comic incredulity of the officials of the 'Nature Theatre' into the theatre itself, but his choice of name has aligned the narrative of the 'Nature Theatre' decisively with the most oppressed 'pariah' group of the United States.

This alignment is intensified by the second main element in the narrative, which is the restitution of a photograph. Karl Rossmann arrives at an abundant welcome feast for the new staff of the Nature Theatre to find a pile of photographic 'views of the theatre of Oklahoma which lay at a pile at one end of the table and which were supposed to pass from hand to hand' (Kafka 2008, 436). Only one reached Karl at the end of the table, and he contemplated it closely. It replaced the lost photograph of his family and his European past and pointed to his American future:

> The Picture showed the box reserved in the Theatre for the President of the United States. At first glance one might have thought that it was not a stage box but the stage itself, so far flung was the sweep of its breastwork. This breastwork was made entirely of gold, to the smallest detail. Between its slender columns, medallions of former presidents were arrayed side by side; one of these had a remarkably straight nose, curling lips and a downward looking eye hooded beneath a full, rounded eye-lid. Rays of light fell into the box from all sides and from the roof; the foreground was literally bathed in light, white but soft, while the recess of the background, behind red damask

curtains falling in changing folds from roof to floor and looped with cords, appeared like a duskily glowing empty cavern. One could scarcely imagine human figures in that box, so royal did it look. (Kafka 2008, 438)

Karl's rapture at the photograph is interrupted by his seeing an old friend, and he is distracted from the photograph. But this view of the 'Nature Theatre' is in a very real sense one of a 'History Theatre' for it is a view of the Washington Theatre, widely circulated as the scene of the assassination of Abraham Lincoln on 14 April 1865 (Figure 1). The 'Nature Theatre' is a scene of execution, but specifically the scene of the execution of the President who emancipated the black slaves. Kafka is aligning the 'Nature Theatre' with the theatre of an event which debatably set back the progress of Black Americans for almost a century. The view of the 'Nature Theatre' also has some peculiar

FIGURE 1 *'President's Box in Ford's Theater Where Lincoln Was Assassinated' (1865). Library of Congress LC-B811-3404.*

formal properties that rehearse a recurrent trope throughout the novel: the place from which to view, the theatre box, becomes the stage itself. The one who gazes, as does Karl at the opening of the novel and as did Lincoln on the evening of his assassination, becomes the object of a harsh, murderous gaze. This view of the 'Nature Theatre' also situates it as a mausoleum or empty tomb. The ambivalence of whether this is a tomb whose occupant has been resurrected or whether it is awaiting an occupant is not settled; it is indeed compounded by the appearance of the portrait of Lincoln among the presidents commemorated in the box, as if this image of the Washington Theatre came from a world and a history in which Lincoln was not assassinated.

Yet this moment of ambivalence is a rare gesture of alleviation in an otherwise bleak scenario, since the gathering of names connected to the history of racial injustice in the United States – 'Negro', 'Lincoln' – is bound together with a third element, the name 'Oklahama'. For a very specific photograph provides the scenario of the Nature Theatre. One of the photographs in Holitscher – Kafka's main photographic source for *Amerika* – is entitled 'Oklahama Idyll' with the misspelling of Oklahoma that Kafka would carefully preserve in his chapter to alert readers to his source (Figure 2). It portrays a racist lynching with the black victims suspended from the bowing branches of a grove of

FIGURE 2 *'Idyll aus Oklahama'. In Arthur Holitscher (1912),* Amerika: Heute und Morgen, *Berlin: Fischer Verlag, 367.*

trees surrounded by an indifferently curious crowd of white spectators posing for the camera before the victims. The photographic image that inspired 'The Nature Theatre of Oklahama' was one of 'strange fruit' – one of the type of images that circulated widely as post cards in the early twentieth century. The 'Nature Theatre of Oklahama' – the 'Oklahoma idyll' – is inseparable from the 'History Theatre of Washington'; it too is a site of execution, the two photographs tied to the same history of racial oppression.

Far from being the utopia believed by Brod, Benjamin and Arendt, the 'Nature Theatre of Oklahama' begins to appear as a site of execution, one inextricably tied to the history of slavery and racism in the United States. In this light, the interruption of the celebratory meal and the behaviour of the nervous official in charge of 'transport arrangements' take on a different significance. This introduces, in the last paragraphs, the fourth element of the 'Nature Theatre' chapter carefully prepared throughout the novel. The loss of the suitcase and sense of dispossession provoked by this loss – the failure to achieve parvenu and the threat of descent into pariah status – that is a *Leitmotif* of the novel now return. The new members of the 'Nature Theatre' are forced to run to the train that awaits them: 'Still, that was no great hardship, for – as Karl only now remarked – no one carried any luggage' (Kafka 2008, 438). The members of the 'Nature Theatre' are the dispossessed, 'destitute, disreputable characters' – pariahs – who, as their train leaves the station, wave and provoke the amusement of the spectators in the station, 'who nudged each other and laughed' (Kafka 2008, 438).

The 'Nature Theatre of Oklahama' joins its contemporary *The Trial* and *In the Penal Colony* as a scene of execution. Kafka uncannily anticipates the process of selection, concentration and transportation later described in Arendt's *The Origins of Totalitarianism*. While the extermination itself is not described by him, it is anticipated in the scenes of violent death that are evoked in the chapter. His view of *Amerika* or the fate of the pariahs or *Verschollene* is one of technological progress allied with exterminatory politics. The parallel between the European Jews and the American Blacks, noted by Sander Gilman (Gilman 1995, 108), is confirmed by the 'Nature Theatre of Oklahama' that can be read as a meditation on a possible outcome to the violent racial history of the United States. Yet this remained invisible to generations of readers of Kafka, including Arendt.

Between 1946 and 1948 Arendt worked as an editor with Schocken Books in New York, where her main task was preparing the translation of Kafka's diaries (Young-Bruehl 2004, 189). From the work on the diaries she would have learnt of the correct order of composition of Kafka's works and realized that this compromised the claims in her 1946 essays for a progression in his writing culminating in the last chapter of *Amerika*. Although she never retracted the readings of 1946, her subsequent readings of Kafka are silent on the 'Nature Theatre of Oklahoma'. Yet more is at stake in the reading of the 1914 'conclusion' to *Amerika* than Kafka's supposed pointing to the possibility of a democratic future for the United States. The novel ends by evoking a violent history of racial injustice, one in which – as in *In the Penal Colony* – juridical considerations of guilt or innocence are irrelevant to the execution of the death penalty. The mistranslation of the passage from the diaries in which Kafka explicitly says that the innocent one – Rossmann – will be executed along with the guilty one K. is indicative of an oversight of Kafka's sombre conclusion. By translating the 'innocent one' [*Unschuldige*] as the 'guilty one', Greenberg/Arendt not only grants the guilty one an easier execution, having him pushed aside, but also undoes Kafka's insistence that both innocent and guilty are executed. The machine of execution is not organized in terms of a juridical logic of guilt and innocence but in terms of the accidents of skin colour and status. The mistranslation implicitly defends the Western jurisprudential tradition organized around guilt and innocence, against Kafka's insight that in modernity such traditional juridical notions no longer apply, even or especially in decisions of life and death.

The overlooking of the racial history that informs the 'Nature Theatre of Oklahoma' leads also to a blind spot not only around this dimension of Kafka's work, but also the specific history of racial injustice in the United States that it works through. Kafka's *Amerika* is one in which this history is prominent; indeed, by the end of his novel this history of injustice has become a central theme. It ends less with a diagram of a just society than with a response to a photomontage of images of racial injustice. In her 'Reflections on Little Rock', Arendt shows how distant she remained from an appreciation of the significance of this history for the American Republic. While I don't wish to review the controversy provoked by this text (Arendt 2003, 193–213), there are a number of features that link it to the limits of her reading of Kafka. The first is the striking coincidence that her reflections, like the 'Nature Theatre of Oklahoma', are provoked and driven by a photographic image of racial injustice in the United States, in her case 'a picture in the newspapers showing a negro girl on her way home from a newly integrated school' (Young-Bruehl 2004, 316). Arendt reads in this image the humiliation of the child, the cowardice of the parents and the poor political judgement of the Supreme Court ruling which initiated desegregation in the schools.

While Arendt is clear and forthright in her condemnation of segregation laws in the name of equality before the law, her argument becomes ambiguous when she deploys her concepts of pariah and parvenu in the context of the categories of the private, social and political. She sees schools and education as a function of the social realm and 'integration' as an example of a parvenu policy in her view almost cynically pursued by the parents. Yet had she been in a position to situate the Little Rock image in a history of such images – in the way that Kafka implicitly juxtaposed images of the Washington Theatre with a racist lynching – then it would have been possible for her to see that a functional political argument according to a diagram/schema of private, social and political spheres was an inappropriate model of judgement. Kafka's 'photomontage' situated his images of injustice within a history, one in which the Little Rock image also finds a place. But it is an image of stoical heroism, not of a victim to oppression but one of resistance. While taking its place within the image-history of racial injustice it also diverted this history away from an inevitable terminus in the 'Nature Theatre of Oklahama' and introduced hope and futurity into this history.

Arendt was very disturbed by the representation of the young woman being escorted out of the school. She saw this as the introduction of politics into the schools, arguing for the protection of children and childhood from the onslaught of politics. Yet the power of the Little Rock image lies in the dignity of the young woman adopting the burden of the history in which she finds herself, and by doing so changing it. Ralph Ellison's later criticism of Arendt's judgement emphasizes the heroism of the Little Rock children and parents: 'in the outlook of many of these parents (who wish that the problem didn't exist), the child is expected to face the terror and contain his fear and anger *precisely* because he is a negro American' (Warren 1965, 343–44). Ellison described the failure of such comportment in terms of 'sacrifice' – the history of injustice demanded these sacrifices. But unlike Kafka, he did not see this history as one of inevitable, interminable sacrifice but sees a heroism emerging from it. Arendt, while touched by the criticism and admitting in a letter to Ellison that she 'simply didn't understand the complexities in the situation', remained unable to recognise the roots of the heroism in the children and parents of Little Rock (Bernasconi 1996, 15). The image on which she reflected was potentially one of sacrifice, but also potentially one of exemplary dignity and heroism. For this to be visible, however, it had to be set within and against the legacy of images of sacrifice and victimhood that document the history of racial injustice in the United States.

It is reported by visitors to her apartment in New York that a photograph of Kafka was one of the most prominent images on the wall in Arendt's study, and indeed his writings presided over her historical and conceptual understanding of modernity. The essays of 1946 were crucial episodes in her developing understanding of the failures and the possibilities of modernity. Her insight into total domination, her appreciation of the resistance strategies of embattled minorities and her judgement of the moral responsibility of bureaucratic officials were forged in the reading of Kafka. So too was her appreciation of the importance of shared narration and spontaneity. And yet her understanding of Kafka, so sensitive in so many ways, remained in other respects bound by the limits of its early reception.

Kafka's bleak jurisprudence, beyond guilt and innocence, his anticipation of photomontage and his putting it to use in the evocation of America's violent racial history in 'The Nature Theatre of Oklahoma' remained beyond these limits. Nevertheless, the strongest moments of Arendt's analyses of the pathologies of modernity – The *Origins of Totalitarianism* and *Eichmann in Jerusalem* – are entirely consistent with the harsh conclusion to *Amerika* that she could not see.

Arendt shared the common view of Kafka as a diagnostician of modernity, one who provided diagrams for interpreting the general characteristics of the epoch. Yet what is driving the narrative in *Amerika* is not American modernity in general, but a specific aspect of its history. The vision of a possible collective and democratic exit from the violent history of modernity that Arendt saw in Kafka's 'Nature Theatre of Oklahoma' was a mirage. She saw in the 'happiness' of the last chapter a realization of the broad aspirations of the American Constitution but could not see the specific history of racial injustice that had from outset betrayed those very aspirations. Her assumptions about Kafka's technique and his understanding of history obscured her judgement when confronted by a text indirectly citing a very specific image-history. It also blinded her to the advent of a new kind of image that challenged the terms of the image-history of racial oppression that haunted Kafka, one in which the fate of the innocent was no longer that of being simply pushed aside as a victim.

Notes

1   Kafka 1964. In the Greenberg/Arendt translation, 'the innocent one' [*der Schuldlose*] is mistranslated as 'the guilty one' – 'the guilty one with a gentler hand, more pushed aside than struck down'.
2   See the account of their differences on Kafka in Wizisla 2009, 164–8.
3   'That *Amerika* is a very special case is indicated by the name of its hero. While in the earlier novels the author never addressed himself otherwise than with a mumbled initial, here, on a new continent, he undergoes a rebirth and acquires a full name. He has this experience in the Nature Theater of Oklahoma' (Benjamin 1996–2003, I, 800).
4   Arendt's first husband, Gunther Stern/Anders, with whom she co-authored an essay on Rilke's *Duino Elegies*, also referred to the 'happy ending' of *Amerika* in *Kafka: Pro e contro*, which began as a lecture given in 1934 to an audience at the Institut d'Etudes Germaniques that included Benjamin and Arendt. However, in the 1951 extended edition of the lecture, Anders, while barely discussing *Amerika*, is well aware that it is an early work but incautiously cites it as a rare example of a 'happy ending' in Kafka (Anders 1989, 70).

5   For a vigorous critique of Weber's notion of the Jews as a 'pariah people' and its adoption by twentieth-century theorists including Arendt see Momogiano 1987, 231–7.

6   For Kant's description of the schema and its place between category and intuition, see *CPR* A137-47/B176-87.

7   See Carolin Duttlinger's outstanding study *Kafka and Photography* (2008).

23

Benjamin's natural theology

I am standing on the threshold about to enter a room. It is a complicated business. In the first place I must shove against an atmosphere pressing with a force of fourteen pounds on every square inch of my body. I must make sure of landing on a plank travelling at twenty miles a second around the sun – a fraction of a second too early or too late, the plank would be miles away. I must do this while hanging from a round planet head outward into space, and with a wind of aether blowing at no one knows how many miles per second through every interstice of my body. The plank has no solidity of substance. To step on it is like stepping on a swarm of flies.

– A. S. EDDINGTON, *THE NATURE OF THE PHYSICAL WORLD*

One of Benjamin's more unexpected citations can be found in his letter to his friend Gershom Scholem, dated Paris, 12 June 1938. As far as I am aware it is the only time that he cites at length from a Gifford Lecture, the distinguished series founded in 1888 and intended 'to promote and diffuse the study of natural philosophy in the widest sense of the term – in other words, the knowledge of God'. I am referring to the citation from Arthur Stanley Eddington's influential presentation of the revolutionary advances in early twentieth-century cosmology (the theory of relativity and subatomic physics) in the Gifford Lectures of 1927 published in 1928 as *The Nature of the Physical World*. Benjamin's extended citation is taken from the 1931 German translation *Das Weltbild der Physik und ein Versuch seiner philosophischen Deutung* and any surprise at his interest in such a text testifies to the widespread critical underestimation of his fascination with contemporary science, especially cosmology, and his sustained efforts to develop a modern natural theology.[1] The significance of Benjamin's interest in cosmology has been obscured by the critical focus on his messianic theology, whose orientation towards the historical world seems at first glance to be wholly incompatible with the cosmological concerns of a natural theology. Yet it can be shown not only that Benjamin possessed and pursued an intense interest in cosmology and natural theology, but also that it served as an indispensable complement to his understanding of the significance of the messianic.

This said, Benjamin's understanding of cosmology and of its role in natural theology might not have been immediately recognizable to Adam Lord Gifford, nor to many of those who lectured on natural philosophy under his auspices. Yet it was not as distant from their concerns as it may initially seem. Benjamin worked with two understandings of the range and character of cosmology: one was largely religious and indebted to Gnostic precedents that were antagonistic towards the created cosmos and its creator God or demiurge; the other emerged from the tradition of natural philosophy that developed into the modern scientific cosmology revolutionized in the early twentieth century by Einstein and Bohr. The two approaches to cosmology enjoyed a perplexing proximity, with the Gifford Lectures founded on an anti-Gnostic position with respect to the relationship between God and his creation and the knowledge of both through natural philosophy. For Gifford, natural philosophy was knowledge of the beneficent creation of the single and benevolent God, not knowledge of the fallen created cosmos and its evil creator. Yet the Gnostic and the scientific understandings of the cosmos were never entirely separate and William Blake was not alone in regarding the Newtonian laws of Urizen as those imposed on a fallen creation by a mad and evil demiurge.

Benjamin's interest in Gnostic religious cosmology was part of a broader, contemporary interest in Gnostic cosmology prompted by Adolf von Harnack's pioneering study of the first-century heresiarch Marcion, *Marcion: Das Evangelium vom Fremden Gott* (1920), that left unmistakable traces in the work of his radical contemporaries Gershom Scholem, Ernst Bloch, Georg Lukács, Hans Jonas and later Jacob Taubes (see Jonas 1963 and Taubes 2010). The Gnostic doctrine shadowing the major monotheisms proposed the existence of two divinities – the evil creator God and the good God beyond creation – and insisted on the unredeemably fallen character of the created world and its laws. It emphasized the rule of the demonic archons over the souls separated from the good but weak God and imprisoned in material creation; in some variants Gnosticism encouraged antinomian behaviour as a form of resistance to the laws of the evil creation, but all Gnostics advocated knowledge or *gnosis* of the God beyond creation. This approach to the cosmos in terms of an ancient religious heresy seems worlds away from the advances in physics and astronomy that allowed the twentieth century to be described as the 'cosmological century' and to which Eddington made distinguished contributions as a researcher and public teacher.[2] Benjamin is perhaps unique in bringing together the two understandings of the cosmos – there is nothing resembling his approach among his contemporaries, with the exception of Eddington himself and perhaps Kafka in whose work he found a similar proximity between Gnosticism and modern cosmology. For Benjamin, the two understandings of cosmology represented negative and affirmative relations to the created cosmos and he understood them as complementary aspects of a broader historical character of the relationship between humanity, the divine and the cosmos.[3]

The Gnostic vision according to which the cosmos stands in a hostile relationship to humanity as the creation of a malevolent divinity is prominent in Benjamin's early writings and receives its most developed expression in *The Origin of German Tragic Drama* (1928) that explicitly discusses the historical character of the 'binding together' of the 'material and the demonic' characteristics of Gnosticism. In one of his many allusions in this book to the historical character of this relationship Benjamin points to the contribution of the Gnostic demonization of nature to the emergence of natural science: 'not only did the middle ages come thus to impose strict limits on the scientific study of nature; even mathematicians were rendered suspect by this devilish essence of matter' (Benjamin 1977b, 227). This reflection on the limits to science posed by the threat of the Gnostic demonization of matter formed part of the larger project pursued in *The Origin of German Tragic Drama*, one of whose objectives was to show how the complex equation of the human, the cosmos and the divine undergoes and has undergone complex and sometimes unexpected historical transformations. Fundamental to the history of this equation is the violent transition from paganism to Christianity described by Benjamin in terms of the conflict between the guilt-laden *physis* of Christianity and the *natura deorum* of the pagan pantheon, a conflict provisionally resolved by the demonization of matter. The ancient Gods were regarded as demonized natural forces with the effect of conceding to Gnosticism a view of the created cosmos as essentially evil. Yet Benjamin wanted to show this resolution was itself historically contingent and unstable, with the Renaissance, Reformation and Counter-Reformation cited as moments of rupture in the Christian relation to the cosmos as modulations in the sense of guilt experienced before nature. The place and character of the cosmos in the history of perdition and salvation provide Benjamin with a methodological key for understanding broader shifts in the relations between humanity, the cosmos and divinity.

The attention to the historical character of the link between humanity, divinity and a fallen cosmos informing *The Origin of German Tragic Drama* is explicitly announced in one of Benjamin's earlier fragments, 'Capitalism as Religion' (1921). While often and not incorrectly understood as an early statement of Benjamin's critique of capitalism, the fragment also provides an important statement of his view of Gnostic cosmology. Its guiding proposition that 'the

Christianity of the Reformation period did not favour the growth of capitalism; instead it transformed itself into capitalism' announces not only an original critique of the Weber thesis concerning the religious origins of capitalism but also a more general historical investigation of a radical change in the relations between humanity, cosmos and divinity (*SW* I, 290). The transformation of the Christian guilt-laden *physis* into a cosmos hostile to both humanity *and* God is understood in 'Capitalism as Religion' in terms of the 'universalization' of guilt up to the point 'where God, too, finally takes on the entire burden of guilt' which is to say the 'expansion of despair, until despair becomes a religious state of the world in the hope that this will lead to salvation' (*SW* I, 290). Although departing from Gnostic premises of a guilty God occupying a hostile cosmos Benjamin does not adopt the bleak conclusions of its soteriology. For him salvation does not come from a God located beyond the cosmos – outside the guilt-laden *physis* of creation – nor from a messianic figure that enters cosmic history from without as an emissary of the remote divinity, but from within the fallen cosmos itself. Benjamin elaborates his soteriology, his view of the salvation of humanity and the fallen creation, by means of an ambivalent confrontation with Nietzsche's thesis concerning the death of God. While conceding that Nietzsche's thesis implies that 'God's transcendence is at an end', Benjamin is careful to note: 'But he is not dead; he has been incorporated into human fate [*Menschenschicksal*]' (*SW* I, 290). The death or rather metamorphosis of the transcendent creator, here the evil God of Gnosticism into human fate – the divinization of historical law – is emphasized in Benjamin's description of the *Übermensch* as the 'passage of the planet Human through the house of despair', where the human incorporates the evil God and becomes an *archon* or ruling planet moving through a fallen cosmos (*SW* I, 290).[4] This election of evil, however, is quickly revealed as being the same gesture as the hope for salvation through the universalization of despair anticipated earlier in the fragment.

Benjamin reads Nietzsche's *Übermensch* in terms of the Gnostic distinction between *psyche* and *pneuma*, between the cosmic and the acosmic bodies of Gnostic soteriology. The first is the body enveloped by corrupt matter undergoing the 'many deaths' assumed by the soul during its descent through the planetary cosmos, while the second is what Hans Jonas described as the 'acosmic principle' or the soul that remains alien to and alienated from the created cosmos (Jonas 1963, 158). For Benjamin, Nietzsche's *Übermensch* emerging after the death or transformation of the evil creator God risks becoming a planet or archon, a shape of the evil creator God who finds himself estranged in a state of 'absolute loneliness' in the alien cosmos of his own creation. It is at the extreme point of this estrangement that Benjamin locates salvation, a place that is at once continuous with and beyond the alien cosmos. Salvation emerges from the *intensification* of the loneliness of the archon 'planet human' or *Übermensch*, through the invention of religious techniques that bring the level of estrangement to the point of explosion: 'The idea of the superman transposes the apocalyptic "leap" not into conversion, atonement, purification and penance, but into an apparently steady, though in the final analysis explosive and discontinuous intensification' (*SW* I, 289). The passing of the creator God renders obsolete the techniques of propitiation and atonement suited to a fallen creature's relationship to its creator and the evil cosmos it is forced to inhabit. As the human approaches the condition of *Übermensch* through an intensification of its solitude in the cosmos and its decision to take responsibility for creation, it breaks with the sense of being a creature inhabiting a created cosmos. In a striking image for this transition Benjamin describes the *Übermensch* as the 'historical man who has grown up right through the sky' and, following this image of continuous intensification, describes this growth as eventually exploding in the 'breaking open of the heavens by an intensified humanity' (*SW* I, 289). In place of the descent of the soul through the levels of the created cosmos until it is incarnated in a human body, Benjamin proposes an ascent of the human and through it the eventual destruction of the fallen cosmos and its evil creator God by the 'intensified humanity' of the *Übermensch*.

With this view of the intensification of humanity and the explosive destruction of the alien cosmos through the breaking open of the heavens, Benjamin parts company not only with Nietzsche but also with Gnostic cosmology. For the intensification of humanity in the *Übermensch* and its estrangement from the created cosmos does not lead to an acosmic contemplation and gnosis of the God beyond creation 'giving it in the beholding of the divine light an acosmic content of its own' but to a historical task (Jonas 1963, 158). Benjamin describes capitalism's unprecedented historical mission as 'not the reform of being but its complete destruction' here understood as the rending of the sky of the created cosmos and overcoming its evil creator (*SW* I, 289). Benjamin's fragment moves to an incomplete conclusion by recognizing a connection between gnosis, or to use Benjamin's terms the 'redemptive and murderous nature of knowledge [*Wissen*], and capitalism' (*SW* I, 290). Both free the human creature from creation and its creator but leave them having to find their own salvation. The murderers of God, according to Nietzsche's classic formulation in the *Gay Science*, murdered the evil creator God but do not yet know or appreciate the import of their deed, nor the more than human responsibility for creation to which it has condemned them. The evil God of creation is dead and the good God beyond creation if not dead is by definition beyond life and death and hence even more remote than ever.

The Origin of German Tragic Drama culminates in a performance of the breakdown of this moment of gnosis, framed in terms of the guilt-laden *physis* of nature announced in 'Capitalism as Religion', but it does so in a way that points towards an alternative, scientific natural theology to the Gnostic demonization of matter. The view of matter absorbing the demonic explored in 'Capitalism as Religion' is now understood in terms of the elimination of the evil of creation and the possible purification of the world: 'According to Gnostic-Manichean doctrine, matter was created to bring about the "de-Tartarization" of the world, and was destined to absorb everything devilish, so that with its elimination the world might display itself in its purity' (OG 227). Both the tearing down of the sky by an intensified humanity described in 'Capitalism as Religion' and the elimination of the demonic aspects of creation allow the cosmos to present itself in its purity. Yet both 'Capitalism as Religion' and to a lesser extent The Origin of German Tragic Drama remain transfixed at this apocalyptic moment of the tearing open of the sky, pointing but not moving beyond it to a description of the cosmos revealed after the death of the creator God. The Origin of German Tragic Drama ends with a suspended apocalypse, at the point where allegory reveals itself to be but an allegory of the 'arbitrary rule in the realm of dead objects, the supposed infinity of a world without hope' (OG 232). This moment of revelation then abolishes itself in the intensified apocalyptic moment of unveiling or the tearing away of the sky and the discovery of a new heaven and a new earth: 'All this vanishes with this one about-turn, in which the immersion of allegory has to clear away the final phantasmagoria of the objective and, left entirely to its own devices, re-discovers itself, not playfully in the earthly world of things, but seriously under the eyes of heaven' (OG 232). The liberation of matter from guilt and from its demonization by the evil creator is certainly a form of gnosis, but one that proceeds under the eyes of a godless heaven in which there no longer dwells even the remote God beyond being of the Gnostics.

The theme of liberation from the gaze of God or the gods would later be central to the thesis of the politicization of art proposed in 'The Work of Art in the Age of Its Mechanical Reproducibility'. There the 'aestheticization of politics' is understood in terms of the gaze of the gods upon the spectacle of human history, following the itinerary of the angel of history from above. The extent of the potential perversity of the divine gaze – that version of the equation of humanity, cosmos and divinity in which the divine spectates and the human is the spectacle – is affirmed in a short and little appreciated text almost contemporary with the Trauerspiel book. In his article 'Books by the Mentally Ill', Benjamin begins by describing the problems of classifying the 'motley collection' that is his 'little library of pathology'. He finds the family resemblance between his books to consist in the elaboration of a theological cosmology, which encompasses an enormous range of perverse and imaginative permutations of the relations between the human, the cosmos and the divine. His collection includes Judge Schreber's celebrated Denkwürdigkeiten eines Nervenkranken, C. F. Schmidt's Leben und

Wissenschaft in ihren Elementen und Gesetzen, a nameless Slavic author, and Carl Gehrman, *Körper, Gehirn, Seele, Gott*. All offer elaborate temperamentally Gnostic cosmologies – reconstructions of the cosmos after the experience of the end of the world characteristic of extreme psychosis. In addition to Schreber's well-known sexualization of the relationship between God and humanity in his person, Benjamin finds in C. F. Schmidt a 'construction of the universe' in the self-image of a God whose 'life-giving gaze' informs the material and intelligible world. These and the cosmopolitical theology of *Der Ganz-Erden Universal Staat* and Gehrmann's 'theological medical science' share a concern with the relationship between the human body, God and the cosmos; each responds to the given historical character of this equation with the invention of deranged variants that Benjamin hints are not so different from the variant that historically we have been called to occupy.

At the same time as writing the historical reflections on the transformations of the relation to the cosmos in *The Origin of German Tragic Drama* and reflecting on the pathological variants proposed by the psychotic theorists of 'Books by the Mentally Ill', Benjamin also completed the remarkable final reflection of *One-Way Street*, 'To the Planetarium'. Here too Benjamin begins with a distinction between the 'teachings of antiquity' and the theology of the now waning Christian epoch. Benjamin encapsulates the former in the formula, 'They alone shall possess the earth who live from the powers of the cosmos'; and he adds: 'Nothing distinguishes the ancient from the modern man so much as the former's absorption in a cosmic experience scarcely known to later periods. Its waning is marked by the flowering of astronomy at the beginning of the modern age' (*SW* I, 486). The final reflection of *One-Way Street* resumes the stalled history of science begun in *The Origin of German Tragic Drama* and maintains that modern astronomy first becomes possible with the liberation from Gnosticism or, in Benjamin's terms, by taking distance from the forces of the created cosmos. Benjamin indeed continues by citing some of the revolutionary figures who like the *Übermensch* literally tore down the sky, observing that their motivation was not simply cognitive: 'Kepler, Copernicus, and Tycho Brahe were certainly not driven by scientific impulses alone' (*SW* I, 486).

Benjamin understood modern astronomy in terms of the emergence of an exclusively optical relation to the cosmos, which differed widely from the *Rausch* or ecstatic trance that characterized the ancient 'absorption in cosmic experience' (*SW* I, 486). The optical connection with the cosmos succeeded the haptic communion with it that was corporeal and ecstatic.[5] *Rausch*, however, is a form of ecstatic gnosis arising from the tension between distance and nearness that would later characterize the phenomenon of aura: it 'gives certain *knowledge* of what is nearest to us and what is most remote from us, and never one without the other' (*SW* I, 486; emphasis added). Such experience, Benjamin underlines, is a 'communal experience' and one whose power should not be underestimated or consigned to 'individual poetic rapture of starry nights' (*SW* I, 486). Benjamin obliquely cites the experience evoked by Kant at the end of the *Critique of Practical Reason*, where the visual spectacle of the cosmos provokes the intensifying *Rausch* of the 'ever increasing awe' – a union of optical perception and physical affect that Benjamin believes points to a closer, corporeal relation between humanity and the cosmos.

For Benjamin, however, the predominance of the optical relation to the cosmos as the object of modern science underestimates the continuing power of the haptic communion with its forces, noting with an enigmatic reference to Nietzsche's eternal return: 'its hour strikes again and again, and then neither nations nor generations can escape it' (*SW* I, 486). The most recent rendezvous was the First World War, which for Benjamin was no less than 'an attempt at new and unprecedented commingling with the cosmic powers' (*SW* I, 486). By 'commingling with cosmic powers' he seems to be referring to the outcome of the electromagnetic scientific and technical revolution inaugurated by James Clark Maxwell that became the acme of twentieth-century modernity.[6] Benjamin described the outcome of this revolution in terms of the difficult birth of a new relation to the cosmos characterized not only by the Gnostic intensification of alienation from the cosmos but also by the hope for a new covenant between God, creation and humanity made possible by technology: 'Human multitudes, gases, electrical forces were hurled into the open country, high frequency currents coursed through the landscape, new constellations rose in the sky, aerial space and ocean depths thundered with propellers, and everywhere sacrificial shafts were dug into mother earth' (*SW* I, 486). Benjamin here describes once again the passage of the 'planet Human' through the cosmos but facilitated this time by technology, a passage that he sexualizes as 'an immense wooing of the cosmos enacted for the first time on a planetary scale' in the 'spirit of technology' (*SW* I, 487). The alienated optical relation to the cosmos bears with the hope of a creative union or *Rausch* whose haptic absorption in its object is figured sexually in metaphors of intercourse, orgasm and birth.

The change in the relation to the cosmos effected by modern technology brought with it radical consequences for human nature: 'Men as a species completed their development thousands of years ago; but mankind as a species is just beginning his. In technology a *physis* is being organized through which mankind's contact with the cosmos takes on a new and different form from that which it had in nations and families' (*SW* I, 487). Just as Christianity created the guilt-ridden *physis* and its correlate cosmos of demonic matter, so now technology is preparing a new *physis* in the technologized body and an appropriate cosmic correlate. The perceptual equivalent of the new *physis* is the expanded sensorium described in 'The Work of Art in the Age of Its

Technological Reproducibility' essay. But just as the powers released by the latter were able to assume a destructive character in aestheticized politics, so too the absorption of Gnostic demiurge or creator God into the technological relation to the cosmos can become murderous. Technology emerges as the mediating term in the equation humanity, cosmos and divinity, substituting for the creator God as the point of negotiation between humanity and the cosmos: 'technology is the mastery not of nature but of the relation between nature and man' (SW I, 487). Benjamin imagines technology making possible a vast expansion of human experience aimed at nothing less than the abolition of time, and with it the resentment (in Nietzsche's view) of the present with respect to the past and with that towards a transcendent punitive divinity. However, his characterization of the new human *physis* as one transformed by 'the experience of velocities by virtue of which mankind in now preparing to embark on incalculable journeys into the interior of time' should be understood not just as a fantasy of time travel but also in terms of the new cosmology released by the establishment of the constancy of the speed of light (SW I, 487). The 'ever-increasing awe' at the 'starry heavens above' evoked by Kant as a spatial spectacle has now become a journey into the 'interior of time' or the remote past of the cosmos that takes place with every glance at the heavens. The tearing open of the sky has revealed a cosmos of far greater power and scale than previously imagined by natural theologians and one for which the Gnostic opposition between the God of creation and the God beyond creation is no longer appropriate. Benjamin thus returns to the ecstasy or *Rausch* that the ancients experienced in their contact with the cosmos.

With the new *physis* the powerful affect provoked by the contact of humanity, cosmos and divinity is understood literally as an unassimilable experience figured by Benjamin in terms of the neural intensifications of epileptic seizure or orgasm. Making a definitive break with the limitation of the cosmos to Latin nature, Benjamin insists on the paroxistic character of our relation to it, substituting paroxism or *Rausch* for gnosis: 'The paroxism of genuine cosmic experience is not tied to that tiny fragment of nature that we are accustomed to call "Nature"' (SW I, 487). The cosmos makes a demand of us that we are scarcely capable of experiencing let alone knowing, one that shakes the very *physis* of the human. The convulsion or seizure occasioned by the technological expansion of the human *physis* – the explosive transition to the *Übermensch* – was for Benjamin experienced pathologically in warfare: 'In the nights of annihilation of the last war, the frame of mankind was shaken by a feeling that resembled the bliss of the epileptic' (SW I, 487). The latter experience is known medically as the aura of a seizure, the sense of wind moving up the body reported by victims of epilepsy or the 'sacred disease'. The sense of a growing estrangement or distance from self and world that is the prodroma of an epileptic seizure is an apt description of the state of unreality that made possible the destruction released by technology in the First World War. Benjamin continues the parallel by describing the revolutions that followed the war as attempts to recover from the paroxysm provoked by technological experience or to 'bring the new body under its control' even describing the 'power of the proletariat' as the 'measure of its convalescence' (*SW* I, 487). Yet beyond this attempt to discipline the destructive energies is the thought of a creative paroxysm with which 'To the Planetarium' and thus *One-Way Street* conclude: 'Living substance conquers the frenzy of destruction only in the frenzy of procreation' (*SW* I, 487). The erotic *Rausch* of creation is Benjamin's understanding of the explosive transition to the *Übermensch*, a transition that can be understood gnostically as the absorption of previously estranged cosmic and divine energies in an act of gnosis, but also in terms of the 'breaking open of the heavens' that has freed space and time for modern cosmology.

The fragment 'Capitalism as Religion' of 1921 and the diptych *Origin of German Tragic Drama* and *One-Way Street* of 1928 situate Benjamin's cosmology within a Gnostic and largely Nietzschean framework. Yet they also announce a growing fascination with the emergence of modern science and in particular the astronomical and the electromagnetic revolutions which together gave birth not only to technological modernity but also to modern cosmology.[7] In this light it should perhaps not be too surprising to find Benjamin using a long citation of Eddington's technical scientific cosmology in his discussion of Kafka. Benjamin recognized not only the theological significance of the scientific and technological relation to the cosmos but also the redemptive significance of the 'paroxysm of genuine cosmic experience' that reverberated in contemporary cosmology. It is a redemption that Benjamin understood in terms of natural rather than messianic theology, that is to say, precisely the conjuncture of contemporary cosmology and mystic theology that he found in Kafka but also in Eddington.

Before looking more closely at why Benjamin thought Eddington's cosmology could help in understanding Kafka, it is necessary to frame a little more explicitly the circumstances of Eddington's entry into his thought. In particular it is crucial to understand how Eddington's cosmology and its affirmative relation to the cosmos – its affirmative natural theology in short – enabled Benjamin to leave the nineteenth-century climate of Nietzsche's thought and to overcome the assumptions of Gnostic cosmology. It might be asked why Benjamin should have been drawn to Eddington's thought in the first place. The explanation is probably independent of Eddington's scientific work and is perhaps related to his political renown (or notoriety) as a pacifist (he came from a Quaker family and was a conscientious objector during the First World War). Eddington's political activity may have brought him and his work to Benjamin's attention as a close follower of pacifist theory and practice. But once he encountered Eddington's *The Nature of the Physical World* he would have been intrigued by its foregrounding of the themes of the void and of the double world as well as by Eddington's claim at the outset of the Gifford Lectures that modern cosmology was initiated by Einstein's theory of relativity and Rutherford's atomic hypothesis. Yet there were also a number of stylistic and metaphorical aspects to Eddington's text that would have specifically fascinated Benjamin and provoked the emergence of the unexpected constellation of his work with that of Kafka.

By way of illustration, consider a fragment from 1938 – the same year as Benjamin's citation from Eddington in his letter to Scholem – on 'Blanqui'. In it Benjamin describes Blanqui's political cosmology *L'Eternité par les astres* as a critique of the nineteenth century 'conceived on a cosmic plane' but also as a Gnostic political cosmology that regards the created universe as hell: 'The conception of the universe that Blanqui develops in this book, taking his basic premises from the mechanistic natural sciences, proves to be a vision of hell' (*SW* IV, 93). Essential to this vision is the 'eternal return' that Benjamin contrasts with the version informing Nietzsche's *Also Sprach Zarathustra*. He offers a long and for him 'depressing' excerpt in which Blanqui suggests that a finite number of elements in infinite space will result in the eternal return of the same. This very moment and point in time has already been and will repeat itself infinitely in the future: 'The universe repeats itself endlessly, marking time on the spot' (Blanqui quoted in *SW* IV, 94). Blanqui illustrates this by reference to his immediate predicament: 'What I am writing at this moment in a cell in the Fort du Taureau I have written and will write throughout eternity – at a table, with a pen, in circumstances absolutely identical to the present ones.' This is followed by a series of claims linking the temporal eternal return with the phenomenon of spatial doubling: 'We have innumerable doubles in time and space … these doubles have flesh and blood, trousers and overcoats, crinolines and chignons' (*SW* IV, 94). Benjamin's attention would have been struck by the curious doubling of Blanqui and Eddington (both of whom he compliments with a lengthy citation) for, like Blanqui, Eddington's cosmological meditation departs from the table on which he writes, in effect doubling Blanqui's obsession with doubling, but from the other side of the cosmological revolution of the early twentieth century. Eddington's understanding of space, matter and the void makes his cosmic plane very different to Blanqui's and far removed from what Benjamin described as the 'mechanistic natural sciences' of the nineteenth century that had been superseded by the electromagnetic and cosmological revolutions of the twentieth century.

Eddington, in characteristically genial vein, begins like Blanqui by evoking the predicament of a man seated at his desk (also important for Kafka), but the differences between their cosmologies become quickly evident. After the electromagnetic and thermodynamic revolutions of the late nineteenth and early twentieth century, Eddington's table looks very different from Blanqui's solid nineteenth-century desk: 'I have settled down to the task of writing these lectures and have drawn up my chair to two tables! Yes; there are duplicates of every object about me – two tables, two chairs, two pens' (*NPW* x). But this is not the same double table that for Blanqui initiates the infernal sequences of the eternal return and repeated spatial doubling. Of Eddington's two tables, only one is inherited from the nineteenth century: 'One of them has been familiar to me from earliest years. It is a commonplace object of that environment I call the world. How shall I describe it? It has extension; it is comparatively permanent; it is coloured; it is above all *substantial*' (*NPW* xi). This same table, however, also doubles as another, twentieth-century or scientific table: 'My scientific table is mostly emptiness' – but unlike Blanqui's eternal spaces this emptiness is not the theatre for a repetition of finite combinations of elements, but something much more random and precarious, for 'scattered in that emptiness are numerous electric charges rushing about with great speed' (*NPW* xi). This table is not made up of substance like Blanqui's but is a dynamic equilibrium of forces, one such that when I lay the paper on it the little electrical 'particles with their headlong speed keep on hitting the underside, so that the paper is maintained in shuttlecock fashion at a nearly steady level' (*NPW* xii). The paper on which he writes is not 'supported because there is substance below it' but is rather 'poised as if on a swarm of flies and sustained in shuttlecock fashion by a series of tiny blows by the swarm underneath' (*NPW* xiii). Eddington explains that the first table inhabits the world of human consciousness and habit while the other is the 'object' of a knowing that is not 'contaminated by conceptions borrowed from the other world'. In departing from the world of consciousness we seem to enter a world of shadows, with Eddington warning us, 'In the world of physics we catch a shadowgraph performance of the drama of familiar life' (*NPW* xiv). But Eddington also imagines a world in the process of emerging from the shadows, a cosmos free of human consciousness, one that is 'far removed from human preconception'. Its indifference to what and how we think challenges our limits and forces us to change our relationship towards it. In place of understanding the world in terms of substance, Eddington proposes that we think of it as the refracted light of the rainbow: 'The sparsely spread nuclei of electric force become a tangible solid; their restless agitation becomes the warmth of summer; the octave of ethereal vibrations becomes a gorgeous rainbow' (*NPW* xv). The emergence of a new cosmos is announced by the rainbow, a phenomenon that for Eddington – as for Benjamin in his 1916 dialogue on the rainbow – announced the promise of a new covenant between humanity, god and nature, even if this new cosmos, for Eddington if not for Benjamin, still contains suffering and evil. Nevertheless, for him as for Benjamin, humanity itself is transformed by its encounter with this new cosmos, which no longer respects the limits of human perception, habit or desire.

Eddington closes his introduction to the lectures by emphasizing that his view of the physical world is different 'from that prevailing at the end of the last century' which as Benjamin noted underlay Blanqui and Nietzsche's views of the eternal return. Such a change in the understanding of the cosmos will bring with it a change in the relation between 'human nature' and the cosmos. Eddington identifies the inauguration of the new cosmos in the 'fundamental changes in our ideas of space and time' introduced by Einstein and Minkowski between 1905 and 1908 and more controversially in Rutherford's introduction of 'the greatest change in our idea of matter since the time of Democritus' (*NPW* 1). It is the latter revolution (paralleled with the Bolshevik Revolution) which Eddington considers most devastating: 'the most arresting change is not the rearrangement of space and time by Einstein but the dissolution of all that we regard as most solid into tiny specks floating in the void' (*NPW* 1). This is literally apocalyptic, a revelation or an unveiling of secrets, for 'the *revelation* by modern physics of the void within the atom is more disturbing than the revelation by astronomy of interstellar space' (*NPW* 1; emphasis added). By way of illustration, Eddington sketched one of his more disquieting images of physical reduction: 'If we eliminated all the unfilled space in a man's body and collected his protons and electrons in just one mass, the man would be reduced to a speck just visible with a magnifying glass' (*NPW* 1–2). If asked what is man or what is the creation, Eddington would answer – a void. But this is not the void of Blanqui, not just the theatre of the eternal return of finite combinations in an immense space: Eddington indeed explicitly criticized theories of eternal return at the end of chapter 4 of *The Nature of the Physical World* from the standpoint of entropy and the second law of thermodynamics.

Eddington's belief that the new cosmology would liberate humanity from its provincial assumptions, humbling and at the same time elevating it, is broadly sympathetic with Benjamin's views regarding the historical character of relations with the cosmos proposed at the end of *One-Way Street*. The new cosmology can potentially liberate us from the phantasms of the fallen cosmos – interestingly proposing a new form of gnosis, but one in which the created universe far exceeds current human consciousness and demands a change in or rather beyond its parochial limits. After ten chapters on the theory of relativity, thermodynamics and particle physics, Eddington arrives at a new alignment between mysticism and modern cosmology, offering a defence of mysticism – as of 1927, he said, it was possible for a scientist to be religious. The traditional scission between an Aristotelian natural theology and a Platonic, Augustinian mysticism no longer holds with respect to the contemporary, atomic and relativistic concept of nature. Both mystical religion and twentieth-century science point to aspects of reality that exceed the substantialist prejudices of traditional natural theology and everyday experience.

Benjamin adapts Eddington's argument for a complementarity between mysticism and cosmology to his description of Kafka's work, precisely pointing to his critique of substance. Benjamin begins his letter to Scholem dated Paris, 12 June 1938, with some critical comments on Brod's biography concluded by 'some of [his] own reflections on Kafka at the end' which he explains subsequently are 'more or less independent of [his] earlier reflections'. It is in this context that he cites Eddington, adapting Kafka's views on the complementarity of mysticism and contemporary cosmology. Benjamin introduces his new reflections on Kafka by describing his work as an ellipse, decisively and deliberately breaking with the figure of the circle and the circular orbits of ancient cosmology and alluding to Kepler's discovery of elliptical orbits: 'Kafka's work is an ellipse whose widely spaced focal points are defined, on the one hand, by mystical experience (which is, above all, the experience of tradition) and, on the other hand, by the experience of the modern city dweller.' Benjamin quickly specifies that the latter experience can mean different things. On the one hand, the 'modern city dweller' is 'the citizen of the modern state, confronted by an unfathomable bureaucratic apparatus whose operations are controlled by agencies obscure even to the executive bodies themselves, not to mention the people affected by them'. This is the spectral realm of the police analysed earlier in the 'Critique of Violence' but this does not exhaust the concept of the modern human. Benjamin insists that 'by "modern city dweller" [he] also means the contemporary of modern physicists'. And it is at this point that Benjamin observes, before proceeding to his citation, 'When you read the following passage from Eddington's *Nature of the Physical World*, it's almost as if you're listening to Kafka.'[8] The tension between reading and listening, and the mistaken listening on which the impact of the citation depends – *reading* Eddington is like *listening* to Kafka – will be picked up subsequently with respect to tradition and the problem of listening. Here it is enough to note that Benjamin is citing the written text of an oral lecture and suggesting that it could be mistaken for Kafka, himself an avid public and semi-public reader of his own and other's work. The predicament is also important for Benjamin, since it points to the problem of the threshold and what it is to pass a threshold.

The passage cited by Benjamin arrives in the fifteenth and final lecture on 'Science and Mysticism' and is indeed the culminating flourish of the entire series of Gifford lectures (*NPW* 242). It is the culmination of Eddington's spirited review of recent cosmological work – from Einstein and Bohr to Schrödinger – that opened with 'The Downfall of Classical Physics' and moved through accounts of relativity, time, thermodynamics, and entropy, gravitation, and quantum theory. It is in the final chapter that Eddington returns to the theme of the Gifford lectures with a reflection on the implications of the new cosmology for the understanding of divinity. The result is very far from traditional natural theology – Eddington does not believe for a moment that contemporary cosmology can make any contributions to arguments concerning the existence of God let alone divine power, goodness and justice. But he does seem to believe that it underlies the importance of faith in the scientific and non-scientific outlooks and implicitly calls for a reconsideration of the relation between science and religion. The entire lecture series is dedicated to undoing the view that the world is made up of solid substances behaving in a law-like manner according to causality; for Eddington the world is more properly understood as a void occupied by a vast, swarming population of elementary particles whose behaviour is a matter of statistical probability rather than causality.

On some occasions Eddington is not very far removed from a crypto-Gnostic or a Manichean understanding of the cosmos. At one point he describes, not without irony, the force of gravity as the work of a demon. Referring to the celebrated Newtonian falling apple, Eddington humorously observes that the deviation (or clinamen) of the apple from uniform motion has to be explained in terms of demonic agency: 'This new phenomenon has to be accounted for by an unimaginable agency or demon called *gravitation* which persuades the apples to deviate from their proper uniform motion' (*NPW* 138). He immediately clarifies that for him the demonic effect is epistemic, an effect of the limits of our perception: 'the demon is simply the complication which arises when we try to fit a curved world in a flat frame' (*NPW* 138). But when we enter the quantum realm the epistemic demon seems even more uncanny, since for Eddington quantum events cannot be described in the substantialist and correlative spatial terms with which we experience the world.[9] In discussing the electron Eddington observes: 'The tossing up of the electron is a conventional way of depicting a particular change of state of the atom which cannot really be associated with movements in space as macroscopically conceived. *Something unknown is doing we don't know what* – that is what our theory amounts to' (*NPW* 291). Confronted with this, Eddington draws two implications from contemporary cosmology for natural theology, the gist of his Gifford lectures. The first is to abandon concepts such as substance and reality and to experience divinity beyond reality and existence; the second is that there is no scientific answer to the Gnostic question of whether creation is divine or diabolic.

Eddington presents the first implication earlier in his lectures by referring to the Quaker idiom of the Inner Light – God is not known but can be experienced through the Inner Light that draws us towards divinity. According to this view, science and mysticism share the pursuit of the Inner Light and its de-substantialization of the world. In one of the many confessional passages of the lectures, Eddington mused:

We all know that there are regions of the human spirit untrammelled by the world of physics. In the mystic sense of the creation around us, in the expression of art, in a yearning towards God, the soul grows upwards and finds the fulfilment of something implanted in its nature. The sanction for this development is within us, a striving born with our consciousness or an Inner Light proceeding from a greater power than ours ... Whether in the intellectual pursuits of science or in the mystical pursuits of the spirit, the light beckons ahead and the purpose surging in our nature responds. Can we not leave it at that? Is it really necessary to drag in the comfortable word 'reality' to be administered like a pat on the back? (*NPW* 327–28)

In this sense, the pursuit of the Inner Light through science or mystical experience is a form of proof of divinity, since the Inner Light proceeds from a 'greater power than ours'. But as it remains unknown even unknowable, there can be no certainty that its pursuit by way of nature is not as diabolic as it is divine, for 'science cannot tell us whether the world spirit is good or evil, and its halting arguments for the existence of a God might equally well be turned into an argument for the existence of a Devil' (*NPW* 238). What science shows us according to Eddington is that we do not live in a world of reliably behaving law-abiding substances but are part of a vast population of atoms and their particles whose behaviours are at best probabilistic outcomes. This, the world of the modern physicist, is also for Benjamin the world of the modern citizen and the world of Kafka's writing.

After citing the passage Benjamin makes two arguments for the proximity of Kafka's writing with Eddington. The first argues for the unique proximity of Eddington and Kafka, with Benjamin confessing that 'I know no passage in literature which displays the characteristic Kafka *gestus* to the same degree' (*SW* III, 325). Benjamin aligns Eddington with Kafka's *gestus* not only in respect to his precarious universe without substance but also in terms of its distance from gnosis: for both Eddington and Kafka to cross a threshold it is better not to know what is involved, better not to know about the subatomic particles or the demonic archons that guard the subsequent gates to the law. Apart from the reference to the *gestus*, Benjamin also argues that Kafka's prose sentences could be juxtaposed with Eddington's physical descriptions of the aporia of the prevalence of accident over substance. Indeed, Benjamin believed that Kafka's most incomprehensible sentences are at home in Eddington. But beyond this complementarity between Kafka and Eddington's cosmology of the accidental universe – which is one focus of the ellipse that is the orbital path of Kafka's writing – is the enormous tension with the other focus, that of mystical experience. The centrifugal and centripetal forces that propel the 'planet Kafka' through the houses of modern cosmopolitical and mystical experience are complementary, but also maddening: the modern comes to Kafka through the mystical. But for this to be possible the mystical experience must have suffered a catastrophe – devastating occurrences that threw it off its proper orbit and brought it into an elliptical formation with modern experience, which has also suffered its own catastrophe not only in the formation of the modern state but also of the modern cosmos which is no longer the creation of a creator God.

Benjamin argues that the shock of modern reality – 'theoretically in modern physics and in practice in military technology' (*SW* III, 326) – is unassimilable by an individual, hence Kafka's recourse to the mystical tradition as a means to shape experience. His writing is understood as the complement of modern experience, which in its nihilistic variant is the reality of extermination or the movement beyond the paired good and evil Gods of Gnosticism to a complete indifference to creation. His surrender of the 'consistency of truth' while maintaining fidelity to 'transmissibility' drove him in Benjamin's reading to a fascination with the 'products of its decomposition', namely the 'rumour of true things' or the 'whispered newspaper of the disreputable and obsolete' (*SW* III, 326). Yet the relationship between the human, the cosmos and the divine that survives in rumour and undergoes the strange variants of folly remains stalled at the same impasse of the end of *The Origin of German Tragic Drama*. The double negation of the allegory of allegory is now seen in Kafka's hope that hope be infinite but not for us. Benjamin takes pains to insist to Scholem that Kafka is the figure of a failure, the chronicler of a fallen world, which even its evil creator God has abandoned.

The devastation of a creation bereft of creator can be experienced as horror and exterminatory, as the ruined gate through which a messiah might pass, or it might be a theatre of transformation. Eddington's cosmos, for Benjamin the vacated cosmos of modern science, cannot offer any reassurance concerning the existence of divinity, but it can challenge its human occupants to change their habits of occupying it. The vision of a transformation of nature and the human envisaged in *One-Way Street* is consistent with Benjamin's anti-Gnostic natural theology in which the cosmos, while bereft of its creator, remains evil. But it is also consistent with war and the view of the cosmos as an anti-creation or theatre of extermination. The negative natural theology of an uncreated cosmos that Benjamin deduced from the collapse of Gnostic cosmology and that he found confirmed in Eddington's vision of modern scientific cosmology can either unleash the forces of extermination or point to new vistas for the relationship between cosmos, human and the divine.

Notes

1 Translated by Marie Freifrau Rausch von Traubenberg und Hermann Diesselhost for the natural science publisher Vieweg Verlag, Braunschweig.

2 Longair 2006. For Eddington's contribution, see North 1965 and North 1994.

3 For an analysis of this equation in terms of the new law following the rainbow – an explicit use of the metaphor of the rainbow as a symbol for a new covenant between God, the cosmos and humanity following the flood, see Caygill 2005.

4 For an analytical description of the planetary doctrine of the Gnostics see Jonas 1963, 156–8.

5 This is the first appearance of the distinction between the optic and the haptic axiomatic for the argument in the 'The Work of Art in the Age of Its Technological Reproducibility', a direct continuation of the themes in 'To the Planetarium'.

6 This recognition also informs Aby Warburg's so-called snake ritual lecture at Kreuzlingen, which shows many similarities with Benjamin's views of cosmology and antiquity.

7 This is Alexander Koyré's description of the achievement of Copernicus and his contemporaries.

8 All excerpts in this paragraph are from Benjamin, 'Letter to Gershom Scholem', in *SW* III, 325.

9 To give just one example of Eddington's sustained critique of substance, one whose affinities with Bergson and Whitehead he explicitly noted: 'So strongly has substance held the place of leading actor on the stage of experience that in common usage concrete and real are almost synonymous. Ask any man who is not a philosopher or a mystic to name something typically real; he is almost sure to choose a concrete thing' (274).

24

Levinas's silence

It is impossible to remain silent. There is an obligation to speak. And if politics, arising everywhere, falsifies the original intentions of the discourse, there is an obligation to cry out in protest.

– LEVINAS, *POETRY AND THE IMPOSSIBLE*, 1969

I will say to you that there are many things about which I cannot speak because I am not in Israel. I forbid myself to speak about Israel not being in Israel, not living its noble adventure and not running this great daily risk.

– LEVINAS, INTERVIEW WITH POIRIÉ, 1987

Levinas's silence

The focus of recent interpretation of Levinas's work has shifted from ethics and its relationship to phenomenology and ontology to the problem of his political philosophy. The change is in many respects motivated by impatience with the degree of political complacency, even sentimentality, which attended the early reception of the ethics of alterity. Indeed, it has become a cathartic necessity to point to some of the more questionable political moments in Levinas's life and thought in order to return to his ethical thought with renewed urgency. Yet once it has been acknowledged that there is a problematic and difficult politics in Levinas's thought, the question of its significance or centrality remains. It might be argued that we know too little about Levinas's empirical politics to arrive at a responsible assessment of its philosophical significance – the archival work on his judgement of the actions of the State of Israel, for example, is still to be done. It might also be argued that even if complete knowledge of his political judgements was ever attained, this would still be irrelevant for appreciating the significance of his ethical diversion of phenomenology. Both positions, however, overlook the importance of Levinas's own philosophical reflection on the question of politics and philosophy, one that issued in a recognition of a 'difficult saying' and a 'difficult silence' beyond the ethical contrast between 'the saying and the said' explored in *Otherwise than Being or Beyond Essence*.

The gravity of the question of the relationship between politics and philosophy is particularly evident in the case of Levinas's judgement of the actions of the State of Israel. The question of the philosophical significance of his judgement in this case can be explored in depth through his published writings, but with important reservations. For there is an immediate hermeneutical problem to be faced when reading these texts that is expressed in Levinas's response in a 1987 interview with Francois Poirié to a question concerning the State of Israel. After a preliminary observation, 'You are touching there on too many strong feelings', he then evokes a right to silence on this question: 'I will say to you that there are many things about which I cannot speak because I am not in Israel. I forbid myself to speak about Israel, not being in Israel, not living its noble adventure and not running this great daily risk' (Poirié 1996, 167). This response is problematic for many reasons. First it seems to imply an abdication of political and ethical responsibility not to speak about a state and its actions on the grounds that one does not live there. Secondly, it also seems to renege on Levinas's own concept of 'Israel' that encompasses both the State of Israel and the diaspora. Thirdly, and perhaps most problematically, the claim to silence seems to turn its back upon the prophetic, universal vocation of human rights central to Levinas's ethics and politics, one that he traced to the Jewish sources of Western culture and according to which *all* rulers may be called ethically to account for their actions.

We know from the case of Heidegger that philosophical silences are both difficult to respect and to understand. And indeed, Levinas did speak often about the State of Israel, but in often tormented and frankly strange ways. Indeed, his evasions and use of indirect speech may be traced back to an ambivalence most clearly expressed in the 1959 essay 'How Is Judaism Possible?' republished in the collection *Difficult Freedom: Essays on Judaism*. The essay opens by invoking the limits of Jewish consciousness in Republican France, limits that Levinas traces to a 'sense of inequality' between Christianity and Judaism. Even a professedly secular state such as France is permeated by a Christian atmosphere that has little room for Judaism, confining it to private worship and works of charity. Before these limits set by the Emancipation, Levinas recognized three 'intermingled events' that were changing the status of Judaism: 'the constitution of the State of Israel and the presence of this state to a consciousness; the appearance and development of youth movements; and the renewal of Jewish studies within these movements' (*DF* 250). They are intermingled insofar as 'The house of prayer coming out into the world is their common significance. A search for space!' (*DF* 250). This observation upon the emergence of the house of prayer into the world is immediately followed by one of Levinas's most considered reflections upon the State of Israel:

> The State of Israel, whatever the ephemeral political philosophy of its greatest workers, is not for us a state like any other. It has a density and depth that greatly surpasses its scope and its political possibilities; it is like a protest against the world. And it reflects our thoughts in the vast culture of the visible, which until then had been subjective thoughts. (*DF* 250)

This passage raises a number of questions. The distinction between the State of Israel and the 'ephemeral political philosophy of its greatest workers' puts into question the identity of the political philosophy in question. Is this the socialist ideology of the founders of the State such as Ben Gurion or is it Zionism? In both cases a distance is established by Levinas between the significance of this State and the ideology of its founders. Then, if it is not a 'state like any other', in what consists its difference, how is it other than 'other' states? Levinas answers in terms of a 'density and depth', one which does not consist in the rootedness in being of the state, as it is described in *Totality and Infinity*, but in being a 'protest against the world'. It is a protest that 'reflects [*répercute*] our thoughts' in the 'vast culture of the visible' – a subjective thought issuing into reality or the 'house of prayer' entering the world. The use of *répercuter* (reflection, deflection, to have a deferred impact) to describe the passage of subjective thought into the visible develops the theme of reflection mobilized immediately before this passage in the text to describe Judaism. Here Levinas insists upon the incommensurability of Judaism – it cannot be defined in the terms of 'confession', 'nation', 'state' or 'race' that were historically applied to it. Levinas describes it as 'the last cold spark of an ancient flame which, for 150 years, has not been fed. All that burns is a strange reflection, lighting nothing and unable to transmit itself: a fire that devours nothing and burns without consuming anything' (*DF* 249). The emancipation has starved the 'ancient flame' of witness leaving a strange play of reflections – 'dense and deep' – lighting nothing, devouring nothing and unable to transmit itself. The State of Israel converts an emancipated Judaism, understood as a light reflected upon itself, into a Judaism that has an impact on the world, but one still guided by the ancient flame.

Already there is something uncanny about the difference that constitutes the State of Israel, a strangeness that is then compounded in the remainder of the essay. Although nothing more is said directly about the State of Israel, with Levinas shifting focus to Jewish educational institutions, it returns in the strange *Aggadah* with which the essay ends. Citing a verse from the Second Psalm – 'Serve the Lord with fear, with trembling kiss his feet' – Levinas meditates upon the significance of trembling. Trembling occurs 'when the foundations of the world are rocked, when the identity of things, ideas and beings is abruptly alienated' (*DF* 254). Trembling occurs when 'A is no longer A, when B is no longer B' and, in particular, when 'Mr B is no longer Mr B'; it occurs when 'the newspaper you buy buys you, when the word you hear signifies neither what it signifies nor what it refutes' (*DF* 254). It accompanies the anti-Hegelian realization that 'the lie that exposes itself lies as it exposes itself, without the negation of the negation becoming an affirmation' and is the salient characteristic of modernity: 'trembling is the whole modern world on both sides of the Iron Curtain, when we see it without curtains or veils' (*DF* 245). It is also finally revealed as the presence of the 'other in the self' and as the condition of Levinas's own silence: with the lie deceptively exposing itself as a lie, there arrives the possibility that it is difficult to judge the world – that it is difficult to speak: 'Trembling is also when we still hesitate to judge the world because – and this is the supreme trembling – through my mouth there perhaps speaks another, an unknown person who has seduced me or bought me, someone I cannot get to coincide with myself' (*DF* 254).

Levinas's ambivalence

The possibility that an other may speak through my voice is not necessarily an argument for silence, as it may have been for Levinas when maintaining silence on the actions of the State of Israel but certainly points to the need for careful, responsible speech. This, however, is not the direction in which Levinas takes his argument. Following the evocation of the supreme trembling, Levinas cites Judaism as promising 'a recovery, the joy of self-possession within universal trembling, a glimpse of eternity in the midst of corruption' (*DF* 254). Strangely enough, Levinas seems here to attribute to Judaism some of the ontological features – self-possession, eternity – that most of his philosophical work was dedicated to undoing. But if, in the opening words of *Totality and Infinity*, we can be duped by morality, perhaps we can also be duped by these aspects of Judaism, and indeed Levinas asks, 'Should we believe it?' Once again, and perhaps surprisingly, we should, but on the grounds that Judaism is a protest against the world: 'Up until now it has been the victim of history; it has not taken on its cruelty.' This protest that is Judaism, and the source of the unique significance of the State of Israel for Levinas, is rooted in the prophetic word: Judaism 'once knew how to speak a word that stands apart from these swarming insinuations, a word that breaks and unties, a prophetic word' (*DF* 254). This word promises self-possession and moral certainty, but it itself is immediately put into question. In so far as Israel *once* knew how to speak this word, with the implication that perhaps it does not know any longer how to do so, should we credit it now? Levinas answers that nothing is certain, but a chance offers itself. The *chance* that modern Israel constitutes a protest against the world – a protest that constitutes the difference of the State of Israel from other states – is all that Levinas permits himself. His closing exhortations – 'Take the chance! Credit it! The signature is not false!' – are desperately ambivalent. Did he not himself just give the anti-Hegelian lesson that a negation of a negation does not constitute an affirmation – that a not-false signature is not necessarily genuine, that trembling continues? The ambivalence that surfaces in 'How Is Judaism Possible?' sways between the poles of trembling and prophetic certainty, and even the attempt to assert the latter trembles at key moments. What is then the proper attitude to adopt towards the chance of prophetic speech? One that neither trembles nor blindly affirms, but which approaches the chance of prophetic speech with responsibility. Yet in what would such a responsible, difficult speech consist when addressed to the State of Israel? Levinas's disingenuous claim to silence on this issue seems closer to trembling than responsibility – suggesting that the reluctance to speak arises from a suspicion that when he says Israel is not a state like any other, he knows that it may be a state like all the others.

The same ambivalence is rehearsed in the essay 'From the Rise of Nihilism to the Carnal Jew' which begins with the Nazi murders and the 'extraordinary fulfilment of the Zionist dream of a State in which to live peacefully is to live dangerously' (*DF* 221). At one point Levinas gives voice to the enemies of the State of Israel and performs the conversion of *their* voice into *our voice* – precisely the terms of the predicament of trembling described in 'How Is Judaism Possible?': 'Our enemies began. They cast doubt on the facts and figures. This continued among ourselves.' The enemy is internalized – first of all he is *our* enemy, the first person plural, raising grave issues of identification – and then the enemy voice is adopted, even to the extent that 'We have reached the stage where Jews are the authors of their own extermination' (*DF* 222). The 'voice of the enemy/self' is not always so unequivocal, more often it produces doubt, fear and trembling, especially with respect to Israel. In the words of Levinas voicing the words of the enemy, 'Israel's independence was called imperialism, the oppression of native peoples, racism ... The eschatological dream was substituted by the seduction of tourism' (*DF* 222). The 'enemy', in other words, denies that the State of Israel is any different from any other state – it is a denial, couched in pseudo-progressive language that leaves youth gnawed by doubt, trembling, leading to the outcome that 'the progressivist language of traitors deceives the traitors themselves' (*DF*

223). The introduction of the term *traitor* in place of that of the *enemy* betrays
a hardening in Levinas's position – traitors are those who adopt the enemy's
voice – Levinas comes close to claiming, indirectly, in the following paragraph
that progressive critics of Israel have been duped by anti-Semitism. After the
assessment of treacherous speech, Levinas moves from trembling to resolute
assertion: against the voice of our enemy he claims, 'The State of Israel, in
this sense, constitutes the greatest event in modern Judaism' (*DF* 225). The
'sense' to which he is referring is the argument – drawn paradoxically from
the early Heidegger – that authenticity is assured by sacrifice or being-for-
death. In Levinas's words, the State of Israel is the 'greatest event in modern
Judaism' because 'once again we have a Jewish value that, to those most
assimilated into it, appears worthy of an ultimate sacrifice'. The willingness to
sacrifice one's life for the existence of the State of Israel – a constant aspect
of Levinas's political judgement – is taken to justify its difference from other
states. But it is probably that which more than anything else identifies it with
them – every state in history, even the most tyrannical, has found citizens and
supporters willing to sacrifice their lives for its continued existence.

The difficulty of speaking responsibly about the actions of the State of Israel
reaches an extreme level of complexity and ambivalence in the Foreword to
Beyond the Verse. Here Levinas approaches the issue of the raison d'être of
Zionism by self-citation from an essay of 1969 'Poetry and the Impossible' on
Paul Claudel, whose Christian view of the *Shoah* as a sacrificial passion he had
largely adopted. At the outset of examining the claim that the existence of the
State of Israel is justified by the Holocaust, Levinas concedes, 'Of course, it
is the West, not the Arab world, which bears the responsibility for Auschwitz'
but then qualifies this political judgement with a universal ethical judgement:
'Unless one accepts that the responsibility of men cannot be divided, and
that all men are responsible for all others' (*BV* xi). He then notes: 'In *Difficult
Freedom* I published the following lines, written more than ten years ago' and
then proceeds to a long self-citation:

> What is the suppression of national distinctions if not an indivisible humanity,
> that is to say, responsible in its entirety for the crimes and misfortunes of
> the few? ... Are all human relations reducible to the calculations of damages
> and interest, all problems to the settling of the scores? Can anyone among
> mankind wash his hands of all this flesh gone up in smoke? ... The gesture
> of recognition which would come to Israel from the Arab peoples would
> no doubt be replied to by a brotherly zeal such that the problem of the
> refugees will lose its unknown elements. (*BV* xi)

He does not, however, alert his readers that the cited passage from 1969
partly comprised him writing *in the voice* of Claudel. The cited paraphrase of

Claudel not only calls for a universal responsibility for Auschwitz but *also* for a 'gesture of recognition' from the Arab peoples that, Levinas adds returning to his own voice, would be met with an *élan fraternel* that would contribute to a solution of the problem of Palestinian refugees. This already indirect speech is further complicated by a number of omissions, some indicated, others not, from the 1969 original. The first omission, signalled by an ellipsis, comprises two sentences in which Claudel/Levinas seems to berate the Arab peoples for their lack of a universal conscience for the crimes committed in Europe:

> The Arab peoples would not have to answer for German atrocities, or cede their lands to the victims of Hitlerism. What deafness to the call of conscience! (*BV* 131)

The Arab peoples in 1969 are accused, with an undeniable hint of irony, of being incapable of universal conscience by not ceding their lands to the victims of the German crime of the *Shoah*. This apparent use of ethical discourse to support a political position seems an example of precisely that political falsification of 'the original intention of the discourse' that Levinas himself berates at the end of 'Poetry and the Impossible' when he claims the obligation to speak. It is further compounded by the invisible deletion of a passage following the sentence on the 'settling of the scores'. This passage opens with a slippery double negative: 'The right to a "birthplace" invoked by Arab refugees can certainly not be treated unjustly'; which does not issue in a Hegelian negation of the negation that the right must be treated justly, but in an ironic aside on the 'nostalgic value of the church tower (or minaret)'. This is followed by a further, invisibly deleted, sentence that asks: 'But can the call of the land silence the cries of Auschwitz which will echo until the end of time?' (*BV* 131). Here, the Levinas/Claudel voice makes a political weighing of suffering, a calculation of relative damage, which colludes in a tasteless and instrumental use of the victims of the *Shoah* in support of a frankly political justification for the expropriation of the Palestinian refugees. The sentence beginning 'can anyone among mankind wash his hands' is followed by a second explicit deletion of two sentences, in one of which Levinas separates his voice from Claudel's, dissociating himself from a 'frightening apostrophe' and 'excessive phrase' of the latter, namely, 'What does all this Bedouin caper matter to us?' (*BV* 131). Yet if this was the attitude of Claudel to the Arab peoples, how was it possible for Levinas seriously to enlist his voice in a universal ethical claim for the latter to sacrifice some of the 'vast spaces' they inhabit to the State of Israel? In sum, the Foreword offers a harrowing example of Levinas's difficulty in achieving responsible speech in the case of the State of Israel. He speaks in the voice of another, owning the voice, but also maintaining a distance from it – speaking through another while remaining selectively silent.

Levinas's adoption of a paraphrase from a writer who displays evident contempt for the contemporary Arab peoples and his carefully selective practice of citation both undermine the validity of the ethical voice that he is trying to introduce into politics. His protest, the impossibility of remaining silent, seems hollow and partisan. It is vital, however, not to lose sight of or underestimate the ambivalence surrounding Levinas's speech. Levinas comments on his citation by saying, 'Today, I will no longer say refugees, but Palestinians', seemingly recognizing the right of the Palestinians to a name (BV xvi). He continues that if the State of Israel is to exist, then it must be recognized by the Arab world and be able to enter into its intimacy. Yet the peace with neighbours that is now evoked takes a further ambivalent twist when the 'inalienable idea' of Zionism is described in terms of the Jewish people 'not to continue being a minority in its political structure' (BV xvii). The implications of this comment are chilling, for what are the ethical limits to a state that is motivated by the idea that a particular people must always form a majority in its political structure?

In 'How Is Judaism Possible?' Levinas appealed to the prophetic word of Judaism as a means of self-possession in the midst of inauthentic trembling; on the issue of the State of Israel, however, his voice was ambiguous, always trembling on the verge of silence. Was this a state unlike any other, a state participating not only in universal but also in holy history, guided by the prophetic word? Increasingly in his later sayings on the State of Israel Levinas introduces an imperative tone. In his response to Sadat's 1979 peace initiative 'Politics After' (one of the three essays collected under the title 'Zionisms' in Beyond the Verse) Levinas said that 'since 1948 this people has been surrounded by enemies and is still being called into question, yet engaged too in real events, in order to think – and to make and remake – a state which will have to incarnate the prophetic moral idea and the idea of its peace' (BV 194). The obligation upon this state to incarnate the prophetic word of peace has within it the possibility that the State of Israel will not observe the prophetic word and, like any other state, put its interests above peace and justice. What would it mean for Levinas if the State of Israel did not live up to its prophetic vocation? Levinas offered a complex answer to this question in what is perhaps the supreme testament to his ambivalence: the notorious 1982 radio broadcast on the occasion of the massacres of Palestinian refugees in the Sabra and Chatila camps by the Christian Falange in Israeli-occupied Lebanon. In response to Shlomo Malka's question whether the Palestinian was the 'Other' for the Israeli, Levinas disturbingly claimed that 'in alterity we can find an enemy' (Levinas 1989, 294). The focus on this moment in the broadcast, however, overlooks the powerful critique of Zionism with which the broadcast ends. Levinas spoke there of the 'calumny' of Zionism or the confusion of its message concerning the 'relationship to the world and to human beings ... with some sort of commonplace mystique of the earth as native soil'. The suggestion that Zionism might be slandered by the territorial ambitions of the State of Israel is confirmed by Levinas's citation of the Talmud's finding that those who malign the land merit death. His reading goes beyond the verse to say:

> if calumny of that which is "but stones and trees" already merits death, then how serious, *a fortiori*, must be calumny relating to human beings ... A person is more holy than a land, even a holy land, since, faced to an affront made to a person, this holy land appears in its nakedness to be but stone and wood. (Levinas 1989, 296–7)

The Holy Land itself is thus an idol when confronted with human suffering. Once again Levinas is speaking by means of covert self-citation, but here to powerful effect. He is referring to his 1965 Talmudic Commentary 'Promised Land or Permitted Land' which offers the most sober judgement on the State of Israel. The reading concerns the law of calumny, of speaking badly. The calumny of the land by the explorers related in the Book of Numbers is likened by Levinas to contemporary critics of Zionism: the explorers, like contemporary critics of Zionism, 'have decided, in the name of truth, to confound the Zionists' (Levinas 1990b, 56). While the calumny merits death, a worse punishment awaits the Zionists who calumny Zionism by not observing prophetic justice, of putting the securing of the land above the life of a person. For Levinas concludes his Talmudic reading by warning that those who would return to the Holy Land must

> not only commit themselves to justice but also apply it rigorously to themselves. Already they are potentially exiled. The date of their exile is fixed before that of their conquest ... They assume a responsibility without indulgence and are summoned to pay for their own injustice with their exile ... You see, this country is extraordinary. It is like heaven. It is a country which vomits up its inhabitants when they are not just. There is no other country like it; the resolution to accept a country under such conditions confers a right to that country. (Levinas 1990b, 69)

What makes the State of Israel different from other states according to this reading is its commitment to absolute justice. Its right to exist issues from its putting human life above the idols of land and statehood – if it does not, then the price for injustice is expulsion from the land, exile, even the end of the State of Israel? The state is ethically and politically obliged. At this point Levinas's politics is closest to his ethics, his voice most full of prophetic responsibility, the least trembling.

25

Tableaux for a Massacre: Shatila, Thursday–Sunday 16–19 September 1982

On Sunday 19 September 1982 an elderly and severely ill Frenchman crossed into the Shatila refugee camp in Beirut to witness the aftermath of what was rumoured to have been an horrific massacre of Palestinian refugees and other inhabitants of the camps. Jean Genet had tried to enter the previous day but had been deterred by the Israeli Defence force which had occupied Beirut on 15 September and had immediately surrounded the refugee camp with a cordon of tanks and control points; now he was among the first group of reporters and photographers to be permitted access. He encountered what the *Daily Telegraph* journalist Ian Glover-James described as innumerable 'tableaux of death', and Bayan Nuwayhed al-Hout as 'various spectacles' or, in short, the deliberate and carefully staged mise en scène of atrocity. The retreat of the Palestinian fighters the previous Monday and the promises of international protection for the elderly, the women and the children they left behind did not protect them from the fury of the Falangist militias admitted to the camp two days after the assassination of their leader Bashir al-Gemayel on Tuesday 14 September. The killing was conducted at close range over three days and nights and estimates of the victims ranged from the 700–800 cited in the Kahane Report (the 1983 Israeli judicial inquiry) (Kahane Commission 2012) to the 1300 named dead and missing collected by Bayan Nuwayhed al-Hout (*SS* 296) to upper estimates of well over 4000 stated immediately after the massacre by Israeli Army Radio and Lebanese police sources (*SS* 295).

Genet set himself immediately to write his testimony and his *Quatre heures à Chatila* (*Four Hours in Shatila*) remains the most poignant act of witness to the dead of Shatila. But he was very aware that he had been given something to see, something that had been prepared very carefully for him and for the other witnesses who came in with him, a spectacle he was expected to relay to the defeated Palestinians and to the watching world. Genet returns repeatedly to the mise en scène that he encountered, whether in the accusation that the nocturnal atrocities had been lit by the Israeli Defence Force flares for the 'voyeurs' in the skyscraper that housed the Israeli military command just north of the camp or in the suspicion that the bodies had been deliberately predisposed in order for him and others to find them. His testimony and that of other first-hand witnesses point, for the latter indirectly and often without their full awareness, to a sustained effort on the part of the assassins to prepare tableaux of the dead: Genet quickly understood that the brutal atrocities encountered in Shatila were meant to be found and to be seen as such. And what is more, it was a spectacle, designed above all, to be filmed and photographed.

Genet's testimony thus begins with a polemic against photography, claiming that it could only see what the killers meant it to see: 'A photograph has two dimensions, so does a television screen; it is impossible to walk through either' (FHS 209). Genet was accompanied into Shatila by the American photographer Mya Shone, referred to in the testimony as 'S'; his own act of witness was thus accompanied by her photographic practice and testimony (which remains an important part of the photo-archive of the massacre). He however distanced himself from the work of his companion. His own report on what he found moves between four and three dimensions: his descriptions of the camp are punctuated by memories of his time with the Palestinians in Jordan ten years before and even more allusively to his time as a young colonial soldier in Syria described elsewhere in his work. By setting the events of the September days within personal and historic time Genet supplied a fourth dimension to what he had been given to see, but his testimony is also important for its allusions to the three dimensional, one might say sculptural quality of his encounters with the forty victims with whom he passed his four hours in Shatila. This testimony also provides a different perspective to the photographic record assembled by photographers and photojournalists including Mya Shone, Ramzi Haydar, Ryuchi Hirokawa, Günther Altenburg and Ali Hassan Salman. Genet frames his description of the massacre in terms of the difficulty of walking through the narrow streets and passages that make up Shatila, now obstructed by the bodies of the victims; they block the streets; he has to step over and around them; the streets are so narrow he is forced to smell, touch and be touched by the corpses while being persecuted by the sound and the attentions of the flies swarming over them. There is, in short, no detached position from which Genet feels able to view the victims and capture his testimony in a two-dimensional frame.

Genet repeatedly refers to the claustrophobic, confined character of the camp and its built environment, starting immediately after the initial questioning of photography. He describes a sculptural scene in which 'From one wall of the street to the other, arched or curved, their feet pushing on one wall and their heads leaning on the other, the blackened and swollen corpses I had to step over are all Palestinians and Lebanese' (*FHS* 209). He likens his progress through the passageways to a game of hopscotch: 'Sometimes a dead child blocked the streets, which were so narrow, almost paper-thin and the dead were so numerous' (*FHS* 209). Returning then to photography, and as if in conversation with his companion Mya Shone, he states simply, 'Photography is unable to capture the flies, or the thick white smell of death. Nor can it tell of the little hops you have to make when walking from one corpse to the next' (*FHS* 210). Photography cannot work in these narrow streets where the proximity of the dead is so close and stifling, and where Genet later imagines that the killers even with the aid of the Israeli flares must have had difficulty in prosecuting their work:

> It is important to know that the Palestinian camps of Shatila and Sabra consist of miles and miles of very narrow alleys – for here even the alleys are so thin and skeletal, that sometimes two people cannot walk together unless one of them turns sideways – alleys cluttered with rubble and debris, stone blocks, bricks, dirty multicoloured rags, and at night under the Israeli flares that illuminated the camps, 15 or 20 gunmen, even if well-armed, could never have succeeded in carrying out this butchery. (*FHS* 222)

The question begins to emerge of how, given these dark and cramped conditions, it was possible to take photographs, for many photographs were to be taken on that Sunday.

Genet's own descriptions of the dead give us a clue. There is first his growing awareness that the dead he is led to see by his enigmatic and taciturn guides are usually children or the very old. The overwhelming visibility of these victims should be set beside Nuwayhed al-Hout's subsequent finding that the largest age group in the global total of victims were young adults (*SS* 345 [Table 4a, Appendix 1]). Why then does Genet repeatedly encounter very young and elderly victims? And not just him, but also the other journalists and photographers who entered the camp at the same time. Robert Fisk in his *Times* article from 20 September for example noted the prevalence of the young and the old: '"That was my neighbour Mr Nouri", a man shouted at me. He was ninety. And there in a pile of garbage on the pavement beside her lay a very old man with a thin grey beard and a small woollen hat still on his head' (quoted in *SS* 204). Genet, too, first encounters the body of an elderly victim: 'The first corpse I saw was that of a 50 or 60 year old man. He would have had a ring of white hair if a wound (an axe blow it seemed to me) had not split open his skull' (*FHS* 209–10). As he passes by the bodies Genet begins to suspect that he is being presented with a carefully contrived spectacle and wonders at the kind of 'artist' capable of producing such horrific ensembles. Who tied the rope to the old man's feet in order to drag him through the passageways, who posed the corpse of the elderly Palestinian woman as if crucified with her fingers cut off? Genet understands that this mise en scène is meant not so much to humiliate the victims as to show the Palestinian fighters the consequences of their retreat and of abandoning their old and their young. The dead in Shatila had been deserted and then desecrated, cut off at once from their community, their nostalgia for the past and their hopes for the future: 'The solitude of the dead in the Shatila camp was even more palpable since they were frozen in gestures and the poses over which they had no control' (FHS 220). In death as in life they had been subject to the will of others, or such is the message that Genet and the other witnesses were supposed to convey to the yet unknowing world. They were supposed to show that this was total defeat, to say that the memories of the past vested in the elderly Palestinians and the hopes for the future held by the young had been blasted and any continuity between past, present and future twisted into bitter and mocking mortuary scenes.

Beyond the grotesque posing of the bodies of the very young and aged victims Genet also remarks on the evidence of demolition confronting him in Shatila. Other witnesses such as Fisk also refer to 'rubble', broken walls and ruined houses. These scenes of demolition are ubiquitous in the images of the photographers at work in Shatila that day, raising the suspicion sensed by Genet on the day that the demolition was not, as many supposed, about clearing the way for the assassins or burying the dead or hiding the evidence of atrocity, but in reality the work of stage-setting in an urban environment of narrow passageways not suited to photographic capture. The demolition served to create spaces for the display of violated bodies; they are repeatedly to be found and photographed on raised piles of rubble set in the open spaces created by bulldozers out of the narrow streets and cramped houses of the camp. The destruction of the physical environment of the camp came after the killings, so it was not meant to facilitate the pursuit of the victims but to display them to the photographic gaze. Indeed the perpetrators had no desire to conceal their crime nor to address a potential public health threat posed by the decomposing bodies; the demolition served to create an environment suitable for the display of the desecrated dead to the camera.

The sound of bulldozers was reported by many witnesses still barred from the camp on the Friday and the Saturday. Crucial testimony is provided by the first photo-reporter to enter Shatila, the Japanese radical photojournalist Ryuichi Hirokawa. Although it seems as if an order had been given to the assassins to retire from Shatila by 10.00 am of the Saturday, sporadic shooting continued during the day accompanied by a constant drone of bulldozers at work within the camp. Ryuichi Hirokawa attempted to enter the camp at 8.30 am on the Saturday morning 'with the sound of gunshots and bulldozers still quite audible' (quoted in *SS* 204). As with Genet, his entry from the north and the east of the camp was barred by Israeli tanks who refused to accept his journalistic credentials. He eventually managed to enter through an unguarded entrance to the south and gave a perplexed testimony of what he discovered. He naturally assumed that the bulldozers had been at work trying to conceal the bodies even though what he reported was not at all consistent with this view. In a contribution to a PLO-sponsored report on the events in Shatila published in December 1982 the courageous Hirokawa describes discovering a murdered family near their home: 'It looked as though a bulldozer had attempted to hide these bodies. The dead body of a child of about two years old was thrown beside the rubble. The child was, I suppose, alive right up to the end, since the killers had not hidden the body beneath the bulldozed rubble' (quoted in *SS* 203). The other explanation of course is that the intention was not to hide the bodies but the precise opposite, namely to create a stage on which they might be displayed. Mention of the victims in the early testimony is almost always accompanied by references to rubble, to ropes being used to drag bodies to their final resting places where they were mutilated and/or posed in elaborate and desecratory scenarios. The journalist Ian Glover-James describes the display of a family with 'Two children aged about eight ... spread-eagled with bullet holes in their heads. Their parents were shot dead in *rubble* alongside' (quoted in *SS* 204). Mya Shone later describing her photographs of that day draws attention to the ropes and to the mutilations: 'Look at those. Ropes were tied to the victims' hands and feet, and then they were dragged. Men were taken around corners, shot, and cut to pieces by knives and axes. Tractors were used to run over them' (quoted in *SS* 204). The radio reporter Loren Jenkins refers to the scene as 'like something out of one's worst dream. Buildings broken, bodies lying in the street, people in alley ways crumpled in great big piles' (quoted in *SS* 203). These features of the demolition accompanying the massacre are corroborated by all the witnesses, but Genet had a different understanding of their significance.

With the exception of Genet, all of the witnesses assume that the tableaux they encountered constituted direct evidence of how the victims died. Their testimony surrounds the tableaux or scenes of atrocity that they discover with imagined narratives of the horrific circumstances surrounding the act of murder and the attempt at flight. They take what they see, in other words, in all its horror and enormity as direct testimony of *what actually happened*. Fisk, after describing Mr Nouri, turns to another elderly victim: 'An old man lay by his front door in his pyjamas, slaughtered as he ran in terror for safety a few hours earlier' (quoted in *SS* 203). The body displayed outside the door is assumed to have fallen there as the victim attempted to escape from his assassins.

Loren Jenkins on witnessing a murdered family adds, 'Obviously the man had come to answer the gate and was shot right there and the woman that was shot right next to him, she still had her dinner plates in her hand crumpled on the ground; babies with diapers next to them with bullet holes in their heads' (quoted in *SS* 203). Once again, a narrative has enclosed the scene of a murdered family, but one for which there can never be any certainty. Similarly Ian Glover-James describes another family that 'had spilled out of their doorway in their last terrified moments of life' and 'five other bodies, some hanging upside down over a broken wall where the killers caught them as they tried to run' (quoted in *SS* 203). In these cases, the witnesses regard the bodies before them as if they were photographs taken at the moment of their death. Genet's critique of photographic witness regards it as unwittingly complicit with the aims of the assassins, for instead of regarding the victims as having deliberately been posed in photographic tableaux, their violated bodies prepared and predisposed for the photographical lens, the photographic witness assumes that they were captured in flight and provokes the invention of narratives of unbearably violent death that will maximize the horror of the spectacle and its impact on the audience.

When he encountered his first victim, the man of 50 or 60, Genet too began to tell a story but quickly breaks it off as if suddenly struck by a suspicion. The victim was lying in a pool of blood, his belt was undone, and 'The feet and legs of the dead man were naked, black, purple and blue; perhaps he had been taken away by surprise at night or at dawn? Was he running away?' (*FHS* 210). But immediately Genet interrupts his 'perhaps' or fictional narrative of a thwarted escape, breaking it off in favour of precise description of the location of the body: 'He was lying in a small alley immediately to the right of the camp entrance across from the Kuwaiti Embassy' (*FHS* 210). This attention to the where and the how of the bodies that have been left henceforth dominates his testimony, lending it an almost forensic tone that enquires into the perpetration not only of the murders but also the horrific ensembles that he suspects have been prepared for him to contemplate and then tell stories about.

With this suspicion Genet attempts to see beyond the framing of the victims, beyond the photographic pose. He is struck by the effort that has been directed towards setting up this mise en scène and tries to understand the purpose of this carefully executed theatre of cruelty. His testimony bears witness less to the event than to the way in which its perpetrators have worked to represent it to the world. He is attentive to the spaces that have been created by demolition and the setting they provide for photographic images. He took refuge from the tableaux of degradation and the place he suspected they occupied in the continuing war against the Palestinians by lending dignity to the degraded bodies as he found them amid the rubble of Shatila but also – through writing – as they continued to live in the memory of the time that he spent with the Palestinians: 'Many people died in Shatila, and my friendship for them and my affection for their rotting corpses was great because I had known them. Blackened, swollen, rotted by the sun and by death, they remained fedayeen' (*FHS* 226). Genet thus accomplished an act of fidelity to the corpses that resisted the lure of the degrading spectacles through which they had been presented to his gaze. On his way out from the camp he is stopped by a Lebanese army control whose commander, fully aware of his identity and at first pretending to speak only English, asks if he has come from Shatila and if 'he has seen it' and whether he will now write about it: Genet answers yes to all his questions, confident that what he saw went beyond what he was meant to have seen and that this would be what he would write.

PART TWO

Resistance

26

Philosophy and the Black Panthers

The vanguard party only teaches the correct methods of resistance.

– HUEY P. NEWTON, 1967

'**H**ey Joe! How many of you motherfuckers are coming out here?' 'Here' was Santa Rita Jail, California, early morning, Thursday 3 December 1964. 'Joe' was Joe Blum, a student radical, and the accompanying 'motherfuckers' were the 814 students who had been arrested for occupying Berkeley the day before in support of the Free Speech and, indirectly, Civil Rights movements. The prisoner who greeted Joe Blum was Huey P. Newton, then in jail for felonious assault. The friendship of Blum and Newton was a cameo for the brief alliance of white radicals and black militants in the wake of the civil rights struggle. Both were students at Oakland City College in 1961 and, on that morning in the bus at Santa Rita, Blum was struck by Newton remembering him. Thereafter he followed closely Newton's development through the foundation of the Black Panther Party with Bobby Seale in 1966 and beyond. He later interviewed Newton when in prison in 1968 on the charge of murdering a police officer and published the conversation as a very influential article in *The Movement*. In 1969 he even named his son Huey. He repented his support when he learnt of Newton's alleged criminal activities, in his article 'The Party's Over' published in *New Times*, 10 July 1978, an article that confirmed the growing eclipse of the Black Panther Party.

At this time of mounting public accusations against Newton and the Black Panthers, in great part seeded by the FBI and its Counter Intelligence Programme of surveillance, infiltration and defamation (COINTELPRO), Newton embarked on a PhD programme in the History of Consciousness at the University of California, Santa Cruz, which he completed in 1980. He wrote a thesis that described the evolution of COINTELPRO and the way it was used against him, an analysis of the sustained and deliberate campaign of defamation conducted in the third person. In the early hours of the morning of 22 October 1989 Newton was gunned down in West Oakland. His assassin remembered his last words, 'You can kill my body, but you can't kill my soul. My soul will live forever,' but he didn't realize the significance of this last of Newton's many paraphrases of Plato's *Phaedo*, which describes Socrates's last hours on death row in ancient Athens.

Much earlier, back in 1970, some representatives of the Black Panthers visited Jean Genet in Paris asking for solidarity; he replied that he was prepared to travel to the United States immediately. His subsequent public statements in support of the Panthers are collected in his book *The Declared Enemy: Texts and Interviews*, but it is in his last book, *Prisoner of Love* (1986), that he proposed a methodology for understanding their struggle, one that links it with the Palestinian resistance, in which he also directly participated. It's a method that appeals to dimensionality, one refined and confirmed by Genet's experience of walking through the Shatila refugee camp in Beirut hours after the murders in 1982. He was struck there by how the killers had taken great pains to create little visual scenarios – little installations of terror – designed to be photographed, televised and disseminated worldwide as a spectacle of humiliation. So at the outset of his 'Four Hours in Shatila' Genet insists:

A photograph has two dimensions, so does a television screen: it is impossible to walk through either. From one wall of the street to the other, arched or curved, their feet pushing on one wall and their heads leaning against the other, the blackened and swollen corpses I had to step over were all Palestinian and Lebanese. (*FHS* 209)

The walk multiplies the dimensions of the experience, restoring depth to the two dimensions of a photographic testimony implicated in a spectacle of terror.

In *Prisoner of Love*, Genet moves between the Palestinians and the Panthers as between two groups of what he calls 'virtual martyrs', reflecting constantly on the politics of their image:

The Whites' recoil from the Panthers' weapons, their leather jackets, their revolutionary hair-dos, their words and even their gentle but menacing tone – that was just what the Panthers wanted. They deliberately set out to create a dramatic image. The image was a theatre for enacting a tragedy and for stamping it out – a bitter tragedy about themselves, a bitter tragedy for the Whites. They aimed to project their image in the press and on the screen until the Whites were haunted by it. And they succeeded.

Genet continues: '"Power may be at the end of a gun", but sometimes it's also at the end of the shadow or the image of a gun.' Genet regarded entry into the spectacle as a plausible tactic of subaltern resistance, but one with its own dangers and risks:

> Wherever they went the Americans were the masters, so the Panthers should do their best to terrorize the masters by the only means available to them. Spectacle. And the spectacle would work because it was the product of despair. ... But the spectacle is only spectacle, and it may lead to mere figment, to no more than a colourful carnival; and this is the risk that the Panthers ran. Did they have any choice? (Genet 2003, 99)

The danger of the Panthers losing position and threat in depth and slipping into a spectacular politics was especially intense given their adversary's mastery of the terrain of the spectacle, especially the FBI and its director, who deliberately set out to transform the Black Panthers' resistance in depth into a revolutionary pantomime of gestural violence. Genet feared that the consequences of this unequal struggle could be devastating and urged in his speeches and writings a return to engagement in depth in the 'metamorphosis of the black community':

> So the Panthers were heading for either madness, metamorphosis of the black community, death or prison. All these options happened, but the metamorphosis was by far the most important, and that is why the Panthers can be said to have overcome through poetry. (Genet 2003, 100)

But this was not the poetry of the spectacle; it was the multidimensional expression of an emergent capacity to resist.

Pantomime villains?

Huey Newton and Bobby Seale with guns and leather jackets in 1966; Huey posed by Eldridge Cleaver with gun and spear in an image he despised; Huey taking his shirt off when leaving prison in 1970 – moments from the escalating spectacle that Genet saw was both weapon and trap. But against this iconography may be posed the photographs of kids eating free breakfasts, community ambulances and the title page of Huey P. Newton's PhD thesis. From one perspective, Newton's doctoral thesis is a devastating confirmation of Genet's concerns, showing how the spectacle was used against the Black Panthers and by extension against any attempt to frame a radical politics in the United States. The FBI wanted to transform the 'metamorphosis of the community' that began not so much with the Civil Rights Movement as with the armed defence of the community pioneered in the South by Robert Williams and the Deacons for Defence and theorized in *Negroes with Guns*.[1] How the authorities in the United States ever expected the black men that they trained to be Marines, like Williams, to then leave the army and meekly return to the humiliations of Jim Crow is beyond belief. The free breakfasts for children, the educational and health initiatives, the sickle cell anaemia screening programme – the FBI set out to convert this capacity, this depth of resistance, into the surface of a 'colourful carnival'. This is confirmed by Hugh Pearson, who in his implacably hostile *The Shadow of the Panther: Huey Newton and the Price of Black Power in America* leaves us with a spectacular portrait of the revolutionary as pantomime villain (Pearson 1996). And he may not be entirely wrong. Yet it is hard to imagine anyone's reputation surviving the manipulations of COINTELPRO intact. (Imagine J. Edgar Hoover's minions getting to work on Socrates: 'Subject is an ex-hoplite with spear and shield training. Mentally disturbed, he maintains a sham marriage while preying on underage males in the agora and at "symposia" … Frequents gymnasiums and bathhouses, where he spreads anti-democratic propaganda that he claims to be "philosophy". Known Associates include declared and potential enemies of the state Alcibiades and Plato … ').

Stepping back from the carnival that swept up, and then swept away, Huey P. Newton, perhaps it is time to look instead at Newton as the revolutionary intellectual who turned away from the religious inspiration of the Christian Civil Rights Movement and the Nation of Islam and looked towards philosophy for strategic and tactical insight. This came at a price. Anyone familiar with the political theology of resistance cannot fail to be struck by a certain thanato-political groundtone resounding from Plato and his scenario of the death of Socrates – his revolutionary suicide – played out in the *Phaedo*. It may be heard in the haunting phrase of the revolutionary Levine, who when on trial for his life after the collapse of the Munich Soviet in 1919 declared to the military court: 'We Communists are the dead on leave.' This thanato-politics obviously informed the writer and the movement that could produce a text with the title *Revolutionary Suicide*, published by Newton in 1973.

This book is many things, one of which is a contemporary rewrite of Plato's *Phaedo*, the story of a condemned criminal on death row who knew he had been sentenced to death long before his trial and execution and who responded, tactically or otherwise, with an appeal to the doctrine of immortality. In place of the immortal soul, however, Newton proposes the immortal revolution that is always to come – in the meantime, though, in this life, there is but resistance. Indeed one of the major and enduring contributions of Newton's *Revolutionary Suicide* to the work of the Black Panthers, and to radical politics generally, is its status as a rare case of theoretical clarity regarding the often blurred distinction between revolution and resistance.

The politics of resistance is generically different from revolutionary politics, a separation that can be traced to a bifurcation in the immediate philosophical succession to Kant's critical philosophy and that was played out through the interpretation of the categories of modality. The dominant lineage passed from an emphasis on the modal category of possibility to the problem of the realization of freedom: Fichte, Schiller and Hegel worked through this revolutionary lineage dedicated to realizing freedom. The other, less well known, line of descent passed through Johann Kiesewetter, Kleist and above all Clausewitz, emphasizing the modal category of actuality and the problem of opposed force or resistance. Sometimes described as 'military Kantianism', it drew upon and refounded the political tradition of resistance, a struggle more sombre and unremitting than temporary enthusiasms of revolutionary freedom. It has its purest expression in Clausewitz's *On War* and its analyses of *Widerstandsfähigkeit*, or the capacity to resist, and in Clausewitz's reader, Nietzsche, with his view of actuality as will to power (see Caygill 2012). From Marx and Engels onwards, Clausewitz and resistant politics occupied the margin – to varying degrees – of revolutionary politics. The by no means self-evident compatibility of revolution and resistance was realized by some revolutionary thinkers, notably Mao in his texts from the mid- to late-1930s on the prolonged war of resistance, which focused on the enhancement of the 'capacity to resist'. Excerpts from the latter (along with embedded quotations from Clausewitz) appear in Mao's *Little Red Book*, closely studied by Newton and Bobby Seale in the mid-1960s.

The theoretical clarity with which Newton and Seale grasped the distinction between revolutionary war and the war of resistance is almost unique and can be traced back not only to the experiences of the struggle but also to Newton's passionate engagement with the philosophy of Plato and Nietzsche, which allowed him to see things in the fragments of Clausewitz passed over by Mao and that were barely visible to his contemporaries. Newton's clarity regarding the distinction between revolutionary war and the war of resistance was evident already in the early position document 'The Correct Handling of a Revolution: July 20, 1967'. The opening proposition of this strategic and tactical reflection locates the black struggle firmly at the level of resistance:

> The Black masses are handling the resistance incorrectly. When the brothers in East Oakland, having learned their resistance fighting from Watts, amassed the people in the streets, threw bricks and Molotov cocktails to destroy property and create destruction, they were herded into a small area by the gestapo police and immediately contained by the brutal violence of the oppressor's storm troops. (*HNR* 141)

Newton here reveals a strategic weakness in the resistance, one that Clausewitz warned against repeatedly. The strategic conduct of resistance is the responsibility of the vanguard party, whose task for Newton ends there: it is responsible for building and sustaining a capacity to resist, hopefully as a prelude to revolution but with clear strategic priority lent to self-defence.

Newton applied Mao's strategy of the prolonged war of resistance, theorized in the context of the resistance to the Japanese invasion of the 1930s, to the circumstances of the black community in the United States. Here, as in Mao's China, 'The primary job of the party is to provide leadership for the people. It must teach by words and action the correct and strategic methods of prolonged resistance' (*HNR* 141). The notion of prolonged resistance points to Mao's temporal inflection of Clausewitz's capacity to resist – a capacity is precisely a prolongation in time – thus the struggle for resistance occupies an extended time horizon, unlike a revolutionary bid for power which thrives on the acceleration of time. Newton also shows an acute grasp of the actuality of war and the vital necessity of preserving capacity to resist in this setting: the strategic priority afforded the preservation of the capacity to resist follows the intuition on Newton's part of Clausewitz's sombre premise of the actuality of opposed forces – war – in which each adversary is dedicated to extinguishing the other's capacity to resist. Consequently:

> The main function of the party is to awaken the people and teach them the strategic method of resisting a power structure which is prepared not only to combat with massive brutality the people's resistance but to annihilate totally the Black population. (*HNR* 143)

The communiqué concludes with one of those moments of clarity regarding the distinction between revolution and resistance that Newton would sustain throughout his career as a revolutionary theorist:

> So if things get worse for oppressed people they will feel the need for revolution and resistance. The people make revolution; the oppressors, by their brutal actions, cause resistance by the people. The vanguard party only teaches the correct methods of resistance. (*HNR* 145)

Yet resistance is always in danger of adopting a purely reactive posture that adapts itself to the initiatives of the adversary – one that is momentary, not prolonged; reactive and not the expression of an affirmative *capacity* to resist. The Black Panther Party for Self-Defense founded in Oakland in October 1966 initiated a programme of building up and sustaining the 'capacity to resist', understood affirmatively, not in responding to discrete acts of oppression but as constituting the visible presence of a capacity to resist present and future threats and attacks.

The rightly celebrated Ten-Point Program of October 1966 is thus not directly revolutionary, but certainly not reformist, as objected by some of its critics. It attempts to theorize an eventual move from resistance to revolution through constituting and augmenting the capacity to resist:

1 We want freedom. We want power to determine the destiny of our Black Community.

2 We want full employment for our people.

3 We want an end to the robbery by the white man of our Black Community.

4 We want decent housing, fit for shelter of human beings.

5 We want education for our people that exposes the true nature of this decadent American society …

6 We want all black men exempt from military service.

7 We want an immediate end to police brutality and murder of black people.

8 We want freedom for all black men held in federal, state, county and city prisons or jails.

9 We want all black men when brought to trial to be tried in court by a jury of their peer group or people from their black communities, as defined by the Constitution of the United States.

10 We want land, bread, housing, education, clothing, justice and peace. And as our major political objective we want a United Nations-supervised plebiscite to be held throughout the black colony in which only black colonial subjects will be allowed to participate for the purpose of determining the will of black people as to their national destiny.

Thomas J. Sugrue perceptively observes in *Sweet Land of Liberty: The Forgotten Struggle for Civil Rights in the North* (2008) that the list of demands emerged from a matrix of radical ideas ranging across the demand for full employment from the 'labor-civil rights agenda of the 1940s', decent housing from Roosevelt's Second Bill of Rights, and the themes of decadence and exploitation of capitalism from Malcolm X and the Revolutionary Action Movement. He also notes the tactic of appealing to the constitution and the UN, supplementing radical demands with an appeal to true constitutional legality and international law (Sugrue 2008).

The syncretic character of the Ten-Point Program was deliberate; it was intended to collect together the experience of over half a century of struggle in a programme dedicated to enhancing the black community's capacity to resist. This strategy would later inspire other resistance movements, such as the Dalit Panthers of the early 1970s in India and the contemporary anarchist movement in Greece. It was meant to serve as a codification of proven tactics. The symbol of the Black Panther Party itself was developed by SNCC workers in the voting registration campaign of Lowndes County Alabama, led by Stokely Carmichael, as a symbol to distinguish the local 'Lowndes County Freedom Organization' from the state Democratic organization, whose symbol was a white rooster. It was readily adopted by the Californian militants, as was the experience of Robert Williams and the Deacons for Defense in Monroe, North Carolina, who armed themselves against the Ku Klux Klan in 1957, an experience narrated in Williams's *Negroes with Guns*, studied closely by Seale and Newton. Williams's experience in resisting racist attacks with the armed Deacons for Defense directly motived the seventh point in the Program, which was implemented by the 'neighborhood watch' of armed Panthers, the 'Police Monitoring Patrols' that observed the behaviour of the police, intervening where necessary and within the limits of the law. This, the most visible of the Black Panthers' actions, formed part of a classic strategy of resistance; however, when it was transformed into the spectacle of militants in black leather jackets carrying shotguns it was open to misinterpretation as a spectacular revolutionary gesture. It was deliberately used in this way on occasions such as the 22 May 1967 siege of the State Assembly Chamber at Sacramento, but the basic strategic justification of the patrols was set in terms of building capacity to resist in depth.

The spectacular invasion of Sacramento by twenty Black Panthers armed with shotguns, M1 rifles and revolvers, dressed in full regalia of leather jackets and berets, was conceived by Newton and Eldridge Cleaver, although Newton was not present. Later, he would severely distance himself from such actions and Cleaver's violent revolutionary rhetoric, which flourished during Newton's imprisonment. In a frequently hilarious television confrontation with William F. Buckley on 11 February 1973, Newton was categorical in taking a distance from Cleaver and the tactics adopted by the Black Panther Party during the latter's ascendancy:

I think that rhetoric ran amok in the Black Panther Party while the leadership was under the influence of Eldridge Cleaver. It caused murders of many of our people. It laid the foundation so that even the black community could say, 'Oh, see those bad guys are out there, you see, they always want violence and robberies and so forth'. This kind of rhetoric can provoke physical conflict. (*HNR* 283)

Newton's critique of Cleaver was even harsher on other occasions, such as his essay on Cleaver's homophobia, 'On Eldridge Cleaver: He Is No James Baldwin'

(1973), but whatever the personal antipathies, the question of political strategy was central to their differences. In a return to the initial inspiration of the Black Panther Party with the departure of Cleaver, laid out in 'On the Defection of Eldridge Cleaver from the Black Panther Party and the Defection of the Black Panther Party from the Black Community: April 17, 1971', Newton claimed that

> the only reason we have been able to survive the repression of the Party and the murder of some of our most advanced comrades, is because of the Ten-Point Program – our survival program. Our programs would be meaningless and insignificant if they were not community programs. (*HNR* 201)

The work of building up a capacity to resist was compromised by Cleaver's rhetoric, Newton now saw. Cleaver's departure was an opportunity to renounce the spectacle of violence and to return, in Genet's words, to 'dimensional' work in the community: 'So the Black Panther Party has reached a contradiction with Eldridge Cleaver, and he has defected from the Party because we would not order everyone into the streets tomorrow to make a revolution.' With this: 'We are now free to move toward the building of a *community structure* that will become the true voice of the people, promoting their interests in many ways' (*HNR* 207). After 1971 the Black Panthers invested a great part of their efforts and resources to the community programmes: free breakfasts for school children (a move that deeply alarmed J. Edgar Hoover, who saw this initiative as the greatest 'long-term threat' to the internal security of the United States), free health clinics, free ambulances, sickle cell anaemia screening, clothing and shoe programmes, buses to prison programmes – all measures consciously directed to building up the community's capacity to resist.

Will to power

Let us turn back to *Revolutionary Suicide*, which is a chronicle of Newton's life of resistance, beginning with his schooldays. Newton ironically thanks his schools for their contribution to his formation as a resistance fighter: 'They never realized how much they had actually educated me by teaching the necessity of resistance and the dignity of defiance.' But what is most remarkable is Newton's narration of how he learnt to read, inspired by his brother Melvin:

> Then I picked up Melvin's copy of Plato's *Republic*, bought a dictionary, and started learning to read things I did not already know. … I spent long hours every day at home going through the *Republic* and pronouncing the words

I knew. If I did not know a word, I would look it up in the dictionary, learn how to sound it out if I could, and then learn the meaning ... I worked on that book, going over it page by page, word by word. (Newton 2009, 50, 54)

Newton took from Plato not only the analysis of the idea of justice, but also the scenario of the public struggle of ideas. He took this lesson first of all to the block: 'Sometimes I got into teaching on the block, reciting poetry or starting dialogues about philosophical ideas. I talked to the brothers about things that Hume, Peirce, Locke, or William James had said.' He particularly recalled the impact of Plato's *Republic* on the street:

I told them about the allegory of the cave from Plato's *Republic*, and they enjoyed it. We called it the story of the cave prisoners. ... The allegory seemed very appropriate to our own situation in society. We, too, were in prison and needed to be liberated in order to distinguish between the truths and the falsehoods imposed on us.

These philosophical debates on the block moved directly into confrontational debates with the police about their individual acts of injustice and their role in a system that perpetuated it, as well as to the study of police science and law, in order to learn how to 'outmaneuver the police' but also 'to become a better burglar' (Newton 2009, 76–9).

Second in importance only to Plato in the formation of Newton, and through him the Panthers' philosophy, was Nietzsche, of whom Newton was a close reader. In *Revolutionary Suicide* Newton observes:

When I read Nietzsche's *The Will to Power*, I learnt much from a number of his philosophical insights. This is not to say that I endorse all of Nietzsche, only that many of his ideas have influenced my thinking. Because Nietzsche was writing about concepts fundamental to all men, and particularly about the meaning of power, some of his ideas are pertinent to the way Black people live in the United States; they have had a great impact on the development of the Black Panther philosophy. (Newton 2009, 173)

Newton goes on to explain how. The first impact was Nietzsche's thought 'that beyond good and evil is the will to power – it is really the will to power that controls our understanding of something and not an inherent quality of good or evil'. He describes how the Panthers tried to apply this theory.

In the early days of the Black Panthers we tried to find ways to make this theory work in the best interests of Black people. Words could be used not only to make Blacks more proud but to make whites question and even reject concepts they had always unthinkingly accepted. (Newton 2009, 174–5)

Newton and the Black Panthers took Nietzsche's *Genealogy of Morals* and his account of the rise of Christianity as a strategic manual in the struggle for power, revaluing words such as 'Black' and using others to compromise the confidence of the adversary by devaluing them. The strongest example was the use of 'pig' for policemen, part deliberate strategy to devalue and delegitimize the police.

Another example of the Panthers' Nietzschean politics was the expression 'All Power to the People': 'that helped to raise Black people's consciousness' and

> has meaning on several levels – political, economic, and metaphysical – it was coined by the Black Panther Party about the same time as pig and has also gained wide acceptance. When we created it I had in mind some distinct philosophical goals for the community that many people did not understand. (Newton 2009, 177)

The political and economic meanings were the actuality of power or the recognition of a state of war and ultimately 'complete control of the institutions in the community' (Newton 2009, 177). The metaphysical meaning was explicitly explained in an earlier position document 'Black Capitalism Re-analyzed I: June 5, 1971'. There Newton comments:

> When we coined the expression 'All Power to the People', we had in mind emphasizing the word 'Power', for we recognize that the *will to power is the basic drive of man*. But it is incorrect to seek power over people. We have been subjected to the dehumanizing power of exploitation and racism for hundreds of years; and the Black community has its own will to power also. ... To us power is, first of all, the ability to define phenomena, and secondly the ability to make these phenomena act in a desired manner. (*HNR* 227)

Power as the ability to define phenomena and to control their action returns to the distinction between resistance and revolution; power becomes the affirmation of a community, not of its freedom, as with the Civil Rights Movement, but of its capacity to resist.

Yet on the other side of Nietzsche's genealogy of morals and will to power is the thought of the more-than-human and its cluster of concepts such as nobility, affirmation and joy. Newton, like Fanon before him, saw a new kind of human emerging from the prolonged and bitter struggles of resistance. He described this in the 1974 article 'The Mind Is Flesh', a rare moment in which Newton looked beyond the thanato-politics of resistance to the revolution and then even further into a post-human communist future that preserves freedom as but one value alongside intellect and character, all of which are second to joy:

As we cross the threshold from the past era of scarcity to the future era of abundance, the mind is learning the controls required to remain zestfully engaged with life, throughout increased longevity devoid of drudgery and poverty. It must also learn to generate a new sort of man, capable of preserving, amplifying, and passing to our human or posthuman followers the striving for mastery of reality, while preserving its elements of intellect, character, freedom, and joy. Especially joy, for we are entering some of the most joyous of all the moments of man. (*HNR* 330)

Note

1   See Lance Hill's *The Deacons of Defence: Armed Resistance and the Civil Rights Movement*, The University of North Carolina Press, Chapel Hill and London 2004.

27

The white mask: Light and shadow in Fanon

'**P**eau noire, masques blancs' – 'Black skin, white masks': four words divided by a comma, leaving behind them an enormous question mark. It is a sentence, if not a grammatical one: there is no verb, just a comma, although it is an important comma dividing and uniting two adjectives and two nouns, one singular, one plural: black/white, skin/masks. It can be read as an opposition, with black skin on one side of the comma and white masks on the other white masks, a classic scenario of the separation of truth and dissemblance with the singular black skin standing for truth and sincerity and the plural white masks for dissemblance and hypocrisy, the whitened sepulchres of St Matthew's Gospel. To read Fanon's title in this way tends towards a black essentialism that is uncharacteristic of his thought; perhaps the title should instead be read as the statement of an Hegelian determination of reflection, with the black skin and the white masks mutually constituting each other, the comma serving as a medium of reflection – there is black skin because there are white masks and white masks because there is black skin (Fanon seems to say this in *Year Five of the Algerian Revolution*: 'C'est le blanc qui crée le nègre', even if he then breaks the symmetry of reflection: 'Mais c'est le nègre qui crée la négritude' (Fanon [1959] 2011, 284) – an apparent interruption of the mutual reflection of black and white that takes him to a discussion of the veil, to which I will return). It can even be read as a statement of identity as in the slang expression for a black person conforming to white expectations as a 'peau noire, masque blanc'. But however the title is understood the masks are not just covers for black skin nor for white colonial violence, but maybe point beyond themselves to another form of relation; Fanon's title in short is itself a mask covering a more fundamental distinction between two forms of occlusion and dissemblance: the mask and the veil.

The mask is not much discussed in Fanon's 1952 *Black Skin, White Masks*, perhaps for the reason that this title is itself a mask for Fanon's own move from the mask to the veil. The title seems to engage with the promise of recognition – the Hegelian master–slave dialectic – but what emerges is less the scenario of recognizing behind the mask the skin, the face or even another mask but rather the absolute resistance of non-recognition. The recognition scenario of masking and unmasking is Manichean, and we will see that Fanon's text drives the mask to its limit, to the point where it becomes something else: the veil or the shroud. While the mask permits and undoes recognition by hiding and revealing at the same time, it does so according to a certain proportion or measure: there are degrees of occlusion and revelation, degrees of recognition and misrecognition. And to work within these degrees, adjusting them, moving within the spectrum of options they provide is to remain within the scenario of recognition. There is a struggle *for* recognition in this mis en scène – classically between master and bondsman – but what is important for Fanon is that if we push these degrees – white on black, black on white, grey on grey – to their extremes – pure white and black – what emerges is no longer a struggle for but one *against* recognition, a refusal to engage with the entire scenario of recognition and its lures. It becomes visible as a scenario, a game of mutual recognition that is not really mutual, in which the masks of master and bondsman are themselves unmasked. Any potential commonality assumed in the struggle for recognition falls away, leaving either enmity, in which the conflict between black and white is no longer motivated by any promise of peace, or (and this will be Fanon's position) a Nietzschean affirmative nobility that does not need or seek the recognition of the oppressor.

There is another more prosaic reason why Fanon does not say much about masks in his book. The reason is apparently quite straightforward: 'Black skin, white masks' is the mask given to a book – a psychiatric treatise – that its author originally entitled 'Essai sur la desalienation du Noir', 'Essay on the Disalienation of the Black'. There is some historical debate about who was responsible for masking the original title, whether Francis Jeanson his editor at Edition de Seuil or more controversially Fanon's adversary Octave Mannoni whose own book *Psychology of Colonization* is vigorously criticized in *Black Skin, White Masks*. In a memoir 'La passion et le Talent' published in *Sans Frontières* in 1989, Mannoni frames his claim to have given Fanon the title in terms of an interesting parallel:

> The first time I met him was in 1949 at Editions du Seuil. We were both publishing our first books. Mine was 'The Psychology of Colonization'. Bad title, the English translated it as 'Prospero and Caliban'. Fanon hadn't found a title for his book. It was me that gave it to him, *Peau noire masques blancs* [Mannoni here apparently forgetting the comma].

> (cited in Chaulet-Achour 2013, 106)

The usual response to Mannoni's memory – and remember, for a psychoanalyst remembering is not uncomplicated – is to point to problems with the timing: Fanon was still dictating his book in 1949 and *Prospero and Caliban* was first published in 1956, but the reference to *The Tempest* is none the less thought-provoking – Caliban Black Skin, Prospero White Mask. However, it also complicates the pairing: Prospero is less the white mask with a 'k' than with 'que', the white masque, the French word when carried over into English having the more specific meaning of a fantastical dramatic performance, practised by the late Shakespeare and of which *The Tempest* is the supreme example. Prospero is the Magician, the master of seeming: he can even make it seem as if there has been a tempest and a shipwreck; and so, omniscient/omnipotent, he sees everything but is not seen; he stages his own overthrow; he inspires doomed conspiracies against himself. He runs his prison island as an elaborate masque apparently having learnt the secrets of the place from Caliban and even having emancipated Caliban only to enslave him anew. He and Caliban perform the master/slave dialectic as masque – black skin, white masque – but he plays it without risk and with nothing to recognize; he merely stages Caliban's recognition of the white masks with which he, Prospero, has surrounded him and brings him at the end to acknowledge Prospero's absolute mastery.

So Mannoni's strange memory teaches us something about why perhaps the phrase 'black skin, white masks' is such an irresistible mask and why Fanon adopted it to cover the more psychiatrically precise previous title as well as some of the unexpected conclusions that he arrives at. The phrase performs a complicity between the two terms – black skin/white masks – through the punctuation mark of the comma. The comma works as a stitch binding the two terms – calligraphically it marks a loop moving back before moving forward, sewing the mask to the face. Fanon's intent in the book, though, is to cut the stitch. Interestingly, when Glenn Coulthard came to publish his devastating critique of the seemingly liberal politics of recognition directed against the indigenous peoples of Canada, he too felt impelled to adapt Fanon's title, now '*Red Skin, White Masks: Rejecting the Politics of Recognition*'. For him, the phrase 'Red Skin, White Masks' proposes a scenario of recognition opposed by 'Against the Politics of Recognition' perceptively suggesting that the politics of recognition is indeed one of red skin, white masks that must be surpassed. In a sense Coulthard is pointing out the truth or rather the irony of Fanon's title: behind the mask of black skin, white masks lies a total opposition to any 'politics of recognition'. Coulthard makes this claim on Fanon's behalf when he says in his introduction: 'unlike the liberalized appropriation of Hegel that continues to inform many contemporary proponents of identity politics, in Fanon recognition is not posited as a source of freedom and dignity for the colonized, *but rather as the field of power through which colonial relations are produced and maintained.* This "is the form of recognition", Fanon suggests, "that Hegel never described"' (Coulthard 2014, 17). Coulthard, like Fanon, Dr King and the Black Panther Huey Newton, replaces Hegelian recognition by Nietzschean affirmation, so permitting a break with the play of masks that Coulthard calls the 'lure of recognition' or the 'necessity on the part of the oppressed to "turn away" from their other-oriented master-dependency' (Coulthard 2014, 43). It is the very possibility of the mask that constitutes the lure, hiding and revealing the temptation of the false promise of mutual recognition.

The preference for the veil over the mask and its dissembled struggle for recognition was clearly stated by W. E. B. Du Bois already at the outset of his 1903 *The Souls of Black Folk.* Du Bois describes his childhood experience of being repulsed in a childhood game and realizing that he was 'shut out from their world by a vast veil' (Du Bois [1903] 2007, 8). His response was not to engage in a battle for recognition, but to refuse to desire the veiled world: 'I had thereafter no desire to tear down that veil, to creep through; I held all beyond it in common contempt, and lived above it in a region of blue sky and great wandering shadows' (Du Bois [1903] 2007, 8). Yet Du Bois also describes how this childhood nobility was reduced by experience: the expansive region of blue sky became the 'streak of blue' above the prison house as the 'vast veil' of the white world became the personal veil of the black subject. In words that anticipate *Black Skin, White Masks* Du Bois describes being 'born with a veil, and gifted with second-sight in this American world, – a world which yields him no true self-consciousness, but only lets him see himself through the revelation of the other world. It is a peculiar sensation, this double-consciousness, this sense of always looking at one's self through the eyes of others' (Du Bois [1903] 2007, 8). The strife he describes is however, by virtue of the veil, not open to any dialectical resolution through recognition, for '[h]e would not Africanize America, for America has too much to teach the world and Africa. He would not bleach his Negro soul in a flood of white Americanism, for he knows that Negro blood has a message for the world' (Du Bois [1903] 2007, 9). The veil allows the dangerous mental state of 'double consciousness' to be contained and held in separation without any movements towards dialectical resolution.

In 1953, a year after the publication of *Black Skin, White Masks*, Fanon took up a position at the legendary mental hospital of Saint Alban, working with François Tosquelles whose thesis/book *Le vécu de la fin du monde dans la folie* (1948) was an important inspiration for *Black Skin, White Masks.* Tosquelles describes the situation when the mask slips and the possibility of recognition falls away as potentially *la fin du monde*, an expression Fanon uses to describe the experience of colonization. If the world is over, how can there be a dialectic of recognition? There can only be a collapse of the terms of recognition. Tosquelles left some interesting memoirs of his time working with Fanon, echoing his own interest in the mask as what enables the mutual recognition of sociality especially between psychiatrist and patient. And à propos of Fanon's gift of his book to him, Tosquelles reflected later, 'Whatever the colour of our face or our skin we all advance masked to meet the others' (Tosquelles 2001, 169). He describes how the mask contains conflict that would potentially end the social world, through an anecdote about Fanon's dancing and the dismay it provoked among his colleagues, who were 'jealous of the extraordinary suppleness he showed when he danced with their wives. The competition that then assumed the mask of professional knowledge sometimes hid this complex conflict of human sexuality represented on the occasion of the dance' (Tosquelles 2001, 170). So the mask allowed for conflict to play out but displaced from its primary source, the mask of racist sexual jealousy and whatever lay behind that; by its means conflict could be recognized and diverted, but never fully recognized. For Tosquelles, thinking as a psychiatrist, as recognition approaches its extreme and the masks are dropped, there is not truth of the skin or the face or of yet another mask but the end of the world, the breakdown of recognition and the beginnings of absolute emnity and for him madness or the barely contained 'double consciousness' described by Du Bois. The discretion entailed in not unmasking changes the scenario of the dissembled conflict of recognition into the refusal to engage that constitutes the veil.

This was also the case for Fanon, but not entirely so. What is certain though is that *Black Skin, White Masks* is less interested in the play of recognition enabled by the donning of masks than in pushing the predicament of the mask to its extreme. And not as a philosophical experiment but as phenomenological description of what had been accomplished in the experience of colonization. So already, early in the second chapter 'The Woman of Colour and the White Man' we find this repudiation of any mutual recognition in an explicit critique of Hegelian subjective certainty. Fanon describes the lived experience of the world of Mayotte Capecias, for whom it seems 'white and black represent the two poles of a world, two poles in perpetual conflict: a genuinely Manichean concept of the world; the word has been spoken, it must be remembered – white or black, that is the question' (Fanon [1952] 1986, 31). Not Hamlet's 'to be or not to be' but Capecias's White or Black is the question. Fanon evoked a Manichean world divided by two poles of good and evil and their struggle: 'I am white ... I am the colour of the daylight ... If I am black, it is not the result of a curse, but it is because, having offered my skin, I have been able to absorb all the cosmic *effluvia*. I am truly a ray of sunlight under the earth' (Fanon [1952] 1986, 31). Mayotte's Manichean experience is important for Fanon because it pulls apart any possible mediation between black and white: the white mask reflects all the light that hits it, remaining impervious to anything outside, while the black skin absorbs it. One repels and remains intact; the other absorbs and is consumed. These are extremes in which the black skin does not enter into a struggle for recognition with the white mask but is consumed, charred by the encounter with glaring, even incendiary whiteness.

Formally, the dropping of the mask brings with it the breakdown of recognition, and not in favour of truth but of bare power. For the scenario of recognition emerges for Fanon as but a masked Manicheanism, as an irreconcilable opposition in which one term has to dissolve into the other. The white mask is untouched and untouchable; it does not recognize or adapt to its encounters – it just reflects light. And in the face of this light, this white, Fanon says, the black 'has no ontological resistance' (Fanon [1952] 1986, 83) since colonial societies have no ontology. Fanon describes this predicament in the crucial fifth chapter of the book 'L'experience vécue du noir' (whose title deliberately echoes Tosquelles's 'l'experience vécue de la fin du monde') when he relates the episode of the frightened boy on a snowy day: 'Maman, regarde le nègre, j'ai peur' (Fanon [1952] 1986, 84). Although the mis en scène is of ice and a world covered in white snow, the experience is incandescent – hot and cold, the experience of the end of a world: 'All round me the white man, above the sky tears at its navel, the earth rasps under my feet, and there is a white song, a white song. All this whiteness that burns me' (Fanon [1952] 1986, 86).

This burning is not part of any struggle for recognition – the icy whiteness burns, leaving a black charred body. For Fanon, to enter into this scene with the desire for recognition can only mean that black will be burnt by white; what is required then is to not enter into this scene, to not enter into relation with the white, but either to acknowledge enmity – 'le beau nègre vous emmerde, madam' he replies to the boy's mother, achieving, he says, two things at once: 'I identified my enemies and created a scandal' (Fanon [1952] 1986, 86) – or to claim independent mastery. That this involves the explicit adoption of Nietzschean nobility becomes apparent at the end of the final chapter 'Recognition and the Black' where Fanon concludes, 'The action of the human is not only reactive. There is always ressentiment in a *reaction*. Nietzsche, in the *Will to Power*, had already warned us' (Fanon [1952] 1986, 173, modified).

This Nietzschean refusal of recognition and the realization that any meeting with white was a battlefield casts a new light on a controversial argument from Fanon's *Year Five of the Algerian Revolution*. It concerns the veil, which Fanon distances from the mask in that it is both a symbol of enmity and the refusal of recognition. Reflecting on the colonial obsession with the veil and unveiling in the chapter 'Algeria Unveils Itself', Fanon observes of the colonial imaginary that 'To unveil this woman, to expose the beauty, to reveal its secret, break its resistance, make it available for an adventure. To hide the face is to conceal a secret, it is to bring into existence a world of mystery and of the hidden ... This woman who sees without being seen frustrates the colonialist. There is no reciprocity. She does not offer or give herself' (Fanon [1959] 2011, 280). This is the refusal to enter into the struggle for recognition intimated in *Black Skin, White Masks*, but it is certainly controversial – for it brings Fanon to the conclusion that 'With every abandoned veil Algerian society seems to accept the tutelage of the master and to change their habits under the patronage of the occupant' (Fanon [1959] 2011, 280). This seems a conservative anti-feminist position, but listen to the *seems*: 'semble accepter'. What will emerge is that for Fanon, what is important is to refuse recognition, either by the veil or by the strategy of *dissembling* entry into the struggle for recognition.

> The veil lifted and then replaced, the veil instrumentalized, transformed into a technique of camouflage, a means of struggle. The almost taboo character of the veil in the colonial situation almost completely disappears in the struggle for liberation. Even Algerian women not actively involved in the struggle adopt the custom of abandoning the veil, although it is true that in certain circumstances the veil reappears ... By now the adversary knows – some militants have spoken under torture, that women apparently very Europeanized play a fundamental role in the battle ... there is disarray among the adversary as they see their own *dispositif* collapse. (Fanon [1959] 2011, 296)

The veil becomes a mask while remaining a veil or is a veil by virtue of assuming the qualities of a mask, refusing recognition while seeming to offer it. The veil is indeed described by Fanon as a second skin, second *peau*, and if carried to the black skin it is adopted as if a mask but in fact is a refusal to enter the scenario of recognition.

With this we have clearly departed from the scenario of the mask, for the veil is not a *prosopon*, person, or theatrical mask but a *gorgoneion*. It is an argument subsequently developed for the case of female suicide bombers by Adriana Cavarero in her *Horrorism* (2007); she suggests that this is a practice of dissemblance founded in absolute hostility and the refusal of recognition. It is a position beyond the mask that Fanon was the first to explore at length and for which there are ever new reasons to understand better and to return to Fanon for help in doing so.

28

The spirit of resistance
and its fate

What place does resistance (*Widerstand*) occupy in the Hegelian system? According to the *letter* of Hegel's work, a very specific and limited one, confined to the analysis of the play of forces and the laws of mechanism. Yet the *spirit* of resistance – technically inadmissible given the external character of the mechanical relation – is barely contained within these confines. It is the elusive motor of the section on 'Force and the Understanding' in the *Phenomenology of Spirit* and serves to vivify the formal definition of resistance presented in the *Science of Logic*. These episodes point beyond themselves to a larger and perhaps not fully recognized spirit of resistance at work throughout Hegel's system. They testify to another force at work, one that resists the mise en scène of *Aufhebung* that casts the absolute alongside freedom and the infinite in a drama of speculation. For while Hegelian resistance always appears on the stage of finite opposition, restricted to an apparently minor role in the Newtonian opposition of mechanical forces, it consistently points beyond mechanism and the external opposition of forces to a thinking of actuality that intractably recoils from any pretention to think the absolute.

The episode 'Force and the Understanding' in the *Phenomenology of Spirit* is well known as the transition from consciousness to self-consciousness but is perhaps not properly recognized as a meditation upon resistance, with implications pointing beyond the opposition of forces that characterize the laws of mechanics. It shows Hegel appealing to infinity as a *deus ex machina* in order to break out of the opposition of resistance and counter-resistance working itself through the play of active and reactive force. It also obscurely indicates the reason for this appeal, which is the need to move from the modal posture of actuality to those of possibility and necessity. This movement is revealed as the *telos* of the chapter of mechanism in the *Science of Logic* that, moving from force to law, arrives at an explicit declaration of 'free necessity'. It is here that Hegel states his formal definition of resistance, in the first chapter of the second section, on 'Objectivity', of the 'Subjective Logic or the Doctrine of the Notion' in the *Science of Logic*.[1] Although located in a seemingly remote and little-studied section of the *Science of Logic*, the definition has a number of properties that point beyond the understanding of resistance as an aspect of the spiritless 'external relation' that usually characterizes the 'mechanical' in Hegel. Prominent among these is Hegel's use of a vocabulary of violence (*Gewalt*), power (*Macht*) and fate (*Schicksal*) that clearly points beyond the discussion of physical mechanism.

In both cases, resistance is revealed in the process of its suppression, accomplished in the departure from the modal stance of actuality to an alliance of necessity and freedom. There remains, however, a lingering suspicion that this fate of resistance is ordained externally, that the move from the actual opposition of forces that constitutes resistance to a self-legislating *revolutionary* subject/substance is the outcome of a prior decision. The elusive and equivocal manifestations of resistance in Hegel's major works may be traced to this decision, which orders the overcoming and suppression of resistance. While it is largely taken for granted in the relegation of resistance to mechanism, the origins of this decision can be traced to his early writings on Christianity, the matrix of Hegel's thought, where the theme of resistance arises at crucial moments of argumentative decision offering an alternative or supplement to the nascent speculative dialectic.

Hegel's early writings on classical culture, Judaism and Christianity attest not only to the presence of a spirit of resistance in his work but also allow a reassessment of its place in the system. Is it the fate of resistance to become a moment successfully surpassed by speculative dialectic – as seems Hegel's intent when he locates it in the discussions of mechanism and thus denies it both spirit and fate – or does it resist, remain to trouble and develop a certain immunity to dialectical capture? Can the possibility be excluded, even within the system, that spirit is necessarily resistant, that it is always the spirit of resistance and as such the fundamental, unsurpassable but suppressed condition of the freedom, infinity and thought of the absolute widely thought to condition and exceed it? Should this seem remotely plausible, then the actuality of resistance threatens to disrupt any actualizing of the alliance of freedom and necessity by means of the infinite that is the destiny of the system. The ambivalent attempts to force resistance into the confines of the discussions of mechanism evident in 'Force and the Understanding' and the definition in the *Science of Logic* then assume a new significance as evidence for the spirit and the fate of resistance under the hostile regime of speculation.[2]

The force of resistance

The section 'Force and the Understanding' seems to mark a crucial transition from 'Consciousness' to 'Self-Consciousness' in the *Phenomenology of Spirit* but also serves to consign the claims of force and law to the outer limits of consciousness, thus clearing the way for an untroubled move to self-consciousness. Hegel tilts the argument in his favour at the outset by situating force within the 'unconditioned universal', which will contain both active and reactive force and which almost by definition allows him to see 'the passivity that is a being for another' and the 'being for self ' as 'essentially self-superseding aspects' posited in their mutual transition (*PS* 81). For the latter is effectively a declaration – at the outset of the discussion of force – of the dissolution of resistance. Although unnamed, resistance remains at stake throughout Hegel's description of the acrobatics of force: it is 'posited as one' and then expresses itself when solicited by an external 'other' that turns out to have always been force itself. These movements describe the workings of a resistance that is constituted as a 'universal medium' in which active and reactive forces appear as 'vanishing moments' (*PS* 83). When Hegel writes that 'the interplay of the two forces thus consists in their being determined as mutually opposed, in their being for one another in this determination' (*PS* 84), this could stand as a definition of resistance and indeed leads with little transition to a deduction of the actuality of force. However, unlike his contemporary Clausewitz, who elaborated this actuality into a philosophy of war as resistance, Hegel seeks to overcome it by dissolving resistance in order to make room for the alliance of necessity and freedom made possible by the notion of the infinite.

The movement beyond the play of resistant forces requires the prior disabling of resistance, and so the 'truth of force' in the thought of force is cast as a transition from force to law: 'the moments of [force's] actuality, their substance and their movement, collapse unresistingly into an undifferentiated unity, a unity which is not force driven back into itself (for this is only such a moment), but its *Notion qua Notion*' (*PS* 86). The suspension of resistance is peremptory, to say the least, but it is necessary to convert force as the source of law into force as its servant. Hegel is hastening the passage to self-consciousness – force and its resistance are but the 'developed negative' whose truth is 'the positive, viz. the *universal*, the object that, *in itself*, possesses being' (*PS* 87). Of course, positivity is as problematic a category as the negative in Hegel and will take us to the abstract opposition of the sensuous and supersensible worlds, but what is most important for him at this point is to leave behind the scenario of the resistant and reciprocally determining forces that make up actuality. In their place emerges the force of law and resistance to the law. And although resistant force returns, it comes only to offer a show of resistance, for the reciprocal and unresolvable force of actual resistance is purged and replaced by a law of force or the 'difference which remains constantly selfsame' (PS 96). The actuality of resistant force is translated into the world and its inversion (Verkehrung) – action in the former is reaction in the latter, where reaction is already action. Resistance in the finite world of actuality here metamorphoses into a distinction between this world and its inversion.

Hegel's examples of this process of inversion range from the opposition of sweet and sour, black and white, positive and negative, magnetic and electrical charges, to vengeance and punishment. But what is most important is that these differences are not mere opposites but stand in a dynamic relation to each other: 'a repulsion of the selfsame from itself, and likeness of the unlike as unlike' (PS 99). Hegel understands this dynamic in terms of the Fichtean Anstoß, translated by Miller as repulsion, but rather than showing that anstoßen is a mode of resistance – negation appearing as position or what is described immediately after as the 'opposite of an opposite' – Hegel suddenly suspends it in the 'absolute notion'. While he intimates the complex topology of resistance as both active and reactive force – 'it is itself and its opposite in one unity' (PS 99) – this description leads not to further reflection on the peculiar properties of resistance but to an upward gaze into infinity. This infinity is far from innocent, since it becomes the means through which 'law completes itself into an immanent necessity' (PS 99); it effectively brokers the transition from the actuality of opposed force to the necessity of law. Hegel then presents properties of resistance as if they were properties of the infinite: the duplication of force that follows from 'the selfsame which repels itself from itself or sunders itself into two' characteristic of actual resistance is infinitized and converted into the necessity of law. In this way, resistance or the doubling of force into action and reaction is stabilized and brought under law, while preserving the possibility that the differences 'can stimulate each other into activity' (PS 99), a stimulus without which everything would grind to a law-abiding halt.

The beautiful but suspiciously rhetorical apostrophe to infinity that immediately follows in 'Force and the Understanding' seems designed to disarm any suspicion that this was always and already the pre-intended destination of the argument: 'This simple infinity, or the absolute notion, may be called the simple essence of life, the soul of the world, the universal blood, whose omnipresence is neither disturbed not interrupted by any difference, but rather is itself every difference, as also their supersession; it pulsates within itself but does not move, vibrates, yet is at rest' (PS 100). Once Hegel is sure that the infinite has filled the field of vision, distracting both natural and philosophical consciousness, he can admit that it had always been there from the start. This principle of method, however, conceals a prior and unthematized decision to move from the actuality of force and resistance to the infinite and the absolute notion. Yet the move from actuality to necessity does not convincingly establish its own necessity. In a key sentence without which the entire phenomenological movement would stall, Hegel writes: 'Appearance, or the play of forces, already displays it [infinity] [*stellt sie selbst schon da*] but it is as explanation that it first freely stands forth; and in being finally an object of consciousness, *as that which it is*, consciousness is thus *self-consciousness*' (*PS* 101). But perhaps it is 'already' there because Hegel took a decision to plant it in advance. The resistance or 'unrest of pure self-movement' does not have to be infinite in order to disturb fixed determinations, nor must the transition to self-consciousness pass ineluctably through infinity. The passage to self-consciousness can be effected from within actuality through the movements of resistance and counter-resistance – there is no inherent necessity to proceed to the infinite. The passage through infinity is required only in order to effect a change in modality, to move from actuality to necessity and ultimately (although this is not explicitly stated in 'Force and the Understanding') to the 'free necessity' of the *Logic*. For as Hegel provisionally concludes, the movement through which law posits unified force and force a unified law is 'necessity'.

Resistance is implied and denied throughout 'Force and the Understanding'. It appears within the actuality of force with active and reactive force each resisting the other. It can also be glimpsed in the relation between law and force, with law anticipating the resistance of the individual and the individual that of law. But the constitutive and unsurpassable role played by resistance is occluded by the appeal to the infinite. The infinite serves to convert actuality into necessity (and later in the progress of the *Phenomenology of Spirit* into possibility, for the infinite is a property of the idea of freedom). However, the relationship between resistance and the infinite remains unanalysed, perhaps because of an assumed imperative to derive the necessity of law from freedom, a movement alien to resistance and its place in the actuality of opposed forces.[3]

Resistance and 'free necessity' in the
Science of Logic

In contrast to 'Force and the Understanding', where the properties of actual resistant forces are surreptitiously transferred to the infinite, the *Science of Logic* is altogether more explicit. It not only proposes a formal definition of *Widerstand* but also explicitly declares its overcoming in a new actuality of revolutionary self-legislation or 'free necessity'. The discussion is located in the chapter on 'Mechanism', the inconspicuous heart of the 'Logic of the Notion' following the logics of Being and Essence.[4] It is to be found in the centre of the section on 'Objectivity', which follows 'Subjectivity' and precedes 'The Idea', as a part of the section on 'The Mechanical Process' framed by 'The Mechanical Object' and 'Absolute Mechanism'. It there forms part of 'The Real Mechanical Process' between 'The Formal Mechanical Process' and 'The Product of the Mechanical Process'. It is thus to be found at the centre of the most highly mediated account of immediacy to be found in the entire *Science of Logic*. This crucial but seemingly remote systemic location is at the extreme limit of the inextricable nexus of immediacy and mediacy pursued throughout the *Science of Logic*. It is an extreme point where the familiar distinctions of subject, object and relation almost lose all their purchase; resistance, in short, explicitly appears at the extreme limit of the *Logic* as both an outcome and condition to be surpassed. This may account for the extreme volatility of the definition and the formulations that prepare and succeed it but also for the critical role played by resistance in sustaining the movement out of mediated immediacy towards life and the absolute idea with which the *Science of Logic* closes.[5]

The chapter on mechanism departs from a 'mediation that has collapsed into immediate identity' (*SL* 712) and that leads to the contradiction (*Widerspruch*) between 'the complete mutual *indifference* of the objects and the *identity* of their *determinateness* or the contradiction of their complete *externality* in the *identity* of their determinateness' (*SL* 714). We are in the realm of external mechanical relation, where objects are both indifferent to other objects and yet bound to them by force and law. Yet, and consistent with the phenomenological method of the *Science of Logic*, this is only in appearance, since 'theoretical or practical mechanism cannot take place without its self-activity, without an impulse and consciousness, yet there is lacking in it the freedom of individuality, and because this freedom is not manifest in it such action appears as a merely external one' (*SL* 711). The transition in this sentence, however, is effected with great haste, since mechanical externality is derived from the *absence* of freedom without any prior evidence for freedom being necessarily present at the outset. The claim that the co-appearance of immediacy and mediacy discloses an immanent process that disrupts immediacy, a process figured in terms of the monad that is immediate and closed upon itself ('windowless') but also open to and limited by others through mirroring and other mechanical operations, coheres without any reference to the postulate of freedom. In the section on 'The Formal Mechanical Process' this immediate mediacy is figured in terms of *Mitteilung* or communication, but it is one accomplished *freely*, or more precisely, *without resistance*: '*Spiritual communication*, which moreover takes place within that element which is the universal in the form of universality, is explicitly an ideal relation in which *a determinateness continues* itself from one person into another unimpaired, and universalizes itself without any alternation whatever

– as a scent freely spreads in the unresisting atmosphere (*widerstandlosen Atmosphäre*)' (*SL* 716). This mediated immediacy is characterized less by the presence of freedom than by the absence of resistance, its relegation from any involvement with spirit, but it risks bringing everything to a halt in an atmosphere of fragrant immediacy.

The absence of resistance is indeed constitutive of the perfumed repose or perpetual peace of the untroubled immediate universal that Hegel conjures up for us at this point of the *Science of Logic*. Yet this mechanical utopia of the senses is destined to be overcome, leaving only a trace of the scent of absolute knowing, but the fantasy of an actuality from which resistance has withdrawn will be carried over into subsequent moments, always under the unproved assumption that absence of resistance equates with the presence of freedom. Hegel executes this movement in 'The Formal Mechanical Process' in terms of the 'universal in and for itself' or the '*objective* as such' (*SL* 716). This state of absorption by the universal is found 'both in the spiritual and in the material sphere; against which the individuality of outer objects as well as of persons is an unessential element that can offer it no resistance (*das ihm kein Widerstand leisten kann*)' (*SL* 716). The universal as medium is constituted by the absence of resistance in both its spiritual and material aspects. Hegel continues to extend his argument from the realm of nature to that of spirit proper: 'Laws, morals, rational conceptions in general, are in the spiritual sphere such communicable entities which penetrate individuals in an unconscious manner and exert their influence on them. In the material sphere the communicable entities are motion, heat, magnetism, electricity and the like' (*SL* 716). In these cases, individuals are absorbed into their mediums as particulars, a movement he describes in terms of two processes – 'the raising of the individual determinateness into universality in communication, and the particularization of it, or the reduction of what was solely a one to a species, in distribution, [that] are one and the same' (*SL* 717). In both cases what occurs is a neutralization of resistance, one that should be distinguished rigorously from its successful supersession.

The distinction between the neutralization of resistance – achieving *Widerstandslosigkeit* – and its overcoming or sublation is critical for Hegel's view of the universal as medium that is developed in the following section of the *System of Logic*, on 'The Real Mechanical Process'. In the immediate run-up to the definition of resistance, Hegel attempts to describe the actuality of resistance in terms of the external relations between objects arrested in a universal medium. Absorbed in the medium, individual objects nevertheless discover 'a *self-subsistence* that is *impenetrable self-subsistence* for other objects'; it is one that leads to 'this more specific opposition of *self-subsistent individuality* and a universal that lacks *self-subsistence*' (*SL* 719). The last steps towards the definition of the resistance that now seems to be emerging between objects in the decaying universal medium pass by way of the real mechanical process of communication. This is no longer governed by the universal medium, but rather through inequalities arising between objects defined by their degree of 'self-subsistence'. However, these inequalities are not simply defined in terms of mutual resistance but also provide the terms through which resistance will come to be defined; resistance, in short, has the important property of appearing as at once prior and posterior to its actions.[6]

In his description of the real mechanical process, Hegel works with a distinction between a resistance of strength and one of weakness, seeing the latter, paradoxically, as being more effective. The weaker can only communicate with the stronger if it enters into a common sphere or medium of communication with it: 'The *weaker* can be seized and penetrated by the *stronger* only in so far as it accepts the latter and constitutes one sphere with it' (*SL* 719). Once within this sphere or shared medium it can of course engage in resistance, but this presumes a prior failure of resistance to even entering the shared sphere in the first place. The prior resistance is explored through a series of analogies ranging from ballistics to zoology:

> Just as in the material sphere the weak is secured against the disproportionately strong (as a sheet hanging free in the air is not pierced by a musket ball, or a weak organic receptivity is less susceptible to strong, than to weak, stimuli), so the wholly feeble spirit is safer from the strong spirit than one that stands nearer to the strong. Imagine if you like someone quite dull-witted and ignoble, then on such a person lofty intelligence and nobility can make no impression. The only consistent defence *against* reason is to have no dealings with it at all. Where the object that is not self-subsistent cannot make contact with one that is and no communication can take place between them, the latter can also offer no *resistance*, that is, cannot specify the communicated universal for itself. (*SL* 719)

The resistance of the weak seems to yield a paradox rather than material for supersession. But as will become evident in Hegel's controversial reading of the 'fate' of Judaism, such resistance to 'communication' with self-subsistent others is not without its risks, and prior resistance can as easily fall to its fate as rise to dialectical supersession.

The resistance of the weak consists in not entering into a common medium or sphere with the stronger, thus neutralizing the strength of the stronger by not, in so many words, engaging in a battle of recognition but in refusing any shared ground or recognition. The bullet cannot penetrate the sheet that resists by refusing to resist it; the weak in spirit are oblivious to the strength of the stronger and thus resist them more effectively than if they tried to be as strong or stronger; and the object that is not self-subsistent resists the self-subsistent not on the terrain of self-subsistency but by refusing to enter that terrain. For the self-subsistent, in the face of the indifference of the former, is defenceless and can offer no resistance to the latter's absence of resistance.

Not only the ancient Hebrews participated in the prior resistance of refusing to enter a shared terrain of resistance and struggle. The Gandhian, originally Christian, practice of *ahimsa* or non-violence relies on the power of the weak to resist through the refusal to participate in resistance on the oppressor's terms. This is clearly intimated in Hegel's discussion of the Sermon on the Mount and his view of Jesus's refusal to resist particular laws as a general indifference to law. Hegel regards resistance to law as opposed to resistance within the law as one of the origins of the resistance he examined earlier in terms of the Christian refusal to lend recognition to the Roman Empire. Confronting the paradox of a resistance all the more powerful for not engaging in a struggle for recognition on a shared terrain finally brings him to his attempt to contrive a formal definition of resistance.

Hegel formally defines resistance as 'the precise moment of the overpowering [*Überwältigung*] of the one object by the other, for it is the incipient moment of the distribution of the communicated universal and of the positing of the self-related negativity, of the individuality to be established' (*SL* 720). Resistance is here described in terms of an object overpowering the resistance of the other in two steps, first by means of bringing it into a common sphere and then vanquishing it according to the terms of the common sphere. Hegel then reiterates the claim that such 'resistance is itself overpowered' when the other object refuses to enter the proffered common sphere, 'where the determinateness of the object is inadequate to the communicated universal that has been taken up by the object and is supposed to individualize itself within it' (*SL* 720). Hegel returns to the resistance that is prior to the resistance provoked by a struggle for recognition: 'The object's relative lack of self-subsistence manifests itself in the fact that its *individuality* lacks the *capacity* for what is *communicated* and therefore is disrupted by it, because it cannot constitute itself as a subject in this universal, or make this latter its predicate' (*SL* 720). Here, resistance appears in the guise of both the object that resists becoming a subject – the sheet with respect to the bullet – and a subject resisting another subject in terms of a shared universal medium. Hegel then reaffirms that there is a resistance that is prior to and perhaps a condition of the second or posterior resistance posed in terms of the shared universal.

At this point, Hegel's lexicon undergoes drastic change as his discussion tips into one of violence and power – *Gewalt* and *Macht*. When an 'object' can or will not assume the shared universal and be constituted as a 'subject' on its terms then violence will be exercised upon it as 'something alien [*fremdes*] to it' (*SL* 720). Violence (*Gewalt*) is thus associated with the first or prior resistance. Power (*Macht*) on the other hand is exercised when an object enters the universal medium, when it is able to constitute itself as a subject for another subject; if it remains outside or is excluded from the universal medium – characterized, it should be remembered, by reciprocity and recognition – then *Macht* will mutate into *Gewalt*. This is in no respect an *Aufhebung*, but rather what Hegel describes as an immediate or more specifically an unreflected negativity: 'What turns power (*Macht*) into *violence* (*Gewalt*) is this, that though power, an objective universality, is *identical* with the *nature* of the object, its determinateness or negativity is not its own *negative reflection* into itself by which it is an individual' (*SL* 720). For Hegel, resistance to power *within* the universal medium is formative; it leads to a determinate negation that constitutes the resistant as a subject. This formative or constitutional resistance is conducted legally in terms of the universal – the previously cited objective universality of 'laws, morals, rational conceptions in general' (*SL* 716). Resistance to power from outside the objective universal is no longer a question of power or the struggle for and within power, but violence, and for Hegel this violence does not issue in a formative struggle or reflected negation that can effect the emergence of a (political) subject, but only in annihilation – it can have no result: 'In so far as the negativity of the object is not reflected into itself in the power, and the power is not the object's own self-relation, it is, as against the power, only *abstract* negativity whose manifestation is extinction' (*SL* 720). If the resistant refuses to accept what would later be termed by Max Weber, in a tacit return to Kant, the *legitimacy* of power and refuses to participate in legitimate resistance, then it is literally outside the pale of law, morals and rationality and will encounter them as a violence dedicated to its annihilation.

Hegel begins the following paragraph by defining the distinction between power and violence as fate: 'Power, as *objective universality* and as violence directed *against* the object, what is called *fate*' (*SL* 720). Fate is a subjection to violence unique to self-conscious beings; beings without self-consciousness 'have no fate; what befalls them is a contingency … the alien power of fate is nothing but their own *immediate nature*, externality and contingency itself' (*SL* 720). Fate, however, belongs to self-conscious beings who refuse to be contained by and to act according to the structures of recognition of power and, by thus refusing, expose themselves to its violence. Hegel sets himself to arguing that self-conscious beings are capable of ceasing to be the objects of fate and of becoming its subject by entering into the objective medium of power. Resistance to power in order to avoid the descent into violence must ultimately enter into complicity and become subject to that power. Resistance to the law, morals and reason must become legal, moral and rational resistance. Hegel's first argumentative step towards this conclusion is to show that resistance to power always already implies a relation to power and that resistance is a mode of this relation: 'Only self-consciousness has a fate in the proper meaning of the word, because it is *free* and therefore in the *individuality* of its ego possesses a being that is absolutely *in and for itself* and can oppose itself to the objective universal and *estrange* itself from it' (*SL* 720). The estrangement can be relative or absolute – it can remain consistent with the objective universal even while resisting it, in which case it is complicit with the exercise of power or it absolutely estranges itself from the objective universal and enters the realm of violence.

Hegel is sceptical about the possibility of a sustained absolute estrangement, since he accepts the essentially reactive posture of resistance. The resistant deed contains within it a recognition – at whatever extreme of negativity – of the 'objective universal' it combats. Hegel tries to imagine the absolute (passive) resistance of a 'people without deeds' (*SL* 721) but concludes that such a people would not be a resistant subject, but purely actual, an object 'without blame' because freedom is not an issue for it. This thought heralds the concluding section of the chapter on 'Absolute Mechanism', which almost exclusively focuses on the resistant power immanent to a structure of recognition and overlooks the resistant violence opposed to the entire structure as such. In the context of power and recognition fate becomes 'rational' or freely chosen, a 'universal that particularizes itself from within' (*SL* 721). As intimated in 'Force and the Understanding', rational fate is in fact law, and from this point forward resistance is always within the law and no longer resistance to law as such. And, as in 'Force and the Understanding', this step corresponds to a modal shift, there to necessity but here to an explicit, freely determined necessity.

Hegel frames his description with reference to the solar system and its heliocentric disposition of forces. Resistance is not so much between individuals – by analogy the planets – as between individuals and the 'centre' or, by analogy, the planets and the sun. Subjection to the law of the centre – in terms of the analogy it is the planets subject to the laws of the sun's gravity – is now the given state of the mechanical system, and 'friction, or whatever other form resistance takes, is only a phenomenon of *centrality*' (*SL* 722). It is a phenomenon that is both mechanical and physical as well as 'spiritual' and which concerns the subjection of the individual within the 'universal power' (there is no longer any talk of resistant violence) of the centre. The centre is explicitly identified with 'government' to which the singulars or 'individual citizens' are subjected, thus 'transposing their ethical essence into the extreme of actuality' (*SL* 724). What is actualized is the relation between the centre and the singulars, one that is expressed in the law which will later be presented as the product of freedom. Also implicated in this are the needs of the citizens: these are not satisfied by mere private exchange relations by property owners in a market, but within the 'universal absolute individuality' of the relation between government and citizens. Hegel then takes the final step that supposedly breaks with mechanism, which is to ground the necessity of the external law that orders particulars in freedom. Freedom is the 'imperishable source of self-kindling movement', and since 'in the ideality of its difference' it has no interest in other differences, it 'relates itself to itself alone, it is *free necessity*' (*SL* 725).

The definition of resistance in the *Science of Logic* travels far from its beginnings as an absolute resistance to any recognition to a resistance within an accepted or legitimate structure. The resistance of violence is surrendered for a resistance of power that accepts to work and struggle, while respecting a given legal structure. This change in the character of resistance is accomplished by moving from the actuality of the first resistance to the actualization of an alliance between freedom and necessity accomplished through 'legitimate' resistance. Yet, as in 'Force and the Understanding', the preference given to the second mode of resistance seems to be the outcome of a prior decision to contain the actuality of resistance within the possibilities and necessities of self-legislating freedom. Putting this decision itself into question – querying the preference given to freedom and law – would be to put into question the suppression of resistance critical for Hegel's wider speculative project.

Hegel's matrix of resistance

The 1796–7 fragment 'The Earliest System-Programme of German Idealism' calls for a rebirth of physics, according to the question of 'how must a world be constituted for a moral being?' (Hegel 2002, 110). Yet this physics will not be a mechanics of opposed forces, neither for the natural nor civil worlds. The author takes distance from both a mechanics of nature and a mechanics of the state – since 'the state is a mechanical thing' – by proposing that 'only something that is an object of freedom is called an idea' (Hegel 2002, 110). The author will expose 'the whole wretched human work of state, constitution, government, legal system – naked to the skin' (Hegel 2002, 111). Yet, with this programmatic leap from physics to the idea of freedom, the realm of opposed forces is abandoned in favour of a 'new mythology' capable of uniting sensibility and reason, enlightened and unenlightened, people and philosophers. The project of 'giving wings' to physics becomes one of escaping a 'mechanics' of force and reactualizing nature and the moral world in an aesthetic philosophy or mythology. Here, indeed, we see one of the first formulations of the decision to abandon the world of opposed and resistant forces for a world transformed by the idea of freedom, one to be repeated with elaborations throughout the *Phenomenology of Spirit* and the *Science of Logic*.

The decision was more than the reassertion of the Kantian primacy of practical reason in which it seems to be framed. In fact, Hegel had been moving steadily away from the Kantian gesture through his philosophical reflections on the Old and New Testaments that make up his so-called *Early Theological Writings*. In the final expressions of a project that occupied him throughout the 1790s, 'The Spirit of Christianity and Its Fate' (1798–1800) and the third part or rewrite of the earlier 'The Positivity of the Christian Religion' (1800), Hegel explores a complex set of relations between the physics of force, mechanism and the idea. These meditations upon the spirits and fates of Judaism and Christianity are indeed elaborate variations on the theme of resistance and its character, limits and consequences. Among the most salient of these is Hegel's repeated view that the fate of the monotheistic spirit of Judaism is *mechanism* and the *mechanical* which, in his eyes, condemn it to perpetual, futile if not self-destructive resistance.

This is apparent throughout Hegel's extended reflections on early Judaism. There can be little dispute about the limited and unsympathetic character of Hegel's understanding of Ancient Judaism in these fragments, but the prominence of the theme of resistance in both the spirit and the fate of Judaism is one of its striking but little-appreciated features. 'The Spirit of Christianity and Its Fate' indeed begins by placing Abraham's creative act of the forging of the 'spirit and fate' of 'his posterity' in a context of fierce military and cultural resistance: 'This spirit appears in a different guise after every one of its battles against different forces or after becoming sullied by adopting an alien nature as a result of succumbing to might or seduction' (*ETW* 182). The spirit emerges through resistance to external forces and eventually succumbs to its fate, in opposition to internal forces that it is incapable of effectively resisting.

After placing the invention of spirit firmly in the context of resistance, Hegel moves immediately to consider a primal act of resistance mounted against the hostility of nature. According to him, the catastrophe of the Flood provoked 'deep distraction' and 'prodigious disbelief in nature' for its contemporaries, including Noah. Nature became an enemy to be resisted: 'If man was to hold out against the outbursts of a nature now hostile, nature had to be mastered; and since the whole can be divided only into idea and reality so also the supreme unity of mastery lies in something thought or something real' (*ETW* 182–3). Hegel then explores three strategies of resistance to inimical nature. The first is the creation of the ideal command through law and self-mastery initiated by Noah and, as we shall see, developed further by Abraham. The second is the unabashedly violent resistance to God and nature mounted by the figure of Nimrod:

> He endeavoured so far to master nature that it could no longer be dangerous to men. He put himself in a state of defence (*Verteidigungszustand*) against it … In the event of God's having a mind to overwhelm the world with a

flood again, he threatened to neglect no means and no power to make an adequate resistance (*genugsames Widerstand*) to him.

In an anticipation of contemporary geo-engineering projects, Nimrod proposed to build a tower that would defeat the floods: 'He defended himself against water by walls; he was a hunter and a king. In this battle against need, therefore, the elements, animals, and men had to endure the law of the stronger, though a living being' (*ETW* 183). The spirit of resistance inaugurated by Nimrod confronted violence (*Gewalt*) with violence, leading, in Hegel's eyes, to fateful tyranny and the open contest of inimical forces.

Hegel then contrasts Noah and Nimrod.[7] The first responded to an inimical power (nature) by 'subjecting both it and himself to something more powerful', to a transcendent God, master of both nature and humans. For Hegel, this is the inaugural gesture of the spirit of Judaism, whose fate was to reduce both nature and humanity to objects of divine command against which there could be little resistance. Nimrod on the other hand sought to tame both God and nature through human powers. Hegel classes both Noah and Nimrod as having made 'a peace with necessity and thus perpetuated the hostility' (*ETW* 183). Both are expressions of incomplete resistance whose strategy contrasted with that of Deucalion and Pyrrha in the Greek myth of the Flood, who after the flood 'invited men once again to friendship with the world, to nature, made them forget their need and hostility in joy and pleasure, made a peace of love, and were the progenitors of more beautiful peoples' (*ETW* 184). In this inaugural moment for Hegel's thought, three possible spirits and fates appear beside each other – two spirits of resistance, one of the covenant and one of sustained resistant enmity – and a third spirit of reconciliation, love and friendship.

Hegel immediately follows this discussion with an account of Abraham and the development of the spirit of Judaism out of Noah. In the remainder of these fragments – and programmatically for his work as a whole – Hegel will set the fate of Judaism against the spirit of love and friendship initiated for Greek culture by Deucalion and Pyrrha. Yet, although the specific history of the spirit and fate of resistance inaugurated by Nimrod ends with these few opening lines of 'The Spirit of Christianity and Its Fate', it of course persists but is always repressed and hardly ever given open expression. In a sense, the explicit hostility of Nimrod becomes the fate of Judaism, buried in the 'peace of necessity' of the covenants with God, first Noah's and then Abraham's. Hegel's extended exposition of the spirit of Judaism is dedicated to showing how the fate of a disowned resistance repeatedly returned in destructive forms; even after the leadership of Moses and the attainment of the Promised Land, the Jews remained 'subjected to the fate against which their nomadic ancestors had so long struggled, a struggle and a resistance in the course of which they had only increasingly embittered their own and the national genius' (*ETW* 194). Hegel sees in the spirit and fate of Judaism the outcome of a disowned resistance, one that for him led to increasing separation and an attempt to govern individual and collective life by mechanical conformity to external command.

Instead of returning to Nimrod and exploring the suppressed spirit of resistance, Hegel rigorously sets himself to exploring the contrast between the spirit and fate of Judaism and Greece. In this exploration, the figure of Jesus is crucial as an attempt to transcend the fate of Judaism towards reconciliation, love and friendship. Although he showed how the spirit of Christianity – universal love and freedom – would be diverted by the fate of Judaism, he considered it to remain a work in progress even to his day and even in the texts he was writing. Yet there was no explicit place in this debate for the spirit of resistance, even though it remained powerfully present. It returns towards the end of 'The Spirit of Christianity and Its Fate' when Hegel reflects on the resistance to fate: 'If a man fights for what is in danger, he has not lost what he is struggling for; but by facing danger he has subjected himself to fate, for he enters on the battlefield of might against might and ventures to oppose his adversary' (*ETW* 233–4). Hegel even contemplates the possibility that the clash of aggressive and resistant forces may never be resolved, that there is only ever an actuality of resistance:

> For even in the struggle for right there is a contradiction; the right is something thought, a universal, while in the aggressor it is also a thought, though a different one, hence there would be here two universals which would cancel each other out, and yet they persist. Similarly the combatants are opposed as real entities, different living beings; life is in conflict with life, which once again is a self-contradiction. (*ETW* 234)

The outcome remains undecided, left either to superior power or to arbitration (the covenant); in both cases, however, the resistance remains even if there has been a renunciation of 'their own mastery of actuality' (*ETW* 234). Yet it is hard to see how Hegel's own solution, the turn to freedom and love and later the infinite, does not also involve some renunciation of the 'mastery of actuality'. The idea that fate could be evaded appears too sudden, as in the sentence: 'A man would be entangled in a fate by another's deed if he picked up the gauntlet and insisted on his right against the transgressor; but this fate is turned aside if he surrenders the right and clings to love' (*ETW* 238). The question remains, however, of whether this 'clinging to love' does not remain a form of resistance, perhaps even a devastatingly effective one, as Ghandi would teach. This question seems to be one of the motivations for Hegel's reflections on Jesus and the question of how far he distanced himself from the spirits of Judaism and resistance.

These questions are explored most consummately in the 1800 rewrite of the earlier 'Positivity of the Christian Religion'. Hegel begins by rehearsing his view that the Jewish people were constituted negatively by their resistance to any contact with surrounding peoples, refusing in the spirit of resistance to enter into relations of mutual recognition with them. Yet such relations were in fact irresistible: 'Multiple relations with others were imposed on it by the situation of its small country, by trade connections, and by the national unifications brought about by the Romans.' Hegel describes the predicament of the Jewish people in terms of 'their mania for segregation' and their 'inability to resist (*nicht Widerstehen können*) political subjection and effective linkage with the foreigner' (*ETW* 178). In what we have seen Hegel subsequently describe as a prior resistance or refusal to enter into a structure of recognition, the Jewish people, for him, exposed themselves to the annihilatory violence of Rome at the same time as developing a loveless and spiritless mechanism based on their resistance to their others (*ETW* 188). Jewish religious practices are described as 'mechanical', driven and shaped by a resistance to external power that in its turn provoked a wide variety of counter-resistances – the Sadducees, the Essenes, Messianic movements and of course the figure of Jesus.

Jesus is described by Hegel as resisting the mechanical spirit of Judaism in the name of the universality of love. For Hegel, his Gospel was an ambivalent fusion of a violent distantiation from Judaism, resisting it by refusing to resist, and a specific engagement with its structures of recognition or discrete laws. In any case, Hegel emphasizes Jesus's own surprise at the 'resistance [*Widerstand*] offered him by the rooted prejudices of his people' (*ETW* 179). One of the most insidious of these, in Hegel's view, is the conversion of his Gospel by his followers into a doctrine or set of commands – for him it is as if the spirit of Christianity was delivered to the fate of Judaism: 'Out of what Jesus said, out of what he suffered in his person, they soon fashioned rules and moral commands, and free emulation of the teacher soon passed over into slavish service of their Lord' (*ETW* 179). Hegel believes that Jesus's specific resistance to aspects of the law were themselves interpreted as commands. For this reason, the Sermon on the Mount was especially important to him as a resistance to law itself rather than particular laws; this resistance that was also indifference could not be commanded:

The whole sermon ends with the attempt to display the picture of man entirely outside the sphere in which it had been sketched earlier, where we had a picture of man in opposition to determinate prescriptions, with the result that the purity of life appeared there rather in its modifications, in particular virtues, as reconciliation, marital fidelity, honesty etc.

(*ETW* 223)

In place of the resistance to individual laws that underwent the fate of becoming laws themselves, Hegel emphasizes Jesus's preaching of the 'extinction of law and duty in love' (*ETW* 223) or a resistance to an entire structure of recognition organized according to the Law of the Covenant.

The spirit of resistance thus reveals its own peculiar fate, which is to have the most devastating effect when most unobtrusively present. For far from being the mechanical property of an external relation, resistance is central to the philosophy of spirit. While it explicitly appears throughout Hegel's work as if subordinate to freedom and infinity – in short, as a servant of the absolute – it nevertheless seems as if its actuality is prior to the modal necessity and possibility of the absolute and has to be converted into them. Resistance in the figure of Nimrod with his enmity to nature and God appears beside the spirits of Judaism and Greece as a shape of spirit in its own right, but one whose fate was to be occluded by the transcendent and immanent absolutes. The spirit of resistance was never given the exposition accorded to the legacies of Noah and Deucalion; it was never recognized as a shape of spirit in its own right. Yet perhaps it is precisely its unrecognized resistance to given and emergent forms of recognition that keeps spirit as a whole vital and restless, resisting even Hegel's own attempts to absolutize it through recourse to the ideas of infinity and freedom.

Notes

1   This part of the *Science of Logic* survives from the 1816 edition; see Di Giovanni's introduction to his translation (Hegel 2010).

2   Even as radically a discursive interpretation of Hegel as Di Giovanni's has to smuggle in resistance in order to progress. His account of the transition to 'measure' in the *Science of Logic* depends on an unthematized appeal to resistance: 'Whatever the qualitative determination of such single terms, their stipulated measure persists, internally resistant to any external manipulation. Because of this resistance, their objectivity (originatively defined as "being") acquires yet another level of formal self-containment, another "for-itselfness"' (Hegel 2010, xl).

3   Hegel's contemporary Clausewitz represents a development of Kant's thought that remains within the realm of actual opposed forces and thus resistance. His emphasis on the modal category of actuality, which he learnt from his teacher, Kant's student and correspondent Kiesewetter, emphasized war as the clash of opposed forces or, in his terms, of resistance and counter-resistance. He does not seek to ascribe any necessity to law nor to defend a Rousseauian notion of the freedom to self-legislate. His approach remains a position immanent to Hegel but diverted into philosophy of the infinite and a notion of freedom as self-legislation or autonomy.

4   To be precise, in the first chapter of the second section of the third division, 'Subjective Logic or Doctrine of the Notion'.

5   It is the point where the Venn diagrams used by David Gray Carlson in his commentary on the *Science of Logic* themselves break down. See Carlson 2007, 533–4.

6   This is noted by Carlson, but without distinguishing between the different modes of resistance Hegel is exploring at this point.

7   For an outstanding discussion of Nimrod and the cynegetic tradition he inaugurates, see Chamayou 2012.

29

Clausewitz and idealism

Hermann Cohen ended his 1883 Marburg inaugural lecture, *On Kant's Influence on German Culture*, with a strong claim for viewing Carl von Clausewitz as a significant heir to Kantian idealism. This is a surprising and at first sight implausible judgement. The author of the classic study of military strategy *On War* is not usually numbered among the heirs of the critical philosophy. Indeed his book and person have a distinctly singular, indeed sulphurous reputation: the ideas of *On War* were considered by the British military historian Basil Liddel Hart as intellectually responsible for the deaths of millions in the First World War while for others such as Lenin and Mao they were a crucial inspiration for theorizing global class war.[1] For Hermann Kahn in *On Thermonuclear War* (1959) and the theorists of the RAND Corporation they provided the intellectual framework for the strategy of nuclear deterrence. Yet Cohen's awarding a pivotal position to Clausewitz within the legacy of the critical philosophy and German culture more generally was not the entirely opportunistic bid to align philosophy with the German militarism of its day that it might seem at first sight. He was indeed very clear that declaring Clausewitz a Kantian entailed the thorough reassessment of the character of the critical legacy and above all its distancing from the idealist philosophy of freedom developed by Fichte, Schiller and Hegel.

Cohen's case for the philosophical significance of Clausewitz's inquiry into war was in fact carefully framed and extensively developed, especially given the limitations of an inaugural lecture. It is based on the historical claim that Clausewitz was taught Kant's philosophy at the Berlin Military Academy by the first-generation Kantian J. G. Kiesewetter, making Clausewitz the only post-Kantian philosopher to have been systematically taught the critical philosophy by a student of Kant's. Cohen detects this proximity to Kant's thought throughout *On War*, observing, 'Actually one cannot read *On War* without feeling the breath of the Kantian spirit in all of its methodological principles' (Cohen 1883, 32). Precisely what Cohen meant by this view of

Clausewitz's methodological debt to Kant is spelt out very clearly in what follows: 'Clausewitz's significance as a theorist of war consists in his freeing strategic genius from the constraints of formulaic thinking; that is to say, in implementing the distinction between determinate and reflective judgement as well as that between constitutive principles and regulative maxims' (Cohen 1883, 32). Referring indirectly to Clausewitz's little-known fascination with Kant's concept of genius, Cohen locates strategic judgement within the distinction from the first and third *Critiques* between determinate and reflective judgement as well as the methodological distinction from the first *Critique* between constitutive and regulative ideas. In the first, Clausewitz's strategic *tact* exemplifies reflective judgement, the rule of judgement adjusts itself to the case – a method indeed practised throughout *On War* which repeatedly confronts the art of war with historical exceptions to its rules. The Commander – whose judgement Clausewitz situates between the passions of the people and the logic of the politicians – practises a *grammar* of violence in which the rules of expression are flexible and adapt to circumstances and precedent. Cohen also focuses on another aspect of Clausewitz's use of reflective judgement, namely its link with Kant's understanding of genius as the capacity to invent the rule for others to follow, which he describes 'as if copied from the *Critique of Judgement*' (Cohen 1883, 32). With respect to constitutive principles and regulative maxims, the most prominent example of Clausewitz's use of this distinction is the repeated and oft-cited 'war is the continuation of politics by other means', a proposition that has been understood as a constitutive principle – most recently by Foucault – but in the spirit of Cohen's observation is one more properly understood as a regulative maxim for guiding research. Clausewitz describes this maxim as a means for reconciling the heterogeneous claims of war and peace, claims that when viewed as constitutive principles must remain irreconcilable.

In spite of its reasoned and precise statement, Cohen's position is often taken as an extreme, even exaggerated statement of Clausewitz's relationship to philosophy. Beatrice Heuser, for example, in her 2002 book *Reading Clausewitz* endorses Peter Paret's now widely adopted view in his classic *Clausewitz and the State* (1976) that 'Clausewitz was a typically educated representative of his generation, who attended lectures on logic and ethics designed for the general public, read relevant non-professional books and articles and drew scraps of ideas at second and third hand from his cultural environment' (Paret 2007, 151). She concludes by agreeing with Paret that Clausewitz was a philosophical dilettante, although not with full conviction: 'He also read Kant, although he might not have been as greatly influenced by him as some would argue' (Heuser 2002, 6). In my view these opinions underestimate not only Clausewitz's understanding of Kant and his idealist legacy, but also the cogency and importance of his critique of it. In fact, I believe Cohen did not go as far or as deeply as he may have in order to discern Clausewitz's profound debt to and differences with Kant. I would like to propose a reading of Clausewitz as representing what became a deviant strain of post-Kantian philosophy distinct from that of Fichte, Schiller and Hegel, one that preserves a fidelity to the actuality of force rather than the possibility of freedom. I will argue that the philosophical contribution of *On War* lies in elaborating a Kantianism without freedom, one whose significance has been obscured by its subsequent notoriety as a disillusioned and even satanic study of modern war and strategy. It can and perhaps should be read as a non-orthodox development of Kantian idealism, one in which, above all, the concept of freedom is toppled from the pedestal it occupies in the Fichtean, Schillerian and Hegelian idealist critiques and extensions of Kant that have become taken for granted and almost unquestionable.

Before looking at this other Kantianism and its technical source in J. G. Kiesewetter's understanding of the modal categories, we can consider Clausewitz's own view of his philosophical accomplishment. This is hinted at in *On War* in two apparently inconsistent passages, one which seems to propose an idealism, the other a realism, of war and its study. In the first, Clausewitz locates his view of the importance of reflective judgement in terms of the distinction between analytic and synthetic methodologies and the types of judgement to which they correspond. Here, what is added in a synthetic judgement is precisely the act of reflection or the adaptation of the rule of judgement to the case before it, an action that Clausewitz understood as the inventive judgement of genius. In Book Two, Chapter Two Clausewitz accordingly complains of existing theories of war:

> All of these theoretical attempts may only be considered as progress in the realm of truth in their analytic part; they are completely useless with respect to their recommendations and rules in the synthetic part. They strive after determinate quantities while in war everything is undetermined and calculations must be made according to variable quantities. These theories too direct their considerations according to material quantities while the entire act of war is permeated by spiritual powers and effects. They consider only one-sided activity while war is a constant interaction of oppositions. (Clausewitz [1832] 1980, 283)

From this we can see that Clausewitz is interested less in the analytical judgement of war – the derivation of rules from the analysis of what was already known from past experience of organized violence – than in the synthetic judgement or their application to new constellations of fact. Consistent with his understanding of Kant, this synthetic part consisted not in the application of secured rules – which was the error of previous theories of war – but in the exercise of reflective judgement. This departs from the presupposition that war is not to be understood according to the model of physical reality in which there are fixed, material magnitudes at play. The exercise of judgement in warfare does not consist in the application of an established rule or procedures as if manipulating material objects but is rather an intervention in an actuality consisting of reciprocal opposed forces in which the rules themselves constitute a dynamic and changeable element.

War, then, is not an exercise in simple calculation but a predicament of judgement in which there are no secured rules. The synthetic part of the theory of war, or the exercise of reflective judgement in contexts of extreme insecurity and conflict, is in short a negotiation with actuality. Already Clausewitz's understanding of Kant shows characteristics and emphases that diverge from the broader consensus existing at his time. Along with his fellow military Kantian Heinrich von Kleist, Clausewitz emphasizes the predicament of insecurity that makes it necessary to secure possession of the categories. Judgement for him does not take place on a previously secured terrain according to constitutionally guaranteed procedures by a fundamentally untroubled subject, but is endangered, whether by chance, by friction or by the efforts of an enemy to dispossess the subject of judgement. Such reflective judgement then is not the work of a subject enjoying its freedom and taking pleasure in the discovery of its conformity to law, but one which is under threat and forced to risk its possession in the very act of defending it. In war, judgement cannot be determinate but is forced into the predicament of reflection. Clausewitz, in short, is not restricting himself to examining that domain of human existence and history that is war, but is making war and its violence stand for the basic predicament of judgement.

For Clausewitz, this means that any act of judgement must reckon with enmity and chance; its objects do not lie tranquilly before it, thing-like and calculable with definite contours, but participate in a complex activity or Act of War (*kriegerische Akt*) that is thoroughly informed by 'spiritual forces and actualities' (*von geistigen Kräften und Wirkungen durchzogen ist*). This passage seems to point to an idealism in Clausewitz, one which would seem to conflict with the chilling realism and anti-idealism for which he was later famed, by Marx and Engels among others.

The idealist claim for the *kriegerische Akt* seems to sit awkwardly with the view expressed throughout *On War* but most explicitly in Book VIII, Chapter 3, that 'the lessons of a war should be drawn not from ideal but from actual relations' (Clausewitz [1832] 1980, 973). The latter passage would seem to support the view that Clausewitz was advocating a realist, anti-idealist even an empiricist approach to war, disdaining 'ideal' circumstances, but such a view would only hold on a hasty reading of the term *wirklich*. We saw in our first passage that forces and actualities make up the 'whole act of war' but the *Wirklichkeit* or actuality here is not the real (as Hegel would make clear in his later lectures on the *Philosophy of Right*: the *wirklich* being rational does not exclude the real being broken and bad). Clausewitz's *wirklich* and *Wirklichkeit* are also something different from the real, but they are not 'ideal' in any conventional sense – his *Wirklichkeit* is linked to *Akt*, to genius and most fundamentally to the modal category of *Wirklichkeit*. Viewed from this perspective there is no contradiction between what would seem to be the idealist and anti-idealist statements in *On War*: both refer to aspects of an actuality.

The key to Clausewitz's Kantianism lies in his referring the fundamental predicament of thinking and judging to the modal category of *Wirklichkeit* rather than the more widely preferred *Möglichkeit*. In order to understand the significance of this interpretative choice it is necessary to look a little more carefully at some of the peculiar properties of the modal categories as they are described in the *Critique of Pure Reason*. They are the fourth of the four groups of categories described in the Transcendental Analytic, following those of quantity, quality and relation. The first group structure the quantity of appearances, the second their qualities and the third their internal relations. The fourth, modal group of categories differ from the others insofar as they involve the relation between the sum of appearances and a subject – in short, they concern the way in which that subject stands with respect to the sum of appearances in general or 'world'. As with the other groups of categories, Kant provides us with three formal options: a subject's relations to appearances may be understood in terms of possibility, in terms of necessity or in terms of actuality. The focus on the relation of the subject to the sum of appearances points to the special character of the fourth group of categories: they involve the basic predicament of the subject with respect to the world as the sum of appearances. When understood in terms of the modal category of possibility, the subject's relation to appearances may be described as 'free'; the subject confronts the sum of appearances as the realm of possibility or as the predicament of the free choice between possibilities. The subject who relates to the sum of appearances as the realm of necessity finds itself under law; it cannot freely select between possibilities but is bound by a prior necessity, a predicament understood by Kant's contemporaries as 'Spinozist'. But the predicament of the subject with respect to the world or sum of appearances for the modal category of actuality is rather more puzzling: what does it mean for the subject's relation to the sum of appearances to be actual?

Overwhelmingly, the idealist reading of Kant, beginning with Kant himself at certain moments then developed by Fichte, and, to varying degrees, Schiller and Hegel, lends weight to the modal category of possibility. Thinking and judgement depart from the predicament of a relation to the world as the realm of possibilities. The subject is free with respect to possible appearances, and as a consequence idealism, as we have heard intoned monotonously for over two centuries, is a philosophy of freedom. The moment of necessity had to wait until the post-war revival of Spinoza and the deeper understanding of what it means for the subject's relation to the world to be necessary. For idealism and the idealist reading of Kant we are ultimately free with respect to the sum of appearances – our relation to them is one of possibility. Appearances do not have to be, or remain, as we *find* them: they are not fixed and necessary but can be changed by our exercise of freedom that is but the other side of their being the realm of possibility. Yet the modal category of actuality or *Wirklichkeit* can be understood to offer another 'idealism', one that is not founded in possibility and in freedom, but which points to the play of forces and actualities. It was this that I think was developed by Clausewitz and that informs his philosophy of war as the fundamental description of the subject's relation to the world or sum of appearances.

An important moment, in which what is at stake in the divergence between the canonical reading of Kant issuing from freedom and modal possibility and another departing from force and actuality becomes momentarily visible, is Schiller's influential *Letters on the Aesthetic Education of Man*. The *Letters* are in many ways the inaugural statement of a view of Kant and idealism founded in freedom and the modal category of possibility. The third letter specifically marks a moment of decision in this respect, one in which we move towards the political constitution of freedom, the aesthetico-political resolution of the conflicting demands of nature and freedom or, in the terms of the third letter, between the physical and the moral subject or *Mensch*. Schiller undertakes this movement by means of an implicit recourse to the categories of modality. In the third paragraph we are introduced to the state of nature (*Naturstaat*), or 'what that political body may be called that derives its original constitution from forces and not laws' (Schiller [1795] 2000, 12). Schiller then makes the portentous step of moving from the state of nature understood as the realm of force, that is, as the world of actuality, to the world understood in terms of possibility and freely posited law, the world of the moral human: 'And so the physical human is actual while the ethical is only problematic. If reason would overcome the state of nature, as it necessarily must if it would replace it, then it has to weigh the physical and actual human against the problematic ethical, and existing society against a merely possible (if morally necessary), ideal of society' (Schiller [1795] 2000, 13). The almost inconspicuous negotiation of the modal categories of actuality and possibility – moving from the actuality of the physical to the possibility of the moral (problematic) human – would be of crucial significance for the future not only of Kant's thought but of idealism more generally. The actuality governed by force that is the state of nature – the world of violence and war – is superseded (*aufgehoben*) through the by now familiar dialectical feint of an opening to possibility, freedom and morality. But this opening to possibility from the realm of actuality cannot be sustained by its own resources but requires an alliance with necessity. What is more, this move from actuality to possibility is not just one possible historical option for Schiller, as this would leave us in a world governed solely by the modal category of possibility, but is necessary: *freedom must be*.

In the Third Letter Schiller enquires into the movement from the actual state of nature to the problematic ethical state of freedom and possibility and affirms with little sense of paradox that the *Aufhebung* of one into the other *must* take place. The ideal of a possible society that emerges here is not just a possibility but is 'morally necessary', with Schiller repeatedly underwriting but also limiting possibility by an appeal to modal necessity, allying in short freedom with law. Schiller concludes this negotiation with the invention of the aesthetic state, but the terms he established for moving from actuality and force to freedom and moral law determined idealism and its political thinking for the succeeding two centuries. There would be very few deviations from Schiller's scenario – the movement out of actuality by means of an alliance between freedom and necessity cloaked in the harmonies of the aesthetic. The striking exception, however, is Clausewitz, who developed a dissenting Kantianism rooted in actuality and immune to the temptations of the paradoxical or dialectically sustained alliance between modal possibility and necessity, freedom and law. While Kant left the relation of moral freedom and natural force largely undetermined and Schiller sought their aesthetic reconciliation in the move out of the predicament of force, violence and war to the realm governed by the laws of freedom, Clausewitz embraced the actuality of force without the comforts of freedom, producing an idealism of actuality that would quickly be mistaken for a regional ontology of war.

To understand this position better it is necessary to turn to Clausewitz's teachers, above all J. G. Kiesewetter. It is in Kiesewetter's exegesis of Kant that we first find the emphasis on the modal category of *Wirklichkeit* and the centrality of the *Akt* that was developed further by Clausewitz in *On War*. As Kiesewetter is to a large degree the forgotten Kantian – unmentioned in most of the histories of post-Kantian philosophy including Eckart Förster's recent *The Twenty-Five Years of Philosophy* (2017) – it is necessary to examine briefly some technical aspects of what would retrospectively come to be viewed as an obsolete, pre-Schillerian version of the critical philosophy. Kiesewetter's 1793 *Grundriß einer reinen allgemeinen Logik, nach Kantischen Grundsätzen* understood itself as a defence of Kantian orthodoxy. Dedicating his book to Kant – his 'Lehrer und Vater' – Kiesewetter is anxious to establish direct legitimacy for his interpretation, sometimes provoking the suspicion that the son is protesting too much: 'Accept this work that in part emerged under your eyes' or even 'Kant himself had seen and approved and even improved some parts of this exposition and I thank him for a large amount of material'

(Kiesewetter 1793, Dedication & Preface). But when we look closely at the *Grundriß*, more closely than perhaps Kant himself did, we see that it is closer to the neo-Leibnizian current of Eberhard and other Leibniz-Wolffians against whose attacks Kant defended the critical philosophy during the 1780s. Kiesewetter's treatment of the four parts of general logic – elements, concepts, judgements and syllogisms – focuses above all on the *Begriff*, reflecting on its clarity, distinctness and completeness – terms central to the Leibniz-Wolffian philosophy with a direct provenance in Leibniz's *Reflections on Knowledge, Truth and Ideas*.

What is distinctive about Kiesewetter's approach is the central role played by the categories of modality and specifically the category of *Wirklichkeit* or actuality. For modal actuality underpins everything that happens in this logic. Kiesewetter is convinced that the origin of the elements, concepts, judgements and syllogisms studied in his logic lies in an *Aktus* or *Akt* of the *Verstand* or understanding: 'Concepts are produced through an act (*Aktus*) of the understanding' (Kiesewetter 1793, xxiv) he says at the outset of his inquiry, confirming that 'concepts can only be produced through an act of the understanding in which a manifold is combined into a Unity' (Kiesewetter 1793, xxiv, 56). This *Aktus* has the strange property of being both a discrete concept – it is one of the three modal concepts – and the condition of possibility of all the concepts, including itself. If we look at the continuation of the first definition, 'Concepts are produced through an act (*Aktus*)' we can see that *Aktus* both produces and is a product, a peculiar concept capable of bringing forth itself and all the others: 'The understanding can undertake such an act (*Aktus*), has undertaken or must undertake it' (Kiesewetter 1793, xxiv). In order for there to be possibility, actuality or necessity there has already to have been actuality. What this means is that predicament precedes possibility – 'A concept is possible when the characteristics from which it will emerge actually allow themselves to be unified in a unity of consciousness; impossible when this cannot take place' – for possibility and, with it, freedom presuppose actuality. The latter is not the actualization of a possibility, but a predicament that precedes possibility: 'A concept is actual when the unification of these characteristics in a unity of consciousness has already taken place' (Kiesewetter 1793, xxiv). This in turn gives us necessity insofar as what has already happened now cannot happen otherwise. In a gloss for his students, Kiesewetter sums up the modal categories as *Kann*, *Ist* and *Muss*, insisting that Can, Is and Must can only be said if there has already been an *Ist* to which they can refer. The *Ist* is the *Aktus* of unifying a manifold before that manifold is unified again in terms of the scenario of the modal concepts.

Let us move abruptly back to Kiesewetter's pupil Clausewitz, who makes liberal use of the *Aktus* and *Wirklichkeit* in *On War*. Kiesewetter's insistence upon the primacy of actuality relegates freedom and possibility to the margins: the *Aktus* is not a free act, it is not grounded in possibility, but rather possibility is grounded in it. This sense for the predicament of actuality as preceding the exercise of freedom in possibility is axiomatic for Clausewitz. It informs *On War,* which we might rename *The Critique of Violent Reason,* for it is not only an original understanding of modern warfare – its limits and conditions of possibility – but also a significant contribution to the history of post-Kantian philosophy. As opposed to the idealist philosophers of the primacy of freedom, Clausewitz remains Kantian in his allergy with respect to the absolute. The experience of the idea of freedom that seemed to be warranted by the postulates of the *Critique of Practical Reason* served Schiller and later Hegel as a means for criticizing Kant's theoretical distinction between the spatio-temporally limited judgements of the understanding and the infinite syllogisms and their objects of the reason. Thinking the absolute on the basis of freedom became the hallmark of Schiller and Hegel's later suspension of the distinction between understanding and reason in the name of Kant's own alleged primacy of freedom and practical reason.

Clausewitz, following the line of interpretation opened by Kiesewetter, remained immune to the temptations of possibility and the primacy of freedom. This also allowed him to maintain fidelity to the Kantian reluctance to leave the spatio-temporal limits of sense for the realm of reason and its infinite ideas. It also allowed him to propose an explanation for why the limits of sense are so frequently breached, one that differs from Kant's own view of the folly of freedom whose property is to exceed all limits. While Clausewitz's analysis of escalation would become part of popular nuclear culture, it was forgotten that in *On War* this served as an orthodox Kantian description of the passage from the spatio-temporally limited to the absolute, one passing through actuality rather than freedom and possibility. Escalation consists of reciprocal actions that intensify each other towards an absolute and unsustainable extreme. In *On War* Clausewitz identified three significant modes of escalation, three reciprocal actions driving themselves towards the absolute. The first is the tendency of an act of violence directed against an enemy to provoke a response that exceeds the ferocity of the initial act (Book I, Chapter 1, §3); the second is the impossibility of leaving the enemy undefeated since this would permit hostilities to reassume, entailing that the enemy must be absolutely defeated (§4); the third is escalation of surveillance and accumulation of the means of violence, the reciprocal effort to know the enemy better than they know you or themselves, hence the need for absolute knowledge of the enemy (§5) (Clausewitz [1832] 1980, 192–5). The three escalations produce the ideas of absolute violence or absolute war, bringing together absolute mastery and absolute knowledge.

Clausewitz's defence of spatio-temporally limited violence, or contained mastery and knowledge is thus consistent with the Kantian distinction between understanding and reason in the first *Critique*. It differs fundamentally from the development of Kant's thought that accepts the primacy of freedom usually associated with German Idealism. René Girard emphasized this in his *Achever Clausewitz*, which confronts Hegelian dialectic and its complicity with the peace of empire with Clausewitz's vision of war and the unavailability of any dialectical resolution of conflict. His political-theological reading of Clausewitz as an apocalyptic thinker for whom escalation is absolute evil – 'Satan is another name for escalation' (Girard 2011, 362) – is set in deliberate contrast with Hegel and dedicated to showing the extreme danger intrinsic to the underestimation of violence in Hegelianism. The lack of a 'radical concept of violence' in Hegel constitutes a fundamental danger for Girard, since it urges the primacy of freedom with little appreciation of its destructive potential. Clausewitz, however, departing from the actuality of war and an extreme sensitivity to violence urges a reassessment of the post-Kantian primacy of freedom, seeing war as actual and omnipresent and replacing the ethics of the realization of freedom with a strategy for the mitigation of the effects of war and the limitation of its absolute manifestations. And as Cohen intuited already in his Inaugural Lecture, this is a rigorously Kantian position, but not at all in the sense that Kant and the critical legacy have come to be understood.

Note

1   Lenin accompanied his study of Hegel's *Logic* and Aristotle's *Metaphysics* while in exile in Bern during the First World War with a close examination of *On War*. He mistakenly considered Clausewitz to be an Hegelian and his work to be of vital importance for prosecuting a revolutionary class war. His study of *On War* contributed significantly to the change of political direction that led to the October Revolution, manifest most prominently in *State and Revolution* and the *April Theses*. In his *Theory of the Partisan* Carl Schmitt went so far as to describe Lenin's notebooks on Clausewitz as 'one of the most remarkable documents of world and intellectual history' (Schmitt 2007, 35) even though they remain little studied. Mao in turn carefully studied Clausewitz – the 'esteemed foreign military expert' – during the mid-1930s while working out the theory and strategy of guerrilla war presented in the lectures 'On the Protracted War of Resistance' and 'Basic Tactics'. Citations and comments on Clausewitz from the former were republished in the *Little Red Book,* making Clausewitz's ideas probably the most widely disseminated of any German thinker.

30

Debt and the origins of obedience

To ask it again: to what extent can suffering balance debts or guilt? To the extent that to make *suffer was in the highest degree pleasurable, to the extent that the injured party exchanged for the loss he had sustained, including the displeasure caused by the loss, an extraordinary counterbalancing pleasure: that of* making *suffer – a genuine* festival …

– NIETZSCHE, *ON THE GENEALOGY OF MORALS*

There is a secret history of debt that follows its passage through the musty corridors connecting the courts and the temples that were traced among others by Nietzsche, Kafka and Benjamin. They saw, or Nietzsche would say smelt, the archaic odour of debt that accompanies, sometimes indiscernibly, sometimes overpoweringly, the legal and liturgical rationalisms in which it dresses itself. It is a quality that Nietzsche called 'cruelty', Kafka 'shame' and Benjamin 'guilt', all three making explicit the ambiguity of the German word for debt: *Schuld* that is also 'guilt'. These archaic qualities to debt have been more than evident in the recent Greek debt crisis in which extravagant displays of cruelty, shame and guilt concerning the issue of national and personal debt adorn the brutal economic management of the structural financial imbalance of the Eurozone.[1] The European debt festival – *Schuldfest* – played out over Greece during the second decade of the twenty-first century confirms Nietzsche's suspicion that 'without cruelty there is no festival' (*GM* II, §6). While we are all aware that the management of debt mobilizes the repulsive affects of cruelty, shame and guilt, sustained reflection upon or inquiry into why and how it does so remains fragmentary. Perhaps part of the current difficulty of developing political strategies for resisting debt is related to the difficulty of thinking debt apart from its archaic residues of 'blood and torture' and to realize that what is at issue is less the restoration of a disturbed economic relation than securing the asymmetries of command and obedience.

Nietzsche's *On the Genealogy of Morals* remains one of the most sustained and influential efforts to track down the role of cruelty in the origins of debt. In the first essay '"Good and Evil," "Good and Bad"' of the *On the Genealogy of Morals*, Nietzsche stages a Dantean descent into the infernal 'dark workshop' – a descent that parallels Marx's descent into the infernal factory in *Capital* – in search of the obscure places where value is created, where *'ideals are manufactured'* (*GM* I, §14).[2] In both descents, the source of value – moral and economic – is found to lie in acts of theft and cruelty that dress themselves in strange forms and disguises, most strikingly, for both thinkers, in the garb of formal equality. In the 'Second Essay' of *On the Genealogy of Morals*, which focuses on guilt and bad conscience, Nietzsche stops to report and reflect on what it was that he discovered in his descent to the factory of ideals, namely the shedding of blood. Descending from the symmetrical world of abstract moral ideals he arrived first at the sphere of law, and then descending further, to a scene of repeated bloodshed:

> It was in *this* sphere then, the sphere of legal obligations, that the moral conceptual world of 'guilt', 'conscience', 'duty', 'sacredness of duty' had its origin (*Entstehungsherd*): its beginnings were, like the beginnings of everything great on earth, soaked in blood thoroughly and for a long time. (*GM* II, §6)

It is important to be attentive to Nietzsche's topographic sequence in this passage. It can be read as a single derivation of the 'moral conceptual world' from the 'sphere of legal obligations' but this would entail that the legal sphere be understood as a scene of bloodshed, tempting but implausible. Yet it can also be read in terms of a movement from the moral conceptual *world* to the legal *sphere* whose *origin* is by no means the same as its *beginnings*. With this reference to beginnings, Nietzsche transforms his topographic scenario into a temporal or historical sequence, with *origin* ramifying into beginnings which then develop into spheres and then finally into worlds. But what cannot be overlooked in Nietzsche's report is that the origin in question involved the shedding of blood, that at a certain threshold in history blood flowed and thoroughly permeated the beginnings of the historical sequences that unfolded in the sphere of law and the world of morality, and not just once but repeatedly, 'for a long time'.

After reporting on this haemorrhage at the origin of debt, law and value, Nietzsche immediately adds that the smell of caked blood still clings to the world of moral ideals, adding that this is the odour of 'torture' and 'cruelty':

And might one not add that, fundamentally, this world has never since lost a certain odour of blood and torture? (Not even in good old Kant: the categorical imperative smells of cruelty.) It was here, too, that that uncanny intertwining of the ideas 'guilt and suffering' was first effected – and now they may well be inseparable – can also be viewed. (*GM* II, §6)

The references to 'torture' and 'cruelty' serve two purposes in Nietzsche's argument: the first is to point to the twisting or creation of an unnatural pressure that forms an origin capable of forcing beginnings – in this case the body that is forced to bleed by a cut or a haemorrhage. Torture and cruelty do not only disrupt and divert a given disposition of forces by provoking suffering, they do not just break, injure and drain the body of life but, by so doing, they also create something new. In this case it is the 'uncanny intertwining', of 'guilt-debt' (*Schuld*) and 'suffering' that Nietzsche takes to have become an irreversible historical fact. With this observation on the creative work of torture and cruelty Nietzsche arrives at the re-statement of the question that has been driving his genealogical investigation all along, the one cited in the epigraph: to what extent can suffering *balance* debts and guilt? Informing the quantitative question of 'to what extent' is the more fundamental one of whether debt is itself the inequality that needs to be balanced; is there an asymmetry at the origin of debt or is this imbalance, but a later translation or expression of it, an historical *beginning*? In Nietzsche's scenario the answer to the question of whether debt is the origin or only the beginning is crucial; is it the original inequality or is it just its subsequent economic expression? If the former, then debt is indeed the origin or inaugural event sought by a genealogy of morals; but if it is the latter, then debt is a mask, a symptomatic expression of an origin yet further removed. The main clue for pursuing an answer to this question is the blood that has been shed and the deeper question: why must the debtor bleed? Nietzsche's answers are deceptively simple: that to cause suffering is pleasurable; that pleasure in shedding blood could compensate for loss of a loan and the displeasure occasioned by that loss; and that causing and witnessing suffering – indulging in cruelty – constituted a 'genuine festival'. But what Nietzsche means by pleasure and how it relates to balance and imbalance is not as straightforward as it seems, and this points to the problem of whether it is possible to think outside of debt, to a cancellation of the very predicament of debt without this being a mere balancing or atonement for it, without it falling back into debt.

The charting of the terrain that surrounds the beginnings of the nexus of debt, guilt and suffering in the 'First Essay' of *On the Genealogy of Morals* is followed in the 'Second Essay' by the hunt through this tormented landscape for the animal able to make promises. On the track of this strange creature Nietzsche scrutinizes an 'entire *prehistoric* labour' dedicated to training this animal, of making humanity (for this animal is the human) 'calculable' or obedient, hypothesizing that 'there was nothing more fearful and uncanny in the whole prehistory of humanity than his *mnemotechnics*' (*GM* II, §3). The uncanny mnemotechnics mentioned here is inseparable from the 'uncanny' intertwining of debt, guilt and suffering involved in the shedding of blood mentioned elsewhere in the 'Second Essay'. Contemplating the spectacle of 'the most dreadful sacrifices and pledges (sacrifices of the first born among them), the most repulsive mutilations (castration for example), the cruellest rites of all the religious cults (and all religions are at the deepest level systems of cruelties) … ' (*GM* II, §3), Nietzsche seems to see a single fugitive figure emerging from all the cruelties: debt. But this figure is elusive and its traces hard to follow, not because they are few and obscure, but because they are many and glaring. Debt seems to loom large, leaving tracks everywhere and in all directions, but precisely this ubiquity makes it elusive and intangible.

For the genealogist, debt seems to lie at the origin of everything: law, religion, philosophy and morality; everything seems to lead to it. It presents itself brazenly as an origin, one that is invested with an uncanny mnemotechnics founded in cruelty that ensures debt is never forgiven or forgotten: all the cruel cuts, mutilations and blows, all the suffering and bloodshed are dedicated to ensuring that the debt is never forgotten. This widely adopted reading of the results of Nietzsche's genealogy puts mnemotechnics to the service of debt; debt is at the origin of the mnemotechnic systems of law, religion and morality that ensure that the debt remains memorable. Indeed, we only remember, Nietzsche seems to say, because there is debt. In Maurizio Lazzarato's terms, Nietzsche's mnemotechnics was and remains dedicated to the creation of 'indebted man'.[3] Yet Nietzsche's genealogical suspicion also alerts him to becoming too indebted to debt: perhaps debt is not so much the reason for the invention of mnemotechnics than one of its more powerful techniques; perhaps debt itself *is* a mnemotechnic and can be located at the beginnings of mnemotechnics, but not at its origin. Debt in short is technical, a powerful means of ensuring suffering and memory rather than the reason for their existence. Faced with all the evidence of debt, Nietzsche begins to suspect that it is but a theatrical persona standing in for a more fundamental problem, that of creating a memorable, obedient and 'calculable' animal.

Perhaps this suspicion is the reason why Nietzsche describes this 'mnemotechnics' or 'intertwining' of suffering and debt-guilt as 'uncanny'. Did he suspect that the genealogical sequence which leads to original debt may be a later elaboration selectively extracted from a more complex original sequence? Debt is undoubtedly a powerful mnemotechnic in that it both provokes suffering and provides a justification for it, but it is at the same time selective, allowing other terms in its own formative sequence to be excluded and forgotten. According to the mnemotechnic of debt, the significant historical sequence departs from incurring debt and then moves through the remembering of this debt until finally arriving at its balancing, in one way or another. This sequence can be applied to a range of experiences – religious, legal, moral – and can even seem constitutive of them, but it always performs a more or less baroque variation on these terms and this sequence. It is a powerful genealogical explanation but one that itself needs to be brought under genealogical scrutiny. Nietzsche's text pushes at these limits, suggesting an alternative sequence in which the invention of the habit of obedience and calculability is inseparable from the constitution of memory, that memory emerges from cruelty and the memory of cruelty is rationalized, legitimated and carried down by means of the mnemotechnical figure of debt. In this alternative sequence debt is not the origin but the outcome of a legitimization of an obedience secured by means of cruelty and its memory.

Nietzsche's genealogical pursuit of the origins of the ideal – 'guilt' – in the material – 'debt' – takes him to 'the contractual relationship between *creditor* and *debtor* which is as old as the idea of "legal subjects" and in turn points back to the fundamental forms of buying, selling, barter, trade and traffic' (*GM* II, §4). This and similar passages from *On the Genealogy of Morals* are used by both Maurizio Lazzarato and David Graeber in their recent speculations on debt to point to the (for Graeber, erroneous) primacy of the economic relation of creditor and debtor. Yet what Nietzsche is describing here is the derivative sphere of law – 'the world of legal subjects' – which is not an origin. It may be a plausible description of a beginning, but it is not an origin. If it is read as such, then Nietzsche's genealogy terminates in the sphere of law, one he has already explained is very late in the historical sequence. It is already an understanding of that sequence in terms of the peculiarity of debt which informs the law of contract and obligation. Roman law recognized that where there is buying and selling there is credit, debt and a contractual relationship that is essentially paradoxical: the parties to the contract are equal and in a symmetrical relationship, but this is also the unequal and asymmetrical relationship of creditor and debtor. Terminating a genealogical investigation at this point forgets that the sphere of law is already structured by the mnemotechnic of debt – but if the terms 'creditor' and 'debtor' are themselves scrutinized, then it becomes possible to discern within their relationship the stabilization of an original inequality of command and obedience: a non-relationship that is only subsequently legitimated in terms of credit and debt. Debt then is the legitimation and rationalization of an inequality, making it appear as but a temporary predicament, one essentially open to future equalization. Command and obedience, however, are not such a relation and cannot be equalized; they can only appear to be equalized if they are translated into terms of debt. The truth of command is not debt, but the singularity of shed blood.

If the hypothesis that debt is a mnemotechnic rather than the origin of mnemotechnics is admitted, then the place of origin must be occupied by something other than debt. One possibility raised by Nietzsche is that of a 'person meeting a person for the first time and *measuring themselves* person against person' (*GM* II, §8). Within the mnemotechnics of debt, this measuring appears as the beginnings of a relation, but from another perspective it can appear as a non-relation in which the other cannot measure up, indeed defies measure. In this view, the relation of debt is another expression for the desire to stabilize and minimize potential outbreaks of refusals to measure up: in other words, of defiance. On this reading of the genealogical sequence, defiance – a refusal to be measured – would be the origin, an upsurge or insurgency whose eruption is met first of all by enforcing measure – a reduction of defiance to the opposition of command and obedience – and then consolidating this reduction by remembering and legitimating it in terms of the mnemotechnic of debt. In this view, it is the memory of defiance and its suppression that must be cruelly expunged and then remembered anew in terms of debt. Expressing considerable repugnance for those of the past 'who created or permitted' the mnemotechnics that sustain contractual (that is to say, debtor and creditor) *relations*, Nietzsche looks more closely at the expressions of cruelty that accompany the apparent equality of debtor and creditor. Within the mnemonic of debt the creditor expects a calculable return from the debtor, and if disappointed then an equivalent pleasure, but crucially, of course, this pleasure is not equivalent – it is a cruel pleasure. This only seems strange if it is assumed that debt is a purely economic imbalance that needs to be redressed; but what is really at issue is not repayment of debt but the application of a sanction for defiance. What appears as the sanction applied in the exceptional case of the non-payment of the debt is in fact the whole reason for the debt. Repayment is literally compliance; it is obedience to a command. The cruel pleasure of applying sanctions for non-payment is a display of command that energizes the mnemotechnic of debt and assures the future compliance/obedience of this debtor and others who witness the festival of cruelty visited on the disobedient: hence the shedding of blood and bodily dismemberments, all signs of the imposition of command.

Nietzsche notes that the debtors' failure to repay required the substitution of 'something else that he "possessed," something he had control over; for example, his body, his wife, his freedom, or even his life' (*GM* II, §5). As David Graeber perceptively shows throughout *Debt: the First 5,000 Years* (2011), debt is indissociable from slavery or the extreme assertion of command.[4] The memory of cruelty and the smell of blood sticking to debt are dedicated primarily to assuring the asymmetry of command and obedience, not their future equalization in repayment. Nietzsche sees this primarily exposed in the idea of the disappointed creditor's 'recompense in the form of a kind of *pleasure*' (GM II, §5), which he traces first to the shame of the debtor and then to the 'foretaste of higher rank' that this shame grants to the creditor. This 'foretaste' is none other than an intimation of assured command, and shame that of guaranteed obedience: the cruel suppression of defiance or non-compliance is here remembered and legitimated in terms of debt but there is always present the smell of cruelty, namely the pleasure of command and the shame of obedience.

Hence the extravagance of the punishments of debtors: what is really happening in these instances is the suppression of their insubordination. If when 'person met person' the one did not measure themselves against the other but shed their blood, they would be refusing all terms of relation. *My blood cannot be recompensed; there is no possible measure; by shedding it you have asserted your command over my body*. Yet there remains the problem of my obedience, which does not display the symmetry or 'relation' that characterizes credit and debt, creditor and debtor. Obedience does not logically follow command, but always remains in question: an upsurge of defiance is always possible and command has repeatedly to assert itself. The translation of this non-relation into the relational terms of debt must sustain the analogy between credit and debt and command and obedience. But as we saw, in these terms my non-payment of a debt should release at most a sanction equivalent to the credit lent and lost, but equivalence is precisely the problem here: what has happened is that the command of the creditor has been defied by the disobedience of the debtor, and it is this defiance that is extravagantly punished in the cruel but festive moralism visited upon the debtor.

Nietzsche is fascinated by the example of Roman law and its evaluations of the limbs and parts of the body as compensation for unpaid debts, a clear case of the cruelty of the creditor visited on the living body of the debtor. Nietzsche considered it 'an advance, as evidence of a freer, *more Roman* conception of law when the Twelve Tables of Rome decreed it a matter of indifference how much or how little the creditor cut off in such cases' (GM II, §6). What is important in short is the bare assertion of command, of possessing the power to mutilate the body of the other or to reduce their insubordination to zero by taking their life.[5] An even more radical escalation of the attempt to secure command over the body extended even beyond death, as in the case of Nietzsche's example from Ancient Egypt, where the debtor was forced to surrender 'his bliss after death, the salvation of his soul, ultimately his peace in the grave: thus it was in Egypt, where the debtors corpse found no peace from the creditor even in the grave – and among the Egyptians such peace meant a great deal' (GM II, §5). This is an observation taken up by Jan Assman in the chapter of his critique of political theology, *Herrschaft und Heil:*

Politische Theologie in Altagypten, Israel und Europa (2000) on 'The Heart on the Balance: Shame, Debt and Sin', which traces the interferences between debt and time. For Assman, debt and shame are opposed concepts which, however, remain capable of alignment: 'Debt belongs to a diachronic space of memory, shame on the contrary in a synchronic space of visibility' (Assman 2000, 134). The two can come together in the visible persistence of the shame of the debtor. On Assman's account, ancient Egypt is the paradigmatic debt culture in which

> immortality is made dependent on freedom from debt, that is to say, the promise of eternal life is tied to freedom from debt. This relationship is regarded as so close and concrete, that debt appears as a form of pollutant that effects putrefaction. The techniques and rituals for debt avoidance through expiation and justification develop in close association with the techniques of embalming and mummification. (Assman 2000, 141)

The putrefying body is the eternal shame of the debtor, for not only as Nietzsche argues is the body of the debtor harried by the creditor after death, but at an even more perverse level of sublimation the debt itself corrupts the body, borrowing from its future integrity. Even when the body is drained of all its blood, it can still be regarded as insubordinate and punished after life itself has ceased.

Nietzsche's *On the Genealogy of Morals* is more than the inquiry into the genealogical descent of moral ideals from the legal and economic relation of debt; it is also and perhaps more pertinently a genealogy of debt, one that pursues law and economy back to the asymmetry of the relation of command and obedience. When the calculable and predictable economic relation of creditor and debtor is superimposed upon the unpredictable non-relation of command and obedience, the attempt at analogy produces effects in the economic relation that are more appropriate to the extravagances of the imposition of command and the efforts to secure obedience through cruelty. Non-payment of a debt becomes an act of defiance to command that is met by escalating efforts to reduce the offender to obedience. Moving back from the world of moral ideas, through the legal and economic sphere to debt, Nietzsche's genealogy then takes a further step and arrives at the problem of securing command and obedience. To see the origin of debt, the sphere of law and the conceptual and moral world in an impossible attempt to secure command over the other not only explains much of the cruel theatre that attends debt, but also shows that at the origins of debt there is not only command but also already defiance and resistance.

Notes

1   For the role of affect in the management of debt, see Elettra Stimili's thoughtful study *Debt and Guilt: A Political Philosophy*, especially chapter 5, 'The Psychic Life of Debt'. Stimilli 2019, 125–58.

2   Stimilli's account of the *Genealogy of Morals* in Stimilli 2017 also notes the parallels with Marx's *Capital* but focuses on the role of debt in primitive accumulation as an origin of capitalism.

3   Lazzarato's subtle description of the relationship between debt and subjectivity remains at the level of Nietzsche's sphere of law. While observing that the 'Second Essay' 'sweeps aside in one stroke the whole of the social sciences' (Lazzarato 2011, 39) especially political economy and symbolic anthropology – a claim sure to annoy David Graeber who objects to Deleuze and Guattari's earlier statement of a similar view (Graeber 2011, 402) – he nevertheless restricts its object to the 'sphere' of law. For him 'debt breeds, subdues, manufactures, adapts and shapes subjectivity' (Lazzarato 2011, 38–9); credit is 'the paradigm of social relations' (Lazzarato 2011, 39) and at the core of this is the ability to promise. While he correctly and pertinently observes that 'making a person capable of keeping a promise means constructing a memory for him, endowing him with interiority, a conscience, which provides a bulwark against forgetting', he is too quick to conclude that 'it is within the domain of debt obligations that memory, subjectivity, and conscience begin to be produced' (Lazzarato 2011, 40). Debt may be a means for that production, but its domain lies elsewhere.

4   Graeber's book analyses a number of historical sequences including among their terms war, slavery, state, markets and debt. In chapter six he proposes an accelerated sequence in the case of Atlantic slavery and in the remainder of the book an extended, global millennial sequence. While Nietzsche is important for his analysis, he underestimated Nietzsche's insight into the use of debt as a means for ensuring command and obedience and the historiographic danger of contriving historical sequences that privilege domination instead of giving normative force to defiance.

5   Graeber regards Nietzsche's reflections on the calculus of debt and the body as 'not a real historical argument' but as a 'purely imaginative exercise' (Graeber 2011, 77). In his interpretation of Nietzsche he underestimates the presence of a problem of command and obedience behind the figures of creditor and debtor and how quickly non-payment of debt became a problem of command and defiance.

FIGURE 1 *The Academia with Athena and Graffiti, Athens, January 2013.*

31

Resisting escalation: The image of Villa Amalias

*The insurrection among the Greek subjects of the Sultan,
which caused such alarm in London and Paris, has now been
suppressed, but its revival is thought not impossible.*

– KARL MARX, *THE GREEK INSURRECTION*

'**N**ot impossible': the double negative used by Marx in his 1854 article on
the Greek insurrection performs a peculiar neutralization of modality; the
revival of the suppressed insurrection is not impossible, but nor is it possible
(the negation of impossibility does not return as possibility) and it is certainly
not necessary or inevitable. It is however consistent with the modal category
of *actuality*, and indeed Marx goes on in his article to show that the Greek
insurrection is actual because it is the expression, sometimes intensified
otherwise subdued, of a Greek capacity to resist. One of the sources of this
view of the actuality of the capacity to resist was the heretical Kantian Carl
von Clausewitz, whose posthumous testament of anti-Hegelianism *On War*
was very early on admired and critically discussed by Marx and Engels and its
lessons concerning politics and war taken further by Lenin and Mao, Debord
and Vaneigem and now perhaps by today's Greek autonomists following
Vaneigem's 2010 *L' État ne plus rien, soyons tout*, written for a meeting of
direct democracy in Salonica.

Wiederstandsfähigkeit or capacity to resist is the principal concept
of Clausewitz's *On War*; indeed *On Resistance* would almost be a more
appropriate title for the book, since the motivation of the text was '*how
to resist*', above all how to resist the armies of the Napoleonic empire.
Clausewitz was inspired by the Spanish guerrilla resistance to the Napoleonic
armies in the Peninsular War and by mountain warfare in the Tyrol to attempt

a philosophical and historical answer to the question *how to resist?* His main contribution was to replace the analysis of resistance as a moral quality with the *capacity* to resist as a material and organizational force. The capacity to resist is indeed the very object of war, whether indirectly when defending my own capacity – what Clausewitz called 'bare resistance' – or by violently attacking and thus compromising my enemies' material and moral capacity to resist. It thus appears in the axiomatic definition of war on the first page of Clausewitz's *On War* where the aim or *Zweck* of war is defined as rendering the enemy 'incapable of further resistance' (*zu jedem fernen Wiederstand unfähig zu machen*) (*OW* 1). *Wiederstandsfähigkeit* or the ability/capacity to resist is thus a differential – expressing itself with varying degrees of intensity according to the pressure of the enemy and ranging all the way to the point of its obliteration in total domination. One of the interesting qualities of the capacity to resist is its modal property of actuality – it is always there, a state of hostility with differing and varying degrees of intensity. The degree of intensity depends on another important element of Clausewitz's conceptual structure, namely escalation. Escalation increases hostility and is dedicated to bringing the opposed capacities to resist to the point of explosion and decision. Strategy rather than logic is the thought of escalation, and is inseparable from considerations of time, position and initiative.

FIGURE 2 *'Villa Amalias Squat Forever' with Flamenco Dancer Throwing off Her Chains, Athens, January 2013.*

Clausewitz's *On War* was misunderstood as making a contribution to international relations with war understood as conflict between nations, while in fact he understood war according to the model of civil war – this is the meaning of his repeated and subsequently much cited phrase: 'war is politics by other means'. Yet the centrality of the capacity to resist in his reflections on war was repeatedly underestimated, although interestingly not in the case of the neo-Clausewitzian Cold War deterrence theory developed by the RAND Corporation strategist Hermann Kahn in *On Thermonuclear War* (1960) and others. Offensive preparation to attack and destroy the enemy's capacity to resist by means of nuclear weapons by the United States and the USSR articulated offensive preparation – nuclear warheads and their delivery systems – with the consolidation of the capacity to resist by surviving a nuclear first strike. We owe the internet as a communications system designed to survive a nuclear first strike to the clear understanding of the Clausewitzian capacity to resist on the part of the RAND Corporation, ARPA and other military research bodies in the United States. But alongside this neo-Clausewitzian doctrine emerged another understanding of Clausewitz associated with Werner Hahlweg and with Carl Schmitt in his late Maoist phase which saw *On War* as a text dedicated to the strategy of resistance by means of guerrilla warfare, one which, unlike Kahn's reading, was fully aware of the strategic dangers of the escalation of conflict and violence. This view and Raymond Aron's attempt to develop a neo-Clausewitzian account of deterrence and a defence of diplomatic and political reason have recently been opposed in Girard's apocalyptic reading of *On War* in *Achever Clausewitz* that seeks to disengage escalation from the capacity to resist and to understand it in theological terms as a name for evil and even Satan.

Which brings me to Greece in the winter of 2012/13 and the suppression and evictions of the anarchist squat at Villa Amalias on Platia Viktorias, close to the iconic site of the Greek capacity to resist during the Dictatorship – the Polytechnic – and adjacent to the now fascist stronghold of Agios Panteleimon.

Let me begin again this time with a *detournement* of Marx's 1854 text: 'The insurrection among the Greek subjects of the Euro, which caused such alarm in Berlin and Paris, has now been suppressed, but its revival is not thought impossible.' Villa Amalias was an occupied building, a squat that lasted over twenty-two years and the site of a vibrant anarchist cultural centre that became representative of the archipelago of squats within Athens and beyond that formed an important locus for the Greek extra-parliamentary capacity to resist. The escalation of the state's attack on the autonomists by the forcible eviction of the Villa in December 2012 was preceded by some mysterious firebomb attacks and the alleged discovery of petrol and bottles in Villa Amalias, all of which served as a pretext for repression and eviction. The closure of Villa Amalias would seem to mark a point of decision for the

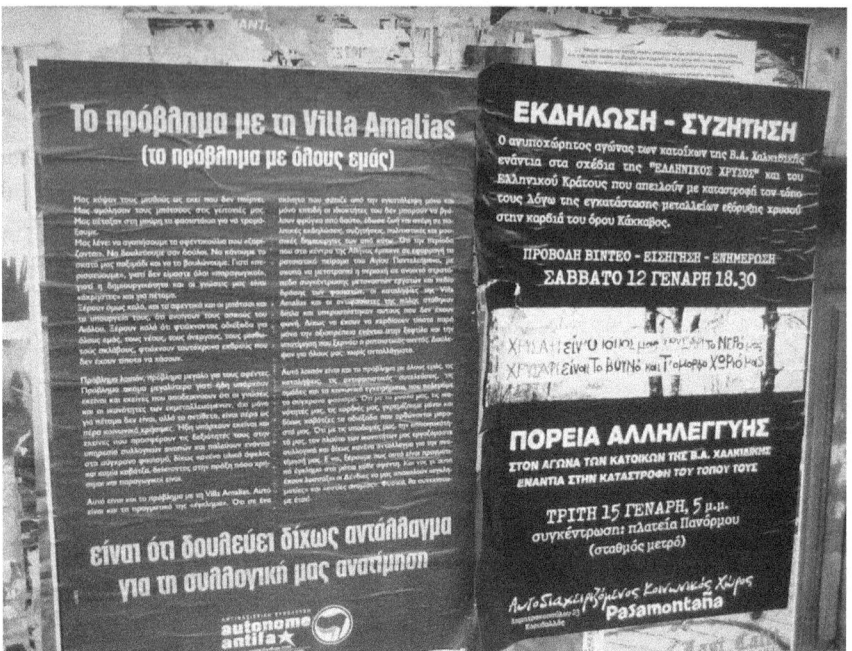

FIGURE 3 *'The Problem with Villa Amalias (the Problem with All of Us) Is That It Works without Exchange for Collective Re-evaluation' and a 'Call for Solidarity', Athens, January 2013.*

survival of the extra-parliamentary capacity to resist, and in many ways the Villa became the shibboleth for this capacity.

Yet as an emblem for the extra-parliamentary resistance, Villa Amalias was vulnerable to manipulation by adversaries seeking to escalate the struggle for resistance for their own ends. The suppression of Villa Amalias was not just the neutralization of an important site for the Greek extra-parliamentary capacity to resist, but the attempt to provoke it to engage in an escalation of violent struggle that would lead to its destruction. Whose interest would such an escalation serve?

In the case of Villa Amalias the green light for the escalation of the suppression of the autonomists was given by the leader of the Parliamentary Left Alexis Tsipras who began publicly distancing the electorally successful Leftist Syriza from the autonomist resistance as part of his conversion, depending on one's point of view, to responsible social democracy or to Leninist internal discipline. In isolating Villa Amalias and in taking distance from the extra-parliamentary Left, Tsipras seemed to be following the ironic advice of his opponent Prime Minister Antonis Samaras, given in an interview in the newspaper *Vima* – calling on him to be more responsible and to abandon the extra-parliamentary resistance: 'Take the example of the case of the Villa Amalias, one would expect that a party that until recently was at 4 per cent and that reached 26 per cent would be more responsible. But they function as a marginal party of protest instead of becoming more responsible and more institutional' (*Vima*, 13/1/2013). Villa Amalias has become the name of a despised margin, a name for irresponsible and non-institutional resistance, and in associating Syriza with this resistance, Samaras hoped to neutralize its electoral threat to the middle-class 'responsible' electorate. In order to bring this message home and to discredit Syriza, a spectacular manifestation of such political irresponsibility would obviously be convenient. The escalation of the struggle with the extra-parliamentary resistance, provoking it to respond violently in turn, would clearly serve to underline the importance of Syriza avoiding any association with the extra-parliamentary margin, accepting institutional responsibility and ceasing to be a focus of resistance.

FIGURE 4 *'You Won't Get Villa Amalias Even in Your Dreams: Villa Amalias Will Remain a Squat Forever'* alongside *'Against the Looting of Nature'*, Athens, January 2013.

Yet contrary to expectations, the evictions of Villa Amalias were met with a disciplined and strategically reasoned refusal of the invitation to escalate on the part of autonomists and extra-parliamentary opposition. This refusal was succeeded by some extraordinary political theatre. In the early hours of Monday morning 14 January 2013, a curious episode took place: the early morning machine-gunning with an unidentifiable Kalashnikov (of course) of the deserted New Democracy headquarters in Athens with the exquisite detail of a single bullet ricocheting into the empty office of the Prime Minister Samaras. The operation was an extremely professional piece of theatre – the controlled simulation of an improbable assassination attempt in response to the eviction of Villa Amalias – which nevertheless served to evoke demonstrations of political solidarity within Greece and internationally. It's hard not to sympathize with the view of the living icon of the Greek capacity to resist, Manolis Glezos – who as a young man with his friend Apostolos Santas on 30 May 1941 replaced the swastika flying over the Parthenon with the Greek flag and who became a member of parliament for Syriza – when he asked in the Greek Parliament on Tuesday, 15 January, 'I want New Democracy to consider whether someone is gaining and who is gaining from these events. In any case it is not the left, someone else is gaining. And whether this gesture comes from para-state organizations friendly to New Democracy?' It was in any case a very professional manipulation of the spectacle, with all the appearances of a simulated escalation of the genre whose most notorious extreme was the burning of the Reichstag by the National Socialists. It led to the call by Samaras for a 'common front' against violence and terrorism, since it was 'necessary for the country to move smoothly towards recovery' – smoothly, which is to say, without undue resistance.

But I'd like to return to the eviction of the autonomist squat at Villa Amalias and the absence of any violent response, the absence of any escalation. This was not a simple sign of defeat or any waning in the intensity of the extra-parliamentary capacity to resist, but the outcome of a reasoned strategic judgement based on a theoretical response to provocation. The elaboration of this response was fly-posted throughout the radical Athenian neighbourhood of Exarchia in the early days of 2013, intensifying over the weekend of the 13th and 14th of January. Accompanying demonstrations and cultural initiatives in solidarity with the evicted squat, the posters and images that proliferated on the walls and lampposts over those critical days were testimony to the sophisticated theorization of resistance emerging from the squats and occupations. The growing pressure of the state – the deliberate escalation of its attack against the extra-parliamentary capacity to resist – was anticipated. A number of posters appeared in Exarchia already early in 2012 that began to sketch a theoretical, strategic response to a predicted intensification of struggle and the state's bid to escalate levels of oppression and thus provoke resistant violence. They appeared alongside some images from the 'Communist

Liberation Youth/Club Anaresis' that propose a Benjaminian constellation of the present with the past and deeply contested resistance of the German Occupation and the Greek Civil War – connecting the current resistance and its occupied territories' of the network of urban squats with the rural and mountain guerrilla of the Second World War resistance and subsequent civil war (Figures 5, 6 and 7). The dialectical image is clear: the war of resistance to Nazism begun in the Second World War resumed against the dictatorship and now again emerging today is the classic case of the Clausewitzian 'protracted war of resistance' revived by Mao in his theoretical and strategic writings and lectures of the 1930s. The central tenet of such protracted war is the *preservation* of the 'capacity to resist' and the refusal to escalate the current

FIGURE 5 *A Partisan Column with the Text: 'We Continue on Their Path to Destroy the Contemporary Junta and Their Neo-fascist Crutches Guerrillas Forever.' Communist Liberation Youth/Club Anaris, Athens, January 2013.*

FIGURE 6 *Dancing Guerrillas with the Same Text, Athens, January 2013.*

specific struggle in any way as to endanger the existence of that capacity at the behest of the enemy. The suppressed Villa Amalias and its near apotheosis into 'Villa Amalias Forever' now become a dialectical image of the survival of the Greek extra-parliamentary capacity to resist – at once an emblem of defeat and victory. Its defence does not entail conflict over the occupation of a dilapidated building on Acharnon Street in Athens but is the manifestation of a capacity to resist whose political and strategic claims and responsibilities exceed the tactical pressures of the present.

The mobilization of such dialectical images aligning past, present and future resistance struggles is accompanied by sustained discursive reflection and

FIGURE 7 *'All Students Death to the Neo-fascist Murderers', Citation of Imagery from the 1940s Youth Resistance Movement EPON, Athens, January 2013.*

invitations to debate, as in the poster issued by the anti-fa which reflects on the danger to the state of constructing an enemy 'with nothing to lose' through escalation and which generalizes the struggle at Villa Amalias into the general problem of resistance. I'd like to look closely at this statement issued by the squat at Lelas Karagianni (a street named after a victim of Nazism) in solidarity with Villa Amalias (Figure 8). The document is accompanied by an image of Villa Amalias with a text written in white on black that is in effect the citation of a document from the previous year – it is signed and dated LK37, January 2012. It presents itself then as a theoretical prediction of the previous oppression but one written in the spirit and letter of Clausewitz's view of politics and war and the dangers of succumbing to escalation.

FIGURE 8 *LK37 Statement, Athens, January 2013.*

The opening proposition is explicitly Clauswitzian in moving directly from a recognition of generalized systemic crisis to a 'continuous intensification of a concerted attack of the rulers on the plebeian and weaker strata of society' – politics has become war. The political crisis is indeed recognized as war and with an identified enemy – not the system but the rulers. It continues to observe that the destruction of what is called elsewhere 'social Europe' leads to the de-legitimation of the system and the multiplication of 'spontaneous and organized political, social and class resistances (*antistasis*)'. The document then introduces the term escalation (*klimakosi*) to link directly the rulers' attack on rights and the standard of living of the Greek population with a 'corresponding intensification and escalation of the state and in many cases the para-state repression of resistances'. This intensification of the attack is reserved not only for institutional resistances, but especially for the attempt at the constitution of a resistance emerging from 'spontaneous protest' and 'rage' of the 'oppressed and exploited'.

The communique continues that an essential part of this resistance is the constitution of a capacity to resist, one that is rooted in spontaneous defiance. The communique concludes,

> The squats and more generally the self-managed spaces are a specific part of this conscious and self-organized resistance, and have played a significant role in the development and evolution of the broader social struggles of recent decades. For this reason the squats always find themselves targeted by state repression and para-state gangs, and especially today are one of the priorities for the repressive operations of the state in view of combatting and eliminating the resistances that spring from below.

The resistances from below that constitute the insurgent capacity to resist are identified as 'demonstrations, strikes and workers struggles, neighbourhood movements, local resistances against the looting of nature, anti-fascist activity, gestures of solidarity to persecuted fighters and immigrants, etc.' The attack on Villa Amalias was indeed expected and to be met with the expression of a capacity to resist 'a wide, massive social front of all the resistances from below', but not the violent defence of a now strategically untenable territory. What is interesting in this document is the theorization of a measured response to the coming attack of the state, an attention to not fall into a reactive response to the state's escalating bid for initiative, but the continued construction of what Villa Amalias stood and stands for, namely the capacity to resist under conditions of civil war.

It is surprising for an observer habituated to the British style of repression through indifference to see the Greek prime minister focusing in his major New Year's press interview on the eviction of an anarchist squat. Of course, as seen, it is a tactic aimed at discrediting Syriza and distracting attention from the Lagarde list, but it is also more: like the Black Panthers in 1967 identified by the FBI's J. Edgar Hoover as the greatest internal threat to the security of the United States (a Greek translation of the Panther Bobby Seale's writings was available on newspaper stands in Exarchia at the beginning of 2013), Villa Amalias has become an icon of resistance. So it has to be de-sanctified by the head of government and its suppression mobilized towards the end of escalation. In a direct response to the accusation of escalating the conflict in the case of Villa Amalias, Samaras replied:

> We are talking about the occupation of public spaces that have lasted decades and that have proven to be centres of illegality. What kind of cultural activities do these thugs with batons, gas masks, and explosives serve, we are talking about dozens of centres of ammunition for illegal activities and even centres of black market. Is that tolerated anywhere in

the world? Is there a democracy that tolerates that? What kind of social spaces are the lairs of those of the balaclavas? Until now the state had to be apologetic for tolerating all that, now that the state is reacting, some will have to be accountable for why they continue to apologize and defend all this, because society does not applaud those with balaclavas, it is on the side of those who want to put an end to their activities. (*Vima* 13/1/2013)

All this is dedicated to neutralizing Syriza and exposing its 'bilingualism' of 'resistance and government' – they have yet to pronounce the shibboleth properly ... While Villa Amalias is being used to apply pressure to Syriza, it is at the same time putting on the agenda the strategic necessity of a concerted parliamentary and extra-parliamentary capacity to resist, one able to meet and counter the concerted and escalating parliamentary and extra-parliamentary offensive against it. As Marx noted, insurrection and the Greek insurrection in particular occupies the mode of actuality, it is important for its capacity to resist to be preserved, for the revival of resistance to be forever 'not impossible'. The suppression of the Greek capacity to resist is escalating, but its survival as 'bare resistance' and its revival is by no means 'not impossible'.

FIGURE 9 *The Villa and the Patriarch. A confrontation of two icons on the wall of Athens University with the graffito 'No nation unites us no state divides us the Villa and the Skaramanga squat forever'. The statue, whose shadow of a pointing finger, resembling a rifle, meets the arrow of anarchy, is Patriarch Gregorious V, executed in Istanbul in 1821 and who subsequently became an icon of the Greek national capacity to resist. He is there to call Greek students to national resistance, but in January 2013 the arrow of anarchy and the finger of the patriarch meet in an impossible unity of national and anti-national resistance.*

32

Strategic intervention and the digital capacity to resist

What is the character of strategic intervention in contexts where there is a claim not only to a monopoly of the use of the means of violence but also to a monopoly of secrecy? What options for resistance are available when the state extends its claim from the monopoly of violence to a monopoly of information? What are the quality and the conduct of resistance – its strategic options – when confronting not only the potential physical violence of state and corporate power but also its *arcanum*, the realm of secrecy and the exclusive control of access to information that it inhabits? Such questions immediately address the case of digital resistance, whether in the use of the internet as a means for coordinating resistance or in resistant interventions carried out on the terrain of the internet. They assume specific urgency when it is understood that the internet is increasingly assuming the character of an *arcanum* or place where states and corporations pursue a monopoly of secrecy, which is to say, the goal of denying citizens their secrecy. What is a strategic intervention in a context where the state's claim to monopolize secrecy or access to information necessarily entails the surrender of any such claim on the part of civil society?

Arcana and the internet

For some, the classic example of a strategic intervention in an *arcanum* is the Second World War. Once the *arcanum* of German and Japanese control and command – the Enigma coding of military communications – had been compromised by the work of Alan Turing and other cryptographers at Bletchley Park (Erskine and Smith 2011), what were the strategic options available for effective intervention? The obvious option was to use the information gained by the breach of military secrecy to secure short-term military advantage: if you know where the U-boats are you warn the ships in the convoys; if you know where enemy forces are and their intentions, you intervene in a pre-emptive response. But such intelligence-directed interventions would immediately alert the enemy that you had broken their codes – entered their *arcanum* – and they would respond by reconfiguring their codes. Another strategy consists of the selective and even disguised use of the information, intervening under the cover of fictions (spies sent and sacrificed, spies invented, bodies floating in the sea bearing false secrets), all designed to prevent the enemy from suspecting that their monopoly of secrecy had been compromised and their codes broken. In this case, strategic intervention becomes a play on appearances – giving any other explanation for operational knowledge than the real one. But this also entailed massive sacrifice – deliberately losing battles, only intervening when the secret of knowing the enemy's secrets is not risked (Sebag-Montefiore 2017). Neal Stephenson's novel *Cryptonomicon* – published in 1999 and widely read within the hacker community – fictionally elaborates on the scenario that the Second World War didn't happen but was a fiction, a cryptonomicon or fictional intervention in the *arcanum*. However extravagant the fiction, it remains the case that the field of operations research in the 1940s was close to the *arcanum* and many of its personnel – John von Neumann, Turing – would be crucial in the pre-history of the internet.

Why Assange missed the point

In his 2012 dialogues *Freedom and the Future of the Internet*, Julian Assange referred to the 'militarization of the Internet', or the 'tank in your bedroom', 'the soldier under the bed'. For him 'the Internet, which was supposed to be a civilian space, has become a militarized space ... [and as] the communications at the inner core of our lives now move over to the Internet ... our private lives have entered into a militarized zone'. 'We can't see the tanks,' he concludes, 'but they are there' (Assange et al. 2012, 33). This view contributes to his scepticism concerning the emancipatory potential of the internet, his view that the possibilities for resistance that it offers are narrow and precarious. Referring to Egypt, but we could now add Turkey, Hong Kong and the United States itself, he warns that digital resistance is a high-risk gamble that, once ventured, has to prevail 'because if it doesn't win then that same infrastructure that allows a fast consensus to develop will be used to track down and marginalize all the people who were involved in seeding the consensus' – the 'critical participants'. But how to win in this *arcanum* where the odds are not in favour of resistance: what would it mean to intervene strategically? Assange's almost intuitive response is to expose and protect – to expose the *arcanum*, state and corporate secrecy at the same time as protecting his own and his whistleblowers' secrecy by intense cryptography.

Assange's scepticism is a salutary warning to any attempt to mount a digital resistance, but it is important to reflect further on its central premise regarding the 'militarization of the Internet' and its implications for an understanding of the limits and possibilities of resistance. My reflections will return obsessively to Carl von Clausewitz and his posthumously published *On War* of 1832; Clausewitz is a central figure both for the development of the internet and for assessing its potential for resistance. Is Assange right when he says that the internet 'was supposed to be a civilian space' but is becoming militarized? Is it not well known that it was always militarized and that its civilian uses were an accidental exception – space wrested from the military, or conceded by it? It is, but without really appreciating the gravity and implications of such knowledge for the capacity to resist, prime among which is that if we move in a space that is a militarized *arcanum*, then our actions have to be guided by the appropriate rules and precautions: strategy.

Clausewitz's war of resistance

Clausewitz is central to the elaboration of a modern theory of resistance. In spite of its title – *On War* – his posthumously published masterpiece is less about war – *Krieg* – than resistance, *Widerstand*, or more precisely the war of resistance. *On War* is not so much an analysis of war than an account of how to resist the emergent military strategy of the revolutionary nation state – France – through what the Peninsular War had called the 'little war' or guerrilla, as opposed to the *grand guerre* conducted by the revolutionary armies. From the outset, Clausewitz offers a conceptual refinement that still in many ways eludes current strategic discussion around the theory of resistance; he is interested above all in the capacity or ability to risk resistance – *Widerstandsfähigkeit* – and not just its performative eruptions. Already on the first page of his first chapter, he defines the two objectives of war as: compromising to the point of destroying the enemy's capacity to resist while enhancing your own. As an idiosyncratic Kantian, his categorical imperative might be phrased, 'act so that maxim of your actions enhances your own and compromises your enemy's capacity to resist'. The rules for ensuring the survival and enhancement of this capacity are what constitute strategy for Clausewitz – it underlies his specific and historical discussion of the disposition of forces and of tactics. It is basically temporal in that it involves the survival or enhancement of the capacity over time and – in pursuit of the strategic aim of enhancement – permits tactical retreat and evasive action. Furthermore, Clausewitz's account acknowledges the centrality of information (and misinformation) for preserving or enhancing the capacity to resist, and in particular the maintenance of secrecy. It was this view that earned him the admiration of Marx, Engels, Nietzsche, Lenin, Mao, Guevara and most recently perhaps his closest and most successful exponent, Nelson Mandela.

But Clausewitz was not only read by the left, his work was also central to nuclear strategy in the Cold War, on both sides, but especially in the emergence of strategic discussion during the 1950s in the United States. There were two opposed positions. On the one hand, nuclear deterrence originally formulated by the mathematician John von Neumann and pursued by President Eisenhower, and on the other, a neo-Clausewitzian position emphasizing survival and the enhancement of the capacity to resist. The latter position was associated with the RAND Corporation and its most prominent exponent was Hermann Kahn, who detailed its execution in an influential theoretical text *On Thermonuclear War* published in 1960. Kahn argued in internal RAND Corporation papers and publicly in his book that the prime strategic objective should be less the avoidance of nuclear war than the enhancement of the possibility of survival and the continued existence of a capacity to resist or, in terms of operations theory, the means of ensuring continuous command and control. His underlying premise was that strategists should prepare the option of launching nuclear war with the security that the capacity to resist would survive a first or retaliatory strike.

Kahn's resistance after nuclear war and the invention of the internet

Kahn's bringing Clausewitz's *On War* into the nuclear age as *On Thermonuclear War* gives an invaluable glimpse into the quality and range of discussions in the RAND Corporation during the 1950s. He focused on the strategic options available under a 'post-attack' scenario, advocating in the name of the RAND Corporation a series of pre-emptive measures to ensure the survival of the capacity to resist after a nuclear attack. He lays out a programme of strategic planning dedicated to ensuring the survival of the United States but most importantly of its capacity to resist in a post-attack environment:

> Our study of non-military defence indicated that there are many circumstances in which feasible cultivation of military and non-military measures might make the difference between our facing casualties in the 2–20 million range rather than in a 50–100 million range. (Kahn 1960a, 98)

The non-military measures include what will later be known as 'civil defence' – fall-out shelters etc. – while the military measures focus obsessively on assuring the survival of the 'command and control' structure vital to order, sanction and execute a counter-attack. A pre-emptive strike on the part of the USSR is assumed to be directed against 'command and control arrangements' in order to disable any possible counter-attack. Kahn predicts that 'the bulk of their blow will be directed towards destroying, crippling or degrading the operation of our retaliatory forces' (Kahn 1960a, 165–6) and in particular the system of command and control. He returns repeatedly to this vulnerability, which he describes as the 'Achilles' heel' of current strategic doctrine, advising that 'we should become more conscious of the central role that command and control is likely to play in the future as a possible Achilles' heel of otherwise invulnerable systems' (Kahn 1960a, 301–2). The latter vulnerability was regarded as critical for the survival of the capacity to resist under nuclear attack and received increasing attention not only from Kahn but also from other researchers within the RAND Corporation.

Kahn's strategic planning focused on putting into place reliable systems of command and control that were guaranteed to survive and continue functioning after a nuclear first strike. The planning entailed putting in place 'some kind of information gathering network of data-processing centers that can receive and evaluate information, make decisions and transmit orders, all in a matter of minutes and even seconds. It seems feasible to build systems that will do this even when under enemy attack' (Kahn 1960a, 187–8). The substitution of 'feasible' for 'desirable' is characteristic of Kahn and the RAND Corporation's can-do ethos – if it was necessary to invent such a network, then it had to be 'feasible'. The only limitation Kahn seemed to place on the network was that it be analog, adding that 'nobody is yet willing to trust the decision of war or peace to a computer' (Kahn 1960a, 188). However, this was precisely part of the pragmatic response of a key technical researcher in the RAND Corporation to Kahn's strategic call for a system of command and control able to continue functioning after a nuclear first strike.

Kahn and the RAND Corporation's strategic requirements for ensuring the survival of the United States' capacity to resist contributed to the thinking that helped lead to the invention of the internet. This is well-known, and a common response to the view of the military, Clausewitzian origins of the internet is to present it as an interesting coincidence with few implications for future developments. However, such a genealogy is important for formulating strategic postures for resistance involving the internet given that its origins were themselves part of a resistance strategy. The contributions of the RAND Corporation researcher Paul Baran are especially important in this respect. His work was dedicated to supplying the network capable of technically delivering Kahn's strategic demand for a survivable system of command and control. In a paper from 1960 prepared for the United States Air Force – *On a Distributed Command and Control System Configuration* (Baran 1960b) – Baran cites Kahn's 1960 RAND Corporation paper *The Nature and Feasibility of War and Deterrence* (Kahn 1960b) as motivation for his invention of a survivable command and control network.

Baran and information war

Baran sought a control and command structure – or capacity to resist – that could survive a nuclear first strike. The option of bomb-proofing physical cables was explored but considered prohibitively expensive and unreliable. Baran focused instead on the idea of decentralized networks – first linking AM radio stations bearing only two messages – initiate and cease attack – then the telephone network, moving finally to theorize a distributed communication network with built-in redundancy and the ability to transmit discrete message packets. Baran later reflected:

> If the strategic weapons command and control systems could be more survivable, then the country's retaliatory capability could better allow it to withstand an attack and still function; a more stable position. But this was not a wholly feasible concept because long-distance communication networks at the time were extremely vulnerable and not able to survive attack. That was the issue. Here a most dangerous situation was created by a lack of a survivable communication system. That, in brief, was my interest in the challenge of building survivable networks. (Baran cited in Naughton 2000, 96)

In a series of RAND Corporation papers ranging from *Reliable Digital Communications Systems Using Unreliable Network Repeater Nodes* (Baran 1960a) in 1960 to *On Distributed Communications* (Baran 1964) in 1964, Baran proposed a distributed, decentralized network as the structure of communications most resistant to enemy attack. He also proposed that it be used to transmit bursts of digital information (later called 'packets') that could arrive by any number of routes across the network to be re-assembled at the receiving station. This would ensure that the network would be neither fatally compromised nor overloaded in the event of an attack. Both the network structure and the digital modality served to enhance the system's capacity to resist.

While it is widely accepted that Baran's work indirectly provided the intellectual inspiration for the internet, it is also held that its implications pointed beyond the military matrix in which it was conceived. It was an example of research of considerable civil import funded by the military but openly published and subject to scientific debate and public applications that far exceeded its contribution to defence (see Warnke 2011). However, as with everything published by the RAND Corporation, even the fact of publication was of strategic significance – and Baran's papers were no exception. The RAND Corporation was happy with the USSR knowing that the United States had theorized and was moving to implement a survivable control and command system. Indeed, the adversary's knowledge of the possibility and existence of such a system was essential to its working as effective deterrence. Even so, it might be argued, the implications of the research into distributed and thus decentralized networks eventually exceeded even this strategic context, providing the conditions for an emancipatory use or resistance of the non-hierarchical network.

Internet as control

This view became a powerful ideological argument for an antihierarchical, even libertarian, view of the net that saw in its decentralized architecture an unanticipated possibility for non-hierarchical exchanges of information. Unfortunately, this view neglects other forms of control over the distribution of information that were also designed into the distributed network. We now know that debates within the RAND Corporation concerning distributed networks were accompanied by research into cryptography and the concealment of message paths and contents in a system with the potential to archive and make available to surveillance all of its communications. Baran's distributed network was also a cryptonomicon since a distributed network had an even greater need for cryptography, building secrecy and the control it afforded into its very architecture. This interest and the research it generated were secret and withheld from the published papers, which were consequently in no respect the unintended 'free gift' from the military to a future non-hierarchical and democratic internet.

The RAND Corporation's proposal foundered in the face of opposition from the telephone companies; however, Baran's papers were noted in the UK in the National Physical Laboratory (Donald Davies and packet-switched networks) and brought to the attention of another US strategic body – the Defence Advanced Research Projects Agency – known as ARPA (dropping the D). The detail of the history is complicated, but the same problem of a survivable network, decentralized but with compensating cryptography to ensure concealed control, persisted in the networks that evolved towards the internet. In spite of their apparently non-hierarchical architecture, the history of these networks and their theoretical inspirations points to the construction of the internet as an *arcanum* or space of secrecy.

How to resist the internet

This brief account of the concealed role secrecy played in the early formulations of the internet puts into question any imprudent use of the internet as part of a resistant strategy. It would not be an exaggeration to regard the internet as one of the most prominent contemporary theatres for the struggle of contemporary resistance movements to invent, maintain and enhance a radical capacity to resist. The struggle is conducted on two main fronts: the first is resistance to the state's claim to a monopoly of information and strategy and the second, resistance to state infiltration and surveillance of social networks and the capacity to resist they have helped bring into existence. The first front is the struggle for and against secrecy – the attempt to sustain powerful encryption on the web against the will of the state and also the effort to compromise state and corporate encryption. This struggle has a history dating back to the 1990s, in which Wikileaks, the Edward Snowden US National Security Agency (NSA) exposures, and Anonymous are but the most recent skirmishes. At stake is the state's claim to monopolize the information transmitted on the web and to archive its movements and content at its openly illegal pleasure. Ironically, Chelsea Manning and Snowden's whistleblowing was made possible by a relaxation of the rules of access to the *arcanum* that was part of the strategic response to 9/11 and the view that the United States' capacity to resist had been compromised by excessive secrecy and the reluctance of the intelligence agencies to share information. The redistribution of the arcana of state secrecy, which was thought strategically necessary to secure the capacity to resist a new kind of enemy, paradoxically undermined it by extending access and making its secrets vulnerable to public exposure.

The other side of the coin of exposing the arcana of state is maintaining oppositional or civil secrecy through encryption. This is a difficult and fallible project, but one which is pursued with great strategic clarity and a keen sense of the paradox involved in protecting civil society (*Öffentlichkeit*) through secrecy. This is an old problem, going back to the publication of Immanuel Kant's essay 'Answering the Question: What is Enlightenment?' (Kant 1784) in the pages of the journal of a secret society – the *Berlinische Monatsschrift*. The strategic stakes involved, however, should not be underestimated, since such efforts on the part of civil society constitute a challenge to the emergent claim to a monopoly of secrecy on the part of the state.

The ability to compromise the state's capacity to resist by weakening its monopoly of secrecy and hence its strategy is an important complement to the ability to use social media in constituting an oppositional capacity to resist on the part of civil society. The two campaigns are usually understood separately, but compromising the state's ability to survey civil society's use of the internet is essential for the latter's ability to resist the state. This is one of the simultaneous strengths and weaknesses of using social media to foster strategic discussion and to organize resistance. They can certainly deliver unprecedented levels of articulated and disciplined mass action, but also every step in constituting the capacity to resist and mounting resistance – as in the Istanbul Taksim Republic for example – can be traced and policed if the resistance is not successful. The very arts that permitted the creation of a capacity to resist on the eve of resistance can also undo it on the day after. Mega-data can be used to trace associations (routine work for the NSA and other intelligence agencies) and to reconstitute with extreme precision the oppositional capacity to resist and its key members – militants and theoreticians – and even to proceed to their physical elimination (see Chamayou 2015). From one point of view, the web can liberate resistance and create a new capacity to resist, but from another it can also serve as the instrument for its decisive repression.

New capacities to resist

Rosa Luxemburg's dictum that resistant struggle itself gives rise to new capacities and constituencies of opposition was vindicated by the resistant actions in Hong Kong. Haunted by the memory of the failure of the Tiananmen Square occupation in 1989, which compromised the Chinese population's capacity to resist for over a quarter of a century, demonstrators associated with the two main strands of the Hong Kong resistance – Occupy Central with Peace and Love and the student Scholarism movement – adopted a strategy that they hoped would ensure the survival of the capacity to resist in the prospect of what Mao himself described in the 1930s as a 'protracted war of resistance'. Alongside the restraint and commitment to non-violence shown by the resistants – by now classical resistance tactics learned from Gandhi and the US civil rights movement – were a number of effective tactical innovations. The most striking was the conscious effort to limit the use of social media for strategic and tactical discussion in order to avoid leaving a record of the constitution of a capacity to resist that would help the authorities to unravel and compromise it at a later date. The demonstrators made wide use of the app FireChat, which makes an off-grid social network possible using Bluetooth and Wi-Fi – ideal for mass gatherings. Over 100,000 copies of the app were downloaded in a day, putting the app to a use that doesn't seem to have been anticipated by its designers (they say on their website, perhaps with faux naïveté, 'Whether you are on the beach or in the subway, at a big game or a trade show, camping in the wild, or even travelling abroad, simply fire up the app with a friend or two and find out who else is there'). The strategic benefit is nevertheless clear: one of the devices connected to FireChat can serve as a portal to the web and to exposed on-grid global social media; this device could employ deep encryption, and the decrypted messages then disseminated through FireChat in a way that left few traces for the state to follow later. This was an example of strategic prudence characteristic of both previous and contemporary resistant politics; it complemented and further mobilized the resistant virtues of a non-negotiable passion for justice and courage. It testified not only to the need for resistance and protest, but also to prudence in the choice of means through which they are pursued, above all through what Clausewitz identified as the prime objective of a resistant politics – the creation and preservation not just of an act of resistance but more importantly of the capacity to resist.

Yet I should end with some comments on the desirability of a resistant intervention that frontally challenges the state's claimed monopolies of violence and secrecy. It brings with it a number of problems that might make us wary of adopting it too enthusiastically as a political philosophy or technique. First of all, the emphasis on strategy and enmity in the theory of resistance brings resistant politics too close to the model of warfare – perhaps politics and political reason are and should be distinct from strategy? In this case, the ever closer relationship between state monopolies of violence and secrecy might provoke disproportionately violent responses to any threat posed to its monopoly of secrecy and an escalation of conflict that can only compromise the capacity to resist. Furthermore, perhaps a resistant politics, however ingenious and imaginative its tactical innovations, is ultimately reactive, reacting against initiatives of its adversaries – as was the case in Hong Kong – and not initiating and guiding political change. Perhaps, too, resistance is too sombre a politics, whose emphasis on the cardinal virtues of courage, prudence and justice limits the emancipatory élan that is characteristic of revolutionary politics to questions of survival under conditions of repression and open attack. And finally, perhaps resistance is less a political philosophy than a politico-military technique, one that can be adopted in the name of emancipation but also in the name of reaction and repression. This leads to the final concern or question – if the *arcanum* is indeed an important site of current interventions and requires an appropriately encrypted resistant strategy, what implications will this have for the existence of a public sphere and even democracy?

33

XR: Thinking resistance at the end of the world

The attitude towards resistance in the recent radicalizations of ecological struggle is strikingly ambiguous. One of the early organizers of Extinction Rebellion – Gail Bradbrook – reported that the emergent movement almost divided on the name for the movement, eventually opting it seems for Extinction *Rebellion* instead of Extinction *Resistance* or other possibilities.[1] And yet she agrees fully with Tukano indigenous nation activist Daiara Tukano's description of 'existence as resistance' (Bradbrook 2019, 185), a view wholly consistent with the theory and practice of total resistance to what Rob Nixon described as 'slow violence' in his now classic reflection *Slow Violence and the Environmentalism of the Poor* (2011). Another organizer, Roger Hallam, describes the careful and deliberate organization of the Extinction Rebellion in terms of a 'civil resistance model' and links the Rebellion to techniques of non-violent resistance pioneered in the Indian Independence Movement and the Civil Rights movement in the United States. And yet, in the movement's 'Declaration of Rebellion' resistance itself is not named, appearing instead as 'rebellion', 'revolt' and 'rising'. Is this reticence in using the term 'resistance' as a motivating term in the open struggle merely verbal, or has the discourse of resistance reached its limit when mobilizing in the face of the grave and increasingly conspicuous threat of incrementally catastrophic climate change?

Resistance and the uprising

One of the main theoretical and organizational sources of the Extinction Rebellion strategy – the Engler brothers' *This Is an Uprising* (2016) – suggests that the problem with the use of term resistance is more fundamental. This reflection on the lessons of US activist movements since the Civil Rights movement in early 1960s and the theoretical work of Gene Sharp, Saul Alinsky and Frances Fox Piven departs from the premise that resistance movements have always involved something more than the reactive stance associated with the term 'resistance'. From the outset, the Englers' discussion of the strategies employed in the Civil Rights campaign of 1963 in Birmingham Alabama insists that it involved more than 'high stakes acts of resistance' or no-saying, however audacious and inspiring these may have been (Engler and Engler 2016, xii). And yet in spite of the Engler's references to 'eruptions of mass resistance' such as 'in Mexico, Turkey, Brazil and Hong Kong' as well as #BlackLivesMatter (Engler and Engler 2016, xxi), it seems as if resistance is a necessary but not sufficient precondition for contemporary activist strategies. The virtue of the Engler brothers' book however is to point beyond an impasse in the theory of resistance that sees acts of resistance as fugitive reactions to momentarily intolerable conditions. From this point of view resistance seems to be reactive and transitive; it is always resistance *to* an intolerable state of affairs comprising sometimes extremely courageous acts that seem destined to leave almost intangible traces. And when this state of affairs is considered to be 'an event unprecedented in [human] history, one which, unless immediately addressed, will catapult us further into the destruction of all we hold dear: this nation, its peoples, our ecosystems and the future of generations to come', then it is easy to see how mere negative resistance may seem insufficient when it becomes a question of affirming the future of life itself on this planet (Extinction Rebellion 2019, 1).

A text squarely in the tradition of the theory of resistance, my *On Resistance: A Philosophy of Defiance* (2013), attempted to escape this theoretical and strategic *impasse* through a number of formal operations, most notably through postulating a Clausewitzian 'capacity to resist' prior to concrete acts of resistance and associated with an appeal to the paradoxical possibility of an 'affirmative resistance'. The object of war in Clausewitz's formulation is not so much the resistance of the adversary as their 'capacity to resist'. Resistance as the enhancement of this capacity ceases to be a reaction to a given state of affairs and becomes a positive end or strategic object in itself. It is possible to affirm the enhancement of the capacity to resist in a number of ways that are not tied to the immediate tactical demands of a given struggle. The capacity to resist is not tied to the present moment of struggle but can also be a legacy from the past to the future; affirming the capacity permits a more powerful, enduring and successful campaign of resistance.

The Englers' reflections on a number of historically specific practices of resistance – the Civil Rights movement in the United States, the Serbian *Otpor* 'resistance' movement, LGBT mobilizations and Occupy Wall Street – seem nevertheless to point beyond even a view of resistance that focuses on the capacity rather than acts of resistance. While paying homage to resistance and some of the logics associated with it, they also discover a number of strategic innovations that enhance its affirmative character and make it appropriate for an action such as Extinction Rebellion. Not only did the Serbian activists appeal to the precedent of historical 'resistance' during the Second World War but they also made a number of strategic innovations in the conduct of resistance struggles that the Englers themselves describe in terms of an emergence of a 'civil resistance' that exceeds the received models of resistance strategy. Yet while the practice is still described as 'resistance', the term itself and its historical resonances are increasingly sidelined: resistance can no longer be carried out in the name of resistance, but better under such titles as 'revolt', 'rebellion' and 'uprising'.

The Engler brothers, building on the work of American theorists Gene Sharp, Saul Alinsky and Frances Fox Piven,[2] point to a number of ways in which the new activist strategic posture seems to exceed the limits of the theory of resistance. The first concerns nonviolence. The theory of resistance does not automatically endorse nonviolence; its most influential modern statement by Clausewitz is indeed framed by the context of violent warfare. While it was innovatively developed by Ghandi and his successors in the direction of a non-violent strategy in an acknowledged state of war, resistance as a tactic is theoretically indifferent to the use of violent or nonviolent means. The classic way of justifying nonviolent resistance – adopted by Ghandi in his notion of the character of the *satyagrahist* – was to appeal to its ethical character as an act of exemplary and unusual moral sacrifice. This position was fundamentally contested by Gene Sharp, whose argument for nonviolence rested less on the grounds of moral value than on those of strategic efficacy – that nonviolent resistance is an efficient and effective strategy for entering into and winning an asymmetrical conflict. This position is adopted by the Engler brothers and is central to their accepting and developing Sharp's term 'civil resistance' as their primary strategic axiom.

With respect to nonviolence, the qualified use of the expression 'nonviolent resistance' as an effective strategic position is certainly justifiable. This is also the case with a second and corollary position held by the Englers, which is that resistance is not just a spontaneous outburst of revolt or defiance. The classic Leninist objection to resistance deriving from *What Is to Be Done* holds that it is largely a spontaneous reaction to insupportable circumstances that flares up and rapidly disappears back into the darkness of subaltern history. The Engler brothers argue against this that resistance can, indeed *must*, be carefully planned and organized, drawing on resources from the past and aiming for sustained action in the future. Their re-invention of Clausewitz's 'capacity to resist' is presented in terms of a mediating position between the primacy of community organization associated with Alinsky and his followers, and the affirmation of spontaneity by Piven; they claim that the future of social change in this country may well involve integrating these approaches ... The emerging field of civil resistance offers considerable potential in addressing this task, providing tools that can help create a synthesis between competing traditions. (Engler and Engler 2016, 32)

Their reading of the cultures of resistance informing and supporting the initiatives of the Civil Rights movement and the resistance movements they study is consistent with the Clausewitzian attention to the capacity or ability to resist (*Widerstandsfähigkeit*), or in their terms the 'skills' of resistance rather than apparently spontaneous acts of resistance. The Engler brothers point to the central role played by organization in apparently spontaneous acts of resistance, and they describe the kinds of organizational structure they deem appropriate not only to mounting but also sustaining resistance. This is certainly confirmed by the carefully planned and executed actions of Extinction Rebellion that succeeded in creating organizational forms that guided their actions, especially their strategic withdrawals, without stifling the joy or initiative of struggle.

While the issues of violence and organization may be contained without compromising the limits of the theory of resistance, the final strategic posture described by the Engler brothers and adopted by Extinction Rebellion does pose a considerable challenge. It concerns the paradox of an affirmative resistance, a resistance that does not react to circumstances but seizes the initiative in shaping them. Clausewitz experienced considerable difficulty in understanding how resistance – by definition reactive and even defensive – could seize the initiative. For him, a condition for success in a conflict consisted in seizing the initiative and defining the character of the battlefield and the terms of engagement. From this perspective resistance, and even the 'capacity to resist', however positively construed, seems always to be already on the defensive and at a disadvantage with respect to its adversary.

The uses of escalation

The response of the Engler brothers is to adopt a term and a practice that was a matter of considerable disquiet to Clausewitz himself: escalation. In their fascinating description of the emergence of strategic positions in the Civil Rights struggle for Birmingham, Alabama in 1963, they describe Dr King's decision to risk jail as a strategic gamble through which 'he could both move others to step forward and reassert a sense of escalating drama in the Birmingham drive' (Engler and Engler 2016, 20). The reference to 'escalation' here is not casual and it recurs throughout the text, even if it is not acknowledged in the admirably full index. Their critique of spontaneous eruptions of defiance is framed in terms of their inability 'to escalate or to sustain multiple waves of protest over a period of years' (Engler and Engler 2016, 28). Dr King's 'Project C' (C for 'confrontation') is an example of a strategy of escalation, which, as the Engler brothers concede, provoked strong criticisms from understandably risk-adverse local organizers and activists (Engler and Engler 2016, 48). However, for the Engler brothers controlled escalation is the means by which a resistance movement is able to seize the initiative, determine the nature of the battlefield and set the terms of its present and future engagements.

For the Engler brothers controlled escalation can overcome the limits of mere resistance and the problems it raises: 'For as long as people have experimented with building movements around strategic nonviolence, they have grappled with a dilemma: how to reconcile the explosive short-term potential of disruptive power with the need to sustain resistance to meet long-term goals' (Engler and Engler 2016, 62). Escalation in other words is the missing term in equating the factors of spontaneity, initiative and a sustainable, organizational capacity to resist. Both the Civil Rights and the Serbian *Otpor* movements provide models for how 'dissidents employing militant nonviolent tactics could gradually increase pressure over time, escalating through multiple stages of uprising that were spread over years' (Engler and Engler 2016, 63). Controlled, phased and strategically planned escalations of resistance could support and enhance both the organization and the constituency of 'civil resistance' by making it strategically effective in Clausewitzian terms and able to seize the initiative and choose the time and place of struggle. In this way it is the adversary who is forced into a reactive, 'resistant' position with respect to the initiative of the resisters. The Engler brothers describe this strategy as 'momentum building' and see it as a movement of intensification that combines action and organization destined to arrive at the 'moment of the whirlwind' that 'is the endpoint of escalation' (Engler and Engler 2016, 189). The 'weapon of resistance', as Subcommandante Marcos once ironically described it, is revealed to be the capacity to escalate in a cumulative and controlled manner.

The resort to escalation as a strategy marks the point where the theory and practice of momentum building exceed or transform the theory of resistance. Clausewitz believed that escalation has to be employed with great circumspection and foresight, for it is intrinsically unpredictable, depending on being able to predict and match the will and the capacity of the adversary to escalate in response. He considered it the resort of gamblers and risk takers, since it would initiate movements that would escape the control of both adversaries. It is the resort of those strategists who have nothing to lose on a final throw of the dice, such as Napoleon towards the end of his military career. It is not something that Clausewitz would associate with the dogged and persistent work of resistance. And yet in the case of civil resistance it does make sense in specific circumstances. One is the scenario of 'slow violence' described by Rob Nixon where the war remains inconspicuous unless it is escalated and driven into visibility, while another is the predicament where the alternative to escalation is mutual assured destruction. The recent mobilizations of Eco-Resistance such as Extinction Rebellion consider both circumstances to be operative: the enemies in the 'climate war' remain inconspicuous and hidden until the struggle against them is escalated, and the failure to escalate in the circumstances of what is believed to be the Sixth (Human) Mass Extinction Event is assured destruction of human life on this planet.

Nixon's analyses of 'slow violence' contrast the rapid, visible violence of open warfare with the slow and inconspicuous violence of daily, routine attrition. Visible violence is fully compatible with slow violence, as in Nixon's analysis of the use Agent Orange in Vietnam that was both an act of extreme visible violence with slow and drawn-out invisible consequences in illness and suffering that last decades. Indeed, Nixon argues, the fast, spectacular violence of war and catastrophe takes place against an almost invisible backdrop of slow, inconspicuous violence:

> By slow violence I mean a violence that occurs gradually and out of sight, a violence of delayed destruction that is dispersed across time and space, an attritional violence that is typically not viewed as violence at all. Violence is customarily conceived as an event or action that is immediate in time, explosive and spectacular in space, and as erupting into instant sensational visibility. (Nixon 2011, 2)

In this respect, the controlled escalation of 'civil resistance' is dedicated to exposing the work of slow violence by accelerating it. The Engler brothers describe the campaign in Birmingham and by extension the entire Civil Rights movement as an attempt to expose the slow violence of routine and thoughtless racism. Dr King's actions were aimed not to engage in uncontrolled escalation but to accelerate conflict sufficiently 'to expose the violence routinely inflicted upon the black community under Jim Crow segregation. "We merely bring to the surface the hidden tension that is already alive," King wrote. "We bring it out in the open where it can be seen and dealt with"' (Engler and Engler 2016, 22). This distinguished the escalation of the resistance in Birmingham, Alabama from the routine daily resistance of the community there; this escalation was driven by the conviction that the truth of slow violence could be exposed through controlled and conscious escalation.

The strategy of controlled escalation is appropriate for contexts that Clausewitz described as those of 'imperial peace' or the peace of the victors. In these contexts the ongoing war is no longer conspicuous and the exercise of violence has de-accelerated to the point of invisibility. The main focus of Rob Nixon's analysis is the environmentalism of the poor, referring to the slow violence of ecological destruction. While the effects of climate change are brutally felt, the causes and the beneficiaries of it remain largely inconspicuous, as does the level of threat under which the world's population now lives. For this reason the approach of escalating civil resistance described by the Englers proved significant for Extinction Rebellion. Theirs was an attempt to make visible the threat of climate change to human life on the planet and to call for immediate radical change. This was not an exercise in resisting the slow violence of climate change on the terms of engagement set by corporations and governments, but seizing the initiative by changing the terrain of struggle and building up a sustained momentum of resistance. Yet perhaps this strategy is too confident that escalation can be controlled by raising or lowering its intensity. Clausewitz warned that because of its dyadic character, escalation was unstable and neither adversary could pretend to be in control of it. And yet the stakes of XR are so high that escalation cannot be avoided with all the risks that an acceleration of violence brings with it.

Extinction Rebellion and the Joyous Revolt

Extinction Rebellion followed the strategic council of the Engler brothers' view of 'civil resistance' by combining organization with a controlled escalation or threat of escalation of the level of struggle. Extinction Rebellion's UK actions included occupations of Oxford Circus, Marble Arch, Waterloo Bridge, Piccadilly Circus and Parliament Square in London in April 2019 with mass actions directed against fossil fuel companies, the Treasury and the Stock Exchange and a threat of sustained action against Heathrow Airport. Their strategic profile conforms both to the drive to make visible an otherwise inconspicuous slow violence – 'Tell the Truth' – and to raise the stakes in a struggle for which its activists are convinced the alternatives are either victory or the end of life on this planet: 'This time, we are literally fighting for our lives' (Burns and Reimann 2019, 108). For this reason Extinction Rebellion are fully prepared to escalate the struggle while building up organizational momentum. And it is for the same reason that they could not adopt the name of Extinction Resistance, since this would concede the initiative to the forces carrying through the Sixth (Human) Extinction Event. The Rebellion does not just say no to extinction, but more affirmatively it says yes to the lives of future generations.

When describing the strategy of Extinction Rebellion, Roger Hallam cites the 'civil resistance model' described by the Engler brothers, but points to a suite of actions that in some respects goes beyond the limits of the theory of resistance. The number of actors required is several thousand and the choice of battlefield is the capital city in order to gain the attention of the elites and their media. So far this is consistent with the Civil Rights precedent, as is the further condition of deliberately breaking the law. The latter is justified in strategic terms of creating the 'social tension and public drama that are vital to create change' (Hallam 2019, 101). After choosing the terrain of struggle the next strategic step is to escalate the struggle by deliberately crossing the border of law-abiding demonstration. With this the movement seizes the narrative: 'It's the great archetypal story in all cultures: against the odds the brave go into battle against evil.' It also serves to show the adversary that 'you are serious and unafraid' and creates 'the necessary material and economic cost' to earn the elite's attention. The actions must also be nonviolent and extended over a long period – they must cease to be an event but become a felt crisis. And finally, the actions must be life-affirming and joyful: 'We are going to show the media that we are not sitting around patiently waiting to die any longer. We're going to have a party. Obviously' (Hallam 2019, 102). With these strategic recommendations Extinction Rebellion set to work on a project of affirmative resistance, making explicit what is often underemphasized in the resistance movements.

One of the most innovative contributions of the first XR campaign was the invention of a strategy for signalling escalation and de-escalation. This was the pink boat, the *Berta Cáceres* – named after the Honduran environmental activist murdered in 2016 – and smuggled by activists into Oxford circus. The *Berta Cáceres* provided an aestheticized focus for the struggle, acting as a way both to initiate and contain escalation. The appearance of the pink boat in Central London provided a joyous visual icon for the rebellion and served to intensify and focus its actions and occupation, but its withdrawal also served as an aesthetic means to signal to activists and the authorities that XR was prepared to de-escalate. It provided a means of strategic retreat otherwise absent in the Engler brothers' theory of escalation. In the words of James and Ruby – XR strategists of the roadblock – it earnt a few days in which 'the police mostly let us be' as well as 'creating a show and a traffic stopping photo opportunity ...' (James and Ruby 2019, 105). The pink boat provided a form of aesthetic immunity for the struggle as well as an all-important exit strategy for an action that deliberately ran the risk of a dangerous escalation of the struggle.

The joy of escalation and saying yes to life marks an intensification of the theory and practice of resistance, releasing it from its often thanatopolitical premises. The appeals to the 'already dead' of the resistance or to 'revolutionary suicide' as a model for resistant action give way to an affirmation of life. This always accompanied resistance movements but, with perhaps the signal exception of the Greenham Common Women's Peace Camp, was never explicitly thematized as an essential strategic posture. Resistance as life is in this case explicit and clear, but it is not so clear whether this 'civil resistance' of joyful, life-affirming escalation can still be categorized as resistance or whether it constitutes a moment or ecstatic point of reference in an extended campaign of ecological resistance. We may conclude that either the forms of resistance currently emerging in the context of ecological struggle mark its radical metamorphosis into a new phase or the perceived stakes of human and wider species extinction remain too high to be left to resistance alone.

Notes

1   'Rebels with a Cause', *Evening Standard Magazine,* 3.5.19, 14.
2   Sharp 1973, Alinsky 1989, Piven and Cloward 1979.

Afterword

In 'The Spirit of Resistance and Its Fate', an essay which comes near the end of this remarkable and much anticipated collection, Howard Caygill argues that Hegel's work is infused with the spirit of resistance, which pushes towards a realm of actuality 'that intractably recoils from any pretention to think the absolute' (391).[1] Caygill is issuing to modern philosophical thought a challenge which picks up and runs with the aporetic moment, the insistence on the trauma of reason, that was central to the philosophical speculation of Gillian Rose, to whose work the opening essay pays tribute. 'Is it the fate of resistance to become a moment successfully surpassed by speculative dialectic,' Caygill asks, 'or does it resist, remain to trouble and develop a certain immunity to dialectical capture?' (392). It is just one instance in the essays where the movement of philosophy seems to mimic, replicate – or even propel and be propelled by – the life of politics on the streets. Does resistance as philosophical concept resist its dialectical capture? Does resistance in the world exceed the forces which array themselves to suppress it, all the more brutally, it seems, with every passing day? What ruse of philosophy and of protest might ensure that resistance is equal to its task, or more simply, survives as a capacity? *Force and Understanding* is best read, I suggest, as Caygill's unique way of asking these questions.

The collection could not be more timely. It arrives in response to the urgency of the hour – climate crisis, genetics, the spreading corruption and capture of the internet, resurgent racism, the crushing of protest across the globe. With exceptional range – and remarkable stamina one might say – Caygill writes on topics that stretch from Kant, Hegel, Nietzsche and Benjamin, through the legacy of colonialism, war in Kosovo and the stranglehold of the Greek debt, to Kafka, the Black Panthers and Extinction Rebellion. It is a book of strange encounters which, sometimes shockingly, always plausibly, manages in the same breath to speak of Deleuze and Darwin, Kant alongside Kepler and Newton, Hannah Arendt and lynching, Bataille and genocide, the British Medical Association and the Pope, Plato and Huey Newton of the Black Panthers (for whom sharing the *Republic* with comrades on the block and reading the famous cave allegory as an allusion to prison changed everything).

'Let me not to the marriage of true minds admit impediments', Shakespeare opens his famous Sonnet 116, lines which came to mind as I read, and which seemed apt for more than one of these pairings (starting with Caygill and Rose). In the quagmire that is so much philosophical disputation, Caygill's writing stands out for its reach, for being bold in readings which are at the same time meticulous to the letter, for its generosity and ruthlessness combined. For example, in an early essay in the collection which returns to his 2001 *Levinas and the Political*, Caygill condemns Levinas without reserve for his refusal to comment in 1967 on the violence of Israel as a nation-state, and for suggesting that the Arab peoples were deaf to the call of conscience after the Shoah in not ceding their lands to the Jews. But he also trawls Levinas's own writing on Judaism where he finds a counter-spirit, for which true Zionism is 'slandered' by Israel's territorial ambitions, and the nation, in failing to be just, betrays the legacy of its own people (Levinas is thus made to embody the 'equivocation of the ethical', which was such an important part of the thinking of Gillian Rose) (359).

One of the main quarries of Caygill's thought throughout this collection is the category of certainty, the idea that doubt can be mastered by philosophy in such a way as to reinforce and permit the expansion of powers that brook no argument or challenge to their authority. Here again Caygill is describing a two-way traffic between philosophy and the world that philosophy both responds to and creates. 'The project of managing the crisis of reason and subjectivity provoked by the violent, imperial expansion of Europe,' he writes in 'Violence, Civility and the Predicaments of Philosophy', which is one of my favourite essays, 'contributed decisively to the development of modern philosophy' (40). Philosophy, one might say, was summoned to the courts of empire to facilitate the expulsion of doubt which nagged at the imperial consciousness while fuelling its ambitions. The newly discovered certainty of the human subject, Caygill argues, arose within the parameters of the burgeoning nation-state whose so-called 'rational' management of violence 'was only possible when potential and actual violence had been displaced to the border' (42). The resonance with the bitter realities of migration today could not be more striking – Trump and the Mexican border, the rising hatred of migrants as cause and effect of Brexit in the UK, the official refusal to acknowledge that it is the legacy of colonialism and the policies of the metropolitan nations that fuels the despair driving migration.

Arguing that such manoeuvres – in the world and in the heart – are doomed to fail, Caygill plucks his support from deep inside his philosophical repertoire. The idea of building a wall against danger is, Epicurus insisted, sheer delusion: 'One can attain security against other things, but when it comes to death all men live in a city without walls' (Epicurus is one of the hero philosophers of the book and Nietzsche an Epicurean, though this is rarely recognized) (142).

Violence located at the border 'recoils', returning in unpredictable ways to the heart of the metropolis in the form of 'traumatized veterans, economic distortion or the effects of environmental damage', to which we could add images of children weeping and drowned (44). Now the border can be seen for what it is, a marker of 'what is possessed by some and not by others' (44). At which point, the space of civility is thrown into crisis since it can no longer hide its own violence from itself. As too is philosophy, which 'has to reorient itself in this new space, beginning with an acknowledgement of the violence of its predicaments' (45). It is just one of the brilliant strokes of this collection to bind philosophy and politics so deeply to each other, while keeping the connection open-ended, to allow for the different, contradictory, paths which that relationship might take: reflective, implicated, at loggerheads, or most devastating perhaps, mutually guilty, that is, morally and historically accountable to and for each other.

'The violent predicaments of philosophy' might in fact have also served as a subtitle to the book, which moves, seemingly without effort, between philosophy's understanding of violence in its historical moment to the violence involved in the very category of judgement (as Caygill indicates, the phrase 'critique of violence' is double-edged, with violence as object of critique but also its attribute) (285). There is, he writes in relation to Kant's concepts of reflection, 'an act of violence without which we would be unable to secure our judgements' (49). 'You must learn', Nietzsche writes in *Human, All Too Human*, 'to understand the necessary injustice in every for and against' (124). Likewise Clausewitz is presented here as not only examining the historical reality of war, but also, since all judgement involves enmity and chance, as making 'war and its violence stand for the basic predicament of judgement' (412). In these readings, civility, judgement, the prized stakes of Western thought and culture – one after the other – fall prey to the cruelties they take pride in disavowing and barring from their remit like barbarians at the gates. Caygill is excavating the philosophical debris of the master nations, exposing the 'unacknowledged violence' lurking behind and deep within our most cherished social arrangements.

We should not be surprised, then, to see the law of contract and the regulation of debt, in which we invest our security, boast our equity, fall at the same hurdle. Amongst the many other things they share, Nietzsche, Kafka and Benjamin all open out the ambiguity of the German word 'Schuld', most commonly translated as 'debt' (for Nietzsche 'cruelty', for Kafka 'shame', for Benjamin 'guilt'). Making one of his many deft moves from then to now, Caygill points out how these archaic qualities of debt have been on view in the recent Greek debt crisis 'in which extravagant displays of cruelty, shame and guilt concerning the issue of nationhood and personal debt adorn the brutal economic management of the structural financial imbalance of the Eurozone'

(419). A veritable *Schuldfest*, not without traces of 'the acts of theft and cruelty', 'the blood and torture' which Nietzsche, in synch with Marx on this matter, traced to the category of debt and to the 'asymmetries of command and obedience' lurking beneath the garb of formal equality which sustains it (420). 'Why must the debtor bleed?' (421). For Nietzsche, law and morality draw their roots out of the same blood-soaked history 'thoroughly and for a long time' (420). Silently, Caygill lets drop the fact that for Nietzsche this has been true for 'everything *great* on earth' (420, my emphasis).

*

Caygill's previous two books, *On Resistance: A Philosophy of Defiance* (2013) and *Kafka: In Light of the Accident* (2017) (a third book on aesthetics and madness will complete the trilogy), are linked by their passionate rejection of the idea that the world can be encompassed and managed by human knowledge. Resistance is a strategy that involves the utmost care and planning, but it also – as Clausewitz was the first to argue – embraces and takes its bearings from the unpredictable moments and opportunities thrown up in the insane and incalculable field of war (which is why guerrilla warfare is the origin of resistance and its prototype). While Kafka, far from offering an allegory of bureaucracy in full mastery of its subjects and itself, as he is so often read, instead portrays a demonic world in which logic and prediction endlessly fall prey to random happenings and a nonsensical, illegible, law. As these essays repeatedly demonstrate, the contingent is a capacious entity that contains multitudes. It can include 'the concussive motion of an all-penetrating matter', which was how Kant described a form of life in excess of his own categories, A. S. Eddington's cosmology of the 'accidental universe' (which he shared with Kafka), and James Clerk Maxwell's view of the telephone as enabling 'the proliferation of new chance encounters' (206, 348, 259). In Maxwell's vision of the future, the human would not become omniscient and omnipotent like the demon, but would always remain 'subject to chance and to the necessity of death' (261). For Aby Warburg, the snake rituals of the Pueblo Indians, through which they summoned rain and lightning, stood out against Uncle Sam's use of technology 'as a precision weapon against the forces of nature', shedding all hubris by recognizing that man was subordinate to nature's capricious laws (257). ('Technology and the Propitiation of Chance' is the title of the essay in which Maxwell and Warburg appear.)

If, in that last example, contingency appears as a concept radically pitted against ecological disaster (to rule is to destroy the world), its political resonance spreads throughout these essays, appearing at moments to be the filter through which they all, or many of them, should be read. Thus in one of Caygill's most striking turns, which was also the starting premise of his book on Kafka, he demonstrates that the common presentation of Kafka's work as a progressive sequence terminating in the utopian vision of community which ends *Amerika* is no such thing (failure to progress as a creative turn in the process of thought is another constant of these essays, something Kafka shares with Kant and Nietzsche) (101). *By accident,* Max Brod published the works out of the order of their original composition, setting in motion a falsely redemptive vision of Kafka's work encapsulated in the advance from *The Trial* to *Amerika* (the sequence was in fact the other way round). Redemption also appears here as the last myth of philosophy which endlessly demonstrates its 'inability to redeem itself from the desire for redemption' (96).

Thus Hannah Arendt, in the footsteps of Walter Benjamin, raised the final scenes of *Amerika*, set in the Nature Theatre of Oklahoma [*sic*] to the status of 'national utopia', a happy ending of collective belonging (also a code for Zionism). In doing so, she ignored the history of racial violence which lurks within and behind its staged veneer, whose unavoidable presence Caygill so cannily demonstrates. Thus Karl Rossman enters the theatre under the assumed name of 'Negro'; he is transfixed by a photo of the Washington theatre that was the scene of Lincoln's assassination; and Kafka's own main photographic source for *Amerika* included a photo of a racist lynching, entitled 'Oklahoma Idyll' (the fact that Kafka preserved the misspelling in his novel suggests he was alerting his reader to this history). 'Far from being the utopia believed by Brod, Benjamin and Arendt', Caygill comments, 'the "Nature Theatre of Oklahoma" begins to appear as a site of execution, one inextricably linked to the history of slavery and racism in the United States' (328). Arendt misses it – in tune with the political blindness on race and segregation that will follow in her own thought. And she does so even as this hidden sub-text places the 'Nature Theatre', alongside *The Trial* and 'In the Penal Colony' which, contra Brod, were its contemporaries, on the path to the processes of selection, concentration and extermination which are at the core of Arendt's own analysis of Nazism in *The Origins of Totalitarianism* (328).

In the name of a non-racist democracy, Caygill exhumes the buried letter of the text. Like philosophy at its best, the world contains multitudes or, to put it another way, must make room for the multitudes it always already contains (like Kant's 'concussive motion of an all-penetrating matter'). The limit to human knowledge is something we should 'mourn and celebrate' because it opens the path of human thought to realms beyond human mastery (165). If today we are threatened by a new 'resentful dictatorship of popular science', it is because the unassailable genetic argument 'for the value of geno- and phenotypical diversity' is being ignored (164). Instead, we are faced with the dictatorship of the philosopher-physician who exerts his crushing rule over life and death, giving rise to a nihilism unable to recognize the sources of its own anxiety. Time and again, the danger is presented by Caygill as a will to control which at once imposes its boundaries and knows no bounds. Nietzsche, for example, was clear that the 'consistent historical tendency towards centralization' of Greece was the result of the lack of a cultural reformation, which allowed Athenian hegemony to establish itself by means of an attack on local myths. Faintly outlined behind his passionate condemnation of Athenian domination, we can see the outlines of the German Reich (106).

If Caygill's range – historical, cultural, philosophical – is vast, his focus, the targets of his greatest discomfort, could not be more steady. Hegemony, centralization, mastery, control are the precepts through which the rulers of science and the world enact their destruction and delude themselves. In each instance, diversity, plurality, multiplicity shadow a system, scientific and/or political, that is veering out of control in direct proportion to the effort of those in power to assert it. But while Caygill heralds plurality and diversity (crushed by genetics, thwarted by Athens), it is not in the name of what has come to be known as 'identity politics'. If freedom is central to his political vision, it is not on behalf of a liberal dispensation that would simply let everyone be whoever they are. Rather, as I read him, he is offering forms of disorientation which leave no form of assumed or assured identity intact (it may be terrifying to think we are no more than bundles of particles, but it is a perfect foil to egoism, dispersing the category of the human as well as deliriously expanding its affinities and reach). When Facebook founder Mark Zuckerberg recently stated that to have different identities was the sign of a 'lack of integrity' – as cited by *New Yorker* writer, Jia Tolentino – he was making it clear that the greatest threat for the powers that be is a form of restless, mobile identity that escapes dominion because it knows that it is more than one (with a quarter of the world's population using Facebook on a monthly basis, Zuckerberg effectively rules over a nation-state) (Tolentino 2019, 170–1).

Zuckerberg is also one of the most brazen representatives of the *arcana* or secrecy which for Caygill resides at the heart of the internet, thwarting its early promise of freedom. Under interrogation by Congress in 2018, he famously refused to disclose anything whatsoever of what is actually going on inside his system, which allows him to go on violating the privacy of his subscribers and globally divulging the information for profit. Who is Zuckerberg? (He also came across as an automaton, his own missing person one might say.) Who are the wizards behind the machine? Caygill takes us back to the pre-history of the internet which tells us much about what has come to be wrongly termed its 'misuse'. As early as the 1950s, the RAND Corporation created an encrypted network system to ensure the survival of the United States in the event of a nuclear attack: 'In spite of their apparently non-hierarchical architecture', Caygill writes in one of the later essays in the collection, 'the history of these networks and their theoretical inspirations points to the construction of the internet as an *arcanum* or space of *secrecy*' (447). The web is a knife that cuts both ways. It can liberate resistance, but it 'can also serve as the instrument for its decisive repression' (449). Caygill never relinquishes his hope for an emancipatory future, but this is one of the very few moments where his disappointment with the present is palpable.

*

If Caygill's movement between hegemony and diversity, doubt and certainty, does not follow the expected pattern, it is also because these now familiar antinomies in no sense set the limits of his vocabulary, which veers way beyond them. Running barely beneath or rather erupting from within his own writing are words which seem to arise from the nether depths of the human mind, what used to be called the 'perplexities of the soul' – precisely, he writes, what 'critical philosophy was supposed to relieve us of' (197). Perversity, turbulence, revulsion, recoil: these are terms resonant of psychoanalytic thought, even if Freud is only mentioned in passing. Thus, to go back to where we started, actuality 'recoils' from any attempt to think the absolute, while the violence expelled to the border from the heart of civility 'recoils', 'and the shock of its return warps the space of reason' (391, 43). What is being described here if not the process described by psychoanalysis as the 'return of the repressed', stretched by Caygill to encompass its broadest historical and social reach? What is being offered if not an image of the human psyche that submits to, and encompasses, no totality because it is not the master in its own home? In fact, the very word 'recoil' might well be poached by the language of psychoanalysis because it so beautifully captures the interminable pull of revulsion and attraction which Freud saw at the centre of the life of the mind. Inside the psyche there lies a demonic impulse which commands and scuppers all human arrangements. We might name it the drives, or the unconscious – indeed, Nietzsche is cited here as comparing the calling of the spirit to freedom with 'an unconscious pregnancy', biding its time, 'dark, questionable, almost untouchable in memory' (122). Both drive and unconscious were central to Freud's thought, though the concept of the drives has been progressively displaced from the centre of many schools of psychoanalysis for nearly half a century because, one suspects, it was simply felt to be too disruptive.

For Caygill, these processes of reason and unreason, the moments when philosophy dips into the life of desire, are crucial in disorienting false knowing even if they are most often overlooked by philosophical argument. A central part of his archaeological endeavour is therefore to lift them from the gutter as fit, indeed indispensable, objects of philosophical speculation. Thus in Human All Too Human, Nietzsche identifies aversion (Abneigung) and partiality (Zuneigung) – the impulse towards or away from something – as intrinsic to the process of evaluation. *Ab* (away) and *Zu* (toward) become operations of a drive or *Trieb* (a word Nietzsche uses). In the process, Caygill suggests, Nietzsche 'drives [*sic*] the notion of human measure to distraction' (125). In this moment, Nietzsche also anticipates Freud's famous 1925 paper on 'Negation' which made judgement an attribute of oral pleasure and displeasure. While for Kant, a 'growing realization that the concept of "life" troubled the representational model of consciousness' was already present in his pre-critical *Lectures on Metaphysics*, it was only in the largely ignored *Critique of Teleological Judgment* that he acknowledged its full implications, as pleasure (desiring) and displeasure (abhorring) become the grounds of activity and its obstruction (179). For both Nietzsche and Kant, Epicurus is key. If he makes more than one appearance in these essays, it is because of the way he plunges philosophy into the realm of revulsion and pleasure, into sensuous, corporal life, whose sublation in death has since Socrates been seen as one of the higher aims of philosophy.

In 'Soul and Cosmos in Kant: A Commentary on "Two Things Fill the Mind"', another stand-out essay for me which focuses on a famous passage from the conclusion of *The Critique of Pure Reason,* a similar pulsatory movement of *Hemmung* (repulsion leading to inhibition) and *Ergießung* (attraction leading to discharge) is lifted from the realm of the sublime into the fraught opposition between the moral law and the starry heavens – these are the two things that fill the mind. While the former allows man to elevate his own worth, the endless expanse of the latter confronts him with the realization of his corporal nature that must 'give back to the planet (a mere point in the universe) the matter from which it came', a recognition that strikes the philosopher with disgust and wonderment almost in equal measure. 'The sight of the starry heavens', Caygill comments, 'intimates the annihilation of this life and the reduction of stargazer to matter' (196). At this point, provided one reads him with the right guide, it seems as if Kant were already telling us that human destiny resides in the ability to see oneself as part of something infinitely vaster than any subject could ever pretend to be: 'The exaltation of personality', writes Caygill, 'begins to be shrouded by the shadows of animal life' (196). This places Kant right into the fractious centre of our modern-day preoccupation with the future of a world we may be destroying and a universe beyond our control. Or, to put it in Kant's words: 'worlds beyond worlds and systems within systems, and then into the limitless times of their periodical motion, their beginning and continuation' – a heretical view of the universe, Caygill tells us, 'which would have been met with sensations of distaste and even horror' (192). In Caygill's hands, Kant – and not only Kant – is gut-wrenching. Philosophy becomes a space of appetites and longings, inhibitions and revulsions, the body a parcel of matter, the cosmos an inspiration, as well as the site of a human and inhuman reckoning, one that is as impossible as it is vital for every one of us to contemplate.

Today these issues have never felt more urgent as we face the possibility of extinction, a prospect addressed by two essays near the end of the collection, as the pressure of the hour on the surface of the writing steadily intensifies. 'What are the conditions of possibility of thinking and talking about extinction violence,' Caygill asks, 'let alone venturing a critique of it?' – a question which seems to bring critical thought to the very limit of its own powers (285; cf. essay 33). Perhaps, then, we need to begin by recognizing that we are not masters of the universe but its 'supplicants': the living carbon based body mass of the planet is 550 gigatons, of which humans constitute a mere 0.06 gigatons, compared with insects at 1 gigaton and mushrooms, amazingly, at 12 gigatons (enough surely to give any of us pause and perhaps to provoke a mix of bewilderment and relief) (292–3). As Kant surmised, we are mere specks of dust. Caygill is unremitting on the scope and damage of human violence, and the moral and political accountability this entails, but it is nonetheless sheer hubris to believe for a second that man has the capacity to destroy the planet. 'While the risk to the survival of human life is undeniable', Caygill concludes from his survey of recent research, 'the inference that this threatens the planet or more modestly life on the planet is unwarranted' (290). Paradoxically, a global catastrophe might be the only way to save the planet from the human: 'We have inadvertently', he writes, 'provided the conditions of possibility for our own supersession as a species' (295).

*

Although there are moments when his spirit clearly falters, on balance I would describe Caygill as a philosophical optimist, always alert to the latent possibilities buried inside scenarios which, at first glance, might seem – in terms of justice and emancipation – to offer no hope. Such possibilities rely on a form of discrimination that seems to be a fine hybrid of judgement and calculating with chance. In December 2012, the anarchist squatters of the Villa Amalias in Greece, the key site of extra-parliamentary struggle for over twenty-two years, were evicted. The green light for further suppression of the activists would be given by Alexis Tsipras, fresh from an electoral surge that would eventually bring his party to power. Cannily, they held fast to their capacity to resist by refusing to be provoked into a violent escalation of the conflict which would most likely have destroyed it. At almost the same time, they staged a simulation of an assassination attempt against Prime Minister Samaras, 'an extraordinary piece of political theatre' which, as theatre, enacted the militant protest which they were neither relinquishing nor submitting to the machinations and blandishments of state authority. This, Caygill comments, was 'the outcome of a reasoned strategic judgement based on a theoretical response to provocation' (434).

On similar ground in the United States in the 1970s, Huey Newton of the Black Panthers distanced himself from a revolutionary rhetoric and performance – militants in black leather jackets and shotguns – which was 'open to misinterpretation as a spectacular revolutionary gesture', too easily diminished and suppressed as political pantomime (378). What matters at each turn – on this Caygill never hesitates – is preserving the *capacity to resist* which was Clausewitz's overarching term, a goal, Caygill suggests 'more sombre and unremitting than the temporary enthusiasms of revolutionary struggle' (375). Even if doing so was, in the case of the Black Panthers, in the eventual service of such struggle. Such a choice also made it possible to work towards the affirmation of black community as the true form of genuine power, because it allowed the space for reflection and judgement. In both cases, the staging of political life is a vital component of strategy. To judge and act as a political subject, whatever the circumstances, you need the keenest eye. Thus, Caygill's perhaps most poignant essay describes the elderly and ailing Jean Genet making his way into the Shatila refugee camp in Beirut the day after the massacre of Palestinian refugees by the Christian Phalange who had been let into the camps by the Israeli army. It did not take long for him to realize – although he appears to have been the sole witness to do so – that the bodies lying in the alley ways were not the authentic relics of the violence, but carefully orchestrated scenes spread across the camp in order to convey, and ensure, the utter, humiliating, defeat of the Palestinian people. You cannot act unless you cut through the crap visibly on offer, dig beneath the surface of the world, teach yourself to read. The capacity to resist relies on a hermeneutics of suspicion (which is also another thing which philosophy, in its uncompromising mode, shares with psychoanalysis).

*

The subtitle of Caygill's book on resistance was 'A Philosophy of Defiance'. Thinking back through these essays, it occurred to me that 'philosopher of defiance' might be a good way to describe Caygill and his project overall, the challenge he is issuing both to modern philosophy and to himself ('radical disobedience' also came to mind). At the heart of that challenge, perhaps its starting premise, is the demand that philosophy itself does not resist, claim immunity from, the turbulence – to use another of his favourite words – of the times. It feels appropriate therefore that this collection should end on a note of radical self-questioning, prompted by the activism of Extinction Rebellion and how it troubles the idea of resistance as capacity, which Caygill's thinking has done so much to sponsor and promote.

In April 2019, Extinction Rebellion provoked a scandal when an image went viral of policemen larking about – dancing and skateboarding – with protestors on London's Waterloo Bridge. The police were of course 'blasted' by the commander of the Metropolitan Police, Jane Connors, who said she was 'disappointed' by their conduct (White 2019). They were failing in their duty to arrest the protestors (getting themselves arrested for breaking the law being one of the protestors' main aims). But these actions by Extinction Rebellion – law-breaking, carnivalesque – must, by Caygill's own account, lead us to reconsider the idea of resistance as a capacity which he has traced from Clausewitz to the world of today. In the light of the urgency – they are after all protesting against the extinction of life on earth – the capacity to resist, precisely as defiance, appears passive, defensive. Its strategy is always somehow dictated by the forces marshalled against it, even when the terms of engagement laid down by those in power are ones which it refuses to recognize (as if alert to this problem, the protesters rejected Extinction *Resistance* in favour of Extinction *Rebellion*). Extinction Rebellion poses 'a considerable challenge', Caygill comments, because it embodies 'the paradox of an affirmative resistance that does not react to circumstances but seizes the initiative in shaping them' (454). 'It is easy to see', he continues, 'how mere negative resistance might seem insufficient when it becomes a question of affirming the future of life itself on this planet ... The new activist strategic posture seems to exceed the limits of the theory of resistance' (452–3).

In his essay on the Villa Amalias protests in Greece, Caygill cites Marx's 1854 comments on the Greek insurrection of the day whose revival, he stated, 'is thought not impossible' (429). From within that double negative – 'not impossible' – Caygill teases out the sliver of hope that keeps resistance, even when up against all odds, alive. In his essay on the Black Panthers, he praised their strategic wisdom in refusing the escalation which the authorities repeatedly attempted to provoke. Now escalation reappears on these final pages as a 'whirlwind' through which resistance joyously affirms its own, and the world's, future. Extinction Rebellion plans with meticulous care (there is no compromise of judgement). It knows when to make strategic withdrawals 'without stifling the joy or initiative of struggle' (454). It is not clear, Caygill concludes, whether this civil resistance of 'joyful, life-affirming escalation can still be categorized as resistance' or whether it signals its 'radical metamorphosis into a new phase' (459). What does however seem indisputable is that the stakes of possible human and wider species extinction 'remain too high to be left to resistance alone' (the last line of the final essay in the book) (459). The risks of the now require us to think again and, in defiance of the darkening skies, never to cease thinking.

Jacqueline Rose, 9 September 2019

Note

1   Parenthetical page references are to the present volume.

References

The following abbreviations are used:

al-Hout, Bayan Nuwayhed
SS: Sabra and Shatila, September 1982, al-Hout 2004.

Arendt, Hannah
RLC: Reflections on Literature and Culture, Arendt 2007.

Bataille, Georges
CH: The Cradle of Humanity: Prehistoric Art and Culture, Bataille 2005.

Benjamin, Walter
OG: The Origin of German Tragic Drama, Benjamin 1977b.
SW: Selected Writings, Benjamin 1996–2003.

Clausewitz, Carl von
OW: On War, Clausewitz [1832] 1984.

Deleuze, Gilles
DR: Difference and Repetition, Deleuze [1968] 1994.
EP: Expressionism in Philosophy: Spinoza, Deleuze [1968] 1990.
SPP: Spinoza: Practical Philosophy, Deleuze [1970] 1988.

Deleuze, Gilles and Félix Guattari
ML: Kafka: Toward a Minor Literature, Deleuze and Guattari 1986.

Eddington, Arthur Stanley
NPW: The Nature of the Physical World, Eddington 1928.

Epicurus
EHU: Epicurea nell'edizione di Hermann Usener, Epicurus 2002.
EO: Epicuro Opere, Epicurus 1973.
ER: The Epicurus Reader, Epicurus 1994.

Genet, Jean
FHS: 'Four Hours in Shatila', in The Declared Enemy: Texts and Interviews, Genet 2004.

Hegel, Georg Wilhelm Friedrich
ETW: On Christianity: Early Theological Writings, Hegel 1961.
HPW: Hegel's Political Writings, Hegel 1964.
PR: Elements of the Philosophy of Right, Hegel 1991.
PS: Phenomenology of Spirit, Hegel 1977.
SEL: Hegel's System of Ethical Life and First Philosophy of Spirit, Hegel 1979.
SL: Science of Logic, Hegel 1969.

Kafka, Franz
JA: 'Jackals and Arabs', in Kafka's Selected Stories, Kafka 2007.
PC: 'In the Penal Colony', in Kafka's Selected Stories, Kafka 2007.
RA: 'A Report to an Academy', in Kafka's Selected Stories, Kafka 2007.
TB: Tagebücher, Kafka 1990.

Kant, Immanuel
CPR: Critique of Pure Reason, Kant [1781/87] 2007.
CPrR: Critique of Practical Reason, Kant [1788] 1993.
CJ: Critique of Judgement, Kant [1790] 1952.
LM: Lectures on Metaphysics, Kant 1997.
OP: Opus Postumum, Kant 1993.
UNH: Universal Natural History and Theory of the Heavens, Kant [1755] 1981.
Levinas, Emmanuel
DF: Difficult Freedom: Essays on Judaism, Levinas 1990a.
BV: Beyond the Verse: Talmudic Readings and Lectures, Levinas 1994.
Maxwell, James Clerk
SP: The Scientific Papers of James Clerk Maxwell, Maxwell 2003.
Newton, Huey P.
HNR: The Huey P. Newton Reader, Newton 2002.
Nietzsche, Friedrich
AC: The Anti-Christ, Nietzsche [1888] 1978.
BGE: Beyond Good and Evil, Nietzsche [1886] 1978.
BT: The Birth of Tragedy, Nietzsche [1872] 1967.
D: Daybreak: Thoughts on the Prejudices of Morality, Nietzsche [1881] 1982.
EH: Ecce Homo, Nietzsche [1888] 1969.
GM: On the Genealogy of Morals, Nietzsche [1887] 1989.
GS: The Gay Science, Nietzsche [1882/87] 1974.
HH: Human, All Too Human, Nietzsche [1878/80] 1986.
KGA III/2: Kritische Gesamtausgabe, Nachgelassene Schriften 1870–1873,
    Nietzsche [1870–73] 1973.
*KGA III/4: Kritische Gesamtausgabe, Nachgelassene Fragmente Sommer 1872
    bis Ende 1874*, Nietzsche [1872–74] 1978.
SSW: 'The Struggle between Science and Wisdom', in *Philosophy and Truth:
    Selections from Nietzsche's Notebooks of the Early 1870s*, Nietzsche 1979.
WP: The Will to Power, Nietzsche 1968.

*

Adorno, T.W. ([1967] 1981), *Prisms*, trans. Samuel Weber and Shierry Weber,
    Cambridge, MA: MIT Press, 1967.
Adorno, T.W. ([1958] 1984), 'The Essay as Form', trans. Bob Hullot-Kentor and
    Frederic Will, *New German Critique* 32: 151–71.
Adorno, T.W. and Max Horkheimer (1979), *Dialectic of Enlightenment*, trans. J.
    Cumming, London: Verso.
al-Hout, Bayan Nuwayhed (2004), *Sabra and Shatila, September 1982*, London:
    Pluto Press.
Alinsky, Saul (1989), *Rules for Radicals: A Pragmatic Primer for Realistic Radicals*,
    New York: Vintage Books.
Allison, D.B. (ed.) (1985), *The New Nietzsche: Contemporary Styles of
    Interpretation*, Cambridge, MA: MIT Press.
Anders, Gunther (1989), *Kafka. Pro e contro*, trans. Paola Gnan, Ferrara: Gabriele
    Corbo.
Angrist, Stanley W. and Loren G. Hepler (1967), *Order and Chaos: Laws of
    Energy and Entropy*, Harmondsworth: Penguin.

Aquinas, Thomas (1975), *Summa Contra Gentiles: Book One: God*, trans. Anton C. Pegis, Notre Dame and London: University of Notre Dame Press.

Arendt, Hannah (1951), *The Origins of Totalitarianism*, New York: Harcourt Brace Jovanovich.

Arendt, Hannah (2003), *Responsibility and Judgment*, ed. Jerome Kohn, New York: Schocken Books.

Arendt, Hannah (2005), *Essays in Understanding, 1930–1954: Formation, Exile, and Totalitarianism*, New York: Random House.

Arendt, Hannah (2007), *Reflections on Literature and Culture*, ed. Susannah Young-Ah Gottlieb, Palo Alto: Stanford University Press.

Aristotle (1941), *The Basic Works of Aristotle*, ed. Richard McKeon, New York: Random House.

Aristotle (1952), *Meteorologica*, trans. H.D.P. Lee. Loeb Classical Library 397. Cambridge, MA: Harvard University Press.

Armstrong, Rachel (1996), *Totally Wired: Science, Technology and the Human Form*, London: ICA.

Assange, Julien, Jacob Appelbaum, Andy Muller-Maguhn, and Jeremie Zimmermann (2012), *Cypherpunks: Freedom and the Future of the Internet*, New York and London: OR Books.

Assman, Jan (2000), *Herrschaft und Heil: Politische Theologie in Altägypter, Israel und Europe*, Munich: Karl Hanser Verlag.

Baran, Paul (1960a), *Reliable Digital Communications Systems Using Unreliable Network Repeater Nodes*, Santa Monica, CA: RAND Corporation: https://www.rand.org/pubs/papers/P1995.html (accessed 9 April 2017).

Baran, Paul (1960b), *On a Distributed Command and Control System Configuration*, Santa Monica, CA: RAND Corporation: https://www.rand.org/pubs/research_memoranda/RM2632.html (accessed 9 April 2017).

Baran, Paul (1964), *On Distributed Communications: I. Introduction to Distributed Communications Networks*, Santa Monica, CA: RAND Corporation: https://www.rand.org/pubs/research_memoranda/RM3420.html (9 April 2017).

Barrow, J.D. and F.J. Tipler (1986), *The Anthropic Cosmological Principle*, Oxford: Oxford University Press.

Bataille, Georges (1979), 'Lascaux ou la Naissance de l'Art', in *Oeuvres Complètes*, vol. 9, Paris: Gallimard, 7–101.

Bataille, Georges (1985), *Visions of Excess: Selected Writings 1927–1939*, ed. A. Stockl, Minneapolis, MN: University of Minnesota Press.

Bataille, Georges (1991), *The Accursed Share: Volume I*, trans. Robert Hurley, New York: Zone Books.

Bataille, Georges (1993), *The Accursed Share: Volumes II and III*, trans. Robert Hurley, New York: Zone Books.

Bataille, Georges (2002), *Tears of Eros*, trans. Peter Connor, San Francisco: City Light Books.

Bataille, Georges (2005), *The Cradle of Humanity: Prehistoric Art and Culture*, trans. Michelle Kendall and Stuart Kendall, New York: Zone Books.

Bauman, Zygmunt (1989), *Modernity and the Holocaust*, Oxford: Polity Press.

Baumgarten, A.G. (1954), *Reflections on Poetry: A. G. Baumgarten's Meditationes philosophicae de nonnullis ad poema pertinibus*, trans. Karl Aschenbrenner and W.B. Holther, Berkeley and Los Angeles: University of California Press.

Baumgarten, A.G. (1973), *Asthetik als Philosophie der sinnlichen Erkenntnis*, trans. Hans Rudolf Schweizer, Basel and Stuttgart: Schwabe.

Baumgarten, A.G. (1983), *Texte zur Grundlegung der Asthetik*, ed. Hans Rudolf Schweizer, Hamburg: Felix Meiner Verlag.

Baumgarten, Eduard (1964), *Max Weber. Werk und Person*, Tübingen: J.C.B. Mohr (Paul Siebeck).

Bellone, Enrico (2004), *Caos e Armonia: Storia della Physica*, Torino: UTET Libraria.

Benjamin, Walter (1977a), *Illuminations: Essays and Reflections*, ed. Hannah Arendt, trans. H. Zohn, London: Fontana.

Benjamin, Walter (1977b), *The Origin of German Tragic Drama*, trans. John Osborne, London: New Left Books.

Benjamin, Walter (1979), *One Way Street and Other Writings*, trans. E. Jephcott and K. Shorter, London: Verso.

Benjamin, Walter (1996–2003), *Selected Writings*, 4 vols., ed. Michael W. Jennings et al. Cambridge, MA: Harvard University Press.

Benjamin, Walter (1999), *The Arcades Project*, trans. Howard Eiland and Kevin McLaughlin, Cambridge, MA: Harvard University Press.

Bergmann, Peter (1987), *Nietzsche: The Last Antipolitical German*, Bloomington: Indiana University Press.

Bernasconi, Robert (1996), 'The Double Face of the Political and the Social: Hannah Arendt and America's Racial Divisions, *Research in Phenomenology*, 26: 3–24.

Blumenberg, Hans (1983), *The Legitimacy of the Modern Age*, trans. Robert M. Wallace, Cambridge, MA: MIT Press.

Bradbrook, Gail (2019), 'What Is Your Place in These Times?' in Extinction Rebellion, *This Is Not a Drill: An Extinction Rebellion Handbook*, London: Penguin Books.

Brainard, Marcus, David Jacobs, and Rick Lee (eds.) (1991), *Heidegger and the Political*, special issue of *Graduate Faculty Philosophy Journal* 14–15 (1).

Brissoni, Armando (2002), *Il De Pulsibus nella Teoria Medica di T. Campanella*, Rome: Internation AM Edizioni.

British Medical Association (1992), *Our Genetic Future: The Science and Ethics of Genetic Technology*, Oxford: Oxford University Press.

Brundage, James A. (1987), *Law, Sex, and Christian Society in Medieval Europe*, Chicago: University of Chicago Press.

Buhr, Manfred (ed.) (1990), *Moderne–Nietzsche–Postmoderne*, Berlin: Akademie-Verlag.

Burns, Danny and Cordula Reimann (2019), 'Movement Building', in Extinction Rebellion, *This Is Not a Drill: An Extinction Rebellion Handbook*, London: Penguin Books.

Calasso, Roberto (2005), *K.*, Milano: Adelphi.

Campanella, Tommaso (1999), *Physiologiae Compendium, Compendio di Filosofia della Natura*, ed. and trans. Germana Ernst and Paolo Ponzio, Santarcangelo: Rusconi libri.

Campbell, David (1992), *Writing Security: United States Foreign Policy and the Politics of Identity*, Manchester: Manchester University Press.

Canguilhem, Georges ([1953] 1965), *La Connaissance de la Vie*, Paris: Vrin.

Cardwell, D.S.L. (1971), *From Watt to Clausius: The Rise of Thermodynamics in the Early Industrial Age*, London: Heinemann.

Carlson, David Gray (2007), *A Commentary to Hegel's Science of Logic*, Basingstoke: Palgrave Macmillan.

Caygill, Howard (1989), *Art of Judgement*, Oxford: Basil Blackwell.

Caygill, Howard (1994), *Hegel and the Speculative Community: Three Essays*, Norwich: University of East Anglia.

Caygill, Howard (1995), *A Kant Dictionary*, Oxford: Blackwell.

Caygill, Howard (1996), 'Gillian Rose, 1947–1995', *Radical Philosophy* 77: 56.

Caygill, Howard (1998a), 'The Broken Hegel: Gillian Rose's Retrieval of Speculative Philosophy', *Women: A Cultural Review*, 9 (1): 19–27.

Caygill, Howard (1998b), *Walter Benjamin: The Colour of Experience*, London: Routledge.

Caygill, Howard (1999), *Philosophy and Cultural History: An Inaugural Lecture Given by Professor Howard Caygill*, London: Goldsmiths College.

Caygill, Howard (2000), 'Surviving the Inhuman', in *Inhuman Reflections: Thinking the Limits of the Human*, ed. S. Brewster et al., Manchester and New York: Manchester University Press, 217–29.

Caygill, Howard (2002), *Levinas and the Political*, London: Routledge.

Caygill, Howard (2005), 'Non-Messianic Political Theology in Benjamin's "On the Concept of History"', in *Walter Benjamin and History*, ed. Andrew Benjamin, London: Continuum Books, 215–26.

Caygill, Howard (2012), 'Also Sprach Zapata: Philosophy and Resistance', *Radical Philosophy* 171: 19–25.

Caygill, Howard (2013), *On Resistance: A Philosophy of Defiance*, London: Bloomsbury.

Caygill, Howard (2015), 'Artaud-Immunity: Derrida and the Momo', *Derrida Today* 8 (2): 113–35.

Caygill, Howard (2017), *Kafka: In Light of the Accident*, London: Bloomsbury.

Chamayou, Gregoire (2012), *Manhunts: A Philosophical History*, trans. Steven Rendell, Princeton and Oxford: Princeton University Press.

Chamayou, Gregoire (2015), *Drone Theory*, London: Penguin Books.

Chaulet-Achour, Christiane (2013), *Frantz Fanon, « Peaux noires, masques blancs »*, Paris: Honoré Champion.

Clausewitz, Carl von ([1832] 1980), *Vom Kriege: Hinterlassenes Werk des Generals Carl von Clausewitz*, vols. 1–3, ed. Marie von Clausewitz, Berlin: Ferdinand Dümmler.

Clausewitz, Carl von ([1832] 1984), *On War*, trans. Col. J.J. Graham, Harmondsworth: Penguin Books.

Cohen, Hermann (1883), *Von Kants Einfluß auf die deutscher Kultur*, Berlin: Dümmler.

Coulthard, Glenn (2014), *Red Skin, White Masks: Rejecting the Politics of Recognition*, Minneapolis: University of Minnesota Press.

Critchley, Simon (1992), *The Ethics of Deconstruction*, Oxford: Basil Blackford.

Crutzen, Paul J. (2002), 'The Anthropocene: Geology of Mankind', *Nature* 415: 23.

Darwin, Charles (1956), *The Origin of the Species*, ed. W.R. Thompson, London: Dent.

Darwin, Charles (1993), *The Portable Darwin*, Harmondsworth: Penguin.

Daube, David (1963), *The Exodus Pattern in the Bible*, London: Faber & Faber.

Deleuze, Gilles ([1962] 1983), *Nietzsche and Philosophy*, trans. Hugh Tomlinson, London: Athlone Press.

Deleuze, Giles ([1970] 1988), *Spinoza: Practical Philosophy*, trans. R. Hurley, San Francisco: City Light Books.

Deleuze, Giles ([1968] 1990), *Expressionism in Philosophy: Spinoza*, trans. M. Joughin, New York: Zone Books.

Deleuze, Giles ([1968] 1994), *Difference and Repetition*, trans. P. Patton, London: Athlone Press.

Deleuze, Gilles and Félix Guattari (1986), *Kafka: Toward a Minor Literature*, trans. Dana Polan, intro. Réda Bensmaïa, Minneapolis: University of Minnesota Press.

Derrida, Jacques ([1967] 1978), *Writing and Difference*, trans. Alan Bass, London: Routledge.

Derrida, Jacques (1981), *Dissemination*, trans. Barbara Johnson, Chicago: University of Chicago Press.

Derrida, Jacques (1982), *Margins of Philosophy*, trans. Alan Bass, Brighton, Harvester Press.

Derrida, Jacques (1987), *Ulysse gramophone deux mots pour Joyce*, Paris: Editions Galilée.

Derrida, Jacques ([1982] 1988), *The Ear of the Other*, ed. Christie McDonald, Lincoln and London: University of Nebraska Press.

Derrida, Jacques (1989), *Of Spirit: Heidegger and the Question*, trans. Geoffrey Bennington and Rachel Bowlby, Chicago: Chicago University Press.

Derrida, Jacques (1992), *The Other Heading: Reflections on Today's Europe*, trans. Pascale-Anne Brault and Michael B. Nass, Bloomington: Indiana University Press.

Derrida, Jacques (2002), *Who's Afraid of Philosophy? Right to Philosophy 1*, trans. Jan Plug, Stanford: Stanford University Press.

Derrida, Jacques (2004), *Eyes of the University: Right to Philosophy 2*, trans. Jan Plug and others, Stanford: Stanford University Press.

Descartes, René (1969), *The Philosophical Works of Descartes*, trans. Elizabeth S. Haldane and G.R.T. Ross, Cambridge: Cambridge University Press.

Dijksterhuis, E.J. (1986), *The Mechanization of the World Picture: Pythagoras to Newton*, trans. C. Dikshoorn, Princeton: Princeton University Press.

Dreyfus, Hubert L. (1991), *Being in the World: A Commentary on Heidegger's Being and Time*, Cambridge MA: MIT Press.

Dubois, W.E.B. ([1903] 2007), *The Souls of Black Folk*, Oxford: Oxford University Press.

Eddington, Arthur Stanley (1928), *The Nature of the Physical World*, Cambridge: Cambridge University Press.

Elias, Norbert (1973), *The Civilizing Process*, trans. E. Jephcott, Oxford: Basil Blackwell.

Engler, Mark and Paul Engler (2016), *This Is an Uprising: How Nonviolent Revolt Is Shaping the Twenty-First Century*, New York: Nation Books.

Epicurus (1973), *Epicuro Opere*, ed. Graziano Arrighetti, Turin: Einaudi.

Epicurus (1994), *The Epicurus Reader*, ed. and trans. B. Inwood and L.P. Gerson, Indianapolis: Hackett.

Epicurus (2002), *Epicurea nell'edizione di Hermann Usener*, ed. Ilaria Ramelli, Milan: Bompiani.

Erskine, Ralph, and Michael Smith (eds.) (2011), *The Bletchley Park Code-Breakers*, London: Biteback Publishing.

Extinction Rebellion (2019), 'Declaration of Rebellion', in Extinction Rebellion, *This Is Not a Drill: An Extinction Rebellion Handbook*, London: Penguin Books.

Fanon, Frantz ([1952] 1986), *Black Skin, White Masks*, trans. Charles Lam Markmann, London: Pluto Press.

Fanon, Frantz ([1959] 2011), *L'an V de la révolution algérienne*, Paris: La Découverte.

Festugière, A.J. (1946), *Épicure et ses dieux*, Paris: Presses Universitaires de France.

Förster, Eckart (2000), *Kant's Final Synthesis*, Cambridge, MA: Harvard University Press.

Freud, Sigmund (1985), *The Interpretation of Dreams*, trans. James Strachey, Harmondsworth: Penguin Books.

Freud, Sigmund (1987), *On Metapsychology: The Theory of Psychoanalysis*, trans. James Strachey, Harmondsworth: Penguin Books.

Genet, Jean (2003), *Prisoner of Love*, trans. Barbara Bray, New York: New York Review Books.

Genet, Jean (2004), *The Declared Enemy: Texts and Interviews*, ed. Albert Dichy, trans. Jeff Fort, Stanford, CA: Stanford University Press.

GEO Kompakt (2014), *GEOkompakt: Der Neandertaler* 41.

Ghelardi, Maurizio (ed.) (2003), *Aby Warburg – Ernst Cassirer: Il Mondo di Ieri*, Torino: Nino Aragno Editore.

Gilman, Sander (1995), *Franz Kafka, The Jewish Patient*, London: Routledge.

Gilsen, Étienne (1955), *History of Christian Philosophy in the Middle Ages*, New York: Random House.

Girard, René (2011), *Achever Clausewitz: Entretiens avec Benoît Chantre*, Paris: Flammarion.

Graeber, David (2011), *Debt: The First 5,000 Years*, New York: Melville House Publishing.

Guidi, Benedetta Cestelli and Nicholas Mann (eds.) (1998), *Photographs at the Frontier: Aby Warburg in America 1895–1896*, London: Merella Holberton.

Habermas, Jürgen (1982), 'The Entwinement of Myth and Enlightenment: Rereading *Dialectic of Enlightenment*', trans. Thomas Y. Levin, *New German Critique* 26: 13–30.

Hadot, Pierre (1995), *Philosophy as a Way of Life*, ed. Arnold I. Davidson, Oxford: Blackwell.

Hadot, Pierre (2002), *What Is Ancient Philosophy?* trans. Michael Chase, Cambridge, MA: Harvard University Press.

Hallam, Roger (2019), 'The Civil Resistance Model' in Extinction Rebellion, *This Is Not a Drill: An Extinction Rebellion Handbook*, London: Penguin Books.

Harf, R. and S. Witte (2014), 'Jäger der verlorenen Schatzes', in *GEOkompakt: Der Neandertaler* 41: 40–49.

Harman, P.M. (1982), *Metaphysics and Natural Philosophy: The Problem of Substance in Classical Physics*, Hassocks/Sussex: The Harvester Press.

Harman, P.M. (1998), *The Natural Philosophy of James Clerk Maxwell*, Cambridge: Cambridge University Press.

Hayman, Ronald (1983), *Kafka: A Biography*, London: Sphere.

Hegel, Georg Wilhelm Friedrich (1961), *On Christianity: Early Theological Writings*, New York: Harper Torchbooks.

Hegel, Georg Wilhelm Friedrich (1964), *Hegel's Political Writings*, trans. T.M. Knox, Oxford University Press.

Hegel, Georg Wilhelm Friedrich (1969), *The Science of Logic*, trans. A.V. Miller, New York: Humanity Books.

Hegel, Georg Wilhelm Friedrich (1971), *Early Theological Writings*, trans. T.M. Knox, Philadelphia: University of Pennsylvania Press.

Hegel, Georg Wilhelm Friedrich (1977), *Phenomenology of Spirit*, ed. J. N. Findlay, trans. A.V. Miller, Oxford: Oxford University Press.

Hegel, Georg Wilhelm Friedrich (1979), *Hegel's System of Ethical Life and First Philosophy of Spirit*, ed. and trans. H. S. Harris and T.M. Knox, Albany: University of New York Press.

Hegel, Georg Wilhelm Friedrich (1991), *Elements of the Philosophy of Right*, ed. Allen W. Wood and trans. H.B. Nisbet, Cambridge University Press, Cambridge.

Hegel, Georg Wilhelm Friedrich (2002), *Miscellaneous Writings of G.W.F. Hegel*, ed. John Stewart, Evanston: Northwestern University Press.

Hegel, Georg Wilhelm Friedrich (2010), *The Science of Logic*, ed. and trans. George di Giovanni, Cambridge: Cambridge University Press.

Heidegger, Martin ([1954] 1968), *What Is Called Thinking*, trans. J. Glenn Gray, New York: Harper & Row.

Heidegger, Martin (1972), *The End of Philosophy*, trans. Joan Stambaugh, New York: Harper & Row.

Heidegger, Martin (1977), *The Question Concerning Technology and Other Essays*, trans. William Lovitt, New York: Harper & Row.

Heidegger, Martin (1978), *Being and Time*, trans. John Macquarrie and Edward Robinson, Oxford: Basil Blackwell.

Heidegger, Martin ([1950] 1984), 'The Anaximander Fragment', in *Early Greek Thinking*, trans. David Krell and Frank A. Capuzzi, San Fransisco: Harper & Row, 13–58.

Heidegger, Martin (1991), *Nietzsche*, 4 vols, trans. D.F. Krell, San Francisco, CA: Harper & Row.

Helmholtz, Hermann von (1971), *Selected Writings of Hermann von Helmholtz*, ed. Russell Kahl, Middletown, CT: Wesleyan University Press.

Hennis, Wilhelm (1988), *Max Weber: Essays in Reconstruction*, trans. K. Tribe, London: Allen & Unwin.

Heuser, Beatrice (2002), *Reading Clausewitz*, London: Pimlico.

Idel, Moshe (1998), *Messianic Mystics*, New Haven, CT: Yale University Press.

Irigaray, Luce (1985), *Speculum of the Other Woman*, trans. G.C. Gill, Ithaca, NY: Cornell University Press.

Irigaray, Luce (1991a), *The Irigaray Reader*, ed. M. Whitford, Oxford: Basil Blackwell.

Irigaray, Luce (1991b), *Marine Lover of Friedrich Nietzsche*, trans. G.C. Gill, New York: Columbia University Press.

Jacob François (1973), *The Logic of Life, a History of Heredity*, trans. Betty E. Spillmann, New York: Pantheon Books.

James and Ruby (2019), 'Cultural Roadblocks' in *Extinction Rebellion, This Is Not a Drill: An Extinction Rebellion Handbook*, London: Penguin Books.

John Paul II (1995), *Evangelium Vitae: Il Valore e l'Inviolabilità della Vita Umana*, Milano: Paoline Editoriale Libri.

Jonas, Hans (1963), *The Gnostic Religion*, 2nd rev. ed., Boston, MA: Beacon Press.

Jones, Howard (1989), *The Epicurean Tradition*, London: Routledge.

Kahane Commission on Sabra and Shatila Massacre report and related documents, Israeli State Archives, released 2012: http://www.archives.

gov.il/NR/exeres/B155D1B7-BA76-4F40-95A5-7B89A4833F,frameless.
htm?NRMODE=Published (accessed 12 November 2014).

Kahn, Herman (1960a), *On Thermonuclear War*, Princeton: Princeton University Press.

Kahn, Herman (1960b), *The Nature and Feasibility of War and Deterrence*, Santa Monica, CA: RAND Corporation: https://www.rand.org/pubs/papers/P1888. html (accessed 9 April 2017).

Kafka, Franz (1958), *Briefe 1902–1924*, ed. Max Brod, Frankfurt am Main: Fischer.

Kafka, Franz (1964), *The Diaries of Franz Kafka*, ed. Max Brod, trans. Martin Greenberg, New York: Penguin Books.

Kafka, Franz (1975), *Metamorphosis and Other Stories*, trans. E. Muir, Harmondsworth: Penguin.

Kafka, Franz (1978), *Letters to Felice*, ed. Erich Heller and Jürgen Born, trans. James Stern and Elizabeth Duckworth, Harmondsworth: Penguin.

Kafka, Franz (1990), *Tagebücher*, ed. Hans-Gerd Koch, Michael Müller and Malcolm Pasley, Frankfurt am Main: Fischer.

Kafka, Franz (1993), *Nachgelassene Schriften und Fragmente*, vol. 1, ed. Malcolm Pasley, Frankfurt am Main: Fischer.

Kafka, Franz (2007), *Kafka's Selected Stories*, ed. and trans. Stanley Corngold, New York: Norton.

Kafka, Franz (2008), *The Complete Novels*, trans. Willa and Edwin Muir, London: Vintage Books.

Kant, Immanuel (1784), 'Beantwortung der Frage: Was ist Aufklärung?' *Berlinerische Monatsschrift* 12: 481–94.

Kant, Immanuel (1902–), *Kants Gesammelte Schriften (Akademieausgabe)*, Berlin: Königlich-Preussischen Akademie der Wissenschaften/de Gruyter.

Kant, Immanuel ([1790] 1951), *Critique of Judgement*, trans. J.H. Bernard, New York: Hafner Press.

Kant, Immanuel ([1790] 1952), *Critique of Judgement*, trans. J.C. Meredith, Oxford: Clarendon Press.

Kant, Immanuel (1960), *Religion within the Limits of Reason Alone*, trans. T. Greene and H.H. Hudson, New York: Harper Torchbooks.

Kant, Immanuel (1968), *Kant: Selected Pre-Critical Writings and Correspondence with Beck*, trans. G.B. Kerferd and D.E. Walford, Manchester: Manchester University Press.

Kant, Immanuel (1977a), *Schriften zur Anthropologie, Geschichtsphilosophie, Politik und Pädagogik*, vol. 1, ed. Wilhelm Weischedel, Frankfurt am Main: Suhrkamp.

Kant, Immanuel (1977b), *Schriften zur Anthropologie, Geschichtsphilosophie, Politik und Pädagogik*, vol. 2, ed. Wilhelm Weischedel, Frankfurt am Main: Suhrkamp.

Kant, Immanuel ([1763] 1979), *The One Possible Proof for the Existence of God*, trans. G. Treach, New York: Abaris Books.

Kant, Immanuel (1980), *On History*, ed. Lewis White Beck, Indianapolis: Bobbs-Merrill.

Kant, Immanuel ([1755] 1981), *Universal Natural History and Theory of the Heavens*, trans. Stanley L. Jaki, Edinburgh: Scottish Academic Press.

Kant, Immanuel (1982), *Vorkritische Schriften bis 1768* 1, ed. Wilhelm Weischedel, Frankfurt am Main: Suhrkamp Verlag.

Kant, Immanuel (1984), *Opus Postumum*, ed. and trans. Vittorio Mathieu, Roma-Bari: Laterza, 1984.

Kant, Immanuel ([1786] 1985), *Metaphysical Foundations of Natural Science*, trans. James W. Ellington, Indianapolis: Hackett Publishing Company.

Kant, Immanuel (1986), *Kant's Latin Writings*, trans. Mary J. Gregor, ed. Lewis White Beck, New York: Peter Lang Publishing.

Kant, Immanuel (1991), *Political Writings*, trans. Hans Reiss, Cambridge: Cambridge University Press.

Kant, Immanuel ([1788] 1993), *Critique of Practical Reason*, trans. Lewis White Beck, New York: Library of Liberal Arts, Macmillan Publishing.

Kant, Immanuel (1993), *Opus Postumum*, ed. E. Förster and M. Rosen, Cambridge: Cambridge University Press.

Kant, Immanuel (1997), *Lectures on Metaphysics*, ed. and trans. Karl Ameriks and Steve Naragon, Cambridge: Cambridge University Press.

Kant, Immanuel ([1783] 2004), *Prolegomena to Any Future Metaphysics That Will Be Able to Come Forward as Science*, trans. Gary Hatfield, Cambridge: Cambridge University Press.

Kant, Immanuel (2007), *Anthropology, History, and Education*, trans. Günter Zöller and Robert B. Louden, Cambridge: Cambridge University Press.

Kant, Immanuel ([1781/87] 2007), *Critique of Pure Reason*, trans. Norman Kemp Smith, Basingstoke: Palgrave Macmillan.

Kant, Immanuel ([1746] 2012), *Thoughts on the True Estimation of Living Forces, and Criticism of the Proofs Propounded by Herr von Leibniz and Other Mechanists in Their Treatment of This Controversy, along with Some Preliminary Observations Concerning the Force of Bodies in General*, trans. Jeffrey Edwards and Martin Schönfeld, in *Natural Science*, ed. Eric Watkins, Cambridge: Cambridge University Press.

Kiesewetter, J.G. (1793), *Grundriß einer reinen allgemeinen Logik, nach Kantischen Grundsätzen*, Frankfurt und Leipzig.

Klibansky, Raymond, Erwin Panofsky, and Fritz Saxl (1964), *Saturn and Melancholy: Studies in the History of Natural Philosophy and Art*, London: Nelson.

Koyré, Alexander (1965), *Newtonian Studies*, Chicago: University of Chicago Press.

Lacoue-Labarthe, Philippe (1990), *Heidegger, Art and Politics*, trans. Chris Turner, Oxford: Basil Blackwell.

Laërtius, Diogenes (1991), *Lives of Eminent Philosophers*, trans. R.D. Hicks, Cambridge, MA: Harvard University Press.

Latour, Bruno (2015), *Face à Gaïa. Huit conférences sur le nouveau régime climatique*, Paris: La Découverte.

Lazzarato, Maurizio (2011), *The Making of Indebted Man*, trans. Joshua David Jordan, Los Angeles: Semiotext(e).

Lehmann, Gerhardt (1969), *Beiträge zur Geschichte und Interpretation der Philosophie Kants*, Berlin: de Gruyter.

Levinas, Emmanuel (1969), *Totality and Infinity: An Essay on Exteriority*, trans. Alphonso Lingis, Pittsburgh, PA: Duquesne University Press.

Levinas, Emmanuel (1987), *Collected Philosophical Papers*, trans. Alphonso Lingis, Dordrecht: Martinus Nijhoff.

Levinas, Emmanuel (1989), *The Levinas Reader*, ed. and trans. Sean Hand, Oxford: Basil Blackwell.

Levinas, Emmanuel (1990a), *Difficult Freedom: Essays on Judaism*, trans. Sean Hand, Baltimore: The Johns Hopkins University Press.

Levinas, Emmanuel (1990b), *Nine Talmudic Readings*, trans. Annette Aronowicz, Bloomington and Indianapolis: Indiana University Press.

Levinas, Emmanuel (1994), *Beyond the Verse: Talmudic Readings and Lectures*, trans. Gary D. Mole, London: The Athlone Press.

Longair, Malcolm S. (2006), *The Cosmic Century*, Cambridge: Cambridge University Press.

Lovelock, James (2006), *The Revenge of Gaia: Why the Earth Is Fighting Back – and How We Can Still Save Humanity*, New York: Basic Books.

Lovelock, James (2019), *Novacene: The Coming Age of Hyperintelligence*, London: Allen Lane.

Lucretius (1976), *De Rerum Natura*, trans. C.H. Sisson, Manchester: Carcanet New Press.

Lukács, Georg (1971), *History and Class Consciousness*, trans. R. Livingstone, London: Merlin.

Lukács, Georg (1980), *The Destruction of Reason*, trans. P. Palmer, London: Merlin.

Lyotard, Jean-François (1988a), *Heidegger et 'Les juifs'*, Paris: Editions Galilee.

Lyotard, Jean-François (1988b), *The Differend: Phrases in Dispute*, trans. G. van den Abbeele, Manchester: Manchester University Press.

Mahon, Basil (2003), *The Man Who Changed Everything: The Life of James Clerk Maxwell*, Chichester: John Wiley and Sons.

Mancuso, Stefano and Alessandra Viola (2013), *Verde Brillante. Sensibilità e intelligenza del mondo vegetale*, Milano: Giunti.

Mancuso, Stefano (2018), *The Revolutionary Genius of Plants: A New Understanding of Plant Intelligence and Behavior*, New York: Atria.

Mancuso, Stefano (2019), *La Nazione delle Piante*, Bari: Laterza.

Mann, G. et al. (ed.) (1985), *Samuel Thomas Sömmering und die Gelehrten der Goethezeit*, Stuttgart: G Fischer.

Marder, Michael (2013), *Plant Thinking: A Philosophy of Vegetal Life*, New York: Columbia University Press.

Marx, Karl (1974), *Grundrisse der Kritik der Politische Okonomie*, Berlin: Dietz Verlag.

Marx, Karl (1977a), *Grundrisse*, trans. M. Nicolaus, Harmondsworth: Penguin.

Marx, Karl (1977b), *Capital: A Critique of Political Economy Volume One*, trans. S. Moore and E. Aveling, London: Lawrence & Wishart.

Maxwell, James Clerk ([1864] 1983), *A Dynamical Theory of the Electromagnetic Field*, Edinburgh: Scottish Academic Press.

Maxwell, James Clerk (2003), *The Scientific Papers of James Clerk Maxwell*, 2 vols, New York: Dover Publications, 2003.

Mazzolai, Barbara (2019), *La natura geniale. Come e perché le piante cambieranno (e salveranno) il pianeta*, Milano: Longanesi.

Mendelsohn, Everett (1964), *Heat and Life: The Development of the Theory of Animal Heat*, Cambridge, MA: Harvard University Press.

Momogliano, Arnaldo (1987), 'A Note on Max Weber's Definition of Judaism as a Pariah Religion', in *On Pagans, Jews and Christians*, Middletown, CT: Wesleyan University Press, 231–7.

Montaigne, Michel de (1938), *Essays of Michael Lord of Montaigne*, trans. John Florio, London: J.M. Dent and Sons.

Moore, R.I. (1987), *The Formation of a Persecuting Society*, Oxford: Basil Blackwell.

Morris, Colin (1989), *The Papal Monarchy*, Oxford: Oxford University Press.

Mortellaro, Isidoro (1999), *I signori della guerra*, Roma: Manifestolibri.

Müller, Michael (ed.) (2003), *Franz Kafka: Romane und Erzählungen*, Stuttgart: Reclam.

Nägele, Rainer (1974), 'Auf der Suche nach dem verlorenen Paradies: Versuch einer Interpretation zu Kafka's *Der Jäger Gracchus*', *The German Quarterly*, 47: 60–72.

Naughton, John (2000), *A Brief History of the Future: The Origins of the Internet*, London: Phoenix.

Newton, Huey P. (2002), *The Huey P. Newton Reader*, ed. David Hilliard and Donald Weise, New York: Seven Stories Press.

Newton, Huey P. (2009), *Revolutionary Suicide*, New York: Penguin Books.

Nietzsche, Friedrich (1962), *Philosophy in the Tragic Age of the Greeks*, trans. M. Cowan, Chicago: Henry Regnery Company.

Nietzsche, Friedrich ([1872] 1967), *The Birth of Tragedy*, trans. Walter Kaufmann, New York: Vintage Books.

Nietzsche, Friedrich (1968), *The Will to Power*, trans. Walter Kaufmann and R.J. Hollingdale, New York: Vintage Books.

Nietzsche, Friedrich ([1888] 1968), *Twilight of the Idols and the Anti-Christ*, trans. R.J. Hollingdale, Harmondsworth: Penguin.

Nietzsche, Friedrich ([1888] 1969), *Ecce Homo*, trans. Walter Kaufmann, New York: Vintage.

Nietzsche, Friedrich ([1870–73] 1973), *Nachgelassene Schriften 1870–1873, Kritische Gesamtausgabe III/2*, ed. G. Colli and M. Montinari, Berlin: de Gruyter.

Nietzsche, Friedrich ([1882/87] 1974), *The Gay Science*, trans. Walter Kaufmann, New York: Vintage.

Nietzsche, Friedrich ([1883/85] 1975), *Thus Spoke Zarathustra*, trans. R.J. Hollingdale, Harmondsworth: Penguin.

Nietzsche, Friedrich ([1886] 1978), *Beyond Good and Evil*, trans. R.J. Hollingdale, Harmondsworth: Penguin.

Nietzsche, Friedrich ([1888] 1978), *The Anti-Christ*, trans. R.J. Hollingdale, Harmondsworth: Penguin.

Nietzsche, Friedrich ([1872–74] 1978), *Nachgelassene Fragmente Sommer 1872 bis Ende 1874, Kritische Gesamtausgabe III/4*, ed. G. Colli and M. Montinari, Berlin: de Gruyter.

Nietzsche, Friedrich (1979), *Philosophy and Truth: Selections from Nietzsche's Notebooks of the Early 1870s*, ed. and trans. D. Breazeale, Hassocks Sussex: Harvester Press.

Nietzsche, Friedrich ([1881] 1982) *Daybreak: Thoughts on the Prejudices of Morality*, trans. R.J. Hollingdale, Cambridge: Cambridge University Press.

Nietzsche, Friedrich ([1873–6] 1983), *Untimely Meditations*, trans. R.J. Hollingdale, Cambridge: Cambridge University Press.

Nietzsche, Friedrich ([1878/80] 1986), *Human, All Too Human*, trans. R.J. Hollingdale, Cambridge University Press.

Nietzsche, Friedrich ([1887] 1989), *On the Genealogy of Morals*, trans. Walter Kaufmann and R.J. Hollingdale, New York: Vintage.

Nixon, Rob (2011), *Slow Violence and the Environmentalism of the Poor*, Cambridge, MA: Harvard University Press.

Norris, Christopher (1985), *The Contest of the Faculties*, London: Methuen.

North, John (1965), *The Measure of the Universe: A History of Modern Cosmology*, New York: Dover Publications.

North, John (1994), *Astronomy and Cosmology*, London: Fontana Books.

Oestreich, Gerhardt (1982), *Neostoicism and the Early Modern State*, trans. David McLintock, Cambridge: Cambridge University Press.

Pääbo, Svante (2014), *Neanderthal Man: In Search of Lost Genomes*, New York: Basic Books.

Papagianni, Dimitra and Michael A. Morse (2015), *The Neanderthals Rediscovered: How Modern Science Is Rewriting Their Story*, London: Thames & Hudson.

Paret, Peter (2007), *Clausewitz and the State: The Man, His Theories and His Times*, Princeton and Oxford: Princeton University Press.

Pascal, Blaise (1909), *Penseés et Opuscules*, Paris: Leon Brunschvicg.

Pearson, Hugh (1996), *The Shadow of the Panther: Huey Newton and the Price of Black Power in America*, Cambridge, MA: Perseus.

Piven, Frances Fox and Richard A. Cloward (1979), *Poor People's Movements: Why They Succeed, How They Fail*, New York: Vintage Books.

Plato (1969), *The Dialogues of Plato*, vol. 1, trans. Benjamin Jowett, London: Sphere Books.

Poirié, Francois (1996), *Emmanuel Levinas Essais et entretiens*, Paris: Actes Sud.

Raeff, Marc (1983), *The Well-Ordered Police State: Social and Institutional Change in the Germanies and Russia 1600–1800*, New Haven: Yale University Press.

Robert, Marthe (1979), *Seul, comme Franz Kafka*, Paris: Calmann-Lévy.

Rose, Gillian (1993), *Judaism and Modernity*, Oxford: Blackwell.

Rose, Gillian (1995), *Love's Work*, London: Chatto & Windus.

Rose, Gillian (1996), *Mourning Becomes the Law: Philosophy and Representation*, Cambridge: Cambridge University Press.

Rose, Gillian (1998), 'The Final Notebooks of Gillian Rose', *Women: A Cultural Review* 9 (1): 6–18.

Rose, Gillian (1999), *Paradiso*, London: Menard Press.

Rose, Gillian ([1981] 2009), *Hegel Contra Sociology*, London: Verso.

Rosenzweig, Franz ([1921] 1988), *Der Stern der Erlösung*, Frankfurt: Suhrkamp.

Roy, Soline (2016), 'Grotte Chauvet: son âge n'a plus de secret', *Le Figaro*, 12 March 2016: 9.

Schiller, Friedrich ([1795] 2000), *Über die ästhetische Erziehung des Menschen in einer Reihe von Briefen*. Stuttgart: Reclam.

Scholem, Gershom (1946), *Major Trends in Jewish Mysticism*, New York: Schocken.

Schürmann, Reiner (1987), *Heidegger on Being and Acting: From Principles to Anarchy*, trans. Christine-Marie Gros, Bloomington: Indiana University Press.

Schmitt, Carl (2007), *Theory of the Partisan: Intermediate Commentary on the Concept of the Political*, trans. G.S. Ulmen, New York: Telos Press Publishing.

Scientific American (2016), *Scientific American* 25 (4), Special Collector's Edition.

Sebag-Montefiore, Hugh (2017), *Enigma: The Battle for the Code*, London: Weidenfeld and Nicholson.

Sebald, Max (1991), 'Das Gesetz der Schande – Macht, Messianismus und Exil in Kafkas Schloss', in *Unheimliche Heimat: Essays zur österreichischen Literatur*, Salzburg: Residenz Verlag, 87–103.

Sharp, Gene (1973), *The Politics of Nonviolent Action*, 3 vols. Boston: Porter Sargent Publishers.

Smith, Crosbie (1998), *The Science of Energy: A Cultural History of Energy Physics in Victorian Britain*, London: Athlone.

Southern, R.W. (1981), *Western Society and the Church in the Middle Ages*, Harmondsworth: Penguin Books.

Spector, Scott (2000), *Prague Territories*, Berkeley: University of California Press.

Stach, Reiner (2006), *Kafka: The Decisive Years*, trans. Shelley Frisch, Orlando, FL: Harcourt.

Stelarc (1992), 'Interview Jean-Yves Katelan', *L'Autre Journal*, 27 September.

Stephenson, Neal (1999), *Cryptonomicon*, London: Arrow Books.

Stimilli, Elettra (2017), *The Debt of the Living: Ascesis and Capitalism*, trans. Arianna Bove, Albany: State University of New York Press.

Stimilli, Elettra (2019), *Debt and Guilt: A Political Philosophy*, trans. Stefania Porcelli, London: Bloomsbury.

Sugrue, Thomas J. (2008), *Sweet Land of Liberty: The Forgotten Struggle for Civil Rights in the North*, New York: Random House.

Taub, Liba (2003), *Ancient Meteorology*, London: Routledge.

Taubes, Jacob (2004), *The Political Theology of Paul*, trans. Dana Hollander, Stanford: Stanford University Press.

Taubes, Jacob (2010), *From Cult to Culture: Fragments toward a Critique of Historical Reason*, ed. Chalotte Elisheva Fonrobert and Amir Engel, Stanford, CA: Stanford University Press.

Thomas, Chris D. (2018), *Inheritors of the Earth: How Nature Is Thriving in the Age of Extinction*, London: Penguin.

Tolentino, Jia (2019), *Trick Mirror: Reflections on Self-Delusion*, New York: Random House.

Tosquelles, François (2001), 'Frantz Fanon et la Psychothérapie Institutionnelle', *Sud/Nord* 14 (1): 167–74.

Tsing, Anna Lowenhaupt (2015), *The Mushroom at the End of the World: On the Possibility of Life in Capitalist Ruins*, Princeton: Princeton University Press.

Van Dooren, Thom (2014), *Flight Ways: Life and Loss at the Edge of Extinction*, New York: Columbia University Press.

Virilio, Paul (1986), *Speed and Politics: An Essay on Dromology*, trans. M. Polizotti, New York: Semiotexte/Autonomedia.

Warburg, Aby ([1923] 1997), *Images from the Region of the Pueblo Indians of North America*, trans. Michael P. Steinberg, Ithaca, London: Cornell University Press.

Warnke, Martin (2011), *Theorien des Internet*, Hamburg: Junius Verlag.

Warren, Robert Penn (1965), *Who Speaks for the Negro?* New York: Random House.

Weber, Max (1977), *The Protestant Ethic and the Spirit of Capitalism*, trans. Talcott Parsons, London: Allen & Unwin.

White, Megan (2019), 'Police Boss Blasts "Unacceptable Behaviour" of Officers Filmed Skateboarding and Dancing at Extinction Rebellion Protests in London', *Evening Standard*, 18 April 2019.

Whitehead, Alfred North (1920), *The Concept of Nature*, Cambridge: Cambridge University Press.

Whitehead, Alfred North (1925), *Science and the Modern World*, Cambridge: Cambridge University Press.

Whitehead, Alfred North (1929), *Process and Reality*, New York: Macmillan.

Whitehead, Alfred North (1934), *Nature and Life*, Chicago: University of Chicago Press.

Whitford, Margaret (1991), *Luce Irigaray: Philosophy in the Feminine*, London: Routledge.

Wizisla, Erdmut (2009), *Walter Benjamin and Bertolt Brecht: The Story of a Friendship*, trans. Christine Shuttleworth. London: Libris.

Wolff, Christian ([1719] 1999), *Vernünftige Gedanken von Gott, der Welt, und der Seele des Menschen, auch allen Dingen überhaupt*, in *Christian Wolff: Metaphysica Tedesca*, ed. R. Ciarfordone, Milan: Rusconi.

Wright, Thomas (1750), *An Original Theory and New Hypothesis of the Universe*, London: H. Chapelle. Reproduced in facsimile edition with introduction by M.A. Hoskin, London: Macdonald 1971.

Wyschogrod, Edith (1986), *Spirit in Ashes: Hegel, Heidegger, and Man-Made Mass Death*, New Haven: Yale University Press.

Young-Bruehl, Elisabeth (2004), *Hannah Arendt: For Love of the World*, 2nd ed., London: Yale University Press.

Zimmerman, Michael E. (1990), *Heidegger's Confrontation with Modernity: Technology, Politics, Art*, Bloomington: Indiana University Press.

Index

9 781350 107861